The Exemplary Society

Studies on Contemporary China

The Contemporary China Institute at the School of Oriental and African Studies (University of London) has, since its establishment in 1968, been an international centre for research and publications on twentieth-century China. *Studies on Contemporary China*, which is edited at the Institute, seeks to maintain and extend that tradition by making available the best work of scholars and China specialists throughout the world. It embraces a wide variety of subjects relating to Nationalist and Communist China, including social, political, and economic change, intellectual and cultural developments, foreign relations, and national security.

Series Editor

Dr Frank Dikötter, Director of the Contemporary China Institute

The Exemplary Society

Human Improvement, Social Control, and the Dangers of Modernity in China

BØRGE BAKKEN

OXFORD

UNIVERSITY PRESS

OXFORD

UNIVERSITY PRESS

Great Clarendon Street, Oxford OX2 6DP

Oxford University Press is a department of the University of Oxford.
It furthers the University's objective of excellence in research, scholarship,
and education by publishing worldwide in

Oxford New York

Athens Auckland Bangkok Bogotá Buenos Aires Calcutta
Cape Town Chennai Dar es Salaam Delhi Florence Hong Kong Istanbul
Karachi Kuala Lumpur Madrid Melbourne Mexico City Mumbai
Nairobi Paris São Paulo Singapore Taipei Tokyo Toronto Warsaw
with associated companies in Berlin Ibadan

Oxford is a registered trade mark of Oxford University Press
in the UK and in certain other countries

Published in the United States
by Oxford University Press Inc., New York

British Library Cataloguing in Publication Data
Data available

Library of Congress Cataloging in Publication Data
Bakken, Børge.
The exemplary society : human improvement, social control, and the
dangers of modernity in China / Børge Bakken.
p. cm. — (Studies on contemporary China)
Includes bibliographical references and index.
1. Social control—China. 2. Social change—China. 3. Moral
education—China. 4. China—Social conditions—1976– I. Title.
II. Series: Studies on contemporary China (Oxford, England)
HN733.5.B36 1999 306'.0951—dc21 99–42802
ISBN 0–19–829523–5 (hb)

1 3 5 7 9 10 8 6 4 2

Typeset in Plantin
by Graphicraft Limited, Hong Kong
Printed in Great Britain
on acid-free paper by
Biddles Ltd, Guildford & Kings Lynn

Preface

THE present project began as an enquiry into the Chinese educational system. It has ended up as a description of what I have called the Chinese 'exemplary society'. The more I delved into the ideas of socialization and education, the more I discovered how the approach of 'exemplary' behaviour and 'exemplary' norms were crucial in Chinese society. The more I looked at human transformation and improvement, the more I was impelled towards theories of discipline and social control. The confines of the classroom and educational institutions soon gave way to the greater perspective of a Chinese educative and controlling society as such, and the powerful pictures of traditional society mingled with the maelstrom of events that characterizes a modernizing China.

I stayed in Beijing from 1983 to 1986, experiencing an early phase of the reforms, and returned in the early 1990s. I recall one episode from the period when the concept of an 'exemplary society' first started to take form. One day in early March I watched the good deeds of the late soldier–hero Lei Feng being rehearsed with gongs and drums and displayed in the streets of Beijing. This 'street theatre' of 'free service' in order to 'serve the people' was a striking demonstration of the spread of the educational, from the classroom to the streets, meant to symbolize the ethos of socialism, collectivism, and—exemplary behaviour.

The exemplary society is all about keeping social order in the midst of change. Here I will concentrate on describing this order as practised in the People's Republic during reform and modernization. Perhaps my story will give the reader an impression like that which often strikes Western tourists visiting Beijing for the first time. The city is too large, they say, the distances too great, and they cannot find the city centre. This will not be a simple story; sometimes it may seem to resemble one of those narrow Beijing lanes—the *hutong*—zigzagging through the inner city. It is my hope, however, that the reader will find in these *hutong* a kind of beauty as well as a way through to the broad avenues that are also Beijing, and in this connection symbols of overview and clarity. It is often difficult to direct a stranger to a certain place through the *hutong*. As a stranger myself—even if I have walked through some of them before—I still have difficulties giving the right directions. It is my hope that I will not send readers into too many detours by my instructions, and also that I have managed to conduct them safely through both the *hutong* and the broad avenues, making for somewhat easier navigation the next time—although the landscape may well change and new maps may be needed in a situation where China changes even faster than the process of printing books.

The present project can be described as an intellectual and geographical journey. I am much obliged to the Research Council of Norway, which financed my journey for three full years, over four continents. I started as a Visiting Fellow at the Contemporary China Centre at the Australian National University in Canberra. I was later hosted as a Visiting Scholar by the John King Fairbank Center for East Asian Research at Harvard University. My host in China was the Beijing Normal University, where I was allowed to conduct interviews with political instructors and class teachers. I then moved on to Munich, where I stayed at the Department of East Asian Studies at the Ludwig-Maximilian-Universität München. I would like to thank Professor Helwig Schmidt-Glintzer and the late Professor Wolfgang Bauer for their *Gastfreundschaft* and for letting me continue my research there. I would further like to thank the Department of Sociology at the University of Oslo, where I obtained my Ph.D. degree, and the Nordic Institute of Asian Studies (NIAS) in Copenhagen, where I finished this part of my journey as a senior researcher in Chinese studies. I am obliged to Jonathan Unger in particular, and to Craig Calhoun, Fredrik Engelstad, Ivar Frønes, Harald Bøckman, Dru Gladney, and an anonymous reader at the Oxford University Press for their comments on the whole or parts of the typescript. A special thank you goes to Beate Geist, who shared her knowledge and research material with me throughout the period of thinking and writing. All were part of my journey.

B.B.

Copenhagen, 1998

Note on Chinese Characters

THE title page of each section features a single Chinese character meant to illustrate the theoretical focus of that section. 'Social Order' (Part I) is represented by *píng*, which encompasses the meanings of 'even', 'equal', 'calm', or 'peaceful'; it indicates 'balance', as in *pingheng*, and even has connotations of 'suppression'. For Part II, 'Education' is *jiào*, 'to teach' and 'to instruct'. 'Discipline' (Part III) is *Lü'*, also meaning 'law', 'rule', 'restrain' or 'keep under control'. 'Modernity, Deviance, and Dangers' (Part IV) is illustrated by *liú*, which implies 'to drift' or 'to flow', 'to move', 'to wander'; the character's connotations of movement can be interpreted both in the positive and in the negative, as it has connotations of 'changing for the worse' or 'degenerating'. 'Theatre' (Part V) is *xì*, meaning 'play', 'drama', 'show', or 'performance'.

To Ragnheiður

Contents

律 III: NORMS, DISCIPLINE, AND THE EXEMPLARY ORDER   211

流 IV: MODERNITY, DEVIANCE, AND DANGERS   315

Figures

Tables

Introduction

IN this book my object of research is Chinese society in the midst of reform and modernization, caught between the problems of order and stability, disorder and danger. I term this society an 'exemplary society', one linked to 'exemplary norms'. It is the character of this 'exemplarity' that will form the essence of my discussion. I have used an inductive strategy in trying to map out this society. Exemplarity itself was not an idea contained in my luggage at the outset of my journey; I picked it up on the way from the rich variety of examples that gradually made its contours distinguishable. My examples represent a pattern discovered during the process of reading and observing. In the face of the variety that is China, I have tried to find clarity through diversity rather than seeing the two as opposed.

This will be a discussion about norms, rules, and strategies, about tradition and modernization, education and morality, socialization and 'human improvement', and discipline and social control. The exemplary society discussed herein can be described as a society where 'human quality' based on the exemplary norm and its exemplary behaviour is regarded as a force for realizing a modern society of perfect order. It is a society with roots and memories to the past, as well as one created in the present to realize a future utopia of harmonious modernity. Exemplarity is in China seen as based on an objective 'moral science', operating as a binding as well as a transforming 'moral force' in society. We might speak of the 'production' of individuals in line with 'objective standards' of exemplarity. The exemplary society is both educative and disciplinary, and we shall look at both its educational methods and its disciplinary techniques or 'technologies' for rewarding virtue and punishing evil. 'Human quality' gradually appears as an object of enquiry, intervention, and surveillance of human behaviour. Morality, politics, and 'human quality' are seen as closely interlinked in the People's Republic of China. Even if the debate has roots in the Chinese tradition, the disciplinary control system described here is made possible by the current power of the state, and is linked to the fortunes of the modern bureaucratic state. People's morality and their physical, mental, and behavioural qualities become important for the sake of state power and the nation: objects for the techniques of social discipline and social engineering linked to the alleged eradication of 'social decay' and the promotion of economic growth. The modern sciences are utilized

in creating a new scientifically based 'exemplary' morality and behaviour. The discipline that is enforced upon the people thus works in
tandem with the disciplines that study them.

The regulatory and disciplinary aspects of this society can be
described, in Foucault's words, as an 'interrogation without end', a 'file
never closed'. The exemplary society, however, is about willed consent
as well as resistance and the erosion of control, and the Foucauldian
approach is insufficient by not seeing clearly enough the importance
of resistance and the strategies of bending exemplary rules and evading power and control. People make of the rules, norms, rituals, and
laws imposed upon them something quite different from the effects
intended. A society simply resists being reduced to the exemplary discipline of its social engineers. I stress the crucial importance of strategies here, since such strategies are about practical ways of operating
within a culture. People have a 'feel for the game', as Bourdieu would
have said,[1] a practical mastery of a society and a culture based on experience with that society or culture. Seeing human behaviour in terms
of strategy is about reintroducing the socialized agent and realizing that
a culture is not a static entity. Culture can instead be understood as a
repertoire of possibilities. It involves a 'mind set' which has the effect
of limiting the repertoire and the full range of alternative possibilities
or behaviours. The dominant mind set, or rather mind sets, are not the
prescribed exemplary one, although one must relate to it. The strategic
uses of exemplary order are described as 'ways of lying' in my concluding chapter. Such 'ways of lying', however, presuppose the knowledge and application of exemplary norms, and the strategies used to
evade power must be based on cultural knowledge about the exemplary
order. Strategies of evasion or resistance are not made at random; nor
are they unlimited, but can be seen as improvizations over well-known
cultural themes. A person's strategic resistance to exemplary norms and
discipline is thus embedded in an intimate experience with or knowledge of the dominating social and cultural patterns. Even if strategy
gives more flexibility and choice to the actors than do assumptions
of structural and cultural determinism, often strategies are 'culturally
coloured' into more or less 'automatic' second natures and are not the
project of a calculating and conscious mind. Strategies are everyday practices, however, and such practices are carved out of necessity without
being determined by forces of culture and tradition. I would like to
emphasize what Elkins and Simeon have claimed, that 'culture does
not explain particular choices which individuals make. Its explanatory
power is rather restricted to setting the agenda.'[2]

Through my discussion, I also hope to shed some light on the general
question of how it is possible to maintain order in a society—particularly

one challenged by the mounting disorder of modernization. My general discussion of norms, order, and modernity will be presented through a cross-cultural and historical approach. Such tools are sorely needed in the social sciences, and we must be aware of the specific historical and cultural foundations of Chinese society if we are to have any hopes of grasping the character of its current development. By using examples from our own cultural sphere, I hope to show that the Chinese example can also shed light on problems of a more general kind. By this I do not mean to indicate that China, as a result of modernization, is 'becoming like us'. We in the West must be sensitive to the differences encountered in the Chinese example, at the same time as we should avoid making China into something inscrutable, impenetrable and exotic, where 'East is East, and West is West, and never the twain shall meet'. Contrary to inclinations of cultural determinism, I hope that, by describing the 'terra incognita' of China, I will also describe something about ourselves.

Let us begin with a brief look at the notions of change, order, and modernity. The Marxist image of modernity is described in the *Communist Manifesto* as a monster, a process where everything stable evaporates (*verdampft*), or where 'all that is solid melts into the air'.[3] Marx further likens modern bourgeois society to a sorcerer no longer able to control the powers conjured up by his spells:

Modern bourgeois society with its relations of production, of exchange and of property, a society that has conjured up such gigantic means of production and of exchange, is like the sorcerer, who is no longer able to control the powers of the nether world whom he has called up by his spells.[4]

Marxism, on the other hand, welcomes the process as historically progressive and holds that the monster can be tamed, since what human beings have created they can always subject to their own control. I do feel that it is important to keep the core of this argument, that the process is not entirely uncontrollable. However, it also seems as if modernization evades the grip of total control frequently propagated by utopian scientism and bureaucratism. Attempts at total control might in fact create another monster, just as ferocious as the one it was meant to control. The sorcerer might prove as dangerous as the monster itself.

Anthony Giddens has questioned the ability to control the modern monster entirely. He has suggested an image of a modernity as a 'juggernaut',[5] not entirely wild, but less controllable than in the Marxist image:

[T]he juggernaut [is] a runaway engine of enormous power which, collectively as human beings, we can drive to some extent but which also threatens to rush out of our control and which could rend itself asunder. The juggernaut crushes those who resist it, and while it sometimes seems to have a steady path, there are times when it veers away erratically in directions we cannot foresee. The ride is by no means wholly unpleasant or unrewarding; it can often be exhilarating and charged with hopeful anticipation. But, so long as the institutions of modernity endure, we shall never be able to control completely either the path or the pace of the journey. In turn, we shall never be able to feel entirely secure, because the terrain across which it runs is fraught with risks of high consequence.[6]

The Chinese programme of modernization can be described as an attempt at taming or binding, of completely controlling the path and the pace of the Juggernaut of modernity. The Chinese regime wants to put brakes on the runaway engine, although it also wants to let it run. These themes are directly addressed in an article by Li Jidong discussing the 'deformation of modernity'. He attacks the loss of conformity and the loss of faith that has spread during the reforms, and explicitly holds that: 'One should control the speed (*sudu*) and the orientation (*fangxiang*) of the modernization process.'[7]

Keeping such control might be seen as a mixed process where both traditional and modern elements play a part. Modernity has been described as a revolt against the normalizing functions of tradition, and is said to live on the experience of rebelling against all that is normative.[8] Tradition, on the other hand, always has a 'binding', normative character. The normative core of tradition is the inertial force which holds society in a given form over time. This force is directed against the dangers or problematics of modernity; and this is one reason why China has experienced an apparent re-emergence of tradition during the recent reforms. In other words, we should judge this phenomenon in terms of the mechanisms of social control, and not in terms of the manifestation of a 'Confucian ethic'. The explanation lies in bureaucracies, social institutions, and social control more than in ideology, and the 'counter-modern' thus becomes part of the modern project itself as we see it in China. The re-emerging 'traditionalization' cannot be explained without taking the expansion of the modern state into consideration, and the eclipse of tradition cannot be understood adequately as the *remains* or rudiments of the past or the pre-modern. This argumentation applies not only to control, but to resistance as well. Mayfair Yang indicates, in her study of Chinese connection building, that even the 'ways of lying' can be described as modern *beginnings*, or rebirths.[9] She describes the art of *guanxixue* as a creative deployment of a 'counter-ethics' which makes room for the personal and the private in a public sphere monopolized by the modern state. Such phenomena can only partly be explained as remains of a pre-modern kinship and locally oriented social system; they are practical answers to the Chinese modern condition.

On the other hand, modernity is not only a rage against order: the overriding emphasis on modernity can also be said to concern control. Implicit in modernization beliefs is a subordination of the world to human dominance. This represents the hope and dreams of modernization, and counteracts the elements of danger and 'evaporation'. In China the first trend is seen as an apparently paradoxical re-emergence of traditional norms and values; the latter trend is expressed in a 'scientific imagination', or rather a scientistic belief in, and enthusiasm about, the possibilities of human transformation and improvement. Improving the 'human quality' (*ren de suzhi*) becomes a core element in attempts to control the Juggernaut. The subordination of the world to human dominance, then, turns into a system of dominating the minds and the bodies of human beings. Such dreams of predictability, of course, have a nasty inclination to end in nightmares. The stability and inertia of tradition, as well as the possibilities of human and social improvement represented by the modern sciences, form the dual basis underlying the Chinese system of social control.

Paradoxically, it is change, understood as human, social, and natural transformation, that is the basic aim of control. However, change has to be combined with stability, and it is important to note that such transformation should first of all be a balanced process and take place within controlled boundaries. The Chinese type of modernization seems to follow a deeply rooted pattern of 'controlled change', with tradition and modernity interlinked in a system of social control where 'tradition' can also serve transforming purposes and 'modernization' can mean stability and order. I will try to show the consequences of these patterns of social control, how they are manifested in theories and ideologies as well as in concrete practices, and how they become institutionalized and bureaucratized. At the same time, the Chinese attempt at human improvement and total control is ridden with its own contradictions. This project is being countered both by the processes of modernization and by the weight of its own rationality or irrationality. We shall see how these contradictions have the effect of ripping the project apart, making an impossibility of the image of total control.

The debate on human improvement and human quality will form a natural starting point for the analysis of what I have called 'the exemplary society'. Here this concept is meant as an alternative to the 'disciplinary society' described by Foucault and theories overemphasizing the image of totalizing 'Orwellian' control. The 'exemplary' is also closely linked to the 'spiritual', and it is precisely here that the Chinese discourse of order begins. It has been important for the current Chinese regime to find out what constitutes the correct understanding of the relation between a 'material civilization' and a 'spiritual civilization'.

Politically and socially, reform appears to offer a means for halting the pressure of social control. On the other hand, the social stability demanded by economic reform strengthens the validity of calls for extending the institutions of social control. A fundamental tenet of the Chinese reforms as seen in the West has been that economic reform brings with it political reform. A great misunderstanding in our Western images of China during 'reform and opening' has been to overlook the fact that social control has been one of the crucial pillars of reform. The brutal crackdown in Beijing in 1989 demonstrated the law-and-order approach to reform, but the silent forms of control that were introduced as parts of the reform programme have long been overlooked in the West. In this context, the Beijing massacre was not a fundamental break in the reform programme: it came as the consequence of one intrinsic part of that programme. Misunderstandings about the 'necessary' connection between market economy and democratic political reforms prevailed before 1989, and still can be heard. Instead of liberalization, we have seen a new regime of social control introduced during the reforms. The picture of Cultural Revolutionary chaos haunts today's Chinese leaders; the result of this revolution has been summed up by Richard Madsen as one where the traditional and populist 'knight-errant ethic' of retribution and retaliation survived and was even enhanced. At the same time, the Confucian ethical solutions to holding that popular ethic in check did not survive the Cultural Revolution.[10] Searching for an alternative ethic during the reform period, the Party has in fact returned to the memories of the Chinese past. Old forms of control have been subsequently modernized and redeployed, augmented and refined in order to 'bind', 'hold', or 'stabilize' a potentially disorderly population.

This sensitivity to traditional cultural forms of control does not imply any cultural determinism, as the old is recreated in the present. Control was strengthened after 1989, but it was a fundamental trait of reform even from the late 1970s. It is a misunderstandig to describe the reform factions in the Party as 'democrats'. Their technocratic and elitist viewpoints are instead manifested in their policy of social control. Even former premier Zhao Ziyang, the leading liberal and symbol of reform values before his political demise in 1989, held that 'the precondition for development is stability'.[11] This technocracy sought legitimacy in the promises of economic growth *and* social control.

It is worth noting that there were at least two words for 'change' in classical Chinese. One—*hua* (𠤎)—had to do with sudden change, or change of substance, and the character is made from the picture of two knives, or coins of knife-money, indicating that currency exchange had given rise to the general idea of change. *Hua* also has a connotation of transforming and improving, and Chinese bureucracy used *hua*—transformation—and *jiao*—education—to strengthen social and moral order.[12]

Also interesting is the existence of a character for change meaning gradual change, and change of form. *Bian* (變) is a character not found in bone or bronze inscriptions; it thus is of a later date, from the late Zhou dynasty (770–221 BC). Its original meaning is somewhat uncertain, but the character is written in the picture of two hanks of silk. In his ancient encyclopedia of classical characters—the *Shuowen jieci*, written *c.* AD 100—Xu Shen claims, or so at least have some of his commentaries understood him, that it meant 'to bring into order', as in spinning or reeling. The radical, the element here placed below, shows a hand holding a stick, signifying 'movement' or 'action'.[13] As I will later show, a hand holding a stick can also indicate discipline. If the character is not a phonetic loan-word, it may have implied change from disorder to order. Of course, this interpretation describes a change entirely different from the change of the modern Juggernaut. This classical picture of change also seems to fit the controlled change that would appear to be the aim of the present modernizers, even if the sudden change found in the pictograph of money '*ex*-change' might be a better indication of where the modernizations might lead in the near future.

It is an obvious characteristic of language itself, and not simply a problem of translation, that for any important concept the dictionary will usually list a variety of meanings. For instance, the 'Encyclopaedic Dictionary of the Chinese Language' (*Zhongwen da cidian*) claims that the character *bian* also has the more 'modern' meaning of *luan*—'disorder'.[14] We thus have a double meaning here, but the *bian* in its interpretation by Xu Shen and his commentaries can at least be seen as a picture of a process highly valued in the general Chinese approach towards change. The change of 'bringing into order', is in fact what the modernizations are meant to be about. The concepts to remember in reading this text, then, are the interpretation of order in the ancient Chinese character *bian* and its contrast, the danger and disorder of the modern monster or Juggernaut.[15] In between these poles lies Chinese contemporary society, and within this span the social phenomena of modernizing China are displayed.

In the Chinese approach to modernization lie both memories of the past and dreams and possibilities of the society of tomorrow. It should be noted that my references to the Chinese past are not so much about schools of ideas as about ways of doing things. 'Confucianism' is used quite loosely in my discussion, and I do not talk of the return of a 'Confucian ethic' to explain today's China. I rather see the return of specific patterns of social control where Confucianism has contributed together with traces of legalism, Mohism, etc. To mention just one aspect, the Mohists' stress on the 'unification of standards' is a central element in the current practices of the exemplary society.[16] Other elements of Chinese traditional philosophy and traditionalism are also parts of this pattern. Memories of the past, however, return not as unreflected traditionalism, but as conscious and calculated ways of controlling the modern. A tradition full of myths and exemplary models is formed into new legitimizing narratives of growth and order to defend the now-fading 'grand narratives' of a once-orderly past. In both memories and dreams there are integrative elements—and in both there are dangers. According to Chinese thinking, the best way to cope with such danger lies in the 'exemplary norm'.

It is one of the fundamental assumptions in the Chinese theory of learning that people are innately capable of learning from models. In addition, rule by morality was more widespread in traditional China than rule by law. Chinese society is undoubtedly a disciplinary society in many senses, but it is also an educational society. A combination of the disciplinary and the educational constitutes the exemplary society of which I speak here. A discipline based on the norm is more durable than one based on outer force only because it seeks to bind people to society with their own ideas. It is linked to power in a way less likely to manifest force or violence. Regulation through the norm is more based on willed consent, and functions more like a positive restraint. The norm is a measurement and a means of producing a common standard, but may be constituted in various ways; it can be linked both to the average and to the exemplary. The special techniques of regulation and control implemented in China are linked to the exemplary norm.

In the West, the meaning of 'norm' slowly changed during the process of modernization. It now refers to a standard measure that allows us to distinguish that which conforms to the rule from that which does not, but this distinction is no longer linked to the notion of rectitude. Even virtue has become normalized. Normalization can be linked to Alphonse Quetelet's early nineteenth-century theory of the 'average man'.[17] Average man does not incarnate a model or an original that can serve as the standard for everyone. Average man is linked to the modern norm, and represents a new way of judging individuals with reference to 'the other' rather than an ideal state of morality. Within this normative system, values are defined not *a priori*, but rather 'through an endless process of comparison'. The exemplary model becomes an extreme on a statistical continuum, rather than the main point of reference in such a context. There is an ambiguity in the concepts of norm and standard that can be illustrated through the concepts of ideal versus typical, conformity versus comparison, moral versus normal, and exemplary versus average. At times the terms refer to models of behaviour, an exemplary type of behaviour towards which all behaviour should be directed. In other words, this represents a moral judgement. The terms, as indicated, also refer to the average, median, or typical pattern of 'normal' behaviour.

My discussion of the origins of the norm of exemplarity is not far removed from Walder's view of the 'neo-traditional'. While stressing here the impact of 'cultural traditions', I do not mean to imply that the exemplary control system is not yet 'modern' or that it has no 'communist' flavour. The control system and its techniques are creatures of the present; much of this controlling structure is even of a fairly recent date and cannot be labelled as 'rudiments' of tradition. I simply hold that the notions of culture and tradition must be used carefully, and not as determinants of development or origin. The system is both 'traditional' and 'modern' at the same time, and without making it a pure 'communist' creation we should recognize the specificity of communist and its modern form of 'reformist' exemplarity. The transmission of culture and tradition is reflexive, not determinist, and there is nothing in tradition that forces the system into the pattern it forms today. I see, however, cultural patterns recurring in the form of 'memories'. Such 'memories' are not only about tradition, but are practical strategies and also concern the adoption of effective mechanisms of control.

The exemplary norm is about guaranteeing order and stability in a society through the prediction of people's behaviour. By focusing on its roots in traditional culture, I merely want to establish a 'practical memory' of behaviour evident also in the practices and ideas of what is today's China. My argument is that, although Chinese 'communism' has defined new forms of exemplarity, communism as such is not a crucial variable in the Chinese cultural undercurrent of exemplarity. 'Communism' merely gives a specific taint or colouring to the main argument of exemplarity. My intention has not been to bind the argument of 'exemplarity' to a certain historical epoch. Through analogies from different periods of the Chinese past, I have tried to illustrate certain recurrent powerful assumptions in the Chinese way of thinking and acting. The alien doctrine of Buddhism was once sinicized, and the modern but equally alien doctrine of communism met with the same fate.

In any given period, Chinese thought and social practices are usually a mixed bag of enduring assumptions and strikingly new ideas. Even the strongest themes often submerge and sometimes disappear, while others reappear in new forms. There is no chronology in the development of such cultural phenomena, and a linear movement of exemplarity is also lacking. Many classical assumptions, however, are still found in official Chinese communist ideology and organizations. I have pointed out the recurring theme of exemplarity as a remarkably strong one without trying to overemphasize the continuity of Chinese ideas in general so as to illude a static development or no development at all.

When I talk of and use examples of exemplarity from different periods of the Chinese past, I do not therefore assume causal links to the present. Rather, I talk of repetitive and imitative cultural processes, and my argument can be summed up in the expression 'repetition with a difference' when classical patterns recur in modern forms. I thus emphasize both repetition and difference. New and modern forms of exemplarity are entangled. I choose to clarify the entanglement in the process by tracing some of the general distinctions that exist rather than mapping out the concrete changes in traditional and communist norms. Of course there is a difference between obedience to the emperor and obedience to the Party, but I rather want to entangle the two by looking at more general processes of differentiation, such as rootedness versus construction, custom versus 'science', and orientation towards the past versus that towards the future.

Memory can be treated as a cultural rather than an individual faculty.[18] Exemplarity as a cultural 'memory' is different from individual memories that merely perish by death. Those cultural memories can be understood as symbols, values, norms, practical strategies, thought patterns, 'ways of doing things', or 'traces' that have materialized in a culture and function as legitimizing factors for acting in society and organizing society. In this specific case, I see such traces materializing in the educational system and its organizations as well as in the organized forms of the disciplinary system and the bureaucratic system. To the individual Chinese mind, these traces are left as the 'learning-how' of a culture, and can be seen as common practice regardless of whether it takes place in a feudal, a 'communist', or a capitalist context.

Structured as well as unstructured and extensive interviews,[19] scholarly as well as popular literature, informal talks, observations from the media and daily life, episodes experienced during my years in China—all were parts of the journey as well as the methodology that made it possible to write this book. Written material, however, has been the main source on which the present work builds. The range of literature used in the present work spans from popular youth magazines to scholarly philosophical treatises; it includes official publications as well as internal (*neibu*) material for limited circulation. *Neibu* is a flexible category. One day I might be allowed to copy material at the National Library in Beijing; the next week that same material was 'non-existing' or 'internal'. Often the whims of the librarian in charge could give me access to or prevent my using certain materials altogether. A wide range of local Chinese survey reports and official statistics has also been used. In general, a sceptical approach to such data is recommended. Frustratingly often, Chinese-made surveys provide insufficient detail on methodology to satisfy the professional sociologist. I advocate an interpretation of the systematic 'cultural bias' found in some surveys. In this regard, there is no reason to turn ethnocentric in our evaluations. Even if the notion of an 'objective culture' is heavily emphasized in the 'moral science' approach of the Chinese intellectual tradition, such culturally biased set-ups of methodology strategies are not a Chinese phenomenon only. We would be well advised to advocate the same scepticism and to realize similar cultural bias in our own schemes and strategies of methodological approach. Chinese sociology and social science in general are still young in China, and are ridden with a great many methodological 'children's diseases' after so many years in the shadows of a 'forbidden area'—or *jinqu*. Sociology was resumed in 1979, after having been banned from the research community for twenty-seven years.[20]

Notes to Introduction

1. See Pierre Bourdieu, *In Other Words: Essays towards a Reflexive Sociology*, trans. Matthew Adamson, Cambridge, Polity Press, 1994, p. 61.
2. David J. Elkins and Richard E. B. Simeon, 'A cause in search of its effect, or what does political culture explain', *Comparative Politics*, No. 11, 1979, pp. 130–1.
3. 'Alles Ständische und Stehende verdampft, alles Heilige wird entweiht, und die Menschen sind endlich gezwungen, ihre Lebensstellung, ihre gegenseitigen Beziehungen mit nüchternen Augen anzusehen.' See 'Manifest der Kommunistischen Partei', in Karl Marx, *Die Frühschriften*, Stuttgart, Alfred Kröner Verlag, 1971, p. 529. The metaphor to 'melt into the air' is used in Samuel Moore's classic translation of the *Manifesto* from 1888, the version authorized and edited by Engels; see 'Manifesto of the Communist Party' in *Capital, the Communist Manifesto and Other Writings of Karl Marx*, ed. Max Eastman, New York, Carlton House, 1932, p. 324.
4. 'Manifesto of the Communist Party', pp. 326–7. See also original text in 'Manifest der Kommunistischen Partei', p. 531.

5. The term comes from the Hindi *Jagannath*, 'lord of the world', the eight incarnation of Krishna; an idol of this deity was taken each year through the streets on a huge car, under which followers are said to have thrown themselves, to be crushed beneath the wheels.

6. Anthony Giddens, *The Consequences of Modernity*, Stanford, Stanford University Press, 1990, p. 139.

7. Li Jidong, 'Fubai yu xiandaihua de bianxing' (Corruption and the deformation of modernity), *Shehuixue yu shehui diaocha*, No. 5, 1989, p. 12.

8. See Jürgen Habermas, 'Modernity versus postmodernity', *New German Critique*, No. 22, 1981, p. 5. Enlightenment thinkers of the cast of mind of Concordet still had the the extravagant expectation that the arts and the sciences would not only promote the control of natural forces, but also would further understanding of the world and the self, and would promote moral progress, the justice of institutions, and even the happiness of human beings. The 20th century would seem to have shattered this optimism (p. 9).

9. Mayfair Mei-hui Yang, *Gifts, Favors and Banquets: The Art of Social Relationships in China*, Ithaca, NY, Cornell University Press, 1994, p. 48.

10. Richard Madsen, 'The politics of revenge in rural China during the Cultural Revolution', in Jonathan N. Lipman and Stevan Harrell (eds.), *Violence in China: Essays in Culture and Counterculture*, Syracuse, NY, State University of New York Press, 1990, p. 183.

11. See interview with Zhao Ziyang in *World Monitor*, January 1989, p. 43.

12. See C. K. Yang, 'Some characteristics of Chinese bureaucratic behaviour', in David S. Nivison and Arthur F. Wright, *Confucianism in Action*, Stanford, Stanford University Press, 1959, p. 141.

13. Xu Shen (ed.), *Shuowen jieci* (Explanations and analysis of characters), Beijing, Zhonghua shuju, 11th printing, 1990, p. 68; and Gao Ming (ed.), *Guwen zi leibian* (The written types of old characters), Beijing, Zhonghua shuju, 1982, pp. 10, 43. See also Colin A. Ronan and Joseph Needham, *The Shorter Science and Civilization in China*, Vol. 1, Cambridge, Cambridge University Press, pp. 129–30; and Bernhard Karlgren, *Grammatica Serica*, in *Bulletin of the Museum of Far Eastern Antiquities* (Stockholm), 1940, Vol. 12, Characters nos. 19 (*hua*) and 1780 (*bian*).

14. *Zhongwen da cidian* (The Encyclopaedic Dictionary of the Chinese Language), Vol. 8 (7th edn.), Taipei, Huakang, Yangmingshan, Chinese Culture University, 1985, no. 36974, p. 1174 (13656).

15. I do not here want to go into a detailed discussion of Chinese etymology as such, a task of which I am not qualified, but I will use etymological interpretations as pictures that can make it easier to understand Chinese society. In this connection, the interpretations of the origins of ancient characters made by Chinese and foreign scholars both in the past and at present are seen as social manifestations in themselves. Such interpretations might be more or less correct from an etymological point of view, but are all generally valid as social data. Etymologists discuss, sometimes quite heatedly, whether a phonetic or an ideographic interpretation of characters is the correct approach. See John DeFrancis, *The Chinese Language: Fact and Fantasy*, Honolulu, University of Hawaii Press, 1984, and Chad Hansen, 'Chinese ideographs and Western ideas', *Journal of Asian Studies*, Vol. 52, No. 2, 1993, pp. 373–99. The latter emphasizes the ideographic approach to Chinese characters.

16. See Yi-Pao Mei (trans.), *The Ethical and Political Works of Motse*, London, A. Probsthain, Hyperion Press, 1929; reprinted 1973. A short overview of the Mohist philosophy is given in Fung Yu-lan (Feng Youlan), *A History of Chinese Philosophy*,

Vol. 1 (trans. Derk Bodde), Princeton, Princeton University Press, 1952, pp. 76–105, 246–78.

17. See Alphonse Quetelet, *Du système social et des lois qui le régissent* (Of the social system and the laws that govern it), Paris, 1848.

18. See Paul Connerton, *How Societies Remember*, Cambridge, Cambridge University Press, 1989.

19. With the help of the Department of Education at Beijing Normal University, I first interviewed seven class teachers (*banzhuren*) and political instructors (*fudaoyuan*) in Beijing. The questions were all written down by me in Chinese and handed over to the respective schools in advance. The answers, however, were given orally, and additional questions to clarify the issue were freely asked and commented upon during the interview sessions. Interviewees 1, 2, and 3 were from the Beijing Normal University (*Beijing shifan daxue*); nos. 1 and 2 were male political instructors (*fudaoyuan*) at the university, while the third was a female class teacher. Both the secondary and the primary school were leading Beijing key-school institutions. Interviewees 4, 5, and 6 were all female class teachers at the Beijing Normal University No. 2 Attached Secondary School (*Beijing shida er fuzhong*). The primary school I visited was the Beijing Normal University Experimental School (*Beijing shifan daxue shiyan xuexiao*). I here interviewed one female model class teacher, listed here as interviewee no. 7. The interviews lasted 2–3 hours each. I have added six unofficial interviewees to my list. For interviewees 8–13 the information is based on several talks and informal interviews over a longer period. While the seven moral educators represented official views of the exemplary society, the unofficial interviewees were of another kind. No. 8 was a former class teacher, now under political surveillance for taking part in the demonstrations in 1989; no. 11 also had a 'political problem' in his personnel file after the Beijing spring demonstrations, and no. 13 had even served one year in jail for copying poems and slogans presented at the Tiananmen demonstrations in 1976. The latter six interviewees were not a representative sample, since they were all intellectuals and males; but they represented resistance towards the exemplary norms, where the first seven had represented obedience to the same norms.

20. See Børge Bakken, 'Kinesisk sosiologi i dag: tiåring med tradisjoner' (Chinese sociology today: ten years after its reintroduction), *Tidsskrift for samfunnsforskning*, Vol. 30, No. 4, 1989, pp. 361–74, with a summary in English.

I

Memories and Dreams of
Social Order

1

Memories
Construction and Structures
of Tradition

BY 'memories' and 'dreams' of social control, I am referring to the control aspect of a culture, and to the fact that, without the precedence of tradition and myth, a culture will be deprived of memory, and thereby also deprived of an important 'binding' element in society. On the other hand, without foresight it will be deprived of its dreams and ideas for a future society: deprived of an idea about where to go. This distinction is crucial also for the narrative of social control, and both elements are mobilized for control purposes. The Chinese reform seems to build on the interplay between the binding force of tradition and the past on one hand, and the promised change to a utopian future on the other. Social control is manifested both as images of memory and as images of dreams. The ideal seems to be to strike a balance between the two. 'Balance' has been a core concept of the Chinese theory and practice of controlled change during the reforms.

Chinese society has seen social formations where both memories and dreams have dominated the scene, each without regard for the other. In the concept of ultrastability I will later discuss Jin Guantao, whose image of China can be regarded as the never-changing culture, as a long and never-ending memory without dreams or hopes for the future. Many have described Chinese tradition as a stagnant society moving in circles, always repeating itself. On the other hand, China also has more recent images of terrifying yesterdays—not only those of dynastic and social breakdown and Western and Japanese imperialism, but in particular those of the Cultural Revolution with its attempts to shatter the traditional mould. This period can be seen as an attempt to cut society off by its roots, to establish a utopian dream unencumbered by memories from the past. This event still haunts the Chinese leadership, many of whom were in some way or other victims of that movement. For them, this brief interlude in the history of the People's Republic is perceived as one where chaos (*luan*) reigned, and party control was lost. Subsequently, in order to overcome such images and prevent their recurrence, the strengthening of control techniques became one of the first tasks to be addressed in the aftermath of the 'ten years of chaos' from 1966 to 1976.

Of course, the memory represented by tradition serves to slow down change, sometimes even preventing it. However, it can also be seen as a necessary brake on a development that is proceeding too quickly. Similarly, the dreams of a new society can be a liberating force and an inspiration, but they can also turn against the existing society in ways that are difficult to mend. Paradoxically, tradition can also be mobilized for the sake of bringing about social change, just as utopias can be used to set boundaries and conserve society in a static and one-dimensional future. I do not therefore see memories of the past solely as binding and cohesive elements. Within this stability there is also change and transformation. On the other hand, dreams of the future are not only about change and transformation: the improvement aspect of such utopias is geared towards adaptation and stability. While the two sources of social control point in different directions, they also tend to move towards each other.

Social control is closely linked to the construction of a culture. It has become common to see culture not as a list of fixed traits inherited passively from the past, but as a set of symbolic representations and expectations that people actively construct to come to terms with reality.[1] In the case of China, we have seen 'culture being worshipped directly in its own name' as national symbols rather than through symbols of religion.[2] In the most extreme form there have been attempts from the Communist Party to 'rehabilitate' the mythical emperor and founder of the Chinese nation, *Huangdi* (the Yellow Emperor), into an historical figure. The Party's general secretary Jiang Zemin wrote inscriptions in his honour, saying 'Chinese civilization, the source is distant and the stream long' (*Zhongguo wenming, yuan yuan liu chang*), indicating continuity with the past.[3] Jiang now officially celebrates Confucius's birthday, thus formally sanctioning the event. Other mythical emperors have been commemorated by the present regime.[4] In one of the most ingenious attempts to bolster feelings of national identity, a project called 'Own a Piece of Chinese Homeland' was started in 1993. The land in question is taken from thirty-six selected scenic or historic spots across the nation. Each of the thirty-six parcels contains 9.6 million square inches of 'homeland' which are for sale, a figure symbolic of China's 9.6 million square kilometres. Each buyer of a 'piece of China' can 'purchase' one square inch of the homeland for US$100. The 'owner' of a square inch of land from one of these 'homeland gardens' is an owner in name only, and one suspects the project of being directed mainly towards the many wealthy overseas Chinese.[5]

While such symbols and constructions of national feeling might be indicative of a trend, there are other types of cultural construction that are geared more directly towards social control than towards mere feelings of patriotism. We have also seen cultural as well as human construction manifested as the construction of tradition and 'human quality'. Both types of construction are preoccupied with the control and prediction of behaviour. The whole society takes part in processes of cultural construction, but the party and the state cadres seem to have perfected such construction into a 'science'. This kind of construction has been turned into a type of social engineering where the 'construction of morality' and the 'construction of civilization' is put on an equal footing with the construction of a 'socialist market economy'. The current regime, engaged in the paradoxical task of a planned transition to an open economy, has become obsessed with a kind of 'moral planning', trying to regulate and control the changing behaviours, norms, and values that follow in the wake of modernization. It is believed that the upheavals of modernization can be effectively tamed through the manifestation of exemplary behaviour. The task thus becomes one of mobilizing morality against the effects of a changing economy.

Economic Growth and Moral Development

In Chinese history some philosophers have opposed the advance of science and technology on the general grounds that the past development of science and the raising of material standards of living have resulted in a decline in morality. The Daoist school of Laozi and Zhuangzi (c. 370–300 BC) was the earliest representative of this viewpoint. The *Daodejing* of Laozi reiterates the view that the discovery of scientific technology, the development of culture and wisdom, and man's pursuit of material desires and expectations are all contradictory to the raising of human morality.

There is, however, another view, which holds that the development of scientific technology and the raising of material cultural life will automatically *raise* the level of morality. During the end of the Spring and Autumn period (770–476 BC), it was said: 'When the granaries are full, ritual and etiquette will thrive. When there is enough to wear and eat, honour and shame will abound.'[6] Mencius and Xunzi also emphasized economic deprivation as a primary external cause of evil conduct. According to Mencius, 'If people have a constant livelihood they will have a constant mind; without a constant livelihood they will not have a constant mind.'[7] In other words, material well-being leads to social order.

Contemporary official comments, however, stress that economic growth has been followed by a deterioration in public morality, the so-called 'spiritual slide' (*jingshen huapo*). Expressions like 'loss of morality' (*daode shiluo*) or 'moral decline' (*daode lunsang*) have also been voiced frequently. A recent article in the party journal *Qiushi* criticizes theories maintaining that negative social and moral phenomena are unrelated to the development of the commodity economy.[8] It draws attention to the spreading tendency to despise social and collective interests and to propagate the supremacy of the individual, to ridicule the finding of pleasure in helping others and assisting the needy. The evils of gambling, prostitution, and corruption have become widespread. These negative phenomena which violate spiritual culture are not dissociated from, but have occurred through, the process of developing a commodity economy. There are two basic misunderstandings about the relation of economic and moral development, according to the article. The first is the 'theory of spontaneity' (*zifa lun*), which maintains that spiritual construction will be achieved spontaneously when material construction has been achieved; the second is the 'ideology of cost' (*daijia yishi*), which maintains that material construction can be achieved only at the expense of spiritual construction. Both are dismissed as harmful.

Supporters of the 'ideology of cost' feel that the 'spiritual slide' is the price that must be paid for developing the commodity economy. It is unrealistic to expect that negative phenomena can be avoided completely during the modernization process, the article maintains; but viewing such phenomena as preconditions for economic development is like a devil's pact issuing a 'permit' for such activities, and the result would be a self-fulfilling prophecy about the inevitability of evil in modernization unless the process can be stopped.

Lu Jian, writing for the sociology journal *Shehui*, presents one variant of the 'theory of cost'.[9] Modernization is always accompanied by the increase of crime, he argues, and his viewpoints come close to a theory about the productivity of crime for economic development. The tight control that kept crime rates down after the 1949 revolution also prevented economic development: 'Behind the extremely low crime rate which people were so proud of, the republic paid a huge price in those years—a growing gap between China and developed countries.'[10] Progress is thus bound to result in certain ethical and behavioural regressions, and modernization is always accompanied by an increase in crime. However, slogans like 'the economy has to go up and crime has to go down' or 'the economy needs to be developed and social security has to be improved' are found everywhere, both in official documents and in the general propaganda. Lu goes on to explain that the pressure towards harsh crime control has considerable grass-roots support, and cannot be seen as a pressure from above only:

Public opinion has put great pressures on government behaviour . . . Ordinary people think that social progress and advancement should include the reduction and disappearance of crime. Otherwise, social progress and advancement would be a failure. Still worse, they often use the growth and decline of crime as a criterion for measuring the success and failure of society. This concept has long dominated the judgement of ordinary people.[11]

The government, Lu further points out, is anxious to put an immediate stop to the increase of crime through 'severe blows' against such phenomena. It also tries to reduce mobile crime by limiting the flow of the population. This theme of social control versus social mobility has in fact a much wider meaning, encapsulating the very dilemma of the relationship between order and development. Many people also unrealistically wish that society would reach a state of ideal and extreme purity, becoming purer as it develops towards its ideal state, but 'the people do not like to see metal doors multiplying and fences getting higher. Still worse, they are afraid of being robbed'.[12] As will be shown, the quest for both more and less control, both purity of behaviour and freedom to choose one's behaviour, characterize the emotions of today's Chinese standing on the threshold between tradition and modernity.

The 'theory of spontaneity' is also officially attacked for bringing harm to spiritual culture. It is said to neglect the importance of ideological and political education. The 'Yan'an spirit' developed in a period of scarcity, but should be carried forward even in today's situation of material well-being. The idea of waiting until material culture has developed before grasping the building of spiritual culture is totally mistaken. 'Only if we seriously grasp the building of spiritual culture at the same time as we grasp the building of material culture, will we truly be able to do well in the building of spiritual culture.'[13]

The development of the commodity economy cannot by itself yield a high degree of spiritual culture in society, it is said. Importantly, the development of the commodity economy can only provide the possibility for developing spiritual culture, and this is not the same as realizing it. Between possibility and realization, a great amount of arduous work remains to be done.[14] In other words, modernization and economic growth form the basis on which a spiritual civilization and a social order have to be built. Both the possibilities of modernization and the dangers of modernity are incorporated into the plan of the reformer. The development of 'civilization' is thus of a dual nature, where economic growth and social order serve the basic foundations of the process. The neglect of either is regarded as harmful to the building of a 'socialism with Chinese characteristics'.

Stability, Change, and the Construction of Tradition

The heavy emphasis on tradition in Chinese modernization might at first sight seem a paradox. Party propaganda as well as the general intellectual debate overflow with analyses of the importance of traditional culture. This clearly represents an important element of legitimation for the regime; but tradition also has to be analysed as an intrinsic part of the reforming and transforming process encouraged by the present regime, at least in its form of memories.

The current Chinese interest in tradition is not without parallels in Western societies. Some analysts have emphasized tradition as a means of creating historical identity. For others tradition has meant a return to the past, even a means of revenge against changes in modern society that are difficult to comprehend or identify with. The theme of tradition, it has been observed, in the Western world is being revived in a cultural climate of disillusionment with social renewal projects.[15] Official Chinese accounts of the phenomenon also stress identity, but otherwise the starting point is entirely different. In China tradition is seen as an integrated part of a renewal project of a technocratic–utopian kind. The project is called 'socialism with Chinese characteristics', and tradition is central in defining these characteristics.[16] Since Friedrich Engels wrote that traditions are a great brake, and the *vis inertiae* of history, it may be difficult to understand that a state socialist regime of today actively uses tradition as part of its transformation project. The answer to the dilemma lies in the question of social order: the great brake of tradition is necessary to stop the 'runaway engine' of modernization.

It has been observed that both the most modernized and the most traditional societies are more stable and less violent, whereas those midway to modernity are most liable to instability and upheaval.[17] China's reformers are very much aware that their reforms might have the same destabilizing effects as those seen in other developing countries. While we have already noted the 'evaporating' effect the modernization process has on norms, values, and the entire social fabric, tradition on the other hand has a fixed, 'binding', and normative character. 'The normative core of tradition is the inertial force which holds society in a given form over time', says Edward Shils.[18] The maintenance of habits and routines is a crucial bulwark against threatening anxieties. 'Normative' here implies a moral component: in traditional practices, the binding quality of activities expresses precepts about how things should or should not be done. Traditions of behaviour have their own moral endowment, which specifically resists the technical power to introduce something new. The fixity of tradition does not derive from its accumulation of past wisdom; rather, coordination of the past with the present is achieved through adherence to the normative precepts that tradition incorporates.

Giddens points out that tradition has to do with the feeling of ontological security in society. Such feelings of ontological security can counteract the anxiety brought about by the process of modernization. He comments on the resurgence of tradition in modern societies:

[T]here would presumably be a renewed fixity to certain aspects of life that would recall some features of tradition. Such fixity would in turn provide a grounding for the sense of ontological security, reinforced by an awareness of a social universe subject to human control.[19]

Giddens discusses both what he calls the disembedding effects of modernity and the re-embedding effects of that process. He clearly sees the importance of tradition as a re-embedding factor, but his answer to how the monster of modernity can be tamed does not at all lie in a traditionalist revival. On the contrary, Giddens's answer is to radicalize modernity. He is concerned first and foremost about destroying the legend of rootlessness in modernity.[20] In the Chinese debate it has been an explicit policy to let tradition represent the re-embedding tendencies of the process. Tradition has been seen as the very force 'binding' the monster of modernity. In some ways—but *only* in some ways—much of the debate in China points in the same direction as does Giddens. The official view in China is to welcome modernization and to see the disembedding effects of this process as avoidable. Tradition is regarded as a useful re-embedding factor, but always *within* the project of modernity. Tradition is the producer of stability within change, order within transformation. The official Chinese viewpoint is similar to that of Giddens in that it refutes the claim about a necessary rootlessness in modernity. It is also similar in not necessarily regarding tradition as 'anti-modern'.[21] The similarities seem to stop here, and Giddens's open society is far removed from the closed Chinese technocratic and exemplary society I will discuss later on. It is not my intention to follow this comparison further here. I have merely wanted to show that, in the official Chinese development model, tradition comes back not as 're-traditionalization' (or 're-Confucianization' for that matter) but rather as a direct instrument of reform and modernization.

There has been much talk in recent years about the re-emergence of the 'Confucian ethic'. This ethic has been compared to the Weberian 'Protestant ethic' and used as an explanation of the success of East Asian capitalism. It has been pointed out that several elements of East Asian culture have been beneficial to development: discipline, respect for authority and education, thrift, cultural homogeneity, etc., are said to have had positive economic effects. On the other hand, it has also been argued that cultural factors have but marginal basis in such phenomena.[22] Such analyses, termed either 'culturalist' or 'institutionalist', might shed light on the Chinese strategy for development. However, I feel that one should not consider Chinese culture as something fixed, some old tradition suddenly turned useful for economic change. There is a great paradox here, since the very same culture has repeatedly been said to have prevented development and change. Peter Berger is obviously right in pointing out that Weber was wrong in asserting that this was the result of Chinese culture as such.[23]

However, it would also be wrong to assume that there has been a fixed and continuous 'Chinese culture' that has suddenly arisen, phoenix-like from the ashes, to become a veritable force of development. There is a very strong element of 'construction' in this alleged 'ethic', and such a construction is concentrated around the issues of social control. Such control aspects might of course be particularly strong in the Confucian ethic, but they will have to be explained as something more than the effects of 'Confucianism'. It has even been shown that the conscious reconstruction of the 'Confucian ethic' might have been inspired by Western analyses of that culture. At least, this seems to have been the case in Singapore, where elements of the Western Confucianism debate have been adopted and applied in society.[24] It would be more correct to say that 'Confucianism' is not re-emerging as ideology or culture as such, but as a theory of social control which is also linked to the understanding of a culture.

To comprehend this process, we need to look more closely at the varying definitions of tradition. Max Weber defined 'traditionalism' as the engagement and belief in the everyday habitual and unswerving norm of behaviour.[25] This type of behaviour describes tradition as a cultural monotone. Traditional behaviour, understood in this sense, is similar to the unreflected observance of a taboo or a dogma that people obey blindly, without any apparent rational justification. Legitimacy is given to forms of control handed down from the past as they 'have always existed'.[26] In a traditional culture, transmitted knowledge was regarded as a continuation and a repetition of the past. Tradition represented the totality of experience, and reflection about it was limited primarily to a clarification of the transmitted past. This we see in Chinese tradition with its all-powerful emphasis on interpretations of the Confucian 'classics', in particular refined in the interpretations of the 'four books' (*si shu*) and the 'five classics' (*wu jing*).[27]

This is not to say, however, that these traditional societies were static societies, seeing time only as static cycles. Rather, they were 'slow moving societies', and their time concept went further than that of cyclical time. What distinguishes them from modern societies is their constant orientation towards the past.[28] This does not mean that people in such traditional societies could not distinguish future, present, and past, and weigh alternative courses of action in terms of likely future considerations. Some historians claim that the ancient Chinese had already developed a linear concept of time, a feeling that human affairs should be fitted into a temporal framework. This is seen in the tremendous and unbroken body of historical literature in China, extending over more than three thousand years. This history served a distinctly moral purpose. The ancients held that by studying the past one might learn how to conduct oneself in the present and the future. The 'timeless Orient' never did exist, even if the focus of attention may have been on the past.[29] The 'compulsion of tradition' that Luhmann talks about was not absolute,[30] even if the Chinese at that time might not yet have reached the point of self-reflection described in Europe by Charles Perrault in 1688 in his polemical statement: 'C'est nous qui sommes les Anciens', where the 'ancients' are for the first time described as something fluctuating with time, and not as a fixed and exemplary point of the past.[31]

We can, however, speak of something like a 'moral time' in the Chinese example. Within tradition there was indeed room for transforming projects like that of human and moral improvement, as well as for renewed constructions of the past. Moral improvement can in fact be said to have represented the core of the traditional Chinese society. Chinese schemes of moral improvement were also very much concentrated on 'man in society', without the religious overtones found in most other cultures. This was a backward-looking process, entailing the seeking of virtuous norms in the exemplary manifestations of the deeds of past sages, and using them as examples for prescribed behaviour for the present and the future. The past was seen as an ideal or a model to be remoulded. Even today, this perspective is very much present in China, as will be shown in the discussion of current heroic myths and models. This is what is meant by the 'memory' of social order, and its binding social effects cannot be underestimated. Such a 'memory' has always been open to renewal and reconstruction. Suffice it to mention the example of filial piety (*xiaojing*) or respect for one's elders, a cornerstone in the Chinese 'familist' traditional society. A Chinese sociologist has summed up the importance of the virtue of filial piety:

Filial piety is the alpha and omega of his [Confucius's] ethics. It includes and logically presupposes every other virtue under heaven. Thus, honesty, justice, courage, self-control, modesty and loyalty, all come under the single rubric of devotion to parents.[32]

Filial piety was not only the core of the patriarchal order in the family or of one's ancestors; from the point of view of the monarch, it was also regarded as the model for loyalty.[33] Filial piety represented the 'cement of society' in a very fundamental way, and was based on assumptions about the ideal human relations among the so-called 'ancients'. However, in sharp contrast to such alleged sagehood, evidence from archaeology as well as from the analysis of oracle bones shows that the custom of killing the aged to prevent them from becoming burdens to society was widespread in ancient China. Thus, the exemplary filial piety of the past also was a constructed entity fabricated for upholding the social and moral order.[34] In this respect, we are dealing not only with the construction of culture, but with the construction of a particular form of social control which is part of that culture.

Tradition, as anthropologists and sociologists have repeatedly noted, is not static and unchanging: it is malleable, not infrequently developed for or adapted to the demands of a new situation by enterprising groups or persons. Craig Calhoun has argued that

The malleability of tradition . . . is wholly relative. It can nowhere be totally absent, or the practices and ideas of communities and societies would become brittle and fail to adapt to changing conditions. On the other hand, where tradition's real links with the past become almost totally lost, it is unlikely to be the source of any enduring consensus. Actual social practice and tradition are constantly interrelated and mutually determining, though the weight of determination may vary.[35]

When the norm is not allowed to fluctuate, or when a norm prescribed from above no longer has a basis in social practice, it turns into what I choose to call a 'super-social norm'. As we shall later see, the inflexibility of the super-social norm builds on the notion of an exemplary norm. This represents a real problem for the regime in its attempts to establish social standards during a period of reform. Instead of having an integrative and cohesive effect, the inflexible and 'super-social' norm becomes a challenge to order. The pragmatic use of tradition that we have seen during reform must have a real social basis to be successfuly implemented. As will be shown, a special form of 'traditional' structure might be helpful in promoting such a process. In China we might still talk of a certain 'segmentary' organization of society, to use the expression coined by Durkheim.[36]

Modern societies do not point towards a 'cultural monotone', but tradition still plays an important role. Chinese scholars point out that tradition is an adapting and changing phenomenon. 'Unceasing change and creativity keep tradition alive and meaningful . . . Tradition includes even what may emerge in the future', the historian Gan Yang claims, and criticizes those who consider tradition as synonymous with the past.[37] Modern societies are not past-oriented: rather than describing a mere future-oriented society, at least in the example of present-day China, they describe past *and* future-oriented societies.

One central characteristic of modern societies is their reflexivity, differentiating them from the backwards-looking societies of the past. Just as we have seen in the example of China, in European tradition it once was of primary importance to look back to the glorious past of antiquity. In China the Confucian classics and the ancient sage-kings represented the 'golden era'. Tradition in the modern era became a process of reflection, a phenomenon to be dissected and weighed, made use of or rejected. We see the same tendencies both in Europe and in China. The process towards a 'reflexive modernity' was succinctly summed up by the German humanist Wilhelm von Humboldt (1767–1835) as the creation of 'double persons'. Humboldt contrasts this modern doubleness with the ancients who 'merely were who they were'.[38] The same 'doubleness' is frequently described in contemporary Chinese accounts of the 'double personality' (*erchongxing de renge*), and the 'marginal person' (*bianji ren*) of modern society. This marginal person is a product of the transition from traditional to modern society, who, confronted by a 'double value system' (*shuangzhong jiazhi xitong*), lives with the contradiction between traditional emphasis on unity and social stability and the modern demands for pluralism and a changing society, the conflicts between a transmitted repetitive past and the modern demand for innovative thinking, experiencing the conflict between thrift and consumerism, ascetism and enjoyment, security and risk.[39] Discussing the concept of 'double personality', some claim that changes in the personality structure among Chinese are today found primarily in the surface structure. In the deeper layers of the personality, hardly anything has changed at all. Many Chinese on the surface can act very modern and progressive, while their real behaviour shows that they are still fundamentally traditional and conservative.[40] Their modernity is manifested mostly in matters of outward expressions of life-style—a liking for modern clothes, modern preferences of recreation, etc. The Chinese person is at his or her most traditional when it comes to concepts of moral values.[41] People have one foot in an unreflected past or habit, and one foot in a reflexive present. Anthony Giddens describes the process of full-fledged reflexivity in the following way:

To sanction a practice because it is traditional will not do; tradition can be justified, but only in the light of knowledge which is not itself authenticated by tradition . . . For justified tradition is tradition in sham clothing and receives its identity only from the reflexivity of the modern. The reflexivity of modern social life consists in the fact that social practices are constantly examined and reformed in the light of incoming information about those very practices, thus constitutively altering their character.[42]

In its modern context, tradition becomes malleable and reflexive in a qualitatively new sense, a far cry from the unswerving, unbreakable whole that dominated conceptions in Weberian traditional societies. It now becomes increasingly possible to choose parts of tradition to use for specific purposes: 'In the past tradition was a whole (*zhengti*), today we pick out moral parts of it that we want to develop further and insert organically into the new social whole.'[43] The Chinese official line about the right way to make use of tradition is summed up in the slogan: 'Throw away the dross, and adopt the essence' (*qi qi zaopo, qu qi jinghua*). Rather than describing the absolute division between tradition and modernity so often seen in Western modernization theories, the Chinese describe tradition and modernity as a 'continuum' (*lianxuti*).[44] Such continua are meant to describe not an evolutionary process where tradition is entirely replaced by modernity, but rather one with a mixture of traditional and modern within modernity. Of course the process of modernization also makes each member of society more uncertain about his or her own identity, making possible a reflexive process of self-identification that is potentially dangerous to the social order. This 'homelessness' of personal identity and the reflexivity of strategies to build new 'homes' represent a potential 'disharmony' that has to be mended in some way or other. For this purpose, the re-embedding effect of tradition is emphasized as a part of the modernization project itself.

Reflection about what is and what is not useful in tradition is not a random process. The construction of tradition in today's China is taking one particular direction. The most important aspect of tradition is said to be its binding and stabilizing elements. Harmony (*hexie*) and stability (*wending*) are seen as the core of traditional Chinese culture in such analyses. Harmony is 'the main value transmitted by Chinese culture to the future world culture'.[45] One article sums up the essence of the recent debate on the 'Confucian ethic' by claiming that 'All factors of Confucianism useful for the stability in family and society, and that can bring about a harmonious environment, can be further developed after getting rid of its feudal dross.'[46] As already pointed out, this pragmatic attitude towards tradition is no ideological revival of Confucianism. Instead, it should be seen in terms of its usefulness for upholding social stability. If tradition once used to be synonymous with the very order of things, it has today changed into a conscious means of preserving the social order. What we see in China today might be described as a 'directed' or 'guided' construction of tradition based on a conception of social stability and order. Predictability has become a key word in the Chinese quest for order. Identity, harmony, stability, and the predictability of behaviour—this is what the construction of 'tradition' is all about in China today. We might say that looking back for the sake of predictability is characteristic of a reflexive use of tradition.

By creating traditions, society builds up patterns of reference aimed at making social interaction predictable. A lack of predictability and tradition not only makes people feel insecure, with nothing to respect and nothing to oppose, but makes it difficult to define one's own position and historical identity. Neither reformers nor revolutionaries can afford to deny the past entirely.[47] In China such arguments have been taken particularly seriously. Tradition is today officially defined as an active part of the national culture which binds together past, present, and future. It represents the identity of the nation. No nation can ignore its 'national self' (*minzu ziwo*) during modernization, but must transform and rebuild precisely from this foundation.[48] In this perspective, tradition is a means to educate and civilize human nature in a period in which human life is in danger of being torn apart by the modern anomic conflict of too many ideals and too many ways of life.

Tradition is mainly about order and identity, but the construction of tradition and culture also involves a more direct economic argumentation of legitimacy. Party commentators say that, if traditions are comprehended and utilized in the right way, they can play a major part in reforming China's political and economic system.[49] The 'essence' of tradition is often presented in the language of a 'moral economy', and seen as a direct input to economic modernization. In a sociological survey carried out in 324 Chinese towns and cities in 1988, respondents were found to hold values like industriousness, thrift, and pragmatism in highest esteem; conservative belief and obedience came next. The researchers comment:

Certain traditional features can help the modernization effort. Industry, thrift and pragmatism can be used in full measure to accumulate and save capital at these early stages of industrialization. We have to encourage and promote these features.[50]

Paradoxically, tradition has become an active part of promoting modernization—not only by 'binding' people to norms, but also as a direct input in the economic sphere. In this respect, there is no contradiction between 'science' and 'tradition'. Both the 'scientific' approach to human and social improvement and the apparent resurgence of tradition must be seen in the same perspective of human and social change within boundaries. Both touch upon the theme of how to transform society while keeping social control.

Structures of Traditionalism and Neo-traditionalism

In China we find both construction and structures of tradition. Chinese tradition is not only embedded in the binding elements of norms and values, but is also inherent in a structure that in many ways appears 'traditional'. There is a resemblance between what Émile Durkheim called 'segmentary societies based upon clans'[51] and the way the Chinese scholar Lu Feng describes today's Chinese work-unit system as a society of 'clan character' (*jiazu xing*).[52] We may also note similarities between the restoration mechanisms of the patriarchal family and the clan described by Jin Guantao and discussed in the following section,[53] the 'familist' Chinese society described by the sociologist Fei Xiaotong,[54] and the society Durkheim termed 'politico-familial'.[55] First, let us look at the roots of the Chinese traditionalist social structure.

The 'familist' type of society undoubtedly goes back to the clan organization, much as in other traditional societies. As Durkheim did in his discussion of mechanichal solidarity, we have to go back to the trade guilds to find the roots of the structure. With the growing transfer of people from the villages into the towns and cities, the village community structure in many ways moved with them. We might say that the villages were moved into the cities. Kenneth G. Lieberthal reports from Tianjin:

A great many peasants who found work in the traditional sector of the economy had entered the city in the first place with the assistance of a fellow villager who had contacts in the city. Once in Tientsin (*Tianjin*), the peasant relied on personal connections, most likely another friend from his village or a relative, to land a job. Almost all of the enterprises in Tientsin's traditional sector required personal introductions before they hired new employees. The importance of personal introductions made the traditional t'ung-hsiang [*tongxiang*] (same locale) ties particularly important and in all probability reinforced these ties in the urban milieu.[56]

The system of recruitment to the trade guilds (*huiguan*) has been termed an 'ethnic division of labour'.[57] Around the turn of the century the guilds in Hangzhou were described in the following way:

Practically all the carpenters, wood-carvers, decorators, cabinetmakers, and medicine dealers are from Ningpo. The tea and cloth merchants, salt dealers and inn-keepers are from Anhwei. The porcelain dealers are from Kiangsi, the opium traders from Canton, and the wine-merchants from Shaohsing . . .[58]

Similar lists could be found for every city in China. A net of relations developed, starting from the principle of a common homeplace, or *tongxiang*. Today, spurred by the increased mobility of economic reforms, the pattern of *tongxiang* is again spontaneously re-emerging. People from different provinces have set up their own 'towns' in Beijing. The sections in the capital where outsiders now live are called Zhejiang, Henan, and Anhui villages. There is also a Xinjiang town. About 60 per cent of the clothes of medium and low quality produced in Beijing are produced in the Zhejiang village. People from Wenzhou have leased almost all the counters in the city's department stores, while people from Fujian province concentrate on selling timber. The Uygur enclave in Ganjiakou has specialized in setting up restaurants.[59] The basic principle for this organization can be found in *tong*, which means 'same', 'alike', 'in common'. *Tong* forms a principle of social organization that builds on common relations of various kinds. We find this character in many connections linking together people of common birthplace, family, work place, school, etc.—*tongxue* (fellow student), *tonghuo* (partner), *tongxing* (of the same surname), to mention only a few. The Chinese 'nets of relationships' (*guanxi wang*), often associated with nepotism and corruption, are frequently organized along such lines.[60] The most important of them all, seen from the socialist point of view, is of course *tongzhi*, or comrade: literally, 'common will'. This 'common will' forms one of the prerequisites for Ferdinand Tönnies's theory of community or *Gemeinschaft*. Tönnies claims that among kinsmen, neighbours, and friends no weighing of advantages is necessary.

They act under the impact of 'a common will (*gemeinsamer Willen*) or spirit which surrounds the individual like a living substance (*ein Lebenselement*)'.[61]

The paradox here is of course that the particularistic value of *tong*, also seen in the 'common will' of Tönnies's traditional community, forms the communist concept of 'comrade'. Instead of the traditional and particularistic value-system of *tong*, communism should, according to all textbooks on communist morality, be imbued with the universalistic spirit of *gong*—meaning 'public', 'collective', and also 'common'. This would clearly represent values closer to those that the communist 'comrade' should hold, and is also recommended as the ideal to teach in schools.[62] Instead, however, the associations we get from the Chinese 'comrade' lead us to the classical utopian societies described throughout Chinese history. Not only do we find the *tong* directly in the classical '*datong*' or 'Great Harmony', but a characteristic trait of Chinese conceptions of utopia in general seems to be the emphasis on community. We find it as the idea of the 'Great Community'; and, in contrast to Western utopias, which were often modelled as ideal city-states, both Confucian and Daoist utopias were always simple, rural communities.[63]

Fei Xiaotong, the grand old man of Chinese sociology, has described the cultural difficulties the Chinese have in relating to a common or public interest, a *gong*. According to Fei, China can be visualized as concentric circles (*tongxin yuan*) of family and social relationships spreading from a centre, which is oneself, to the surrounding society. In the traditional structure, each family takes its position at the centre, and draws a ring around itself. This ring is the 'neighbourhood'. But there is no fixed group, and the rings are better characterized as spheres (*fanwei*). Social relations resemble the ripples from a stone thrown into water. Spreading outward, the further out they go the more faint they become, says Fei, describing the phenomenon as the basic characteristic of Chinese social structure. Within this 'differentially ordered configuration' (*chaju geju*) it becomes difficult to distinguish between selfishness (*si*) and the common interest (*gong*).[64] Anything within the circle can be called *gong*. Chinese can sacrifice their family for themselves, their party for their family, their country for their party, and so on. The logic can be extended to more and more distant ripples.

What is common interest under such a formula is not easy to judge in any universal way. When sacrificing the party for the family, the family is defined as the common interest; when sacrificing the nation for one's small group, this is done for the public interest of the group. The *tong* and the *gong* continuously change position in such a system.

They become relative concepts, making it difficult for any universalistic norm to strike root. True common interest seems to be pushed somewhere into an exemplary utopia.

The term '*tongzhi*' takes us back to where we started this discussion. *Tongzhi* concerns the socialist promise of a development combining the memories and the securities of the past with the utopian dreams of a future society. Peter Berger has pointed out that socialism is a faith in renewed community, and that in its mythic form it has the capacity to combine modernizing and counter-modernizing traits.[65] This socialist myth absorbs central themes of modernity, among them the progress of history and the changeable character of man, as well as a utopian view of the socialist society as a renewed community pointing back to the memories of the past. Socialism also presents itself as a solution to the problem of *anomie*, as it 'promises to reintegrate the individual in all-embracing structures of solidarity'. And further, 'If modernization can be described as a spreading condition of homelessness, then socialism can be understood as the promise of a new home', Berger and his associates claim.[66]

It is precisely here that we should search for an answer to the paradox of the apparently particularistic meaning of 'comrade' and the tradition-like traits of Chinese social organization. The very social fabric in China builds on traditionalistic structures with a promise and the practice of community. However, Tönnies makes a distinction between community or *Gemeinschaft* as '*Herrschaft*' and '*Genossenschaft*'. By *Herrschaft* he means authoritarian domination; by *Genossenschaft*, egalitarian fellowship or comradeship. Both are possible sub-types of *Gemeinschaft*. *Herrschaft* operates as a communal kind of authoritarian domination as in vassalage, contrary to the contract defining a *Gesellschaft*. These are all forms of social relationships. *Genossenschaft* is, according to Tönnies, repressed in the factory system, but regains some of its power within the trade unions and the workers' movement. Even here, *Genossenschaft* is confronted by the powerful bureaucratic influence of a *Herrschaft*-like structure.[67] The Chinese work-unit (*danwei*) can be defined in the picture of *Herrschaft* and *Genossenschaft*.

A work-unit is the place where the entire urban population, with few exceptions, lives and experiences their everyday lives—a factory, a school, a hospital, a university, a government bureau, etc. The system is seldom found in the countryside, but entirely dominates the scene in the cities. The *danwei* is an organization under the leadership of the State and the Party. One Chinese scholar, Lu Feng, sees the entire Chinese society in the picture of *danwei*, and claims that the entire society has a 'work-unit character' (*danwei xingzhi*).[68] It represents the central nerve system of society, and can be described as a 'multifunc-tional' (*duozhong gongneng*), non-mobile unit with administrative, productive, social, and cultural tasks. It represents a society in itself controlling important goods and services like work, including the sys-tem of job security, education, housing, etc. It also provides the all-powerful household registration (*hukou*), defining place of residence, as well as a wide range of welfare services including pensions, medical services, holiday arrangements, kindergartens, shops, schools, cinemas, and the exercise of public security. Birth control and the allocation of birth certificates are handled by the *danwei*, and even funerals take place through the *danwei*. It is said that the work-unit is with a person *sheng-lao-bing-si*—in birth as in old age, in illness as in death. Even identity is linked to the work-unit; if you leave it you cannot move a single step. In Lu's words the *danwei* 'owns' you, and you simply 'belong to' your *danwei*.[69] The work-unit is a closed system, led by 'non-contract con-nections' (*fei qiyue guanxi*), a trait typical of traditional patterns of organ-ization. In this connection Lu also mentions the 'clan character' of the work-unit, describing the system as a paternalistic power structure based on approvals and 'letters of introduction' (*jieshao xin*) from work-unit cadres who control and allocate resources. In this system the indi-vidual becomes dependent on interpersonal relations. In this respect Lu emphasizes the importance of distinguishing between formal and informal power structures.[70]

While Lu talks about the thousands of years of bureaucratic rule, other analysts of the system have taken care to point out that the system is not a traditional one. The most influential analysis has been given by Andrew Walder, who terms the special type of authority represented by the work-unit system 'communist neo-traditionalism'. Without implying that one cannot talk of the impact of 'cultural traditions' in a meaning-ful way, Walder explicitly states: 'Communist neo-traditionalism is a modern type of industrial authority.' Still, he uses the term 'traditional' because it 'has come to be associated with dependence, deference, and particularism, and the term *modern* with independence, contract, and universalism'. He further points out that neo-traditionalism does not signify a social pattern that is not yet 'modern', and in my view cor-rectly points out that there is 'no implied universal scale of modernity'.[71]

The two principal aspects of the type of control manifested through 'neo-traditionalism' are 'organized dependence' and 'principled par-ticularism'. The first process describes the comprehensive and mono-polistic control of workers by work-unit cadres. Like Lu's argument of non-mobility of resources, the theory focuses on the non-market char-acter of the work-unit, in which labour is assumed to be immobile and all goods or services are provided through the work-unit under party leadership. The worker is, as Lu mentioned, dependent on his or her unit, and in this respect 'belongs' to the unit.

Principled particularism describes how the work-unit leadership exercises power through its control of goods and welfare services, building up networks of loyal 'activists' (*jiji fenzi*) who do the leaders' bidding in exchange for preferential treatment, thereby becoming a source of envy and dissent among the other workers. Organized dependence, in other words, describes the structural character of the work-unit, while principled particularism describes the type of rational behaviour that follows from that structure.[72]

These aspects describe how a system of authority and control is implemented within the work-unit. The system breeds personal rule, making it resemble the patriarchal systems of the past. Walder strongly refutes the criticism that he has described a system of total control.[73] His theory is formulated in opposition to any kind of theory that implies 'totalitarianism'. Nor is workers' dependence total. In a system of particularistic control, management can also become dependent on its workers. The point is, however, that 'Chinese firms have a wide variety of benefits that can be used as powerful tools in the exercise of authority.'[74]

This aspect of the work-unit as a tool of authority and control might also explain why it has 'survived' in such a 'tradition-like' manner. Walder's assertion that the system is a 'modern' form of authority is shared by his critics, such as Brantly Womack. The latter, however, seems to put more stress on mass welfare functions, in particular the aspect of job security, or 'work-unit socialism'. The work-unit community seems to operate midway between state and society, as control is both willed by and imposed on its members. On the question of whether this type of system is traditional or modern, however, Womack holds that:

work-unit community is not a traditional community. It is already part of a rational, future-oriented, differentiated, technological structure, and it has been effective in important modernization tasks. It is community within modernity, within a division of labour—a transfigured community.[75]

Walder emphasizes the tools of authority inherent in the system, and Lu the 'strong bureaucratic control' of the work-unit system, both describing it in the shape of a *Herrschaft*. Womack seems to emphasize more the work-unit traits of *Genossenschaft*.[76] I think that both considerations of control and comradeship once shaped the system, and that we still see elements of both. In many ways, the market reforms are about to weaken the authority structures of the work-unit. Seen from a strictly economic point of view, the system might even be an obstacle to reform, and political control through the work-unit is waning. After the Beijing massacre the units' 'struggle sessions' used to target the politically suspect no longer worked properly. Co-workers, often with the complicity of the work-unit's party leaders, offered protection to each other by insisting that nobody in the unit had taken part in the demonstrations.[77] The work-unit provides security and identification in a rapidly changing society. While very few feel any identification with the state apparatus, many Chinese still see their unit as a second home. Its patriarchal structure cannot be seen only as repression, but also as a willed and consented authority. The work-unit with its 'traditional' structure is a vital binding force in Chinese society, providing identity for its members.

Durkheim's description of the segmentary society in some ways resembles Lu Feng's description of the work-unit system. Lu described the system as 'a small society' in itself, while Durkheim described the segmentary organization as 'a small society within the larger one'. Durkheim, however, saw these structures in a strictly evolutionary manner, predicting 'the progressive disappearance of the segmentary organization'.[78] At the same time, Durkheim was preoccupied with the social control aspects of segmentary organizations, claiming that

this particular structure enables society to hold the individual more tightly in its grip, making him more strongly attached to his domestic environment, and consequently to tradition . . . [T]he disappearance of the segmentary type of society would be accompanied by a steady decline in morality. Man would no longer be held adequately under control. He would no longer feel around him and above him that salutary pressure of society that moderates his egoism, making him a moral creature.[79]

The strong side of the segmentary organization in terms of integration lies of course in the possibilities it provides for close surveillance. The presence of the 'social gaze' and the fact that every member is always 'seen' within such an organization Durkheim described in the following way: 'When everyone's attention is constantly fixed upon what everyone else is doing, the slightest deviation is remarked upon and immediately repressed.'[80] Durkheim linked the segmentary organization to the traditional form of mechanical solidarity, and held that, where the segmentary structure remained pronounced, there would be reproduced only societies of a 'very inferior type'. He also claimed that the segmentary organization increasingly loses its contours as societies develop.[81] He further held, however, that even traditional structures could persist over time, claiming that 'mechanical solidarity persists even in the highest societies'.[82] Raymond Aron notes that, according to Durkheim, 'in certain societies which have very advanced forms of economic division of labour, segmental structure may still persist in part'.[83] In this 'survival of segmental structure', as Aron calls it, we may also place the Chinese work-unit. I am not thereby suggesting that what we see are residues of the past. Instead it is the conscious calculation of the effect of certain structures of social control that has made these control patterns persist. In contrast to Durkheim, I think that these structures do not necessarily represent a gradually fading organizational structure. There is no blueprint or universal scale of modernity, and 'neo-traditionalism' might seem a 'reconstruction' of tradition representing a pattern of control not so easily eliminated by the 'invisible hand' of market socialism. At least thus far, the 'visible hand' called 'social stability' might be the stronger of the two. The 'segmentary' reality of today's China could also be a model for the control pattern of tomorrow.

The 'Ultrastability' of Chinese Culture

Jin Guantao's theory of 'ultrastability' (*chao wending*) could be seen as reflecting the ossifying, never-ending memory dominating a culture, but it also attacks the problem of the interrelationship between stability and change.[84] Jin's basic question was why Chinese feudalism had persisted for more than two thousand years with such remarkable stability. He turned to cybernetics (*kongzhi lun*), information theory (*xinxi lun*), and systems theory (*xitong lilun*) in his attempt to find an answer. In Chinese the term *kongzhi lun* for cybernetics directly translated means 'control theory'. This Chinese expression has been tempting for people preoccupied not only with the problems of explaining control, but also with maintaining control. In line with cybernetic reasoning, Jin claims that stability does not mean motionlessness. Far from being a static and motionless society, Chinese feudal society was repeatedly shaken by social upheavals; violent and apparently successful rebellions repeatedly made old dynasties collapse and new ones appear.

The typical historical scenario described by Jin Guantao is that, after a period of rest, the bureaucratic apparatus is gradually blown up. Corruption, disintegration, and finally great chaos set in, leading to rebellion and total collapse. A new emperor then ascends the throne, and the crisis is met by a reform. The bureaucracy is simplified, and a restoration of the authority of the dynasty takes place. The peasant uprisings get rid of bureaucracy's power-mongering in the end, but then start to restore the same structure, trying to build the new with the old. Thus, the periodic change and upheaval in this system paradoxically contributed to the perpetuation of the old order.[85]

A remarkable stability based on internal resilience and the capacity for continuous readjustment characterized this society. Mechanisms of internal adjustment restored stability in times of upheaval. A great unity (*da yitong*) characterized the Chinese feudal system, which Jin describes as 'ultrastable'. This 'ultrastable structure' could be said to consist of three major parts, represented by political, economic, and cultural relationships. A system of control described as 'supra-economic coercive control' (*chao jingji de qiang kongzhi*) dominated all walks of life. The 'centre of control' (*kongzhi zhongshu*) was the mechanism of feudal centralized power, the feudal court state apparatus. On another level, the patriarchal clan functioned as a mediator between the state and the individual, perfecting the control. When things went wrong, the second regulatory mechanism came into play—the periodic oscillations of major peasant rebellions. In Jin's theory, instead of representing a challenge against the system as such, these peasant rebellions effected a regulation by 'violent control' ('*qiang kongzhi*' *tiaojie*).

How does Chinese society always manage to return to its original shape after collapse? *Yitihua*—'unification'—is the core of the system, says Jin. Everything is similar, and functions according to the same principles. As long as society—or the 'system' (*xitong*)—is stable, the information input (*xinxi luzhi*) from the structure of this system can be transmitted down to the sub-systems or 'same structure systems' (*tonggou xitong*). If the system collapses, a process of restoration takes place through the so-called 'restoration mechanisms' (*xiufu jizhi*). The traditional state is anticipated by the patriarchal family and the clan, and builds on the feudal family system.[86]

In the case of such a collapse, information about the system is still contained in its sub-systems. Thus, the sub-system can re-establish the state system after its collapse. In the feudal state this process of 'collapse-restoration' (*bengkui-xiufu*) occurred at repeated intervals. The state was crushed in the rebellion, while the clan and the patriarchal family were in principle left unharmed. Those who built up the new dynasties usually came from patriarchal rich families closely connected to the old system. Even among peasants, the 'information' from the state system was incredibly strong. The peasants were themselves imbued with 'imperial authoritarianism' or 'emperorism' (*huangquan zhuyi*) when they rebelled, and thus they too contributed to the re-establishment of the previous system.

According to Jin's calculations, major uprisings have occurred at intervals of about 200–300 years in China. However, it has taken only about ten to thirty years after an uprising to consolidate a new restoration.[87] Edward Shils warns against looking at traditional societies as unchanging societies, but his description of families and clans having their own recuperative power points in the same direction as does Jin's theory: 'The family manifests a greater resiliency and recuperative power than corporate bodies which are not centered on primordial qualities.'[88]

Before major breakdowns there is also considerably more influence from other cultures. In such periods the inner forces of the system are too weak to fend off these outside influences. Here the digesting (*xiaohua*) and assimilating (*tonghua*) tendencies or abilities of the Chinese cultural system are used to explain how, despite such strong influences, Chinese society was able to maintain an uninterrupted culture for so long: these mechanisms simply assimilated influences from abroad and sinified them. The Mongols of the Yuan dynasty (1271–1368) as well as the Manchus of the Qing (1644–1911) are examples of such processes.[89] Jin's underlying issue is to show that Chinese society has been highly resistant to change, even to the point of assimilating the change brought about by regimes that conquered the country.

Jin's theory can easily be seen not only as an explanation of Chinese feudalism, but also as a comment on China's contemporary problems. The points made by Jin on the blown-up and corrupt bureaucracy, the general inertia of Chinese culture, and the authoritarian systems of control could be interpreted as a direct criticism of the present regime and its monopoly of control. The government was quick to sense this, and refuted the theory altogether. The Party regards Jin's theory as 'typical historical idealism'.[90] An ultrastable, unchanging state has never existed, it claims. But Jin's point is that ultrastability does not necessarily mean unchangeability. Society is more than mathematics, and Jin's work is rightfully attacked for its scientistic bias. The restorative aspect of peasant uprisings and peasant wars suggested by Jin is also a central point of the attack against the theory. In the official Marxist interpretation it was precisely such uprisings that had promoted the development of Chinese society, rather than causing feudal society to fall into an historical cycle of constant return.

Parts of this critique seem sound. It might appear that Jin has at times become too preoccupied and locked into his own theory, trying to force too much into his explanations. Jin's theory also seems too closed and claustrophobic.[91] It is probably too weak to account for the historical realities it is meant to describe. On the other hand, one does not have to buy the whole theory to see some very distinct values in it. Jin describes very well certain traits of a social control system that I will discuss in detail later. In particular, I would emphasize the importance of the restoration element (*xiufu*) in his theory. This is a useful concept which describes basic patterns of how the Chinese control system functions. Its usefulness probably also goes much further than just describing this particular system. The *fu* in *xiufu* corresponds to the prefix re- in restoration. In Chinese, *fu* is a character meaning 'to turn around', 'to turn over', 'to recover'. It appears not only in the word for restoration, but also in words like repetition (*fuxi*) and rehabilitation (*fanfu*). These are aspects central to social cohesion. I will try to show that repetition and rehabilitation are basic elements in a control system that is far more than merely a description of the historical restoration of imperial dynasties. The word itself is a picture symbolizing important processes of control. It belongs to the microeconomy of control, and gives us insight into the processes that hold societies together. *Fu* as it is used in the present work might be seen as a principle of cohesion.

The model of ultrastability can be seen as a theory where culture operates like a black hole, sapping all the energy out of any and every force of change. There might be rebellions, there might be conquering states ruling the country: but everything ends up the same, turning the forces of change into restoration. It is obviously wrong, however, to assume that the China of Confucius and the China under Deng are one and the same. Rather than assuming a non-changing society, Jin's system can be interpreted as a theory explaining change within stable systems, a theme central to the dilemma of the reform policy itself. Cadres on all levels are grappling with the problems of creating change within controlled boundaries, and they are preoccupied with the task of creating growth while maintaining social order. Elements of the past return as controlling elements in society with a regularity as certain as that of the cat that always lands on its feet. In Jin's theory we can see Chinese culture not only transmitted through a binding 'segmentary' structure, but as a self-perpetuating system of order in itself. We do not have to incorporate this fully into the picture of cultural determinism. Instead, I suggest that the elements of culturally constructed order are products of a planned and conscious policy in today's China. Tradition is re-emerging as a mechanism of social control, not as a repetition of history. Obviously there is repetition, but this is 'repetition with a change'.[92] Old forms of control come back, but in a modernized and redeployed form, augmented and refined in order to 'bind', 'hold', or 'stabilize' a potentially disorderly population. Jin's concepts are suggestive of general Chinese thought-patterns, like those of creation within imitation, and balance within imbalance.

Balance and the 'Unstable Equilibrium'

The problem of combining the change of economic growth with the stability of social order was widely discussed in China during the reforms. Yuan Huayin and Pang Shuqi identify the aim of reform as a search for a 'rational social equilibrium' (*heli de shehui pingheng*).[93] To achieve this aim, it is necessary to get rid of the former non-rational equilibrium. The problems of reform can be seen as a result of a society in conflict between a rational and a non-rational balance. There are two kinds of social equilibrium: static and dynamic, normal and abnormal. The first type is passive, the second active; the first stable, the second unstable. The society of stable equilibrium as described here possesses some of the same characteristics as that described by Jin Guantao. Jin's concept of 'ultrastability' is also used by Yuan and Pang, who talk about an 'ultrastable equilibrium' (*chao wending de pingheng*). The reforms are still struggling with a passive, abnormal, and ultrastable equilibrium. It represents a development spiral starting with non-equilibrium, and developing into equilibrium; then it consolidates and rests in a high degree of equilibrium (*bu pingheng – pingheng – gaoji pingheng*). Making class struggle the key link simply makes society unstable (*bu pingheng*), and has nothing to do with attempts to achieve change within controlled boundaries. The Cultural Revolution was a disaster in which the state system itself was destroyed. A similar loss of control and a loss of equilibrium might also be the results of reform, unless strict measures can be taken against such developments. The state must uphold social control during reforms, the reforms must not destroy the state system, and destabilizing elements must not be allowed to get the upper hand, argue Yuan and Pang.

There do exist such dangers of destabilization, however. In the stage of lost equilibrium (*shiheng*) between tradition and modernity brought about by the reforms, some individuals are not able to adapt, while others go from one extreme to the other. On the one hand, a feeling of alienation (*geshigan*) spreads. Others seek even faster change. These attitudes are equally harmful to reform. Both the outer control by the state and the inner control of the people have been weakened. Lost equilibrium and lost control are experiences characteristic of the reforms. But the lost equilibrium is not necessarily only a bad thing. Negating non-balance altogether means negating changes and progress. By some a moderate loss of balance can be accepted, but one should guard against the loss of control: 'The loss of balanced behavioural patterns and relations are often the step before control is lost . . . we have to establish systems to maintain control', Yuan and Pang maintain.[94] As we shall later see, such systems of control have been established on many levels.

Some hold that law, discipline, and the disciplinary power of morality should actively be used to maintain control: 'The socialist system of control is an active control system, it brings about change.'[95] This transformative, improving character of control is seen by Anthony Giddens as a sign of modernity itself:

The idea of secular correction emerged only gradually and should be understood as part of broader processes whereby the social and natural worlds came to be seen as transformable rather than merely given. 'Social control', therefore, was not primarily a means of controlling pre-existing forms of 'deviant' behaviour. 'Deviance' was in fact largely created by the imperatives brought about by the transmutation of naturally given conditions into manageable ones.[96]

The point about the creation of deviance is correct, but the assumption about correction being a modern way of thinking does not seem to fit the Chinese example. Giddens in this case seems to rely too strongly on the European example described by Foucault.[97] Improving and corrective practices have been employed in China for centuries. As early as the Zhou dynasty (1100–221 BC), correction through labour was explicitly mentioned as a method for reforming prisoners.[98] The close relationship between social order and human rectification was also a basic idea of Confucianism. The classical values of 'self-cultivation, family regulation, ordering of the state, and bringing tranquility and order under heaven' (*xiu shen, qi jia, zhi guo, ping tian xia*) have dominated Chinese culture for centuries. This has served as a founding principle for creating the ideal personality and the ideal society for ages, and it still finds resonance in the theories of social engineering to which I will later return. The principle originates in a famous passage in the Confucian classic 'Great Learning' (*Daxue*):

The ancients who wanted to illustrate illustrious virtue throughout the kingdom first ordered well their own states. Wishing to order well their states, they first regulated their families. Wishing to regulate their families, they first cultivated their persons. Wishing to cultivate their persons, they first rectified their hearts. Wishing to rectify their hearts, they first sought to be sincere in their thoughts . . . From the Son of Heaven down to the mass of people, all must consider the cultivation of the person the root of *everything besides*.[99]

The first line of the Chinese text about how the ancients 'illustrate illustrious virtue' (*ming ming de*) is a crucial point for the discussion on how exemplary virtue is displayed or in fact paraded. The principle constitutes a founding pillar of the present Chinese version of what I call 'exemplary society'. As I have already indicated, Chinese historical writing served a distinctly moral purpose, aiming at the creation of exemplary morality. The social world was also seen as potentially transformable, not merely a given. This tradition-based interest in improvement or transformation, however, was oriented towards an assumed ideal past.[100] Though the orientation went back in time, the concern was with present control through human correction and improvement. Whether the orientation is towards the mythical past of 'Great Harmony', or towards the the the equally mythical and technocratic future of the modern state, balance and social order remain at the core of the argument.[101] The control described in the following chapters is that of the modern state, although it is based on memories of the past.

Notes to Chapter 1

1. See e.g. Clifford Geertz, *The Interpretation of Cultures*, New York, Basic Books, 1973; Clifford Geertz, *Negara: The Theatre-State in Ninteenth-Century Bali*, Princeton, Princeton University Press, 1980; Marshall Sahlins, *Culture and Practical Reason*, Chicago, Chicago University Press, 1976.
2. I have borrowed the phrase from Ernest Gellner, *Culture, Identity, and Politics*, Cambridge, Cambridge University Press, 1987, p. 16.
3. *Renmin ribao (haiwai ban)*, 9 April 1993, p. 1.
4. On Jiang Zemin attending the celebrations of Confucius's birthday, see *Renmin ribao (haiwai ban)*, 9 October 1989, p. 1. On the construction of a new grave for Yandi, see *Renmin ribao*, 10 March 1993, p. 1.
5. *China Daily*, 1 May 1993, p. 5.
6. Liu Guojie, 'Lun kexue zhishu, wuzhi shenghua yu daode de guanxi' (The relationship of scientific technology and material life to morality), *Zhexue yanjiu* (Philosophical research), No. 6, 1980, pp. 12–18; trans. in *Chinese Studies in Philosophy*, Vol. 13, No. 1, 1981, pp. 3–21.
7. In Legge's translation of Mencius's text, 'constant mind' (*hengxin*) is replaced with 'fixed heart': 'The way of the people is this. If they have a certain livelihood, they have a fixed heart. If they have not a certain livelihood, they have not a fixed heart.' See 'The Works of Mencius', bk III, pt I, ch. 3, in *The Four Books (Sishu)* (in Chinese and English), trans. James Legge, Taipei, Culture Book Co./Wenhua tushu gongsi, 1983, p. 611. On Xunzi, see Donald J. Munro, *The Concept of Man in Early China*, Stanford, Calif., Stanford University Press, 1969, pp. 89–90.
8. Zhang Xiaolin, 'Zhangxue bawo jingshen wenming yu shangpin jingji de jiu ge lilun wenti' (Several theoretical questiuons on correctly grasping the relationship between spiritual civilization and commodity economy), *Qiushi*, No. 9, 1990, pp. 38–43.
9. Lu Jian, 'Crime: a dilemma in the course of modernization', *Shehui*, No. 78, July 1991, pp. 44–6; also in *Joint Publication Research Service Report* (hereafter *JPRS Report*) *JPRS-CAR-91-061*, 4 November 1991, pp. 37–9.
10. Ibid., p. 44 (37).
11. Ibid.

12. Ibid.

13. Zhang Xiaolin, p. 43.

14. Ibid., p. 42.

15. Simonetta Tabboni, 'A configurational approach to the study of traditional behavior', *Research of Social Movements, Conflicts and Change*, Vol. 10, 1988, pp. 225–33.

16. In China there is also a process of 'real' restoration of tradition, for example in the increasing power of clans in the countryside. Traditional ways of organization have re-emerged as the collective organizational structure represented by the communes was dismantled following economic reform. I will here, however, focus on the 'reconstruction' of tradition promoted by the regime as a part of its scheme to reform society on the basis of upholding 'unity and stability'. For an account of the re-emergence of clans, see Qian Hang and Xie Weiyang, '"Zongzu wenti": Dangdai Zhongguo nongcun yanjiu de yige shijiao' (The question of clans: a view from today's Chinese rural studies), *Shehui kexue*, No. 5, 1990, pp. 21–4, 28.

17. Rosalind Feuerabend and Ivo Feuerabend, 'Aggressive behaviour within politics, 1948–1962: a cross-national study', *Journal of Conflict Resolution*, No. 10, 1966, pp. 249–71.

18. Edward Shils, 'Tradition', *Comparative Studies in Society and History*, Vol. 13, No. 2, April 1971, p. 145.

19. Anthony Giddens, *The Consequences of Modernity*, Stanford, Stanford University Press, 1990, p. 178.

20. For such an interpretation of Giddens, see Ulrich Beck, 'How modern is modern society?' *Theory, Culture & Society*, Vol. 9, 1992, pp. 163–9.

21. See Anthony Giddens, 'Commentary on the reviews', *Theory, Culture & Society*, Vol. 9, 1992, p. 174.

22. For a presentation and discussion of these theories, see Peter L. Berger and Hsin-Huang Michael Hsiao (eds.), *In Search of an East Asian Development Model*, New Brunswick, NJ/Oxford, Transaction Books, 1988.

23. Peter L. Berger, 'An East Asian Development Model?' in Peter L. Berger and Hsin-Huang Michael Hsiao (eds.), p. 7.

24. Beng-Huat Chua, '"Konfuzianisierung" in der Modernisierung Singapurs', in Joachim Matthes (ed.), 'Zwischen den Kulturen?' *Soziale Welt*, Vol. 8, Göttingen, Verlag Otto Schwartz, 1992, pp. 249–69.

25. 'Das alltäglich Gewohnte als unverbrüchliche Norm für das Handeln' (Max Weber, *Gesammelte Aufsätze zur Religionssoziologie*, Vol. 1, Tübingen, J. C. B. Mohr (Paul Siebeck), 1986, p. 269; first published in 1922).

26. See Weber's discussion of 'traditional authority' in Max Weber, *The Theory of Social and Economic Organization*, New York, Free Press, 1964.

27. The 'four books' were *Daxue* (The Great Learning), *Zhongyong* (The Doctrine of the Mean), *Lunyu* (The Confucian Analects), and *Mengzi* (The Works of Mencius). The 'five classics' were *Yijing* (The Book of Changes), *Shijing* (The Book of Poetry), *Shujing* (The Book of History), *Liji* (The Book of Rites), and *Chunqiu* (The Spring and Autumn Annals).

28. Jon Elster has suggested a distinction between 'tradition' and 'traditionalism': 'Tradition I understand as mindlessly repeating or imitating today what one's ancestors did yesteryear . . . Traditions are subject to drift, by the cumulative result of many imperfect imitations . . . By contrast, traditionalism—the deliberate imitation of some original model—is not subject to drift' (Jon Elster, *The Cement of Society: A Study of Social Order*, Cambridge, Cambridge University Press, 1989,

p. 104). While Elster is right in pointing out a difference between these two processes, he underestimates the 'drift' of the traditionalist model. Even 'traditionalism' is open to change through constant reinterpretations of what characteristics constitute the 'original model'.

29. Joseph Needham, *Science in Traditional China: A Comparative Perspective*, Hong Kong, Hong Kong University Press, 1981, p. 131.

30. See Niklas Luhmann, 'Sinn als Grundbegriff der Soziologie', in Jürgen Habermas and Niklas Luhmann, *Theorie der Gesellschaft oder Sozialtechnologie: Was leistet die Systemforschung?* Frankfurt am Main, Suhrkamp, 1971, pp. 57 ff. Luhmann talks about a '*Zwang der Tradition*'.

31. Charles Perrault, *Parallèle des anciens et des modernes en ce qui regarde les arts et les sciences*, ed. Hans Robert Jauss, Munich, Eidos Verlag, 1964, p. 113; first published in 1688–97.

32. *China Critic*, Vol. 3, No. 4; quoted from Chen Jingpan, *Confucius as a Teacher*, Beijing, Foreign Languages Press, 1990 (original Univ. of Toronto Ph.D. thesis 1940), p. 278.

33. Cheng Zhongying, 'Lun rujia xiao de lunli jiqi xiandaihua: zeren, quanli, yü dexing' (On the Confucian ethic of filial piety and its modernization: responsibility, authority and virtue), *Hanxue yanjiu*, Vol. 4, No. 1, 1985, pp. 83–106.

34. That beating to death was a means of 'spirit release' is suggested by the oracle bone graph (inscriptions of the first Chinese characters inscribed on tortoise shells for divinitory purposes)(𣏚) (in modern Chinese, *wei* (微), which consists of a hand holding a cudgel in close proximity to the depiction of a person with long hair, connoting old age). See James C. H. Hsü, 'Unwanted children and parents: archaeology, epigraphy, and the myths of filial piety', in Julia Chang and R. W. L. Guisso (eds.), *Sages and Filial Sons: Mythology and Archaeology in Ancient China*, Hong Kong, Chinese University Press, 1991, p. 27.

35. Craig Calhoun, *The Question of Class Struggle: Social Foundations of Popular Radicalism during the Industrial Revolution*, Chicago, University of Chicago Press, 1982, p. 156.

36. Émile Durkheim, *The Division of Labour in Society*, trans. W. D. Halls and with an introduction by Lewis Coser, London, Macmillan, 1984.

37. Gan Yang, 'Chuantong, shijianxing yu weilai' (Tradition, temporality and future), *Dushu*, No. 2, 1986, pp. 3–10.

38. 'Sie waren bloß, was sie waren. Wir wissen noch, was wir sind, und blicken darüber hinaus. Wir haben durch Reflexion einen doppelten Menschen aus uns gemacht' (Wilhelm von Humboldt, *Ansichten über Ästhetik und Literatur: Seine Briefe an Christian Gottfried Körner*, ed. Fritz Jonas, Berlin, 1880 (letter from 30 April 1803); quoted from Hans Ulrich Gumbrecht, 'Modern, modernität, moderne', in Otto Brunner, Werner Conze, and Reinhart Koselleck (eds.), *Gesellschaftliche Grundbegriffe*, Vol. 4, Stuttgart, Klett-Cotta, 1978, p. 106.

39. Wei Lei, *Zhongguo ren de renge: cong chuantong dao xiandai* (The personality of the Chinese: from traditional to modern), Guiyang, Guizhou renmin chubanshe, 1988, p. 184; Qiao Lin, 'Gaige kaifang yu shehui xinli' (Opening, reform, and the social psychology), *Shehui*, No. 3, 1988, p. 11; Ye Nanke and Tang Zhongxun, 'Lun xiandai renge zhuanxing' (On the changing character of Chinese personality), *Shanghai shehui kexueyuan xueshu jikan*, No. 1, 1990. p. 128; also in *Fuyin baokan ziliao*, C4 *Shehuixue*, No. 3, 1990, p. 33.

40. Bai Yuntao, *Dangdai Zhongguo qingnian suzhi lun* (Discussions on the quality of contemporary Chinese youth), Shenyang, Liaoning renmin chubanshe, 1987, p. 113.

41. Wei Lei, p. 183.
42. Anthony Giddens, p. 38.
43. Zhang Mingyuan, *Zhongguoren de rensheng quxian* (The lifeline of the Chinese), Beijing, Zhongguo renmin daxue chubanshe, 1989, p. 153.
44. Professor Luo Rongqu suggests this concept in *Renmin ribao*, 26 February 1989, p. 6.
45. Feng Zusheng and Lin Yingnan, *Kaifang yu fengbi: Zhongguo chuantong shehui jiazhi quxiang ji qi dangqian liubian* (Openness and closedness: the value orientation in traditional Chinese society and its present change), Shijiazhuang, Hebei renmin chubanshe, 1987, pp. 90–1.
46. Li Jinquan, 'Zhengque dudai chuantong wenhua daode yichan he jianshe shehui zhuyi jingshen wenming de guanxi' (The relation between correctly handling the moral heritage of traditional culture and the construction of socialist spiritual civilization), *Zhongshan daxue xuebao (Zhexue shehui kexue ban)*, No. 1, 1990, p. 36.
47. Simonetta Tabboni, p. 228.
48. Chen Chuancai, 'Zhongguo minzu wenhua de tezhi yu biange' (The characteristics and change of Chinese national culture), in Zhang Liwen *et al.* (eds.), *Chuantong wenhua yu xiandaihua* (Traditional culture and modernization), Beijing, Zhongguo renmin daxue chubanshe, 1987, p. 56.
49. Wang Xingguo, 'Tantan chuantong yu gaige' (Discussing tradition and reform), *Hongqi*, No. 12, 1987, pp. 28, 30.
50. *Zhongguo wenhua bao*, 6 and 16 September 1987, trans. in *Beijing Review*, No. 5, 2 February 1988, p. 25.
51. Émile Durkheim, *The Division of Labour in Society*, p. 127.
52. Lu Feng, 'Danwei: Yizhong teshu de shehui zuzhi xingshi' (The work-unit: a specific form of social organization), *Zhongguo shehui kexue*, No. 1, 1989, p. 79.
53. Jin Guantao, *Zai lishi de biaoxiang beihou: dui Zhongguo fengjian shehui zhao wending jiegou de tansuo* (Behind the phenomenon of history: a discussion of the ultrastable structure of the Chinese feudal society), Chengdu, Sichuan renmin chubanshe, 1983.
54. Fei Xiaotong (Fei Hsiao-tung), 'An interpretation of Chinese social structure and its changes (1946)', in Fei Hsiao-tung, *Chinese Village Close-up*, Beijing, New World Press, 1983, p. 127. On Chinese familism, see also Lin Yueh-Hwa (Lin Yaohua), *The Golden Wing: A Sociological Study of Chinese Familism*, London, Kegan Paul, Trench, Trubner, 1948.
55. Émile Durkheim, *The Division of Labour in Society*, p. 128.
56. Kenneth G. Lieberthal, *Revolution and Tradition in Tientsin, 1949–1952*, Stanford, Calif., Stanford University Press, 1980, p. 13.
57. G. William Skinner, 'Introduction: urban social structure in Ch'ing China', in G. William Skinner, *The City in Late Imperial China*, Stanford, Calif., Stanford University Press, 1977, p. 544.
58. Frederick D. Cloud, *Hangchow: The 'City of Heaven'*, Shanghai, Presbyearian Mission Press, 1906, p. 9; quoted from G. William Skinner, p. 538.
59. Wang Chunguang, a sociologist at the Chinese Academy of Social Sciences in Beijing, has studied the new local communities inside Beijing. See two articles by Cai Hong in *China Daily*, 2 July 1993, p. 4, and 3 July 1993, p. 4, for further details on the re-emergence of the *tongxiang* principle.
60. For a discussion of the *guanxi* concept, see J. Bruce Jacobs, 'The concept of *guanxi* and the local politics in a rural Chinese setting', in Sidney L. Greenblatt *et al.* (eds.), *Social Interaction in Chinese Society*, New York, Praeger, 1982, pp. 209–37;

J. Bruce Jacobs, *Local Politics in a Rural Chinese Cultural Setting: A Field Study of Mazu Township, Taiwan*, Canberra, Contemporary China Papers, Australian National University, 1980.

61. 'Unter den sozialen Bedingungen ist aber keine bedeutender als die objektivierte Gestalt des vorhandenen, beharrenden, gemeinsamen Willens oder Geistes, der das Individuum wie ein Lebenselement umgibt und durch Sinne wie Verstand in unzähligen Eindrücken sich ihm mitteilt' (Ferdinand Tönnies, *Soziologische Studien und Kritiken, Dritte Sammlung*, Jena, Verlag von Gustav Fischer, 1929, p. 195).

62. Chinese schools stress the benefits of having a universalistic public morality in general. The positive value of impartiality (*gongzheng*) is also opposed to that of favouritism (*piansi*) in the schools. See *Zhongxue zhengzhike shouce*, 'qingshaonian xiuyang' bufen (Political class manual for middle schools, 'youth self-cultivation' section), Beijing, Shifan daxue chubanshe, 1984, p. 3.

63. Hsü Cho-yün, 'Comparisons of idealized societies in Chinese history', in Julia Chang and R. W. L. Guisso (eds.), *Sages and Filial Sons: Mythology and Archaeology in Ancient China*, Hong Kong, Chinese University Press, 1991, pp. 43–63.

64. Fei Xiaotong, *Xiangtu Zhongguo–Xiantu chongjian–Chongfang jiangcun* (Rural China–Rebuilding the countryside–Revisiting a village by Changjiang), Hong Kong, Wenxue chubanshe, 1948 (facsimile of the Shanghi edition from 1947), pp. 22–30 (particularly pp. 25, 29). Excerpts have been translated as 'Chinese social structure and its values' in J. Mason Gentzler (ed.), *Changing China: Readings in the History of China from the Opium War to the Present*, New York, Praeger, 1977, pp. 210–14. For translation see Fei Xiaotong, *From the Soil*, Berkeley, University of California Press, 1992.

65. See Peter L. Berger, *Facing up to Modernity*, New York, Basic Books, 1977.

66. Peter L. Berger, Brigitte Berger, and Hansfried Kellner, *The Homeless Mind*, Harmondsworth, Penguin Books, 1973, p. 124.

67. The concepts are discussed in more detail under 'social relationships' in Ferdinand Tönnies, *Einführung in die Soziologie*, Vol. 2, Stuttgart, Ferdinand Enke, 1931, pp. 34–73.

68. Lu Feng, p. 71.

69. Ibid., p. 72.

70. Ibid., pp. 76–7, 79–80.

71. Andrew Walder, *Communist Neo-Traditionalism: Work and Authority in Chinese Industry*, Berkeley, University of California Press, 1986, p. 10.

72. Ibid., particularly chs. 1 and 4.

73. See the critique by Brantly Womack, 'Review essay. Transfigured community: neo-traditionalism and work-unit socialism in China', *China Quarterly*, No. 126, 1991, pp. 313–32; and Andrew G. Walder, 'A reply to Womack', *China Quarterly*, No. 126, 1991, pp. 333–9.

74. Andrew G. Walder, 'A reply to Womack', p. 333. See also Andrew Walder, *Communist Neo-Traditionalism*, p. 2, and Andrew Walder, 'Factory and manager in an era of reform', *China Quarterly*, No. 118, 1989, p. 252. Lu Feng's analysis also accepts that leaders have a limited power, and that they are dependent in some respects on their workers (see Lu Feng, p. 79).

75. Brantly Womack, p. 330.

76. Womack does mention Tönnies in his article. Unfortunately, Womack's conception of Tönnies does not go further than the common misunderstanding that his theory represented a 'nostalgic' and 'romantic pessimism' (Brantly Womack, p. 330).

77. Jon Unger, 'Internal change in China: commentary', in Stuart Harris and James Cotton (eds.), *The End of the Cold War in Northeast Asia*, Melbourne, Longman Cheshire, 1991, pp. 72–3.
78. Lu Feng, p. 77; Émile Durkheim, *The Division of Labour in Society*, p. 168.
79. Émile Durkheim, *The Division of Labour in Society*, pp. 242, 333.
80. Ibid., p. 239.
81. Ibid., pp. 204, 136.
82. Ibid., p. 135.
83. Raymond Aron, *Main Currents in Sociological Thought*, Vol. 2, *Durkheim; Pareto; Weber*, Harmondsworth, Penguin, 1968, p. 22.
84. See Jin Guantao, *Zai lishi de biaoxiang beihou*.
85. Ibid., pp. 34–83.
86. Ibid., pp. 115–17.
87. Ibid., pp. 93, 105.
88. Edward Shils, p. 158.
89. Ibid., pp. 182–6.
90. Liu Xiuming, 'Ping Jin Guantau de "chao wending jiegou" shiguan' (Evaluating Jin Guantao's 'ultrastable structure' view of history), *Qiushi*, No. 11, 1990, p. 13.
91. I think much can be gained towards understanding the weaknesses of Jin's theory by looking at the position of Jin Guantao himself. His theory must be understood from the situation in which it was created. As Alvin Gouldner pointed out that Talcott Parsons's theory emerged in the USA as a conservative's reaction to social unrest during the Great Depression of the late 1930s (see Alvin Gouldner, *The Coming Crisis of Western Sociology*, London, Heinemann, 1970, p. 169), we must also understand Jin's theory as it appears during the reform era in China. It reflects the pessimism of a marginalized and sceptical intellectual attacking an ossified system of bureaucratic socialism. The theory about the restorative impact of peasant uprisings can also be interpreted as an intellectual's alienation from his potential allies in an attack against the system, the peasants, workers, and the more populist part of resistance. Such alienation became evident during the 'Beijing spring' of 1989 for all those who wanted to see—although some refused to.
92. The expression is suggested by Dutton in his explanation of the re-emerging and seemingly traditional patterns of social surveillance in China (Michael R. Dutton, *Policing and Punishment in China: From Patriarchy to 'the People'*, Cambridge, Cambridge University Press, 1992.
93. Yuan Huayin and Pang Shuqi, 'Tantan tizhi gaige yu shehui pingheng wenti' (On the problem of system reform and social equilibrium), *Shehuixue yanjiu*, No. 5, 1987, pp. 76–9; also in *C4 Shehuixue, Fuyin baokan ziliao*, No. 5, 1987, pp. 87–91.
94. Ibid., p. 90.
95. Wang Ge, 'Gaige yu shehui kongzhi' (Reform and social control), *Shehui kexue*, No. 9, 1987, pp. 34–8; also in *C4 Shehuixue, Fuyin baokan ziliao*, No. 5, 1987, p. 95.
96. Anthony Giddens, *Modernity and Self-Identity: Self and Society in the Late Modern Age*, Cambridge, Polity Press, 1991, pp. 157–8.
97. See Michel Foucault, *Discipline and Punish*, New York, Vintage Books, 1979.
98. See Michael R. Dutton, p. 106.
99. The rest of the quotation goes: 'Wishing to be sincere in their thoughts, they first extended to the utmost their knowledge. Such extension of knowledge lay in the investigation of things. Things being investigated, knowledge became complete. Their knowledge being complete, their thoughts were sincere. Their thoughts being

sincere, their hearts were then rectified. Their hearts being rectified, their persons were cultivated. Their persons being cultivated, their families were regulated. Their families being regulated, their states were rightly governed. Their states being rightly governed, the whole kingdom was made tranquil and happy' (*Daxue*, The Great Learning, 4–6, in James Legge (trans.), *The Four Books (Sishu)*, pp. 4–7).

100. Joseph Needham, pp. 129–30.
101. The value of *he*, or harmony, was emphatically stressed at the family level. Indeed, family harmony itself became a goal. Given the primacy of family models throughout society, harmony became the touchstone for all interpersonal behaviour. See Ambrose Y. C. King and Michael H. Bond, 'The Confucian paradigm of man: a sociological view', in Wen-Shing Tseng and David Y. H. Wu, *Chinese Culture and Mental Health*, London, Academic Press, 1985, p. 34.

2

Dreams: Technocracy, Social Engineering, and 'Human Quality'

AN underlying assumption in Chinese analysis seems to be that behavioural factors and the value concepts that support social practices are fundamental in explaining both social change and social stability. The same assumptions seem to haunt a frustrated opposition as well as the power-holders. Cultural factors, and especially value concepts, constitute that area of a nation's development that is the most stable and whose influence is longest lasting, and hence the most conservative. Jin Guantao's discussion shows clearly a tendency towards cultural determinism. Culture is seen as a submerged dimension which controls behaviour through the operation of value concepts. Such a cultural approach could in theory 'soften' the often hard technocratic assumptions of the relationship between individual and society. In the Chinese debate, however, such culturalist assumptions are combined with a strong inclination towards scientism. Human behaviour, values, and norms are incorporated into a system of cultural and social engineering that is meant to fit the development of and linked to the fortunes of the modern state and Chinese modernization. Tradition, culture, and human life itself are subsumed under a system of social control and turned into objects for the techniques of social discipline and social engineering linked to the alleged eradication of 'social decay'. It is a technology of modern mass manipulation, and the logic of this system is strictly technocratic.

'Social engineering' (*shehui gongcheng*) has become a popular concept among the Chinese political and technocratic elite, and the expression used by the scholar Qian Xuesen at the initial stage of his theory of 'spiritual wealth'. As I shall later show, this theory was intended to be integrated into the very development model of Chinese reform and modernization. The theory represents the core of the 'Chinese characteristics' promoted as a central theme in that new model of socialism.[1] Here 'social engineering' was explained in cybernetic terms as a 'small range' (*xiao fanwei*) of systems engineering controlled by the larger system of society.[2] The term 'moral construction' (*daode jianshe*), also used in the party press, illustrates the importance of such theories, as 'construction' is normally a word associated with the great narratives of progress and production in the language of the regime.[3] Thus, from the onset of reform, human behaviour was part of a system of control thoroughly integrated in the overall plan for development and 'socialist construction'.

Technocracy and the Belief in Scientism

Here a broader introduction to Qian Xuesen is appropriate because he represents the highly influential elite of Chinese technocrats. Qian earned a Ph.D. in aerodynamics at the California Institute of Technology, and taught at MIT as a professor of aerospace engineering in the 1940s. He returned to China in 1955, later serving as China's leading expert on guided missiles and space technology. He also has been a member of the Central Committee of the Chinese Communist Party, and in 1990 became Vice Chairman of the National Committee of the Chinese People's Political Consultative Conference, as well as Chairman of the Chinese Association for Science and Technology.[4]

Qian is an outstanding representative of the Chinese technocratic elite, an elite of vast importance in today's China. These are the very sorcerers about whom Marx once spoke, the men who by their spells have conjured up 'the powers of the underworld'. They are also the ones who believe they can control the same powers. Qian Xuesen is representative of leading factions in the Party who hold similar technocratic viewpoints. This technocratic elite has been inspired by the belief that national progress depends on science and technological development. The elite dominates both power-holders and dissidents. CCP General Secretary Jiang Zemin and Premier Li Peng are both engineers by background. Dissidents like the astrophysicist Fang Lizhi and the former leader of the dissidents in exile, mathematician Yan Jiaqi, as well as many of the student leaders, can with some modification be said to belong to the same category. Leaders such as Deng Xiaoping, Hu Yaobang, and Zhao Ziyang have also largely shared Qian's views.[5]

After the Cultural Revolution there was much talk among the political leadership and intellectuals about a 'new technological revolution' that should bring about fundamental change in China. As an aftermath of the 'ten years of chaos', it seems almost natural that much of the technocrats' credo should focus on control technology. Li and White have pointed out that one of the common propositions among these technocrats is that all '[m]odern problems, which sometimes originate in technological change, can only be reduced by the application of more advanced technology'.[6] Qian's theories prove that such technology is not understood solely in terms of machines and 'hardware'. Included in the vision of Chinese technocracy is a human 'software' of disciplinary technology of an even wider range. As we shall see, the technocrats are as much concerned about the 'spiritual' as the 'material' improvement of the nation. When Qian and the technocratic elite he represents are such optimists with regard to development, it is because they are believers in science who hold that 'All aspects of the universe are knowable through the methods of science.'[7] Today's Chinese scientists are also preoccupied with culture, even to the point of defining their ideas as 'culturology'. A kind of scientism that 'stresses science's role as a cultural system and as a model for general social values' is described by Christopher Buckley as a 'scientific imagination'.[8] This 'scientific imagination' is a part of the Chinese political culture, 'a view of "science" as a value-neutral instrument capable of reconciling the values of "tradition" and the demands of the modern world'.[9] Such viewpoints represent the beliefs or imaginations of a technocracy or a 'technical intelligentsia'.

In China this 'technical' intelligentsia also increasingly defines the domain of the 'humanistic' intellectuals.[10] Even so, and with dominant political circles also subscribing to such technocratic thinking, such descriptions of Chinese scientism are shared among some Chinese intellectuals. Yu Wujin points out that a basic characteristic of scientism is a belief that natural science and technology can solve all issues in society, and that the conclusions of natural science could be applied to all aspects of social life. Yu thinks this tendency has already gone too far, and that China is now experiencing a form of 'techno-humanism' (*jishu rendao zhuyi*).[11] As Feng Youlan has pointed out, a particularly strong trend in the development of Chinese science was that techniques were developed not only 'for knowing and controlling matter', but for 'knowing and controlling mind'.[12] Feng's words are important not only as a description of historical trends: we should also bear them in mind in analysing the techniques of socialization and discipline in today's China.

We can see the phenomenon of scientism in the picture of the larger issue presented by Marx, writing about the 'evaporation' of all that was solid. The process of 'calling back' the differentiation of past sureties brought about by the modernization process has led to the quest for new sureties. Richard Baum claims that science was made into 'a secularized surrogate religion' to compensate for the lost certainties of Confucianism.[13] Chinese scientism has a strong moralistic bias. 'A

traditional definition of morality as a code of cognitively known, objective truths has been owerwhelming for nearly all Chinese intellectuals',
Thomas Metzger points out.[14] The ancient phrase *tian fa*—meaning 'Laws
of Heaven'—does not refer to a law of nature in a scientific sense, but
concerns social affairs, and indicates a fixity or objectivity of social conduct. It was thought that human conduct and moral order somehow
had a superhuman, but not necessarily supernatural, authority.[15]

At the opening speech at the National Conference on ethics in 1980,
it was argued that, 'As a branch of the sciences, the study of ethics
must have its own scope, principles, rules, and theoretical systems, and
its own corresponding research methodology.'[16] The 'exemplary' is in
such a moral–political climate not only 'exemplary', but also 'objectively correct'. We have here the paradox that modernity itself imposes
constraints of a traditional kind based on a new quasi-religious modern icon of science. Its cultural form is scientism, and this culture of
scientism imposes identity even upon social actors who have to follow
the countless 'rational' frames of modern social control.[17] Under the
protection of the magic spell of 'science', the sorcerers of modernity
seem to make norms stop fluctuating, morality freeze, and 'correctness'
flow abundantly in a kingdom of reason. The kind of social and cultural engineering and disciplinary technology found in China today
describes a mixture of moralism and scientism. Both can be seen as
instruments to control and bring order into the modernization process. Ulrich Beck has suggested that we should 'install brakes and a
steering wheel into the "non-steering" of the racing techno-scientific
development that is setting explosive powers free'.[18] He also speaks of
the 'myth of superiority of science', arguing that science is increasingly
concerned with the distribution of errors and risks produced by itself,
rather than being concerned about 'liberation' from old bonds.[19] In
China, however, the myth of science has become the legitimating myth
behind the recent reforms. Both 'liberation' and the 'brake and the steering wheel' are associated with science. The process of 'scientification'
itself becomes the answer to the problems of modernity.

'Culturology' and 'Spiritual Civilization Studies'

Before returning to the roots of Qian's theory, we need to move on
to the higher levels of political decision-making, and specifically Hu
Yaobang's report at the 12th National Congress of the Communist Party
of China in September 1982. In this report, the theory of the 'two

civilizations' (*liang ge wenming*) was first presented in its official form. Socialist construction, according to Hu, depends on the building of both 'material civilization' (*wuzhi wenming*) and 'spiritual civilization' (*jingshen wenming*).[20] Roughly, 'material civilization' represents the growth aspect of the model, and 'spiritual civilization' the social control aspect of it. The regime bases its policies and derives its legitimacy from these two sources. Here let me concentrate on the 'spiritual' side. In their often economistic understanding of the Chinese reform model of development, Western observers tend to overlook the strategic importance of the spiritual element. After having emphasized material civilization and the development of productive forces, Hu shifts his attention to spiritual civilization. His remarks present an initial outline of an 'exemplary' society:

In the process of transforming the objective world, people also transform their subjective world, and the production of spiritual values and the spiritual life of society also develop. The latter achievement is what we call the spiritual civilization, as manifested in a higher educational, scientific and cultural level and in higher ideological, political and moral standards. The transformation of society or the progress of a social system will ultimately find expression in both material and spiritual civilization. As our socialist society is still in its initial stage, it is not yet highly developed materially. However, the establishment of the socialist system makes it possible for us to build a high level of socialist spiritual civilization while striving for a high level of material civilization . . . Socialism must possess one more characteristic, that is, socialist spiritual civilization with communist ideology at its core. Without this, the building of socialism would be out of the question. The view that communism is but a 'dim illusion' and that it 'has not been tested in practice' is utterly wrong. There is communism everywhere in our daily life, of which it forms an inseparable part. Inside and outside our Party there are so many heroic and exemplary People, so many who are ready to give their all, including their very lives, for the realization of revolutionary ideals. Do they do all this for material rewards? Does not a lofty communist spirit guide them? Socialism is advancing steadily towards the goal of its higher phase—communism. This advance depends not only on the increase of material wealth but also on the steady growth of people's communist consciousness and revolutionary spirit.[21]

Hu is not merely talking about ideological education in the same way as countless cadres had done before him in an endless stream of official rethoric: no, he bases his speech on a refined theory of social engineering. Many of his phrases can be traced directly back to the theoretical writings of Qian Xuesen. Hu goes on:

Roughly speaking, socialist spiritual civilization consists of two aspects, the cultural and ideological permeating and promoting each other. The cultural aspect refers to the development of undertakings such as education, science, art and literature, the press and publication, broadcasting and television, public health, physical culture, and libraries and museums, as well as raising the level of the general knowledge of the people. It is an important requisite both for the building of a material civilization and for the raising of people's political consciousness and moral standards. To build a socialist spiritual civilization is a task for the whole Party and the common task of our people in all fields of endeavour. Ideological education in the Party is the pillar for building spiritual civilization in the whole society, and party members should, first of all, play an exemplary role morally and ideologically. Ideological and political workers, workers in culture, in the sciences and in education of all types and levels from kindergartens to graduate schools—all shoulder especially heavy responsibilities in building a socialist spiritual civilization.[22]

The 'exemplary' is here linked to the discussion of moral order. According to Hu, a 'planned economy' of moral order should be implemented for the next five years—a 'moral five-year plan', in other words. His speech formed the basis for the anti-crime campaigns that as early as 1983 were to send so many criminal youths to the scaffold:

The Central Committee of the Party is determined to effect a fundamental turn for the better in standards of social conduct in the next five years. This includes, in the main, the achievement of markedly better public order, generally improved attitudes towards all types of work and a marked decline in the crime rate. It also means putting an effective check on, and arousing universal contempt for, such unhealthy tendencies and practices as benefiting oneself at others' expense, pursuing private interests, loving ease and despising work, putting money first in everything, unscrupulous pursuit of personal enjoyment and attempting to isolate and attack advanced elements. It also includes resolutely eliminating all the vile social evils which had been stamped out long ago by New China but have now cropped up again.[23]

In short, Hu's speech was a battle-cry for taming the monster of modernization, and bringing control into the chaotic process. Social order was of strategic importance to the whole Party—'left' as well as 'right', 'hard-liner' as well as 'reformer'. Hu Yaobang, whose death initiated the demonstrations that ended in the Beijing massacre in June 1989, was a liberal and a reformist, but he was as concerned about the social order as anyone else in the Party. Hu's contribution to the upholding of such order was to perfect the control apparatus; for that purpose he used the theories of Qian Xuesen and the intellectual milieu around him.

In 1981 Qian Xuesen wrote that culture should no longer be regarded as a mere reproductive activity. Not only science and technology, but also literature and art and other expressions of culture should be looked upon as productive activities. Qian developed the concept of culture as a 'fourth industry', or 'quaternary industry' (*di si chanye*) to stress its productive functions. According to this theory, this quarternary industry of culture means the 'preparation' (*zhunbei*), or the preparatory stage of production.[24]

Qian later came to the conclusion that the term was insufficient, and that he had been too preoccupied with the economic and material side when he formulated his theory. Consequently he developed the longer concept of 'the industry of creating socialist spiritual wealth' (*shehui zhuyi jingshen caifu chuangzao shiye*), this time even proclaiming it a new discipline of social science, 'exploring the creation of socialist spiritual wealth'. He dubbed the new science of such spiritual production 'culturology' (*wenhuaxue*) corresponding to economics, which he saw as the social science engaged in studying the production of material wealth.[25]

Qian first sets out to 'firmly establish' the importance of his theory for the whole project of socialist construction. He criticizes earlier practices, where the undertaking of spiritual wealth was assigned to the category of education, science, and culture, and thus regarded as consumptive financial expenditures. As a consequence, there had been less motivation for spiritual creation than for material production. 'It is the people who create history', Qian continues, and this creation is both a material and spiritual process. Socialist spiritual wealth is not the creation of any single person, but the achievement of humanity through thousands of years of labour. In modern society, a person must first possess an education and knowledge to be able to add even the tiniest bit to this wealth, Qian contends. 'Culturology' was later defined as one of two main branches for the study of spiritual civilization.

There are three aspects of people's knowledge of the objective world. First comes the person (*ren*), the subject of knowledge. Second comes the objective world, the object of knowledge; and third comes spiritual wealth, the means of knowledge created by mankind. The objective world is material and primary. People's consciousness is spiritual and secondary. Spiritual wealth is the creation of human beings; reflecting man's knowledge of the objective world, it too is secondary. Despite this, Qian regards the creation of spiritual wealth as 'an undertaking or industry' (*yi zhong shiye huo chanye*) of science and culture. He explains how his theory represents a development of classical Marxist philosophy. To the objective world and the individual it adds spiritual wealth, a third category differing from the first two. The Marxist principle remains: matter is primary and consciousness is secondary.[26]

In an article in the Party's theoretical journal *Qiushi*, Qian, together with Sun Kaifei, sums up developments from both the 12th and the 13th Party Congresses, and elaborates further on the theory.[27] The authors address Marx's concepts of 'social formation' (*shehui xingtai*) and 'social economic formation' (*jingji de shehui xingtai*) to develop their points of view.[28] They introduce the term 'ideological social formation' (*yishi de shehui xingtai*), indicating what they regard as an extension and improvement of Marxist theory. Research in this field should improve and perfect the system of social engineering and social control that was scientifically defined and politically implemented during the party congresses. The development of the theory shows that the circle of theoretical reflection and political implementation has been tightened. The authors take care to point out that their perfection of the theory now builds on the political movement of the 'two civilizations'. Material civilization cannot be achieved without simultaneously building spiritual civilization; growth cannot be achieved without social and moral order.

Here, the vital theme of 'human quality' (*ren de suzhi*) is also introduced. The quality of workers and people in general should be improved. Such quality concerns not only their cultural level of knowledge, but also ideological, political, moral, and behavioural aspects. This is a crucial task for building the four modernizations and developing socialism with Chinese characteristics. Human improvement is thus linked with the development of the productive forces in general, and theories of 'human perfection' are added to the Marxist argument. Ideological 'improvement' is thus elevated to a higher status:

The basic task in the preliminary stage of socialism is to develop the productive forces . . . Man is the most important and the most revolutionary factor of the productive forces. The crucial point of whether the role of man is fully developed and how it is developed lies in the ideological and educational level of man.[29]

Along with this crucial transformation of man comes an improvement in the tools of production, which relies on the development of culture, science, and technology. According to analyses in other countries, Qian and Sun claim, as much as 60–80 per cent of labour productivity and economic growth depend on cultural development. The Western concepts of Taylorism and 'scientific management' (*kexue guanli*) are introduced as a matter of great importance for a nation's development.[30] As we shall later see, the moral and behavioural aspects of such scientific management in practice go further in China than in perhaps any other country.

Moral degeneration is getting worse day by day, and can do more harm to the country than inflation, Qian and Sun contend. 'Inflation can be remedied in a short time, but it could take more than a generation to rectify immorality'.[31] Without a scientification of the system of social and moral order, the further advance of modernization is in danger, and modernity will lead to a return to chaos (*wenluan*). In short, the issue is human transformation and 'quality' on the one side, or chaos on the other.

The answer to these problems of order is to establish a 'macro study of ideological social formation and spiritual civilization'.[32] Qian and Sun immediately distance themselves from the Chinese debate on the 'culture fever' (*wenhua re*) that dominated intellectual circles at the time.[33] Their study is not a culturalist one, they maintain. 'Culture' (*wenhua*) and 'civilization' (*wenming*) should not be mixed up: the latter concept is broader than the former, and also indicates a higher order of development;[34] 'civilization' also has a connotation of order and improvement not necessarily found in the concept of 'culture'. They term their theory a 'sociology of ideology' (*yishi shehuixue*), or more specifically refer to it as 'spiritual civilization studies' (*jingshen wenmingxue*): the study of the relations between human consciousness, changes in thinking and culture, and the general change in society's development as a whole. It is concerned with the rapidly changing norms and values represented by the process of modernization, and the improvement of the behavioural quality of the population. Development is given a strong connotation of ideological and moral order, with the stress explicitly on social 'guidance' (*yindao*) and 'control' (*kongzhi*).[35] Civilization theory might be described as a planned system of spiritual and cultural control.

The division of socialist spiritual civilization into two aspects, cultural and ideological, as mentioned in Hu Yaobang's speech at the 12th Party Congress, is also used in the theory of 'spiritual civilization studies'. Cultural construction (*wenhua jianshe*) refers to the development of education, science, literature and art, press and publication, radio and TV, public health and physical culture, libraries, museums, and recreation and other activities and institutions for raising the educational level of people. Under ideological construction (*sixiang jianshe*) is listed Marxist world outlook and scientific theory, communist ideals, beliefs and morality, a sense of mastering one's own affairs, collectivism, a sense of rights and duties, a sense of organization and discipline, a spirit of sacrifice in serving the people, a communist attitude towards work, socialist patriotism and internationalism, and other means of improving the people's moral standards. Under 'spiritual civilization studies' there should thus be two main fields of study. Cultural construction, led by the study of 'culturology', and ideological construction should both be defined as branches of the behavioural sciences (*xingwei kexue*). Under this final heading come phenomena like ideological and political education, moral education, ethics, social psychology, and so-called talent studies (*rencai xue*). Again, the stress is on behavioural and moral control.

A discipline of cultural systems engineering (*wenhua xitong gongcheng*) should be established to build up a system of cultural construction. A sociology of science studying the relation between science and social development should also be an integrated part of such studies. Literature and all kinds of art forms and expressions belong to 'cultural system theory' (*wenhua xitongxue*). In addition to the aspects formerly mentioned, this includes phenomena like architecture and landscaping, physical culture, dress, and cosmetology. Socialist cultural development also covers seven other aspects, somewhat confusingly categorized as: '1, parks (historic sites); 2, exhibition halls, museums, and science and technology halls; 3, tourism; 4, flowers, birds, insects, and fish; 5, cooking; 6, mass organizations; and 7, religion'.[36] To explain the role such phenomena are alleged to have on the improvement of people's quality, we will later have to introduce the concept of 'environmental moulding' (*huanjing taoye*) or simply 'environmentalism'.

This mixture of cultural studies and behavioural science describes a process of social systems engineering. Qian's image of Chinese society is an 'open, complicated, and gigantic system'.[37] It is bursting with technocratic optimism about the possibilities for transforming society and people, improving their social and moral quality, and creating '*genuine* cultural revolutions'. Qian's system is aimed at mapping out the developmental laws of spiritual civilization.

'Human Quality' as Human Modernization

We have seen that the construction of tradition served to uphold the social and moral order in society. If this represented the 'memory' of social control and a starting point for controlled change, then social engineering and in particular the policy of improving 'human quality' represent the 'dream' of control in all its utopian fervour. It describes a human technology closely linked to both the material and the spiritual side of 'civilization'. Not only does the improvement of human quality represent a brake on social disorder, it also has to be seen within a context of economic growth and national progress. Such human 'improvement' is not an end in itself, but is geared towards the very aim of Chinese reform described by Deng Xiaoping and added to the Constitution in March 1993: 'making the country rich and strong'.[38]

The classical Chinese characters for quality, *suzhi*, was *su* (素), meaning pure or simple, beginning or root, and *zhi* (質), meaning intrinsic quality, or innate character. The meaning was slowly transferred from things to persons.[39] This sense of purity and naturalness of quality has also been replaced by a concept of the conscious manipulation, formation, and fostering of quality. Indeed, this change in meaning might encapsulate the whole debate on human quality as something changing from the naturally given to the manageable and administrative. In recent years the concept of 'human quality' has been linked to modernization and reform, describing it as a human input of this process. There are countless descriptions of its importance.

Several sources describe the ideal modern development as one where material and spiritual quality form a unity. In 1988 this ideal was summarized as follows. Modernization consists of more than material modernization (*wu de xiandaihua*): the relationship between material (*wu*) development and human (*ren*) development is crucial. The process of modernization must also include human modernization (*ren de xiandaihua*).[40] Some have suggested that an entire science should be predicated to research the question of personal modernity and individual modernization. A group of Chinese scholars has established a so-called 'science of personality' (*renxue*) that is to deal with what they call 'modern personality studies' (*xiandairen xue*). This new branch of science is meant to bring together different sciences to cope with the problems of individual modernization at all levels of society.[41] A crucial task here is to set up a guiding 'personality model' (*renge moshi*) to cope with the 'violent resocialization process' of material and spiritual modernization.[42] This introduces an issue of immense importance in Chinese thinking about socialization and social control. Throughout Chinese history, models have been presented to the people for emulation. These models were the sages and exemplary men of the past; now they also represent the ideal personality of the future. The 'personality model' is a model of the anticipated future developed for the sake of controlling the present. It is one of the fundamental assumptions in the Chinese theory of learning that people are innately capable of learning from models. Munro has outlined the dilemma of the ancient Chinese ruler:

How does one induce compliance with the body of prescriptions one wishes to enforce? Should a ruler control the people through fear of punishment for transgressing a penal law, or should he urge them to develop the right habits through the emulation of models . . .[43]

I will later describe the present regime's use of both methods in detail. Here, it suffices to point to the elements of stability represented by the emulation of modern personality models.

Harmony and stability are set up as explicit prerequisites for modernization in most of the Chinese literature on the subject. It is necessary to achieve a 'harmonized development' (*xietiao de fazhan*) throughout the entire society, if one is to have any hope of solving the emerging social problems.[44] There is also a strong emphasis on stability. Some even claim that the whole process of improving and modernizing human quality can be defined as the gradual development of a person's stable character (*wengu xingzhi*).[45] Now there is talk of 'stability in movement'.[46] Things change, and stability should change with them.

In terms of the 'personality model', the theme of controlled change has been described as the dual competence of initiative (*nengdong xing*) and adaptability (*shiying xing*). Both are important characteristics of the modern personality, representing two sides of the same process. Initiative is described as the motive force for recognizing and changing the objective world. Adaptability is defined in terms of conscious change of self in order to adapt to changes in the natural and social surroundings.[47] In many comments on socialization and modernization theory, such 'self-change' is paradoxically described in the language of classical 'self-cultivation' (*xiuyang*).[48] One commentator sees adaptability as the most central modern value of them all. Such adaptability must be seen in connection with competition and choice when describing the controlled change needed for coping with the 'rapidly changing character' (*duanzan xing*) of modernization.[49]

A nearly unavoidable aspect to be described in the process of socialization is that of gradual personal improvement. 'Human life is a continuous process of perfection', and a process of gradually 'completing' one's physiology and psychology.[50] The aim of such perfection is to achieve a 'striving forward' (*jinqu xing*), embedding values like risk-taking (*maoxian*), innovation (*chuangxin*), competition, and independence.[51] It has been extremely popular in China over the last few years to compile lists and even whole catalogues of modern 'concepts' and prescribed modern behaviour. Among the endless lists of such alleged modern concepts, the title of one book—'One Hundred Concepts of Modernity'—sums up this trend.[52] There is also a streak of social Darwinism running through the entire discourse on individual modernity. Competition is defined as the striving for superiority and the right to exist according to the rule of the 'survival of the fittest'. Competition is necessary in order for people to feel under sufficient pressure to strive harder. Everyone who competes wants to be superior, and to avoid losing out. This process produces a 'feeling of stress' (*weiji gan*). The inferior ones experience an 'existential stress' (*shengcun de weiji*), while the stress experienced by the superior ones is the risk of losing their positions of superiority (*shiqu youshi de weiji*). This feeling of stress produces in everyone a will to strive continuously. No one dares to be lazy, and competitive psychology in modern society becomes a highly effective motivating force for producing superior talents as well as superior products.[53]

Human quality has been viewed as synonymous with human modernization during the reforms. A Youth League propaganda department writer claims that modernization has three aspects: economy, politics, and human quality, with the last the most important.[54] The crucial task for China is to raise the spiritual quality of the whole nation, in particular the quality of youth. In today's China, however, there are too few people with the correct 'modern spiritual qualities'. The function of a reform of the political system is restricted; it can only create the *conditions* for the realization of modernization, not modernization itself. The road to national prosperity is thus the modernization of spiritual human qualities. Only the creation of the modern person can promote modernization. There is a dialectic between the spiritual quality of the individual and the spiritual civilization of society.[55] Political reform is described as a phenomenon of the superstructure, but no such restriction is put on the concept of 'human quality'. Rather, human quality in this and other accounts seems to incorporate both superstructure and base in the Marxist sense, since man is also a decisive part of the means of production. In this sense human quality is superior compared with the third element in the three aspects of modernization, the economy. Young people may dance at discos, wear modern clothes, and follow fashion, he points out, but the inner world has not discarded the fetters of agrarian society. Such people are at most a mixture of new and old.[56] Economic development is dependent on the quality of the work-force.

Peter Berger has argued that 'it is relatively easy to teach people with . . . a medieval self-image to fly jet planes; it is more difficult to build medieval notions of personal loyalty and obligations into bureaucratic institutions'.[57] The issue illustrates the modern problem of double or dual personality. This duality results in imbalance, which has to be brought back into balance if the economy is to prosper. Even if the useful parts of the past are carefully selected and included, people's minds should be consolidated into one unified and balanced individual modernity.

The literature on modern human quality is very wide, and various authors point to many aspects that need modernizing. Some put the emphasis on the modernization of feelings, often using the arguments of the US futurologist John Naisbitt about the combination of 'high tech and high touch'.[58] Naisbitt comes close to the definitions of material and spiritual civilization, even if it is unclear whether he himself is aware of the technocratization of spirit represented by that Chinese concept. Naisbitt has in fact visited China; he has been translated into Chinese, and is widely read. He uses another keyword to explain some of his popularity in China, *balance*, and goes back to its Greek traditions rather than to its Chinese:

The great lesson we must learn from the principle of high tech/high touch is a modern version of the ancient Greek ideal—*balance*. We must learn to balance the material wonders of technology with the spiritual demands of our human nature . . . The principle symbolizes the need for a balance between our physical and spiritual reality.[59]

Some sources also stress the modernization of our way of thinking,[60] while others define human modernization as the cultural and psychological quality of thinking, value orientations and feelings, locating the concept well within the 'building of a spiritual civilization'.[61] 'The future of mankind depends on the quality of mankind', according to Li Boxi, who describes the modernization of thinking and behaviour as the most important aspect of the modernization process, more important than the material and the organizational aspects of modernization. 'Quality' is here defined as a combination of intellect and spirit, capability and value concepts.[62] Even among the rebellious students, the language of 'quality' and 'improvement' seems part of the standard vocabulary, although intellect prevails over spirit in their definitions.[63] As we shall soon see, efforts have been made recently to bring the different aspects of human quality together into one comprehensive system.

Alex Inkeles's theories of the modern personality have had considerable influence in China during the reform period. He is frequently quoted in works on modernization theory which talk of modern psychological (*xinli suzhi*) and spiritual quality (*jingshen suzhi*),[64] and some of his books are now available in Chinese. However, his most often quoted work is the early short article called 'The Modernization of Man'. In this article, his view of the modern factory as a 'powerful example of the principles and practices of modern living' would seem dear to the heart of a Chinese technocrat bent on practising 'social engineering' of the type already outlined.[65]

The many Chinese studies on 'talent' (*rencai*) normally take care to point out that talent is achieved; it is also historically and socially determined and thereby 'fostered'. Here we find an orientation towards the problems of 'material civilization'. A talent's quality should be geared mainly towards production, but there are also 'spiritual talents' of moral and ideological quality.[66] Quality is a concept geared to technological and economic development and the very key to developing society. The 'quality' concept includes individual as well as collective quality, quality of body as well as of mind, quality as innate as well as learned. Schools have a particular responsibility for developing the quality of moral character.[67] While many see this discussion as a pretext for adopting an elitist educational system in China,[68] others lean towards arguments for public education.[69]

The technocrats, however, seem to have gained the upper hand in such questions. In particular, the 'cultural quality' of the ruling elite has been emphasized. Qian Xuesen again emerges as an important figure. In something nearly resembling a recreation of the imperial system, he proposed in 1983 that by the year 2000 all cadres should be college graduates, all leaders at the county or bureau level should hold MA degrees, and all full or deputy ministers and provincial governors should hold Ph.D. degrees. Government should be composed mainly of scientists and engineers. In 1988 he again argued that, since the top priority for China was to meet global scientific competition, engineers should lead the state. Goverment was seen as strictly a problem of technical design.[70] This policy seems partly to have been implemented at the higher levels. It was reported that nearly 84 per cent of members of the new 14th Central Committee in 1992 had received higher education, compared with 26 per cent of the 11th Central Committee in 1977, 55 per cent of the 12th in 1982, and 73 per cent of the 13th in 1987.[71] Among Chinese mayors, only 2 per cent had received a college education in 1981; by 1986 the figure had risen to 78 per cent, and three-quarters of these had majored in engineering or natural science.[72] The level of higher education on a national scale is about 1 per cent. Some even openly advocate 'elitism' (*jingying jingshen*) as a solution to China's problems, noting that talented people have always been overwhelmed by large masses.[73]

The modernization of the human quality is presented mainly in the form of a theory of national development. The debate on re-Confucianization might be characterized as a variant of such a theory. Some, like the sociologist Li Qiang, have approached the human quality argument from a Weberian point of view, claiming that China needs a 'Protestant ethic' for its reforms to succeed.[74] This theme has also been taken up by the philosopher and regime protagonist He Xin, but in his version Marxism has taken over from Protestantism. In a remarkable interview in the Youth League's central newspaper in December 1989, he suggested that China needed a 'revolutionary religion' (*geming de zongjiao*), combining the binding elements of spiritual civilization into an ethic of development and production much like the one Weber spoke of in the West. This is perhaps the most clearly formulated example of the 'cohesive marxism' and 'socialist order' that dominates the debate on controlled modernization in China.[75] In many ways He Xin's suggestion resembles Kang Youwei's attempt to establish a Confucian religion (*kongjiao*) at the beginning of the century.[76]

The Chinese discourse on modernization and human quality is a version of the theory of individual modernity. While such theories might yield interesting data about differences between 'traditional' and 'modern' cultural traits, the importance of the theory as an explanation of development and underdevelopment is at best limited. Central to this kind of theory is the assumption that modern concepts or values of a psychological kind lead to modern behaviour, which again contributes more or less directly to the development of societies.[77] Armer and Isaac have looked at the validity of such theories and the national development implications of individual modernity and conclude:

[T]he results undermine confidence in the modernity thesis regarding the importance of modern attitudes and values in producing behaviour identified as instrumental for modernization of society . . . Those who use the concept of individual modernity in their research or theory should note the lack of evidence regarding the significance of modern attitudes for either national development or underdevelopment.[78]

Their evaluation reflects the overall weak position of this theory in Western development research today. Its relative weakness in explaining development stands in sharp contrast to the enormous popularity of such theories in China. The popularity of this type of thinking is rooted in Confucianism itself. In the rich tradition of Chinese sayings, there is the expression: 'Everybody is responsible for the rise and decline of the empire' (*tian xia xing wang, pi fu you ze*). More important, however, such theories are rooted in the modern state itself and represent crucial ways of constructing a Chinese modernity similar to but different from the memories of tradition. It is another map for understanding and controlling problematic social reality, bringing order into the process of modernization. In the picture of the 'two civilizations' it may belong more to the 'spiritual' and social control side of that model than to the 'material civilization'. At least in real life the control of social behaviour seems more directly related to such theories than does economic growth. 'Being modern' is a behaviour to be learned and fostered, and gives important signals and guidelines about the 'correct' way to conduct oneself in a modern society. New 'objective' standards for modern norms and behaviour are mapped out, and it is stressed that this process of value change should take an orderly form. There are also utopian promises of development and prosperity in the narrative of modern human quality that can act as motivating forces for adapting to the realities of reform.

On 'Fostering' the Human Body and Population Quality

The discourse on human quality is clearly disciplinary and regulatory. At the core lies a strong pedagogical intention. The concept of 'fostering' (*peiyang*) human beings describes the essence of the matter. Through the improvement of human quality, the regime seeks to educate and administer life itself. This process resembles what Foucault has described as 'biopower'—the development of disciplines of the body and of attempts to regulate the population.[79] The first of these Foucault calls an 'anatomo-politics of the human body'. This type is 'centered on the body as a machine: its disciplining, its optimization of its capabilities . . . the parallel increase of its usefulness and its docility'. The second type of discipline he calls the 'bio-politics of the population'. This is about regulatory controls; it is 'centered on biological processes, births and mortality, the level of health', etc.[80] He sees the emergence of biopower as the outcome of a historical process, where '[t]he old power of death that symbolized sovereign power was now carefully supplanted by the administration of bodies and the calculated management of life'.[81] Instead of regulating society through negative sanctions alone, power had given itself the function of administering life through a range of new techniques: 'Hence there was an explosion of numerous and diverse techniques for achieving the subjugation of bodies and the control of populations, marking the beginning of an era of "biopower".'[82]

The power to 'foster' life is addressed by Foucault: 'One might say that the ancient right to *take* life or *let* live was replaced by the power to *foster* or *disallow* it to the point of death.'[83] Power here is not seen in its negative sense of taking away the right to life, but rather in its 'positive' sense as the power to form and 'improve' life. It is about 'generating forces, making them grow', rather than destroying them.[84] In short, it is a means of both transforming and controlling people. Foucault here discusses the power aspect of the social engineering project. His description further touches upon the 'adjustment of the phenomena of population to the economic process'.[85] In China today, this forms the very foundation for the discourse on human quality, modernization, and reform. Biopower is the power concerned with 'distributing the living in the domain of value and utility. Such a power has 'to qualify, measure, appraise, and hierarchize, rather than display itself in its murderous splendour . . . '.[86] The issue of measurement and appraisal of 'human quality' runs through the entire discussion on the 'exemplary' society that is today's China. It is precisely here that the administrators, bureaucrats as well as technocrats, reveal their own talents in forming and cementing the norms and dreams of the regime to achieve the aims of controlled change. The 'murderous splendour', however, has not disappeared in China. I will later show that where the 'improving' forces fail, and deviance is too obvious, the execution ground replaces the classroom. Even this is seen as a means of improving the collective human quality.

The production of a healthy offspring was of ultimate importance in imperial China.[87] In late imperial China medical knowledge constructed a whole range of prohibitions and restrictions around the foetus. The concept of human quality today must be seen in close connection with this tradition and with the Chinese population policy and its emphasis on eugenics. The control of sexual desire, the regulation of reproductive behaviour, and the disciplining of emotions belong to this discourse.[88] Human beings are ranged after a hierarchy of 'quality'. At the lower end of the quality scale there is inferiority. Statistics from the Ministry of Health show that in 1989 China had nearly 52 million disabled people and over 10 million mentally retarded people: more than 30 million people are officially defined as 'defective' in China.[89] The eugenic narrative of inferiority and the inferior (*lie*) represents another side of the human quality discourse, summed up in the much quoted myth of the 'idiot village' (*shazi cun*). In one such account the 'idiot village' is described as a small mountain village where 150 out of 200 inhabitants are mentally retarded, or simply 'idiots' (*shazi*), in the language of the narrator. Typically, he can only tell us that 'the name of the village is almost forgotten'. They have schools there, but some of its pupils take ten years to get as far as second grade in primary school. Some of the peasants can only count to four, and cannot cope with the concept of five oxen. The place lies isolated up in the mountains and intermarriage is usual. Constantly the rate of idiocy is growing. The moral of the story is summed up as follows:

To have good offspring not only creates happy families, but also influences the growth of the state and the prosperity of the nation. For plants and animals we already have good seeds and breeds: should we also not use such methods on mankind itself to improve the quality of the population?[90]

While the government has set a ceiling target for population growth, particularly well propagated through the 'one-child policy', some observers complain that such a policy focuses on quantity only and has seriously ignored the question of quality.[91] Controlling the 'quality' of newborns gradually became as important as the control of their quantity. This trend was strengthened by the introduction of the 'Eugenics Law' in 1995 (later renamed the 'Maternal and Infant Health Law'), a law particularly aimed towards preventing 'inferior births'. Such 'inferior births' have 'no quality' (*ling suzhi*), and can make no social contribution.[92] The eugenic narrative of inferiority and that of productivity and prosperity are often combined in such discourses of human quality. Gansu, described as 'a parched, desolate province on the edge of the Gobi desert and plagued by poverty and disease for centuries', is now used as a model example of the implementation of a policy of population quality in China. The province was the first to pass a new law in 1988 that forbids people with 'severe hereditary retardation' from having children.[93] Mental retardation in the province is said to be caused by inbreeding, endemic and congenital diseases, and malnutrition.

This debate has been taken further to illustrate the rural–urban contradiction and the urban elitism of human quality discourse even more clearly. Zhou Xiaozheng criticizes the population policy from an urban point of view. 'Educated people in the cities have the highest quality [of life]', he bluntly states.[94] Their marriage and birth rates are fairly low, moreover, while the rural population in the educationally stagnant countryside has much higher birth rates (see Table 1). The one-child policy has only served to restrict people of relatively high quality and in relatively superior environments from having children: there has been no control of those with low quality or from relatively backward environments. It is claimed that as a result the total Chinese human resources and their overall quality have been deteriorating. Statistics are produced to underline the point.

The strictest supervision over the one-child policy is found in the urban areas. In the populous low-quality rural areas more children are allowed. This affects the total health quality of the country. Using the argument about abnormal births, Zhou suggests the active use of

TABLE 1   Birth rates from different districts, 1980–1987

	No. of children per married couple
Total	2.47
Cities (*chengshi jiedao*)	1.33
State farming and forestry areas (*nonglin chang*)	1.47
Suburban districts and villages (*jiaoqu xiang*)	2.39
Rural towns (*zhen*)	2.43
County administered villages (*xianshu xiang*)	2.84

Source: Zhou Xiaozheng, 'Renkou suzhi shi wo guo renkou wenti de guanjian' (Population quality is the key to the problem of China's population), *Keji daobao*, No. 4, 1989, p. 15; also in *Renkouxue*, C5, *Fuyin baokan ziliao*, No. 5, 1989, p. 84.

eugenics principles. An additional problem is the rural 'marriage connection nets' (*lianyin wang*). The frustration we found in Jin Guantao's account of ultrastability is here repeated in connection with population policy. Rural marriage customs are products of an ultrastable feudal society, Zhou claims. People of inferior quality are multiplying in a vicious circle, preventing the prosperity and growth of the Chinese nation. The more people there are of a lower quality, the more inferior is the overall quality. The 'administration of life' described by Foucault fits neatly into this picture. The 'adjustment of the phenomena of population to the economic process' is also clearly mapped out in the Chinese human quality debate. Biopower was expected to be concerned with 'distributing the living in the domain of value and utility'. Zhou Xiaozheng's debate has already shown us the geographical site of human value and human quality. The discourse leaves us with no doubt about the conclusion: rural is inferior. Some 'population experts' have recently suggested that intellectuals be allowed to have a second child, while the illiterate, semi-illiterate and handicapped should be strictly prevented from having a second child, and absolutely stopped from having a third. Noting that the number of children of illiterates is increasing and that of intellectuals is decreasing, they use the same arguments about rural population growth preventing the population from 'improving'. To 'improve the quality of the population and prepare talented people for the next century', by 'using the eugenic principle of bringing up "scientists" with scientists', a vast number of home-trained intelligent children can be produced. These suggestions have allegedly 'drawn the close attention of China's supervisory departments and feasible research can now proceed'.[95]

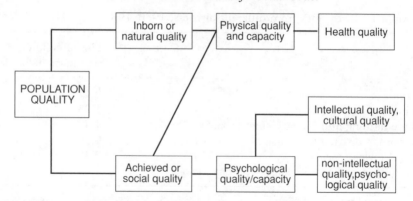

FIGURE 1   Human quality model as suggested by Mu Guangzhong
Source: Mu Guangzhong, 'Renkou suzhi xinlun' (New discussion on human quality),
Renkou yanjiu, No. 3, 1989, p. 56, in *Fuyin baokan ziliao, Renkouxue, C5*, No. 5, 1989,
p. 91.

Attempts have been made to construct an overall index of population quality in China. Mu Guangzhong's discussion of such a national
'population quality index' (*renkou zhiliang zhishu*) makes the biopolit-
ical issue of 'value and utility' even clearer.[96] First is the economic aspect:
human quality or population quality represent hidden productive
forces (*qianzai de shengchanli*). The population quality criterion focuses
on health, both physical and psychological, in a broad sense. From the
cultural point of view, the individual cultural development index is the
basis of judging the capability of the population. The development of
human resources is concerned with both open and hidden capabilities.
Having defined human quality as concerning mainly education, health,
and moral/ideological issues, Mu focuses on whether or not the moral–
political quality factor should be included. He favours the introduction
of moral and ideological criteria in an overall human quality index, con-
sidering that 'this concrete understanding is more complete than a concept of population quality including physical and cultural quality only'.[97]

Mu's explanation of the different aspects of the population quality
index is set out in Figure 1. Both inborn or natural quality (*ziran suzhi*)
and achieved quality (*houtian suzhi*) should be listed in the index.
'Biology' (*shengwu*) criteria should be used to describe physical properties, while 'work' (*laodong*) criteria should be used for social properties.
Human quality, however, is defined as being mainly of an 'historical
and relative character', open to manipulation and 'improvement'.

Physical quality is defined as height, weight, speed, stamina, etc. Psychological quality includes feelings, consciousness, memory, imagination,
and thinking. Under psychological quality and capacity, Mu distinguishes

between intellectual and cultural quality on the one hand, and non-intellectual, psychological quality on the other. Intellectual quality includes creative capacity, adaptability to one's surroundings, and capacity of judgement. Such qualities and capacities closely correspond to the 'modern concepts' described in the 'concept-catalogues'. Intelligence has five basic components: observation, memory, thinking, imagination, and manipulation. Intellectual quality is a broader concept than cultural quality, which takes time of schooling as its index basis. Further, there are numerous psychological and non-intellectual quality aspects. Non-intellectual quality includes morale, sentiments, feelings, will, and interests. Mu claims that attempts to set up a population quality index were unsuccessful because they did not include non-intellectual qualities. One cannot ignore the population's moral and ideological quality (*renkou sixiang daode suzhi*) in preparing such an index.

Mu rejects suggestions to use the crime rate to measure moral quality in society, because that might give the reforms low marks for quality. The crime rate is thought to be too limited a measure, and does not necessarily measure the moral and ideological quality of a population. Moreover, crime is defined differently in different cultures; it can be linked to economic development, etc. Mu is obviously right in pointing out that crime rates are bad comparative measures of morality, but he entirely lacks the same critical attitude towards the even more confused moral and ideological criteria that he does include in the index.

Mu's figure includes a line indicating a connection between the upper 'biology-ruled' part of his model and the lower 'work-ruled' part. In other words, not only do social engineering techniques operate in the social quality area of achieved capabilities, they also move into the biological sphere of physical quality. The figure seems to indicate that inborn/natural quality is not directly manipulable, but that the fostering of quality found in the social sphere can also contribute to the improvement of physical quality. Concepts from the 'biology' sphere also intrude into the social quality sphere. Mu argues that the eugenics concept of a disabled or deformed population (*canji renkou*) must also include spiritual and psychological deformities, and he uses a 1987 Chinese sample survey to prove the importance of such a policy. Out of a population sample of 51 million, 1.94 million people were mentally ill (*jingshen bing canji*); 'double or multiple physical deformities' (*liangchong huo duochong canji*) were found among 6.73 million. The first figure constitutes nearly 4 per cent of this sample and the second, more than 13 per cent. Mu describes the latter as people of 'low intelligence quality' (*fei zhili suzhi*). According to the already quoted statistics from the Ministry of Health from 1989, however, China had about 4.5 per cent disabled people and less than 1 per cent suffering from mental retardation. Mu does not specify the detailed definitions used in the sample survey, but one is left with the impression that new definitions have since been introduced that decrease the numbers of 'the deformed and the mentally ill'. Mu's moral–ideological definition of 'low intelligence quality' is naturally disturbing seen against the background of these perspectives.

Mu belongs to the reform-minded fraction of the Chinese technocracy.[98] The 'population quality index' is but another indication that social engineering and human technology are seen as important means of order and reform, supported and promoted by the reform ideologues. It warns us against putting the labels of 'liberalism' and 'democracy' on this faction, as their stand is part of the repressive technocratic dreams of the future. It would also be wise to bear in mind that dreams may turn into nightmares. One should also remember, however, that despite the cultural specificities, eugenics in China is not significantly different from twentieth-century movements of racial hygiene in Europe. The PRC is, however, the only powerful country still officially promoting such ideas on a wide scale.[99]

It is claimed that all the traits of modern human quality reflect the degree of 'civilization' that a person possesses. Outward expressions and appearances are the visible indications of a person's inner quality, the externalization of personal quality.[100] As we shall see, it is in this 'visibility' that human control technology establishes its kingdom. Here lies also the material for judging and measuring 'objective' morality.

'Exemplary Society': A Utopia of Reconstruction

We have seen that traces of the exemplary society can be found in the balance between the memories of the past and the dreams of the future. Let me clarify the part about the dream. To what extent is this exemplary society a utopia? Lewis Mumford has pointed out that utopias, from Plato's Republic via the Utopia of Sir Thomas More and up to modern times, have been trying to 'face the difficult problems of transition'.[101] The problem of transition cannot be identified as the transition between traditional and modern society alone. Even the classical Confucian ideal society with its ideal men had as its starting point a similar concern for the problems of transition.[102] The modernization process represents a qualitatively new form of transition, and the new 'projects of perfection' or 'utopias' are concerned with this particular historical transition as other historical societies were concerned about theirs. What remain are the fears and concerns about transition. The social and cultural engineering I have outlined is part of something that might be called a utopia of progress and a utopia of control, described as utopias of 'quality' or 'perfectability'.

Here another paradox about the Chinese modernizations is found, again bringing us back to the difficulty of drawing up a boundary between traditional and modern. The very project of 'perfectability' is said among anthropologists to be a typical traditional trait. Max Gluckman has pointed out that in non-industrial societies people rebelled not to revolutionize society, but to install better men as rulers.[103] The line of argument is related to Jin Guantao's descriptions of Chinese history. The 'emperorism' he describes was very much about installing a 'good emperor' to replace a bad one. In traditional societies what is demanded is not only a 'good emperor', but the reform of *all*, since the burden of order rests on all. Both Colson and Mair find in traditional witch-hunting movements some of the clearest examples of attempts to perfect social life by perfecting the individuals. Such movements deal with individuals as members of communities where individual redemption is not an end in itself: the aim is a communal reform through the reform and perfection of those who do evil. The guiding principle for witch-hunting movements is that, if only all could be made perfect, then evil would lose its grip and the ideal world would come into existence.[104] Unfortunately, the prerequisite for a witch-hunting movement is still intact in today's China.

Mannheim held that a utopia came about only by shattering order. He saw a distinction between an integrating ideology, which he related mainly to dominant groups, and revolutionizing utopias, which were said to be promoted by ascending groups and the lower strata in society.[105] Paul Ricoeur has questioned this attempt to connect utopias to social strata, and I think his critique of Mannheim is correct on this point.[106] It might be true that lower social strata, at least among the Chinese urban population, support the utopias of 'quality'. At least, this 'consent' is a very important factor in maintaining control and maintaining the rule of the technocrats. In many ways the fact that the 'exemplary' needs such consent to exist might be a factor that can potentially break down the 'totality' of power. Even if the exemplary utopia is about the attempts at total control, I see the exemplary society in opposition to such 'totalitarianism'—a point to which I later return. However, it is the technocratic power-holders who press forward with their utopian schemes of control. The technocrats might be said to be 'ascending', but their *power* is the main force behind the utopia of total control. That such a utopia is about keeping control and building power questions Mannheim's assumption that utopia is about shattering order. Qian Xuesen's theories describe a scientistic utopia where scientists are meant to rule. This has been a characteristic also of a Western utopian tradition,[107] and in China the scientist is increasingly becoming a part of the ruling elite that can realize the utopian dream. Utopias thus are not dreams only. In his discussion of Mannheim, Ricoeur points out the importance of the realizability of utopias: 'a utopia is not only a dream but a dream that wants to be realized'.[108] Mumford has taken this aspect further, categorizing utopias into two types. The first type he calls 'utopias of escape'—mere daydreams, not to be realized— and the second type is called 'utopias of reconstruction', representing programmes wanting to be realized. While the first type leaves the world as it is, the second seeks to actively change society.[109] The exemplary society that we find in China is definitely of the latter category, with its plans for ethical and technocratic perfection. It is definitely not a daydreaming individual's utopia of escape, but a collective project supported by a vast bureaucratic and technocratic machinery for its realization. It is a 'market-socialist' utopia, far removed from the original socialist utopia of freedom; indeed, the Party seems to have designed this utopia as a conservative one. Mannheim has discussed this paradox, pointing out that after the revolution, a conservative trend seems to dominate the socialist utopia. The Party in power wants to control what it has already achieved, and to preserve all its gains.[110]

Since control is combined with change, as we have already seen, the conservative trend represents not only control, but also progress. Control is upheld in the picture of a technocratic utopia and an ethical utopia as well. Both seem designed within the overall picture of scientism. A utopia can have both disintegrating and integrating functions; it can mean both a shattering of the old order and the maintainance of new control; it can be both dream and reality, and can include aspects of both memory and dream. Thus, Mannheim's idea that ideology represents integration and utopia stands for change cannot be upheld in its strict form. The picture is far more complicated. Memory might be identified with ideology and manifested as the 'traditional' aspect of social control, while the dreams paradoxically coming back as the utopian 'objectivity' of scientism might be identified with change. However, in both processes there are integrating and disintegrating aspects, and we can only generally and vaguely identify the first with integration and the second with change. The politics of controlled change further cannot be made into a system of total control. I will maintain that the dream of total control is mainly a dream, and that it contains its own contradictions that make its realization impossible.

Regarding the memories and dreams of social control, the utopias of the past sometimes bear striking resemblances to the realities of the present. Lewis Mumford sums up one of the great utopias of the Western tradition, Plato's *Republic*, by saying that in order to perpetuate his ideal construction Plato relied on three methods: 'breeding, education, and a discipline for the daily life'. The 'biopower' of Foucault, in other words, was already anticipated; Plato advocated the elimination of those who were too deformed, whether spiritually or physically.[111] The educative and disciplinary aspects of the 'Republic' comprise the other two methods of modern ideal Chinese society as well. The 'exemplary society' has distinct educative and disciplinary aspects that manifest themselves in real life. Let us first look at the educative aspects of this phenomenon. Social control is a pedagogical project in China.

Notes to Chapter 2

1. Qian Xuesen and Wu Jiapei, 'Zuzhi guanli shehui zhuyi jianshi de jishu: shehui gongcheng' (Social engineering: a technique for the organization and administration of socialist construction), *Jingji guanli*, No. 1, 1979, pp. 5–9.
2. Ibid., p. 5.
3. Song Huichang, 'Daode jianshe zhong de jige lilun wenti' (Some theoretical questions on moral construction), *Hongqi*, No. 10, 1987, pp. 34–40.
4. Li Cheng and Lynn T. White III, 'China's technocratic movement and the world economic herald', *Modern China*, Vol. 17, No. 3, 1991, pp. 342–88. For a more thorough presentation of Qian Xuesen, see Iris Chang, *Thread of the Silkworm*, New York, Basic Books, 1995.
5. Ibid., pp. 345, 362.
6. Ibid., p. 368.
7. D. W. Y. Kwok, *Scientism in Chinese Thought, 1900–1950*, New Haven, Yale University Press, 1965, p. 3.
8. Christopher Buckley, 'A new May Fourth: the scientific imagination in Chinese intellectual history, 1978–1989', unpublished paper, Australian National University, Canberra, 1989, p. 2.
9. Ibid., p. 5.
10. I here use the distinction suggested by Alvin Gouldner, *The Future of Intellectuals and the Rise of the New Class*, New York, Seabury, 1979.
11. Yu Wujin, 'Lun dangdai Zhongguo wenhua de ji zhong beilun' (On some controversies in contemporary Chinese culture), *Renmin ribao*, 22 August 1988, p. 5.
12. Feng Youlan, 'Why China has no science: an interpretation of the history and consequences of Chinese philosophy' (in Chinese), *Zhongguo zhexue shi bu* (Further historical studies of Chinese philosophy), Shanghai, Wang ling wu, 1924, p. 10; quoted from Christopher Buckley, pp. 12–13.
13. Richard Baum, *Scientism and Bureaucratism in Chinese Thought: Cultural Limits of the Four Modernizations*, Lund University Research Policy Studies Discussion Paper No. 145, Lund, Lund University Research Policy Institute, 1981, p. 16.

14. Thomas Metzger, *Escape from Predicament: Neo-Confucianism and China's Evolving Political Culture*, New York, Columbia University Press, 1977, p. 222.
15. A feudal leader as early as 515 BC is reported to have said: 'If you, my kinsmen by birth and marriage, will rally around me according to the Law of Heaven (*tian fa*)'. (Colin A. Ronan and Joseph Needham, *The Shorter Science and Civilization in China*, Vol. 1, Cambridge, Cambridge University Press, 1978, pp. 294–5).
16. Speech at the opening of the National Conference on Ethics, 'Jiji kaizhan lunlixue de yanjiu' (Actively develop the study of ethics), *Zhexue yanjiu*, No. 6, 1980, pp. 3–5; trans. in *Chinese Studies in Philosophy*, Vol. 13, No. 1, 1981, pp. 37–44.
17. For a sociological analysis of such phenomena in a Western setting, see Ulrich Beck, *Risikogesellschaft: Auf dem Weg in eine andere Moderne*, Frankfurt am Main, Suhrkamp, 1986; trans. Mark Ritter as *Risk Society: Towards a New Modernity*, London, Sage, 1992.
18. Ulrich Beck, *Risk Society*, p. 180.
19. Ibid., p. 158.
20. Hu Yaobang, 'Create a new situation in all fields of socialist modernization: Report to the 12th National Congress of the Communist Party of China, 1 September 1982, *Beijing Review*, Vol. 25, No. 37, 13 September 1982. On the theory of spiritual civilization, see particularly pp. 21–6.
21. Ibid., pp. 21–2.
22. Ibid., pp. 22–3.
23. Ibid., p. 26.
24. Qian Xuesen, 'Zhongshi kexue wenhua fazhan "di si chanye" ' (Pay attention to science and culture and the development of a 'quaternary industry'), *Renmin ribao*, 17 June 1981, p. 3.
25. Qian Xuesen, 'Yanjiu shehui zhuyi jingshen caifu chuangzao shiye de xuewen: wenhuaxue', *Zhongguo shehui kexue*, No. 6, 1982, pp. 89–96; trans. as: 'Culturology: the study of the creation of socialist spiritual wealth', *Social Sciences in China*, Vol. 4, No. 1, 1983, pp. 17–26.
26. Ibid., pp. 18, 20 (90, 92). Popper develops a similar theory about the 'three worlds'. According to Qian, he operates with the objective world (world 1), the subjective world (world 2), and the social world of science, technology, art, and literature (world 3). Qian links his theory to Popper, but criticizes Popper's theory, claiming that Popper mistakenly thinks world 3 has a 'reality' and an 'autonomy' of its own. See Qian Xuesen, 'Yanjiu shehui zhuyi', p. 21 (92). In Popper's own words, '[W]e may distinguish the following three worlds or universes: first, the world of physical objects or physical states; secondly, the world of states of consciousness, or mental states, or perhaps of behavioural dispositions to act; and thirdly, the world of *objective contents of thought*, especially of scientific and poetic thoughts and works of art' (Karl R. Popper, 'Epistemology without a knowing subject', in *Objective Knowledge: An Evolutionary Approach*, rev. edn., Oxford, Clarendon Press, 1979, p. 106.
27. Qian Xuesen and Sun Kaifei, 'Jianli yishi de shehui xingtai de kexue tixi' (Build a scientific system of ideological social formation), *Qiushi*, No. 9, 1988, pp. 2–9.
28. The two also employ the original German expressions *Gesellschaftsformation* and *Ökonomische Gesellschaftsformation* to avoid any misunderstanding about their intentions (Qian Xuesen and Sun Kaifei, p. 2).
29. Ibid.
30. See Pat Howard and Roger Howard, 'China's enterprise management reforms in the eighties: technocratic versus democratic tendencies', paper presented at the

Sino-Australian conference on 'China 40 Years after the Revolution', Research Institute for Asia and Pacific, University of Sydney, September 1989.

31. Qian Xuesen and Sun Kaifei, pp. 3–4.
32. Ibid., p. 5.
33. On the Chinese 'culture fever', see Wei Xiuyi (ed.), *Zhongguo wenhua re* (The Chinese culture fever), Shanghai, Shanghai renmin chubanshe, 1988.
34. Qian Xuesen and Sun Kaifei, p. 5. On the difference between culture (*wenhua*) and civilization (*wenming*), as well as the origins of the concept of 'culturology', see also Liu Wei, *Yi ge sifenkesi zhi mi de qiujie* (Striving to understand the mystery of a sphinx), Beijing, Renmin chubanshe, 1988, pp. 21–5, 33. Liu claims that Qian Xuesen's culturology concept is a recapitulation and a renewal of a theory popular before the revolution.
35. Qian Xuesen and Sun Kaifei, pp. 5, 7.
36. Ibid., pp. 6–8.
37. Ibid., p. 9.
38. *Renmin ribao (haiwai ban)*, 30 March 1993, p. 1. Deng Xiaoping thus repeats the reformist slogan from the turn of the century about Chinese 'wealth and power'. See Benjamin Schwartz, *In Search of Wealth and Power: Yen Fu and the West*, Cambridge, Belknap Press, 1964.
39. Xu Shen, *Shuowen jiezi* (Explanation and analysis of characters), Beijing, Zhongua shuju, 1990, pp. 130, 278. See also Xin Yang (ed.), *Zhongguo banzhurenxue* (Chinese class teacher studies), Changchun, Jilin jiaoyu chubanshe, 1990, p. 84.
40. *Guangming ribao*, 10 January 1988, p. 3.
41. Liu Yuelun, Li Jiangtao, Chen Zhenhong, and Guo Weiqing, *Xiandairen xue* (Modern person studies), Guangdong, Guangdong renmin chubanshe, 1988, p. 4. The group suggest that the content of the new science should include: (1) the characteristics of modern people, (2) the modernization of people's values, (3) the structure of modern personality, (4) the thought patterns of modern people, (5) the relations between modern people, (6) the life-styles of modern people, (7) the question of scientific–technical revolution and the moral responsibility of modern people, and (8) independence and overall development.
42. Ibid., p. 8.
43. Donald J. Munro, *The Concept of Man in Early China*, Stanford, Calif., Stanford University Press, 1969, p. 97.
44. Ibid., p. 227.
45. Yu Qiding, 'Zai lun suzhi—jian ping Hong Baoshu tongzhi de "shangque"' (Discussing quality again—and evaluating comrade Hong Baoshu's 'Discussion'), *Jiaoyu lilun yu shijian*, No. 10, 1990, p. 47.
46. Liu Yuelun *et al.*, p. 198.
47. Ibid., pp. 22–3.
48. Zhang Mingyan, *Zhongguoren de rensheng quxian*, (The lifeline of the Chinese), Beijing, Zhongguo renmin daxue chubanshe, 1989, p. *v*.
49. Bai Yuntao, *Dangdai Zhongguo qingnian suzhi lun* (On the quality of contemporary Chinese youth), Shenyang, Liaoning renmin chubanshe, 1987, p. 7. Others speak of 'conscious self modernization'; see Liu Shugong, 'Yanjiu xiandaihua lilun, tansuo xiandaihua daolu' (Researching modernization theory, approaching the road of modernization), *Lilun yu xiandaihua*, No. 1, 1989, p. 21.
50. Liu Yuelun *et al.*, p. 26.
51. Ibid., p. 68.

52. Wang Guorong (ed.), *Guannian xiandaihua yi bai ti* (One hundred concepts of modernity), Beijing, Yejin gongye chubanshe, 1988.

53. Liu Yuelun *et al.*, p. 71.

54. Liu Binjie, 'Ren de jingshen suzhi xiandaihua', in Gongqingtuan zhongyang xuanchuanbu (Propaganda department of the Youth League Central Committee) (ed.), *Dangdai qingnian lilun dachao* (Theoretical waves on contemporary youth), Beijing, Nongcun duwu chubanshe, 1989, pp. 12–25.

55. Ibid., pp. 12–15.

56. Ibid., p. 20.

57. Peter L. Berger, *Facing up to Modernity*, New York, Basic Books, 1977, p. 75.

58. Ding Dong, 'Qinggan lungang' (Outline of discussions on feelings), *Jinyang yuekan*, No. 6, 1987, pp. 95–103; also in *Fuyin baokan ziliao, B4 Xinlixue*, No. 1, 1988, p. 28.

59. John Naisbitt, *Megatrends: Ten New Directions Transforming our Lives*, New York, Warner Books, 1984, pp. 40, 53.

60. Li Guoshi, 'Siwei fangshi yu xiandaihua' (Modes of thinking and modernization), *Lanzhou xuekan*, No. 4, 1988, pp. 50–5; also in *Fuyin baokan ziliao, B4, Xinlixue*, No. 10, 1988, pp. 19–24.

61. Xu Sumin, 'Ren de xiandaihua' (The modernization of man), *Qingnian luntan*, No. 1, 1984, p. 10.

62. Li Boxi, 'Peiyang qingnian ren: yingjie ershi yi shiji' (Educating young people: welcoming the 21st century), in Gongxingtuan zhongyang yanjiushi (ed.), *Zhongguo daqushi yu dangdai qingnian* (Chinese megatrends and contemporary youth), Jinan, Shandong renmin chubanshe, 1989, pp. 125–33.

63. An investigation of students' attitudes towards quality *(suzhi)* in 1988 found that 80% think that ability *(nengli)* is the most important human quality to strive for (*Zhongguo jiaoyu bao*, 7 July 1988, p. 3).

64. Bai Yuntao, pp. 18–25; see also Alex Inkeles and David H. Smith, *Becoming Modern: Individual Change in Six Developing Countries*, London, Heinemann, 1974.

65. Alex Inkeles, 'The modernization of man', in Myron Weiner (ed.), *Modernization: The Dynamics of Growth*, New York, Basic Books, 1966, pp. 138–50; see also Alex Inkeles and Donald B. Holsinger (eds.), *Education and Individual Modernity in Developing Countries*, Leiden, E. J. Brill, 1974; Alex Inkeles and David H. Smith, *Becoming Modern*; Alex Inkeles, *Exploring Individual Modernity*, New York, Columbia University Press, 1983. Excerpts from Inkeles's works have been compiled and translated into Chinese: Yin Lujun (trans.), *Ren de xiandaihua* (The modernization of man), Chengdu, Sichuan renmin chubanshe, 1985.

66. See e.g. Xu Zhangsong (ed.), *Daxuesheng chengcai xiuyang* (Self-cultivation for university students to grow into useful timber), Shanghai, Fudan daxue chubanshe, 1988, pp. 214–15.

67. Yu Qiding, pp. 46–7.

68. Two scholars even wanted to adopt the elitist Singaporian school system of 'three different classes' to 'raise the quality of the whole nation'; apart from regular classes (*putong ban*), they advocate special classes (*tebie ban*) and fast classes (*kuaijian ban*), and in addition, university preparatory classes (*daxue yuke ban*) for the elite 'to develop outstanding talents' (Zhu Ruoqian and Xu Jiangjia, 'Jiaoyu shi tigao quan minzu suzhi de zhongyao shouduan' (Education is an important method of raising the quality of the whole nation), *Xiandaihua* (Modernization), No. 11, 1988, pp. 19–20; also in *Jiaoyuxue, G1 Fuyin baokan ziliao*, No. 1, 1989, pp. 53–4).

69. One such suggestion in particular emphasizes the importance of raising the quality of rural workers, and the argumentation is one benefiting 'material civilization'. The crux lies in raising the quality of the peasants. See Chen Zhexian, 'Zai tigao nongcun laodongzhe suzhi shangxia gongfu' (Put all efforts into raising the quality of rural workers), *Qiushi*, No. 16, 1990. pp. 36–8.
70. *Shijie jingji daobao*, 10 October 1983, p. 2; 9 April 1984, p. 8; 28 March 1988, p. 1; quoted in Li Cheng and Lynn T. White III, p. 362.
71. Graham Young, 'The 14th Congress of the Chinese Communist Party: consolidation of reformist orthodoxy', *China Information*, Vol. 7, No. 3, 1992–3, p. 7.
72. Li Cheng and D. Bachman, 'Localism, elitism and immobilism: elite formation and social change in post-Mao China', *World Politics*, No. 42, 1989, pp. 64–94.
73. *Shijie jingji daobao*, 1 May 1989, p. 7; quoted in Li Cheng and Lynn T. White III, p. 375.
74. Li Qiang, *Zhongguo dalu de pinfu chabie* (Differences between rich and poor in mainland China), Tianjin, Zhongguo funü chubanshe, 1986, p. 159.
75. Wu Huijing and Fu Wen, 'Jisi zhi luan hou de lengjun fensi: He Xin fang tanlu' (Stern reflections on the chaos of 1989: notes from a talk with He Xin), *Zhongguo Qingnianbao*, 6 December 1989, pp. 1, 3.
76. See Wing-tsit Chan, *Religious Trends in Modern China*, New York, Octagon Books, 1969, pp. 6–10. This connection has been pointed out by Geremie Barmé, 'Travelling heavy: the intellectual baggage of the Chinese diaspora', *Problems of Communism*, Nos. 1–2, 1991, p. 106.
77. See Alex Inkeles and Donald B. Holsinger (eds.), *Education and Individual Modernity in Developing Countries*; Alex Inkeles and David H. Smith, *Becoming Modern*; Alex Inkeles, 'The modernization of man'; Alex Inkeles, *Exploring Individual Modernity*; Joseph A. Kahl, *The Measurement of Modernism: A Study of Values in Brazil and Mexico*, Austin, University of Texas Press, 1968; Alan Peshkin and Ronald Cohen, 'The values of modernization', *Journal of Developing Areas*, No. 2, 1967, pp. 7–21; Daniel Lerner, *The Passing of Traditional Society*, Glencoe, Ill., Free Press, 1965.
78. Michael Armer and Larry Isaac, 'Determinants and behavioral consequences of psychological modernity: empirical evidence from Costa Rica', *American Sociological Review*, Vol. 43, No. 3, 1978, pp. 331, 333.
79. Michel Foucault, *The History of Sexuality*, Vol. 1, *An Introduction*, New York, Vintage Books, 1990, particularly pp. 135–45. The Chinese 'village compacts' (*xianggui minyue*) have been described in the perspective of Foucaultian biopower. These compacts are engaged in the improvement of 'quality' in Chinese society, and describe a special case of the Chinese 'improvement' strategy; see Ann Anagnost, 'Socialist ethics and the legal system', in Jeffrey N. Wasserstrom and Elizabeth J. Perry (eds.), *Popular Protest and Political Culture in Modern China: Learning from 1989*, Boulder, Colo., Westview Press, 1992, pp. 177–205.
80. Michel Foucault, *History of Sexuality*, Vol. 1, all quotations p. 139.
81. Ibid, pp. 139–40. One does not necessarily have to follow Foucault's assumptions of historical development here. It has been claimed that the neat juxtaposition of the punishment of pain (traditional) and the punishment of regulation (modern) is not possible in the case of China. See Michael R. Dutton, *Policing and Punishment in China*, Cambridge, Cambridge University Press, 1992. I think the development of biopower can be seen in the same perspective. The administration of life and the improvement of human quality have deep roots in Chinese history, even if the modern version is different and refined.

82. Michel Foucault, *History of Sexuality*, Vol. 1, p. 140.

83. Ibid., p. 138.

84. Ibid., p. 136.

85. Ibid., p. 141.

86. Ibid., p. 144.

87. See Charlotte Furth, 'From birth to birth: the growing body in Chinese medicine', in Anne Behnke Kinney, *Chinese Views of Childhood*, Honolulu, University of Hawaii Press, 1995, pp. 157–91.

88. For a more detailed account of the historical and intellectual roots of the Chinese eugenics debate, see Frank Dikötter, *The Discourse of Race in Modern China*, Hong Kong, Hong Kong University Press, 1992; Frank Dikötter, *Sex, Culture and Society in Modern China*, London, Hurst, 1994; Frank Dikötter, and *'Imperfect Conceptions': Medical Theories and Birth Defects in Late Imperial China*, forthcoming.

89. About 380,000 babies with physical effects and mental retardation are born in China yearly, *China Daily*, 4 July 1991, p. 4. The 30 million figure is taken from the Eugenics Symposium in Beijing in 1989. See Frank Dikötter, *Imperfect Conceptions: Medical Knowledge, Birth Defects, and Eugenics in China*, London, Hurst, 1998, p. 162.

90. Wang Guorong (ed.), p. 31.

91. Zhou Xiaozheng, 'Renkou suzhi shi wo guo renkou wenti de guanjian' (Population quality is the key to the problem of China's population), *Keji daobao*, No. 4, 1989, pp. 14–19, 28; also in *Fuyin baokan ziliao, Renkouxue, C5*, No. 5, 1989, p. 84.

92. Dikötter translates *ling suzhi* as 'zero worth'. He describes the compulsory character of eugenic legislation and points to the lack of clear definitions of what constitutes a 'severe' handicap or who are 'defective' persons. He instead paints the picture of an overdetermined universe of categories of deviance bent on creating social order and avoiding 'deviance' in its many forms and definitions. Frank Dikötter, *Imperfect Conceptions*, pp. 161, 175.

93. *China Daily*, 4 July 1991, p. 4. The marriage law has already banned the marriage of people with blood ties and infectious diseases.

94. Zhou Xiaozheng, p. 83.

95. All quotations from *SWB-FE*/1685, 11 May 1993, p. B2/4.

96. Mu Guangzhong, 'Renkou suzhi xinlun' (New discussion on human quality), *Renkou yanjiu*, No. 3, 1989, pp. 55–8; also in *Fuyin baokan ziliao, Renkouxue, C5*, No. 5, 1989, pp. 90–3.

97. Ibid., p. 56 (91).

98. Arguments like 'the "iron rice bowl" weakens the psychological quality of the Chinese people', and the praise of the controversial TV-series *'Heshang'* (River Elegy) that is here said to have 'cried out in alarm over the psychology of a weak nation' are sufficient clues to enable such a conclusion. The 'iron rice bowl' is the usual picture used for the welfare functions in Chinese society, while the highly controversial 'River Elegy' was the perhaps best known product of the movement to re-examine the foundations of Chinese cultural identity. The series criticizes the 'yellow culture' of traditional China, and describes a utopia of the 'blue culture' based on distinct myths about the modern and the Western (Mu Guangzhong, p. 57 (92)). For the full text of the TV-series, see Su Xiaokang and Wang Luxiang (eds.), *Heshang* (River elegy), Beijing, Xiandai chubanshe, 1988. See also the extensive discussion on the series over three issues in *Chinese Sociology and Anthropology*, Vol. 24, Nos. 3, 4, 1991–2; Vol. 25, No. 1, 1992.

99. See Frank Dikötter, *Imperfect Conceptions*, p. 165.

100. Li Xiulin *et al.* (eds.), *Zhongguo xiandaihua zhi zhexue tantao* (Approaching the philosophy of Chinese modernization), Beijing, Renmin daxue chubanshe, 1990, p. 368.

101. Lewis Mumford, *The Story of Utopias: Ideal Commonwealths and Social Myths*, London, George G. Harrap, 1923, p. 114.

102. Mencius (372–289 BC) describes the age of Confucius in the following words: 'Again the world fell into decay, and principles faded away. Perverse speakings and oppressive deeds waxed rife again. There were instances of ministers who murdered their sovereigns, and of sons who murdered their fathers . . . Confucius was afraid' 'The Works of Mencius', bk III, pt II, ch. IX, §§ 7, 8, in James Legge (trans.), *The Four Books (Sishu)*, p. 676.

103. Max Gluckman, 'Tribalism in modern British Central Africa', *Cahiers d'Etudes Africains*, Vol. 1, 1960, pp. 55–70.

104. Elizabeth Colson, *Tradition and Contract: The Problem of Order*, Chicago, Aldine, 1974, p. 95; Lucy Mair, *Witchcraft*, New York, McGraw-Hill, 1969, pp. 171–9.

105. Karl Mannheim, *Ideologie und Utopie*, 3rd edn., Frankfurt/Main, Verlag G. Schulte-Bulmke, 1952; quotations in English from *Ideology and Utopia*, trans. Louis Wirth and Edward Shils, New York, Harcourt, Brace & World, 1936.

106. Paul Ricoeur, *Lectures on Ideology and Utopia*, New York, Columbia University Press, 1986, pp. 274, 285.

107. Nell Eurich, *Science in Utopia: A Mighty Design*, Cambridge, Mass., Harvard University Press, 1967.

108. Paul Ricoeur, pp. 276, 289.

109. Lewis Mumford, p. 15 ff.

110. Karl Mannheim, p. 241. This conservativeness of the ruling party is also observed by Alvin Gouldner in his discussion of Soviet approaches to change and control. Gouldner notes the paradox that the essentially change-oriented Marxism had become a troublesome factor for Soviet rulers, and that the emphasis on integrating forces was propagated in the social sciences as well as in the pictures of society painted by the ruling elite (Alvin Gouldner, *The Coming Crisis of Western Sociology*, London, Heinemann, 1971, pp. 454–5).

111. Lewis Mumford, pp. 44, 48, after Plato, *The Republic*, trans. Benjamin Jowett, Oxford, Oxford University Press, 1894.

II

*Education, Society,
and Morality*

3

Socialization, Moral Education, and 'Moral Science'

ALL persons are potentially perfectable through education: this is a strong assumption in Chinese philosophy and culture. The educational environment determines whether or not an individual will be good or evil, and educational reform is a key to solving urgent social and political problems. Some observers have even pointed out that the tendency to regard a person's social behaviour as his essence caused Confucians to overestimate the extent to which human beings are malleable through education.[1] Morality was the core of education; and Xunzi (298–235 BC), like Mencius (fourth century BC) before him, used the virtuous rulers Yao and Yü and the evil rulers Jie and Zhi as his examples:

A person can become a Yao or a Yu [Yü]; he can become a Ch'ie [Jie] or a Chih [Zhi]; he can become a day laborer or an artisan; he can become a farmer or a merchant; it depends on what training he has accumulated from his ways of looking at things and his habits.[2]

Even today, moral education represents both binding and building forces in Chinese society. The theme of controlled change comes back in a compressed form in moral education. We find the themes of discipline and control in both 'moral' and 'education'. Although they are different entities, education and discipline are intermingled and closely interlinked. In education there is discipline, and in discipline there is education. Michel Foucault describes the 'carceral' or the 'prison-like' as a process engulfing every sector of society, including the educational sector.[3] We might turn this picture on its head and also claim that the educational spreads throughout all sectors of Chinese society, including prison. Whether the disciplinary infiltrates the educational or the educational infiltrates the disciplinary is hard to distinguish. Chinese society is a disciplinary society in many senses, but it is also an educational society. A combination of the disciplinary and the educational constitutes the exemplary society of which I speak here, and the 'exemplary' is also made up of morality.

Discipline, education, and morality thus constitute the three pillars of Chinese exemplary society. Education promises continuity with the past while also upholding the dreams of the future. Moral education (*deyu jiaoyu*), including its more recent variant, political–ideological education (*sixiang zhengzhi jiaoyu*), has in various forms been given enormous weight in China—not only during communist rule, but generally throughout history. Mannheim's claim that ideology has an integrating effect in society is fully shared by today's Chinese moral educators. In fact, ideology (*sixiang*) describes a state of harmony and discipline; it seeks to make thoughts alike to achieve harmony.[4]

Moral education has to do with the upholding of moral and social order, and in China the discourse on moral education touches more directly on sociological aspects than in perhaps any other culture. The Party views moral and ideological education precisely from its integrating and social control perspective.[5] Courts, prisons, and the police are important tools of control. They punish the already deviant minority, but they also frighten (*zhenshe*) the majority—those who are not criminals. The tools of control have the effect of frightening people, but they also have an educating effect. As we shall later see, the techniques of both 'pain' and 'spectacle' have definite educational purposes in China. Courts and prisons are the outward signs (*biao*) of control, while moral or ideological education is the basis (*ben*) of social control. The other side of the coin with regard to punishing a small number of people is that it can create good people (*zuo haoren*) through ideological transformation. The most effective type of control comes through the internalization of social norms and rules, but even without such internalization the process of moral education binds individuals to society. Customs, habits, morals, laws, art—all are forces of social control.

It is worth noting that in our own cultural setting 'moral' derives from the Latin '*mores*', meaning social customs, accepted usages, and common behaviour patterns among people, rather than connoting 'ethical'. In China this understanding of 'morality' as a social entity has strong traditions. Chinese discussions on morality and moral education in fact come close to the ideas of Durkheim, who believed that in society he had discovered 'the source and the end of morality'.[6] The classical Chinese character for virtue or morality—*de*—in its old form (德) shows this social connotation. The character on the left-hand side shows a diagram of a crossroads, meaning to go or to move, indicating transformation. The most conspicuous part of the character is a primitive anatomical representation of the eye and the heart, referring to seeing and thinking, respectively. The left-hand component refers to the social matrix.[7] As we shall see, the social element of seeing constitutes a crucial aspect of Chinese socialization theory as well as accentuating the social connotation of morality in Chinese. While the heart symbolizes the 'inner' aspect, the eye symbolizes the 'outer' aspect of socialization. Internalization has to do with the heart, while the externalization of moral rules is transmitted by the proper conduct of an outer kind, observable to the eye.

Contemporary Chinese moral education comes very close to what Durkheim termed a worshipping of society. In *Les formes élémentaires de la vie religieuse*, he tried to demonstrate that throughout history the human race has never worshipped anything other than its own society.[8] The very goal of the educational system was thus to bind individuals to the collectivity, and to persuade them to choose society itself as the object of respect and devotion. In many ways, Chinese moral education resembles Durkheim's ideal of a 'secular morality'. The following description rotates between the texts of Durkheim and the practices of contemporary China. This is not done at random, as there are indeed some striking parallels here. We may start with a passage from David Chu about the relevance of applying Durkheim to the Chinese example:

Durkheim's works had been translated into Chinese and available since before 1949 . . . To my knowledge there is no evidence of Chinese social scientists attempting to elaborate on or to apply the Durkheimian notion . . . One might foresee, however, that as China modernizes in an era that places a premium on order, stability, and reforms—the essential ingredients in the post-Mao strategy of development—gradual change and evolutionary mechanisms may replace rapid transformations by radical, revolutionary means—the hallmark of Maoist strategy. Consequently, Durkheimian concepts may become more attractive, relevant, and therefore, applicable than Marxian ones.[9]

At times Durkheim's viewpoints are strikingly similar to the Chinese official view on moral education, even if in some instances this may differ considerably from Durkheim's own theories. In both cases there is talk of a 'moral science' meant to bring harmony and stability to a changing society. In the following I will use Durkheim's definition of moral education as a phenomenon consisting of three main elements: discipline, attachment to the group, and autonomy. Both education and morality should be seen in a social perspective.

Education, Discipline, and Socialization

The Chinese character *jiao* means 'to teach', 'to instruct', or 'to educate', but it can also have the meaning 'to restrain' and 'to discipline'.

1 First example of the character from the Shang dynasty (1600–1100 BC)
2 Example from Zhou dynasty's Spring and Autumn periods (700–476 BC)
3 Example from Zhou dynasty's Warring States period (475–221 BC).
4 Example of seal character (*zhuan shu*) still used in seals: the character
   represents the first standardized Chinese writing during the Qin dynasty
   (221–207 BC).
5 The character as it is used in today's Chinese writing.

FIGURE 2   The development of the character *jiao* (to teach)

Source: adapted from Gao Ming (ed.), *Guwen zi leibian* (The written types of old characters), Beijing, Zhonghua shuju, 1980, p. 78.

Characters are catalysts of culture; we might also analyse them as living social fossils of history. Words and phrases are small windows that make us familiar with the people of the past and thereby also people of the present. Our interpretations of the meaning sedimented in old character inscriptions might add to our understanding of the social processes behind them. In the particular case discussed here, the matter concerns the disciplining and integrative functions of education.

These aspects of education can be illustrated by the etymology of the character *jiao* (教). This character is remarkable for its stability. Versions of it over three thousand years old have been found inscribed on tortoise shells from the Shang dynasty, and the different elements of the character have been nearly identical ever since (see Figure 2). Although today's character looks somewhat different from the original one, this is a mere change in the design of the strokes: all the elements are fully intact. We know of no other written signs or characters that have been in use as long as some of these Chinese characters without considerable change.

The character *jiao* consists of three basic elements. The first resembles two letters 'x' written one over the other (爻). In the *Yijing* (The book of changes) this was originally one of the divinitory symbols. It was later spelled '*yao*' and came to stand for written educational material, or the contents of education; it also stood for change (*bianyuan*), showing the transformative element of education through educational material.[10] To the right in the character we find the second element, '*pu*' (攴), depicted by a hand holding a whip or a person holding a whip in his hand, representing the teacher as well as the method of education and reflecting the ancient idea of discipline.[11] *Pu* also has a

connotation of movement and action.[12] A Chinese proverb still emphasizes 'making the hand grasp the whip' (*yi shou zhi bian*) as the best
method of education. Even if the official line is today to ban corporal
punishment from schools, reports about its practice both in families
and particularly in rural schools are still frequent. The third element,
the character *jiao*, further represents the integrating element of education by describing the respectful and submissive, particularly emphasized in the element under the '*yao*'—the '*zi*' (♀). *Zi* stood for the person
who is being whipped (educated). This '*zi*' still stands for 'son' or 'child'
in Chinese. It was written in the picture as a small person with his
arms apparently stretching upwards. Even the position of this element
placed under the other elements in the overall character has been understood by some as signifying the underdog position of the whipped one—
the student or pupil—signifying subordination.[13] The disciplining effect,
however, lies both in the educational material and in the educational
method. The element of morality is also strong. Submission and
obedience to one's elders were to represent the core of Chinese social
relations for thousands of years. The principle of *zhong jiao hou de*—
'emphasizing education and morality'—has been a stable element in
Chinese culture for over three thousand years. The stability of these
aspects is remarkable. Education, morality, and discipline are closely
connected in this tradition, and education still fluctuates around the
same themes as when the character *jiao* was inscribed on a tortoise shell
sometime during the Shang dynasty.

Not only does education contain discipline. Michael Dutton claims
that the educative element of discipline can be found in the development of the characters for 'prison' or 'confinement'.[14] Early meanings
of 'prison' were linked to connotations of discipline and confinement
only, like the term *huantu* (圜土). This can be rendered as 'circular city
of earth', and it was this form of mud-walled compound that characterized the shape of a prison at that time and up to the Han dynasty
(206 BC–AD 220). The same can be said of the character *qiu* (囚), a very
simple and clear picture signifying a person surrounded by an enclosure,
indicating detention. This character appeared during the Zhou dynasty
(1100 BC). Even during the Zhou, however, the term *lingyu* (囹圄) was
used, later to reappear in the Qin. This, too, was dominated by the
enclosure radical (囗), but indicated something new, and far removed
from a mere enclosure. For inside the first enclosure we now find the
character *ling* (令), to command, order, or decree, while the other has
wú (吾) at its centre (reading as *wù* (悟)), to realize or awaken. Hence
lingyu can be rendered as the place where one is ordered to realize one's
errors.

It is in the domain of actions and behaviour that we find the basic elements of Chinese moral education. Morality in China is a social form of morality, based largely upon the gaze of the other. The fear of what others might say about you is the greatest fear in Chinese society, says Sun Longji, quoting the Chinese saying that 'gossip is a fearful thing' (*renyan ke wei*).[15] To a great extent, morality is about how you adapt to outward rules. 'Doing' seems to be the main principle here, more important than 'being'. In China a person can be realized only in his or her social connections: there is no personality (*renge*) behind these connections, as Sun sees it. Chinese culture emphasizes the bond to the group, and a Chinese person is expected to be 'utterly devoted to others without thought of self' (*hao bu li ji, zhuanmen li ren*). This is not a principle originating in Marxism, even if it dovetails nicely with the collectivist ethos propagated in socialist China, but is a traditional way of 'being a person'—literally, 'doing a person' or 'making a person' (*zuo ren*). Here the 'doing' or 'making' means to behave in a certain prescribed way in society.[16] 'To make a person' resembles the expression *zuo xi*, playing theatre, or 'making' theatre, and thus indicates a certain level of 'acting' or even inauthenticity in the process. One may also recall Goffman's 'presentations of self', although in China the 'performance' normally does not take place in the random 'encounters' described by him, but rather in a structured and well-defined hierarchy of social connections led by strict rules and norms. The classical themes of self-discipline, loyalty, and obedience are strong in this Chinese conception of being a person, and a person's social attachment is incorporated in the very definition of what it means to be a person. The distinctions between 'individual' and 'society' tend to be diminished, if not to disappear entirely. Such a viewpoint of course has consequences for the socialization practices followed in a culture.

Durkheim once pointed to the limits of discipline by claiming that discipline could only 'train mechanically (*dresser*); but it cannot educate, since it produces no inner effects'.[17] In Chinese pedagogy this phenomenon of the 'mechanical' has also been observed. However, it has been given a different interpretation from that in Durkheim's works, and not as a negative trait only. Even if Chinese pedagogy, like Durkheim, sees the internalization (*neihua*) of social values as the highest stage of the socialization process, it seems to accept the not-so-ideal facts of mechanical training and outward control as building bricks and important steps in the hierarchy of socialization. By 'doing the right thing', you also influence others who will tend towards emulating and imitating what is seen and experienced around them.

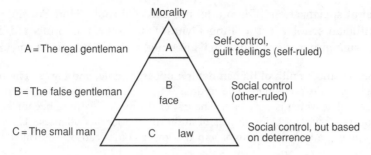

Non-formal control rules A and parts of B; formal control rules parts of B as well as all of C.

FIGURE 3   The Chinese 'pyramid of morality' or 'pyramid of socialization'

Source: Chen Zhizao, 'Mianzi xinli de lilun fenxi yu shiji yanjiu' (The theoretical analysis and practical study of the psychology of face), in Yang Guoshu (ed.), *Zhongguo ren de xinli* (The psychology of the Chinese), Taipei, Guiguan tushu gongsi chubanshe, 1989, p. 176.

Durkheim's *dresser* has an integrated part to play in the overall picture of socialization, since, by showing proper conduct without necessarily internalizing it, you also contribute to the improvement of others. In this respect the collective social setting is more important than individual inner thoughts. In Chinese socialization theory and practice, we might thus talk of a type of *externalization* contrasting the ideal of internalization.

According to Donald Munro, the actual process of human cultivation has two sides. One can be identified as 'inner' (*nei*), and the other as 'outer' (*wai*). The first is related to techniques of introspective self-examination, 'looking within', while the latter is related to the emulation of the attitudes and outward behaviours of models.[18] Instead of the 'looking within', we here see a 'looking at others' defining the socialization process. The latter is also the most frequent way of socialization, even if it might be far more 'mechanical' than the introspective internalization of norms. Rather than saying that mechanical discipline cannot educate, the Chinese operate with levels of discipline where such methods of externalization stand below internalization, but above the techniques of coercion and deterrence.

This phenomenon is indicated by Chen Zhizhao's 'pyramid of morality' or 'pyramid of socialization', set up to explain the traditional as well as the current hierarchy of morality and socialization practices in China. In Figure 3 he distinguishes three main steps in the hierarchy of morality.[19]

Chen, a contemporary scholar based in Taiwan, typically uses the classical expressions of the Confucian 'gentleman' (*junzi*), also translated as 'man of noble character' or 'ethically cultivated person', as the ideal of socialization. The model has classical roots. Han Yu, the great Confucian scholar in the Tang Dynasty (618–907), commented upon the original nature of individuals as taught by Confucius by saying:

> There are three ranks of human nature: upper, middle, and lower. The upper is that which is only good. The middle is that which can be led upwards, the lower is that which is only bad. The upper degree by learning becomes intelligent, the lower by being in fear of authority reduces its offenses. Therefore, the upper grades can be taught and the lower grades can be controlled.[20]

We find frequent references to a similar model both in the People's Republic and on Taiwan. In theory, any person can be improved and 'fostered' into perfectability. Today's Chinese educators and social engineers view the phenomenon more as a continuum than as a model with fixed stages. Socialization cannot change all people into one type. The 'degree of socialization' (*shehuihua chengdu*) reflects degrees of the ideal or model personality of a nation or a cultural environment, according to one commentator.[21] But there are some who seem to fall outside the sphere of education—the small group of deviants who can no longer be cured. In such extreme cases, where improvement is impossible, capital punishment is the only remaining option. As I will later explain, capital punishment has an educative effect by parading vice to others in order to demonstrate retributive justice. The 'educational' follows us on to the scaffold itself, infiltrating the 'carceral'. Roughly put, the Chinese process of socialization can be seen as a theatre in which the minority of upper and lower levels parade virtue and vice for the wavering but educable majority of the middle. But first, more on the pyramid of morality in Figure 3.

The 'real gentleman' (*zhen junzi*) is of course like the classical sage, and stands far above the intermediary stage of the 'false gentleman' (*wei junzi*). The real gentleman is characterized as having internalized the social rules, making them a part of himself. According to Chen, this is the socialization by 'self-rule' where social rules and norms are intrinsically understood and followed out of an autonomous insight into necessity. Self-rule often means self-cultivation (*xiuyang*) and self-reflection—*neixing* in the Confucian vocabulary. Confucius also used the expression *shendu*, often translated as 'to be watchful over oneself when alone'. Mencius advocated similar techniques and talked about self-examination (*fanshen*) or introspection (*fanxing*).[22] In another repetition of traditional techniques of control, the same expressions can be read in today's educational textbooks and self-cultivation manuals. The real gentleman is the ideal personality of an exemplary society; the model for others to emulate. The degree of socialization is in fact identical to the degree of exemplary personality. The real gentleman is 'watchful over himself when alone'; he follows the rules and norms even when the social gaze of others cannot reach him. This is the highest stage.

The false gentleman, as the expression indicates, is in part a 'gentleman', possessing the potential to reach the level of a real gentleman. 'False' here has to do with the fact that the adaptation to social rules is not entirely internalized: rather, moral conduct is upheld out of fear for what those close to one would say and do if rules and norms were broken. The Chinese concept of 'face' (*mianzi*) is important in this respect. The concept is broad and touches many aspects; suffice it here to indicate its effects on '*dresser*', and the fact that order is upheld only under the social gaze of others. When not observed, false gentlemen would break the rules, and one can say that they are led by 'falseness' rather than by internalized autonomous insight into the rules. This is the 'normal' way of *zuo ren*, or 'doing/making a person'. The most important thing is what the other thinks about you. Sun Longji explains that 'moral character' in Chinese is *renpin* (人品). *Ren* is 'man' or 'person', and since *pin* is the picture of three mouths, the Chinese character indicates 'what three mouths say about you'.[23] One can say that *zuo ren* is about surface, but that the process concerns not only oneself. It rather means that if you behave well, you will also give face to the other. There is social reciprocity in the act, and to 'make a person' entails 'self' as well as 'other'. The false gentleman is 'other-ruled', doing what he expects others want him to do when he is watched. Some claim that, if this category of socialization is allowed to reign, one might develop a lackey character (*nucai xing*) characterized by overt agreement but covert opposition (*yangfeng-yinwei*) against what is said and done. This is the case of the 'false gentleman' (*wei junzi*), or the hypocrite. The remedy for such tendencies is to implement a strong guidance function (*daoxiang gongneng*) actively directing the socialization process. This view is blind to the possibility that cementing inflexible rules and norms might in fact strengthen phenomena like the false gentleman.[24]

The false gentleman is deemed to represent the situation for the vast majority of people, and here we also find the main arena of education as the Chinese have traditionally seen it. Perfection originates in imperfection, and conscious understanding in mechanical acceptance. Positioned between the real gentleman and the 'small man' (*xiaoren*), the most advanced elements of this group can reach the highest level, while the lowest elements can at least be educated to abide by the law. In traditional China the law had a low standing, viewed only as a last resort for upholding order. The law was for the 'small man'; and the small man, according to this model, was educated into a better level if ruled by falseness rather than by law. The doing of the right thing is an improvement to the lawlessness that is its alternative, and as long as this falseness leads to correct outward behaviour it also has a positive effect on the social order. 'Falseness', in other words, is not all that bad when seen in its social rather than its individual context. Donald J. Munro has remarked that in both Confucian and Daoist thought, behavioural implications count more than the truth or falseness of a statement:

In China, truth and falsity in the Greek sense have rarely been important considerations in a philosopher's acceptance of a given belief or proposition; these are Western concerns. The consideration important to the Chinese is the behavioral implications of the belief or proposition in question. What effect does adherence to the belief have on people? What implications for social action can be drawn from the statement?[25]

Normally, the small man can understand only the language of force and deterrence. This level of the socialization hierarchy is about instilling fear in the subject. Only the real gentleman can rely on self-control or non-formal control, while both false gentlemen and small men have to be kept in check by different means of social and formal control. Even if the model builds on traditional thinking, it defines quite precisely the way moral educators think in China today. The model explains that discipline is part of the whole education or socialization process, but that it develops from its low stage of law and deterrence, via the intermediate level of 'face' and 'falseness', to the high level of self-discipline. There is more identification and 'understanding' of society the higher up we move in the pyramid, whereas the lowest level is that closest to the natural or unsocialized person.

In this brief outline of the pyramid of morality, we should touch on the questions of morality (*de*) and law (*fa*) that have dominated Chinese debates on social control for centuries. Law is indeed less important than morals in Chinese tradition: law should be used to punish the evil, not to encourage the good; law is able to punish men, but unable to make men kind. All good behaviour is derived from education, and only when people are led by virtue will they have a sense of shame and become good.[26] Virtue is closely linked to the following of rules in Chinese tradition, as shown by the concept of *li*. The following passage in Confucius's *Analects* addresses this problem:

If the people be led by laws, and uniformity sought to be given them by punishments, they will try to avoid *the punishment*, but have no sense of shame. If they be led by virtue, and uniformity sought to be given them by the rules of propriety (*li*), they will have the sense of shame, and moreover will become good.[27]

The *li* of which Confucius spoke so positively, and which Legge has translated as 'rules of propriety', may be better translated as 'rules of proper conduct'.[28] This is what is meant by virtue in China, and the rules of proper conduct have been said to constitute the very core of what it means to be Chinese: 'From the perspective of ordinary people, to be Chinese was to understand and accept the view that there was a correct way to live one's life', says James Watson. '[P]ractice rather than belief was what made one Chinese in the eyes of others.'[29] In the rituals of daily life, 'orthopraxy' (correct practice) rather than orthodoxy (correct belief) has been the most important part of the construction of 'Chineseness'. Interviews with Cantonese villagers revealed that they knew a lot about *li*, and talked extensively about it. Without *li* there was improper behaviour, impoliteness, uncivilized actions, and disorder (*luan*).[30] The rules of proper conduct are very much connected to the discipline of education and morality; they represent the core of moral education today as in traditional society. *Li* provides integration as well as identity, and the control function of *li* is a more effective one than that of law alone, goes the argument. The primary function of *li* is to prevent human conflict; the superiority of *li* is that it not only constrains, but also 'ennobles' human beings.[31] In other words, *li* represents not only the disciplinary and binding elements, but also the improving element in society. The distinction between *li* and *fa* also had a class perspective, *li* being the code of honour among the ruling group, while *fa* was valid only for the common man.[32]

Xunzi comments on the ennobling effect of *li*: 'To display sincerity and take away falseness is the law of the rules of proper conduct.'[33] Several commentators, however, have pointed to the exact opposite effect, showing that *li* might instead have constituted a founding element of the very same falseness. By emphasizing *li*, the Chinese have paid a considerable price. Donald Munro claims that, since so much of human conduct is dictated by *li*, behaviour tends to degenerate into formalism and mere habitual practice of the customary norms.[34] I will return to these problems in my concluding chapter.

The distinction between rule by virtue and rule by law has been widely debated during the present reforms. Many voices of reform have emphasized law as a modern answer to the less exact and more particularistic entity of virtue. However, they are negotiating from a position of weakness. An official article written in the aftermath of the 1989 Beijing massacre blamed the unrest on the neglect of moral education, and claimed that moral education had become a mere appendage to the school system. The so-called 'subordination theory' (*congshu lun*) was said to have been dominant in the late 1980s, diminishing the role of moral education. Stress had been on 'replacing morality with law' (*yi fa dai de*) and 'replacing morality with intellectual [education]' (*yi zhi dai de*). According to the article, an even more extreme standpoint was represented by the 'cancelling theory' (*dixiao lun*), which stood for getting rid of moral education, claiming that such education had simply been a waste of energy. Certainly, one should now step up the use of moral education.[35] Recent reports emphasize that the 'development of a market economy demands not only legal but moral support', and a quotation from Deng Xiaoping stressing moral education, saying that 'the decline in moral standards will affect the economic performance', is again much referred to.[36]

Morality has always been seen as a more important aspect of social integration and control than has law. Thus, moral education has been institutionalized to a degree and in a way that perhaps no other cultures have experienced. Sun Longji has remarked that in China there is often no distinction between government administration (*zheng*) and the education represented by the *jiao*, which we have already discussed.[37] The bureaucratization and instrumentalization of education is closely connected to the control aspect of education. In my opinion, much of what has been called pedagogy in China has been less preoccupied with methods of creative learning than it has been directed towards finding methods of effective control. Education has mainly been about the ways to rule rather than about the ways to teach. Discipline, loyalty, submission, control—these are some of the most important 'synonyms' of the Chinese word for education. The same administration, bureaucratization, and instrumentalization of morality are found in Chinese society even today, making the talk of a 'construction' of morality nearly literal through large-scale campaigns to encourage moral deeds and the exhibition of correct behaviour.

The disciplinary elements of education and the educative elements of discipline form an important basis for today's exemplary society. But the discipline of education is not enough to constitute 'exemplarity'. As we have seen, discipline is linked to morality, and this connection has to be further explored before we can understand the importance and meaning of Chinese moral education.

Morality, Regularity, and Constraint

What, then, does morality entail? According to Durkheim, it involves consistency and a regularity of conduct. It also invariably involves some sense of authority constraining us to act in certain ways. These two features of morality—regularity of conduct and authority—are both aspects of discipline. 'The fundamental element of morality is the spirit of discipline', says Durkheim.[38] Both 'moral' and 'education' must be seen as strong integrating forces in society. Durkheim, like the Chinese moral educators of today, was very concerned about how to reactivate integrating forces in a period of violent change. Much as in today's official Chinese theories, he was also preoccupied not only with the problem of order as such, but with the problem of the changing nature of order.[39] In that sense, Durkheim's standpoint is very close to the Chinese model of controlled change, and the allegedly Marxist Chinese regime is much more Durkheimian than Marxist in this respect. It would be misleading to claim that either Durkheim or today's Chinese regime are arch-conservatives, cementing the memories of the past at any cost. In both conceptions there is considerable understanding of the fact that society is changing. Durkheim points this out explicitly by maintaining that control must adapt to as well as contribute to change. As in the Chinese theories discussed earlier, the important question is not change versus non-change, but the speed and direction of change:

[W]e must not see in the preference of control certain indescribable tendencies toward stagnation . . . It is not a matter of knowing whether one must move or not, but at what speed and in what fashion.[40]

Instead of seeing morality as something fixed and static, emphasis is on the disciplining and integrating aspects of morality and moral education in their changing surroundings. There is also in both conceptions a clear understanding of the social aspects of morality. Just as the Chinese of today as well as yesterday see morality in the 'rules of proper conduct', and as a social rather than a transcendental phenomenon, Durkheim too sought the origins of morality in the social sphere: 'In a general sense, morality begins where and when social life begins.'[41] Morality varies from society to society; in this, Durkheim sees a proof that morality is a social product: 'it is impossible to desire a morality other than that endorsed by the conditions of society at a given time'.[42] Roman society would not have survived if, through some miracle, it had suddenly been exposed to the morality of Western Europe in the late nineteenth century: 'Each social type has the morality necessary to it, just as each biological type has a nervous system that enables it to sustain itself.'[43] Morality also has to be sufficiently flexible to adapt to the changing conditions: 'Society is continually evolving; morality itself must be sufficiently flexible to change gradually as proves necessary.'[44] Since morality is in a process of gradual and slow change, 'we shall feel it our duty to combat moral ideas that we know to be out of date and nothing more than survivals'. The most effective way to do this is to deny such ideas not only in theory but also in action.[45]

In Chinese moral education we find the same argument. The methods of moral education should 'fit the times' (*shidai xing*). If in moral education the 'key' does not fit, the 'lock' of peoples' ideological problems will not open.[46] The need for flexibility in 'fitting the times', however, runs the risk of being stifled by a too rigid process of planning. The planned or 'guided' change of which the Chinese speak might thus turn into an obstacle to change rather than a promotion of it. More specifically, the 'exemplary key' might not fit the 'lock of market socialism'. The Confucian roots of such thought are obvious. Zhu Xi (1130–1200) held that the *li*—the rules of proper conduct—in principle were subject to revision or even elimination. Commenting that the ancient rules of proper conduct did not fit needs in the Song dynasty, Zhu Xi advocated 'upholding the essential and practical' only, and felt free to make deletions and additions to the rules as he saw fit. One must reject rules that are burdensome and superfluous, and retain those that are practicable and essential to the maintanance of the social order, he claimed.[47] In principle, then, *li* is open to great flexibility. As we shall see, however, the formalization of rules represents a counter-trend, ossifying and 'fixing' exemplary norms.

Yun Pengju maintains that mankind not only recognizes the world, but actively changes it by transforming it. Not only do we receive social experiences, social culture, and social rules, we also reproduce the social system. By transforming our own experiences, we form our own values and aims.[48] Recognition and knowledge, however, constitute the foundation on which such transformation rests in most of the Chinese literature on the subject. As I have already shown, the planned and thereby harmonized way in which such transformation is thought to occur, for example by introducing and fostering allegedly objective 'modern values', characterizes the mainstream Chinese approach. Again we have a case of 'controlled change' in contrast both to more violent change and to mere stagnation and passivity. An important point about moral education is that it consists of a system of rules of behaviour that predetermine conduct, just as in the case of the Chinese *li*. Such rules state how one must act in certain given situations. Even if morality is a changing social entity, the important thing is that it is a basically constant, integrating force. 'Morality . . . implies a certain ability to develop habits, a certain need for regularity', and habit formation constitutes a 'binding advice', as Durkheim puts it.[49]

Regularity and predictability are central aspects of the system of modern 'moral planning' in China, and the formation of habits is regarded as one of the most important fundaments of the social order. An important aspect in all Chinese education is practising over and over again (*fanfu*) to change individual habits.[50] The integrating functions of habit formation were among the concerns at the fifth Chinese National Morality Conference in 1990, and is a theme frequently addressed by moral educators.[51] There must, however, be more to morality than regularity. Rules and customs must have a firm foundation, and this can be secured only through authority from some superior power. Besides regularity, there must be authority:

[T]hese two aspects of morality are closely linked, their unity deriving from a more complex idea that embraces both of them. This is the concept of discipline. Discipline in effect regularizes conduct. It implies repetitive behavior under determinate conditions . . .[52]

One of the most crucial insights to be learned from the Durkheimian analysis is that discipline is not to be viewed as sheer constraint, neither in its foundations nor in its consequences. Discipline builds upon education and morality, and thus, contrary to an understanding merely emphasizing an outer type of coercion, or some external, palpable police force, it resides in social life itself: 'authority does not reside in some external, objective fact . . . It is the judgement of the group.'[53] In its consequences, discipline also contributes to more than sheer coercion: it offers security and restraint against limitless aspiration. In the first place, discipline predetermines appropriate modes of response without which order and organized life would be unthinkable. It frees us from the need to grope *de novo* for an appropriate response to every stimulus from the environment, and provides ontological security for each individual. Without such limits, we suffer the inevitable frustration and disillusionment entailed by limitless aspiration.

That the Chinese control system is not based on sheer constraint has been pointed out by many observers. Walder, commenting on dependency relations in the work-unit, remarks that behaviour stemming from such dependency relations 'become habitual, almost second nature to employees'.[54] Anagnost too points out that the Chinese system of control leans heavily on willed consent.[55] In this sense, the Chinese practice fits neatly in with the concept of hegemony: 'The "normal" exercise of hegemony . . . is characterized by the combination of force and consent, which balance each other reciprocally, without force predominating extensively over consent', Gramsci sums up in his *Prison Notebooks*.[56] In many ways, the exemplary society comes close to the Gramscian description of willed consent.

The moral control found in the exemplary society is a powerful control indeed, in many ways more resistant to upheavals and break-downs than systems based on sheer coercion. Still, it is incorrect to describe the exemplary society as an example of total control. Michel Foucault's theory seems to me to be too closed, leaving no potential for evasion from or rebellion against total disciplinary control. His views, however, are highly relevant for the Chinese example, and I agree with Alberto Melucci when he claims that 'Foucault's arguments over-emphasize the image of a totalizing "Orwellian" control, yet they point correctly to the diffuse and less visible forms of system integration.'[57] It is precisely in describing these forces of disciplinary system integration that Foucault fits the Chinese reality but this disciplinary society is different from the exemplary society I discuss here. I think it is precisely in the social origins of discipline that we find the limits of total control. An exemplary society that leans heavily on mechanisms of morality and education might in some ways be more flexible than the Orwellian models of societies that are mere fictions and impos-sible models of total control. 'Community control' based on social rules and norms of proper conduct is a more realistic and effective system of control than 'Big brother' models of outer repression. Why is it still not total control? Despite its potentially greater flexibility, an exemplary society also tends towards inflexibility in a technocratic and illusory ideal of total predictability and thereby towards another form of inflexibility and 'supersociality'. Its alleged predictability was, however, presented as the very 'scientific' foundation for such a society. Here we may quote Alasdair MacIntyre about the generally meagre possibilities of total social control:

Since organizational success and organized predictability exclude one another, the project of creating a wholly or largely predictable society is doomed, and doomed by the facts of social life. Totalitarianism of a certain kind, as imagined by Aldous Huxley or George Orwell, is therefore impossible. What the totalitarian project will always produce will be a kind of rigidity and inefficiency which may contribute in the long run to its defeat.[58]

The experiences of the twentieth century, however, must make us ask how long that long run is, without changing our main theoretical argument about the faint possibilities of *total* control. A 'science of moral-ity', as seen in today's China with its positivist quest for total predictability and social and moral engineering, does not become much prettier by our rejection of the argument about total control. Fortunately how-ever, this gives us a more positive perspective on the future than do theories of total control.

On Limitlessness, Self-Restraint, and Attachment to the Group

Moral education is fundamentally about drawing boundaries and setting limits. Throughout his academic career, Durkheim emphasized the dangers of limitless aspiration. Limitless aspiration is found in the *anomie* of modern society. Reaction to the confrontation with rapid changes in values, life-styles, consumption patterns, work methods, forms of social contact, etc., produces a feeling of insecurity among people about what rules to follow. The sociological concept of *anomie* has become well-known in Chinese sociology in recent years. A Chinese glossary of sociological terms gives several translations for *anomie*. The expression *shifan*—meaning to 'lose limits'—reflects the Durkheimian emphasis on the dangers of limitlessness. Another translation is *wu guifan*, meaning 'without norms' or 'without standards'; a third one is *fanchang*, meaning 'unusual', 'perverse', 'strange', or 'abnormal'.[59] The last translation has contributed to an inflated use of the concept, giving it a missionary-like interpretation about fighting modern spiritual pollution in general, linking that which is modern to that which is deviant. Moral education is intended to oppose such effects of the modernization process, to create a preference for balance and moderation as well as some feelings of moral limits, so as to prevent the pessimism, frustrations, and disorders that follow from insatiable aspirations.

The limitlessness of human desire is an old theme in Chinese philosophy. Xunzi's discussion of *li* makes the point that *fen*—setting limits—is of utmost importance for upholding order in society. Xunzi's discussion on the theory of *li* (*lilun*) touches upon many problems that will later be central to Durkheim:

What is the origin of the rules of proper conduct (*li*)? Humans are born with desires. When desires are not satisfied, they cannot but seek some means to satisfy them. When this seeking has no measure and limits, there will be contention. From contention comes social disorder (*luan*); from social disorder comes poverty. The former kings hated such disorder, and hence they established *li* in accord with their sense of rightness (*yi*), in order to set limits (*fen*) to this confusion, to educate and nourish (*yang*) human desires, and to provide opportunity for this seeking of satisfaction.[60]

Durkheim describes the abnormality of 'insatiable society' in the picture of a bulimiac:

With a certain amount of nourishment a normal man is no longer hungry; it is the bulimiac who cannot be satisfied . . . In order to have a full sense of self-realization, far from needing to see limitless horizons rolling before him, in reality he finds nothing as unhappy as the indeterminate reach of such a prospect ... [H]e can only be happy when involved in definite and specific tasks.[61]

Such specific tasks, Durkheim is quick to point out, do not limit us to a fixed position where we will find ultimate tranquility: there is movement also on the other side of limitlessness. In China this phenomenon is expressed in the combination of moderation and modernization. Moral rules limit the insatiability of the modernization process, and these rules are 'still more invariable than all the others; to learn to act morally is also to learn conduct that is orderly'.[62]

Durkheim saw the learning of school rules as an important part of education. By respecting such rules, the child was to learn respect for rules in general and thereby also to develop the habit of self-control.[63] The same assumption is a main dogma of Chinese moral education. The importance of learning school rules by heart is the starting point of every lesson in political and moral education. The repetitive aspect is again crucial.[64] The authority of rules and regulations is necessary to halt and contain rebellious forces, and 'to prevent the individual from encroaching on forbidden territory'.[65] In the setting of rules and drawing of boundaries for social life, and in preventing the consequences of limitlessness, we can talk of morality as a 'moral force' in the way both Durkheim and the Chinese moral educators do. In this way morality operates as a binding force—but, as we shall later see, also as a building force.

Today the theme of limitlessness in China is taken up in kindergartens as well as on the macro level of national politics. Some months before the Beijing spring of 1989, the theme of limitless expectations was discussed by the State Institute of Systemic Reform as a potential time bomb ticking towards social explosion. Their researchers warned against a too high or 'premature consumption' (*chaoqian xiaofei*). People had become used to growth during the 1980s, and expectations were ever higher. When setbacks (*cuozhe*) then suddenly occurred in the late 1980s, an explosion was predicted. The 1988 report showed with the help of statistical material that more people felt it was getting harder to survive in 1987 and 1988. Curves for the discrepancy between expectations and real development from 1984 to 1988 indicated the setback of reform, but also illustrated the theory of the danger of unrealistically high or limitless expectations.[66] This theory is a plausible one, and similar variants have also been discussed in the West, at least since de Tocqueville. The gap between reality and expectations certainly seems to have been an important factor in the incidents in

China the following spring. This late 1988 warning is bound to have impressed cadres who tried to put brakes on the Juggernaut of modern consumption in the years following the 1989 crackdown.

Thrift has always been an important theme of moral education. Even in a future developed China, such values are to be adhered to; and Deng Xiaoping is quoted as having said after the 1989 crackdown that 'the education on hard work and plain living will continue in the coming 60 to 70 years'.[67] Again and again now, it is claimed that the consumption needed for market reforms to work in no way is contradictory to the old virtues of 'plain living and hard struggle' (*jianku pusu jianku fendou*)—an old core concept in the vocabulary of Chinese moral education.[68] On the contrary, one should now practise plain living and hard struggle more than ever before. A high standard of living should still be combined with thrift and plain living since such virtues are to be regarded as a life-style and a moral culture in itself.[69]

My own interviews with class teachers in a Beijing primary school in 1991 confirmed such views. Parents were discouraged from giving pocket-money to children. Being gluttonous (*tanzui*) was regarded as a very negative trait, and was seen as one of the dangers of modern society.[70] Thrift is seen as an economic input in much the way Benjamin Franklin explained it in early capitalist America. Attacks against the 'theory of high consumption' (*gao xiaofei lun*) are combined with suggestions that tempering and improving oneself will make China strong. One might say that the massive propagation of thrift represents a particular form of 'moral economy'.[71]

The enticements of limitlessness are constrained through the ability of self-control. To halt the dangers of limitless aspiration, one has to 'bind' individuals. Of course, such restraint is to some degree an external restraint forced upon us, but it should also be reflected as an internal expression. In fact, 'the most essential element of character is this capacity of restraint or—as they say—of inhibition, which allows us to contain our passions, our desires, our habits . . . '.[72] From this follows a recommendation that moral education should be concerned primarily with the fostering of self-restraint and self-control. '[T]his capacity for self-control is itself one of the chief powers that education should develop', according to Durkheim.[73] If I should choose one theme where Durkheim and today's Chinese moral educators are fundamentally in agreement, it would be this emphasis on self-restraint and self-control. Chinese textbooks in pedagogy and moral education are full of references to this central theme. 'Self-control [*ziwo kongzhi*] is the basis of all education', say educators Wu and Chen, who proceed to several core arguments on moral education which we also find in

Durkheim's theories. Self-control represents a conscious process of internalization of moral rules and norms to be changed into action. It helps create identity (*tongyi xing*) between self and society, and makes the 'natural person' (*ziran ren*) develop into a 'social person' (*shehui ren*).[74]

The identity between individual and society, and the change from natural to social persons, originates in the capacity for self-control. This theme seems a universal one in moral education. In America during the period of transition to modern industrial society, a quite similar emphasis on self-restraint was witnessed.[75] The 'real gentleman' was of course the master of this game in ancient China, and self-control was then regarded as the highest stage of discipline. Individual harmony affects social actions and promotes the stability of society. Self-control manifests the moral and social order. Even modern values are often combined with the emphasis on self-control in the 'modern concept' literature from which I have quoted earlier. One commentator links the creative character of talent, a strictly modern value concept, to a self-controlling character (*zikong xing*). Being good at independent thinking—another modern concept—is also the result of self-control.[76] Others see self-control as a prerequisite for modern values such as adaptation to mobility.[77] The stress on self-cultivation was the basic theme of Confucian ethics, and we have seen a revival of stress on self-cultivation techniques during the reforms. These attempts to revive the traditions of self-restraint and self-cultivation have been met with hostility, however. Several reports indicate the extreme unpopularity of themes of self-sacrifice and self-control among youth.[78]

In times of flux and rapid change, the disciplining effect of rules and norms is shaken. The era in which Durkheim lived was precisely an era in which the 'constancy' of morality was being challenged and often no longer seemed valid. It becomes important to bind discipline to mechanisms that will carry human solidarity through the trauma of such changing social conditions. It is not enough to talk of the boundaries of society alone: the process of taming modernity must be linked to a discussion of the bonds between individuals and their society. This bond is represented by the collective interest and the group. The answer to the problem of social order is a strengthened emphasis on matters of collective solidarity and sacrifice. In other words, self-restraint has to reach a higher level of self-sacrifice, indicating solidarity to something outside and higher than oneself:

In times of flux and change, the spirit of discipline cannot preserve its moral vigor, since the prevailing system of rules is shaken, at least in some of its parts. At such times, it is inevitable that we feel less keenly the authority of a discipline that is, in fact, attenuated. As a result, it is . . . the spirit of sacrifice and devotion . . . that becomes the province, par excellence, of morality. Now . . . we are going through precisely one of these critical phases. Indeed, history records no crisis as serious as that in which European societies have been involved for more than a century. Collective discipline in its traditional form has lost its authority.[79]

It is precisely in the self-sacrifice that Durkheim mentions that the highest principle in Chinese moral education can be found. Chinese culture emphasizes selflessness, and the moral–political educators have merely extended an already established cultural trait by following up this line of thought. A Chinese person is expected to be, as in the saying, 'utterly devoted to others without thought of self' (*hao bu li ji, zhuanmen li ren*). An article in the Party's theoretical journal *Qiushi* discussing socialist morals uses Confucian morality to underline the point of self-sacrifice. Starting with the Confucian principle of benevolence (*ren*), the article maintains that the core principle of socialist ethics includes the need for individuals to make necessary self-sacrifice (*ziwo xisheng*) for the overall social interests: 'A person who can truly be selfless will, when necessary, make self-sacrifices, even when this means sacrificing one's own life.'[80] As we shall later see, sacrifice and death for the common good are the main ingredients in the heroic narrative of the exemplary model person. We are now already discussing the second element of morality according to Durkheim. Whereas discipline was the first element, the second element is the individual's attachment to social groups. This social type of solidarity is connected to the self-control and the self-discipline of moral education. To be able to attach himself to a group, man must leave his animal instincts and be fully socialized:

It is not given to man then, to develop his nature but, on the contrary, he must triumph over it, he must vanquish it, silence its demands. It only provides him the occasion for a beautiful struggle, an heroic effort against himself.[81]

In Chinese moral education, the same development of 'conquering natural instincts' is seen as crucial for the socialization process. The dangers of human desires were already described by Xunzi, who held that if individual desire is followed 'impurity and disorder results', and the rules of proper conduct would be destroyed.[82] In a recent Chinese dictionary, under 'social control' (*shehui kongzhi*) and 'social restrictions' (*shehui yuezhi*), we can read that both have the meaning of 'controlling people's animal instincts', and of seeking to restrict individual tendencies to seek self-interest (*zili*). A process of restriction (*yueshu*) keeps people within bounds, and restrains and punishes human behaviour.[83] According to the typical textbook discourse, education in a broad sense is about inculcating in the raw and primitive 'natural person' the rules and regulations of human society, teaching knowledge, values and morals step by step so as to develop the 'social person'.[84] This 'social person' is also a social being in the sense that his or her individual 'little me' (*xiaowo*) subordinates itself to the 'big me' (*dawo*) that constitutes the totality of the state. The metaphor has led some to conclude that the self is weakly developed in China.[85] Durkheim, for his part, propagated an ascetic discipline where the self is restrained. He totally excluded individual behaviour directed towards personal ends from the sphere of moral behaviour. Such behaviour has no moral value whatsoever as Durkheim saw it. Moral behaviour is instead linked to collective behaviour: 'To act morally is to act in terms of the collective interest'; and 'There is no genuinely moral end except collective ones.'[86]

My interviews with class teachers confirmed such viewpoints. Collectivism is set before individuality, it was stressed, and 'the contributions you make to your country determine your moral level'. Collectivism was also geared towards the aim of developing the productive forces.[87] An individual acts morally only when he works towards goals superior to himself and beyond individual goals, Durkheim continued. He ruled out the religious sphere, maintaining that beyond the individual only a single empirically observable 'moral being' exists: society.[88] He draws his pedagogical conclusions from this premiss. From childhood on, each individual should be linked to the group:

To bind the child to the social group of which he is a part, it is not enough to make him feel the reality of it. He must be attached to it with his whole being. There is only one effective way of doing this, and that is by making his society an integral part of him, so that he can no more seperate himself from it than from himself.[89]

This means, above all, nourishing the capacity for personal sacrifice and for giving and devoting oneself. Durkheim sees it as necessary to involve individuals in the pursuit of 'great collective ends' to which they can devote themselves, and to train them to cherish social ideals. If attachment to the group is not strongly emphasized, nations will fall into moral debility, entailing danger even for their very existence.[90] Devotion of self and sacrifice for collective and society stand in sharp contrast to what was already described as individual non-moral behaviour. 'There is pleasure in saying "we" rather than "I", because anyone in a position to say "we" feels behind him a support, a force on which he can count.[91] The 'we' totally dominates the 'I', and signifies the social bond. The 'we' is an integrating force in society, while the 'I' might be seen as a disintegrating entity. Anyone who breaks this social bond linking him with something other than and superior to himself has an inferior capacity for committing himself. In Durkheim's view, this is in the last instance what immoral behaviour is all about.

This again finds resonance in contemporary Chinese practices. Selfishness is regarded as a cardinal evil, and selfless dedication to society as the greatest virtue in traditional Chinese culture.[92] Kenneth Abbot has observed that China sees an enduring influence from a common cultural heritage rooted in collectivism, and that 'collectivism and harmony' are the supreme values of Chinese culture. He goes further in indicating that in China 'social change gains strength through maintaining a continuity with traditional collectivist values'.[93] In other words, he sees collectivism not just as part of a traditional culture, but as a cultural form of organizing society that could very well define a modern type of society as well. Such assumptions are confirmed by other researchers. Hofstede found that there exist both 'I' and 'we' types of culture; normally the 'I' type is found in modernized capitalist *Gesellschaft* type societies, while the latter dominates *Gemeinschaft* type traditional societies. However, modern capitalist societies like Singapore and Taiwan stand out, showing a value set of the 'we' type.[94] The rapid transformation of Japan into a modernized nation also has proceeded without involving the full process of 'individualization' of the people or a breakdown of the cohesive traditional culture.[95] Durkheim held that individualism would develop as modern society developed. Such an assumption might in fact be a biased and probably Eurocentric standpoint. Recent theories about the 'globalization' of modernity have shown that the necessary connection between development and individualism is not an iron law of development.[96] China is not very likely to give up its 'we' type culture during modernization, even if that type of culture has also come under pressure during the reforms.

In socialist societies, collectivism seems to have formed a core of the social ethic along with attempts at modernization. Song Huichang, writing on the 'Marxist scientific theory of morality', states that the fundamental principle of Marxist morality must be collectivism. 'To develop collectivism we must eliminate individualism.' He maintains that individualism works contrary to the integrating forces in society: 'Reality has told us that egoism and individualism are not coagulating forces [*ningju li*]'. Only collectivism has the ability to function as a unifying or integrating force in society.[97]

In moral education the theme of collectivism is very explicit, both in the People's Republic and on Taiwan, thus indicating a cultural core value rather than a mere political value imposed on people from outside. If the pictures and images in which collectivism is propagated are different, the message is the same: attachment to the group is a most important value for moral educators to transmit, socialist and capitalist alike. For instance, Richard Wilson comments that in an elementary level textbook used on Taiwan there is a story of a small goose who flies away from the rest of the flock:

Twice the small goose does this and twice other members of the flock fly after him to attempt to persuade the small goose to return. The third time that the small goose departs, however, a hawk spies and seizes him. The admonitions given by other members of the flock of the small goose during this story contain injunctions such as, 'such wild flying is not permitted', 'you must follow the rules of the group', 'being with the group is most important', and, of course, the tragic ending is designed to provide confirmation that departing from group rules and norms is highly undesirable and dangerous.[98]

Stories such as this are not simply childhood parables. The parable about the small goose had been deliberately chosen since the formation that geese fly in is roughly the same as the Chinese character for 'person' or 'people'—*ren* (人). In class, therefore, the teacher could use this character as a simple device to bring the story of the small goose into a human context and thus make the children understand the importance of proper group behaviour.

During the reform period in the People's Republic there have been many attacks on the collectivist ethos. It has been attacked both as a remnant of feudalism and as a remnant of Maoism. In an official attack on this ethos, some of the arguments are summed up. Collectivism was accused of stressing submission and suppression of the individual, and showing a hostile attitude towards individual needs and wants. Critics confounded the collectivist principle of socialist ethics with the feudal and patriarchal principle of ethics, and negated socialist collectivism in the name of criticizing feudal autocracy. Some of the critics simply regarded collectivist ethics as 'blockhead ethics' (*caonu daode*) and 'cannibal ethics' (*chiren daode*), asserting that 'selfless devotion' (*wusi fengxian*) was an 'extremist and one-sided dogma'.

To refute accusations about collectivism being a 'feudal' remnant, the counterattack argues instead that 'collective' is a scientific condensation of the concept 'society' (*shehui*) and 'the whole' (*zhengti*). What it refers to is the 'true collective' (*zhenshi de jiti*), which represents the unity of overall social and personal interests, and does not cover the unreal (*fei zhenshi*) or false collective (*xuwei de jiti*). The relationship between society and the individual is seen as identical to that between a living organism and a cell.[99]

The distinction between 'true' and 'false' collectives is an important one in a China riddled by group chauvinism and *danwei* (or work-unit) socialism. In reality, the universalistic morality described as the aim of all moral education might remain only an exemplary ideal. Even in less particularistic cultures than China, morality is coloured by a tendency towards locality. 'Morality is always to some degree tied to the socially local and particular and . . . the aspirations of the morality of modernity to a universality freed from all particularity is an illusion', says MacIntyre.[100] As the Chinese themselves correctly sum up, the virtues are part of a tradition. What they incorrectly believe is that tradition can be manipulated and 'planned' in a rational manner, making people see 'correct' ways of behaving as defined from an ideal of 'selfless' rational modernity.

In present-day China, as in Durkheim's theories, moral education lies between disintegrating selfishness and integrating sacrifice. In China, as in other collectivistic cultures or political systems, the collective has been used for controlling and disciplining functions. Criticisms of such uses of the collective are many and varied. Lily Chu Bergsma claims that the Western critique of collectivism is biased and ethnocentric, and attacks US culture for its 'competitive and aggressive individualism', which makes it impossible to see the virtues of other alternatives. Conformism does not come as an automatic effect of group attachment, she claims, pointing to the assets of group learning and group attachment.[101] In China the collective has obvious disciplinary functions, and this phenomenon has met with some harsh criticism over the last several years. So, too, in the former socialist countries there were attacks against the tradition of using collectivism as a means of discipline and regulation only.[102] In collectivism, however, there is the possibility for different tendencies. Dutton has pointed out that a repressive regime is not a function of a collectivist culture, but that collectivist and individualist cultures alike can both end in repression. Rights cannot be secured by reference to a higher-order morality, be that individualism or collectivist socialism. Instead, rights must be made secure by definitive and concrete social practices.[103] He thus attacks Western cultural chauvinism, but also issues a warning to those Chinese scholars who see a panacea for all problems of socialism in adopting full-fledged individualism. Durkheim sought a solution to the problem of repression in his concept of 'autonomy', but the explicit scientism in the approach of both Durkheim and the Chinese seems ill-suited to solve the problem of repression.

'Autonomy': An Exercise in 'Moral Science'

The third and last element of morality, according to Durkheim, is autonomy. If strictly self-centred conduct is regarded as immoral, that
which denies autonomy is equally so. Controlled behaviour also is not
good behaviour. Having strongly emphasized the coercive character of
the first two elements of morality—discipline and commitment to the
group—Durkheim holds that autonomy is meant to 'open' the coercive system by the help of a 'moral science' based on *reliable knowledge*
about the moral order. Thus, in addition to the disciplinary and binding elements of moral education, there is autonomy, representing the
element of 'objectivity' in morality. Durkheim showed an interest in the
'positive science of morality' early on, and in the preface to the first
edition of his *Division of Labour* he was already programmatically stating: 'This book is above all an attempt to treat the facts of moral life
according to the methods of the positive sciences.'[104] According to Steven
Lukes, Durkheim never gave up this positivist position about a science
of morality, although he never finished more than a few pages of a theoretical introduction to his final work on morality. In part, the recurrence of the word 'moral' in Durkheim's works adopted the virtual
interchangeability of the concepts of the 'social' and the 'moral' in much
of eighteenth- and nineteenth-century French thought. Much more than
in England or Germany, the 'moral sciences' and the 'social sciences'
were equivalent terms in French writing from at least the time of
Montesquieu down through Durkheim's works.[105] In linking the moral
to the social, not only the Chinese intellectual tradition but also
Chinese culture as such seem to resemble the French approach that is
so evident in Durkheim's writings.

The Durkheimian assumption that there is an objective, scientific way
to 'know' the right morality of a society is shared by Chinese scholars,
moral educators and political powerholders alike. Xu Weicheng, in his
speech at the fifth National Morality Conference in 1990, might stand
as a representative of this widely held view in China. Xu takes up the
suggestion that the Party should elaborate an overall ethics plan to be
linked to the question of spiritual civilization, and comments that 'the
idea is quite correct', but unfortunately impossible at the present time
because 'we have not yet reached a clear understanding of this'. Xu
hopes for more investigation and study on the topic. After all, he comments, 'This is an ethical and moral system for 1.1 billion people, not
a book-bound system. That is, what are 1.1 billion people supposed to
use as the norm for their personal conduct?' The ethical and moral

system must 'be beneficial to our nation's modernization and development' and compatible with the politics of reform.[106] In other words, a planned and scientific 'ethical system' is in principle a feasible policy, but the necessary tools for reaching that aim are 'not yet' adequate. Such a system rests on two important elements. Both are attached to the binding force outside oneself that was also described by Durkheim. According to Xu, this higher force is first of all represented by patriotism and collectivism. These values represent not only the 'morally good' alternatives, but the 'scientifically correct' values—which of course is quite another thing.

Xu discusses the options for a scientific understanding of the 'laws of social norms' as a means to uphold order in society. The task of moral educators and politicians is to conduct research on how society's actual moral norms are formed, and to take practical steps to implement the findings. The question is, where do these concepts come from, and why is it that everyone happens to think in this or that way? One has to study the real history of social morality, that is the history of the development and changes in people's moral concepts, to reach a scientific conclusion about how to make use of social morality and transform it into the type of 'moral force' of which Durkheim spoke. In one passage of his speech, Xu addresses the not yet understood 'laws' of this development:

In a society, a group of people, everyone considers a certain mode of conduct as honourable, and a different mode of conduct as dishonourable: How does this come about? What is the mechanism of its formation? These rules would be of immense use to us. If we understood these rules we could finally realize a whole series of explosive, effective, and stable measures. We would not be launching movements, but would step by step, through a hundred million billion repetitive actions . . . truly build up a socialist morality in the real world.[107]

Xu addresses the problem of social and moral 'understanding' by saying that, because of the mode of production and the limits of a person's capacity for understanding, it is still a difficult task for a person to understand himself. To be able to understand oneself, one must have the ability to see oneself in one's own necessary social context. Since this is still difficult, individualism will continue to exist for a long period to come. Individualism, in other words, is seen as an immoral, immature and unscientific conception of the objective relations between individual and society. Individualism reflects ever so clearly that we still lack an adequate understanding. Xu subsequently refutes the idea of self-value or self-realization as a principle of social existence. Self-realization simply means a kind of self-inflation. At the present stage of experience and scientific development, however, each person is regarded as existing as an individual, and this individual existence makes it appear as if each individual body can be separated from the social body. Xu refutes this view as wholly unscientific, and with metaphors—not at all accidentally borrowed from the natural sciences—describes why one cannot be separated from one's social body:

Naturally, in actuality he cannot leave it, for if he were completely divorced from it, he would die. However, he can still believe that he can set himself up in opposition to all of society. It is just like a cell which is unable to entirely leave the body; although it is capable of becoming cancerous, of unlimited enlargement of itself; in the end it destroys the entire body, and loses the basis of existence itself.[108]

As we have seen, one of Durkheim's premises is that the realm of the moral is the realm of the social, and that 'morals are in the domain of action'.[109] Durkheim's ambitions went further than simply stating the social roots of morality. Throughout most of his academic life, Durkheim sought to outline a science of secular morality built on reason. A *'sciences des moeurs'* would, according to Durkheim, make it possible for the social scientist to understand the objectively correct moral order. 'We can only conquer the moral world in the same way as we conquer the physical world: by building a science of moral matters.'[110] At least in theory, this would be possible if the scientist only knew enough about his object of study. The difficulty lay merely in finding what constituted the essential morality of a given society or culture, and what tendencies and ideas were 'required' by a certain process of change. Since morality was based on the social, and the social was open for investigation, rational understanding and practical manipulation, there would also be a way to analyse both the world of the 'is' and that of the 'ought' with equal scientific accuracy. A scientific approach to morality would liberate mankind from the direct dependence on things, and thereby set us free. Durkheim undoubtedly saw this as a very liberating and modern thought, as something extending the reflexivity of the modern person. Social adaptability would be merely a question of having enough knowledge about the physical world. According to this line of thinking, there would be a correct way to find the correct conclusion about which moral conduct to follow in a particular situation, just as a mathematician can arrive at his conclusions by the means of his science. Such knowledge would free us from social constraint. Our 'autonomy' thus rests with adequate knowledge:

Conforming to the order of things because one is sure that it is everything it ought to be is not submitting to a constraint. It is freely desiring this order, assenting through an understanding of the cause. Wishing freely is not desiring the absurd. On the contrary, it implies wishing what is rational—that is to say, it implies the desire to act in agreement with the nature of things.[111]

We can investigate the nature of scientific moral rules through education to arrive at a scientific understanding of the moral order. Once we have enough knowledge about moral precepts, how they originate and how they work in society, we will be in a position to conform to them. We will know why we follow these precepts, and therefore such conformity has nothing of constraint about it, according to Durkheim. Consent, in other words, is based on 'scientific' understanding. Following the attachment to the group and the understanding of the social bond, we consciously and willingly understand that it is in our nature to be controlled by forces outside us, and we accept this limitation freely. This is not a passive conformity that constitutes a reduction of our personality, Durkheim continues, since we understand why we conform.[112] To act morally, then, it is not enough only to respect discipline: we must also have knowledge about ideals and rules, and how to adapt to them.

To sum up, Durkheim claims that the third element of morality is to have rational understanding of one's relationship to society. To be able to accept the rule, one has to see it as a moral fact to be grasped through reason like other natural phenomena. The taste for regularity, the preference for moderation, the need for limits, self-restraint, a spirit of devotion and sacrifice—all these constitute elements of a 'rational morality'.[113] 'Rational knowledge' dominates Durkheim's thinking about 'autonomy'. He also addresses the question of aesthetic education, mostly because of the widespread belief that it played a very important part in the formation of moral character. Durkheim allots to aesthetics only a secondary role:

Art does not contribute to the formation of moral character. It does not commit one to activities moral in themselves. It is not a positive factor in morality. It is a means of preserving us against certain evil influences once the moral character is formed . . . [W]e are led to the conclusion that aesthetics is not of central significance.[114]

Durkheim, however, sees certain positive influences from aesthetics education, even if he does not regard it as essential. When we awaken the taste for the beautiful, we open the mind for the ability to sacrifice. Art can extend morality into our hours of leisure, and this is why it would be good to give all children an education in aesthetics.[115] In contrast, Chinese moral educators put more stress on aesthetics and 'feelings'. Is it possible, asks Xu Weicheng, by planning according to objective rules, to foster in people a certain type of emotion so that everyone likes one type of thing and dislikes another? The answer is affirmative, and the means to achieve it seems to lie in a further study of the 'people's customs, habits [and] the beauties of their country'.[116] 'One can foster the moral feelings of children, [and] one can learn moral feelings', it is claimed.[117] Feelings like patriotism can be learned because they possess objectivity and truth. The 'moral science' is based on both knowledge and aesthetics, on both reason and feelings.

Textbooks on moral education mention several methods through which the instruction of correct moral feelings could be given a scientific expression. The 'moulding character' (*taoye xing*) of moral education is emphasized in Chinese moral pedagogy. The different 'methods of moulding feelings' (*qinggan taoye fa*) are meant to work through suggestive education (*anshi jiaoyu*) or through unconscious psychological activity (*wu yishi xinli de huodong*), instead of relying on the transmission of rational knowledge. The moulding process has to be a relatively long-term and directed process, working through the principle of exerting a subtle influence on character, thinking, etc. Artistic moulding (*yishu taoye*) is another moulding technique often mentioned. Songs, dance, music, and images of morality through the pictures of heroes' deeds and thoughts are among the things that silently enter the students' spirits. Both knowledge and morality are received through artistic moulding. The moulding of feelings is an important element in the overall moral education, 'bringing thoughts away from the self, binding the young to the correct and the beautiful in society'.[118]

Socialization and the Institutionalization of 'Moral Science'

The 'moral science' of autonomy solved one important theoretical question for Durkheim. Correct knowledge about the relationship between individual and society seems to open the way for a willed and rational solution to the problem of passive adaptation or outright repression. Each individual can actively and consciously take part in social life according to his or her level of insight into the rules through which this society functions. Sacrifice for and devotion to society does not mean a repression of the individual: instead, it means the culmination of the individual's knowledge. In China we have already seen how the regime seeks the same explanation through theories of the objective norm.

Chinese socialization theory has had a vast range of approaches in recent years. Central to most of these theories is the creation–adaptation dichotomy.

'Youth adapt to social life as well as they create social life', runs a typical passage in a Chinese Dictionary of Sociology.[119] There are, however, different interpretations of this line of thought. Some stress that socialization means adaptation to society. Socialization is then mainly seen as passive; the stress is on inculcation (*guanshu*) of behavioural norms, and on the fostering of social roles. It is usual to stress the importance of childhood experiences. 'First impressions are strongest' (*xian ru wei zhu*) is an important principle in much of this socialization theory, and children are seen mainly as passive objects of mechanical inculcation. If the child is a *tabula rasa*, family education is the first brush to paint the picture of who the child will later be. In this literature, we have seen a revival of the traditional role of the family, even if it has been presented in the form of 'scientific family education'.[120]

Others put more stress on the active potential of the individual. Individuals are shaped by their environment, Yun Pengju claims, but Marxism also contends that individual consciousness subjectively reflects the objective world.[121] This means that, not only do we receive social experiences, social culture, and social rules, but we also actively reproduce the social system, by transforming these experiences, forming our own values and aims. Work creates the person, and the essence of socialization is to make a person change from a non-working to a working person. The new persons (*xin ren*) made by the new times will create a new world. It seems to be a widespread assumption, however, that such creative abilities rest on a foundation of mechanically inculcated truths. More specifically, it means that there are no contradictions between individual development and the ideology of the reform era.

This description of 'creative adaptation' to official reform values and the necessity of the new norms fits neatly into Durkheim's discussion of 'autonomy'. The active process is about knowing the rules, and knowing how to adapt to their changing forms and conditions. Since the process of active adaptation between individuals and society is a never-ending process, socialization is also never fully completed. Yun's article is kept within a Marxist framework, and the Durkheimian 'autonomy' could possibly be expressed only with the help of Engels's view on freedom as insight into necessity. What makes Durkheim relevant here is that the argument on necessity is extended into the realm of morality.

After the correct knowledge has been transmitted, a basis is created on which creative adaptability can unfold. While primary socialization is passive, secondary socialization is an active process, says Shen Jianguo. This assumption is typical of most of the literature on socialization. Shen maintains that it is one-sided to hold that culture, state, and individual are identical (*yizhi*) entities. Such theories see the process of socialization as a mere adaptation to culture and its values. Instead, Shen adopts something resembling the theory of imperfect reproduction as a cause of change. During socialization, when adapting to the norms and rules of society, people act differently and reproduce (*zai chengchan*) the social rules and norms differently. A person actively takes part in social life, continually changing and recreating personality as well as society. Shen holds that socialization is a life-long process.[122] Such descriptions of slow or evolutionary change seem quite popular in China today.

In his last work, the unfinished introduction to 'La Morale', Durkheim made a new and interesting distinction between '*morale*' and '*moeurs*'. While the first concept connotes ideals, values, and norms, the second describes practices, or rule-governed behaviour. Durkheim contrasts the ideal morality (*morale*), which is over and above human behaviour, with the 'deformations' of real existing practices among people (*moeurs*):

Doubtless the morality (*morale*) of the time is to be found in social practices (*moeurs*), but in a degraded form, reduced to the level of human mediocrity. What they express is the way in which the average man applies moral rules, and he never applies them without compromising and making reservations. The motives on which he acts are mixed: some are noble and pure, but others are vulgar and base.[123]

This distinction between the ideal morality and the base morality of everyday life is interesting in the Chinese context. Towards the end of his life Durkheim wanted to develop a 'science of morality' or 'a science of moral facts', which built on ideal morality and its function as a 'mental, moral force' in society. It is precisely this ideal morality, the *morale*, that stands in the foreground in the exemplary society. To anticipate our discussion on norms, it seems as if prescribed conduct focuses on the exemplary norm, and that it is the exemplary norm that defines this society. This also distinguishes the exemplary society from the disciplinary society. Foucault's disciplinary society focuses on the average norm and the process of 'normalization', rather than on the exemplary. The preoccupation with the exemplary and the ideal has important consequences for the way in which this society functions.

A party journal article brings together the themes of improvement, 'moral science', and the exemplary in a discussion on communist ideals.[124] The article seeks a scientific meaning and significance of communist ideals, and looks at the alleged laws governing such ideals. An ideal is a belief, but a belief that has the possibility or the hope of being realized. Ideals must be based on reason, and should represent a unification of wishes and possibilities. To realize such wishes, one must understand the 'objective laws' governing them. An ideal starts from reality but aims to achieve goals that are not yet reality. Ideals are thus 'improvements on reality'. They also represent 'the future of reality and the reality of the future'. The prescribed utopias, in other words, should be based on realizability or feasibility. Here we see a perfect example of what Mumford called a 'utopia of reconstruction'. The ideal constitutes a 'moral force', and such ideals will become powerful driving forces (*jinqu de liliang*) for social progress and historical development as well as spiritual pillars (*jingshen zhizhu*) of social change and reform.[125] The discussion describes the building element of the 'moral force' and the important task to bring this force under institutionalized 'scientific control'.

In the new Chinese 'moral science' of spiritual civilization, Durkheim's intentions might seem to have been implemented in practice. I do not mean to give Durkheim any responsibility whatsoever for that theory: I simply point out that the programme of a secular 'moral science' seems to have become a reality in today's China. This 'science' differs in many fundamental ways from the outline Durkheim made. The distinction between the ideal and the mediocre is an important one. While the Chinese exemplary society is directed towards the ideal *morale*, it seems to grapple with problems of vulgar human behaviour, the *moeurs* of the mediocre. The question of how to implement rewards and punishments in moral education follows as a natural question about how to implement a 'science of morality'.

Rewards 'are used primarily in the school as a means of stimulating the qualities of intelligence, rather than those of the heart and the character', remarks Durkheim.[126] The schools have placed more emphasis on academic success than on moral merit. Good marks, prizes, and class honours are reserved for the most intelligent students rather than for the most virtuous. In addition, the part played by punishment has been much greater than that of rewards. Acts infringing on the rules are frequently punished, but only the most exeptional manifestations of virtue produce any sign of reward. Durkheim is however sceptical when it comes to amending this practice. He sees praise as 'a narrowly egotistical sentiment', as something diverting the individual from collectivist sacrifice.[127] Durkheim asks whether a system of rewards parallel to the penal code could be established in society, to encourage and extend virtuous behaviour; he answers in the negative in a passage that is worth quoting at length:

It is impossible to have a system of rewards parallel to the penal code. Moreover, such behaviours have their full worth only insofar as they are performed without the actor anticipating any regular reward. It is this uncertainty, this indeterminacy of the sanction, its insignificance from a material point of view, which makes for its value. Were there a price tag on such behaviours, they would promptly acquire a degrading commercial air. Therefore it is normal that offenses have more precise, certain, and regular sanctions than genuinely meritorious behaviour; and on this point the discipline of the school must resemble that of life.

This is not to say, however, that there is nothing of merit in the criticisms we have discussed. Certainly it is not a question of making the students compete in honesty, veracity, etc. The idea of a prize for virtue makes us smile, not because we hate innovation, but because the ideas thus paired contradict each other. We feel an aversion to recompensing moral merit in the same way as we do talent. There is an opposition here which not unreasonably shocks us. The true reward of virtue is found in a state of inner tranquillity, in the feeling of esteem and sympathy that it brings us, and in the resulting comfort. But there is reason to believe that prestige may attach too exclusively, in school life, to intellectual merit, and that a greater share should be accorded moral value.[128]

A moral reward system clearly did not fit into Durkheim's idea of a 'moral science'; instead, he regarded such ideas as totally unrealistic. In China, however, such a reward system has become the logical result of society's traditional roots as well as its 'scientific' perceptions of an ideal future society. The Chinese go further in their ideas about establishing an institutionalization of 'moral science' than did Durkheim, at least in the way they measure their morality, and they place it within a system of checks and balances. In China moral measurement has come to represent the very 'scientification' or 'objectivity' of the system. It is one of the main characteristics of the exemplary society that it so thoroughly emphasizes the reward of virtuous behaviour. Later I will show in greater detail how this system spreads during the current reforms. It might be said that, while the material civilization focuses on the production of goods, the spiritual civilization focuses on doing good. We have already seen the stress on moral knowledge and moral feelings. The good deed occupies an important position and represents the third element of Chinese moral education, the importance of 'moral practice'. At the National Morality Conference, Xu Weicheng suggested the following about the reward of good deeds, holding up the system of rewarding 'advanced persons' at the Changchun department store as a meritorious example:

Seven levels of activities are commended as advanced, from advanced section to national model worker; they are commended at each level, and additionally, each step is taken very seriously, with meetings organized, report meetings held, posters put up. It takes only a small exhibition of goodness to reach a different level of advancement, and so everyone has a chance. Having become advanced one cannot be complacent, because there are more levels above. Our whole society should be this way, not just seven levels, but 99 levels, so that every individual has a hope of exhibiting himself, to use his own effort to win over the honour of other people, and to advance unceasingly.[129]

The bureaucratization and the hierarchization seem to me more obvious than the scientific character of such a system. In the case of China, the reward of virtue at least in theory equals the punishment of vice. The practice is developed and refined into 'science' to serve the needs of the modern state. The 'science' of knowing the objective rules, however, also seems to have clear parallels in Chinese tradition itself, with its emphasis on unification (*yitonghua*). Not only do we find such traits in Chinese tradition, but other traditional types of society have seen similar developments, again indicating the traditional roots of scientism. Alasdair MacIntyre has pointed out that such practices in fact dominated in the 'heroic societies' of the Western tradition, like Homeric Greece, Saga Iceland and in pagan Ireland:

[M]orality and social structure are in fact one and the same in heroic society. There is only one set of social bonds. Morality as something distinct does not yet exist. Equivalent questions *are* questions of social fact. It is for this reason that Homer speaks *always* of knowledge of what to do and how to judge. Nor are such questions difficult to answer, except in exceptional cases.[130]

Even the exemplary society has in it traits of heroic society, and the hero plays an important part in the narrative of exemplary norms. Paradoxically, the 'moral science' in today's China is one of the clearest examples of the 'repetition with a difference' and the redefinition and redeployment of traditional patterns discussed earlier. The differentiation of modernity again seems tamed by the sureties of traditional times, even if the form is claimed to be modern and 'scientific'. The 'moral' in 'moral science' seems better translated as 'moralist', and 'science' is better described as 'scientism'. Moral science thus seems to be nothing but 'moralistic scientism' as practised in China today.

It has been claimed that social order is not an end in itself in China because it is placed within a narrative of progress that aims to channel and magnify an ethic of production. While this focuses on an obvious tendency within Chinese society, I would like to modify that assumption. I have argued that 'socialism with Chinese characteristics' is based both on growth and order, and that both represent pillars of legitimacy and can be regarded as ends in themselves. Stability and order are preconditions for development and progress, but the narrative of order is not always subordinated to the narrative of progress. The relationship is not that of horse and carriage. When the former reformist premier Zhao Ziyang once said that 'the precondition for development is stability', this meant a whole lot more than paying lip service to some conservative faction in the Party. Order is of strategic importance for the whole reform process, and the aim is to create both a prosperous and a harmonious country. Where the traditional Chinese once said that 'the gentleman seeks moral principles instead of food' (*junzi mou dao bu mou can*), it is now suggested that the proverb, rather than being put on its head, should read that the gentleman 'seeks moral principles *and* food' (*ji zhong dao, ye mou can*). Morality has, however, admittedly become more and more coloured by the narrative of progress. This particular form of 'moral economy' can be found even in expressions like 'moral investment' (*deyu touzi*), referring to the usefulness of moral education for development in general and for business in particular, and 'moral efficiency' (*deyu de xiaolü*), indicating the need for more moral guidance in schools so that students will better understand the objective laws of morality. Only communist morality suits the needs of the development of the socialist mode of production, Wang Xingzhou maintains. Such morality is a progressive morality and an important factor in promoting the development of society. And most important, this progressive morality is built on a scientific foundation: 'Its benefit for social development is the basic and objective standard for the moral evaluation of people's behaviour.' The SONY company uses the so-called 'seven spirits' system to make employees work harder, and in China the example is used to point out the economic benefit of moral education. 'Civilized work-units' (*wenming danwei*) in China have already introduced bonuses and money awards for showing spiritually civilized conduct and good deeds defined according to fixed criteria, and a system of moral 'evaluation points' (*pingfen*).

The Encyclopedia of Education discusses the concept of 'moral quality education'. The core of moral belief is to sacrifice one's body or life for the collective. 'Moral behaviour' (*deyu xingwei*) is, however, defined in terms of methods of achieving such behaviour, rather than the behaviour itself. Like the ancient Confucianists, the modern regime seems to expect miracles of moral education. The educational method is regarded as the scientific educational foundation for the 'moral science' of adapting individuals to society.

Notes to Chapter 3

1. Donald J. Munro, *The Concept of Man in Early China*, Stanford, Stanford University Press, 1969, p. 83.

2. Homer H. Dubs (trans.), *The Works of Hsüntze*, Taibei, Ch'eng-wen, 1966, pp. 60–1. Xunzi, totally refuting Mencius's philosophy that all men are originally good, fully shared Mencius's view that human beings were essentially educable and malleable. Xunzi builds directly on Mencius here, as the latter was once asked: 'Cao of Jiao asked Mencius, saying, "It is said, 'All men may be Yaos and Shuns';—is it so?" Mencius replied, "It is"'. 'The works of Mencius', bk VI, 2,2,1, in James Legge (trans.), *The Four Books (Sishu)*, Taipei, Culture Co./Wenhua tushu gongshi, 1983, pp. 894–5.

3. Michel Foucault, *Discipline and Punish: The Birth of the Prison*, New York, Vintage Books, 1979, pp. 271, 293–308.

4. Sun Longji, *Zhongguo wenhua de shenceng jiegou* (The deep structure of Chinese society), Hong Kong, Jixian she, 1983, p. 314.

5. Zhu Genxiang, 'Lun shehui kongzhi yu sixiang zhengzhi gongzuo' (On social control and political/ideological work), *Hubei dangxiao xuebao*, No. 6, 1987, pp. 44–6; also in *Sixiang zhengzhi jiaoyu, G2, Fuyin baokan ziliao*, No. 2, 1988, pp. 30–2.

6. Émile Durkheim, *Sociology and Philosophy*, trans. D. F. Pocock, London, Cohen & West, 1965, p. 59.

7. See Bernhard Karlgren, *Grammatica Serica*, No. 919k, here quoted from Colin A. Ronan and Joseph Needham, *The Shorter Science and Civilization in China*, Vol. 1, p. 140. See also Gao Ming (ed.), *Guwen zi leibian*, Beijing, Zhonghua shuju, 1982, p. 118.

8. See Émile Durkheim, *The Elementary Forms of Religious Life*, trans. Joseph W. Swain, London, George Allen & Unwin, 1976.

9. David S. K. Chu, 'Social problems in contemporary Chinese society: editor's introduction', *Chinese Sociology and Anthropology*, Vol. 17, No. 2, 1984–5, p. 18.

10. *Ciyuan* (The origin of words), Vol. 3, Beijing, Shangwu yinshuguan, 1984, p. 1969; *Zhongwen da cidian* (The encyclopaedic dictionary of the Chinese language), Vol. 6, no. 20187, p. 52 (8902); and Hao Zhilun, 'Lun "jiao" zhi chuantong wenhua yiyun' (Discussing the meaning of '*jiao*' (to teach) in traditional culture), *Jiaoyu yanjiu*, No. 3, 1990, p. 49.

11. *Zhongwen da cidian*, Vol. 4, no. 13415/16, p. 860 (6066), and Hao Zhilun, p. 49.

12. See Colin A. Ronan and Joseph Needham, p. 129.

13. This particular interpretation by Hao Zhilun might be an over-interpretation. See Hao Zhilun, p. 49.

14. Dutton's interpretations are, however, based on speculation, as there were no written sources as far back as the Xia dynasty (2100–1600 BC), where he finds the origin of the term *huantu*. Dutton further claims that later etymological indications fit in well with the arguments that suggest that confinement in Zhou-dynasty China actually included concern for prisoner reform. It is, however, wise to note that such findings are indications only. See Michael R. Dutton, *Policing and Punishment in China: From Patriarchy to 'the People'*, Cambridge, Cambridge University Press, 1992, p. 106.

15. Sun Longji, p. 36.

16. Ibid., pp. 11–12.

17. Émile Durkheim, *Moral Education*, trans. Everett K. Wilson and Herman Schnurer, New York, Free Press, 1973, p. 202.

18. Donald J. Munro, p. 95.

19. Chen Zhizhao, 'Mianzi xinli de lilun fenxi yu shiji yanjiu' (The theoretical analysis and practical study of the psychology of face), in Yang Guoshu (ed.), *Zhongguo ren de xinli* (The psychology of the Chinese), Taipei, Guiguan tushu gongsi chubanshe, 1989, p. 176.

20. Han Yu, *Yuan Xing* (An inquiry into human nature), quoted from Chen Jingpan, *Confucius as a Teacher*, Beijing, Foreign Languages Press, 1990 (originally U. of Toronto Ph.D. thesis, 1940), p. 409.

21. Yun Pengju, 'Guanyu qingnian shehuihua de ji ge wenti' (On some problems concerning the socialization of youth), in Gongqingtuan zhongyang xuanchuanbu (The Propaganda Department of the Communist Youth League Central Committee) (eds.), *Dangdai qingnian lilun dachao* (The theoretical spring tide of modern youth), Beijing, Nongcun duwu chubanshe, 1989, p. 165.

22. Zhou Dechang, *Zhongguo gudai jiaoyu sixiang de piping jicheng* (Criticizing and inheriting ancient Chinese educational thinking), Beijing, Jiaoyu kexue chubanshe, 1982, pp. 87–121.

23. It is also an old Chinese principle that 'In private one's behaviour is different from what it is in public' (*yin yi tao, yang yi tao*). See Sun Longji, pp. 155, 157, 159–60.

24. Cui Dashan, 'Xuesheng pinde pingjia chutan: xingzhi, gongneng he biaozhun' (Preliminary discussion on students' moral character evaluation: nature, function, and standard), *Jiaoyu yanjiu yu shijian*, No. 3, 1986, p. 71.

25. Donald J. Munro, p. 55.

26. T'ung-Tsu Ch'ü, *Law and Society in Traditional China*, Paris, Mouton, 1961, p. 248 ff.

27. *Confucian Analects (Lunyu)*, bk II, ch. III, 1,2, in James Legge (trans.), p. 135.

28. Chen Jingpan, *Confucius as a Teacher*, p. 249, discusses the different translations of the concept. Suggestions in addition to the above mentioned have been 'what is proper', 'regulations', 'ceremonies', 'rituals'.

29. James L. Watson, 'The renegotiation of Chinese cultural identity in the post-Mao era', in Jeffrey N. Wasserstrom and Elizabeth J. Perry, *Popular Protest and Political Culture in Modern China*, Boulder, Colo., Westview Press, 1992, p. 73.

30. Watson translates *li* with 'proper form': ibid., pp. 73, 75.

31. See Antonio S. Cua, 'The concept of *li* in Confucian moral theory', in Robert E. Allinson (ed.), *Understanding the Chinese Mind: The Philosophical Roots*, Hong Kong, Oxford University Press, 1989, p. 214.

32. Roonan and Needham remark: 'The full significance of the interplay between *li* and *fa* can . . . only be understood with reference to their relationships to social classes. In feudal times, for instance, it was natural enough that feudal lords should not consider themselves subject to the positive laws that they promulgated. *Li* was therefore the code of honour among ruling groups, *fa* the ordinances to which the common people were subject' (Colin A. Roonan and Joseph Needham, p. 284).

33. Homer H. Dubs (trans.), p. 254.

34. Donald J. Munro, p. 92.

35. Yang Deguang, 'Gaoxiao deyu ying juyou xiangdui duli diwei' (University moral education should have an independent status), *Renmin ribao*, 1 July 1989, p. 5.

36. *Liaowang*, quoted from *China Daily* 11 May 1993, p. 4.

37. Sun Longji, p. 295.

38. Émile Durkheim, *Moral Education*, p. 35.

39. An interesting interpretation of Durkheim that points in the same direction is made by Anthony Giddens, *Capitalism and Modern Social Theory: An Analysis of*

the *Writings of Marx, Durkheim, and Weber*, Cambridge, Cambridge University Press, 1971.

40. Émile Durkheim, *Moral Education*, p. 50.
41. Ibid., p. 79.
42. Émile Durkheim, *Sociology and Philosophy*, p. 38.
43. Émile Durkheim, *Moral Education*, p. 87.
44. Ibid., p. 52.
45. Émile Durkheim, *Sociology and Philosophy*, p. 61.
46. Yang Wenrong, 'Xin shiqi deyu fangfa de tedian' (Characteristics of moral education methods in the new period), *Banzhuren*, No. 4, 1990, p. 5.
47. Zhu Xi's remarks were made in his 'Preface to family etiquette', here quoted from Kao Ming, 'Chu Hsi's discipline of propriety', in Wing-tsit Chan (ed.), *Chu Hsi and Neo-Confucianism*, Honolulu, University of Hawaii Press, 1986, p. 324.
48. Yun Pengju, p. 164.
49. Émile Durkheim, *Moral Education*, pp. 27–8.
50. Zhang Nianhong (ed.), *Jiaoyuxue cidian* (Dictionary of education), Beijing, Beijing chubanshe, 1987, pp. 450–1, 472.
51. Xu Weicheng, 'Create a socialist moral system with Chinese characteristics', *Sixiang zhengzhi gongzuo yanjiu* (Research in ideological political work), No. 11, 1990, pp. 8–12; Part I in *JPRS Report*, *JPRS-CAR*-90-086, 21 November 1990, pp. 6–9; Part II in *JPRS Report*, *JPRS-CAR*-91-005, 31 January 1991, p. 61; see also Wang Ge, 'Gaige yu shehui kongzhi', *Shehui kexue*, No. 9, 1987, pp. 356; also in *Fuyin baokan ziliao, C4 Shehuixue*, No. 5, 1987, pp. 92–3.
52. Émile Durkheim, *Moral Education*, p. 31.
53. Ibid., p. 91.
54. Andrew G. Walder, 'Communist social structure and workers' politics in China', in Victor C. Falkenheim (ed.), *Citizens and Groups in Contemporary China*, Ann Arbor, Michigan Monographs in Chinese Studies, Vol. 56, 1987, p. 74.
55. Ann Anagnost, 'Socialist ethics and the legal system', in Jeffrey N. Wasserstrom and Elizabeth J. Perry (eds.), pp. 177–205.
56. Antonio Gramsci, *Selections from Prison Notebooks*, New York, International Publishers, 1971, p. 80.
57. Alberto Melucci, *Nomads of the Present*, Philadelphia, Temple University Press, 1989, p. 48.
58. Alasdair MacIntyre, *After Virtue: A Study in Moral Theory*, 2nd edn., Notre Dame, Ind., University of Notre Dame Press, 1984, p. 106.
59. *Yinghan shehuixue cihui* (English–Chinese glossary of sociology), Nanchang, Jiangxi renmin chubanshe, 1983, p. 23.
60. Li Tisheng, *Xunzi zhishi*, Taibei, Xuesheng 1979, p. 417. The translation here is based on a modified verson of Dubs and Watson made by Antonio S. Cua, p. 215. Cua, however, does not translate *li*. I have used Dubs's 'rules of proper conduct'. Watson uses 'rituals' or 'rites'. Instead of 'rightness' for *yi*, Dubs uses 'justice'. I have kept Cua's translation here. See Homer H. Dubs (trans.), p. 213, and Burton Watson (trans.), *Hsün Tzu: Basic Writings*, New York, Columbia University Press, 1963, p. 89.
61. Émile Durkheim, *Moral Education*, pp. 38, 40.
62. Ibid., p. 46.
63. Ibid., p. 149.
64. The alleged influence from rote learning is assumed to operate among kindergarten children when they learn the 'rules and regulations over and over again' (*fanfu*

xuexi guicheng), according to one typical report: Wang Banghui and Zhang Zhifen, 'Zhuzhong deyu de qianyi mohua yingxiang' (Pay attention to the imperceptible influence of education), *Zaoqi jiaoyu*, No. 3, 1991, p. 2.

65. Émile Durkheim, *Moral Education*, p. 42.

66. Guojia tigaisuo (State Institute of System Reform), 'Zhi you tongguo gaige gongjian: caineng huan lai shehui wending' (Only through reform one can assault fortified positions: ability brings social stability), *Shijie jingji daobao*, 29 August 1988, p. 7.

67. *China Daily*, 6 October 1989, p. 4. After the crackdown in 1989, the old models of development through thrift, the Daqing oilfield, and the Yan'an revolutionary base area were again promoted as models.

68. *Renmin ribao*, 6 March 1993, p. 1.

69. *Zhongxue zhengzhike shouce*, 'qingshaonian xiuyang' bufen (Political class manual for secondary schools, 'youth self-cultivation' section), Beijing, Beijing shifan daxue chubanshe, 1984, p. 247.

70. One class teacher at the Beijing Normal University Experimental (Primary) School claimed that 'the life style of hard living and not indulging in pleasures should be upheld despite the fact that living standards were rising' (interviewee 7). Even at the university level, this theme was an integrated part of moral education (interviewees 1, 2, 3): Beijing 1991. See also Zhang Mingyuan, *Zhongguoren de rensheng quxian*, Beijing, Zhongguo renmindaxue chubanshe, 1989, p. 15.

71. Zhang Boxing, 'Yongyuan jicheng fayang jianku fendou de Yan'an jingshen' (Forever carry on the Yan'an spirit of plain living and hard work), *Qiushi*, No. 19, 1990, p. 5.

72. Émile Durkheim, *Moral Education*, p. 46.

73. Ibid., p. 45.

74. Wu Xinjuan and Chen Ziliang, *Xuesheng xinli yu banji guanli* (Student psychology and class management), Beijing, Zhongguo kexue jishu chubanshe, 1991, p. 96.

75. Paul Boyer quotes a speech given to Boston sunday school teachers in 1837 by the Unitarian leader William Ellery Channing. The aim was not to impose external conformity upon the scholars, he said, but 'to train them to control themselves', not merely 'to form an outward regularity, but to touch inward springs' (Paul Boyer, *Urban Masses and Moral Order in America, 1820–1920*, Cambridge, Mass., Harvard University Press, 1978, p. 51.

76. Zhao Xuehua, 'Xin shiqi peiyang mubiao de tedian' (The characteristics of fostering objectives in the new period), *Beijing jiaoyu*, No. 12, 1986, p. 6.

77. Gu Shudong, 'Dui peiyang xuesheng sixiang suzhi de yizhong renshi' (On understanding the fostering of students' ideological quality), *Shanghai jiaoyu*, No. 1, 1985, pp. 13, 25.

78. A survey from 1986 found that Beijing students had no sympathy for a lifestyle 'controlling one's impulses, (showing) self-control, and ascetism'. See Bai Yuantao, *Dangdai Zhongguo qingnian suzhi lun*, Shenyang, Liaoning renmin chubanshe, 1987, p. 68. Very low scores were given to the value of self-control among 2,125 Chinese undergraduate students. See Huang Xiting, Zhang Jinfu, Zhang Shulin, 'Wo guo wu chengshi qingshaonian xuesheng jiezhiguan de diaocha' (Investigation of the values of Chinese adolescent students in five cities), *Xinli xuebao*, No. 3, 1989, pp. 274–83.

79. Émile Durkheim, *Moral Education*, p. 101.

80. Song Xiren, 'Lun shehui zhuyi daode de jiben yuanze' (On the basic principles of socialist morals), *Qiushi*, No. 4, 1990, p. 23.
81. Émile Durkheim, *Moral Education*, p. 50.
82. Homer H. Dubs (trans.), p. 301.
83. Zhang Nianhong and Leng Hong'en (eds.), *Rencaixue cidian* (Dictionary of talent studies), Beijing, Nongcun duwu chubanshe, 1989, p. 176.
84. Zhu Genxiang, 'Lun shehui kongzhi yu sixiang zhengzhi gongzuo', p. 30.
85. Sun Longji, pp. 11, 229.
86. Émile Durkheim, *Moral Education*, pp. 59, 82.
87. Interviewee no. 6, Beishida no. 2 attached secondary school, Beijing, 1991.
88. Émile Durkheim, *Moral Education*, pp. 60–1; see also *Sociology and Philosophy*, p. 51.
89. Émile Durkheim, *Moral Education*, p. 277.
90. Ibid., p. 102.
91. Ibid., p. 240.
92. David Y. F. Ho, 'Psychological implications of collectivism, with special reference to the Chinese case and Maoist dialectics', in Lutz H. Eckensberger, Walter J. Lonner, and Ype H. Poortinga (eds.), *Cross-Cultural Contributions to Psychology*, Lisse, Swets and Zeitlinger BV, 1979, pp. 146–7.
93. Kenneth Abbot, *Harmony and Individualism*, Taipei, Orient Cultural Service, 1970, pp. 148–9, 196.
94. Geert Hofstede, 'Value systems in forty countries: interpretation, validation, and consequences for theory', in Lutz H. Eckensberger, *et al.* (eds.), pp. 389–407.
95. Iwao Munakata, 'The distinctive features of Japanese development: basic cultural patterns and politico-economic processes', in Peter L. Berger and Hsin-Huang Michael Hsiao (eds.), *In Search of an East Asian Development Model*, New Brunswick, NJ, Transaction Books, 1988, p. 155.
96. See Anthony Giddens, *The Consequences of Modernity*, Stanford, Calif., Stanford University Press, 1990, p. 175. Modernization is not necessarily 'westernization', and China can find its own path towards modernization, says Luo Rongqu, one of China's leading scholars on modernization theory: see Luo Rongqu, 'Lun xiandaihua de shijie jincheng' (On the world-wide process of modernization), *Zhongguo shehui kexue*, No. 5, 1990, p. 115, and Luo Rongqu (ed.), *Cong 'xihua' dao xiandaihua* (From 'westernization' to modernization), Beijing, Beijing daxue chubanshe, 1990.
97. Song Huichang, 'Daode jianshe zhong de jige lilun wenti', *Hongqi*, No. 10, 1987, pp. 34, 36.
98. Richard W. Wilson, 'Conformity and deviance regarding moral rules in Chinese society: a socialization perspective', in Arthur Kleinmann and Tsung-Yi Lin (eds.), *Normal and Abnormal Behaviour in Chinese Culture*, Dordrecht, D. Reidel, 1981, pp. 123–4.
99. Song Xiren, pp. 21–2.
100. Alasdair MacIntyre, pp. 126–7.
101. Lily Chu Bergsma, *A Cross-Cultural Study of Conformity in Americans and Chinese*, San Francisco, Robert D. Reed and Adam S. Eterovich, 1977, p. 72.
102. 'Sie betrachten das Kollektiv einseitig oder vorzugsweise als Diziplinierungs- und Regulierungsmittel und weniger als unerläßliches Milieu für die Entwicklung starker Individualitäten': see Gerhart Neuner, 'Kommunistische Erziehung der Persönlichkeit', *Sitzungsberichte der Akademie der Wissenschaften der DDR Gesellschaftswissenschaften*, No. 5/G, 1976, pp. 11–12.

103. Michael R. Dutton, p. 353.
104. Émile Durkheim, *The Division of Labour in Society*, London, Macmillan, 1984, p. *xxv*.
105. Robert Nisbet, *The Sociology of Émile Durkheim*, New York, Oxford University Press, 1974, p. 187.
106. Xu Weicheng, p. 61.
107. Ibid., p. 60.
108. Ibid., p. 58.
109. Émile Durkheim, *Moral Education*, p. 271.
110. Ibid., p. 120.
111. Ibid., p. 115.
112. Ibid., p. 118.
113. Ibid., p. 122.
114. Ibid., p. 274.
115. Ibid., p. 269, 273–4.
116. Xu Weicheng, p. 61.
117. Zhang Nianhong (ed.), p. 451.
118. Hu Shoufen, *Deyu yuanli* (Principles of moral education), rev. edn., Beijing, shifan daxue chubanshe, 1989, p. 167.
119. Zhang Guangbo (ed.), *Shehuixue cidian* (Dictionary of sociology), Beijing, Renmin chubanshe, 1989, p. 362.
120. Zhou Lu, Yang Ruoquan, and Hu Ruyong, *Qingshaonian fanzui zonghe zhili duice xue* (Studies in how to deal with comprehensive control of juvenile crime), Beijing, Qunzhong chubanshe, 1986, p. 166 ff.
121. Yun Pengju, pp. 164–73 passim.
122. Shen Jianguo, 'Guanyu ren de shehuihua de ji ge wenti' (Some questions on the socialization of man), *Fujian luntan: jingji, shehui ban*, No. 5, 1987, pp. 47–50; also in *C4 Shehuixue, Fuyin baokan ziliao*, No. 4, 1987, pp. 47–8.
123. Émile Durkheim, 'Introduction à la morale', *Revue Philosophique*, Vol. 89, p. 96; trans. quoted from Steven Lukes, *Émile Durkheim: His Life and Work*. London, Penguin, 1973, p. 420.
124. Yan Zhimin, 'Guanyu lixiang de jiu ge bianzheng guanxi' (On some dialectical relations concerning ideals), *Hongqi*, No. 16, 1986, p. 39.
125. Ibid., p. 40.
126. Émile Durkheim, *Moral Education*, p. 204.
127. Émile Durkheim, *The Evolution of Educational Thought*, trans. Peter Collins, London, Routledge & Kegan Paul, 1985, p. 212.
128. Ibid., p. 206.
129. Xu Weicheng, p. 61.
130. Alasdair MacIntyre, p. 123.

4

The Educational Method:
A Sociological Interpretation

THE educational method should be analysed not only as a method of pedagogy, but as a method of understanding how Chinese society functions in general. The themes of the educational method are the same themes as those we have already discussed in analysing the relations between tradition and modernization, integration and disintegration, etc. In particular, the themes of imitation and repetition appear to lie at the core of thinking about education and society in China. These seem to be thought patterns or 'mind sets' of a far more wide-reaching type than strictly pedagogical methods. Yando, Seitz, and Zigler have tried to develop what they have called a 'two factor theory' of imitation, viewing imitation in the perspective of both a theory of learning and a theory of social bonds:

In this theory, we have argued that imitation serves two major functions—that of enhancing intellectual competence in the species and that of serving as a mechanism for affecting the strength of attachment bonds among human beings.[1]

It is precisely in the latter sense that the theory of imitation has gained importance in China far beyond educational circles. Not only are educators preoccupied with imitation; the bureaucrats of social order are equally intensely involved in this discourse. In the case of repetition, we have noted the binding and ordering element of *fu*. Repetitiveness is seen as a guarantor for stability, and as a reminder of the right way of conduct so eagerly promoted in moral education. Confucianism held that only repeated practice of the rituals or the rules of proper conduct (*li*) would eventually result in good morals. I have already quoted Chinese observers claiming that education has become synonymous with social control in China, that administration and education have become identical throughout the centuries. In fact, imitation and repetition have been important instruments in this process of instrumentalization of education, and there has been an educational and administrative institutionalization of imitative and repetitive practices. Let us reflect on these assumptions as we consider the educational method. The methods reflect the structure of the society and culture in which they originated, while also forming that culture in very obvious ways. Imitation has become a cultural truism in China, and there is much talk about the 'laws of imitation' in matters concerning socialization and social order.

Imitation in Western and Chinese Thought

Imitation has been discussed widely in Western social science. In sociology it was a core concept at the turn of this century, although it lost much of its explanatory power as sociology developed. Historically, the concept of imitation was undoubtedly an improvement compared with the many biological explanations current in the social sciences at that time. A good example is the influence of imitation in sociology and criminology, where Charles H. Cooley stressed the imitative and emulative man in contrast to the biologically defined criminal of Lombroso.[2] Today, however, works like Gabriel Tarde's *Les lois de l'imitation*, where Tarde believed he had found the elementary social fact and the cornerstone of sociology in the phenomenon of imitation, seem half-forgotten in the West, and attract interest mainly among historians of sociology.[3] In psychology and pedagogy, the concept of imitation regained strength with the introduction of behaviourism and developmental psychology. Bandura and Walters's work on imitation is but one example of the re-emergence of the concept in the social sciences, a literature only recently appearing in China.[4]

Just as the 'moral sciences' survived in the East, the power of imitation seems one of the main sources for explaining society in the newly re-emerging Chinese social sciences. Not only are the works of behaviourism and developmental psychology on imitation frequently quoted and referred to in China, but Gabriel Tarde seems to be treated as one of the central 'classics' of sociology and is frequently quoted. This admiration cuts both ways: Tarde was impressed by the 'eminently Chinese and Japanese faculty of speedily adapting themselves to their environment'.[5] Chinese references to the sociological 'classics' on imitation, however, seem to lie on the surface as modern 'scientific proof' of a thoroughly imitative type of culture, where imitation has formed part of central thought patterns for centuries. To understand the powerful role of such thought in the Chinese cultural setting, we again have to look at tradition. Although certain general traits of Chinese traditional society are also found in the Western tradition, the survival of traditional forms and thought-patterns seems to be more striking in China.

In traditional society, imitation was not merely a method of learning: imitation of the past was understood as imitation of something superior, and this was seen as the only way in which society could continue being a society. The traditional and retrospective-looking society imitated 'what had always been' in order to preserve the ways of the past in the present, perpetuating the past into the future. Gumbrecht uses the concept for historical periodization in his discussion of the emergence of modernity. In the early renaissance, he claims, *imitatio* was the principle of organizing society. At the end of the late renaissance, the *imitatio* was replaced by the *aemulatio* and by the hope of emulating and recreating the greatness and the cultural blossoming of the Greeks and the Romans.[6] Still retrospective, but with an alternative tradition in sight, the methods of emulating the past thus dominate society.

The imitation of models has deep roots in traditional societies. It is practised in all cultures to promote the acquisition of socially sanctioned behaviour patterns, and there need not be any particular theory about imitation for such behaviour to take place. The cultural importance of such observational learning seems to be a ubiquitous phenomenon in traditional societies of all kinds. Anthropologists have observed that in many languages the word for 'teach' is the same as the word for 'show'. Children often do not do what adults *tell* them to do, but rather what they *see* adults do.[7] 'Seeing' and 'being seen' constitute important aspects of the Chinese socialization strategy.

Margaret Mead used the distinctions 'postfigurative', 'cofigurative', and 'prefigurative' to describe what she saw as three different kinds of culture and three kinds of socialization process. In a 'postfigurative culture', children learn primarily from their forebears; in a 'cofigurative culture', both children and adults learn from their peers; while 'prefigurative culture' describes a socialization process in which adults learn from their children.[8] Traditional societies are primarily postfigurative, deriving their authority from the past. In more developed societies, with their need to incorporate change, we see the emergence of a stronger form of cofigurative learning from peers, playmates, fellow students, fellow workers, etc. The modernization process can be described as a process of socialization where the young take on new authority with their prefigurative apprehension of the still unknown future.

This rather rough-and-ready description of the historical process of socialization must not be taken as more than an idealistic description, indicating a tendency or a movement in socialization. It might nevertheless shed light on the situation in traditional as well as in present-day China. In the Chinese example we see the limits of Mead's concepts. Chinese society seems to have preserved postfigurative structures during modernization to a greater extent than has occurred in modern Western societies. Nevertheless, Mead's theory might illuminate the conflict between mainly postfigurative and traditional methods of socialization, and the emerging prefigurative demands of socialization found in modern society.

An attempt to understand the Chinese quest for the modernization of moral education will reveal some interesting paradoxes in Chinese educational practice. The 'feudal' tradition embodies a particular form of education in which imitation and repetition lie at the core of the educational process. This basic approach is typical of the kind of postfigurative society described by Mead, in which the child obeys the father and the apprentice copies the master. A non-changing society naturally encouraged this kind of education, as the mode of life lived by the parent generation would be repeated by younger generations in a seemingly endless continuity.[9] Not only traditional China but traditional European society as well was dominated by such postfigurative and imitative socialization practices. The widely read devotional work 'The imitation of Christ' (*De Imitiatione Christi*) by the Dutch monk Tomas Kempis (1379–1471) stood for the imitation of eternal truths. In Kempis's book the Lord urges his followers to 'mould your desires entirely after my pleasure, and be no lover of self, but an eager imitator of my will', because 'I am the way unchangeable, the truth infallible, the life unendable'.[10] This quotation not only fits the needs of a belief, it describes a society and a way of organizing it as well. Repetition of the eternal Truth contained in the catechism was central to the 'feudal' educational systems of the West, and the tradition goes even further back.

Imitation had a central place in Western educational tradition. Most ancient and many modern educators considered imitation the methodological *sine qua non* of classical teaching, and they were determined to be true to the past. Plato (427–347 BC) said: 'The well-regulated man . . . will imitate the good man most of all',[11] and in educational theory imitation has dominated the scene at least since the time of Plato and his contemporary, the orator Isocrates (436–338 BC). In China, Confucius had been dead for less than fifty years when the two Athenians were born. Isocrates based his entire system of teaching on the principle of imitation—a principle neither invented by him nor ceasing with his retirement. But in the Western tradition educators have constantly voiced warnings against purely mechanical imitation and rote learning. Neither Isocrates nor Quintilian (AD 35–96), who compiled his twelve-volume pedagogy in Rome nearly two thousand years ago, regarded imitation as superficial copying or mere rote. According to

Quintilian, repetition is an important technique, but needless repetition is deadening. It only saps the energy and curiosity, and leads students to doubt the significance of an educational process that places a premium on teaching students things they have already mastered.[12] Later Thomas Aquinas (*c.* 1225–74) advocated the method of 'discovery' (*inventio*), which he held to be the basis of good instruction. Erasmus von Rotterdam (1466–1536) saw the love of imitation, the *imitandi libido*, even in infants. He saw in this love to imitate the eagerness to be taught.[13] Western tradition warned with ever-increasing urgency against mechanical copying, and stressed the discovery method earlier than did the Chinese.

However, the history of educational thought as discussed thus far might also be misleading. The method of 'copying the classics' (*yinjing judian*) has undoubtedly haunted the Chinese educational system for centuries. Not only were methods of imitation used in an academic context: moral education in ancient society also preserved the imitation method as its core. Despite the massive use of mechanical imitation and methods of rote learning that characterized ancient China,[14] Confucius is said to have advocated 'elicitation methods' (*qifa shi*), and the Daoists were more critical of the methods of imitation than of any tradition in the West. Guo Xiang (died AD 312) sounds surprisingly modern in his critique of the imitation of the classical Chinese sages Shun and King Wu. In his comments on Zhuangzi, he claims:

Those who imitate the sages imitate what they have done. But what they have done is something already passed, and therefore cannot meet the present situation. It is worthless and should not be imitated. The past is dead while the present is living. If one attempts to handle the living with the dead, one certainly will fail.[15]

Far from seeing society as a timeless repetition of the past, Guo Xiang saw it changing with the circumstances. When circumstances change, institutions and morals should change with them. If such movement is obstructed, both institutions and morals become artificial and false. Guo sees it as natural that new institutions and new morals will spontaneously produce themselves—sounding more like a modern philosopher than one who has been dead for 1,700 years. When mechanical imitation nevertheless prevailed, it is important to understand that bureaucracy rather than the ideas of pedagogy ruled the Chinese educational system.

Western tradition has seen many examples of mechanical imitation and slavish copying in the past. The Latin schools of Europe stressed imitation as the most vital part of the learning process. There were three steps to education. First there was *praeceptum*, which meant that rules were learnt from the book. Second was *exemplum*, where examples or models were used to illustrate the application of rules. The third step was *imitatio*, where the things learnt from the two first steps were to be imitated by the students.[16] A sixteenth-century manuscript on pedagogy is typical in describing 'memory and imitation' as the 'salient signs of an able mind'.[17] By extension, behaviour should be similarly manageable; for, when the will has been trained by systematic habituation, actions should cease to be erratic. Thus, the entire chain of psychological responses, from perceiving to learning, judging, knowing and acting, was seen as an orderly, controllable and more or less predictable process. Students were expected to imitate the rules presented to them in the classroom. Moral education was seen as the most important part of education; it was also assumed that by learning moral rules by heart one would learn to behave correctly. The *imitatio* of the old Latin schools finds its equivalent in the Chinese *mofang*—to imitate—as contrasted to *chuangzao*—to create.

We saw in Chapter 3 that today's Chinese moral educators have sought to bring about a positive process of habit formation. Already Quintilian said that 'repeated imitation passes into habit' (*frequens imitatio transit in mores*).[18] Imitation was thought to be particularly well suited to bring about such results, and we find exactly the same insights in sixteenth-century Europe. Directed imitation passes by frequent repetition into habit, and moral character was defined as 'habit long continued'. The power of habit had developed into dogma. Few words turned up with greater frequency in the educational regulations of the Reformation than 'habituation' (*Gewöhnung, consuetudo, usus*). Another widespread precept was that comprehension was built on drill: 'For the young cannot grasp our teachings unless they are first habituated to them by means of verbatim repetition.'[19]

A person's nature might tend to move him in a certain direction, but only habit could make this tendency continuous and predictable. The 'genealogy of predictability' in today's China has to be sought in these traditional characteristics. Inculcation of habit was necessary for the stability of individuals and society alike. Left undirected, the soul would always follow its perverted inclinations. Raw nature could be habituated to approved conduct, most easily during the early years; for, as the old German proverb says, 'Bent in youth, inclined for life' (*Jung gewonet, alt getan*).[20] Strauss sums up the view of sixteenth-century educators by saying:

To sixteenth-century pedagogues, therefore, the constraining and directing power of habit over life was much more than a fond hope, a rhetorical commonplace or a rule of thumb taken from experience. They accepted it as a scientific doctrine, one that explained the operation of the mind and the process of learning, offered them an instrument of indoctrination for remaking their fellowmen into decent Christians, and even promised to bring within their reach the truly formative kind of education of which Plato had written that it 'leads you always to hate what you ought to hate and love what you ought to love from the beginning of life to the end'.[21]

Habituation is the theory of imitation put into practice, for at the bottom of this theory lies an assumption of imitation as the cement that holds society together. In imitation lies the copying of social rules, of what is already there, of what is contrary to innovation. Imitation is on the side of tradition, and, as Paul Ricoeur has pointed out, 'innovation remains the pole opposite to that of tradition'.[22] The rules change under the pressure of innovation, but they change slowly and even resist change, he continues, thus pointing to the conserving effect of imitation. Foucault has remarked that the panoptic system of surveillance made it possible to observe performance without there being any imitation or copying, thereby pointing to the surveillance effects that are inherent in the methods of imitation.[23] In other words, imitation stands for a particular view of social cohesion and order, rather than a method of education only. Gabriel Tarde is so often quoted in China today because he saw imitation as a social tie which binds people together, and thought that imitation should therefore be regarded as the basic principle of social development.[24] Tarde claims that society 'began on the day when one man first copied another', and he repeatedly uses the expression 'society *is* imitation'.[25] If we add to the last sentence 'and imitation is integration', we have also summed up the basic value of imitation in Chinese education and society. We remember Durkheim's emphasis on the regularity represented by morality. The same effect of regularity is implicit in imitation, and Tarde at the start of his book describes a society without imitation or repetition as a society without a memory:

But let us imagine a world where there is neither resemblance nor repetition . . . a world where everything is novel and unforeseen, where the creative imagination, unchecked by memory, has full play, where the motions of the stars are sporadic, where the agitations of the ether are unrythmical, and where successive generations are without the common traits of an hereditary type.[26]

Tarde further maintained that the social being, to the degree that he is social, is essentially imitative, and imitation plays a role in societies analogous to that of heredity in organic life.[27] Imitation follows a social logic. Tarde did not, like Ricoeur, necessarily see imitation and innovation as opposites. Rather, he viewed tradition and custom as the conservative forms of imitation, while innovation or imagination was seen as a unique but necessary event for the social progress. For the innovative event to take root, however, it must be transmitted to society by the acts of imitation. 'This original act of imagination and its spread through imitation was the cause, the *sine qua non* of progress,' Tarde explained.[28] Innovations, in other words, could be imitated, and only through such imitation would they gain social significance. Innovation belongs to the individual, while imitation represents what is truly social: 'The laws of invention belong essentially to individual logic; the laws of imitation belong in part to social logic.'[29] Since individualism was regarded as 'non-moral' behaviour by both Durkheim and the Chinese moral educators, we can also see a moral connotation in the 'social logic' of imitation. The theory about a transmission of innovation through imitation lies close to the adaptation–innovation thinking of controlled change. This is also the usual way Tarde's 'law' of social development is understood by contemporary Chinese sociologists. On the basis of adaptation, human beings can make new inventions, and a new process of imitation can start.[30] Imitation must be seen in connection with the 'moral science' of objective norms. The 'mechanical' character of imitation is thus no problem. Mechanical imitation is merely a building stone and one form of imitation—the most basic and objective form.

'Imitation is the natural instinct of the child, the world of a child is the world of imitation,' Wu Zhen explains.[31] In the process of growing up, imitation is the very first method of obtaining knowledge about the world, and the first form through which children can grasp the real world. By imitating adults, children develop from 'living beings' to 'social beings'. The process starts in the realm of the 'mechanical', and the development goes from blind (*mangmu*) to reasoned (*liyou*) imitation. Before they are 5 years old children imitate the cooking of food without understanding the meaning of 'work'. Later, selective imitation takes place, and children start evaluating morally what is right or wrong. Rules are transmitted by selecting the right kind of imitation game for children, says Wu. Role playing is used. Through the game 'catch the train' (*cheng huoche*) they learn to respect rules such as queuing up and buying a ticket, and they come to understand what a 'driver' and a 'passenger' are, and the relationship between them; in playing 'catch the spy' (*zhua tewu*), they learn the basic meaning of 'good person' and 'bad person'. Through such imitation of real life in games, children also come to understand the basic meaning of 'work', as well as social and moral concepts, rules, and customs; and they learn to regulate their self-control according to the correct rules. Children gradually understand society and its social activities as imitation develops from external (*waibu mofang*) to internal imitation (*neibu mofang*).

The imitativeness of behaviour is particularly strong. The germination period of a child's individuality and the establishment of moral concepts and their 'plasticity' (*kesuxing*) is at its greatest when the child is 3–6 years old. Moral and disciplinary concepts are said to take root most easily in this period and to provide a firm foundation for later improvement of their human quality.[32] Imitation is a basis for moral education, according to educators Jiang and Zhang.[33] The sequence goes from unconscious to conscious imitation, from game imitation (*youxi mofang*) to practical life imitation (*shenghuo shijian mofang*). From modelling the superficial outer characteristics of the model and acting similarly, the child develops an ability to imitate the inner characteristics of the model. Jiang and Zhang are representative of the view that originality and creativeness lie on a continuum of imitation: 'In the end imitation leads to original behaviour and one develops an individual creative character (*duchuang xing*).' One should therefore produce an imitation consciousness, seek imitation targets, analyse the targets, decide on their contents, then repeatedly (*fanfu*) imitate, thereby forming habits. Habit formation is thus seen as a necessary prerequisite not only for control, but also for creativeness. Only by imitating can one achieve a basis on which creativity can be built, and such creativity starts in mechanical copying. This belief also explains the immense importance given to mechanical imitation and methods of rote learning. The superficial and the mechanical are the basic building materials of knowledge and innovation. This belief is one of the basic cultural truisms of Chinese society. The argument is repeated over and over again in all kinds of literature, and is applied to all kinds of situations. Innovation is also described as rule-governed behaviour. The Chinese are obviously right about that, but the emphasis on 'guidance' tends towards ossification and obstruction of innovation.

Class teachers in Beijing said explicitly and without hesitation: 'To be able to create you first have to be able to copy (*mofang*) well.'[34] A handbook of practical and theoretical knowledge for youth states that 'Creation lies in imitation as a possibility.' The book goes on to explain that many creative personalities have started out by imitating. Creation, however, is not the necessary outcome of imitation. There are three types and two steps of imitation. First there is simple imitation (*danchun mofang*), then refined imitation (*tilian mofang*), and finally comprehensive imitation (*zonghe mofang*). The process goes from low-grade to high-grade imitation, ending in 'trail-blazing consciousness' (*chuangxin yishi*), the creation of new ideas. Imitation and creation are not opposites: they are extremes on a continuum where the basic root lies in imitation gradually reshaped into creation.[35] 'Imitation does not remain at the level of mechanical copying . . . If you want to create you have to be able to imitate well, this is the dialectical relation of inheritance and innovation.'[36] To imitate is to follow the example of exemplary models. Creativity is learned from imitating the practical actions of models.[37] The task of creating modernizing talents is directly connected to the methods of imitation.

Even at the macro level of development strategy, the techniques of imitation are heeded. The Youth League's central newspaper discusses the different imitation strategies (*mofang zhanlüe*) of economic development. It states that the strategy of development should be learned from Japan. The Japanese adopted the method of digestion (*xiaohua*), reform (*gaizao*), and improvement (*tigao*). Such imitation is a combined process of imitation and creation, and the article says that such a process should form the basis of China's development strategy.[38]

'No matter how much a new organization's founders may want to build an exact copy of a model drawn from another society, they can never replicate it completely in the new setting,' says Eleanor Westney.[39] Copies are nearly always caricatures of the original model. Both conscious and unconscious innovations produce departures from the original model. Since imitation is never perfect, it always moves; thus, it does not lead to total stagnation. Imperfect attempts to imitate others might in fact lead to innovative mistakes. The imitation–adaptation model is a model for, if not slow, then at least controlled change. Even if imitation can point out directions for change, the process is in itself slowed down by imitation. We might say that imitation is based on memories, making the process of change an orderly one. At the same time, models of change might be prescriptions for future development through a process of selective imitation. They operate as planned, ordered and limited standards for change.

Imitation belongs to a traditional conception of time and society. In Chinese as well as Western art theory, important information can be found about how traditional societies viewed processes of change and imitation. The strong tendencies towards reproducing the past in traditional societies have been described in Chapter 1. In art this was manifested in the fact that no higher praise could be meted out than to say of a painter that he entered completely into the spirit of some old master. This succession of teaching from a master-teacher to his disciples was called *shicheng*, and characterizes the imitative type of transmission typical of China.[40] Since the old masters were held to be creative geniuses, there was a debate about whether spontaneity and creativity could be copied at all. It was of course right and proper to imitate the ancients because they were spontaneous, but the copying of spontaneity represented a paradox. Ouyang Xiu (1007–72) held that 'In ancient painting, they painted *yi*, the idea, not *xing*, the mere outer appearance.' Only a spark of intuitive insight, not a copyist's talent, could bring an artist close to the works of ancient genius. Creation is here seen as a communication with a master. Creativity is found in a representation of an idea and in a specific social relationship rather than in individual genius. In copying the old masters, artists were supposed to copy in a manner called *linmo*, which means to copy a model of calligraphy or painting in a special way. Characteristic of this method of copying was that it was meant to divine the spirit of the master-work, not to repeat the letter of that work. One Ming critic mentioned four great painters who had each studied the painting of Dong Yuan, copied it in the *linmo* way, and produced works quite dissimilar among themselves. If 'vulgar men' had been set this task, the critic said, their works would all have been quite the same as the original model.[41]

The power of memory dominates the process of change in traditional societies, but the *linmo* method of imitation once again illustrates that this need not mean total stagnation. In Europe similar methods were used. The medieval copyists were thoroughly medieval in their willingness to imitate. Typically, these copies are not signed, and the copyist was anonymous, a person without individuality. The medieval copyist worked within a set of values and conventions unlike ours. This was a world where imitation was not pejorative, but rather was the handmaiden of creation. The concept of *imitatio* permeated medieval life; it was a common ethical practice in the visual arts, just as in music, in literary production, and in spiritual and everyday matters. James Farquhar has described the life and concepts of artists in general at that time, taking as examples the nameless copyists, the so-called 'Arsenal 575 Master', the 'Fastolf Master', the 'St. Maur Master', etc. The miniatures are reproduced in Farquhar's book for comparison, and illustrate clearly what the Chinese must have meant by *linmo* imitation:

An artist was not expected to overthrow tradition; that is a post renaissance value. Rather he was impelled to work within it . . . Superior models, whether the work of a great master or one with the greatest reputation, were essential; through imitation one grasped the work of the master and developed an individual style. Creation involved imposing one's own style on accepted iconography. Thus the Arsenal 575 Master often displayed a fidelity to his models in terms of iconography and composition, but he created the work in his own style; his *Nativity* could not be mistaken for that of the Fastolf Master, nor his *Virgin and Child* from that of the St. Maur Master, or his *Finding of the True Cross* for the *Turin–Milan Hours* miniature. In this way continuity was maintained between past and present, tradition and innovation. Through imitation, beautiful aesthetic forms were created without disrupting the essential element of meaning.[42]

'Working within tradition'—the expression paradoxically can be used to describe today's Chinese attempts at reform. In the West, from antiquity to the late medieval period—from Homer to Aeschylus, Horace, Ovid, Virgil and Christian de Pizan—creativity often consisted in retelling the old myths in an attractive way to interest the audience. Critics did not praise originality as such; instead, they reserved their paeans for beauty, phrasing, skill, and the ability to move the emotions, to give pleasure, and to instruct.[43] In Chapter 5 I will take the theories of imitation further, and show that it is precisely in the skilled retelling of myths that imitation is most useful from the perspective of social and moral order. The myths are retold with the help of exemplary models within the grand narratives of Chinese culture, socialism, order, and progress. These are the exemplary models that represent the 'objective standards' of society, fixing the exemplary to the equally 'objective' narratives of modern China.

Of course, even the limited creativity of the copyist can be constricted. This happened for example during the Ming (1368–1644) and the early Qing (1644–1911) periods. These were ages of intellectual corruption of creativity when rules were imposed on everything. Art had to follow detailed, prescribed rules. Mountains, rivers, grasses, trees, birds, animals, fishes, and insects had fixed forms. It was held that if these were thoroughly studied, one could successfully reproduce them through rules. Only the human face escaped being copied according to fixed rules in painting, because it had so many various forms that it would be impossible to provide stereotypes of it. Faces could be understood only spiritually. However, portraiture followed certain rules anyway, such as how to paint the so-called five 'mountains' of the face.[44] We also find this 'rule imperialism' in the famous 'eight-legged essay' (*bagu wen*)—the formalized style in which all essays for the imperial examinations were to be written after 1487. This formalization caused examination essays to deteriorate into sterile exercises of form, removing all creativity from them. The eight-legged essay is an example of how education more and more became a means of exercising order, and schools more and more became agencies of surveillance. The entire society seems to have been led through the terror of the rule. It often seems as if formalized imitation and rule-making have a tendency towards self-perpetuating processes of routinizing all kinds of human expression.

This is not merely the result of a traditional society: a bureaucracy must be present to fix the rules into this state. Such fixed forms of rules and norms thus become increasingly alienated from real life, and turn into phantoms or 'supersocial norms' because they do not follow the changed social circumstances. They lose their flexibility and turn into absolute things-in-themselves. To press for the absolute is obviously counter-productive unless there is some social cement to hold the rules together. In the form of institutionalization, the binding elements of imitation might be bound too tightly, stopping the circulation of change and innovation.

Not only is imitation institutionalized; processes of imitation have come to represent a particular imitative culture or even a kind of habitus in China. Even modernity takes place in a climate of imitation. Tarde has pointed to the relations between tradition and modernity with regard to imitation.[45] While the traditional form of imitation focuses on custom, Tarde chooses fashion as the modern form of imitation. He seems to focus on the traditional and binding elements of imitation rather than its modern forms. Imitation can explain change, in Tarde's opinion, but in a passage about the imitation of custom and fashion his definition resembles the picture of slow or controlled change so often discussed in China. He talks of the 'currents of fashion', claiming that such currents represent a very feeble stream compared with the 'torrent of custom' represented by imitation. Periods dominated by the view that 'everything new is admirable' are essentially externalized, on the surface, while those epochs whose maxim is 'everything antique is good' live a life wholly from within. Tarde touches on the social logic of imitation by pointing out that the binding elements of patriotism were diminished by periods dominated by fashion:

In periods when custom is the ascendant, men are more infatuated about their country than about their time; for it is the past that is pre-eminently praised. In ages when fashion rules, men are prouder, on the contrary, of their time than of their country.[46]

The coercive side of the binding character of imitation is but one side of it. We should also recognize the spontaneity of popular credulity and docilility. There are two ways of imitating: to act exactly like one's model, or to do exactly the contrary:

A society is (therefore) a group of people who display many resemblances produced either by imitation or *counter-imitation*. For men often counter-imitate one another, particularly when they have neither the modesty to imitate directly nor the power to invent. In counter-imitating another, that is to say in doing or saying the exact opposite of what they observe being done or said, they are becoming more and more assimilated, just as much assimilated as if they did or said precisely what was being done or said around them. Next to conforming to custom . . . there is nothing more imitative than fighting against one's natural inclination to follow the current of these things, or than pretending to go against it. In the Middle Ages the black mass arose from a counter-imitation of the Catholic mass.[47]

Tarde adds that we must be very careful not to confuse counter-imitation with invention, its dangerous counterfeit. Much of what goes under the heading of innovation in contemporary China might in fact be such counter-imitation. There is considerable talk of the psychology of blind defiance in China today, and that phenomenon can be explained in the light of counter-imitation. The tendency towards doing *das ganz Andere* is widespread. According to one book, this defiance expresses itself in a craze for reading prohibited books, and in the reluctance to see officially praised films.[48] Cursing the Party and socialism has also become popular. The massive doses of 'imitate rule' that we see throughout China have their counter-expression in *nifan xinli* or the 'psychology of defiance', said to constitute an important element of the emerging youth culture. Young people simply do not want to listen and obey (*tinghua*) any longer.[49]

At times, moral appeals may have counter-productive effects. Instead of greater obedience and a higher moral level, it turns out that defiance might be the by-product of the process. In a Western experiment about cheating on exams, Tittle and Rowe speculated as to whether moral appeals not to cheat could in fact lead previously honest students into cheating. The assumption in this particular experiment was that the moral appeal suggested to the honest students that cheating had become so customary that it was out of control and that the norm against it had lost its moral force. Tittle and Rowe's experiment was designed to show the relative effects of sanctions on moral appeal and college classroom cheating. The moral appeal was found to have no effect on the level of cheating, but a clear and substantial impact was observed for the sanctions.[50] Interestingly enough—and potentially devastating for the moral appeals approach of exemplary societies— results appear to support the deterrent argument, and to demonstrate that fear of sanction is a more important influence than moral appeal in generating conformity to the norm of classroom honesty. Tittle and Rowe, however, claim that it would probably be a mistake to attribute all conformity to fear of sanction: 'Moral commitment was no doubt operative to some extent . . . [I]t would be a mistake to draw sweeping conclusions from these results.'[51] In China, during the 1950s and

1960s moral appeals seem to have been far more effective, indicating that a positive overall 'social climate' has to exist before such appeals can be succesfully utilized.

The speculations of Tittle and Rowe find some support in Chinese practices. A small-scale survey based on questionnaires and conducted at a secondary school in Beijing showed that cheating on exams was widespread, and that even students who were praised for their high moral level took part in the cheating. The 39 respondents included Youth League members, class cadres, and good as well as poor students. It was found that all the students had cheated by copying homework from others, or cheating on tests and exams. Some of the cheaters got excellent marks and were even praised for their achievements by the teacher. Some had even become 'three-good students'—a title of honour including high morality—by means of cheating.[52] Under certain circumstances the appeals to high moral standards seem to have turned into a ritual, and my point here is that the widespread ritualization of morality is connected to the imitative culture itself.

We get a hint about the social effects of exaggerated imitativeness in the very word 'imitation'. One of its connotations indicates falseness; another has to do with play-acting. It is related to words like 'mime' or 'mimicry', with further links to 'simulation'. We here see the contours of the 'culture of falseness' (*xuwei wenhua*) or 'hypocrisy' that plagues the Chinese even today, and that some find to be an obstacle to modernization. This is a point to which I shall return in the final chapter.

The Social Significance of Repetition

The repetition and memorization (*shiji*) that have dominated Chinese education for centuries, as in the Western tradition, seems closely knit to a traditional time-concept. The 'natural rhythms' of agrarian life were based on the repeated cycles of nature. With Lévi-Strauss, we could talk of a cyclical or reversible time, governed by the logic of repetition, and where the past is a means of organizing the future.[53]

In Western tradition, a psychology of learning inherited from the ancient world underlay the emphasis on repetition and memorization. Renaissance educators never worried that the child's memory might become saturated. On the contrary, they held that constant practice enlarged memory capacity. Guarino Guarini, one of the most famous teachers of the Renaissance, in 1425 quoted Vergil: 'I will repeat and repeat again, and recommend many many times' that teachers must exercise the student's memory.[54] Repetition was more important than explanation. To the charge that this type of education trained memory more than understanding, a Renaissance teacher might have replied, 'Yes, and so much the better!'[55]

In his *The Art of Memory* from 1697, the Hugenot Marius d'Assigny devoted much space to explaining the means of achieving or maintaining bodily equilibrium and the need for repetition. Memory, *recordatio*—remembrance—and *reminiscentia*—recovery of ideas—were seen as the most important elements in education. The heroes of his book are persons of extraordinary memory. Some carried with them whole libraries in their memory.[56] Nor is the theme of self-control forgotten, and d'Assigny combines our point about the connection between memory, order, and the perfectability of human beings:

A too frequent and violent use of Venus, when the Stomach is altogether empty, or too full, or contrary to the Rules of Conjugal Chastity and Religion, is very dangerous, not only to the Body, but also to the Soul, and all its Faculties . . . A moderate Joy and Contentment of Mind is very profitable for the preserving and fortifying of this Ability of Memory.[57]

These themes are found in Chinese education today—not only in regard to the importance of memory and repetition, but also, as we shall later see, relating the importance of sexual chastity to promote general human quality and to uphold social and moral order.

It was Zhu Xi's brand of Confucianism that institutionalized the methods of repetition and memorization in Chinese schools. It was his methods that were taught in the schools, in the Imperial University, and even in the imperial household. And it was his understanding of Confucianism that served as the basis for the prestigious civil service examinations. From the fourteenth century until the early decades of the twentieth, Zhu's teachings constituted a sort of orthodoxy. Although some scholars rejected the system constructed by Zhu, none could avoid reading or memorizing his works, for the entire educational structure of later imperial China was built on them. At that time, few books were available, so Confucianists of the Han period (206 BC–AD 220) just recited the classics from memory. Zhu Xi held this to be an ideal, even if during his time books were readily available. He advocated that students recite each text over and over again until they no longer saw it as an 'other', and he was fully convinced that every reading would produce a deeper understanding; even fifty or a hundred readings should not be regarded as too many. Zhu did not recommend any fixed number of times for books to be read; he simply advised that 'when the number is sufficient, then stop'. The ideal reader should read the book from front to back over and over again, to the point of 'intimate familiarity'.[58]

It has occurred to me that recitation (*du*) is learning (*xue*) . . . [and] learning is reciting. If we recite it then think it over, think it over then recite it, naturally it'll become meaningful to us . . . I used to find it hard to remember texts. Then I simply recited them aloud. What I remember now is the result of recitation. Old Su simply took the Book of Mencius, the Analects, the Han Feizi, and the writings of the various sages and for seven or eight years sat quietly reciting them. Afterward he wrote a number of things that were very good.[59]

Reading made individuals achieve not only knowledge, but also constancy of mind and self-control. In reading a text, there was no other way than to recite it aloud, stated another of Zhu's dogmas of learning.[60] It serves to clear one's mind, and to make the social rules a part of oneself and one's own body:

If a man's mind is always clear, his body will follow the accepted rules without any external compulsion. It's only because there are times when man's mind becomes distracted that we set up the many rules to regulate it. If we are ever vigilant, so that our bodies follow the accepted rules, our minds will not become lost and will endure in their brightness. To keep the mind constantly alert, then to regulate it with rules as well, is the way to nurture the mind both from within and without.[61]

Reading and recitation in the old society had a moral and ordering function which has been retained to the present day despite violent attacks from people like Mao Zedong, who was in theory an educational reformer in this sense, but who started the Cultural Revolution based on excessive moral recitation in the reading of that Little Red Book. The themes of habit and constant repetition that I earlier quoted from Xu Weicheng's speech at the morality conference still fit the orthodoxy of the eight-hundred-year-old maxims of Zhu Xi.

Zhu Xi institutionalized the method of recitation and rote learning, but the roots go much further back. There has been considerable speculation as to the origins of the traditional emphasis on these methods. In China, obvious social reasons dictated the use of recitation. Surprisingly enough, parts of the explanation can be found in the realm of politics and poetry. Recitation of poems became a matter of diplomacy, of stability and order, peace and war, life and death. Rote learning and recitation were highly important social phenomena. Harmony itself, the very heart of the Chinese cultural concept, depended on such methods.

At the time of Confucius, there was a certain collection of songs very similar to the classic *Book of Poetry*. These songs were widely used on important occasions, such as feasting and ritual sacrifice, and were also frequently used as a medium of exchange of opinions in diplomatic relationships. Much of the diplomatic exchanges were carried out during feasting, and it was common to have singers sing songs to entertain the guests. Individuals at the feast were often asked to select one or more songs from the collection, to be sung by professional singers. It was of utmost importance that these songs suited the situation. They should express the desires of those who chose them, without offending others. Serious national disgrace and calamity could result from the inability to select the appropriate songs. Under the sixteenth year of Duke Xiang (557 BC), Zuo Zhuan stated:

The Marquis of Jin feasted with other princes in Wen, and made their great officers dance before them, telling them that the songs which they sang must be befitting the occasion. Those sung by Gaohou of Qi were not so, which enraged Xunyan, so that he said, 'The states are cherishing a disaffected spirit', and proposed that all the great officers should make a covenant with Gaohou who, however, stole away back to Qi. On this, Shu Sunbao, Xunyan of Jin, Xiangxu of Song, Ningzhi of Wei, Gongsun Jie of Zheng, and a great officer of Little Zhu, made a covenant engaging that they should together punish the state which did not appear at the court of Jin.[62]

The diplomats were always carefully chosen to be those who were most skilled in using the songs. On the social value of poetry, Confucius claimed that the songs 'serve to stimulate the mind . . . teach the art of sociability . . . [and] show how to regulate feelings of resentment'. He also held that they aided the moral purposes of serving one's father and one's prince, and even taught the names of birds, beasts and plants.[63]

Poetry (*shi*) at the time of Confucius, then, can be seen as a 'proto-science' covering lessons in psychology, sociology, political science, and natural sciences. Confucius endorsed a type of 'applied poetry', finding real uses for the verses in specific life situations. The aim of most of Confucius's students was to enter politics. Confucius maintained that the mere ability to recite these songs had no practical value if one had not acquired the art of using them with tact in practical situations. He was preoccupied with the social effects of a skill, and not the skill itself.[64]

Intelligence is often measured by a scale of 'memory power' (*jiyi li*),[65] but the methods are first of all meant to serve a moral purpose. By continually accumulating good acts, everyone can become a sage; but to do 'good acts', one has to know the text prescribing them. In imperial China the classics were said to represent the truth about morality and society. The person who had memorized the texts, in other words, knew the rules of proper conduct, and would later be able to use this knowledge. This theme has never faded: today in China, knowing the texts is as important as it was back then. It is one of the central mechanisms in acquiring the knowledge necessary for grasping the 'moral science' that defines the truth. 'The repetitive character of moral education' is one of the reference-words in modern encyclopaedias of education.[66]

The method of repetitive education is used in normal schools every day, but it is also much used in prison rehabilitation or redemption work. In an article on 'help-education' (*bangjiao*), a method of legal surveillance and support for former juvenile criminals, the importance of 'repeated education' (*fanfu jiaoyu*) is emphasized. This is a slow-working but effective method, best described by the proverbial wisdom that 'It takes more than one cold day for the river to freeze three feet deep' (*Bing dong san chi, fei yi ri zhi han*). As the formative process of wrong ideas has taken a fairly long time to develop, there must also be a long-term process of combating and correcting wrong ideas. This process of ideological transformation (*sixiang zhuanghua*) does not come about easily, but takes a tortuous course on its road to successful transformation. Ideological relapses (*sixiang fanfu*) will occur during the process. One should 'grasp such relapses over and over again by grasping repeated education' (*zhua fanfu, fanfu zhua*). Methods of such help and understanding should be used repeatedly to prevent erring youth from writing themselves off as hopeless.[67] The following story relates how deviant persons are led on to the right path with the help of such repeated education.

Xiao Liu used to be called the 'great fighting king'. The story is about the hooligan who became an exemplary student, then relapsed into fighting, and again became the exemplary student and later a writer and editor. This success is said to have come about because of constantly repeated learning, and the *fu* of which we earlier spoke is here highly operative in the discussion of *fanfu* (relapse) and *fusu* (recovery). The process is said to be one of 'repetitive treatment (*yizhi*), relapse, and renewed treatment (*zai yi*)'.[68] The method of constant repetition should not only correct, but should also improve, and it represents the basic method of what is called the crime pedagogy (*fanzui jiaoyu*) of prison reform. One should 'repeatedly educate, repeatedly consolidate, and repeatedly raise' (*fanfu jiaoyu, fanfu gonggu, fanfu tigao*), and thereby transform the human quality level of the offender. Repetitive education represents a principle of order on which prison reform as well as social stability rests.[69]

In the schools, methods of rote learning and memorization still represent the order of the day. Memorization is still used to measure the effectiveness of the teaching process. An often-made distinction between 'concentrated review' (*jizhong fuxi*), a method where the class reviews all the lessons at the end of the semester, and 'dispersed review' (*fenbu fuxi*), where the texts are reviewed after each lesson, shows the effectiveness of constant review and repetition. The method of dispersed review is found to be more effective in consolidating the texts, thus giving a scientific proof of the old argument of constancy.[70] Such measuring of memory is typically seen as an objective proof of learning, and there is seldom any question about what is actually measured in these investigations.

A most draconian method of repetition and constant review is found in the method of 'over-learning' (*guodu xuexi*). An article in the pedagogy volume of the authoritative *Great Chinese Encyclopaedia* describes this as a method where by it is not enough merely to learn a text by heart: one should then start reciting the text over and over again. Over-learning is said to be the best way to remember the texts and 'consolidate' (*gonggu*) them in one's mind. It is added that children normally do not appreciate the method, but that once they are able to use it they become enthusiastic about it.[71] Memory and consolidation of the teaching material were said to be important aims of education among nearly all the class teachers I interviewed in Beijing in 1991, with the dispersed review method used and defended in the schools I visited. It was my impression that concentrated cramming before exams comes in addition to the constant practices of dispersed review.[72] The only critical voice was a young former class-teacher who held that the 'repeated repetition method is injuring the students'.[73]

Even educational articles that display a quite liberal view on educational methods tend to keep intact their belief in rote learning and recitation. An advocate of 'amusement education', emphasizing that amusement and playfulness should be the media of learning (*yu jiao yu le*), does not fail to suggest that reviewing lessons is a crucial point of education.[74] Another article on the use of 'self-exploring repetition' (*zizhu tansuo fuxi*), suggests as an improvement that the pupils themselves choose which texts from the textbook to learn by heart; the fact that a fixed number of texts should and must be learned by heart is not challenged at all.[75] Even those who advocate methods of exploration end up defending the values of repetition. More varied forms of exercise are suggested, but this does not challenge the method of recitation and repeating the text from memory (*beisong*), which is said to be among the most important methods in language learning. The time spent on such recitation should be checked, and students should be drilled in the basic methods of recitation. Reading aloud (*langdu*) is also important. It should be fostered and combined with repetition.[76]

Thus, there seems to be much tolerance for the 'mechanical' approach to learning, for which we recall Durkheim had little praise. In the discussion of memorization, this is expressed in the belief that 'conscious memorization' (*yiyi shiji*) can develop only on a foundation of 'mechanical memorization' (*jixie shiji*). The latter process is mere cramming without understanding the text, while the former includes understanding and meaning, enabling the student to interpret the texts. Conscious memorization builds on mechanical memorization, which is extremely important for early education. As to the weight of the different methods in practical teaching, the authoritative answer is that understanding and interpretation should take about 20 per cent of the time, while the repeated reviews of a mechanical kind should take as much as 80 per cent.[77]

Repetition and review methods focus on the long-term process of education. Time and routine, as we have seen, are important elements of moral education, and seem to constitute core concepts of morality in China. Nor is it any accident that the very word for 'routine' (*changgui*) also means 'rule' in Chinese. Fixed rules have been important guiding elements in a long range of discourses on morality in both ancient and contemporary China. This theme is addressed in a book by Wen Hanjiang, who emphasizes that time and routine are important elements of education in general and of moral education in particular.[78] This is also evident from the rich lore of Chinese proverbs. A much-quoted proverb used today in educational literature claims: 'It takes ten years to grow a tree, and a hundred years to foster [good] people' (*Shi nian shu mu, bai nian shu ren*). And one should 'work day in and day out, year in and year out' (*ri fu yi fu, nian fu yi fu*) with one's studies. Master Zhu Xi himself would undoubtedly have been pleased by the fact that 'elder statesman' Deng Xiaoping often cited these maxims. In a much quoted passage, Deng advocates 'working day and night, seven days a week' with one's reading.[79] Such persistent work, and in particular the observation of time and routine, is necessary to develop feelings of responsibility among students, according to Wen Hanjiang. For instance, it is highly important that students do not come late to class, that they do not leave early, that they respect the time schedule as well as their teacher and fellow-students. This brings about good morality in the long run, Wen claims, again stressing the importance of repetitiveness in the process of moral order. The training of students' morality and ideology is a task that proceeds bit by bit (*diandian didi*). Repetition means intellectual systematization; memory and consolidation of knowledge are crucial elements of order. Strict surveillance should be maintained, and routine is emphasized as being particularly important in such surveillance: 'This routine resembles a silent order (*wusheng mingling*) that makes students exercise and practise over and over again, making them study and live in an orderly way, and develop good behaviour and habits.'[80] The repetitive order of time and routine thus brings about harmony in both individuals and society at large. This 'silent order' of which Wen speaks can be compared to the 'hidden curriculum' of Western educational theory. The stress on order in education takes many forms, but it is often linked to the importance of setting standards.[81]

Memorizing Power and the Repetitive–Imitative Culture

This rigid system of repetition and memorization has grave consequences for the students who are subjected to it. The press has even carried accounts about suicides resulting from the rigid system of education.[82] Despite such dramatic reports, however, it has also been noted that the repetitive methods of cramming and rote-learning enjoy mass support among teachers, parents, and students. Jonathan Unger has observed that:

[M]any students felt comfortable with rote learning. They had been taught to memorize by heart in primary schools, and found it still provided a safe and methodical method when in doubt or nervous about a test. A correct answer, after all, was equally a correct answer whether derived through comprehension or memory. It was the not-too-good conscientious students' means to overcome their more academically competent classmates' advantages.[83]

These strict methods were also strongly defended and held as 'special Chinese methods' and thereby alternatives to the system practised in 'capitalist countries', by the delegates at an educational conference in Hubei, indicating that we are here touching upon a deeply rooted cultural phenomenon.[84] Repetition constitutes a certain thought pattern; and China may be said to be both an imitative as well as a repetitive culture. In his book on Chinese culture, Wu Shenyuan has claimed that a creativity-suppressing culture has developed to perfection through the specific Chinese 'power of memorization'. As a prototype of this culture, he refers to the text-critic Shen Tao from the Qin dynasty who could recite by heart the three classics. 'To transmit but not to create' (*shu er bu zuo*) has become the norm that everybody is following.[85]

Wu's criticism of Chinese culture is an interesting contribution to the flowering culture critique that has appeared in China in recent years, and his suggestion deserves a closer look.

An interesting analysis of Chinese cognition has been carried out by Liu In-Mao, discussing the concept of 'Chineseness' from the standpoint that the Chinese have received a unique set of external and internal experiences distinguishing their culture from others. This culturally unique set of experiences determines behaviour in certain fields that have to do with cognition. If this is true, then it will be necessary to specify the exact nature of the past experiences that Chinese have had and that differentiate them from other people and cultures.[86] Although Liu's article concentrates on problems of cognition, there is a social aspect in the argumentation that should be developed further. Interestingly, Liu's analysis of cognition takes as the starting point of analysis the same culture of memorization discussed above.

Let us suppose, like Gilbert Ryle, that there are two types of knowledge. First there is procedural knowledge, that is, knowledge about how to do something; next there is declarative knowledge, meaning knowledge of facts about the world. Ryle speaks of 'knowing how' and 'knowing that'. He talks in terms of intelligence, arguing that some 'reassimilate the knowing *how* to knowing *that* by arguing that intelligent performance involves the observance of rules, or the application of criteria'.[87] *That* things are the way they are thus includes the procedural *how*. This applies in a cultural context as well. Procedural knowledge of knowing how to learn and behave follows prescribed rules and becomes second nature—a culturally coloured 'script' that limits choice. If you learn *how* by repeated practice and habit, you also learn *that* things are the way they are by the same methods.

Liu was led by assumptions about cognition to identify distinct sets of behavioural rules acquired by the Chinese. There are both higher-order and lower-order behavioural rules which the Chinese acquire in childhood. The declarative knowledge about rules is propagated in the family, in schools, and in society. Some of these rules are written, some are not. Procedural knowledge lies in the general approach to these written or unwritten daily rules, and they are closely connected to identity per se.

'Chineseness', in my opinion, lies in what James Watson termed 'orthopraxy'—in 'doing the right thing'. Adhering to this 'doing' are the cultural ways in which things are done. Liu finds three basic rules of behaviour among the Chinese that determine their approach to their ways of thinking and—I would add—to their social surroundings. First, from childhood the Chinese are taught to respect and be obedient to their superiors. In ancient China all human relations were organized in the 'five human relations' (*wu lun*), which hierarchically regulated relations between high and low. These five relations were those between the ruler and his subordinate, the father and son, the older and younger brother, husband and wife, and between friends.[88] Rules of filial piety and, as we have seen, relations between teacher and student were characterized by subordination to the superior. This is a rule deeply ingrained in Chinese society. Liu shows, with examples from linguistics and other sources, how 'loyal' and 'filial' are very much emphasized in the Chinese language and culture. This first rule can be called the 'respect superiors' rule. It be formulated as: '*If your superiors are present, or indirectly involved, in any situation, then you are to respect and obey them.*'[89]

Next comes what we could call the 'memorize lesson' rule: '*If the purpose is to acquire the knowledge contained in an article, then the best strategy is to memorize the article.*'[90] Liu has found empirical material backing this rule in examples drawn mainly from Taiwan. In this sense, both the capitalist and the communist flags are definitely coloured by the same culture, and the same rule applies in the People's Republic. The third rule is closely connected to the second. It can be called the 'practise skill' rule: '*If the purpose is to acquire any new cognitive skill, then the best strategy is to practise repeatedly.*'[91]

Using the language of cognition, it is easy to see that the main cognitive skill required by the two last rules is memorization. As already noted, both Western and Chinese traditions have been dominated by a pedagogy of 'memory power', where the cultural heroes of high intelligence were those who could memorize vast amounts of information and retain it in their memory: Cyrus the great, knowing the names of all his soldiers; Seneca; the Han Dynasty Confucians praised by Zhu Xi; and Shen Tao from the Qin Dynasty as critiqued by Wu Shenyun. There was even a Western influence on China in this regard. The Chinese of the Ming dynasty were impressed by the mnemonic techniques and methods of memorization presented to them by the jesuit Matteo Ricci, a man of great 'memory power'.[92] In ancient Europe as well as in various non-European cultures, the rule of memory power seems to have had strong moorings. Anthropologists report similar characteristics even today.[93]

Liu refers to several cross-cultural studies about cognition. As a consequence of having acquired the 'respect superiors' rule from their childhood, Liu concludes from these findings that the verbal and ideational flow of the Chinese is less smooth than that of Westerners. On the other hand, because of the 'memorize lesson' and 'practise skill' rules, the Chinese excel in tasks requiring memorization, and Chinese schoolchildren score highly not only on language but also on mathematics achievement tests. Liu goes on to speculate about whether the 'respect superiors' rule can contribute to the emotional stability of individuals as well as to the stability of family and society. I think it is precisely here that we see the main significance of these rules. If we leave the scene of cognition, we see that not only the 'respect superiors' rule but all three of the basic rules have a similar and obvious social significance. They are closely interlinked, because on the social level all three rules concern matters of social order. The deeper layers of the script tell a story about how to be Chinese, and the central meaning of the rules is about the way to achieve harmony and social stability. Memorization is here not primarily about cognition, but about a social approach to rules and proper conduct in general. The 'memorizing power' gives direction to 'identity' as well as 'order' in a wide sense. It represents an important part of a higher-order rule that governs rules of a lesser order. We might compare the rules and thought patterns described here with Bourdieu's concept of habitus as something largely unconscious and unquestioned representing a source of durability and reinforcing social order and stability.[94]

We started out with social memory in the first chapter. Now we have come to the point where memorization and what I have called an imitative–repetitive culture give new meaning to that memory. The observed tendency to perpetuate or prolong certain structures and patterns normally associated with the 'traditional' can be explained by this emphasis on the imitative and the repetitive. The 'neo-traditional' or the 'repetition with a difference' are structures recreated in a modern context. I agree with authors like Walder and Dutton that seemingly traditional structures represent something new; but this 'new' has a continuity built into it—it is not an entity without a memory. Such techniques might be productive for the instigation of an 'orderly modernization' or a 'controlled change'. The Chinese imitative–repetitive pattern thus influences both the micro level of educational methods and socialization practices and the macro level of organizational and material culture. It defines both socialization and development strategy.

Elicitation or Inculcation—Education or Politics?

While truths can be imparted, procedures can only be inculcated, says Ryle.[95] Inculcation methods are best suited for strengthening processes of 'knowing how'. Inculcation is therefore not so much about the particular knowledge in question as it is about the general approach to the problems. Inculcation is precisely the gradual process needed to secure the imitative–repetitive culture described here. To be trained or fostered is thus more and different from merely being informed. That brings us to the heated debate about which educational method is best suited to serve modernization and reform. This debate has a sociological interest apart from its obvious educational points. An interesting aspect is the high political temperature of the debate. A main point of disagreement has been whether to follow the 'elicitation method' (*qifa shi*) or the 'inculcation' (*guanshu*) method. At times this debate seems to revolve around definitions of words and concepts, but at the root lie clear social and political considerations.

Before 1989 the advocates of the elicitation method clearly tended to see their pedagogical preferences in a political light. Elicitation is not only a 'form' or a 'method' of education, says Wang Ziguang: it presupposes a democratic attitude and a democratic atmosphere in which to function. Among other things this concerns the teacher–student relationship. The teacher should be the leader, but the relationship should be a democratic one. For thousands of years, the spoon-feeding method dominated. Wang feels that the time ought to be over when teachers' words were absolute, and when the outmoded educational form of 'teachers pass on knowledge, while students merely receive it' (*shi chuan sheng shou*) was all-embracing.[96] Some argue that the method of elicitation reflects the correct relationship between teacher and students. Elicitation is opposed to inculcation (*guanshu*) and cramming (*zhuru*), which are mere coercive methods of learning, based on giving orders. Both Confucius and Mao advocated the elicitation method; Mao actually said that schools should 'promote elicitation methods and abolish the spoon-feeding method (*zhuru shi*)'. Methods of inculcation and elicitation are not merely two forms or methods of education, but two entirely different ideas of education.[97] The method of elicitation is described as the very method of modern societies.[98] The confused, comprehensive, rapid flow of information in modern society demands elicitative education. Inculcation is defined as a traditional method opposed to modern methods of education. Traditional education is confined to the narrow circle of classrooms and books. It regards pupils as empty containers (*rongqi*) into which knowledge can simply be poured.

This 'pouring' of knowledge is what has been in focus in recent years. Both the *guan* in *guanshu*—inculcation—and the *zhu* in *zhuru*—cramming—mean 'to pour', or 'install into'. In my English–Chinese dictionary of education, *guanshu* and *zhuru* are treated as identical words; both are translated as 'indoctrination'.[99] One of my Chinese interviewees did not feel there was any difference in meaning between the two words; then, thinking over the matter, he opined that *guanshu* has an aim, that one should understand the correctness of the principles suggested. In *zhuru* it is indicated mechanically that an A is but an A, with no deeper understanding of principles involved. The first has more to do with moral education, and the second with intellectual learning.[100] Zhou Luming emphasizes that the *guan* in *guanshu*, the element of 'pouring in', is the most dominant element of the process, and that such elements should be avoided.[101] Other educators hold that the methods of cramming are not good for student initiative and creativity since knowledge is 'poured' but not 'entered into'. Many stick to the old ways of '*wo jiang ni ting*' ('I talk, you listen'), simply because the elicitation methods do not provide good results. However, it is also claimed that students get fed up, and that inculcation produces resistance and immunity (*kangyaoxing*) among students,[102] while others simply claim that inculcation, used correctly, will 'arouse the students' motivation and positive character'.[103] In kindergarten, however, the 'pouring' of rules and regulations allegedly makes children adopt good habits and ideas. The message seems to be that inculcation perfectly fits in with the mechanical way children learn.[104]

Many commentators seeking to defend the inculcation method are at pains to explain that *guanshu* is not like the traditional 'mechanical copying' (*shengban-yingtao*), 'the method of force feeding' (*tianya shi*), or the 'cramming method' (*zhuru shi*).[105] Opinion seems to differ widely on this particular question. While some see inculcation as a traditional and negative method, others maintain that tradition is the strong side of it: that traditional moral education was based on inculcation, but did not represent a totally oppressive (*yayi*) or constraining way of education. One should develop what is useful and healthy and discard the unhealthy from such methods. The main healthy part of inculcation is its effectiveness in bringing about good moral behaviour. Those favouring inculcation hold that the method is necessary to dam up the modern 'overflow of freedom' (*ziyou fanlan*), the 'grand landslide' (*da huapo*) of public morality, and the 'crisis of faith' (*xinyang*) among the younger generation. People lose their strength and capacity for self-restraint, their feeling of shame, and show contempt for the social norms. This rapid deterioration of social norms is why inculcation methods should be used despite some drawbacks.[106] It is impossible to make use of basic Marxist knowledge without a good basis of inculcation; Jiang Jiqing claims that 'Only when there is inculcation can there be elicitation (*you guanshu cai hui you qifa*).'[107] First comes the mechanical, and only then there is a possibility for innovation.

The word *guanshu* is often explained with reference to a Lenin quotation that originally appeared in his *What Is To Be Done?* from 1902. Lenin here explains that proletarian communist consciousness does not come automatically or spontaneously to the working class.[108] The English translation of Lenin's collected works goes as follows: 'We have said that there could not have been Social-Democratic consciousness among the workers. It would have to be *brought* to them from without.'[109] Zhang Zhilun is one of those who quote Lenin, bringing the quality of society into the debate. Inculcation is an important 'lever' (*ganggan*) of society, raising it to a higher level of moral perfection.[110] Quoting the same passage from Lenin, the Party's theoretical journal claims that inculcation has become particularly important since 4 June 1989.[111] Not only in schools, but in factories, rural areas, neighbourhoods, and research units it is necessary to provide systematic ideological education. Inculcation of Marxist ideology aims to make people believe in and accept. The 'rigid inculcation methods of "force feeding"' ('*tianya shi*' *de yingxing guanshu*) are however ineffective, and should not be applied.[112]

An official attempt to sum up the debate was made by Wang Zongzhu in 1990. The article's main purpose was to rehabilitate methods of inculcation, and to describe their correct form.[113] *Guanshu* also means 'irrigation', and Wang discusses the relation between the 'irrigating' form of inculcation and the methods of 'dredging' (*shudao*). The dredging method can be described as the elicitation method best adapted to moral education. In addition to 'pouring in' the rules and truths, there is also a process of 'digging out' obstacles in individuals. The process of dredging should be used to counter the psychology of defiance among youth. Dredging is attached to internalization, and describes a self-aware process. Good inculcation depends on good dredging. Mediation or guidance is meaningless without a good foundation of dredging.[114] Wang says that before the 'political disturbances' (*zhengzhi fengbo*), the dredging method was held in high esteem, while the inculcation method was overlooked. Afterwards some cadres felt that the dredging method was unsuitable. Some think that the method of inculcation is valid for certain revolutionary situations only. However, Wang concludes that inculcation is a 'means' (*shouduan*), and not merely a 'method' (*fangfa*); it is thus appropriate for all situations.

Wang disagrees with those who see the *guan*, meaning 'to pour into, to instil into, to fill up', as the central character in *guanshu*. Instead he believes that the *shu* signifies the basic meaning of the concept. *Shu* has the same connotation as in *shusong*—'to carry', 'to transport'—or as in *shuru*, meaning 'input' or 'import'. The *guan* merely underlines and strengthens this meaning. Lenin, in Chinese translation, uses *guanshu*, and Wang's explanation seems to fit the English Lenin translation: 'to be brought to'. The *guan* has a purpose (*zhi*), distinguishing it from mere mechanical inculcation; it also has a limit (*du*). By stressing the limit of the 'pouring', Wang seeks to promote a moderated form, distancing the concept from the slavish rote learning of ancient China. Commenting on the unstable situation during modernization, he concludes that inculcation should function as mental 'flood irrigation' (*manguan*).[115] In addition to having a purpose and a limit, inculcation also has a 'constant' (*heng*). The meaning of constancy here refers to the theme of constant and repeated effort, but also has connotations relating to the constancy of the moral norm. One does not change people into 'new persons' in a day, Wang adds.

The meaning of 'irrigation' is exploited to the full. Inculcation is the 'source' or the well from which the water is taken to nurture the young plants. Dredging refers to the 'canal' through which the water is conducted; it should be used in combination with inculcation. Mediation and guidance are important elements for solving contradictions. Marxism, patriotism, and collectivism represent the source of Marxism–Leninism–Mao Zedong's thought that should be brought in through inculcation. One first has to implement mediative dredging (*paijie xing shudao*) to get rid of obstacles. Then water can be poured in (*guanshu*) from the source, and the sprouts—the students—will receive the life-giving water of ideological maxims.

Wang warns against a one-sided focus on the dredging method. During the 1980s, the Youth League turned away from politics and became an organization of welfare and entertainment to put a damper on the *Sturm und Drang* of the increasingly oppositional students.[116] Some claimed the 'canal' only got filled with more mud because of these approaches to 'opening up' and 'digging out'. Those who arrange dancing parties to pacify (*anfu*) the mood of students have not been made aware of the guiding function of dredging, comments Wang. To solve the problem, one has to go one step further and let in the flow of Marxist ideas. If the mud in the river is not taken away in time, it will block the flow of water from the source. One has to get rid of the obstacles by grasping political education. Harmony will make the sprouts grow, and later society can harvest the fruit of 'new persons'.

Another important aspect of the educational method is infiltration (*shentou*).[117] Infiltration is the method of 'exerting a subtle influence on a person's character'—translated as *qianyi mohua*. Such methods of infiltration are not as conspicuous as the planned methods of inculcation. They work imperceptibly or silently.

Moulding, Environmentalism, and the Imperceptible Influence of Education

Methods of 'infiltration' are known as 'methods of moulding' (*taoye fa*). They have also been called 'unconscious education' (*wu yishi jiaoyu*)[118] or 'silent education' (*wusheng zhi jiao*).[119] There are numerous expressions describing the effects of such influences of education and socialization. In addition to *qianyi mohua*, there is *erru-muran*, meaning 'to be imperceptibly influenced by what one constantly sees and hears'. Socialization is everywhere around us, spontaneously and constantly exerting an influence. The roots of such thoughts are age-old in China. Well-known is Mencius's remark from the fourth century BC: 'Near vermillion, one gets stained pink; near ink, one gets stained black' (*jin zhu zhe chi, jin mo zhe hei*). The quotation is still used as an example of the importance of the educational surroundings and the effect of imperceptible education. The process is said to form part of the foundation for so-called 'student quality development work'.[120] *Xuntao* is another important word in the vocabulary of Chinese pedagogy. It means to 'nurture', 'edify', or (better) 'to exert a gradual, uplifting influence'. The expression reflects the themes of both the slow, gradual influence of education, and the aspect of improvement. The process can be reversed: *Xunran* means 'to exert a gradual, corrupting influence' on somebody.

Educational literature abounds with concrete examples of how to use such processes, and they are closely connected to the discourse on human quality. In particular, parents' quality exerts an imperceptible influence (*qianyi mohua*) on the development of their children.[121] Teachers I interviewed supported explanations of the unconscious influence of one's surroundings; this was described as a constant process. Educators as well as criminologists discuss the silent corrupting influence of the so-called 'yellow' or pornographic literature on the behaviour of children.[122] Television and all kinds of modern social phenomena are said to have a creeping negative influence on young people in particular.[123]

To make use of unconscious or imperceptible influences, a 'carrier' (*zaiti*) is needed. This means a model or an activity which can be used to strengthen the influence. As early as kindergarten, children are set to practise good deeds. Such methods are thought to help the formation of a noble mind and good behaviour and promote polite language among children. Activities such as 'Uncle Lei Feng smiles at us' use the soldier hero Lei Feng to lecture kindergarten children in communist morality. 'Making a holiday present for mama' is about upholding the traditional value of filial piety. This ancient value has recently been upgraded in kindergartens and schools as education in 'respecting the elder generation' (*zunjing zhangbei*), thus supporting harmony between the generations. Another activity, 'the motherland is in our hearts', is meant to build up feelings of patriotism in children. These are all 'courses' in kindergarten classes. To study 'Uncle Lei Feng' involves constant training in doing good deeds. Education in being thrifty follows the principle of 'doing one good deed every day, saving one *fen*, one drop of water, and one grain of rice every day'. Such practice is repeatedly emphasized in the hope that children's deeds later in life will be imperceptibly influenced by their early training in thrift.[124] This type of education should be carried out by 'gentle restraint' (*ruan yueshu*) and constant practice. By constant practice and constant exposure to edifying 'carriers', a 'sudden realization of the truth' (*dunwu*) may appear.[125] This sudden realization is seen as the most successful result of the method, and also describes the hope of the repetitive efforts so often used in moral education in general. The repetitive, quantitative effort, in other words, can turn into qualitative improvement. The ability to apply rules is the product of practice, and 'learning by doing' in moral education is based on the 'exercise method' (*duanlian fa*).[126]

Imperceptible influence is associated mostly with methods of elicitation, and is often regarded as a method of education in aesthetics which supposedly exerts a favourable influence on people's character, and appeals to feelings and values much more than does the inculcation approach. The imperceptible influence of aesthetics education is one not of persuading (*shuofu*), but of influencing (*ganran*). It does not openly reason (*mingle*), but gives expression to one's emotions (*shuqing*). It arouses feelings and stimulates (*jifa*) people; these feelings are of a principled and orderly character which counteracts the alleged unhealthy stimulation (*ciji*) so often discussed in connection with the emerging youth culture. Appreciation of natural beauty builds on a series of small, unconscious, imperceptible influences. The creation of 'stable and high-quality feelings' is the result of such education.[127] It leaves impressions and imprints on students that conscious control, adjustment, and guidance cannot achieve for a long time. Conscious and unconscious psychological mechanisms are mutually dependent, with the unconscious producing the basis for the conscious. This is why one should stress 'campus culture', and the construction of a hidden curriculum (*qianzai kecheng*).[128] The concept of 'campus culture' (*xueyuan wenhua*) belongs to that part of educational theory known as environmentalism. This is a theory based on the assumption of the edifying invisible strength (*wuxing de liliang*) of the environment, and is central in the ongoing efforts to create a 'spiritual civilization'.

Environmentalism, or 'environmental moulding' (*huanjing taoye*), has had considerable influence also in Western theory. In the old 'moral sciences', architecture was in part a branch of ethical theory. The idea of moral reform through environmental improvement was highly valued by the US reformers of the 1890s. Positive alternatives were provided to the allegedly morally degenerating dance-halls and saloons: the reformers saw the development of parks and playgrounds, public baths, facilities for concerts and art exhibits as important to the development of human character. These were held to promote both the physical well-being and the 'moral health' of the poor, and to counteract 'tendencies to vulgarity and dissipation and immorality' in the cities.[129] The new outlook that a 'bad physical environment means a bad moral environment' gradually spread through urban America in an attempt to solve the chronic problem of moral breakdown in the cities. Environmentalism turned into a technique of urban moral control. John Dewey, with his insistence on the central role of environment in shaping human behaviour, claimed that the most effective social control was 'not merely physical or coercive, but moral'.[130] The American 'park movement' was another result of the environmentalist trend. Paul Boyer comments:

Today, parks are so ubiquitous and familiar a feature of the urban scene that we give little thought . . . to their social significance. Thus, it takes a considerable imaginative leap to realize that the park movement once had the force of a fresh social discovery that could arouse intense and passionate commitment, and that its moral implications were carefully explored and debated by moralists, urban reformers, social critics, landscape designers, and municipal authorities alike.[131]

Parks were to provide grassy meadows that would bring 'tranquility and rest to the mind'; it was argued that they would exert upon the urban masses a 'harmonizing and refining influence, favorable to courtesy, self-control, and temperance'.[132] The moral significance and social control function of parks seemed to arise from a belief in the elevating power of grass and foliage. The park movement can be interpreted as a 'traditional' counterweight to the morally destructive pressures of urban life, and as a nostalgic longing for a pre-urban model of social homogeneity. American reformists at the end of the last century, like the Chinese reformers of today, seem to believe that the key to social stability lay in somehow re-creating a cohesive community bound together by an enveloping web of shared moral and social values. The moral effect of the environment was heavily stressed in ancient China, as exemplified in the story about Mencius's mother who moved house three times to find the right educational environment for her son. Mencius imitated his surroundings: when they lived near a cemetery, the boy played at building graves and conducted burial ceremonies. They then moved near a marketplace, and Mencius played at being a merchant. Finally they moved near a school, and Mencius started to imitate the rules of proper conduct and respectful behaviour.[133]

The family and school atmosphere are seen as particularly important. The alleged power of grass and foliage is an important part of Chinese assumptions about environmentalism. At school green trees, fragrant flowers, clean classrooms, famous paintings, etc., have an improving effect. A relaxed and receptive state of mind and a will to strive are the fruits of such surroundings. A creative environment produces creative students, and both knowledge and morality are said to be improved through such environmental moulding. The language environment is also important.[134] The narrative of environmental improvement, however, not only has nostalgic overtones with the aspect of cohesive community a central element: in line with the overall narrative of progress, a competititive environment is also emphasized in today's China.[135] This environmentalism builds fundamentally on the perceptions of a social engineer, and the improvement of the environment is in the final instance about improving human beings.

It is necessary to improve the environment (*gaizao huanjing*), says Guo Zhao, but this also means transforming people's spiritual or mental outlook. Such transformation is applied not only on the individual level: efforts are linked to the strategy of creating a spiritual civilization, and are said to have a social effect of a much larger scale. Guo claims that in Sanming city in Fujian province a successful beautification campaign brought down the crime rate.[136] Improvement alone is not enough. China's criminology literature reflects the anti-crime campaigns launched during the 1980s; instead of 'improvement' there is often talk of a 'purification' (*jinghua*) of the environment, a process through which all kinds of evils and obscenities are to be be wiped out and banned.[137]

After the student unrest of the 1980s, 'campus culture' has become the very focus of the debate of environmental moulding. It is emphasized that the principles of education through imperceptible influence must be grasped if one is to build a 'spiritual atmosphere' (*jingshen fenwei*).[138] To create such a spiritual atmosphere, one has to pay heed to both its material and spiritual aspects. A campus possesses both material and spiritual culture; its material culture constitutes three main elements. First, there is an 'environmental culture' (*huanjing wenhua*). This includes the whole design of the campus, the overall architectural structure, the beautification of the interior of the buildings, and the purification of the surroundings. Next comes the so-called 'facility culture' (*sheshi wenhua*)—the administrative equipment, teaching facilities, lecture halls, laboratories, libraries, logistics equipment, and so on. Last there is the 'style culture' (*fangshi wenhua*); this involves erecting memorial stone tablets, sculptures of famous persons, exhibition halls, etc., on campus. All three types of culture will have a positive influence on students: 'feelings will be controlled, behaviour will be restrained, conduct will be moulded, and one's intellect will be enlightened and awakened. Intellect and feelings will be influenced.' Feelings like loyalty, love, responsibility and a sacrificing spirit are strengthened through the correct handling of the material culture of campuses.[139]

This theory of environmentalism and of a material element of spiritual civilization influences the top of the party leadership. In an authoritative speech on spiritual civilization, one of the top party leaders, Li Ruihuan, has linked the problems of 'environmental sanitation, civility, manners and social conduct' as follows:

For example, the sky is clearer and brighter, the landscape cleaner and greener, the roads are broader and smoother, the people are dressed better and smarter, and they get along with one another with greater civility. The people recognise and appreciate all these changes. If there ever was some disagreement several years ago over the questions of cleaning up, afforestation, and beautifying the environment, most of the people approve them now . . . Fujian and Shashi city are quite clean. A common practice adopted by them is to pave the ground, particularly roads and courtyards, with either soft or hard cover. Soft cover refers to grass and plants. Hard cover means paving the road with bricks, asphalt or cement.[140]

Here we immediately recognize the American reformers of the last century, with their concern about a grassy environment. Paving the roads and covering the courtyards with grass is a matter of moral improvement and spiritual civilization. Li Ruihuan promises that research on spiritual construction is to be intensified, suggesting that there should be 'a general plan'.[141] In addition to a material culture, there is also a spiritual culture on the campuses. Here the principles of imperceptible influence should be exploited to the full. To educate people, particular emphasis should be given to educational organization, to latent study (*qianzai de xuexi*), and to unconscious education (*wu yizhi jiaoyu*). One must create a consciousness of 'belonging' among the students. The spiritual atmosphere of the school and class, its traditions, its collective spirit—all make up a 'hidden culture' (*yinxing wenhua*) to which everybody on campus belongs. This hidden culture is expected to improve the political, ideological, moral, and scientific quality of the students, and to represent a 'national culture' countering 'total Westernization'.[142] The improvement of campus culture is thus both about 'binding' and 'belonging', both social order and national identity.

Notes to Chapter 4

1. Regina Yando, Victoria Seitz, and Edward Zigler, *Imitation: A Developmental Perspective*, New York, John Wiley, 1978, Preface.
2. Charles H. Cooley, '"Nature versus nurture" in the making of social careers', in *Proceedings of the National Conference on Charities and Correction*, 1896, pp. 399–405.
3. Gabriel Tarde, *The Laws of Imitation*, New York, Henry Holt, 1903 (originally published in French in 1895 as *Les lois de l'imitation*). Durkheim devoted considerable energy to refuting the findings of Tarde in his *Division of Labour in Society*, while a sociologist like Simmel seemed to have more sympathy for the concept of imitation, or '*Nachahmung*'. See Georg Simmel, 'Fashion', in *On Individuality and Social Forms: Selected Writings*, ed. Donald N. Levine, Chicago, University of Chicago Press, 1971, pp. 294–323.
4. See Albert Bandura and Richard H. Walters, *Social Learning and Personality Development*, New York, Holt, Rinehart & Winston, 1963. Bandura and Walters make the point that in many cultures the use of models and imitation has been an important part of the socialization process (see pp. 47–50). However, they seem unaware of the vast importance the theory has had in Chinese culture, as no reference is made to this in their book. For an example of a Chinese implementation of Bandura, see Zheng Xinran, 'Bangyang huodong yu ren de xinli fenxi' (A psychological analysis of the education by model activities), *Qingnian chao*, No. 3, 1990, pp. 17–20. As usual, Bandura merely seems to be added to the rich lode of Chinese material on the subject.
5. Gabriel Tarde, p. 86.
6. Hans Ulrich Gumbrecht, 'Modern, Modernität, Moderne', in Otto Brunner, Werner Conze, and Reinhart Koselleck (eds.), Gesellschaftliche Grundbegriffe, Vol. 4, Stuttgart, Klett-Cotta, 1978, p. 99.
7. Gladys A. Reichard, 'Social Life', in F. Boas (ed.), *General Anthropology*, Boston, Heath, 1938, pp. 409–86. Reichard is one of the anthropologists on whom Bandura and Walters build their analysis.
8. Margaret Mead, *Culture and Commitment: A Study of the Generation Gap*, New York, Natural History Press/Doubleday, 1970, p. 1.
9. The close connection between imitation and generation was pointed out by Tarde, who held that 'there is not only an analogy . . . between Generation and Imitation, but a fundamental identity' (Gabriel Tarde, p. 34).
10. Over 2,000 editions of Tomas Kempis's manuscript are known, and, next to the scriptures themselves, it is probably the most widely used religious work of all times: Tomas Kempis, *The Imitation of Christ*; trans. of the MS 'De Imitatione Christi' (1441) by Edgar Daplyn, London, Lakeland, 1979, bk III, ch. 11, p. 87; bk III, ch. 56, p. 145.
11. R. L. Nettleship, *The Theory of Education in Plato's Republic*, Oxford, Clarendon Press, 1935, p. 56.
12. Edward J. Power, *Evolution of Educational Doctrine: Major Educational Theorists of the Western World*, New York, Appleton Century-Crofts, 1969, p. 112.

162   *Education, Society, and Morality*

13. Gerald Strauss, 'The state of pedagogical theory ca.1530: what Protestant reformers knew about education', in Lawrence Stone (ed.), *Schooling and Society: Studies in the History of Education*, Baltimore/London, Johns Hopkins University Press, 1976, pp. 78, 83.
14. Miyazaki explains that the rule used in the schools was to review the text 100 times: 50 times by reading from the book, and 50 times by reciting the text by heart. It has been estimated that it took rote learning of a passage of 200 characters every day for six whole years to master the material needed for the imperial examinations (Ichisada Miyazaki, *China's Examination Hell: The Civil Service Examinations of Imperial China*, New York Tokyo, Waetherhill, 1976, pp. 15–17). Moreover, the Chinese system of characters sets tougher demands on memorization than does a language built on an alphabet. It has for example been found that it takes over two years to bring an illiterate to literacy in China, three months in North Korea, and nine months in Russia. (Chao Lin, *A Survey of Chinese (Han) Characters*, Hong Kong, Universal Book Company, 1968, p. 34).
15. Fung Yu-lan (Feng Youlan), *Chuang Tzu: A New Selected Translation with an Exposition of the Philosophy of Kuo Hsiang*, Beijing, Foreign Languages Press, 1989 (enlarged from the Commercial Press edn. of 1931), p. 123. For further discussion see also Fung Yu-lan (Feng Youlan), *A History of Chinese Philosophy*, Vol. 2, Princeton, Princeton University Press, 1952, pp. 219–20.
16. Friedrich Paulsen, *Geschichte des gelehrten Unterrichts auf den deutschen Schulen und Universitäten vom Ausgang des Mittelalters bis zur Gegenwart*, 2 vols., Leipzig, 1919, 1924, Vol. 1, p. 345, and Wolfgang Dreßen, *Die pädagogische Maschine: Zur Geschichte des industrialisierten Bewußtseins in Preußen/Deutschland*, Frankfurt, Ullstein Materialen, 1982, p. 42.
17. Gerald Strauss, *Luther's House of Learning: Indoctrination of the Young in the German Reformation*, Baltimore/London, Johns Hopkins University Press, 1978, pp. 82–3.
18. Gerald Strauss, 'The state of pedagogical theory', p. 83.
19. Ibid., pp. 83–4.
20. Gerald Strauss, *Luther's House of Learning*, pp. 83–4.
21. Ibid., p. 84.
22. Paul Ricoeur, 'Life in Quest of Narrative', in David Wood (ed.), *On Paul Ricoeur: Narrative and Interpretation*, London/New York, Routledge, 1991, p. 25.
23. Michel Foucault, *Discipline and Punish: The Birth of the Prison*, New York, Vintage Books, 1979, p. 203.
24. One book typically praises Gabriel Tarde for being the founder of an evolutionary theory of social imitation: see *Shehui xinlixue jiaocheng* (The educational process of social psychology), Lanzhou, Lanzhou daxue chubanshe, 1986, p. 390.
25. Gabriel Tarde, pp. 74, 87, 28.
26. Ibid., p. 5.
27. Ibid., p. 11.
28. Ibid., p. 43.
29. Ibid., p. 382.
30. See Zhang Guangbo (ed.), *Shehuixue cidian* (Dictionary of Sociology), Beijing, Renmin chubanshe, 1989, p. 571.
31. Wu Zhen, 'Ertong mofang de tezheng yu jiaoyu' (The characteristics and education of children's imitation), *You'er jiaoyu*, No. 10, 1986, p. 5.
32. Deng Hongxun, 'You'er jiaoyu shi peiyang yi ge xinren de dianji gongcheng' (Child education is an old process of fostering a new person), *Hongqi*, No. 11, 1987, p. 30.

33. Jiang Haohua and Zhang Lin, 'Dui bangyang jiaoyu fangfa de zai renshi' (Towards a new understanding of model education), *Qingnian yanjiu*, No. 2, 1987, p. 8.
34. Interviewee no. 7, Beijing, 1991.
35. Tianjin qingnian bao (ed.), *Qingnian shouce* (Youth handbook), Beijing, Zhongguo zhanwang chubanshe, 1986, pp. 148–9.
36. Zhang Nianhong and Leng Hong'en (eds.), *Rencaixue cidian* (Dictionary of talent studies), Beijing, Nongcun duwu chubanshe, 1989, pp. 80–2.
37. Zheng Xinran, 'Bangyang huodong yu ren de xinli fenxi', p. 19.
38. Liu Bo, 'Xuehui "mofang"' (Learn 'imitation'), *Zhongguo qingnianbao*, 19 April 1991, p. 4.
39. Eleanor D. Westney, *Imitation and Innovation: The Transfer of Western Organizational Patterns to Meiji Japan*, Cambridge, Mass., Harvard University Press, 1987, p. 25.
40. Hao Zhilun, 'Lun "jiao" zhi chuantong wenhua yiyun' (Discussing the meaning of *'jiao'* (to teach) in modern culture), *Jiaoyu yanjiu*, No. 3, 1990, p. 50.
41. See Joseph R. Levenson, *Confucian China and its Modern Fate: The Problem of Intellectual Continuity*, Vol. 1, Berkeley/Los Angeles, University of California Press, 1958, pp. 28–9.
42. James Douglas Farquhar, *Creation and Imitation: The Work of a Fifteenth-Century Manuscript Illuminator*, Fort Lauderdale, Fla., Nova/NYIT University Press, 1976, pp. 73–4.
43. Ibid., p. 73.
44. See Victoria Contag, 'Das Mallehrbuch für Personenmalerei des Chieh Tzü Yüan', *T'ong Pao*, Vol. 33, No. 1, 1937, pp. 16, 20–1.
45. Gabriel Tarde, p. 244.
46. Ibid., p. 247.
47. Ibid., p. *xvii*. In developing the concept of counter-imitation, Tarde was inspired by Darwin, who also dwelt on the need of counter-expression.
48. See Xu Ming, Chu Xian, Song Defu and Qiang Wei (eds.), *Sixiang zhengzhi gongzuo daoxiang* (Guidance in ideological–political work), Beijing, Kexue chubanshe, 1990.
49. A typical although fairly innocent example is that of young people taking up the habit of smoking 'through anger' and to 'defy the social norm': see *China Daily*, 5 June 1991, p. 6.
50. Charles R. Tittle and Alan R. Rowe, 'Moral appeal, sanction threat, and deviance: an experimental test', *Social Problems*, Vol. 20, No. 4, 1973, pp. 489–92.
51. Ibid., p. 496. In using Tittle and Rowe's example, Elster fails to quote the authors' warning against making too much out of their example. See Jon Elster, *The Cement of Society: A Study of Social Order*, Cambridge, Cambridge University Press, 1989, p. 212.
52. Qiu Ling, 'Yi zhong burong hushi de xianxiang' (A phenomenon one is not allowed to ignore), *Beijing jiaoyu*, No. 4, 1986, pp. 20–1. Copying of homework had occurred in 103 cases among these students throughout the school year, while cheating on exams had occurred in 83 cases. The cheating was most frequent in mathematics (25, 14), followed by physics (22, 13), Chinese (16, 17), chemistry (18, 11), foreign language (11, 13), politics (8, 6), and biology (3, 9).
53. Claude Lévi-Strauss, *Structural Anthropology*, Naumburg, Allen Lane Penguin Press, 1963, p. 301.
54. 'Unum tibi repetam "repetensque iterumque iterumque monebo" ut puerorum memoriam exerceas', from Vergil, *Aenid* III, 345. See Paul F. Grendler, *Schooling*

in Renaissance Italy: Literacy and Learning 1300–1600, Baltimore, Johns Hopkins University Press, 1989, p. 196.

55. Paul F. Grendler, p. 197.

56. 'Great Cyrus had so large a Memory, that he could call every Soldier of his numerous Army by his proper Name . . . Likewise Seneca tells us of himself, that he could repeat 2000 district Names that had no dependence' (Marius d'Assigny, *The Art of Memory*, New York, AMS Press, 1985, pp. 19, 26–7; originally published 1697).

57. Marius d'Assigny, pp. 47, 51.

58. Chu Hsi (Zhu Xi), *Learning to Be a Sage: Selections from the Conversations of Master Chu, Arranged Topically*, trans. with a comment by Daniel K. Gardner, Berkeley, University of California Press, 1990 (Zhu 4.34, 5.35, 5.36), pp. 45–6.

59. Ibid., p. 138.

60. Ibid., pp. 139, 143, 147.

61. Ibid., p. 164.

62. See Chen Jingpan, *Confucius as a Teacher*, Beijing, Foreign Languages Press, 1990, pp. 329–30 (Pinyin added).

63. Confucian Analects (*Lunyu*), bk XVII, ch. IX, in James Legge (trans.), *The Four Books* (*sishu*), Taipei, Culture Book Co./Wenhua tushu gongshi, 1983, p. 383.

64. See Chen Jingpan pp. 331–2. In the Analects we can read: 'The Master said, "Though a man may be able to recite the three hundred odes, yet if, when intrusted with a governmental charge, he knows not how to act, or if, when sent to any quarter on a mission, he cannot give his replies unassisted, notwithstanding the extent of *his learning*, of what practical use is it?" ' (Confucian Analects (*Lunyu*), bk XIII, ch. V, in James Legge (trans.), p. 300.

65. Xin Yang, (ed.), *Zhongguo banzhurenxue* (Chinese class teacher studies), Changchun, Jilin jiaoyu chubanshe, 1990), p. 103.

66. 'The repetitive character of moral education is one of the characteristics of the moral process' (Hangzhou daxue jiaoyu xi (ed.), 'Deyu de fanfu xing' (The repetitive character of moral education), in Hangzhou daxue jiaoyu xi (eds.), *Jiaoyu cidian* (Encyclopaedia of Education), Nanchang, Jianxi jiaoyu chubanshe, 1987, p. 828).

67. Zhang Shaoxia, 'Wo guo bangjiao gongzuo de lilun yu shijian' (The theory and practice of Chinese help-education work), in Yantai daxue faxuesuo (ed.), *Zhong Mei xuezhe lun qingshaonian fanzui* (Juvenile delinquency and its treatment by Chinese and American scholars), Yantai, Qunzhong chubanshe, 1989, p. 87.

68. Liu Ruifeng, 'Lun gongdu xuexiao dui qingshaonian fanzui de zaoqi ganyu' (On the early intervention of the work–study school on juvenile delinquency), in Yantai daxue faxuesuo (ed.), p. 98.

69. Li Junjie, *Fanzui jiaoyuxue* (Criminal pedagogy), Beijing, Qunzhong chubanshe, 1986, p. 75. For methods of redemption work used in the so-called work–study schools, institutions for petty criminals and juveniles with special problems, see also Li Guangda, 'Wanjiu jiaoyu gongdu xuesheng de wu ge jieduan' (Five stages of redemption education for work-study schools), in *Zhongguo qingshaonian fanzui yanjiu nianjian 1987* (Yearbook on Chinese juvenile delinquency studies), Beijing, Chunqiu chubanshe, 1988, pp. 764–6.

70. The concentrated review (1) was far less effective than the dispersed review (2) in the following survey: after a comparison of two groups using the different methods marks were excellent for (1) 9.6%, (2) 31.6%; marks were good for (1) 36.6%, (2) 36.8%; marks were average for (1) 47.4%, (2) 31.6%; marks

were bad (the students flunked) for (1) 6.4%, (2) none. See Tianjin qingnian bao (ed.), *Qingnian shouce* (Youth handbook), Beijing, Zhongguo zhanwang chubanshe, 1986, p. 121. In another investigation, Pan Shu found that the dispersed review method has a long-term effect. Those having used the method remembered 60% of the texts after one year, while those practising the other method could remember only 38% after that time; see Pan Shu (ed.), *Jiaoyu xinlixue* (Educational psychology), Beijing, Renmin jiaoyu chubanshe, 1982, pp. 118–19.

71. Xiao Yuxiu and Yan Guocai, 'Shiji' (Memorization), in *Zhongguo dabaike quanshu: jiaoyu* (The great Chinese encyclopedia: education), Beijing, Zhongguo dabaike quanshu chubanshe, 1985, p. 322.

72. Interviewees nos. 4 and 5, Beijing, 1991. The over-learning method was not practised in this key school, but the class teachers I interviewed told me that the review of the whole school period before exams could be regarded as such since they spend half a semester on this. The students were said to gain knowledge on a higher level when they repeated what they had learned and already reviewed before, and they were also expected to become more mature because of this cramming.

73. Interviewee no. 8, Beijing, 1991. This interview was made unofficially, without the help of the school authorities, and the interviewee was a former class teacher who had run into 'political problems' after June 1989 because of his involvement in the demonstrations in Beijing. This interviewee saw educational methods in a broader perspective, linking questions of democracy to the practice of such methods.

74. Zhang Deqing, 'Zou chuqu, chengshou meihao huanjing de xuntao: xuesheng suzhi peiyang gongzuo zhi yi' (Go out, inherit the edifying effect of a beautiful environment: student quality development work, part 1), *Beijing jiaoyu*, No. 7–8, 1987, p. 46; 'Zou chuqu, chengshou meihao huanjing de xuntao: xuesheng suzhi peiyang gongzuo zhi er' (part 2), *Beijing jiaoyu*, No. 9, 1987, pp. 14–15. The rest of the article follows in Nos. 10 and 11, 1987.

75. Zhang Zongke, 'Wo zheyang jinxing qimo fuxi' (This is how I conduct end term reviews), *Xiaoxue jiaoxue yanjiu*, No. 6, 1991, p. 2.

76. Ning Decong, 'Zai fuxi zhong gonggu zhishi, peiyang nengli, fazhan zhili: yuwen di ba ce de fuxi yaodian he jianyi' (Consolidate knowledge, foster abilities, develop intelligence through repetition: Suggestions on the main points of repetition for Chinese language textbook no. 8), *Beijing jiaoyu*, No. 2, 1986, pp. 38–9.

77. Xiao Yuxiu and Yan Guocai, 'Shiji', p. 322.

78. Wen Hanjiang, *Xiandai jiaoxue lun yinlun* (Guiding discussion in educational theory), Tianjin, Tianjin jiaoyu chubanshe, 1988, p. 237.

79. Deng Xiaoping, *Selected Works of Deng Xiaoping (1975–1982)*, Beijing, Foreign Languages Press, 1984, p. 67; Chinese edition: *Deng Xiaoping wenxuan (1975–1982)*, Beijing, Renmin chubanshe, 1983, p. 51.

80. Wen Hanjiang, p. 237.

81. For instance, the 'standard answers' (*biaozhun da'an*) taken from successful previous exam papers are enormously popular among upper secondary students cramming for the university entrance exams: see *China Daily* 18 April 1985, p. 4.

82. The emphasis on tests and exams is perhaps more severe in China than in any other country. In one secondary school there were reported to be 46 exams each semester, and in addition there were three quizzes a week. The students were said to be 'very nervous' (*Renmin ribao*, quoted from *China Daily* 5 July 1986, p. 3). Reports on suicides among pupils and students and killings by parents of their offspring because of unsuccessful academic achievement have stirred up many

commentators. On suicides among school pupils, see *Guangming ribao*, 24 April 1988, p. 2, about the death of Xu Xiapei; see also Xu Yinglong, 'Ba meihao de qiwang zhuanhua wei haizi shangjing de lizhong', *Qiushi*, No. 16, 1988, pp. 10–12, on the death of Xia Fei. I have discussed the effects of cramming, memorization and exams in Chinese schools in more detail elsewhere. See Børge Bakken, *Kunnskap og moral: Om utdanningsreformer i dagens Kina* (Knowledge and morality: on educational reforms in today's China), Department of Sociology, University of Oslo, Report no. 1, 1989, particularly pp. 116–43. On memorizations and tests in China see also Jonathan Unger, *Education under Mao: Class and Competition in Canton Schools 1960–1980*, New York, Columbia University Press, 1982, pp. 66–83.

83. Jonathan Unger, p. 75.

84. *Zhongguo jiaoyu bao*, 11 January 1986, p. 3.

85. Wu Shenyuan, *Zhongguo chuantong wenhua de yichuan he bianyi* (Change and heritage in Chinese culture), Changsha, Hunan wenyi chubanshe, 1988, p. 46.

86. Liu In-Mao, 'Chinese Cognition', in Micheal Harris Bond (ed.), *The Psychology of the Chinese People*, Hong Kong, Oxford University Press, 1986, pp. 73–105.

87. Gilbert Ryle, *The Concept of Mind*, London, Hutchinson, 1958, p. 29; see also pp. 25–61.

88. The fifth relation between friends shows no distinction between superior and inferior. Xunzi omitted this relation since he did not see it as fundamental to the social order. See Homer H. Dubs (trans.), *The Works of Hsüntze*, Taibei, Ch'eng-wen, 1966, p. 135.

89. Liu In-Mao, p. 78.

90. Ibid., p. 80.

91. Ibid., p. 82.

92. Jonathan D. Spence, *The Memory Palace of Matteo Ricci*, Harmondsworth, Elisabeth Sifton Books/Viking, 1984, pp. 20–3.

93. An example is Botswana, where it appears that ratings of intelligence were related to the recall of stories. See E. F. Dube, 'A cross-cultural study of the relationship between "intelligence" level and story recall', unpublished doctoral thesis, Ithaca, NY, Cornell University, 1977, quoted from Liu In-Mao, p. 88.

94. Pierre Bourdieu, *Outline of a Theory of Practice*, trans. Richard Nice, Cambridge, Cambridge University Press, 1977, p. 189.

95. Gilbert Ryle, p. 59.

96. Wang Ziguang, 'Ye tan qifa shi jiaoxue' (On teaching by elicitation), *Beijing jiaoyu*, No. 7, 1986, p. 40.

97. Wen Hanjiang, pp. 221–3.

98. Feng Quanxin, 'Chuantong jiaoxue yu qifa shi jiaoxue shi maodun de' (Traditional education and elicitation education are contradictory to each other), *Zhengzhi jiaoyu*, No. 3, 1986, p. 37.

99. *Yinghan jiaoyu cidian*, (English–Chinese dictionary of education), Beijing, Jiaoyu kexue chubanshe, 1982, p. 91.

100. Interviewee no. 11, Beijing, 1991.

101. Zhou Luming, 'Ba gaoxiao sixiang zhengzhi gongzuo zuowei yi men kexue lai yanjiu' (Study ideological–political work in universities as a science), *Gaodeng jiaoyu yanjiu*, No. 4, 1985, p. 88.

102. Ye Zheng, 'Zhuru shi jiaofa fei gaibian bu ke (Cramming methods of education must be revised), *Zhengzhi jiaoyu*, No. 5, 1986, p. 39, and Hu Shoufen, *Deyu guanli*, (Principles of moral education), rev. edn., Beijing, Beijing shifan daxue chubanshe, 1989, p. 168.

103. Shen Furong, 'Guanshu jiaoyu "zhuru shi"' (Inculcation education is different from the 'spoon feeding method'), *Zhengzhi jiaoyu*, No. 4, 1986, p. 36.

104. Wang Banghui and Zhang Zhifen, 'Zhuzhong deyu de qianyi mohua yingxiang' (Pay attention to the imperceptible influence of education), *Eaoqi jiaoyu*, No. 3, 1991, p. 2.

105. Zhu Jiang and Zhang Yaocan, *Daxue deyu gailun* (Introduction to university moral education), Wuhan, Hubei jiaoyu chubanshe, 1986, p. 239.

106. Wang Fengxian, 'Xuexiao deyu de zhudao zuoyong yu shehui huanjing de youhua wenti' (The leading role of moral education in today's schools and the perfection of environment for social education), *Jiaoyu yanjiu*, No. 8, 1989, pp. 3–8.

107. Jiang Jiqing, 'Guanshu shi he qifa shi ying you ji jiehe' (Inculcation and elicitation must be organically combined), *Zhengzhi jiaoyu*, No. 3, 1986, p. 38.

108. Gu Mingyuan (ed.), *Jiaoyu da cidian* (Great encyclopedia of education), Vol. 1, Shanghai, Shanghai jiaoyu chubanshe, 1990, pp. 136.

109. V. I. Lenin, 'What is to be done?' in *Collected Works*, Moscow, Progress Publishers, 1975, p. 375 (italics added); originally published between 1901 and 1902.

110. Zhang Zhilun, 'Shilun "guanshu"' (Tentative discussion on 'inculcation'), *Pujiao yanjiu*, No. 2, 1991, p. 26.

111. Benkan Pinglunyuan (Commentator's article), 'Lun guanshu' (On inculcation), *Qiushi*, No. 21, 1990, p. 3. A 'commentator's article' might indicate that it is written by a leading political figure.

112. Ibid., p. 6.

113. Wang Zongzhu, 'Guanshu–shudao–xunlian' (Inculcation–dredging–drill), *Pujiao yanjiu*, No. 5, 1990, pp. 23–4. My own material indicates that articles with an entirely negative view on inculcation appeared before the summer of 1989; after that date more positive accounts of inculcation were heard.

114. Zhang Zhilun, p. 27.

115. Wang Zongzhu, p. 23.

116. Based on talks with students at Beijing University in 1986.

117. Zhang Zhilun, p. 33.

118. See *Guangming ribao*, 20 March 1991, p. 3.

119. See *Zhongguo qingnianbao*, 8 June 1991, p. 3.

120. Zhang Deqing, 'Zou chuqu, chengshou meihao huanjing de xuntao: xuesheng suzhi peiyang gongzuo zhi yi' (part 1), p. 46. The rest of the article follows in Nos. 9, 10, and 11, 1987.

121. Tao Xincheng, 'Fumu suzhi yu jiating jiaoyu' (Parent quality and family education), *Fumu bidu*, No. 12, 1989, p. 4.

122. Mu Shuhuai, 'Zhengque duidai zhongxuesheng lian'ai xianxiang' (Correctly handle the phenomenon of premature love among secondary school students), *Ningxia jiaoyu*, No. 1–2, 1989, pp. 15–16.

123. On the dangers of modern society and its influences, see *Zhongguo jiaoyubao*, 9 April 1991, p. 3.

124. Wang Banghui and Zhang Zhifen, pp. 2–3.

125. See *Guangming ribao*, 21 March 1991, p. 3.

126. See Wen Hanjiang, p. 237.

127. Song Xuewen, 'Meiyu dui fazhan qingshaonian xinli suzhi he renge wanshan teshu jiezhi' (The special value of aesthetics education in developing the psychological quality and the perfection of personality among youth), *Jiaoyu luncong*, No. 1, 1991, p. 27.

128. Ibid., p. 28. Sometimes the educational effect is not too clearly defined. For example, some teachers from Beijing went to the bathing resort Beidaihe with their pupils to look at the sunrise for 'unconscious education' reasons. This 'amusement education' has an educational effect, through an imperceptible influence, an influence that it is not possible to estimate or appraise (*wufa guliang de*). See Zhang Deqing, p. 46.

129. Paul Boyer, *Urban Masses and Moral Order in America, 1820–1920*, Cambridge, Mass., Harvard University Press, 1978, p. 180.

130. John Dewey, 'Intelligence and morals' (1908), in John Dewey, *The Influence of Darwin on Philosophy*, Bloomington, Indiana University Press, 1965, p. 74. Dewey's insistance on moral control over legal control appealed Chinese intellectuals as well, and partly explains the enormous popularity that Dewey later gained in China.

131. Paul Boyer, p. 236.

132. Ibid., p. 238.

133. Liu Xiang, *Gu lienüzhuan*, bk 1, ch. 1 (*Zou Meng Ke mu*), in *Congshu jicheng*, Shanghai, Shangwu yinshuguan, 1936; trans. in A. R. O'Hara (trans.), *The Position of Women in Early China according to Lieh nü chuan, 'The Biographies of Eminent Chinese Women'*, Washington DC, Catholic University of America Press, 1965, pp. 39–42. The family discipline of the clan of Yan Zhihui, the Confucian, is also often quoted as an example of such environmental moulding.

134. Hu Shoufen, pp. 169–70.

135. Xu Zhangsong (ed.), *Daxuesheng chengcai xiuyang* (Self-cultivation for university students to grow into useful timber), Shanghai, Fudan daxue chubanshe, 1988, p. 263.

136. Guo Zhao, 'Shilun huanjing yingxiang yu diling fanzui' (A tentative discussion on the influence of the environment on minors' crime), *Qingshaonian tantao*, No. 4, 1990, p. 20. Sanming municipality in 1982 had 2.34 m inhabitants, the city proper had 230,000; see *Zhongguo 1982 nian renkou pucha ziliao* (Materials from the 1982 population Census of China), Beijing, Zhongguo tongji chubanshe, 1985, p. 467.

137. See e.g. Bai Gang and Jin Yonghua, 'Fanzui dilinghua yanjiu zongshu' (Summary of the research on the decreasing age among juvenile delinquents), in *Zhongguo qingshaonian fanzui yanjiu nianjian 1987* (Yearbook on Chinese juvenile delinquency studies), Beijing, Chunqiu chubanshe, 1988, pp. 316–22.

138. Wei He, 'Guanyu xiaoyuan wenhua de jiu qian tantao' (Study on campus cultures), *Jiaoyu yanjiu*, No. 2, 1992, p. 31.

139. Chen Kuiyan, 'Guanyu xiaoyuan wenhua de sikao' (Thoughts about campus culture), *Jiaoyu yanjiu*, No. 2, 1992, p. 21.

140. Li Ruihuan's speech, 'Suggestions on the question of building socialist spiritual civilization', was held on 9 November 1991 for cadres in Changsha. The speech was originally published in *Sixiang zhengzhi gongzuo yanjiu zazhi* (Journal of ideological–political work research), No. 1, 1991, and quoted in *SWB-FE/0969*, 14 January 1991, p. B2/1–6 (B2/1–2).

141. Ibid., p. B2/6.

142. Such spiritual culture consists of four main elements: a curriculum culture (*kecheng wenhua*), a course extension culture (*keyan wenhua*), a system culture (*zhidu wenhua*), and an organization culture (*zuzhi wenhua*) (see Chen Kuiyan, pp. 22–5).

5

On Models, Modelling, and the Exemplary

WE may recall the statement that to imitate is to follow the example of exemplary models. The method is a central characteristic of the exemplary society. But learning from models is more than a simple pedagogical method. It represents the culmination of an imitative–repetitive culture. The Confucian view assumes that men are drawn to virtuous models, and that social stability results from their emulation of those models. Confucian thought prefers social control through the presentation of virtuous models. By emulating them, people will develop a constant attitude towards the norms, thus ensuring proper conduct even in the absence of direct surveillance.[1] Modelling becomes an important technique of upholding order. Indeed, Chinese modelling theory still holds that 'a model is a silent order'.[2] Armen Alchian's remark that 'modelling is a response to uncertainty' fits Chinese reality.[3] Models represent order and counteract uncertainty. The constancy of norms represented by the modelling philosophy of a Confucian cultural setting is confirmed in modern Western modelling theory. Models draw attention to particular courses of action and increase the salience of social norms. Further, they supply information about the appropriateness of certain actions by setting an example and creating a normative standard for action. Models supply definitions of the situation and give clear signals about the consequences.

It is not only on the individual level that models and modelling operate. Virtuous models and exemplary persons also represent the grand narratives of society—here the stress is on society as opposed to the individual. Joseph Campbell has argued that throughout human history the imitation of heroes has represented an effective annihilation of the human ego and a strengthening of the social bond. Society has achieved a cohesive organization through the celebration of its cultural heroes.[4] The cultural hero provides identity, linking individuals to a collective memory. MacIntyre has observed that traditional society has utilized the telling of stories as the chief means of moral education, and that 'such narratives did provide the historical memory, adequate or inadequate, of the societies in which they were written down'.[5] Memories are transmitted via models. Pointing out that such narratives provided a moral background to the contemporary debate in classical societies, he describes them as 'an account of a now-transcended or partly-transcended moral order whose beliefs and concepts were still partially influential, but which also provided an illuminating contrast to the present'.[6] In today's China we see the same traditional traits repeated. Even if they represent a 'partly-transcended moral order', the stories of virtuous and exemplary models establish standards of social behaviour and still represent the grand narratives of society. That narration has roots in the culture, and even if the narratives are withering, they are not phenomena of a transcended social order. They preserve the collective memory linking reality to the repetitive movements already described. Paul Ricoeur has defined the narrative of traditional models as closer to the pole of repetition than to that of deviance, thus emphasizing its cohesive element:

It is tied in one way or another to the models handed down by tradition. But it can enter into a variable relation to these models. The range of solutions is broad indeed between the poles of servile repetition and calculated deviance, passing by way of all the degrees of ordered distortion. Popular tales, myths, and traditional narratives in general stick closer to the pole of repetition.[7]

Although Ricoeur is here talking about literature and poetry, the issue is not one of poetry only, but of society as well, and his remarks are highly relevant to an examplary society in general. By juxtaposing repetition and deviance, Ricoeur correctly emphasizes the cohesive and integrating element of repetition and model learning alike. I will later show that deviance breaks the repetitive logic, thus representing danger. We can look at the exemplary model as a 'narrative' or a 'myth' serving social memory and social cohesion. Such models, like the Homeric epics or the Nordic sagas, not only represent the social memory, but also provide the moral background for the present. The Chinese narrative of the exemplary person is a modern variant, with themes we have already noted in the debate on moral education. Harmony, stability, cohesion, constancy, sacrifice, control of self, and attachment to the group are story-lines again and again in this narrative. But, as Ricoeur is quick to point out, stories are recounted, and life is lived. The exemplary person is partly a recounted person—in China this is often the story of the sacrificing hero. The hero (*yingxiong*) is with few exceptions a real person even if the story makes him or her greater than life. The texts of the exemplary vacillate between myth and biography. Not only does the hero spread virtue by personal example, the text about the hero is a minutely constructed text, intended to magnify the effect of exemplarity.

The gap between fiction and life represents a problem for moral educators. If the world of the reader and the world of the text seem too far apart, the expected exemplary effect might not take place. The horizon of personal experience and the horizon of the text confront each other continually. The problem becomes acute when the text is too far removed from the life of the reader, listener, or spectator. This problem has confronted Chinese ideological–political propaganda workers more than once during modernization and reform. As norms and values change, the conception of the exemplary also changes. The text has difficulties following the pace of real life, leading to a sharpened conflict between the two. The Chinese answer has partly been an attempt at rationalization or 'scientification' of texts and models. The issue of exemplary models has thus been moved from 'poetry' to 'science', preserving elements of both. This might be seen as an attempt to demystify myth at the same time as myth is prolonged as biography. Such a process is not entirely unproblematic; the alleged 'scientification' runs the risk of turning counterproductive, adding a beginning 'traditionalization' as an alternative way of firming up the loosening grip of the modelling text. Both memories and dreams are involved in the modelling project. As will be shown, the issue resembles what Weber called the 'routinization of charisma'.

The Emulation and Parading of Models

There is evidence that the idea of modelling and moral emulation goes at least as far back as the Western Zhou dynasty (1100–771 BC). Munro mentions bronze inscriptions where two terms, *xing* and *shuai*, both mean 'to emulate'. These appear most frequently in conjunction with the term *de*, usually translated as 'moral' or 'virtue'. The statements refer to one person emulating the *de* of another. For example, one inscription reads: 'I now earnestly imitate (*xing*) Wen Wang's political *de*.' Another: 'I do not dare not to emulate (*shuai*) the *de* reverently held by my refined ancestors and august father.'[8] Also famous is Mozi's (*c.* 480–390 BC) remark about the efficacy and necessity of 'appropriate' modelling. Mozi was impressed by the capacity of dyes to transform white pieces of cloth. 'Dyed in blue, they become blue, and dyed in yellow they become yellow. If one changes [the colour] in which they are dyed, they also change their colour. When dyed in five different colours, they are five times coloured.'[9] Particularly interested in 'good ruler' models, Mozi concluded that the same principle applied to human beings, and he went on to talk about the right or wrong colouring of kings and dukes. The learning paradigm adduced was that association with good people would make a man good, while association with evil would inevitably lead to bad character. By his example, the ruler was radiating virtue throughout society, and the idea represents the core of the imperceptible influence the exemplary model has on the entire population. The ruler was the person who could spread his virtue or evil down to the population most effectively or fatally.

The classical 'good ruler' syndrome is evident also in present-day China. The importance of model education is institutionalized in the regulations for party members who should strive to be exemplary persons. In the party statutes it is stated that a party member should 'have a model function for the masses', and the seventh duty for party members stipulates that they should be 'models in production, work, study, and social life, and in preserving the social order. They should also develop the new socialist habits and promote communist morality.'[10] A recent commentary on the party statutes, meant as teaching material for aspiring members, emphasizes modern values and adds that through their behaviour party members should 'strengthen the commodity economy and the concept of competition among people'.[11] In other words, the exemplary behaviour of the party member is meant to preserve both of the party's legitimating foundations—growth and stability.

The idea of model emulation was of utmost importance in Chinese philosophy. As already mentioned, law (*fa*) came second to morals (*de*) in the debate on social control. It is interesting to note that one meaning of the character for law—*fa*—is in fact 'model'. In some archaic variants, *fa* was made up of the symbols 'to adapt' (*chi*) and 'uprightly' (*zheng*), hence the meaning of 'law', 'rule', or 'a model for behaviour'.[12] The Chinese have a faith that positive models and good morality will naturally attract people. In early texts there is talk of a magnetic attraction towards people to virtue. For example, Confucius compares the ruler of exemplary virtue with the Pole star: 'He who exercises government by means of his virtue may be compared to the north polar star, which keeps its place and the stars turn towards it.'[13] Mencius said: 'The people turn to a benevolent rule (*ren*) as water flows downward, and like wild beasts fly to the wilderness.'[14] Beliefs seem to follow the very same pattern today. A political inspector I interviewed illustrated the point by quoting a proverb: 'Peaches and plums do not have to talk, yet the world beats a path to them' (*Tao li bu yan, xia zi cheng xi*).[15] The meaning is that people are naturally led towards virtue,

re-establishing the classical theme. In reality, sin might be more pro-
ductively modelled than virtue and self-control.[16]

The belief in the powerful educational effect of emulating the good
deeds of exemplary persons is demonstrated in the current pedagogical
literature, and would appear to be another cultural truism that modern
China seems to be redeploying from the past.[17] In the late 1960s,
Donald Munro pointed out that in China 'assumptions about model
emulation dominate social control theory'.[18] These words seem equally
apt today. The phenomenon is not only seen in schools, but spreads
throughout society. The imitative–repetitive culture is largely a modelling culture. Top party leaders repeatedly advocate the learning from
models and the rewarding of models, and Deng Xiaoping approves
of awarding lavish premiums to model people who make outstanding
contributions to the building of the 'four modernizations'.[19] Large-scale
celebrations of exemplary people in both material and spiritual civilization
activities are also arranged. Over 9,000 workers from industrial, commercial, and transport sectors in Beijing were cited as 'model workers'
at a meeting in 1991. A total of three million workers, accounting for
90 per cent of all the workers in Beijing's state-owned enterprises, par-
ticipated in the drive.[20]

The Chinese language is rich in words for 'model'. Some of the most
common are *mofan, dianxing, bangyang,* and *shibiao*. The last word—
shibiao—indicates a person of exemplary morals and learning, and is
often used to honour outstanding teachers or parents. *Mofan* refers to
exemplary persons or matters, and is often used in titles of honour like
'model-worker' (*laodong mofan*), 'model-teacher' (*mofan jiaoshi*), etc. The
word has the same *mo* as in *mofang*—imitation. The two characters *mo*
and *fan* in *mofan* as well as the character *xing* in *dianxing*, all today meaning 'model', in classical Chinese originally stood for moulds made of
various materials.[21] We have already noted the importance of 'moulding' techniques in education; the meaning reflects a fundamental belief
in the Chinese theory of modelling: the unlimited malleability and edu-
cability of human beings. Today the *mo* can also mean 'standard', or
'to imitate', both meanings suggestive of the process and functions
of models and modelling. Further, *bangyang*—an exemplary person or
matter worthy of emulation—is the word most often used in the volu-
minous pedagogical literature on models and modelling. It can also refer
to the method of modelling.[22] In every textbook on pedagogy there
are references to, and nearly always a separate chapter about, the
great importance of *bangyang jiaoyu*—'model education', or 'education
through examples'. The *bang* in *bangyang* is also interesting for our purposes. It originally stood for the list of names posted up to announce

the successful candidates for the imperial exams. We still find this meaning in *rongbang*—honour roll—and such honour rolls are still displayed to praise worthy students or model workers. The honour roll examplifies the vital process of parading, and the modelling process builds on both imitation and parading of skill and virtue. Virtuous examples should be adopted not only through imitation: one should also extend the model by displaying its virtue to a greater public. Not only individual improvement through imitation, but the active improvement of all should be made possible through parading exemplary deeds.

When models are established, the educational techniques of commending (*biaoyang*) are always emphasized. Through commending, the exemplary deeds of the model are proven and rewarded.[23] Rewards should also be given in public, for maximum effect. Perhaps the earliest mention of awards for virtue comes in 'The Mandate Given to Prince Bi', a chapter in *The Book of Documents*:

Award insignia to the virtuous and set apart the vicious. Give honorific emblems to their houses and villages, so making illustrious the good and imposing affliction upon the evil. Establish the influence and reputation (of the good).[24]

Scholars of a later era tended to see in these practices something similar to what Cai Chen in the thirteenth century called 'subsequent generations placing insignia of virtue on the doors of houses and the gates of villages'. During the Later Han period (AD 25–220) a system of honours was introduced. Later, in 515, it was decreed that in order to promote good behaviour 'insignia shall be placed on the dwellings of filial sons, obedient grandsons, righteous heads of families (*yifu*) and faithful widows in order to make manifest their excellence'. Mark Elvin remarks that this imperial recognition of virtue was seen as a semimagical means of remedying the unpropitious political situation and the dwindling charisma of the dynasty.[25] This remark seems to fit perfectly the picture of today's China, and the campaigns of spiritual civilization can be seen as attempts to uphold a charisma now about to be lost.

During the Ming period the aim was 'respect and encouragement for moral norms'. The Qing statutes speak of 'the education . . . [and] transformation of the [moral] atmosphere'. The virtuous deeds must be paraded in front of a public, and recipients of moral awards were meant to be 'exemplars' and 'models to their communities'. According to the Yongzheng emperor, if there is confusion, and no behaviour is marked with awards for approval and shown to the people, then those who perform good acts will not know what they are to do, and will become negligent, while those who perform ill deeds will not know what they must not do, and will daily grow more reckless.[26]

These historical examples are strikingly parallel to the system used during the present 'building of the two civilizations'. In 1990 there was much talk of the spiritual example of Xinyang County of Suzhou municipality, where the leadership started building socialist spiritual civilization through the 'drive to become ten-star civilized peasant households' (*zhengchuang shixingji wenming nonghu huodong*), or the 'ten-star-grade movement' (*'shixingji' huodong*) for short.[27] Households were selected—'five good families' (*wu hao jiating*), 'good mother-daughter-in-law relations' (*hao poxi*), 'double civilized households' (*shuang wenminghu*) of high standing both economically and morally, 'law-abiding households' (*zunji shoufa hu*), etc. This drive was inspired by the grading into 'four-star' or 'five-star' hotels, and the county administration decided to divide educational elements into ten parts and marking each with a red star. On the board showing the star grades, each star had a fixed position and acquired a particular connotation.[28] An educational campaign was launched; to sum up and show the results of the educational evaluation process (*jiaoyu pingding*) a 'civilized-star grade-board' (*wenming xingjipian*) with red or yellow five-pointed stars was hung up at the main gate of every household. The board clearly showed the household's strong points and defects, implying commendation and criticism according to the principle of 'carrying out education through positive examples and self-education'. Those who met the educational requirements received a red star to affirm their achievements and commend them, while those who failed were given a yellow star for encouragement. According to the report, in just over half a year the administration carried out 'ten-star-grade' assessment activities in 303 villages across the county, solved many difficult problems, and made remarkable achievements. In the end every peasant household had a 'star grade-board' over the main gate, just as in imperial times. The important effect of these star grade-boards is said to be that they differentiate, and in particular that they make clear the features or (moral and material) appearance of each household. Apart from manifesting the standards of society, the parading through stars also strengthens social control (*shehui jiandu*).[29]

The star grade-board illustrates in a very direct way the aspect of parading of virtue, so important in the overall educational strategy of modelling. The system allegedly improved the spiritual civilization and purified (*jinghua*) the social atmosphere in many ways. Birth control used to be difficult, but during the campaign people in Xinyang became more motivated to follow the Party's one-child policy. Education was taken more seriously, and girls were no longer taken out of school. Family trouble and neighbour quarrels were solved, and

78.6 per cent of the non-harmonious families became harmonious. Among those who had been unfilial against elders, 93.4 per cent had corrected their mistakes. Criminal cases decreased by 90 per cent during the first half-year of the campaign. A gang of hooligans decided to stop doing evil; superstition was nearly eradicated; temples were dismantled; gamblers overcame their addiction to the habit; relations between cadres and people improved; rich people gave donations for public purposes; etc. Not only civilized peasant households (*wenming nonghu*), but civilized villages (*wenming cunzhen*) were elected and promoted, and the campaign 'raised production and improved the collective spirit'.[30]

'Civilized cities' (*wenming chengshi*) are also promoted according to the principle of parading virtuous behaviour. During 1990–1, some 5,000 work-units and 300,000 employees took part in a large-scale moral competition campaign in Harbin; 100 work-units were awarded a gold medal, while 200 obtained a silver medal. In addition to the work-units, 300 individuals were awarded gold medals and 3,000 got silver medals. The emphasis was on being service-minded, and the newspaper *Harbin ribao* was the most outstanding example of all the units in the city. To illustrate the exemplary effect (*shifan zuoyong*) of parading, the newspaper was declared a 'window work-unit' (*chuangkou danwei*) to serve as a window for others to learn to behave in the same virtuous way. The campaign is meant to be based on participation, and should inspire and control (*jiandu*) public opinion; it is said to 'defend unity and stability' and to 'accelerate the civilization of people's quality'.[31]

The exemplary person represents the standard (*biaozhun*) and personification (*renge hua*) of moral norms and values.[32] A model person is characterized by virtuous behaviour. But the manifestation of this behaviour is what is central—it does not necessarily have to be imitated to the point of internalization. Such internalization is for the 'sage' only. The sage puts virtue on display, and the display of virtuous behaviour as such can then be acted out by most people. The parading of virtue can be described by the theatre metaphor. On a stage of virtue, the task of the virtuous (and not so virtuous) agent is to spread the example of virtuous behaviour, even if they themselves should not be 'honest' in their display. The transmittor of virtue can 'act out' the exemplary norm without standing fully behind that behaviour, since role-playing has a moral educative value in itself. It is often openly admitted that the exemplary display is 'acted' behaviour. In a recent commentary to a television show displaying the deeds of model husbands, this aspect is illustrated:

Even if the men are not such models as they pretend to be on television, it is still good for the TV-viewers to watch how the men play their role. This activity alone should promote a more desirable husband-wife relationship.[33]

The theme of environmental 'imperceptible influence' underlies this type of argumentation. The term 'typical example' (*dianxing*) is often used as a synonym for 'model'. The 'typical' refers to the display of the exemplary rather than to the statistically most frequent behaviour. Often the exemplary person has been made into a very atypical person with skills or virtues hard for the common man to emulate and attain. In Chinese modelling theory the *dianxing* is typical in that it demonstrates a certain appropriate characteristic easy for others to grasp, if not exactly equally easy to emulate. These are often to be propagated on a large scale, and could be not only individuals but also examples of how to do certain things, how to organize society, etc.[34]

We can distinguish between functionally diffuse and functionally specific models.[35] By functionally diffuse I refer to the models symbolizing the grand narratives of society in its most general form. The texts are about stability, order, thrift, sacrifice, and attachment to the group. These great integrative texts are the most important general contributors to the overall process of socialization and cultural identity. The functionally specific models can be models for learning a specific task, or they may give important clues about a specific and limited area of information. Model-workers and production models promoting certain effective methods or attitudes towards work are examples here. There are also, however, mixed texts, like that of the 'good entrepreneur'. Entrepreneur models are often specific models, for example showing how to cultivate mushrooms, or some other specific technique. In this respect they can be seen as part of a general information technology.[36] But the stress is here both on 'good' and on 'entrepreneur', for spiritual as well as material civilization, order as well as growth. The 'good' symbolizes attachment to the group, willingness to share their knowledge with others, etc. To be materially rich without being spiritually rich is actually to be poor—that is the message often transmitted.[37] These texts are partly of the diffuse, partly of the specific kind, and represent the narratives of both progress and order.

Very common today is the 'story of the happy and stable family'. Articles on happy family models, scores of model husbands and model daughters-in-law, and articles on filial and dutiful children and youth, all emphasizing the traditional themes of family harmony, filial piety, and social peace, have been presented in recent years. The picture leaves no doubt that social stability and harmony have been emphasized in the extreme.[38] Filial piety and respect for the old, core issues of traditional morality and society, are again described as the 'flowers of spiritual civilization'.[39] One should foster good family members who are also good members of society to uphold social order and stability. The so-called 'five good families' (*wu hao jiating*) campaign started back in 1976, and selections of 'good mothers' (*hao mama*) were implemented to stress exemplary upbringing of children in order to prevent crime.[40]

Stability and exemplarity begin in small things. Within the cell of the small good deed lies the potential unfolding of a real exemplary society. If in Marxist theory the commodity represents capitalist society in its cell form, one might say that in today's China the good deed represents the exemplary society in its cell form. At least this is the 'spiritual cell' of moral and exemplary society, according to the theory of moral order prevalent during the reform period. There exists a hierarchy of exemplary conduct, starting from the small and everyday good deed. Doing good deeds (*zuo haoshi*) is a milder form of exemplary everyday behaviour prescribed for campaigns where the ordinary imitates the exemplary and its heroic deeds (*yingxiong shiji*). As the heroic deed is the ultimate proof of the exemplary, acts of heroism are often used as examples in moral education.

The theme of imitation moving from mechanic copying to creative innovation is important in this respect. True modelling is meant to transcend mimicry in implying the adoption of behaviours that are symbolic equivalents of the behaviour of the model. It implies the capacity not merely to copy behaviour mechanically, but also to learn and support the cultural values that legitimize a given action, so that explicit modelling becomes no longer necessary as an antecedent to a given type of response.[41] The 'true gentleman', in other words, learns 'true modelling'. Models symbolize and reflect the meaning and demands of society. The method is said to be the most effective way of producing attachment to social norms. *Xiao*, as in *xiaofa* (to model oneself on, to learn from), means to 'imitate' or to 'follow the example of', but it also means 'to prove effective'. The greater moral effectiveness is shown by the greater proximity between imitator and society. The aim is said to be 'to lead [the students] on the way to society' (*zouxiang shehui*).[42]

True modelling also involves having an insight into 'moral science' as the perfect knowledge of the objective social norms. True modelling lies in understanding the 'objectivity' of the model. Apart from having educating and guiding functions, the numerous stories about model persons are also to have an encouraging (*jili*) function.[43] Individual socialization is to be strengthened, and social responsibility feeling and cultural quality (*wenhua suzhi*) raised, through such objective model learning, according to Jiang Haohua and Zhang Lin.[44] These authors discuss a new and modern understanding of model education, in which the theory of unity between knowing and doing should be utilized. The student must be taught good habits by transforming his knowledge (*zhi*) about models into doing (*xing*) like them. Effective control of behaviour lies in the perfection of 'objective knowledge' about models and what they symbolize.

This is what is meant by identity or at least proximity between 'text' and 'life'. The grand narratives represented by models are to be turned into a real life of exemplary behaviour. In the aftermath of a campaign arranged to learn from the soldier model Lei Feng, Wu Zhuo is overtly optimistic concerning the text; and succumbs to wishful thinking when he describes the morality formed and developed under socialism: 'So many advanced exemplary figures have emerged one after another that they have become common practice (*weiran cheng feng*).'[45] His wishful thinking, however, represents the exemplary ideal. Even if it is an obvious exaggeration to claim that the exemplary text has become common practice, it is assumed that models represent the best way to make people grasp the demands of society. Lenin's statement that 'the power of models is endless' is often used in pedagogical as well as political literature. Models are also linked to the issue of self-cultivation, and personal behaviour should be adjusted in line with the model's behaviour. A model is regarded as a mirror where one can see one's own insufficiency and shortcomings, one's strong points and achievements. Such social correction and guidance is said to 'uninterruptedly strengthen the confidence in going forward'.[46]

The Moorings of Models and Modelling

Models can be part of a culture, and models can be imposed from above. The ideal of modelling theory, however, is still that models should emerge from below and not from above.[47] Models coming from below have social and cultural moorings making them extremely stable and effective in holding society together. The imposed model, by contrast, lacks such moorings: it is a figure constructed 'outside' society itself. In China, we can find examples of both these approaches of models and modelling. Tracing the cultural basis of educational development, LeVine and White have explored the roots of what they call the 'agrarian concept of virtue'. In the process, they come close to Chinese thinking about morality and model learning:

What is most important about agrarian concepts of virtue, is not that they are used to punish deviants and reward conformists to community standards in the manner of a legal code that is being enforced, but that they offer rich models of the good life and the good person that inspire identification in boys and girls and motivate adults to realize the cultural ideals in their own lives.[48]

These cultural influences are effective because the models are reinforced by experience, and are so deeply grounded in the pragmatics of the agrarian family situation as to be consistent with common-sense conclusions of nearly any member of that community. The symbols contained in traditional models are also more elaborated conceptually and more appealing emotionally than those of an ideology coming from outside the community itself. It is vital that the ideals embodied in such local models can be viewed as locally realizable. Without this concrete and realistic approach, models can actually become counterproductive.

In China, models have long been real cultural exemplars in this sense. For centuries the Chinese have had recourse to dramatic personifications of good and evil, familiar as ancient models of virtue and vice, inspiring social identities committed not only to virtuous activity, but also to the struggle against vice. While some contemporary models might be short-lived and episodic, some traditional cultural heroes live on for centuries.[49] In this way, many were effectively motivated in their economic, moral, and political activities. The culturally rooted, locally realizable models are best suited for, if not an agrarian society, then at least a community-based society. If modelling is more effective in small-scale social surroundings, as LeVine and White seem to assume, then the segmentary structure of China will probably also render such methods more effective than in a more impersonal modern society of what Durkheim called 'organic solidarity'. This assumption also admits the possibility that models and modelling might fade as modernization progresses. Models are found not only in traditional societies, but they seem to fit best in community-related surroundings. The cultural hero became a hero precisely because of the strong social and cultural moorings surrounding his or her image. Dorothy Norman speaks of the heroic deeds of those great moments in history where 'performer and performance are one; when the hero himself is not even conscious that his act is heroic'.[50] This ideal is far removed from the Chinese reality of today, even if it is still regarded as an ideal. Taking another perspective, we can say that text and reality are no longer identical. In fact, the two are gradually moving further apart as society turns more complex and the modern Juggernaut moves faster.

There are still in Chinese society cultural moorings that render the model images effective. The imitative–repetitive approach already described fits well into the overall picture of a modelling culture. The belief that people learn from models has become an important characteristic of Chinese culture. The Chinese process of socialization is still followed by massive doses of model learning, and people know their models as an obvious part of their cultural knowledge and identity. The current emphasis on model learning and the 'imitation of sages' from classical times build on the same principles. Model emulation seems part of the script about 'learning how' that constitutes Chinese identity; it is not just something imposed from above.

Interestingly, an investigation on changing student concepts published in late 1988 showed that heroes played an important role in students' thinking despite the new trends towards self-expression and independence, a finding tragically demonstrated at Tiananmen during the spring of 1989. The report concludes:

The traditional idea of modelling after the old still affects the youth . . . As for heroes who sacrifice their own interests, even their lives, for the benefit of others, 2.6 per cent of the total said these people were silly. Another 4.5 per cent said they would never do such things. But 76.6 per cent still answered that they would not hesitate to do them.[51]

Stories of soldiers who sacrificed themselves in the struggles of war and revolution have been very popular in the period of the People's Republic, and some have represented real cultural heroes. The Tiananmen 'soldier hero' models promoted after June 1989, however, are the most counterproductive models seen in China so far. They represent a striking example of models without popular roots, and display a text that breaks radically with reality—as it was perceived by the vast majority of the Beijing population.[52]

That models and modelling are still very prevalent in China despite the wear and tear of modernization might be linked to China's imitative–repetitive pattern of thinking. Particular models might have lost their ability to influence people, but the general approach towards modelling seems to have kept much of its original educational effect. A child's readiness to adapt to a model is based on the former history of reinforcement experienced by the child. Through childhood imitation of significant others, a 'learning how' to imitate exemplary models seems to be inscribed into the developing cultural 'script' of the individual. Studies purporting to demonstrate what Urie Bronfenbrenner calls a 'generalized imitative set' of responding have done so by showing that non-reinforced imitative responses are often acquired once an imitation–reinforcement sequence has been established. Even if more research is needed to clarify this issue, it is not unlikely that children differ in their susceptibility to modelling as a function of their prior history of reinforcement from models.[53] 'An individual's past history of social reinforcement influences his present receptivity to social reinforcement', explains Rueben Baron.[54] The social reinforcement history, e.g. 'the frequency, intensity, and variability of past social rewards', he refers to as an individual's 'social reinforcement standard'. Subjects most responsive to reinforcement are those who experienced considerable reinforcement in the past. If Baron is correct, and imitation is strengthened by experience, an imitative culture like the one we find in China, which systematically rewards model behaviour, will make methods of imitation and the modelling of exemplary persons all the more easy to apply effectively.

Model learning is today one of the most common methods of moral education in China. The current discussions on models, however, are increasingly becoming pedagogical discussions of the general effect of modelling. The obviousness of the cultural hero is replaced more and more by discussions on techniques and effects. We have seen a rationalization of the model image. The scope and importance of model learning has been shown in analyses of children's books, where exemplary models dominate the stories.[55] It has been shown that, if a moral model person's behaviour is known and discussed in class, the moral knowledge and ability among secondary schoolchildren improves markedly. But such moral learning is not left at the stage of mimicry only. If understood, the model's deeds might improve general moral behaviour among students also in other moral situations. Simple or forced behaviour training does not necessarily have a great positive influence on moral behaviour on a short-term basis, but is useful in the light of long-term behaviour training.[56]

The potency of the model also increases with the extent to which the model is perceived to possess a high degree of competence, status, and control over resources. The most 'contagious' models for the child are likely to be those significant others who provide support and control in the child's environment, such as parents, playmates, older siblings, and children and adults who play a prominent role in the child's everyday life.[57] There is often a hierarchy of models with local imitations of the general national model. The local model is often selected from the unit itself, and becomes the transmitter of the higher-order model.

This principle of social proximity in modelling is related to the principle of local realizability. A community is still the best breeding grounds for modelling; when the general development moves towards more 'organic' ways of organizing social life, the segmentary structures of familism and *danwei*-ism define the background of the growing ratio-nalization of the model discourse. Significant others, as defined here, are thus not only parents and friends: they are also persons in author-ity who control the resources of individuals. The petty bureaucrat is an important model upholding authority in Chinese society, as is the teacher. The latter has been described as the generalized model in schools, a 'moral entrepreneur' whose model effect is again given much con-sideration in Chinese pedagogy.

Administering the Model Image

An article compiled by the Department for Propaganda in the Army confirms the strong emphasis on the modelling of the exemplary. In particular, heroes of the People's Liberation Army 'radiated the glory of communism . . . and thereby formed a gigantic spiritual driving force for hundreds of millions of people'.[58] The 'Resolution of the CPC Central Committee regarding the guiding principles for building socialist spiritual civilization' in the Army states that:

[T]he basic task of building socialist spiritual civilization is to meet the needs of socialist modernization; to cultivate socialist citizens who . . . emphasize moral-ity, are educated, and observe discipline; and to improve the quality of think-ing and standards of morality, as well as the scientific and cultural education, of the whole Chinese nation . . . mobilize people's positive factors through pub-licizing new models and new deeds, and guide the people to draw a clear line of demarcation between good and evil, beauty and ugliness, and honour and disgrace. It should propagate . . . heroes who devoted their lives to the liber-ation cause of the Chinese nation, so that their examples will influence later generations and will encourage people to emulate their deeds, to follow their footsteps, and to score heroic achievements.[59]

The theme of which values and norms are promoted through the texts on models is far too broad to be dealt with in a few examples only, and it is impossible to reflect the great variety and the many faces of models and heroes in a few lines.[60] Certain typical characteristics of these texts, however, can be used as examples. One core element of the text is that of sacrifice and the shedding of blood for the cause or the collective. Sacrifice, stability, and harmony are the central arche-types of the present exemplary text. This text, however, can be revised and rewritten in many different ways and can serve many different purposes. Social stability has not always been the core of the Chinese grand narrative. During the Cultural Revolution there was an all-out attack on the stability of the model. There were then even models of disorder, the so-called 'going-against-the-tide' (*fan chaoliu*) models attacking officials, teachers, and other persons of authority.[61]

Sacrifice and the control of self seem to be crucial themes in all social myths. In her book on the hero in mythology, Dorothy Norman focuses on the theme of self-love. In many traditional myths, self-love is seen as the first and primary cause of evil, the mother of all passions, and of all vices.[62] This is typical of a traditional society facing uncontrollable dangers, whether real or imagined. Joseph Campbell, emphasizing the integrating elements of myth in modern society, points out the difficulty of upholding those great coordinating mythologies which have now gradually come to be known as lies. Under traditional social forms, society was kept together by a collectivity that has now disappeared: 'Then all meaning was in the group, in the great anonymous forms, none in the self-expressive individual; today no meaning is in the group—none in the world: all is in the individual.'[63]

Myths have long addressed the dangers of self, and the virtue of the group and the collective. They represent the forces that stand outside oneself and are superior to oneself—as described by Durkheim and the Chinese moral educators. The Chinese mythology of the exemplary hero touches upon these same integrating myths. Self stands against sacrifice and the collective. The myth of the exemplary hero serves as a cohesive myth of solidarity, defending the morality of a culture. There are the good forces fighting against the evil forces. This theme—of good against evil, virtue against vice, and order against disorder—has been described as man against beast, saints and good spirits against demons and evil spirits. It is within this classical tradition that we should view the Chinese exemplary hero, even though in recent times the Chinese texts have been closer to life than to the ancient myths. In China the good and heroic deeds of exemplary models find their opposite in evil deeds (*lieji*). Many commentators repeat that the socialist ideal is to sacrifice oneself to realize social values, and that the socialist hero represents such values. On the other hand, they note, the hooligan or *liumang* seeks only the values of self, even if these can be obtained only by improper means. Thus, the hero and the hooligan represent pure social and pure selfish values, respectively.[64] The texts on heroic deeds in China are also interesting because they come so close to a direct Durkheimian 'worshipping of society'—without any supernatural embellishment of the text.[65] The exemplary hero might be said to represent a type of 'secular saint'. If the secular saint is not a supernatural figure, his or her exemplary conduct can in fact be seen as super-social acts. A text becomes super-social when it is too remote from real life and sentiments in a society and a time epoch; and this might under certain circumstances in fact lessen the effect of the model. I will return to this problem below.

There are various types of model and hero. The most persistent model of all is Lei Feng. Apart from being a model for collectivism, loyalty and stability, he is first and foremost a model for doing good deeds. The good deed must be seen as a 'small beginning' of more heroic deeds and behaviour. In contrast to Lei Feng, heroes like Dong Cunrui, Wang Jie, Lai Ning, and numerous others are models of heroic deeds which make them into martyrs. They all gained their fame after death. In fact, most of the great exemplary models are dead models, martyrs for the collectivity and the cause. Even if Lei Feng was a typical do-gooder, making small contributions of helpfulness and thrift, bent on 'serving the people' (*wei renmin fuwu*) in everyday life situations, he sprang to fame after being killed 'on duty' in a motor car accident in 1962.

Dong Cunrui is another type of model—a sacrificing hero, typical of the period of war and revolution. Dong, a soldier in the Eight Route Army, died in 1948 at the age of 19 when he sacrificed himself by holding explosives in his own hands in order to blow up a bridge and prevent the enemy from passing it; there was no time to fasten the explosives, and Dong saved his comrades and secured the advance of the Red Army through his heroic sacrifice.[66]

Such heroic deeds have also been reported in times of peace. Wang Jie is one of the best-known examples here. Wang died in 1965 at the age of 23 during a military exercise when he saved his comrades from the army and the militia by covering detonating explosives with his own body; by his heroic deed Wang saved twelve soldiers and cadres. He was later made a model for his selfless and determined sacrifice for the revolution and the socialist cause.[67]

Even today, new sacrificing soldier-heroes are propagated. Su Ning died at the age of 37 in April 1990 while rescuing two other soldiers from a hand grenade explosion. This hero was intellectually outstanding as well, and had made valuable contributions to military theory and computer science. Su Ning was thus a modern sacrificing hero, one who combined the themes of modernization and sacrifice.[68] Such 'scientific and technological deeds of talents' (*keji rencai de shiji*) have been promoted during the reforms.[69]

Altruistic suicide seems a sure way of gaining model status. Most of the major nationwide 'diffuse' models are dead persons. One reason is quite pragmatic: dead models never err, they remain fixed in their exemplarity. It has been explained that, while this may be one factor in selecting models, it does not mean that all models should be dead and buried before they can gain the status of a hero, since living models can often have stronger educational effect.[70] The strong emphasis on blood sacrifice is illustrated by a debate in 1992 about a soldier who saved three children who had fallen into the Yellow River.[71] Since he did not risk his life by jumping into the river, but saved the children with a rope and was not hurt, some were against recording a merit for him; by not risking his own life, he had merely done a good deed, and should only be praised for that. Form seems more important than results in such cases, and consequence more important than intention.

We can note the theme of blood sacrifice also in recent stories of models of filial piety. Shen Wengui, a Shanghai worker who adopted a poor elderly couple as his own parents, repeatedly sold his blood to a hospital in order to get enough money to support them.[72] One of the more recent well-known heroes of sacrifice is Zhang Hua, a student who died in 1982 after having tried to save a peasant who had fallen into a manure pit.[73] Zhang Hua died in this attempt, while the person who finally dragged both of them out of the pit and survived was not accorded much attention. After his death Zhang was used as an example in a drive to curb growing individualism, in particular among youth at the outset of reform.

The importance of protecting public property is another popular theme in the model texts on sacrifice. Xiang Xiuli, a Guangzhou factory worker who in 1959 died from the burns she sustained in trying to save public property during a fire at her factory, is an earlier typical example. She was brought to hospital and briefly regained consciousness before she died, only concerned whether the factory had been saved.[74] The sacrificing and heroic deed of Lai Ning is another one now widely proclaimed in the schools. Lai, a secondary school pupil, was killed in a fire trying to save public property. As he was a schoolchild himself, it was thought that the effect of his sacrifice would have a stronger impact on other schoolchildren. Even the Party General Secretary, Jiang Zemin, made a speech to his honour, 'canonizing' him by talking about a 'Lai Ning spirit' (*Lai Ning jingshen*) to inspire people to strive for the benefit of society.[75]

Recently, however, many educators have been asking themselves why these exemplary models no longer seem to hold any appeal. Despite the innovations found in recent Chinese theories on modelling, the models have become increasingly unpopular. Some claim that it is because of the dead and ossified style used in establishing and propagating the models. There are too many perfect paragons of virtue. Instead, the model should be limited in scope and should 'make up a much more colourful crowd' than before.[76] Models should reflect modern values, with the fixity of the traditional exemplary model loosened up in order to adapt to the changing times.

A 'scientific determination of model images' is now propagated.[77] For a long time models have been robot-like creatures without individuality. It is now felt by some that a new and more scientific five-step approach should be implemented in making a model. First, one should determine an image (*queding xingxiang*) to establish a clear model; the needs of the students should be evaluated. Second, one should find or discover a model (*faxian bangyang*). Then comes the fostering of the model (*peiyang bangyang*). After these three steps, one should start promoting the model (*xuanchuan bangyang*); an important aspect here is to grasp the 'degree' (*du*), meaning that one should not make the model too perfect. The fifth aspect is guidance (*yindao*) of the students to help them learn from the model.

In discussions on modelling during the 1980s, the value of immediate (*zhijie*) models was increasingly emphasized as an alternative to the many revolutionary martyrs. 'Immediate' models can be seen as identical with the 'contagious' models mentioned by Bronfenbrenner. In the pedagogical literature of the 1980s parents were termed the 'first models', and teachers became more and more valued as models of spiritual civilization.[78] These models also signified that family and teacher authority was now reintroduced after the Cultural Revolution. This trend has been strengthened in the 1990s. The inclination towards familism and 'feudal' authority figures might be seen as an attempt to redesign the lost community support of the modelling process.

A new flexibility has also been introduced in model-learning pedagogy. Models should be 'stratum-specific' (*cengci xing*)[79] and time-specific to fit the style of reform.[80] Introducing pluralism in the image of models has also been recommended.[81] Model education should further pay heed to age differences. Models should fit the development of youth, and the changed value concepts of young people.[82] All these suggestions for the organization and hierarchization of the model are aimed at making the model more effective, more credible, and more attainable. Exemplary models should be less like 'sculptures' or 'monuments', and more lively.[83]

Not all commentators support the new trend in model pedagogy, however. Qian Mingfang claims that 'the tendency to let the model change its role with the political wind in order to be fashionable has been taken to extremes'.[84] According to Qian, the confused condition among youth in general should rather be countered with the stable goals of models. Such stability is no longer to be found; instead, 'everybody takes what they need when learning from models. Even some opportunists and adventurers have become . . . "models"', Qian indignantly maintains. One should instead strive to uphold the gradually uplifting and edifying influence of models. An exercise (*fanfu duanlian*) in learning from exemplary models should also be constantly repeated to strengthen this effect.[85] The traditional exemplary figure signals fixity, and in that fixity lies also the salience of the norm. Qian's point is that the norm becomes less salient when the exemplary adapts to the rapidly changing situation in modern society. As I pointed out earlier, there is a struggle between fixity and adaptation here. Such a fixity might lead to rigidity, however, and the alleged effectiveness of the fixed exemplary model might get lost on the way. As was the case with inculcation versus elicitation, the struggle of the definition of model images is as much a political struggle as it is one of educational methods. The group that attains hegemony over the modelling texts is also the group in power. Since the mechanical moorings of the model are disintegrating, the growing discrepancy between text and reality becomes increasingly evident. This has led to a stepped-up emphasis on the administrative side of modelling. The construction of models is less and less of a self-evident process, and evokes an ever-increasing number of questions concerning administration and technique.

We have noted the beginnings of a crisis in the construction of models during the reforms, and it has become increasingly difficult to fit the cohesive text to the changing realities of reform. Even the biographies of old and well-known models have been changed in order to accord with the changing reform values. Since these texts are rooted in traditional narratives of order, modern twists have not been entirely successful. In much of Chinese modelling pedagogy, however, the problem of the modelling text seems to be reduced to a problem of mirroring reality in the best way possible. It is directly stated that the principles of selection, commending, propagating, and emulating models should be based on reality. The exemplary deeds should be taken from real life, and the exemplary person should be described as he or she is. Methods of perfecting already exemplary deeds and personalities in order to increase the authority of models should not be resorted to. A basic principle is that models should be realizable and attainable for normal people.[86] The model should be 'selected' (*xuanze*) rather than 'established' (*shuli*). To establish models is to exaggerate model characteristics in order to make them more perfect. Such models will not prove effective because they are not credible, and their image is unattainable.[87]

In an interesting analysis of the soldier model Lei Feng, the best-known model of them all over the last thirty years, Beate Geist points out that the values being attributed to him seem to be changing with the changing political needs of the Party.[88] Basically, the 'Lei Feng spirit' has been associated with the 'respect superiors' rule in Chinese culture. Lei Feng embodies the 'spirit of a screw' (*luosiding jingshen*). In his diary, Lei compared the role of a person in society to that of a screw in machinery. His wish was to be a 'never-rusting screw' in this machinery, and his remarks lie close to the 'spirit of sacrifice and devotion' as well as the collectivistic 'attachment to the group' rules so important in the Chinese version of 'moral sciences'. But among the more liberal echelon of reformers, Lei Feng's deeds of collectivist morality have been associated with a loss of individuality. The Lei Feng spirit was criticized for being a 'tool theory' (*gongju lun*), established for the purpose of making people into 'docile tools' (*xunfu gongju*).[89]

The Party has tried to counter these attacks by adapting Lei Feng to the changing times. During the 1980s, passages inappropriate to the current image of the soldier model were omitted altogether from editions of his diaries. Among the entries omitted are references to serving Mao Zedong; as a reaction to criticism, the expression 'always be a docile tool of the Party' was also omitted.[90] Values of modernization have been launched as a part of the Lei Feng image. There have been attempts to transform him from a pure model of thrift into 'Lei Feng the consumer', to make his image more in tune with the emerging commodity economy. He was suddenly said to have had 'material as well as spiritual needs'.[91] Today the emphasis on 'stability' (*wending*) seems to be the most important part of the Lei Feng spirit. Such adaptation of a model to changing circumstances may be in line with the flexible adaptation to change advocated in the theory of controlled change, but it has failed to strengthen the model's credibility. Lei Feng has been rendered impossible and now even appears ridiculous to young people; a symbol of a dubious character. He is, however, still used with some effect in the model learning of small children, and, despite the recent ridicule and doubt, also represents a model image for some of the older generation. Many view Lei Feng with nostalgic feelings for a past that was characterized by honesty, innocence, and order.

The Devaluation of Models

Despite the cultural basis for model learning, there has recently been a severe crisis of faith in the exemplary model. In particular, revolutionary leaders and heroic models are reported to be unpopular among students.[92] The community-based 'natural' model described by LeVine and White has been severely challenged by modernization, and the motivation in learning from models has deteriorated. According to worried educators, 'a devaluation [*bianzhi*] of models has taken place',[93] while the more cynical ones claim that 'now it's the slack season for heroes'. These cynics see the exemplary heroes as 'cold blooded animals of a lonely and aloof world', far removed from the lives of ordinary people.[94]

This issue became well known through an important debate on youth work started by the paper *Shekou Tongxunbao* after a turbulent meeting in 1988 of famous Beijing educators and youth representatives from the new economic zone in Shekou—a meeting later referred to as the 'Shekou storm'.[95] One of the attacks made by Shekou youths was that all models during the past thirty years had been 'gods'. Learning from exemplary heroes had virtually turned into a 'culture of gods' (*shen de wenhua*), it was claimed; living people of flesh and blood have human desires and emotions, and nobody could be expected to imitate such gods. The 'storm' turned into an all-out attack on the exemplary model. Since people have weaknesses, and can never be perfect, what we need instead is a culture of human beings (*ren de wenhua*), it was claimed. The youth educators expect everybody to behave like one or several models: what China needs most is not millions of duplicates of one model, or many in the form of one (*'duo' biancheng 'yi'*)—on the contrary, what China needs now is one in the form of many (*'yi' biancheng 'duo'*), and the trend towards deification (*shenhua*) should no longer be used.[96] A poem published in the journal 'Young People' typically describes the model person as seen by the younger generation: 'People tear off his god-like veil . . . He is no sage, he is no superman.' The commentator remarks that models should be not only *moral* personalities, but also *normal* personalities. This theme, as we shall later see, is an important one for distinguishing the exemplary norm from the average norm.[97]

Often the pressure of the model text has become too heavy a burden for the real-life heroes, and there have been numerous reports of disillusionment among such models selected to represent the exemplary person. In a letter to the 'People's Daily' from the All-China Workers' Federation, we can read that twenty-one model workers had been admitted to a sanatorium, all with various disorders caused by overwork. 'The model workers have been overworked for years,' the letter stated, adding that the same could probably be said of model workers all over the country.[98] In several cases model workers have become alienated from their colleagues, and many have turned down their titles of honour. Such resistance among workers against the 'model worker' cannot be explained as a turn towards individualism among workers only. Parts of what we see here must be interpreted as a clash between two types of collectivism. The unofficial workers' collectives must have regarded the model worker as a 'rate buster'. In Western industrial sociology, such a rate buster is the factory leadership's Trojan horse within the workers' informal community, and a person to be frozen out of this collective.[99]

As the reforms progress, 'market' is proving more forceful than 'socialism' in the new Chinese concept of 'market socialism'. It is becoming increasingly difficult for the factory leadership to resort to the incentives of the 'model worker' in order to increase production. The informal workers' collectives seem to be confronting the image of 'model worker' with collectivist egalitarianism. Reports say that 'the good standing of a model worker has been reduced greatly due to malpractices in their selection'.[100] In many units, the selection of model workers has deteriorated into a system of mere rotation. Fixing the numbers of model workers is another practice criticized in the same report for being ridiculous; the very title of 'model worker' is about to lose its meaning. These examples indicate that, when the model is defined from without, the community structure that would normally strengthen the effect of the model instead turns against it. The trend might be interpreted as a 'weapon of the weak' among a working class deprived of the right to form autonomous unions or other interest groups. Here we see the 'small' and particularistic collective turning against the 'big' and universalistic collective.

Today there are few young people who would actually like to be selected as models of any kind, unless for instrumental reasons of benefit or profit. A survey among 600 young people in Tianjin, 63 per cent of them young workers, found that as much as 91 per cent had no interest whatsoever in becoming model workers.[101] Just as there seems to be a norm against the 'rate buster', so there would also seem to be a norm against the 'do-gooder' in general. China has institutionalized the good deed, but attacks on the 'do-gooder' have reached a level seldom seen in other cultures, and administrative countermeasures have been implemented. Several incidents have been reported where exemplary models have been harassed and ridiculed, attacked and isolated. A survey among 108 'advanced workers' (*xianjin gongzuo zhe*) from all over China showed that 73 had been met with ridicule or had been attacked because of their model status.[102] There are also examples of heroes being taken advantage of and discriminated against, after being crippled through their heroic deeds.[103]

It has been proposed that society should have a 'mechanism for the protection of heroes' (*jizhi baohu yingxiong*).[104] The problems encountered by do-gooders as well as models and heroes are varied, and numerous. Children who stand up and give their seats to elders on the bus are ridiculed; those who help others are criticized. An article in the journal 'Political education' states that one should guarantee the rights of those who are bullied in public places, because this behaviour is injurious to the moral quality in society. Such attacks discourage children from doing good deeds, and lead them to doubt their own good habits of exemplary behaviour. Some even develop a defiant psychology instead. The attacks on models and communist moral education are destroying the edifying influence of the environment; one thus has to guard against criticism of the good in society.[105]

Seen in this perspective, the criticism of models and model deeds is an attack on the very foundation of spiritual civilization, and should be regarded as a violation against the social order. Li Weiwei, a Communist Youth League secretary, has requested welfare guarantees for heroes, and in addition some kind of secular paragraph of 'blasphemy' to guarantee that heroes' rights should be established. Some call heroes 'stupid things' (*shashi*), but they should rather be seen as 'spiritual pillars of society', Li says. They are 'idols to be worshipped at all times', and society needs heroes. It is not enough to rely on heroic deeds spontaneously appearing. Society needs an environment and a mechanism for training and fostering heroic figures, and yet there is no mechanism protecting their deeds. Steps should be taken to guarantee that they are not discriminated against, and a mechanism based on politics and law should be put in place to ensure this. Society should give protection to heroes, and guarantee that their payment in blood is compensated for.[106]

A youth magazine presents the complaints of a disillusioned young worker who tried to take literally the call to follow exemplary persons. Instead of feeling spiritual enlightenment, he reports that he feels spiritually tired. For every sentence he utters and everything he does, there is the model and himself fighting with each other. Sometimes the model in him takes the upper hand, sometimes his own nature (*tianxing*) is in command. To begin with he tried to emulate exemplary models with enthusiasm, whether it was a Lei Feng, a Zhu Boru, or a Zhang Haidi.[107] He would give up his seat on the bus, send money to disaster areas, and practise good deeds all the time. He even started to walk like the Laotian heroes (from the Vietnam border war), and tried to imitate their deeds. He imitated Li Pengli, a crime-fighting model, and openly challenged local hooligans. The result was that he could not afford to pay his hospital bills. In the end he felt like an ascetic monk. He was rejected by those around him, and was called an idiot and a narrow-minded person, an inflexible nitpicker and a strange fellow. He came to the point where life had lost its flavour because of his attempts to be an exemplary model. Some people told him he was a traditional person in wanting to learn from old models. Others told him that, by trying to imitate the traditional heroes, he instead became like 'Dong Shi knitting her brows' (*Dong Shi xiao pin*). This ancient story is a well-known cultural mockery of blind imitation. The ugly Dong Shi used to frown in imitation of beauteous Xi Shi in order to become as beautiful as she. Instead it made her even uglier. 'Some say imitating models makes your life more meaningful', sighs the former exemplary model. 'I think it just makes life more miserable.' The influence of models in society is restricted:

If everybody liked to help other people, then society would be such that you help others to do everything, and rely on other people to do your own things. When you give something to beggars, you only help them become dependent. I don't mean to say that we should take away all guidance, but that such guidance should . . . not be the method of learning from the spirit of heroes.[108]

The frustrated person quoted here seems to have fallen prey to the instrumentalization of the good deed. In the ridiculing and the hatred of the do-gooder, there lies an assumption that a good deed is done in order to achieve personal profit of some kind. Activists working their way up in the hierarchy of power have to pay heed to the ideal of the good deed to get their career started. The good deed thus becomes a means to an end outside the realm of moral virtue and altruism. This phenomenon has been described by many observers. Susan Shirk has studied the apple-polishing process of fakes and favours in Chinese schools, and describes the situation of a 'virtuocratic' competition where good deeds turn instrumental because they are rewarded and used as a ladder in a career system. What counts in such a virtuocratic system is the profit of the good deed rather than the deed itself.[109] Martin King Whyte has described the ambivalence towards the good deed as it was experienced in the competitive moral atmosphere of Chinese schools. This ambivalence was a reaction to a deed perceived as an effort of do-gooders to put the ones they were 'helping' into a bad light, thus 'undermining their own special prestige'.[110] The instrumentalism of the 'good deed' is closely connected to the phenomenon that Durkheim warned against. Precisely because good deeds are commended and rewarded, a degrading commercial air is bound to surround them. This is the 'price tag' of a moral reward system, predicted by Durkheim. It is also the price tag of an exemplary society.

It is therefore no more than a logical consequence that with the reforms have come real price tags on model honours. A recent article in the magazine *Liaowang* stated that the honour of 'model worker' could now be purchased on the market. Donors of 50,000 yuan can be awarded the honour of all-province model worker; those giving 30,000 yuan can be awarded a model status on the city level.[111] Despite devaluation, the titles are still investments in social capital.

The Loss of Charisma: Models between Myth and Biography

Attempts at the differentiation and democratization of models and the texts of modelling are new approaches to coping with the fading images of exemplary persons and heroes. At the same time, and paradoxically, the changed image of heroes might have contributed to the further breakdown of the exemplary text. The rewritten texts show a many-faceted picture, but basically they represent a gradual change in the model image from myth to biography. The 'secular hero' might be closer to reality, but the effectiveness of modelling depends on more than mere proximity to reality. Something obviously has been lost on the way towards 'scientification'. The 'crisis of faith' has now caught up with the secular hero. Even the new democratic models seem associated with party authority, and are often mocked among the young. Some students, commenting on one of the most famous models of the 1980s, Zhang Haidi, say: 'First we would admire her, then we became more and more fed up, and in the end we were annoyed by and disgusted by her.'[112] From the educators' point of view, the tragedy is that Zhang Haidi, a partly paralysed girl born in 1955, was one of the new models embodying the values of reform, a 'Lei Feng of the 1980s', with 'individuality, thirst for knowledge, and social responsibility', very different from the political activists promoted a decade earlier. Her model status, however, bore the stamp of officialdom, and that destroyed her credibility in the eyes of many young people. The attitude towards Zhang Haidi sums up a general trend towards models over the last decade. The official model image is rapidly fading; instead, young people are seeking their own models to emulate.

Certain flaws in the new strategy of modelling have to be taken into consideration. The fading of model power is linked to the general crisis of power and problems of legitimacy for the present regime. At the same time, both the modernization process itself and the sometimes contradictory use of models lessen their effects. The growing discontinuity between private and 'outside' worlds represented by modernization of course poses a threat to the traditional stability of the family, and the strong emphasis on family models might be a counterattack against such threats. At the same time, youth sociology has pointed out that the same process leads to relatively autonomous youth groups and youth cultures. 'There is a growing gap between generations, and a weakening of direct guidance by parents and teachers, and thereby of the relevance for youth, of adult models.'[113]

Another negative side of models is the double message they signal. Outbursts of emotion used to restrict emotions, and the violent suppression of violence seen in legal reactions, are both paradoxes of model learning. The parallel to the Tiananmen 'soldier martyrs' of June 1989 is obvious. Very few people are likely to believe the message about 'serving the people' when the 'serving' actually means shooting at the people. The most obvious effect of such heroes is their ability to strengthen resistance against officially designed heroes in general.

There might also be another reason for the crisis of faith in heroes. When the text of exemplary and heroic deeds leaves the mythology and becomes biography, the charismatic power of the hero fades. The most important function of the models has been to represent an alternative to bureaucratic authority. Modelling in itself is a technique for achieving authority based upon the charismatic character of the model and the hero. Models represent charismatic authority in Chinese society. What is happening in China today is an example of what Weber characterized as the 'routinization of charisma'. As we can see, Weber's basic description of charisma in certain respects goes against the new image of the rationalized hero:

The term 'charisma' will be applied to a certain quality of an individual personality, by virtue of which he is set apart from ordinary men and treated as endowed with supernatural, superhuman, or at least specifically exceptional (*außeralltäglich*) powers or qualities. These are such as are not accessible to the ordinary person, but are regarded as of divine origin or as exemplary (*vorbildlich*), and on the basis of them the individual concerned is treated as a leader. In primitive circumstances this peculiar kind of deference is paid to prophets, to people with a reputation for therapeutic or legal wisdom, to leaders in the hunt, and heroes in war. It is very often thought of as resting on magical powers.[114]

China's 'model person' is indeed exemplary in many ways: but the point about model emulation now is that models are to be designed on the principle of recognition and attainability. With the fading of the grand narratives of society, it seems doubtful whether the ordinary hero, based on such principles, can have the power to move people any longer. Of course, this represents a dilemma for the designers of model images. Myth can no longer be reproduced in a society where it has become more and more obsolete; but the means to cope with the problem might not have much chance to succeed either. Weber has described the general routinization process that befalls charismatic authority thus:

In its pure form charismatic authority has a character specifically foreign to everyday routine structures. The social relationships directly involved are strictly personal, based on the validity and practice of charismatic personal qualities. If this is not to remain a purely transitory phenomenon, but to take on the character of a permanent relationship forming a stable community of disciples . . . it is necessary for the character of charismatic authority to become radically changed. Indeed, in its pure form charismatic authority may be said to exist only in the process of originating. It cannot remain stable, but becomes either traditionalized, rationalized, or a combination of both.[115]

The last sentence above is particularly important. The charisma of the exemplary model has not proved stable in today's China. In traditionalized charisma emerges the memory or nostalgia of order of which I earlier spoke, while the rationalized charisma represents the dreams of future order. The exemplary model has been both rationalized and traditionalized. As in Weber's description of charisma, in Chinese propaganda circles one is now grappling with the problem that charismatic authority seems to exist only in its process of originating. In traditionalization we can now see a reintroduction and a look back at this 'process of originating' or the 'moments of creation'. Before turning to the traditionalization of the exemplary model, let us look at its rationalization. The 'scientification' of model images represents what Weber called a 'rationalization of charisma'.

Dorothy Norman has described the hero as myth: the hero represents one of the great basic myths of society. 'Heroes do not represent definable human figures, but rather mythological ideals to be achieved'; the hero as myth appears in countless guises, 'freeing us from the tyranny of darkness'.[116] Heroes represent symbols that bind people together. Symbols, however, are susceptible to change, as Norman makes it clear: 'Symbols that have satisfied for centuries may quite suddenly appear devoid of meaning; those images most lacking in the power to move us can, to our surprise, possess the greatest import when rediscovered at crucial moments or in fresh garb.'[117] During the Chinese modernization old symbols seem to be fading, and the model constructors are at a loss as to what to do. The emulation of modern heroes has not been a success, and the sudden diversity of models might have led to a certain cacophony instead of having the expected stabilizing effect.

Norman's description of heroes or models suddenly devoid of meaning certainly fits the Chinese example. This is not to say that the power of the exemplary model is dead. Like Freud, Jung, and their followers, the Chinese pedagogues and political educators of modelling have demonstrated that the logic, the heroes, and the deeds of myth survive into modern times. But the Chinese rationalization of myth has done something crucial to its effects. Joseph Campbell has summed up this effect in the following way:

Wherever the poetry of myth is interpreted as biography, history, or science, it is killed. The living images become only remote acts of a distant time or sky. Furthermore, it is never difficult to demonstrate that as science and history mythology is absurd. When a civilization begins to reinterpret its mythology in this way, the life goes out of it, temples become museums, and the link between the two perspectives is dissolved.[118]

The exemplary model still has a strong influence in Chinese culture, but there are signs that the power of the exemplary is fading, that the god-like heroes are losing their motivating and inspiring power. In line with Durkheim, we could argue that the sacred has no need for religion. Maintaining a balance between rationality and myth, however, might indeed be difficult in a system based on rational heroes only. In some ways, the 'magic' of the supernatural can have a greater effect on social control than that which is rational but super-social. The supernatural can have cultural moorings that the super-social lacks. Chinese modelling is about myth, but it is also about rational techniques of education. The exemplary model's dual character of myth and educational technology, and the turn towards the technological end of the spectrum, illustrate the point made by Lyotard, that the grand narrative has lost its credibility. 'The narrative function is losing its functors, its great hero, its great dangers, its great voyages, its great goal.'[119] He sees the decline of narrative as an effect of the development of techniques and technologies that has taken place in recent decades. The emphasis has been changed from ends to means. With the fading of the grand narrative, its unifying and legitimating power is also lost. This is precisely the issue now facing China's reformers and educators. The grand narrative of socialism in China has been reduced to technique, and the prescribed ends of that narrative live on merely as a ghost of 'spiritual civilization' built on the same technocratic means as in the Western capitalism it was meant to challenge.

Many Chinese model constructors and propaganda workers have understood the dangers of pure rationalization. They now seem to be reaching back towards tradition in order to grasp those crucial 'moments of originating' or 'moments of creation'. In many ways, this type of traditionalism is artificial. It is obviously wrong to contend that the step back into the myths of past represents any pure kind of traditionalization. Rather, what it reflects is the phenomenon addressed in Chapter 1: that traditionalism is no longer a 'whole', but that useful parts of tradition can be carved out for the sake of constructing stability-conjuring images. The process might be seen as a rational way of reconstructing tradition, and as a hope that the links of cultural memory will mend the perceived instability. In that sense, what is described here is not entirely the traditionalization of charisma as described by Weber. The logic of the argument, however, remains valid. Both rationalization and traditionalization of the exemplary model image are being used, even if this is more of a 'performance' of traditionalism than the real thing. Again, tradition is recreated in the present for reasons of upholding order.

I have mentioned the reintroduction of the element of pure myth in Chinese propaganda through the reconstruction of a unifying past represented by the ancient mythical 'yellow emperor' and the equally mythical model emperors Yao and Shun.[120] Shortly after the 4 June massacre of 1989 came another reconstruction of former worn and well-known socialist models of growth and 'socialist creation'. Party General Secretary Jiang Zemin started the nostalgic trend of recirculating old socialist models in the early autumn of 1989 by praising Yan'an, the revolutionary base area and the values of thrift and hard work that had dominated at that moment of creation.[121] Later that autumn Deng Xiaoping again hailed the spirit of thrift, hard work, and plain living. Daqing oilfield, a previous model of socialist construction, was once again held up for praise. The renewed strength in promoting the 'Daqing spirit' included the element of learning from its Stakhanov-like worker hero, Wang Jinxi. The country needs such a spirit 'because the national economy is still weak', ran propaganda.[122] The reintroduction of 'the honest and hard-working cadre' took as its example a model cadre from an earlier period. Jiao Yulu, a county party secretary who worked himself to death serving the people in 1964, regained fame during the early 1990s, and Jiao clones have reappeared in the media ever since; the Kong Fansen campaign of 1995 is just one example.[123] Use of the old socialist models of Yan'an, Daqing, Wang Jinxi, and Jiao Yulu might be an attempt to exploit the wave of nostalgia that received much popular support. The 'Mao Zedong-fever' (*Mao Zedong re*) is one example of a popular nostalgic trend in Chinese society that has been taken up by the regime and adapted by official propaganda.[124]

The nostalgia centres on a 'golden age' of order, stability, and a solidaric community now associated with the 1950s and early 1960s. The contrast is of course the growing disorder, fading solidarity, and rampant corruption of today's reform period. The return to the old Stakhanovite myth also issues a signal of hard times to come despite economic progress and growth. The confused wavering between all types of model is also certain to signal some confusion about which image will prove effective in keeping stability and order in the era of 'socialist market economy'. The use of such models might have been an attempt to 'rediscover at crucial moments' effective myths that had been lost. Whether they also represented that 'fresh garb' of which Norman wrote is highly doubtful.

In reality, the busy administration and construction of heroes in China has made heroism into an instrumental act. The instrumental approaches to heroic deeds have contributed greatly to the present cynicism to such deeds. Charisma is hard to find when it is the bureaucrats who administer heroism. Often the rationalization of modelling the good deed has turned into sheer enumeration. At one point a movement to 'establish the model in one's heart' (*shuli xinzhong kaimo*) was launched in Henan. Small groups were organized to study models, and it was enthusiastically summed up that 'more than 520,000 good deeds have been done' and that petty crime was nearly wiped out as a result of the campaign.[125] The bureaucratization of model learning is also well illustrated by an article in the journal 'Political Instructor' arguing that model learning should be conducted by an organization led by the Youth League. To lead the 'learn from Lai Ning' campaign, a backbone 'model education guidance team' (*bangyang jiaoyu zhidao duiwu*) of Youth League cadres, political instructors and class teachers should be set up, its aim 'to change the very spirit and behaviour of society', using the media, mass organizations, etc. The use of the word *hui*—in the meaning of 'meeting'—characterizes the bureaucratic logic behind the idea. Report meetings (*baogui hui*), lecture meetings (*yangjiang hui*), and informal discussion meetings (*zuotan hui*) were to be held to discuss and consolidate the model. Models were to be promoted on a large scale and in a planned way and through mobilization meetings (*dongyuan hui*).[126] As so often in China, such an 'organizational fix' is prescribed to mend problems of quite another order. The uprooting of models is a matter that goes far beyond the techniques and organization of modelling. The problem is fundamentally linked to the process of modernization itself.

The 'traditionalization' of model charisma can be seen both in the reintroduction of ancient myth and in the nostalgia for the moments of socialist creation, and for traditional figures of authority such as the family and the teacher. The reintroduction of such models represents another 'repetition with a difference', where traditionalism comes back as a rational way of upholding social stability through the augmentation of traditional authority figures. In this project, the immediate model has proved the most effective, and the class teacher, or *banzhuren*, has been seen as the crucial figure in moral education. In the language of spiritual and material civilization, the *banzhuren* can be described as the 'spiritual entrepreneur'.

In the following chapters we shall see that not only the techniques of modelling, but also the bureaucratic administration of the good deed, have been subsumed under a technocratic logic of minute observation and 'scientific measurement'. Even the class teacher has turned into a bureaucrat administering that particular logic. Spiritual civilization and its cultural heroes are highly dependent on the technologies of the 'moral sciences'. If the myth is gone, the technology of control at least prolongs the control of the withering narrative; for, even if the decline of the grand narrative is linked to the development of techniques and technologies, such technologies can also uphold some of the discipline contained in the narrative. The effect is paradoxical. Even if the exemplary narrative has lost many of its cultural moorings, it still serves an important role in Chinese society. Exemplary models might be ridiculed, but they have not yet lost their grip. If the exemplary model is no longer able to stand on its own feet, the 'learning how' to act is supported by a range of disciplinary techniques now being implemented to administer the exemplary. It is not possible to halt the start of the breakdown of the grand narrative of exemplarity by this disciplinary technology, but the process can be slowed down. *Ratio* is thus paradoxically used to compensate for the loss of *credo*. This would seem to apply even if elements of traditional myth are introduced as part of that *ratio*.

Notes to Chapter 5

1. See Donald J. Munro, *The Concept of Man in Early China*, Stanford, Calif., Stanford University Press, 1969, pp. 14, 111.
2. Gu Mingyuan and Huang Ji (eds.), *Jiaoyu xue* (Pedagogy), Beijing, Renmin jiaoyu chubanshe, 1987, p. 306.
3. Armen Alchian, 'Uncertainty, evolution and economic theory, *Journal of Political Economy*, Vol. 58, No. 1, 1950, pp. 211–21.
4. Joseph Campbell, *The Hero with a Thousand Faces*, Bollingen Series 17, Princeton, Princeton University Press, 1973, p. 390.

5. Alasdair MacIntyre, *After Virtue: A study in Moral Theory*, 2nd edn., Notre Dame, Ind., University of Notre Dame Press, 1984, p. 121.

6. Ibid., p. 121.

7. Paul Ricoeur, 'Life in Quest of Narrative', in David Wood (ed.), *On Paul Ricoeur: Narrative and Interpretation*, London, Routledge, 1991, p. 25.

8. Donald J. Munro, p. 99.

9. *Mozi jian gu* (Mozi with separate explanations), Beijing, Zhonghua shuju, 1986, pp. 10–11.

10. *Zhongguo gongchandang zhangcheng* (The regulations of the Communist Party of China), Beijing, Renmin chubanshe, 1982, p. 21.

11. Zhonggong zhongyang zuzhibu zuzhiju (ed.), *Ru dang jiaocai* (Teaching material on entering the Party), 11th edn., Shanghai, Shanghai renmin chubanshe, March 1991, pp. 153–4; first published in 1989.

12. Wang Zhiping, 'Explicating "law": a comparative perspective of Chinese and Western legal culture', *Journal of Chinese Law*, Vol. 3, No. 1, 1989, p. 58.

13. Confucian Analects (*Lunyu*), 2,1, in James Legge (trans.), *The Four Books (Sishu)*, Taipei, Culture Book Co./Wenhua tushugongsi, 1983, p. 134.

14. Legge's translation 'benevolent rule' can also be translated as 'humanheartedness': see *The Works of Mencius* (*Mengzi*), bk IV. I.9.2, in James Legge (trans.), p. 705. The Taoists, however, held nature as a better teacher than the virtuous models and also held that: 'Those who can think learned from themselves, and not from the sages' (Joseph Needham, *Science in Traditional China: A Comparative Perspective*, Hong Kong, Hong Kong University Press, 1981, p. 119.

15. Interviewee 2, Beijing, 1991. The interviewee was a political inspector (*fudaoyuan*) for students at the Beijing Normal University.

16. See Aletha Huston Stein, 'Imitation of resistance to temptation', *Child Development*, Vol. 38, No. 1, 1967, pp. 157–69.

17. In schools the principle is practised in many different ways. One method is to increase the number of good students by establishing friendship ties between good and bad students. In a reported example from one class, Xiao He liked to do good deeds, while Xiao Li was a naughty boy. Xiao Li changed entirely after a friendship was established with good Xiao He, and he later got a good evaluation. See Tan Guangrong, 'Banzhuren gongzuo zhaji liang ze' (Two standard rules for class teacher work), *Zhengzhi jiaoyu*, No. 9, 1987, pp. 38–9.

18. Donald J. Munro, p. 168.

19. For example, Li Tieying recommends the cultivation of advanced models in society for teachers; Zhu Rongji calls on the Shanghai press to make known illustrious cases and model persons. See *SWB-FE*/0844, 16 August 1990, pp. B2/4 and B2/5. Deng Xiaoping was reported to have expressed appreciation for the decision to give an outstanding medical researcher in Zhuhai an award of 1 m yuan (US$180,000) (*China Daily–Business Weekly*, 13 September 1992, p. 1). The list could be made very long indeed, quoting from the abundant material on such examples.

20. *SWB-FE*/0989, 6 February 1991, p. B2/6.

21. In the *Shuowen jiezi* it says: 'Made from earth it is called *xing*, made from metal it is called *rong*, made from wood it is called *mo*, made from bamboo it is called *fan*. It is the same object, only the material is different.' See commentary to the character *fan* in Xu Shen (ed.), *Shuowen jieci zhu* (Explanations and analysis of characters with commentaries), Shanghai, Shanghai guji chubanshe, 1981, p. 191.

22. One dictionary of education defines *bangyang* as an educational method of using people's good thoughts, morals, and actions to influence students. It is also said to be one of the most important methods of moral education. See Zhang Nianhong (ed.), *Jiaoyuxue cidian* (Dictionary of education), Beijing, Beijing chubanshe, 1987, p. 463.

23. See Sun Xiting, Jin Xibin and Chen Xiaobin, *Jianming jiaoyu xue* (Concise pedagogy), Beijing, Beijing shifan daxue chubanshe, 1985, p. 230; Zhang Nianhong (ed.), p. 143.

24. S. J. Couvreur, *Chou king*, Hejianfu, 1897; reprinted Taibei, 1971, pp. 264–6, quoted from Mark Elvin, 'Female virtue and the state in China', *Past and Present*, No. 104, August 1984, p. 115. Elvin remarks that this part of *The Book of Documents* is almost certainly a forgery of post-Han (206 BC–AD 220) times.

25. Wei Shou, *Weishu* (History of the Wei) (sixth century AD), quoted from Mark Elvin, pp. 115–16.

26. *Qinding Da Qing huidian zeli* (Imperially sanctioned collected statuses and precedents of the great Qing), quoted from Mark Elvin, pp. 135–6.

27. Qin Shuli, 'Nongcun shehui zhuyi jingshen wenming jianshe de yi zhong hao xingshi: Xingyang xian "shixingji wenming nonghu" huodong diaocha' (A good way of building socialist spiritual civilization in the rural areas: investigation of 'ten-star-grade civilized peasant household' activities in Xingyang county), *Qiushi*, No. 17, 1990, pp. 30–6; Ma Shaoning (ed.), 'Wenming cun jianshe de yige chuangzao: henan sheng Xingyang xian kaizhan zhengchuang "shixingji wenming nonghu" jiaoyu huodong de jingyan, zhi yi' (A creative way to build civilized villages: experiences from the educational activities on carrying through the competition in creating 'ten-star-grade civilized households', Part one), *Jingshan wenming jianshe*, No. 10, 1990, pp. 15–16; and Ma Shaoning (ed.), 'Wenming cun jianshe de yige chuangzao: henan sheng Xingyang xian kaizhan zhengchuang "shixingji wenming nonghu" jiaoyu huodong de jingyan, zhi er' (. . . Part two), *Jingshan wenming jianshe*, No. 11, 1990, pp. 18–19.

28. The stars symbolized the following aspects: the first star: Love the party, the country, socialism, and the collective; 2, Pay great attention to cultural education to improve man's quality; 3, Apply scientific and technological achievements to agricultural production and try to become prosperous through labour; 4, Acquire knowledge of and observe the law; 5, Eradicate superstition and change prevailing habits and customs; 6, Late marriage and childbirth and good prenatal care; 7, Family harmony and good relations between neighbours; 8, Be industrious and thrifty in managing a household and build an enterprise through arduous effort; 9, Be benevolent and willing to bring benefit to fellow villagers; and 10, Protect the environment and pay attention to hygiene. Qin Shuli, p. 31, Ma Shaoning (ed.), Part one, p. 16.

29. Ma Shaoning (ed.), Part one, p. 16.

30. Qin Shuli, pp. 31–5; Ma Shaoning (ed.), Part two, p. 18.

31. The campaign was launched in order to show 'three civilizations': 'speaking a civilized language', 'setting up civilized things', and 'making civilized people'. See Ha'erbin shi jingshen wenming jianshi huodong weiyuan hui, 'Kaizhan "san wenming" huodong: tuijin wenming chengshi jianshe' (Develop 'three civilizations' activities: carry forward the building of civilized cities), *Wenming xiangdao*, No. 1, 1991, pp. 21–2.

32. See Zhonggong zhongyang Mao Zedong sixiang yanjiushi bianxiezu (ed.), *Sixiang zhengzhi gongzuo jiaocheng* (Lectures in political–ideological work), Beijing,

Zhonggong zhongyang dangxiao chubanshe, 1987, p. 178; Sichuan jiaoyu xueyuan (ed.), *Jiaoyu xue* (Pedagogy), Chengdu, Sichuan jiaoyu chubanshe, 1984, p. 306.

33. The programme was broadcast on the Beijing TV station's Channel Six. Contestants were nominated by the neighbourhoods and townships where they lived, as well as by their wives. See *China Daily*, 9 July 1991, p. 6.

34. Dazhai and Daqing, for example, for a long period were examples of places that organized agriculture and industry in an exemplary way. They were promoted as examples for others to learn from and emulate. It was later revealed that these were to a certain degree staged and constructed examples, and the Dazhai model in particular has been associated with the strategies of the Cultural Revolution. The Daqing oilfield, however, has been re-utilized as a model during the reforms.

35. The distinction is used by Donald Munro, and I have adapted the concepts somewhat to my own thinking on this matter. See Donald J. Munro, p. 168.

36. Charles P. Cell has seen the Chinese 'campaign' (*yundong*), the large-scale model emulation drives, in the picture of such information technology. See Charles P. Cell, *Revolution at Work: Mobilization Campaigns in China*, New York, Academic Press, 1977.

37. The stories about the 'good entrepreneur' were also aimed at reducing the unpopularity of the newly rich. The party campaigns propagating 'getting rich' (*fa cai*), and the benefits of 'ten thousand yuan households' (*wanyuanhu*) have been summed up as one-sided, and it was admitted that these campaigns led to much resistance among people. See Yi Changtai, 'Jingji gaige yu shehui xinli' (Economic reform and social psychology), *Zhongguo jingji wenti*, No. 3, 1987, pp. 1–6, 21; also in *C4 Shehuixue, Fuyin baokan ziliao*, No. 4, 1987, p. 81.

38. A look through the *China Daily* from 1990 to 1992 reveals a wide range of articles on models. The articles from this and other sources are too numerous to be quoted, but a selected clutch of articles on family harmony is worth mentioning. On happy family models, see *China Daily* (*CD*), 3 March 1990, p. 3; on a young man adopting two elderly people and sacrificing himself for their happiness, see *CD*, 28 February 1990, p. 6; on 50 women being awarded the title of 'virtuous daughter-in-law'; *CD*, 8 April 1991; on dutiful girls, *CD*, 24 February 1992, p. 6, and *CD*, 24 September 1992, p. 6; on model husbands, *CD* 25 April 1991, p. 4, and *CD*, 9 July 1991, p. 6. This impression of the new strong emphasis on family harmony was underlined in my interviews with Beijing class teachers. The interviews showed that emphasis on family and filiality had in recent years become quite a common aspect of the school curriculum, sharing the spotlight with patriotism and collectivism. Still that omnipresent soldier of good deeds, Lei Feng, dominated the picture. A presentation of Lei Feng and the different models of the 1980s is given in Beate Geist, 'Lei Feng and the "Lei Fengs of the Eighties"', *Papers of Far Eastern History*, No. 42, September 1990, pp. 97–124.

39. Zhang Xuemin, 'Zun lao jing xian yingdang chengwei shidai fengshang' (Respecting the old and the virtuous should become the practice of the times), *Shehui kexue jikan*, No. 4, 1989, pp. 29–32.

40. To give an impression of the scale of such campaigns, it is worth noting that as many as one-tenth of the 42,000 households in Huang county were elected 'five good families'. See Zhou Lu, Yang Ruohe, and Hu Ruyong, *Qingshaonian fanzui zhonghe zhili duice xue* (Studies in how to deal with comprehensive control of juvenile crime), Beijing, Qunzhong chubanshe, 1986, pp. 167–9.

41. On symbolic equivalents in modelling theory, see Urie Bronfenbrenner, *Two Worlds of Childhood: US and USSR*, New York, Simon & Schuster, 1972, p. 130.

42. Zheng Xinran, 'Bangyang huodong yu ren de xinli fenxi' (A psychological analysis of education by model activities), *Qingnian chao*, No. 3, 1990, pp. 17–20.

43. Huazhong shifan xueyuan jiaoyuxi *et al.* (eds.), *Deyu xue* (Moral education), Xi'an, Shaanxi jiaoyu chubanshe, 1966, p. 173.

44. Jiang Haohua and Zhang Lin, 'Dui bangyang jiaoyu fangfa de zai renshi' (Towards a new understanding of model education), *Qingnian yanjiu*, No. 2, 1987, p. 7.

45. Wu Zhuo, 'Guanyu xuexi Lei Feng de jiu ge shiji wenti shiyi' (Clearing up some practical questions about learning from Lei Feng), *Zhongguo gaodeng jiaoyu*, No. 10, 1990, p. 24.

46. Zhu Jiang and Zhang Yaocan, *Daxue deyu gailun* (Introduction to university moral education), Wuhan, Hubei jiaoyu chubanshe, 1986, p. 242.

47. Sun Xiting, Jin Xibin, and Chen Xiaobin are among those who advocate this approach from below; see p. 231.

48. Robert A. LeVine and Merry I. White, *Human Conditions: The Cultural Basis of Educational Development*, New York/London, Routledge & Kegan Paul, 1986, p. 35.

49. Cultural heroes can live for centuries, and reappear in the strangest circumstances. For example, in 1943, when Joseph Needham visited peasants in Sichuan, they had already identified the principal participants in the war: Mao Zedong, Chiang Kai-shek, and the Japanese invaders. 'It will happen as it did before, the North will win', the peasant explained, talking about the incidents of the Three Kingdoms (*San guo*) from the period AD 220–65. Mao, situated in Yenan in the north, represented for them the cultural hero Cao Cao, the leader of the northern and then victorious state of Wei; Chiang Kai-shek represented Zhuge Liang of the Shu kingdom in the west; and the Japanese ally Wang Jingwei was sitting in Nanjing in the west, like the ruler of the ancient kingdom of Wu. The peasants were talking about the heroes of virtue and vice of the third century as if it were only a few years ago, Needham observed, somewhat shocked. See Colin A. Ronan and Joseph Needham, *The Shorter Science and Civilization in China*, Vol. 1, Cambridge, Cambridge University Press, 1978, p. 43.

50. Dorothy Norman, *Hero: Myth/Image/Symbol*, New York, Anchor Books Doubleday, p. 5.

51. A presentation of the research report conducted by the Institute of Sociology of the Chinese Academy of Social Sciences is given by one of the researchers, Wang Zhenyu, in *China Daily*, 20 August 1988, p. 4. Indeed, the point of heroism and 'blood sacrifice' made by certain student leaders was to become a tragic reality only a few months later, in the spring of 1989 as shown in Carma Hinton's TV documentary, 'The Gate of Heavenly Peace'.

52. Among those having spilled their blood during that night, only the 'soldier martyrs' qualified for the notion of 'heroic sacrifice' in the official propaganda. On the 'soldier martyrs' of the Tiananmen massacre, see Beate Geist, pp. 110–12. The campaign of learning from these alleged soldier heroes was very short indeed, and probably wrought more havoc to the picture of 'heroic deeds' than any other incident and campaign before it.

53. Urie Bronfenbrenner, p. 131.

54. Rueben M. Baron, 'Social reinforcement effects as a function of social reinforcement history', *Psychological Review*, Vol. 73, No. 6, 1966, pp. 527–8. Baron uses the abbreviation 'SRS' for social reinforcement standard.

55. Eileen Polley Blumenthal, 'Models in Chinese Moral Education: Perspectives from Children's Books', Ph.D. dissertation, University of Michigan, 1976.

56. In one Chinese survey among 88 secondary schoolchildren, Kohlberg's methods were used to test the effects of model learning. A story about stealing in order to help a sick person was evaluated after seeing a film about the soldier model Lei Feng. According to the report, the children's moral knowledge and behaviour improved after a short period. Zhang Jilian, 'Bangyang jiaoyu youxiao tujing de bijiao yanjiu' (Comparative research on the effective ways of model learning), *Xinli xuebao*, No. 1, 1984, pp. 27–33.

57. See Urie Bronfenbrenner, pp. 132–3. For an account of the importance of a model's competence in effecting children's imitative behaviour, see James H. Thomas, Kathleen M. Due, and Diane M. Wigger, 'Effects of the competence and sex of peer models on children's imitative behavior', *Journal of Genetic Psychology*, Vol. 148, No. 3, 1987, pp. 325–32.

58. Zhongguo renmin jiefangjun zong zhengzhibu quncong gongzuobu (ed.), 'Jinyibu gaohao junmin gongjian jingshen wenming de huodong' (Do a still better job in building a spiritual civilization with army–people joint activities), *Qiushi*, No. 15, 1990, p. 18.

59. Ibid., p. 19.

60. For a more detailed account of models and heroes in Chinese society and their uses, see Beate Geist, 'Vorbilder in Revolution und Reform: Die Modellierung des Menschen in der Volksrepublik China', unpublished manuscript, Ludwig-Maximilian-Universität, Munich, 1989. Geist presents a short biography of 90 named models and heroes, giving a good picture of the norms and values represented by the texts of exemplary models. See also Betty Burch, 'Models as agents of change in China', in Richard Wilson *et al.* (eds.), *Value Change in Chinese Society*, New York, Praeger, 1979, pp. 122–37; Mary Sheridan, 'The emulation of heroes', *China Quarterly*, No. 33, 1968, pp. 47–72; Donald J. Munro, 'The Chinese view of modeling', *Human Development*, Vol. 18, No. 5, 1975, pp. 333–52; and Donald J. Munro, *The Concept of Man in Contemporary China*, pp. 135–57. On the models of the reform period, see Beate Geist, 'Lei Feng and the "Lei Fengs of the Eighties"', pp. 97–126, and Stanley Rosen, 'Prosperity, privatization, and China's youth', *Problems of Communism*, March/April 1985, pp. 1–28. There are also several biographies and diaries of exemplary models published in Chinese: see e.g. Wang Jie, *Wang Jie riji* (Wang Jie's diaries), Beijing, Renmin chubanshe, 1965; Lei Feng, *Lei Feng riji* (Lei Feng's diaries), Beijing, Jiefangjun wenyi she, 1966; and another version of his diaries in Zong zhengzhibu (ed.), *Lei Feng riji xuan* (Selections from Lei Feng's diaries), Beijing, Jiefangjun wenyi chubanshe, 1989; Qiu Shaoyun, *Jiti zhuyi de yingxiong* (Heroes of collectivism), Shanghai, Renmin chubanshe, 1971; and *Qingnian yingxiong de gushi* (Stories about young heroes), Beijing, Zhongguo qingnian chubanshe, 1978. There are also short biographies of a great number of heroes and models in the encyclopedia *Cihai* (The ocean of words), Shanghai, Shanghai cishu chubanshe, 1985.

61. These models of disorder were used in a political power struggle during the Cultural Revolution. Some of them even became prominent political figures, like Zhang Tiesheng, who allegedly handed in a blank examination paper to protest against the methods of university entrance examinations. In another example, primary school pupil Huang Shuai was made into a model for protesting teacher authority. Both models were later condemned for having been used in the power struggle by the so called 'Gang of Four' faction in the party leadership. On Zhang Tiesheng, see *Renmin ribao*, 10 August 1973, p. 1, and 6 January 1976, p. 1. Zhang was later called a counter-revolutionary element, and was arrested in 1977. See *Renmin ribao*

28 December 1978, p. 2, *SWB-FE*/5466, 18 March 1977, p. B2/1-2; see also Jonathan Unger, *Education under Mao: Class and Competition in Canton Schools 1960–1980*, New York, Columbia University Press, pp. 198, 288. On Huang Shuai, see *Renmin ribao*, 28 December 1973, p. 1, and Stanley Rosen, 'Education and the political socialization of Chinese youths', in John Hawkins (ed.), *Education and Social Change in the People's Republic of China*, New York, Praeger, 1983, p. 109.

62. Dorothy Norman, p. 139.
63. Joseph Campbell, p. 388.
64. Tan Zhen and Hu Shouhe, 'Lun shehui jiazhi he ziwo jiazhi' (On social value and self value), *Wuhan daxue xuebao (shehui kexue ban)*, No. 3, 1988, pp. 46–51.
65. See Émile Durkheim, *The Elementary Forms of Religious Life*, trans. Joseph W. Swain, London, Free Press of Glerncoe, 1948.
66. *Qingnian yingxiong de gushi* (Stories about young heroes), Beijing, Zhongguo qingnian chubanshe, 1978, pp. 34–72; *Cihai* (The origin of words), Vol. 3, Beijing, Shangwu yinshuguan, 1984.
67. See *Cihai*, p. 1194.
68. Wu Naitao, 'Su Ning: a pace setter', *Beijing Review*, Vol. 34, No. 28, 1991, pp. 27–8.
69. Duan Mingjun, 'Peiyang xuesheng zijue zili zixue' (Foster students self-consciousness, abilities in taking care of themselves, and self-studies), *Nei mengge jiaoyu*, No. 1, 1988, p. 11.
70. Gu Liping, 'Shi lun bangyang zai jiaoyu zhong de zuoyong' (On the effect of models in education), *Jiaoyu yanjiu*, No. 5, 1988, p. 42.
71. The debate took place in the Army paper *Jiefangjun bao* in April 1992. In another incident, an official who captured two murderers with guns did not shed any of his blood in the process; again, the deed did not qualify as heroic, in contrast to the many heroic models who were killed or crippled struggling against criminals (from *China Daily*, 11 July 1992, p. 4).
72. *China Daily*, 28 February 1990, p. 6.
73. See presentation of Zhang Hua in *Zhongguo baike nianjian 1983*, Shanghai, Zhongguo da baike quanshu chubanshe, 1983, pp. 15–16.
74. *Cihai*, p. 83.
75. Jiang Zemin, 'Xiang Lai Ning xuexi: zuo shehui zhuyi shiye jieban ren' (Learn from Lai Ning: become successors to the socialist cause), *Fudaoyuan*, No. 11, 1990, pp. 4–5. A long range of articles on learning from Lai Ning can be found in the journal *Fudaoyuan* (Political instructor) in 1989–91. The Beijing schools I visited in the summer of 1991 also ran campaigns in learning from both Lei Feng and Lai Ning.
76. Cui Chunbao, 'Cong chuantong guannian zhong jiefang chulai' (Liberation from traditional concepts), *Qingnian shidai*, No. 4, 1985, p. 7.
77. Jiang Haohua and Zhang Lin, p. 6.
78. Huadong liu sheng yi shi jiaoyu xueyuan xiezuo (ed.), (*Xuexiao jiaoyuxue* (School pedagogy), Zhejiang jiaoyu chubanshe, 1987, p. 174; Hu Yinsheng and Wang Li (eds.), *Jiaoyu xue* (Pedagogy), Beijing, Renmin chubanshe, 1987, p. 286; Gu Mingyuan and Huang Ji (eds.), p. 281.
79. Gu Liping, p. 42.
80. Liu Ke *et al.* (eds.), *Deyu zhishi cidian* (Dictionary of moral knowledge), Shanghai, Shanghai jiaotong daxue chubanshe, 1987, p. 190; Zhonggong zhongyang

Mao Zedong sixiang yanjiushi bianxiezu (ed.), *Sixiang zhengzhi gongzuo jiaocheng* (Lectures in political–ideological work), Beijing, Zhonggong zhongyang dangxiao chubanshe, 1987, p. 170.

81. Gu Liping, p. 43.
82. Infants (*you'er*) can imitate only in a mechanical way, and their imitation is not based on choice. The child (*ertong*) period represents the gradual introduction of evaluative abilities; here one should take care to foster the ability to differentiate between right and wrong. During the adolescent (*shaonian*) period, normally described as the 10–16 year age group, the young are capable of self-conscious seeking of images, and this is where correct guidance is needed. In the youth (*qingnian*) period models should be rich and many-sided. See Jiang Haohua and Zhang Lin, pp. 6–7.
83. Zhang Lifu, 'Xianjin yinggai shi huoshengsheng de' (Advanced [persons] must be lively), *Zhongguo qingnian bao*, No. 20, 1981, p. 11.
84. Qian Mingfang, 'Bangyang jiaoyu xiaoying ruohua de yuanyin yu duice' (The weakening of the model education effect and its countermeasures), *Pujiao yanjiu*, No. 3, 1990, p. 13.
85. Ibid.
86. Huazhong shifan xueyuan jiaoyuxi *et al.* (eds.), *Deyu xue* (Moral education), Xi'an, Shanxi jiaoyu chubanshe, 1985, p. 177; and Zhonggong zhongyang Mao Zedong sixiang yanjiushi bianxiezu (ed.), p. 179.
87. Gu Liping, p. 42.
88. Beate Geist, 'Lei Feng and the "Lei Fengs of the Eighties"', pp. 97–124; Lei Feng, *Lei Feng riji*, pp. 8–9.
89. Fang Lizhi has called the Lei Feng spirit a 'tool theory', indicating that persons become tools for a state machinery instead of developing their own individuality if they follow the prescribed spirit: see Zhang Yusheng, 'Lei Feng jingshen shi yongheng de' (The Lei Feng spirit is eternal), *Hongqi*, No. 7, 1987, p. 47. In his criticism of the campaigns for learning from Lei Feng, Liu Binyan has seen the same spirit as an attempt to make people into 'docile tools' for the Party: see *Renmin ribao*, 25 January 1987, p. 1.
90. See Lei Feng, *Lei Feng riji shi wenxuan* (Selections of Lei Feng's diaries and poems), Beijing, Zhanshi chubanshe, 1982, p. 15, and Lei Feng, *Lei Feng riji*, p. 10.
91. Among other things, it was revealed that Lei Feng, the leading model of thrift, actually had woolen trousers and a Swiss watch, symbols of luxury during the years of poverty in the late 1950s and early 1960s: see *SWB-FE* 0095, 9 March 1988, p. B2/3, and *China Daily*, 12 January 1989, p. 4.
92. Huadong liu sheng yi shi jiaoyu xueyuan xiezuo (ed.), p. 174.
93. Qian Mingfang, p. 13.
94. Shen Xiping, 'Xue yingxiong, xuyao yizhong jiankuang de shehui daoxiang' (Learning from heroes needs healthy guidance by society), *Nianqing ren*, No. 9, 1989, p. 5.
95. The debate soon spread to the People's Daily, and was of its most intense in August and until mid-September 1988. After the People's Daily's opening article (*Renmin ribao*, 6 August 1988, pp. 1, 3) came scores of articles on the issue on page 3 during this period.
96. Zhong Peizhang, 'Qingnian jiaoyu de kunhuo' (The perplexity of youth education), *Qiushi*, No. 5, 1988, p. 24.
97. Cao Jiongfang, 'Bangyang: daode renge yu pubian renge' (Models: moral personalities and normal personalities), *Nianqing ren*, No. 10, 1989, p. 41.

98. The letter was originally published in *Renmin ribao* in August 1988 and was quoted in *China Daily*, 12 January 1989, p. 4.

99. The classical definition of the 'rate buster' is: 'You should not turn out too much work: if you do, you are a rate "buster" '; it is found in F. J. Roethlisberger and William J. Dickson, *Management and the Worker: An Account of a Research Program Conducted by the Western Electric Company, Hawthorne Works, Chicago*, Cambridge, Mass., Harvard University Press, 1947, p. 522. The informal collective in the Hawthorne research programme also had norms against working too little ('chiseller'), and against reporting to the supervisor anything that would react to the detriment of an associate ('squealer').

100. *China Daily*, 8 January 1987, p. 4.

101. Chen Sheng and Zhao Li, 'Dangdai qingnian de sixiang daode tedian jiqi chengyin' (The ideological and moral characteristics of modern youth and their cause of formation), *Jiaoyu yanjiu*, No. 7, 1990, pp. 61, 63.

102. *Radio Beijing*, 16 February 1982, in *Foreign Broadcast Information Service: China*, (hereafter *FBIS-CHI*) 82-035, 17 February 1982, p. K2.

103. One example is Dai Birong, who was crippled in the 1960s while rescuing three children from drowning; she got her titles of honour, but lost her right to study or lead the life she wanted. Another is Zhu Guo'an, who was stabbed in the eyes trying to safeguard state property. On Dai Birong, see editorial comment in *Nianqing ren*, No. 8, 1989, p. 22; on Zhu Guo'an, see *China Daily*, 3 June 1989, p. 4.

104. See editorial article in *Nianqing ren*, No. 12, 1989, p. 12.

105. Lai Yangchun, 'Xuexiao daode jiaoyu yu shehui daode pingjia de fancha' (The contrast between moral education in school and moral evaluation in society), *Zhengzhi jiaoyu*, No. 11, 1987, p. 44.

106. Li Weiwei, 'Shehui xuyao yingxiong, yingxiong xuyao shehui baohu' (Society needs heroes, heroes need society's protection), *Nianqing ren*, No. 9, 1989, p. 4.

107. Zhang Haidi, a paralysed girl, was also one of the top exemplary models first promoted in 1983. See *Renmin ribao*, 8 March 1983, pp. 1, 3. Zhu Boru, a soldier in the Wuhan airforce, was like Zhang Haidi one of the new models promoted in 1983. He had saved several people in danger, and helped others economically. Among other things, he paid the medical expenses for an old man who fell ill, and whom he did not know; he even gave a blood donation to the man in the hospital. Zhu was praised as a 'contemporary Lei Feng' (*dangdai Lei Feng*), and a 'living Lei Feng' (*huo Lei Feng*) and used as a model for 'serving the people'. See *Zhongguo baike nianjian 1984*, Beijing/Shanghai, Zhongguo dabaike quanshu chubanshe, 1984, p. 14; *Guangming ribao*, 2 March 1983, p. 4; *Renmin ribao*, 5 March 1983, p. 4. For further details on Zhu Boru and Zhang Haidi, see Beate Geist, 'Vorbilder in Revolution und Reform', pp. 130–3, 142–4.

108. Yang Ye, 'Ku a! Zai ouxiang guanghuan li' (Oh bitterness! Inside the halo of an idol), *Nianqing ren*, No. 8, 1989, pp. 22–3. Yang Ye claims to be writing on behalf of a young factory worker in Xiangtan.

109. See Susan Shirk, *Competitive Comrades: Career Incentives and Student Strategies in China*, Berkeley/Los Angeles, University of California Press, 1982.

110. Martin King Whyte, *Small Groups and Political Rituals in China*, Berkeley/Los Angeles, University of California Press, 1974, pp. 122, 124.

111. *Liaowang*, quoted from *China Daily*, 11 May 1993, p. 4.

112. Jiang Haohua and Zhang Lin, p. 8.

113. Sergei N. Eisenstadt, *From Generation to Generation*, New York, Free Press, 1971, p. *xviii*.

114. Max Weber, *Grundriss der Sozialökonomik*, Vol. 3, *Abteilung: Wirtschaft und Gesells-chaft*, 3rd edn., Tübingen, Verlag von J. C. B. Mohr, 1947, p. 140; trans. taken from Max Weber, *The Theory of Social and Economic Organization*, trans. A. M. Henderson and Talcott Parsons, New York, Free Press, 1964, pp. 358–9.

115. Ibid., pp. 142–3; English edn. pp. 363–4.

116. Dorothy Norman, pp. 3, 7, 23.

117. Ibid., p. 4.

118. Such a blight has certainly descended on the Bible and on a great part of the Christian cult, says Joseph Campbell, p. 249.

119. Jean-François Lyotard, *The Postmodern Condition: A Report on Knowledge*, Manchester, Manchester University Press, 1984, pp. *xxiv*, 37.

120. On emperor Shun (*Shundi*), see *Renmin ribao (haiwai ban)*, 8 April 1993, p. 3.

121. On Jiang Zemin promoting the Yan'an spirit, see *China Daily*, 15 September 1989, p. 1. The deeds and thrift of revolutionary leaders like Mao Zedong, who was 'dressed shoddily and had simple vegetarian meals', Zhu De, 'who was already in his fifties then, still cultivated land, collected manure, and walked rather than rode in cars', and Zhou Enlai, who 'wove yarn and cloth and took part in production', are emphasized in an official party propaganda article on the Yan'an spirit. In propagating the spirit, 'one should use typical examples of plain living and hard work that appear in the course of reform and opening up' (Zhang Boxing, 'Yongyuan jicheng fayang jianku fendou de Yan'an jingshen' (Forever carry on the Yan'an spirit of plain living and hard work), *Qiushi*, No. 19, 1990, p. 6.

122. On Deng Xiaoping praising Daqing, see *China Daily*, 6 October 1989, p. 4; on the Daqing spirit, see *China Daily*, 28 September 1989, p. 1. Wang Jinxi, the 'iron man' (*tieren*), was one of the most used models of socialist construction in the 1960s. See also Leslie W. Chan, *The Taching Oilfield: A Maoist Model of Economic Development*, Canberra, Australian National University Press, 1974, and 'The Man of Iron': Wang Chin-hsi', *China Reconstructs*, No. 5, 1966, pp. 2–5.

123. Jiao Yulu was secretary of the Communist Party Committee of Lankao County, Henan Province, from 1962 to spring 1964, during a period when China was plagued by natural disasters and famine. Despite a serious illness, he worked day and night to help those who suffered. He was finally overcome by illness and died in May 1964 at the age of 42. A film about Jiao Yulu became a big hit in China in 1991. See *China Daily*, 16 March 1991, p. 4, and *Renmin ribao*, 27 February 1991, p. 1. On the Kong Fansen campaign see *Renmin ribao*, 8 April 1995, p. 1.

124. Mao Zedong appeared as a popular symbol of the orderly society of the 1950s, and also as a protest symbol against the upheavals of the ongoing reforms. The Mao fever, which originated at the grass-root levels of civil society, was rapidly utilized from above and made into a symbol of unity and stability, as well as a legitimating symbol of reform. On the Mao fever, see Zhang Zhanbing and Song Yifu, *Zhongguo: Mao Zedong re* (China: the Mao Zedong fever), Beijing, Beiyue wenyi chubanshe, 1991; and Liu Feng, 'Shehui huaijiu xintai toushi' (Perspectives on the nostalgic mentality in society), *Shehui kexue*, No. 7, 1990, pp. 21–8. Geremie R. Barmé's anthology, *Shades of Mao: The Posthumous Cult of the Great Leader*, Armonk, NY, M. E. Sharpe, 1996, is an informative and read-able work on this topic in English.

125. *Zhongguo jiaoyubao*, 7 July 1988, p. 2.

126. Shi Jinyao, 'Qiantan bangyang jiaoyu ying zunxun de yuanze' (On the principles to be followed in moral education), *Fudaoyuan*, No. 4, 1991, p. 24.

III

律

*Norms, Discipline, and the
Exemplary Order*

6

Discipline and the Exemplary Norm

THE dichotomy between morality and law has been seen as a dichotomy between traditional and modern forms of organizing and establishing order in society. Such a dichotomy, however, does not quite seem to fit the reality of order. In China there have been attempts to strengthen law during the reforms. But this tendency is a very uneven one, and, as we have seen through the emphasis on spiritual civilization, morality has maintained a strong position throughout the whole period of reform, and has even been considerably strengthened in the 1990s.

The emphasis on law during the reforms has not been developed in opposition to morality. Rather, law has been intended to underline the moral approach to order. Chinese criminology and jurisdiction are full of moral considerations. The dichotomy between law and morality in China is a parallel to the relationship between law and norms in Western development. Foucault has pointed out that modernity does not mean the strengthening of the law at the expense of the norm. The juridical mode of order and governance characterized by confinement and repression has increasingly been replaced by the building character of 'bio-power', and this type of power has imposed upon life a system of regulations and detailed inspection:

Another consequence of this development of bio-power was the growing importance assumed by the action of the norm, at the expense of the juridical system of the law . . . The law operates more and more as a norm, and . . . the judicial institution is increasingly incorporated into a continuum of apparatuses . . . whose functions are for the most part regulatory.[1]

While the law always refers to the sword, corrective and regulatory mechanisms dominate the disciplinary sphere of the norm. In *Discipline and Punish* Foucault argues that discipline is not concerned primarily with prison and confinement, but that prison is rather the purest expression of the disciplinary order. Prison, confinement, and lastly death are preceded by the norm and its regularization. Norms lead and transform the negative restraints of the juridical into the more positive controls of normalization. The effectiveness of the norm in regulating society is obvious. A discipline based on the norm is more durable than one based on outer force only because it seeks to bind people to society with their own ideas. It is linked to power in a way that is less likely to manifest force or violence. Regulation through the norm is based more on willed consent, and functions more like a positive restraint. In China, regulation through the norm is of strategic importance for the programme of spiritual civilization, and defines a main approach in the regulation of order. The norm, however, can be linked both to the average and to the exemplary. In the following paragraphs I will trace the differences between the average or the normalized on the one hand and the exemplary on the other. The special techniques of regulation and control implemented in China are linked to the exemplary norm in ways that form the basis of Chinese social engineering practices. The exemplarity of norms has many paradoxical consequences for the implementation of discipline and order.

On Average and Exemplary Norms

The norm is a measurement and a means of producing a common standard, but such a standard may be constituted in various ways. Models have been used to set standards and to increase the salience of norms. Norms can be enormously durable. Here we may recall Shils's remark that the normative core of tradition is the inertial force which holds society in a given form over time. That the norm is linked to inertia and durability, however, does not necessarily mean that norms will remain consistent over time. On the contrary, norms are inconsistent almost by definition. Even if norms might have moved slowly in a traditional context, their inconsistency wins out in the long run. A norm cannot bind anyone for an indefinite period, as a law (in principle) can.[2] Norms are social entities: they do not exist in isolation. The norm is open to active manipulation and construction, and persistent efforts have been made to spread the constraining effects of the norm throughout society, both in China and in the West. Norms are embedded in the memories of the past, but are actively constructed to serve the dreams of the future. The norm establishes itself as an order, and the whole society is defined by this order. Norms are not coercive in themselves, but, linked to coercive techniques, they constitute a basic element of order. The norm must be distinguished from, as well as linked to, the techniques of discipline and power that follow in its wake.

The point to emphasize is that there exists a disciplinary technology that builds on the norm, and is linked to the norm in different ways.

Foucault has claimed that the 'disciplinary society' obeys the logic of the norm at the level of 'micro power'. There are various approaches to such micro power, and in Chapters 7 and 8 I will discuss some aspects of it, such as evaluation and registration. The difference from Foucault's European example is that in China the disciplinary technology is linked to the exemplary norm rather than to the average.

Georges Canguilhem's remarks on the etymology of the word 'norm' link the norm to the 'square', opposing the 'twisted, crooked, or awkward'. The norm was thus originally linked to the notion of rectitude:

When we know that *norma* is the Latin word for T-square and that *normalis* means perpendicular, we know almost all that must be known about the area in which the meaning of the terms 'norm' and 'normal' originated, which have been taken into a great variety of other areas. A norm, or rule, is what can be used to right, to square, to straighten . . . The concept of right, depending on whether it is a matter of geometry, morality, or technology, qualifies what offers resistance to its application of twisted, crooked, or awkward.[3]

Canguilhem sees the norm as a mediator between the myth of a golden age and that of chaos. From a golden age, a paradise of guiltlessness without need for correction, the norm develops as a means of correction, preventing the other mythical state of total chaos. In China similar notions of memories of a golden past are linked to fears of a chaotic future and memories of a chaotic past. A norm offers itself as a possible mode of unifying diversity, resolving a difference, settling a disagreement. In the West, the meaning of norm has changed. It still refers to a standard measure that allows us to distinguish that which conforms to the rule from what does not, but this distinction is no longer linked to the notion of rectitude. François Ewald has pointed out that 'its essential reference is no longer to the square but to the average; the norm now refers to the play of oppositions between the normal and the abnormal or pathological'.[4] Even virtue has become normalized. Ewald links his argument to Alphonse Quetelet's theory of the 'average man'. Quetelet defines average man as a 'fictional entity': there is simply no 'average 25-year-old Frenchman' or any other average man, although such a person figures in the mirrors of probability and statistics.[5] Average man does not incarnate a model or original that can serve as the standard for everyone. Average man is linked to the modern norm, and represents a new way of judging individuals. With Quetelet a new means of specifying individuals appears with reference to their position in a group rather than to their essence or ideal state of being. 'The other', rather than an ideal state of morality, becomes the standard of measurement for individuals. Within this normative system, values are not defined a priori, but rather 'through an endless process of comparison'.[6] The exemplary model thus becomes an extreme on a statistical continuum, rather than the main point of reference.

The idea of perfection is not involved in the process of modern standardization,[7] a process quite different from the Chinese production of standards where the details of exemplarity and perfection are mapped out. In Chinese the word for norm or standard—*guifan*—also means 'pattern', 'model', or 'example'. The notion of rectitude and exemplarity is included in the term, and their present rule of the norm is still closely connected to the idea of exemplarity. In the exemplary society the norm is still linked to the ideal or exemplary more than to the average. Exemplarity describes a tighter definition of behaviour than does normality, so an exemplary society represents a 'tighter' type of society. The scepticism towards the average norm is outlined by Durkheim, and also illustrates the Chinese approach to the 'moral sciences'. One simply cannot let the average define the standard of morality in a society. 'No individual can be completely in tune with the morality of his time,'[8] Durkheim claims: there must be a standard higher than the minds of individuals which regulates the order of society:

There is . . . an enormous gap between the way in which values are . . . estimated by the ordinary individual and the objective scale of human values which should in principle govern our judgements. The average moral conscience is mediocre; it feels only slightly the commonest duties and hence the corresponding moral values; it is as though it were blind to some of them. We cannot therefore look to the average for a standard of morality.[9]

There is an ambiguity in the concepts of norm and standard that can be illustrated through the concepts of ideal versus typical, and conformity versus comparison. At times the terms refer to a model of behaviour, an exemplary type of behaviour towards which all behaviour should be directed. In other words, it represents a moral judgement. The terms, as indicated, also refer to the average, median, or typical pattern of 'normal' behaviour. *Webster's Collegiate Dictionary* shares this ambiguity when it defines 'norm' both as 'a rule or authoritative standard . . .' and as 'a set standard of development or achievement, usually the average or median achievement of a large group'. The concept is here used sociologically as both 'ideal' and 'typical'.[10]

'Standard' also has a dual meaning. In the *Encyclopedia Britannica* the article on standardization stipulates that 'a standard is that which has been selected as a model to which objects or actions may be compared.' In the *Collins National Dictionary* a standard is described as 'a model to which others must conform', as an 'established rule, model, etc.', and as 'having a fixed value'.[11] The *Encyclopedia Britannica* definition does not refer to the production of objects that all confirm to a model type. In this sense it is less a question of conforming to a standard model, and more a question of a distribution around an average. When conformity is stressed as the main criterion, then the definition leans more towards the exemplary. The *Encyclopedia Britannica* definition gains in flexibility, while the one in *Collins National Dictionary* lies closer to fixity. There is also comparison in the exemplary regime, but here comparison is made to measure the distance from exemplary norms. A standard might be defined as a criterion established by an authority, custom, or general consent. When the exemplary is rooted in a culture as described earlier by LeVine and White, then standards lie closer to custom or general consent. The more the exemplary is detached from its social and cultural moorings, the more standards are established 'from above' by an authority.

The production of norms and the establishment of standards is a major task of moral–political education in China. In one article on the importance of research in spiritual civilization, Dai Mucai revisits the theories of Qian Xuesen. Since Qian's contributions and program for research on spiritual civilization, no penetrating study has been done in this field. Dai argues for the scientification of exemplarity, for the production of norms and standards to be carried out in a far more systematic and scientific manner:

No perfected or scientific evaluation of standards or particular index system of norms has been set up, except for the establishment of civilized work-units (*wenming danwei*), hygienic work-units (*weisheng danwei*), 'three-good' (students), and 'five-good' (families).[12]

Dai's article is an attempt to build up a methodology of spiritual civilization based on the scientific production of norms and standards. Moral indexes should be established to bind the norm into an effective system of control; thus, the measurement of order and exemplarity is placed on the agenda.

Establishing standards for people is seen as crucial in halting the growing scepticism towards the social practices of reform: 'More and more people are discontented. First the reforms were received with enthusiasm, then perplexity, fear, and alarm set in, and now there is silence', says one textbook of ideological–political work in the aftermath of 1989.[13] On a lower level—in schools—the importance of fixed standards is repeatedly emphasized. A university teacher stresses that the first thing to do in moral education is 'to establish a clear standard for evaluation'.[14] Learning the written official 'Standards for daily student behaviour' is regarded as a basis for moral education. Such standards give a direction to moral education, and are important for the so-called directed leadership (*daoxiang*) in schools. They are used for examining and evaluating the students' moral behaviour and quality, helping them to set their own standards.[15] These rules are equally important for primary school children and university students alike. Shortly after June 1989 the code of conduct for students was reformulated and promoted at the universities.[16] The minute construction of standards is explicitly linked to the discourse on human quality, in particular moral ideological quality. There should be fixed standards about 'what is true and false, what is right and wrong, beneficial or harmful . . . good and evil, sincere and false, beautiful and ugly, honourable and dishonourable, high and low . . . The genuine, the beneficial, the good, and the beautiful should be standards of quality.'[17]

There are also warnings against letting standards drift. Objective criteria should be found; 'vague standards (*mohu biaozhun*) and evaluation by words only (*wenzi biaozhun*) should be avoided'.[18] Dangerous also are the alternative standards of those youths who seek 'the new, the beautiful, the different, the first' in contexts other than those prescribed.[19]

In traditional Chinese society, norms and nature were parts of the same system. Aberrations in the natural order, like changes in weather, earthquakes, floods, and so forth, were seen as occurring in response to human transgressions of social norms, and as willfully commanded by a displeased 'good' Heaven.[20] Today norms and standards are repeatedly described in the language of 'law' and 'necessity'. Individuals are said to be both active and intentional, but their activity takes place within the frame of necessary and objective norms. The unity of norms, self, and society stands as a basic dogma in the literature on moral evaluation. One book on self-cultivation of talents typically states that talents create their own environment, and that people are not slaves of their environment. However, they are not the masters of their environment, either, but only a part of it. To change society, talents must first adapt to it, understanding and respecting that both natural and social change develops according to certain laws. Social norms seem to be included in this scheme of objectivity and law, and the 'insight in necessity' is extended to the norm and normative entities.[21]

The exemplary standard is more inflexible than one based on the average. Even if standards are produced for the sake of controlling or 'holding' society within a certain order, the nature of standards is such that they are constantly fluctuating. According to Ewald,

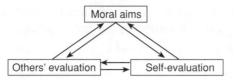

FIGURE 4   The process of evaluating behaviour as described in a Chinese textbook on moral evaluation

Source: Yuan Zhenquan, *Zhongxiaoxue deyu pingjia* (Moral evaluation in primary and secondary schools), Kaifeng, Henan daxue chubanshe, 1988, p. 114.

A standard may become stable or regular, but it is only temporarily so. The standard is a form of compromise, the common denominator, a point of reference that is destined to disappear—a measurement that expresses the relation of a group to itself.[22]

Norms and standards are created by the collectivity, which finds its own twists and turns when the construction of exemplary standards and norms becomes too tight. Standardization cannot be implemented by decree: it constantly escapes the grip of any self-declared standard-bearer. As in the example of the withering exemplary hero, any exemplary standard will exist for a certain period only. A norm can be seen as a river which forces its way through any obstacle that tries to control it or obstructs its path. Exemplarity can be seen as an instrument to dam up this river of social norms. In contrast to the fixity of the exemplary norm, the modern norm is characterized by relativity, contradicting the idea of absolute norms. The notion of 'objective' norms returns as alleged scientification. This modern concept of scientification of course covers up for the reality of renewed absoluteness.

Even if the exemplary is far stronger in Chinese society than in the Western context, there is no 'pure' exemplarity. The evaluation of behaviour takes as its starting points both 'the other' and fixed exemplary standards described as 'moral aims' or 'moral objectives' (*deyu mubiao*). The endless process of comparison of which Ewald spoke is part of the disciplinary use of the norm in today's China. In the techniques of mutual assessment and evaluation, 'the other' is an important part of the moral evaluation system. As shown in Figure 4, the connections between self-evaluation (*ziwo pingjia*), others' evaluation (*taren pingjia*), and the development of moral aims or objectives define the process of evaluation. Both the average and the exemplary lie at the root of the process.

The difference between modern Western societies and modern Chinese society is not that distributions around the average norm do not exist in China, but rather that the average is embedded in a much tighter jacket of exemplarity. This tightness of exemplarity has import-ant and paradoxical consequences for the evenness of norms, and for social order in general.

Dilemmas of the Exemplary Norm

In China setting up standards of conduct, establishing exemplary norms, and enforcing rules has been the natural way of doing things for millennia. The cultures of both China and Japan lie outside the Western tradition and have made strict rule obedience central to their way of life. Strict rules even regulated how people should smile, stand, walk, sit and rise, forming a rigorous etiquette of expression and deportment. In the words of Robert Edgerton in Japan in particular there were 'not ten commandments, but hundreds'.[23]

Some exemplary norms can find grotesque expression. In its most extreme form, the exemplary norm has been linked to the imperative of sacrifice and the morality of filial piety, which even led to *gegu*, the practice of a filial devotee's cutting a piece of flesh from his or her own body for an ailing parent to eat as a specially restorative medicine. There were also several cases of *gegan*—cutting off a piece of one's own liver. This practice became popular in the twelfth century and was seen as the highest expression of virtue.[24] Such exemplary behaviour was hon-oured and rewarded in public, to give it a greater audience.

The more a society is led by such exemplarity, the more it will pro-duce its own counter-effects. Instead of recognizing that the exemplary norm produces its own resistance, in China there still seems to be a strong assumption that the stricter the rule and the more exemplary the norm, the more optimal will be the effect of upholding social order, and the more smoothly will society be expected to develop. Without rules, it has often been said, human life would be chaotic, and no one could be either free or safe. But here agreement stops, and a debate on the nature of norms and rules starts. Edgerton, in discussing rules, exceptions, and social order, asks whether freedom and security are best achieved by rules that are flexible enough to accommodate the com-plexities of human living, or whether rules should be inflexible and rig-orously enforced. Philosophers, scholars, and theologians, he claims, have never ceased debating the proper place of rules in human society, while practical men and women have attempted to find rules that would allow them to cope with their environments and with one another. He also asks why some rules are inflexible while others are flexible, quoting Robert Burton's 'No rule is so general which admits not some exception.'[25]

All cultures have numerous alternatives and flexibilities in their effective norms, even the Chinese exemplary society of seemingly fixed norms. In extreme situations of exemplarity, exceptions even seem to be the rule—as when large segments of the population support standards more honoured in the breach than in their performance. In such cases, the norm itself might lose its controlling authority in general.[26] In China, rules and norms do tend to be inflexible and rigorously enforced. Flexibility thus lies in the breach of the norm. Optimal order does not lie in the exemplary norm, however. Such norms even produce disorder. Exceptions to rules may turn into resistance to rules; as Durkheim observed, 'discipline . . . runs the risk of creating more rebels'.[27] This definitely applies in today's China, as well as in traditional Confucian society. Despite the emphasis on order in Confucian philosophy, it has been argued that a potential of disobedience is evident in Confucianism.[28] I would hold that some of this potential is rooted in the inflexibility inherent in the exemplary norm.

Modernity represents upheaval and violent change of norms and values. Social norms lose their grip as increased social and geographical mobility constantly redefine situations that were once constant. Norms are weakened because of the incessant change in modern society, and norms that once served to regulate human action no longer have an effect. The pace of change has left society in a moral void characterized by a confusion between the old and the new. Along with modernization, society is moving from a situation where social relations operate within tight groups to one in which social relations are increasingly directed towards strangers. This trend is evident in China, even if attempts are made to prolong the segmentary structure of traditional society as a means of ordering the modern. New norms spontaneously emerge to regulate relations among strangers, but such norms need time to become established, and confusion occurs.

Queuing is a good example of what happens when norms regulating action are left in a void. In northern China the expression *jia sair*— to 'jump a queue'—is often used, describing an irritating and recurrent phenomenon. This expression is not found in classical Chinese, whether in dictionaries or in the classical literature.[29] *Jia sair* first appears in the dictionaries of modern Chinese from our own century. The expression as well as the practice are products of modern society. There are several ways of jumping a queue. The 'soft' way involves finding a friend somewhere at the front of the queue. You then start talking, 'forgetting' to step out of it when you arrive at the counter. The 'hard' way is also often used. Here you do not need a friend at all; arriving on the scene, you simply force yourself into line. If you have muscles, or rely on a loud voice and an ugly face, the people behind you are sure to 'remain as silent as a cicada on a winter's day', fearing the consequences of interfering. The modern principle of 'first come, first served' has not yet been established in China. The phenomenon is evident in the most developed parts of China, but rarely found in the marketplace of a traditional village. The practice is especially widespread among the most modernized sections of people; in particular, university students take pride in jumping any queue. Old people complain that the traditional virtues are not heeded any longer, or that the collectivistic style has disappeared, to be replaced by the perils of Western individualism. But Western students do not have the same problem, and when they queue up, disorderly scenes are seldom seen. Both collectivism and individualism seem to be against the jumping of queues.

Norms and morality are not something physical. You cannot just go and get a new one to replace the old. In China there is a story from Zhuangzi (*c.* 370–300 BC) called 'Learning from Han Dan's gait' that illustrates the general problem. Some young people heard that Han Dan walked with an extraordinarily beautiful gait, and went abroad to study the technique. Three years later they returned, but without having been able to learn the beautiful gait. Indeed, they had even forgotten their own, and came back crawling on all fours. In China today, one has as yet failed to learn the modern individualist ways of dealing with strangers in a queue; at the same time, the old collectivism has been lost, leaving the actor with no orderly way to regulate the action. The story has many layers. One of them is about flexibility: that new norms are not allowed to develop spontaneously, and that old and often exemplary norms cast their shadows over new situations. The moral void, as illustrated by the example of the queue, renders the process of modernization even more unstable and uneven. But here such unevenness lies in the process of transformation between the old and the new, and not in the modern norm itself. Even if queue-jumping also occurs in the West, boarding a bus in Beijing at rush hour has convinced me that the problem is real. The word 'jumping' could easily be exchanged for 'fighting'.

As we have noted, an important part of the Chinese strategy for halting the dangers of modernity has been to revisit the memories of order, and to redeploy and use traditional ways of control in the new and modern context. In the Confucian tradition, fixed rules were held up as a remedy for individual confusion. In a classical text, Zhu Xi explains: 'It's only because there are times when man's mind becomes distracted that we set up the many rules to regulate it.'[30] The exemplary norm is meant to produce a fixity that can prevent this distraction and preserve the social order. Now, however, the alleged controlling effect of this fixity is breaking up, and this trend is evident also in the constitution of norms. Exceptions to the exemplary norms and rules become more and more frequent. As the fixity of the exemplary norm no longer seems able to cope with the new situation, the 'looseness' of the average norm more and more seems to take its place. Despite the modern upheaval, however, norms can paradoxically be characterized as more 'even' under modern regimes than in traditional contexts. The point about the modern norm is the relative evenness and stability of emotional restraints. Traditional society is not necessarily the 'static' or 'even' society of popular conception.

Norbert Elias claims that 'the expressions of feeling of medieval people are, on the whole, more spontaneous and unrestrained than in the following period'.[31] The case of medieval Europe is far too complex to be discussed in detail here. Of course, there were vast differences between the sexes, between secular and clerical society, between classes and social strata. The point is that in medieval Europe one found both freer emotional expression and greater repression of anger than tends nowadays to be the case. The 'unevenness' is directly linked to the 'tightness' of a society. Traditional segmentary societies are tighter and more closed than their modern counterparts. In general, 'hate as well as love is more likely to emerge in small, tightly knit communities'.[32] The very segmentary structure that is meant to maintain—and in many ways *does* maintain—social order in China has a two-fold effect, nuancing the picture of control. Restriction and control are produced, but the system also produces its own deviance and resistance. Norms will be 'even' only when they have been established in a way that regulates the new order. Norms are social processes and cannot be contained in fixed rules over time.

The marginal social situation of China, where the old is not yet gone and the new has not yet been introduced, might strengthen the effect of unevenness contained in the traditional. Traditional forms of regulation and control might not adapt to modern society as easily as the technocrats of control have expected. The exemplary pushes society into a memory of order and action that is no longer there, thereby adding to the unevenness of norms. The tightness of exemplary society and the construction of fixed exemplary standards are meant to check the uncertainties of modern society; but the 'traditionalized' approach to norms leads to unevenness, and the inflexibility of the exemplary norm leads to resistance. Instead of strengthening unity and stability, the exemplary norm works against such order. This argument will be further underlined because it shows the vulnerability of exemplary order, and explains how the underlying disciplinary structure is not a system of absolute discipline. When rules and norms are fixed in an exemplary system, flexibility is no longer found in the system itself, but floats on the outskirts, or finds its way entirely outside of it. Chapter 4 described the 'psychology of defiance', and mentioned the fact that moral appeals might have counter-productive effects; Chapter 5 described current resistance against the exemplary do-gooder. Such phenomena form a pattern, strengthened by the inflexibility of the exemplary norm.

The emphasis on precise definitions of the exemplary norm also reflects a misconceived idea of the omnipotence of rules and norms. With their emphasis on rules as social control mechanisms, Chinese theorists of socialization tend towards an 'oversocialized' view of man, even without the heavy emphasis on 'internalization' in Dennis Wrong's critique of functionalist sociology. Writing in 1961, Wrong argued that 'man is social but not entirely socialized', while the scholarly opinion was that people were firmly devoted to their rules and norms and easily socialized to follow the cultural rules.[33] Functionalism has not been blind to the problem of cultural resistance. Malinowski showed that 'primitives' were not slaves of their rules, but could use their rules to their own advantage. Merton's concept of 'negative reference' also points out that 'the negative type involves motivated rejection, i.e., not merely non-acceptance of norms but the formation of counter-norms'.[34] This is what has happened to the Chinese exemplary model. For many it has turned into a negative reference, a model of what not to do. Robin Williams says that such regularized avoidances or violations of utopian and 'heroic' standards are themselves variations in normatively oriented behaviour.[35] Others have described the phenomenon as 'a customary way of not conforming to custom'.[36]

In China there is certainly an awarance of counter-norms and behaviour strategies. On the other hand, surprisingly little of the sociology from Simmel to Goffman or similar lines of thought has been utilized, even if Chinese society in many ways confirms their views of man as an actor, skillfully taking account of the social context in ways calculated to achieve personal advantage. In the corridors of power, the Chinese regime has been skilful in adapting techniques similar to those of the father of such theories, Niccolò Machiavelli. In a Machiavellian 'seeking the practical truth of things',[37] the regime is effectively freeing political action from moral considerations, while the common man is put under the heavy moral surveillance of spiritual civilization.[38] The common man, however, hits back: within a culture there is not only 'transmission of culture' but also resistance to culture. Human action lies in between these two poles of transmission and resistance. China adds to the growing body of empirical evidence from societies throughout the world the fact that strategic interaction is an integrated part of action rather than an exception. It is not only in the West that Goffman-esque individuals manipulate flexible rules for their strategic purposes; strategic interaction is not only a modern phenomenon, but can be found in traditional societies as well. The inflexible rule and the fixed norm also produce their own strategies, as people are forced to improvise action in order to go around the inevitable and impenetrable 'great *Boyg*' of exemplarity, to use Henrik Ibsen's metaphor. In strategic interaction theory, rules are *used*, not followed, and exceptions to rules are natural, even inevitable. In the discussion of *li* and law in China, this flexibility lies right on the surface, but Chinese socialization theory closes the eyes to that fact, proceeding as if nothing had been heard or seen about the use of rules and norms.

In the enthusiastic spirit of crushing the paternal home of functionalism, Lyman and Scott embrace the theories of strategy, claiming that in modern complex societies there are few binding values, and that individuals incessantly 'search for adventure, thrills, novelty'.[39] In modern urban society, people are confronted by such a variety of rapid social changes that meanings are no longer stable. The old forms of social organization break down and new meanings are created. Machiavelli's prince and Goffman's social actor have no interior specifications—situations specify them. The point made by Machiavelli is extremely important for understanding the realities of Chinese socialization. Performance should be ahead of reality. It does not matter whether men are virtuous: what counts is whether they can appear to be so when it matters.[40] The Machiavellian concept of 'man-in-episodes' challenges the rule of the norm, and also finds resonance in Goffman's theories emphasizing the manipulation of rules in an idiom of 'encounters', 'moves', 'ploys', 'gambits', and 'openings', using the theatre or game as his metaphor.

The emphasis on strategies, however, must not replace an 'oversocialized' conception of man by an equally mystifying 'undersocialized' one. While Lyman and Scott come close to such a view, Goffman, despite his main emphasis on strategy, documented the constraints that rules impose on the strategic moves available to actors. He also noted that some rules were so 'incorporated' into the person that they could not be broken, not even for strategic advantage.[41] A 'man-in-society' must be supported by theories of 'man-in-episodes', without replacing society by those episodes. Lyman and Scott argue that the social world is continually created and recreated by man. In this statement lies a fundamental truth that should not be understood or applied one-sidedly. In making their point, they deny the existence of any social world that influences or channels the behaviour of people. In reality, however, people are linked not only to the social norms, but to their own individual narratives, constraining the scope of their strategies. The Chinese approach can be criticized for making the norm, and in particular the exemplary norm, into an omnipotent explanation of socialization and order. Although action is undoubtedly a result of intention and subjective meaning, one should still not underrate or negate the contributory influence of social norms, standards, values, habits, routines, agreements, contracts, and rituals in determining social behaviour. Strategy often takes place against the background of strict social norms. To 'present self', 'select masks', 'save face', etc., are not strategies that exist in a state of meaninglessness and disorder. To state that the world is 'essentialy without meaning', as Scott and Lyman do, fails to grasp the complexity of human action.

'Saving face' is one good example of a strategy highly regulated by strict norms and embedded in the Chinese culture in ways vastly different from the approach of 'meaninglessness'. The concept of 'face' is Chinese in origin, and a translation of *lian* or *mianzi*. Owing to the hierarchical structure and the group-relatedness of Chinese society with its built-in permanency of statuses and hierarchies, face has become a skill based on thorough knowledge of social guidelines. *Lian* is even characterized as a moral face whose dictates are typically internalized.[42] According to David Yau-fai Ho, face is never a purely individual thing, and it does not make sense to speak of a person's face as something lodged within his person: 'it is meaningful only when his face is considered in relation to that of others in the social network'.[43]

On the one hand, Chinese society is regulated by strict norms; on the other, a more leisurely attitude towards the norms can be seen. One of my interviewees, a Beijing intellectual, told me that in China rules are rules only. This means that in China people don't act according to the prescribed rules even though they know them well: they do things in the way they think best for themselves.[44] What he meant was that rules might be followed on the surface, but that people use their own strategies to beat the rules when these are too strict. Everybody knows that rules can be broken, and that flexibility lies in breaking a rule. A. C. Scott's description of the classical Chinese theatre is a good picture of Chinese society as such:

When an actor makes an entry or an exit he obeys a certain procedure in his speech and movements which never varies and is governed by the particular role he plays. This formality is extended throughout the play; the actors use certain movements of their heads, hands and feet to accompany their narration and singing as the plot of the play is unfolded both visually and vocally to an audience primed and fully conversant with dramatic symbolism . . . While the strictest formality controls the actor's performance in the Chinese theatre, the reverse is true of the orchestra and the stage assistants who look after the actor's needs during the course of a performance. The orchestra is placed on the stage . . . but . . . the ceremony and costume which is seen on the Japanese stage is absent altogether in the case of Chinese theatre musicians. They come and go as they please between scenes, show a catholic taste in the costume they wear and in general display a nonchalant attitude to their whereabouts. This attitude is deceptive however and in no way interferes with the precision of their playing. So too with the stage assistants, who leisurely perform their duties in full view of the audience, while the play is proceeding, and remain on the stage throughout. Their attire is often quite informal, particularly in hot weather.[45]

The classical theatre expresses traditional Chinese society in stylized and symbolic yet surprisingly detailed ways. In China great emphasis was laid on ceremony and the punctilious observance of an etiquette covering all aspects of daily living. Ranks of society were strictly distinguished by certain styles of clothing or objects for everyday use. There were standard forms of address between superiors and inferiors. Greetings, the reception and seating of guests, and a host of other matters were all bound by formal rules. This regard for the ceremonial is clearly expressed in the etiquette of former times; in the classical theatre it is also crystallized in the formal speech and gesture of the actor and the costumes he wears. Forms of etiquette and formal rules have changed; but from moral rules and norms down to the small details of etiquette, there have always been strict definitions and standards. Scott emphasizes a sharp difference between the theatres of China and Japan. In the latter everyone, from the actors down to the stage hands, obeys convictions which add to the pattern of movement and stage design as an entity. In China the common man can be seen both as the actor in a strictly regulated play, and as the theatre musician or stage assistant in informal attire, ignoring the play of rules. In China there is flexibility within inflexibility.

Lily Chu has experimented with cross-cultural differences in imitation and conformity between American and Chinese children.[46] Since one of the assumptions about Chinese culture is that it breeds conformity, Chu's findings that Chinese are as frequently non-conformers as they are conformers might surprise us. This anti-conformity is not dictated by sheer strategy alone, and Chu's experiment indicates a core of cultural learning in conformist as well as anti-conformist behaviour. Her findings must be seen in the perspective of a two-dimensional model of conformity that builds on insights from what I have called the imitative–repetitive culture of China. Assumptions about conformity and non-conformity must be linked in with the process of imitation and model learning. Conformity, however, has often been contrasted with non-conformity or independence, the assumption being a continuum with conformity at one end and non-conformity or independence at the other. Such uni-dimensional formulations are inadequate, says Chu, because conformity, independence, and anti-conformity are related to each other as the apexes of a triangle. At least two dimensions are involved here: conformity/anti-conformity, and independence/dependence. The two-dimensional conception emphasizes that both conformers and anti-conformers are similar in the sense that both accept the collective norm to an unusual degree—the conformers in order to agree with the norm, the anti-conformers in order to disagree. The collective norm is not given any weight in the judgement of the independent person. In other words, the latter differs from both the conformer and the non-conformer. The logic is that followed by Tarde in describing the process of counter-imitation. The 'doing or saying the exact opposite' he described as an equally imitative behaviour as yes-saying itself. The behaviour or psychology of defiance so much discussed in Chinese pedagogy and the moral–political literature can in many ways be seen as an acceptance of the cultural 'learning how' without accepting the 'what' of that learning. The 'generalized imitative set' or the 'script' mentioned in Chapter 4 also seems to form the framework of resistance, without preventing that resistance from occurring. For example, learning from models is accepted as such, but the values transmitted by this or that model might be either accepted or rejected altogether. The Chinese seem to be less independent of the model than do Americans.

In Chu's study, experiments with various types of model were used, showing that more Chinese were either conformers or anti-conformers, and more Americans were independent of the model's choice. Chu's findings also indicate the greater meaning and effect of the collective in Chinese society as compared with the greater role played by individualism in American culture. It was predicted and shown that, since Chinese were more sensitive to their surroundings than Americans, the Chinese conformed to the model's choices when the model either had high status or was competent, or when material reinforcement was utilized. Conversely, they showed anti-conformity to the model's choices when the model either had low status or was incompetent, or when there was no material reinforcement. Americans, on the other hand, responded more independently of the model's choices and were more indifferent to the experimental manipulations.[47] While this experiment can explain the duality of conformity and non-conformity in Chinese culture rather than indicating that Chinese are conformers, it also underlines the arguments of dependence dominant in both social psychological theories and sociological theories of 'organized dependence'.[48] Dependence and conformity are two different processes.

The exemplary norm does not bring about the expected optional state of order. Order does not lie in exemplary norms and behaviours alone. Instead, a mixture of factors, including behaviours that are not at all of an exemplary character, contribute to order. Jon Elster is probably correct in asserting that 'Altruism, envy, social norms and self-interest all contribute, in complex, interacting ways to order, stability and cooperation.'[49] Each society and each community will be glued together by a particular, idiosyncratic mix of these motivations. The main ingredients that go into what Elster calls the 'cement of society' seem basically the same in all societies, even if they appear in innumerable combinations.

Reformalization and the Micro Penalty of Discipline

We have seen several examples of how the standards of exemplarity make Chinese individuals into actors in the strictly regulated play. Even the rules of etiquette are subsumed under the ever-present motto of spiritual civilization, and are integrated as a part of the exemplary operating as non-coercive control. China, however, saw an earlier unprecedented attack on the formal rules of society during the reforms that followed the early 1980s. This process is characterized by 'informalization', which has been defined as 'a process in which dominant modes of social conduct, symbolizing institutionalized power relationships, tend towards greater leniency, variety and differentiation'.[50] The regime's strategy for spiritual civilization might in this context be seen as an attempt to reformalize society. Even if formalization has been associated with the traditional, and informalization with the modern, the juxtaposition is impossible to make. Periods of formalization and informalization occur more rapidly, and can be found as waves of shorter duration within traditional as well as modern societies. Cas Wouters sees the waves of informalization as parts of more comprehensive processes of democratization and social equalization carried forward by upwardly mobile groups violating the dominant code of conduct. In the West, striking waves of informalization characterized the turn of the century, the 1920s, and the 1960s and 1970s; the most recent era of informalization ended in the late 1970s. A new phase of stabilization follows informalization periods, and thereafter a formalization process gains the upper hand, with the dominant modes of social conduct tending towards greater strictness, hierarchy, and consensus. One indication of this change can be seen in the popularity of new books on manners and etiquette. During periods of informalization, etiquette books are discarded as handbooks for the perpetuation of social inequality and superficial and hypocritical manuals of snobbery. When formalization again sets in, such books tend to represent regained securities. One such book quoted by Wouters represents a yearning for more formal, stricter codes:

Unlike the legal world, the social world has no coercive measures to put people on the right track and keep them there. But society does see to it that anyone who does not adhere to the proper rules of conduct—whether due to ignorance, a lack of understanding or even unwillingness—puts himself outside the social borders. He is out of the running, he barely counts any more.[51]

In China the *luan*—or chaos—associated with the informalization of reform has led to a similar return to formalization. In many ways the trend has been a spontaneous movement, a nostalgia for order from below, but it has also been directed in campaign-style manner from above. Etiquette has become an integrated part of 'civilization work'. Competitions of 'professional etiquette and bearing in daily life' are arranged, aimed at 'improving youngsters' manner and behaviour', and winners of 'deportment competitions' are now celebrated in the press.[52] Etiquette books promoting the formal rules of the past are also back on the shelves in China, and are selling extremely well. The foreword to one such book states that etiquette can be used to bring order into the confusions of reform:

Today's society is a very confused society owing to the differences in economic status among people and their different lifestyles. Our ways of arranging social relations need to fit these [new] circumstances.[53]

There may be talk of adapting to the changing times, but the rules of etiquette presented in the book are taken from the traditional popular repertoire of etiquette. Again, the securities of tradition are used to mend the scars of modernity. Sometimes, however, a flair of the 'Western' is presented, and translations from Western etiquette manuals are often found in youth magazines and other publications. In part, these present the exotic aspect of westernization, but they also formalize its dangers, thus making the phenomenon less dangerous. In one such article rules for setting the table are given:

There should be thirty centimeters between the knife and the fork. Both should be three centimeters away from the plate on each side as the plate is placed in the middle . . . You should leave your chair on the left side, and push it forward until it nearly touches the tablecloth . . . The man has to get up first and take the chair of the woman . . .[54]

The point about 'civilization' made by the Chinese is interesting in terms of Norbert Elias's theories on the 'civilizing process'. He claims that in Europe ever since the Middle Ages a wide range of natural 'animalistic' acts such as eating, drinking, and sleeping have become increasingly subjected to more and more differentiated regulations, standardized as 'good manners'. We shall later see that habits of eating and drinking are parts of the danger-signs that make up the Chinese continuum of deviance. The dangers of social living are countered by good manners and formal codes of behaviour. In China the standards of good manners and good deeds form the core of the exemplary norm. This development can be viewed as a long-term process of formalization. In Europe, it is only since the end of the nineteenth century that the dominant formalization seems to have been overshadowed by a longer-term process of informalization.

Formalization also seems to describe the main direction of Chinese culture. During the Chinese reforms the dominant formalization has been challenged by the informalization brought about by modern mobility. The upwardly mobile and aspiring reform elite now see the rules of the conservative elite as 'superficiality, ceremony, and formal conversation', and as going against the 'development of the individual personality'—in much the same way as in Elias's description of the bourgeois view of nobility in eighteenth-century Germany.[55] Here we should note, however, that today's reformalization does not only come from the conservative elite. While some of the aspiring elite might be sceptical, and even antagonistic, towards the conservative factions in the Party, many support reformalization as a means of inflicting order upon the people. Tendencies towards reformalization also come from the depth of popular sentiments; indeed, this populist trend is even more important for the stability of Chinese society than any officially orchestrated process.

The reformalization of society through etiquette is but a mild breeze of correction compared with the apparatus of discipline that is linked to the norm and geared towards the production of individuals. The production of exemplary norms has been illustrated through the production of norms and standards, which is again closely linked to the production of individuals along the lines of spiritual and material civilization. A system of disciplinary techniques is mobilized in order to supervise, transform, correct, improve, 'hold', punish, reward, cure, or educate individuals. Foucault has stated that the main function of the disciplinary power is to 'train'—an argument much in accordance with the Chinese expression to 'foster' (*peiyang*). The idea is to 'multiply and use' individuals. Discipline represents a developing and building power. Foucault repeatedly returns to the idea that discipline 'produces' or 'makes' individuals: not only does discipline manage and make use of individuals, it represents a power that constitutes them as its object.[56] This idea is reflected in the Chinese literature on discipline and human improvement. 'The Party and the nation needs qualified talents and should not produce [*chu*] "defective goods" [*cipin*] or "damaged articles" [*canpin*]', according to one book on social control theory.[57] The expression 'qualified talents' is here linked to the 'human quality' of spiritual and material civilizations. Discipline is a part of such quality itself; and 'discipline is the most important trait of the new socialist man'.[58]

We have noted the importance of constructing and upholding standards—*biaozhun*. While the production of norms and standards is concerned with the social body, the techniques of discipline extend further, to controlling individual bodies. Central here is *biaoxian*, which means 'to show, display, manifest, express', or even 'show off'. It concerns moral conduct, but is best translated as 'moral–political manifestation' or 'moral–political expression'. Walder has used the concept in his discussion of industrial sociology, and explains that it describes 'a subjective quality of employees evaluated continuously by leaders . . . It describes a broad and vaguely defined realm of behaviour and attitudes subject to leadership evaluation.'[59] It is especially important to stress the relational aspect of this concept. *Biaoxian* concerns loyalty and other types of behaviour worthy of reward from an authority, or 'the task of selecting good people and good deeds [*haoren haoshi*]'.[60] The concept forms the core of moral and ideological–political education, and also serves as a core concept for the whole disciplinary system in China. Through *biaoxian* one can check each individual's attitude towards the prescribed norms. *Biaoxian* is a way to compare individual behaviour against the prescribed standards. Through *biaoxian*, the category of punishment can be extended to cover anything capable of impressing on the errant individual his or her non-observance of a norm. Every non-observance of the exemplary standards can be punished by an authority. The phenomenon comes close to what Foucault describes as the 'disciplinary penalty of non-observance', that which controls behaviour that does not measure up to the rule or departs from it.[61]

The concept of *biaoxian* is a loose one. It can refer to political ideas only, stressing the degree of patriotism and activities of formal character in moral–political campaigns and the like. It can also be used in a broader meaning, referring to all aspects of individual performance. The concept is in this sense flexible, but the background of judgement is meant to be the inflexibility of the exemplary norm. Good *biaoxian* involves acting in accordance with exemplary norms, or rather in accordance with the definition of such norms as they are held by those in authority. The universality of the exemplary norm is always evaluated from the particularistic view of a person of authority. Blecher and White express this aspect of *biaoxian* by quoting a Chinese interviewee saying that *biaoxian* 'in practice . . . tended to manifest itself or be associated with good relations with cadres'.[62] Paradoxically, then, the alleged universality of the exemplary norm is always filtered through the particularistic reality of a segmentary society.

Biaoxian can also mean to show off. Good *biaoxian* involves the showing off of virtue manifesting these views or values, and thus describes a behaviour that contributes to the overall spectacle of virtue. Bad *biaoxian* is showing off self, disregarding the rules and norms of exemplarity or personal authority. In *biaoxian* we find the cell of the disciplinary system. It becomes the means through which the disciplinary individual is produced. Through *biaoxian*, all kinds of 'little things' come under the surveillance of the norm, and discipline can be exercised over all types of behaviour. A regime of disciplinary power is established, and the issues of reward and punishment spread into the banalities of everyday life and matters of otherwise little interest to the law. Discipline submits a whole mass of behaviour—like the utilization of time and space, speech, physical deportment and cleanliness, sexual activity—to exhaustive, detailed inspection and disciplinary punishment or reward. The situation is summed up by Foucault in his description of 'micro penalty':

The workshop, the school, the army were subject to a whole micro-penalty of time (latenesses, absences, interruptions of tasks), of activity (inattention, negligence, lack of zeal), of behaviour (impoliteness, disobedience), of speech (idle chatter, insolence), of the body ('incorrect' attitudes, irregular gestures, lack of cleanliness), of sexuality (impurity, indecency).[63]

Within such a system of micro penalty, no behavioural phenomenon is too minute or trivial for a norm not to be erected about it, and the slightest departures from the norm are open to surveillance. The building and improving character of discipline enlarges the category of an offence. It is no longer a question merely of infractions of rules: there can even be failures to fulfil a task or to fulfil it in the right spirit. I will in the following chapters show how this phenomenon is paid enormous heed in China, with infractions and the fulfilling of tasks neatly measured. The power of discipline is productive, so one point about this system is that human energies are not so much repressed as they are channelled into more productive directions, making man calculable and useful at the same time.

Discipline here exists in a systematic combination of rewards and punishments. We may also speak of a 'micro penalty of privileges and impositions', an expression used by Foucault to describe the system utilized by the Brothers of the Christian Schools. For example, a pupil was given four or six catechism questions to copy out as a penalty. He could, however, gain exemption from this by accumulating a certain number of privilege points. Rules for obtaining such points were defined as strictly as the penalties for breaking the rules of correct behaviour. For example, the pupil has a penalty of six negative points; he earns a privilege of ten, leaving him with a merit of four points; and so on. Foucault observes that what we have here is a transposition of the system of indulgences. Through the use of awards and debits, thanks to the continuous calculation of plus and minus points, the disciplinary apparatus hierarchizes the 'good' (*hao*) and the 'bad' (*huai*) subjects in relation to one another. A similar system of indulgences is frequently practised in today's China. Evaluation and assessment are important in this overall system of discipline:

Through this micro-economy of a perpetual penalty operates a differentiation that is not one of acts, but of individuals themselves, of their nature, their potentialities, their level or their value. By assessing acts with precision, discipline judges individuals 'in truth'; the penalty that it implements is integrated into the cycle of knowledge of individuals.[64]

Foucault here writes of a 'perpetual penalty', describing a system where each individual 'finds himself caught in a punishable, punishing universality'.[65] My emphasis has rather been on the impossibility of a punishing universality of total control. The production of resistance through the exemplary at least points in that direction. The attempt at perpetual penalty is bound to be unsuccessful, and the exemplary norm can regulate only to a certain extent. Norms also live their own lives outside any attempts at construction.

Opacity, Visibility, and the Exemplary

The constant examination of each individual's *biaoxian* resembles what Foucault calls a 'normalizing gaze', and represents a surveillance that makes it possible to qualify, to classify, and to punish. The concept of visibility is important here. The disciplinary regime of evaluating *biaoxian* represents a visibility through which each individual is differentiated and evaluated. Foucault's argument is that historically the examination of individuals transformed the economy of visibility into the exercise of power. Traditionally what was seen, what was shown and manifested, was power itself. Power was spectacular, while the individual was hidden away. Disciplinary power, on the other hand, is exercised through its invisibility at the same time as it imposes on those subjected to it a principle of compulsory visibility. In discipline, it is the subjects who have to be seen. Their visibility assures the hold of the power exercised over them. Foucault sees the development of discipline as a juxtaposition between the traditional spectacle of pain and power that physically mark the body, and a disciplinary regime based on hidden regulation and the 'marking' of the file emerging with the coming of the modern. Dutton has refuted the argument of such historical juxtaposition and says that there exists 'any neat geometry of transition to be evidenced through transitions in technologies of punishment and social regulation'.[66] While contemporary techniques clearly differ from those of the past, there is no single dividing line which separates these practices from those of the present. This is not to suggest that past and present practices are the same, but it is necessary to counter the argumentation that certain disciplinary techniques represent the modern. The Chinese example shows that Foucault simplifies the argument. There is no simple narrative history of regulation and punishment, and the categories of spectacle and regulation are intermixed, as we shall see.

There are examples of traditional spectacles of public executions in China like those in the West. Since the punishments for crimes were aimed as much to terrify the public as to injure the prisoner, brutal torments were publicly inflicted on the convicted. Whippings and beatings were the order of the day. Forms of execution included decapitation, cutting in half at the waist, lopping off the four limbs, slicing to death, beating to death, driving a wedge into the skull, pulling apart by horses, burying alive, boiling alive, skinning alive, drowning, strangling, and smothering. The worst spectacle of pain of them all was called the Five Penalties. First the victim's nose was cut off, then the limbs, and finally the victim was beaten to death, then decapitated, and chopped into mincemeat, and the remains displayed in the marketplace.[67] Such spectacles of pain were supported by the spectacles of virtue. In particular, the virtuous suicide was put on display. Here is an account of a widow's suicide by hanging in Fuzhou in the mid-nineteenth century:

She was borne to and fro through the streets, seated in a sedan carried by four men, dressed in gaudy clothing, and holding in her hand a bouquet of fresh flowers. After burning incense and candles before the tablets in this temple . . . she returned home and in the afternoon took her life, in the presence of an immense crowd of spectators.[68]

A widow was expected to take her own life instead of being touched by another man after the death of her husband. At least, this was the exemplary norm of traditional Chinese society. The proselytizing biographical sketches of females who had committed suicide to save their honour in times of calamity became standard models in the dynastic histories. In the late Qing dynasty of the past century platforms of virtuous suicides were even erected in the main street. In another account of a virtuous suicide, it is told that after the widow's death 'the spectators cheer uproariously in praise of her virtuous deed. The corpse is then taken home, paraded through the streets with music.'[69] Such spectacles of pain and virtue are not seen today, but the basic theme of visibility and spectacle is maintained in present-day China, as will be shown in Chapter 11. For instance, the practice of street parading (*youjie*) is still followed. To parade through the streets to exhibit someone before the public (*youjie shizhong*) is another technique of parading, making justice visible to the public.

In the following two chapters I will talk more of the disciplinary techniques of regulation. Through techniques of evaluating *biaoxian*, 'human quality' is dissected and 'produced', and in the end 'frozen' into files. Evaluation is about seeing and being seen, evaluating oneself and being evaluated by others. Both introspection and the social gaze are involved in the process. At the same time, the regulator is able to make the disciplinary subjects more visible. The files can in one sense be said to be hidden from view, but as we shall see there is also a central element of spectacle even in the files. Foucault is mistaken in using the file as the prototype of discipline hidden from view, as the regulation juxtaposed to the spectacle.

There are, however, obvious signs of the 'panopticon' described by Bentham and Foucault. The panoptical principle is explained in detail and applied in the telling example of the prison regime of Mao's wife Jiang Qing, in a report only months before she committed suicide in her prison in May 1991:

Jiang Qing is now detained in a room approximately twenty square meters in size. The room is fitted with a special door and windows. One can see the inside clearly from the outside through the door and windows, while one cannot see the outside from the inside. Light can pass through the door and windows, so the room is not dark.[70]

Discipline assumes that social and political unruliness lies in the 'opacity' of the populace to the forces of order. The populace is opaque in the sense that people's lives are unknown to those concerned with their governance. Disciplinary regulation seeks to make the 'opaque' populace visible in many ways. During the Chinese modernization, social mobility represents one way in which disciplinary opacity grows and develops. The changing values that are being experienced represent another aspect of such opacity. Discipline is linked to, and is meant to have the same effect as, the exemplary norm: it fixes, it arrests, or it regulates movements. Discipline is used to prevent opacity in the 'floating population' who wander about the country at random. It makes them visible, which helps to dissipate modern dangers. A highly bureaucratic logic underlies this disciplinary system and the disciplinary techniques aimed at maximal visibility. The disciplinary regime can be seen as an historical movement aimed at transforming highly disruptive economic conflicts and political forms of disorder into quasi-technical or moral problems for social administration.[71] In the final instance, this concerns the administration of modernity itself, and explains why a modernizing regime is not necessarily a more democratic regime. At least there is no automatic response in such a development.

In Foucault's description, discipline is based on the norm, but its influence is invisible and anonymous, and power is hidden from the individual. In China, where the norm is linked to the exemplary model, things are different. The exemplary norm is prescriptive rather than normative, and it lies in the nature of the prescriptive that it should and must be visible. Discipline is linked to a prescribed and consciously willed idea of how society should be. The disciplinary regime thus comes fully equipped with memories of the past and dreams for the future describing a conscious transformation of society. 'Civilized' society, broken down into civilized cities, villages, families, and individuals, is contrasted to its 'uncivilized' counterpart. Power is not spread throughout society in the same way as in Foucault's description of Europe. Nor does visibility operate first and foremost as a panoptical principle: it forms a far more open model where power is characterized more by proximity than by distance. Power is not entirely hidden from view: on the contrary, it is actively and consciously promoted. In China power still explodes into 'moments of truth' on the scaffold and in the heroic deed. The parading of vice and virtue illustrates both dying by the axe of power and sacrificing oneself for the same power. Anagnost has even described the Chinese brand of power as 'extravagantly visible':

It is not anonymous, invisible, and silent, but personal, extravagantly visible, and accompanied by the hushed buzz of voices or the clamor of gongs and drums. The disciplines of the body—its bearing and demeanor, its productivity and reproductivity—are influenced by means of a direct 'address' by the Party as a transcendent authority that bears a recognizable face in the person of the local Party secretary.[72]

A discipline accompanied by gongs and drums is a logical result of the exemplary norm and signifies the very educative effect of the norm. Prescribed exemplarity must be followed, but it is not only the party secretary who represents the transcendent authority controlling whether the norm is followed: the petty bureaucrat, the head of the personnel office keeping the files, the class teacher in charge of moral evaluation, etc.—they are all there, representing a highly visible authority. Each individual knows the norms and the rules, which are recognizable as well as visible. The exemplary norm and the stress on a prescribed order does not make the exemplary society into a society of absolute discipline. The visibility and paradoxically also the very inflexibility of that norm make disciplinary order particularly vulnerable to conscious resistance and change. In many ways this describes a more 'open' system than its Foucaultian counterpart. In some ways the techniques of exemplary discipline serve to strengthen control, but they also undermine it in the long run.

The exemplary norm can never be reproduced in its ideal form, but human quality can always be compared to this ideal. The minute measuring of disciplinary order and human quality found in today's China is a 'permanent measure of a gap in relation to an inaccessible norm and the asymptotic movement that strives to meet in infinity'. The ideal of disciplinary order, as described by Foucault, would certainly be acclaimed by the executors of the Chinese disciplinary system as well. It is described as 'an interrogation without end', and a judgement that would be 'the constitution of a file that was never closed'.[73]

Let us now turn to both these characteristics of disciplinary regulation. The interrogation or the evaluation indeed seems without end, and the file is literally never closed in China. Together these describe the core of the disciplinary technology of human quality.

Notes to Chapter 6

1. Michel Foucault, *The History of Sexuality*, Vol. 1, *An Introduction*, New York, Vintage Books, 1990, p. 144.
2. See François Ewald, 'Norms, discipline, and the law', *Representations*, No. 30, Special issue: 'Law and the Order of Culture', ed. Robert Post, Spring 1990, p. 156.

3. Georges Canguilhem, *On the Normal and the Pathological*, Dordrecht, D. Reidel, 1978, p. 146.
4. François Ewald, p. 140.
5. See Alphonse Quetelet, *Du système social et des lois qui le régissent*, Paris, 1848, and *Sur l'homme et le développement de ses facultés; ou, Essai de physique sociale*, 2 vols., Paris, 1835, quoted from François Ewald, p. 145.
6. François Ewald, p. 152.
7. See Norman F. Harriman, *Standards and Standardization*, New York, 1928, quoted after François Ewald, p. 151.
8. Émile Durkheim, *Sociology and Philosophy*, p. 40.
9. Ibid., p. 83.
10. *Webster's Collegiate Dictionary*, 5th edn., p. 677. See also Philip Selznick, 'Sociological theory and natural law', *Natural Law Forum*, No. 6, 1961, pp. 84–108.
11. *Collins National Dictionary*, rev. edn., London, Collins, p. 474.
12. Dai Mucai, 'Lüelun jingshen wenmingxue' (Brief discussion on spiritual civilization studies), *Shehui kexue jikan*, No. 2, 1991, p. 15.
13. Xu Ming, Chu Xian, Song Defu, and Qiang Wei (eds.), *Sixiang zhengzhi gongzuo daoxiang* (Guidance in ideological–political work), Beijing, kexue chubanshe, 1990, p. 194.
14. Interviewee no. 1, Beijing, 1991.
15. Shanghai shi jiaoxian zhongxiaoxue deyu xiezuo yanjiu hui, *Nongcun zhongxiaoxue banzhuren gongzuo zhidao* (Directions for class teacher work in rural primary and secondary schools), Shanghai, Shanghai kexue jishu chubanshe, 1990.
16. The 'Code of Conduct for Implementation' formulated by the State Educational Commission became effective on 17 November 1989, and contains a mixture of political and moral rules. Among the many points: (1) Students should defend the interests of the motherland; they should not take part in any activity that will damage the motherland's dignity and honour, violate the four cardinal principles, endanger public order, or undermine stability and unity. (8) Students should pay close attention to the cultivation of a fine moral character. They should be clean and dress neatly, and be honest and creditable, modest and prudent, soft-spoken and courteous. They should conduct themselves properly in dealing with the opposite sex; they should respect teachers and fellow students, care for the aged, protect children, and be ready to help others at any time; and they should dare to fight against evil practices. (13) They should observe the dormitory regulations . . . They should not ask people of the opposite sex to stay overnight, and they should not let persons who are not from the college stay overnight in the dormitory without approval. (See *SWB-FE*/0626, 29 November 1989, p. B2/4.)
17. Xin Yang (ed.), *Zhongguo banzhurenxue* (Chinese class teacher studies), Changchun, Jilin jiaoyu chubanshe, 1990, pp. 90, 92.
18. Ibid., p. 185.
19. Peng Xincai, 'Shimao yu qingshaonian weifa fanzui' (Fashion and juvenile criminal offence), *Qingshaonian fanzui yanjiu*, No. 10, 1988, p. 24.
20. Donald J. Munro, *The Concept of Man in Early China*, Stanford, Calif., Stanford University Press, 1969, p. 41.
21. Xu Zhangsong (ed.), *Daxuesheng chengcai xiuyang* (Self cultivation for university students to grow into useful timber), Shanghai, Fudan daxue chubanshe, 1988, pp. 256–7. See also Hu Wei, 'Xiandai deyu pingjia de tedian ji gongneng' (The characteristics and functions of modern moral evaluation), *Shanghai jiaoyu*, No. 7–8, 1987, pp. 16–17.

22. Hu Wei, 'Xiandai deyu pingjia de tedian ji gongneng', pp. 16–17.
23. Robert B. Edgerton, *Rules, Exceptions, and Social Order*, Berkeley, University of California Press, 1985, p. 175.
24. The origin of this cannibalistic practice has been generally ascribed to the *Bencao shiyi*—the classical Chinese Materia Medica published by Chen Zangchi in 739 AD, which listed human flesh as an effective medicine for the physical and mental decay of senility as well as for consumption, thereby seeming to promote this medical cannibalism in China. Examples of fake *gegu* and *gegan* were also discovered as people inflicted smaller wounds on themselves in order to gain the honours prescribed for the real act. See T'ien Ju-K'ang, 'Male anxiety and female chastity: a comparative study of Chinese ethical values in Ming-Ch'ing times', *Monographies du T'oung Pao*, Vol. 14, No. 14, Leiden, E. J. Brill, 1988, esp. pp. 152–9.
25. Robert B. Edgerton, p. 1.
26. Robin M. Williams, Jr, *American Society: A Sociological Interpretation*, New York, Alfred A. Knopf, 1951, pp. 355–6.
27. Émile Durkheim, *Moral Education*, trans. Everett K. Wilson and Herman Schnurer, New York, Free Press, 1973, p. 202.
28. Ambrose Y. C. King and Michael H. Bond, 'The Confucian paradigm of man: a sociological view', in Wen-Shing Tseng and David Y. H. Wu, *Chinese Culture and Mental Health*, London, Academic Press, 1985, pp. 29–47.
29. He Bi, 'Lun jia sai' (On jumping the queue), *Daxuesheng*, No. 11, 1990, pp. 42–3; also in *JPRS-CAR*-91-007, 8 February 1991, pp. 72–4.
30. See the classical text of Chu Hsi (Zhu Xi), *Learning to be a Sage: Selections from the Conversation of Master Chu*, trans. Daniel K. Gardner, Berkeley, University of California Press, 1990, p. 164. The full passage goes: 'If a man's mind is always clear, his body will follow the accepted rules without any external compulsion. It's only because there are times when man's mind becomes distracted that we set up the many rules to regulate it. If we are ever vigilant, so that our bodies follow the accepted rules, our minds will not become lost and will endure in their brightness. To keep the mind constantly alert, then to regulate it with rules as well, is the way to nurture the mind both from within and without' (12.Ib:6/200:3).
31. Norbert Elias, *The Civilizing Process*, Vol. I, *The History of Manners*, trans. Edmund Jephcott, Oxford, Blackwell, 1978, p. 215. Elias's views have been critiqued by Anthony Giddens, *The Constitution of Society: Outline of a Theory of Structuration*, Cambridge, Polity Press, 1984. For a discussion and critique of Giddens's viewpoints in this debate, see Eric Dunning, 'Comments on Elias's "Scenes from the Life of a Knight"', in *Theory, Culture & Society*, Vol. 4, 1987, pp. 366–71.
32. Jon Elster, *The Cement of Society: A Study of Social Order*, Cambridge, Cambridge University Press, 1989, p. 286.
33. Dennis H. Wrong, 'The oversocialized conception of man in modern sociology', *American Sociological Review*, Vol. 26, No. 2, April 1961, p. 191.
34. Robert K. Merton, *Social Theory and Social Structure*, rev. edn., Glencoe, Ill., Free Press, 1957, p. 300.
35. Robin M. Williams, Jr, pp. 355–6.
36. James S. Slotkin, *Social Anthropology: The Science of Human Society and Culture*, New York, Macmillan, 1950, pp. 81 ff.
37. See Niccolò Machiavelli, *The Prince*, Toronto, Bantam Books, 1981, p. 7.
38. The name of the Party's theoretical journal 'Red flag' (*Hongqi*) was changed into 'Seeking truth' (*Qiushi*) in 1988. I choose to see this as a symbol of exactly this way of 'seeking the practical truth of things' in the strict Machiavellian spirit.

39. Stanford M. Lyman and Marvin B. Scott, *A Sociology of the Absurd*, New York, Appleton-Century-Crofts, 1970, pp. 4, 18.

40. See Niccolò Machiavelli, pp. 63–4.

41. Erving Goffman, *The Presentation of Self in Everyday Life*, Harmondsworth, Penguin, 1969; see also Erving Goffman, *Strategic Interaction*, Oxford, Basil Blackwell, 1970.

42. Hsien Chin Hu, 'The Chinese concept of "face"', *American Anthropologist*, Vol. 46, No. 1, 1944, pp. 45–64.

43. David Yau-fai Ho, 'On the concept of face', *American Journal of Sociology*, Vol. 81, No. 4, 1976, p. 882.

44. Interviewee no. 10, Beijing, June 1991.

45. A. C. Scott, *The Classical Theatre of China*, London, George Allen & Unwin, 1957, pp. 18–19.

46. Lily Chu, 'The sensitivity of Chinese and American children to social influences', *Journal of Social Psychology*, Vol. 109, 1979, pp. 175–86.

47. The number of Chinese and American children in three categories was significantly different. Further analysis showed that more Americans (89%) than Chinese (76%) were independent and that more Chinese (24%) than Americans (11%) conformed to the model's choices. More Americans (71%) than Chinese (44%) were independent and more Chinese (56%) than Americans (29%) were classified as either conformers or anti-conformers. Further, it was shown that more Chinese seeing a competent model (41%) than seeing an incompetent model (8%) conformed, and more Chinese seeing an incompetent model (92%) than seeing a competent model (59%) showed anti-conformity. No difference was found between the number of Chinese who saw a competent model (45%) and those who saw an incompetent model (35%) classified as independent, and the number of Chinese who saw a competent model (55%) and who saw an incompetent model (65%) classified as either conformers or anti-conformers (see Lily Chu, pp. 175–7, 181–2).

48. For an interesting social–psychological approach to Chinese dependence, see Richard H. Solomon, *Mao's Revolution and the Chinese Political Culture*, Berkeley, University of California Press, 1971. The 'classical' work on organized dependence theory is of course Andrew Walder, *Communist Neo-Traditionalism: Work and Authority in Chinese Industry*, Berkeley, University of California Press, 1986, see also Andrew Walder, 'Organized dependency and cultures of authority in Chinese industry', *Journal of Asian Studies*, No. 1, 1983, pp. 51–76.

49. Jon Elster, p. 287.

50. Cas Wouters, 'Developments in the behavioural codes between the sexes: the formalization of informalization in the Netherlands, 1930–85', *Theory, Culture & Society*, Vol. 4, No. 2–3, 1987, p. 405. See also Cas Wouters, 'Formalization and informalization: changing tension balances in civilizing processes', *Theory, Culture & Society*, Vol. 3, No. 2, 1986, pp. 1–17.

51. Cas Wouters, 'Developments in the Behavioural Codes between the Sexes', p. 408.

52. A competition held to 'improve youngsters' was held at the Sixth Youth Cultural Festival in Beijing (*China Daily*, 27 April, 1990, p. 3). Zhang Mengxi and Zhou Yun were the first male and female champions of a 'deportment competition' in Shanghai in 1992. The competition lasted for four months, with more than 1,000 participants of both sexes. Categories included carriage, bearing, shape, make-up, and foreign language ability. Half of the participants were college graduates, and 85% could speak English (*China Daily*, 6 May 1992, p. 6).

53. Yang Fan and Lin Xiao (eds.), *Zhongguo minjian shejiao tongyong quanshu* (Encyclopedia of China's popular rules for social relations in common use), Nanning, Guangxi renmin chubanshe, 1990, p. 1.

54. Jun Feng and Yu Miao, 'Xican de zhishi yu lijie' (Etiquette and knowledge of Western food), *Shidai qingnian*, No. 2, 1991, p. 38.

55. Norbert Elias, p. 19.

56. Michel Foucault, *Discipline and Punish: The Birth of the Prison*, New York, Vintage Books, 1990, p. 170.

57. Zhou Lu, Yang Ruohe, and Hu Ruyong, *Qingshaonian fanzui zonghe zhili duice xue* (Studies in how to deal with comprehensive control of juvenile crime), Beijing, Qunzhong chubanshe, 1986, p. 214.

58. Ding Xiaodong, 'Jiaqiang jingshen wenming jianshe zujin daju wending' (Strengthen and promote the stability of the overall situation through the building of spiritual civilization), *Jingshen wenming jianshe*, No. 5, 1990, pp. 6–7.

59. Andrew Walder, *Communist Neo-Traditionalism*, p. 132.

60. Ding Xiaodong, p. 6.

61. Michel Foucault, *Discipline and Punish*, p. 178.

62. Marc J. Blecher and Gordon White, *Micropolitics in Contemporary China: A Technical Unit during and after the Cultural Revolution*, London, Macmillan Press, 1980, p. 41.

63. Ibid.

64. Ibid., p. 181.

65. Ibid., p. 178.

66. Michael R. Dutton, *Policing and Punishment in China: From Patriarchy to 'the People'*, Cambridge, Cambridge University Press, 1992, p. 5.

67. See Sidney Shapiro, *The Law and Lore of China's Criminal Justice*, Beijing, New World Press, 1990, p. 32; and Ernest Alabaster, *Notes and Commentaries on Chinese Criminal Law*, Taipei, Changwen Publishing Company, 1968, pp. 57–8.

68. Justus Doolittle, *Social Life of the Chinese*, 2 vols., Singapore, Graham Brash, 1986, Vol. 1, p. 109; originally published in New York in 1867.

69. T'ien Ju-K'ang, *Male Anxiety and Female Chastity: A Comparative Study of Chinese Ethical Values in Ming–Ch'ing Times*, Monographies du T'oung Pao, Vol. 14, Leiden, E. J. Brill, 1988.

70. *Hainan ribao*, 16 January 1991; also in *SWB-FE*/0989, 6 February 1991, p. B2/5.

71. Both Michel Foucault, *Discipline and Punish*, and Jeffrey Minson, *Genealogies of Morals*, London, Macmillan, 1985, argue in line with this logic.

72. Ann Anagnost, 'Socialist ethics and the legal system', in Jeffrey N. Wasserstrom and Elizabeth J. Perry (eds.), *Popular Protest and Political Culture in Modern China: Learning from 1989*, Boulder, Colo., Westview Press, 1992, p. 196.

73. Michel Foucault, *Discipline and Punish*, p. 227 all quotations.

7

The Disciplinary Techniques of Evaluation

EVALUATION is the main way in which exemplary society links people's behaviour, or rather brings their *biaoxian* closer to the exemplary norm. The Chinese ancients said 'promote the good, suppress the evil' (*yang shan yi e*), and 'only by comparison can one distinguish' (*bi ze ming qi li*). The way to achieve all this is still through evaluation. While binding individuals to norms, evaluation at the same time improves 'human quality'. The process of evaluation inspires and develops individuals of all sorts, according to Xie Hongmao and Chen Weifen; the process also represents a 'restraining or binding force (*yueshu li*)'.[1]

Evaluation makes visible the exemplary norm, and each individual in relation to it. It pushes individual 'black spots' to the foreground against an exemplary background of white. Evaluation is an integrated part of collective life, a way of linking individuals to the greater society, a way of being. Through evaluation, the individual 'small self' is lifted up to the level of the collective 'great self' that is society. Evaluation is there to improve human quality, to halt the modern Juggernaut. In the words of one moral educator, 'Evaluation will prevent the bad influences coming in the wake of opening up and reform.'[2] If one catchword of evaluation is visibility, another catchword during the reforms has been objectivity. The chaotic change of values must be held together throughout the so-called objective evaluations. As we shall see, such alleged objectivity leads to a detailed measurement of behaviour, subsuming individual behaviour under the logic of a strict exemplary standard.

Evaluation is knowledge, knowledge about individuals, and thereby power in the hands of the regime. But evaluation also makes individuals understand the social values, giving them knowledge about those values.[3] Without evaluation one cannot know what is right or wrong. Wang Keqian's definition leads right to the question of the objectivity of norms: 'Evaluation is a subject's attitude towards objectively existing values'; it is about 'the objective character of objective values [*keti de jiazhi de duixiang xing*]'. One must not break the connection between evaluation and objective knowledge. 'Direction' is an often-used expression in the vocabulary of the Chinese 'moral sciences'; evaluation should also have a directional character (*zhixiang xing*). 'Direction' or 'guidance' should be used to lead the populace on the right path to exemplary, objective order.[4] It has been claimed that the guiding function (*daoxiang gongneng*) of evaluation will raise moral efficiency (*deyu de xiaolü*).[5] The movement of spiritual civilization is often expressed in the language of such 'moral economy', as the administration needs exact measures to legitimize a campaign that cannot match the hard facts of output and profit found in the prestigious movement of enhancing material civilization. Since norms are seen as objective entities in the Chinese moral sciences, however, such strict measures must also be found for spiritual civilization. Evaluation offers such a possibility. Wang uses the concept of 'value objectivity' (*jiazhi duixiang xing*) in characterizing the evaluation process. 'Value judgements are subjective reflections of objective practice', and combine knowledge with 'an essence of rich emotions'. There are both internal and external yardsticks for evaluation: the internal yardstick (*neizai chidu*) lies in conscience (*liangxin*), while the external yardstick (*waizai chidu*) is social intelligence, social opinion, and the objective standards of society.[6] As indicated in Chapter 2, both internal and external yardsticks are subsumed under the disciplinary concept of human quality. Self-evaluation is held to be the best form of evaluation, while that coming from the outside is far less effective.

Organizing the Evaluation Process

There exists a range of evaluation techniques, including oral and written types of evaluation, open and hidden ways of judging individuals. Evaluation concerns education and improvement, discipline, rewards and punishment. Zhang Yutian's 1987 textbook on evaluation work focuses on three main effects of evaluation: improvement, knowledge, and selection. First, evaluation is helpful in correcting people's behaviour; second, it helps us understand people; third, it should be used to 'select talents for society'. The corrective and improving effect of evaluation is its most important characteristic. Evaluating moral behaviour is a process of carrying out ideological and moral education among students. Understanding and knowledge have a two-fold meaning. From the viewpoint of the evaluator, knowing and understanding people involves making them visible and susceptible to improvement. For the

evaluated individual, the evaluation involves understanding the objective norms. The selection function is often described through the picture of a universalistic ideal of equitable allocation for jobs, education,
and other scarce resources. The particularistic reality of China, however, turns evaluation into a very subjective way of controlling such
resources. This particularistic reality forms the background to the
repeated talk of objectivity in the evaluation process. It is said that 'fixed
norms' (*kebi zhibiao*) should be established, and one should 'make objective evaluations through seeking truths from facts'.[7] Evaluation also concerns cultural collectivism; cultural critic Sun Longji claims that the
constant process of evaluation reflects the fact that the Chinese cannot define their value from themselves only.[8] The Chinese see themselves and learn about themselves only from other persons, a relational
approach expressed in the Chinese concept of '*talü*', which can be translated as 'other-ruled'. In China extreme importance has always been
attached to outer norms: indeed, Liu Guangming claims that an outer
social ethic is more strongly developed than an inner personal morality.[9] Liu links this outer ethic to authoritarian structures, and calls it
a 'non-individual patriarchal ethic' (*fei geti de zongfa lunli*). The control
exercised through public laws, norms, and moral standards is thus particularly strong and evident in China. There is also a strong cultural
acceptance of evaluation in a society where the concepts of 'other'
and 'outer' are so central. The Chinese must be the most thoroughly
evaluated people of us all.

The modernizer's classical theme is the freeing of individuals from
the inertia of their primary ties. Instead, in the organization and techniques of evaluation, we see primary ties utilized for the sake of modernizing. Here I am thinking primarily of the small group (*xiaozu*). The
exemplary norm is built into informal and not-so-informal social networks of various types, with the *xiaozu*—the small group—as the core
of these new primary networks. Within such groups, social norms are
'held' and individuals 'improved' under conditions of maximal visibility through constant evaluation. The small group is an immediate face-
to-face organization, but it represents the collective, the force 'outside'
so important in Chinese moral education.

There are rules for the correct division of small groups, supervised
by teachers or class cadres who represent the outer exemplary norms
in a particularistic context. A textbook on evaluation techniques suggests that one should 'carry out evaluation in a group with no less
than five members'.[10] In one of the schools I visited in Beijing, there
were six small groups per class, normally with six to eight members in
each group.[11] The small group forms the front line of a moral battle.

Large parts of society are organized into such small, informal groups. Classrooms, factories, neighbourhoods, prisons, military camps—all are formed and supervised by higher authorities through small groups. Within these groups each person is expected to analyse his or her attitudes, to reconsider values in the light of an exemplary collectivity. Self-evaluation and self-criticism go hand in hand with the criticism of others' viewpoints. In small groups the social gaze is represented by mutual evaluation (*huping*), and is meant to be concerned with the 'gaze from within' through self-evaluation (*ziping*). The technique of repeated evaluation (*fuping*) is also a link to the theme of repetition—or *fu*— discussed earlier.[12]

The small group is the core of evaluation, but since evaluation is an ever-present and all-round process, it does not stop at the confines of the small circle. The small-scale network opens up to a society outside classrooms and work-units; it is often heard that school, family, and society should all form a mutual network of evaluation touching on all walks of life. Knowledge of evaluation is not only knowledge of self: it is the authorities' knowledge about all individuals. The process thus entails considerable investigation and surveillance. Both the aspect of all-round evaluation and the gathering of knowledge is exemplified by the home visit (*jiafang*), a method often used in evaluation work. This is the expression used for a visit to the parents of school students or young workers. In the character *fang* there is a connotation of investigation as well as visit. In schools the home visit should be linked to the establishment of a 'student family file' (*xuesheng jiating dang'an*); in the work-unit the regular personnel file is used for this purpose. All kinds of background information on workers or students should be gathered by unit cadres or class teachers. During a home visit, the teachers should gather information not only on the students or young workers, but also on their parents. The parents should be questioned about their formal schooling, their impressions about their nature or disposition, and note should be taken of parents' methods of family education. Furthermore, the evaluator should 'thoroughly observe the arrangement of the room, how the household duties are arranged, the relations between the family members, and other factors helping to explain the situation at home'.[13] Here the ideal is face-to-face relations, where the evaluator's task is openly revealed to those who are evaluated. This is no 'panopticon', since power is highly visible. Some parents even discuss personal frustrations in their everyday lives with visiting teachers and cadres. Knowledge is sought on all levels, and, as one class teacher remarks about parents during home visits, 'They show full confidence in us by telling about their family disputes.'[14] Home visits may aim at evaluating parents directly, even if they are also evaluated in their own work-units. Class teachers are also asked to visit the parents' work-units and ask their leaders for help. Both the home gate (*jiamen*) and the factory gate (*changmen*) should be used. The distribution of titles of honour forms an important part of the evaluation process. In some schools, not only the students but also parents become part of this system of evaluation for honour, with 'best parents' (*zui jia jiazhang*) elected by public appraisal after thorough evaluation reports.[15] The home visit has its equivalent in the parents' school visit (*xiaofang*), and parents are encouraged to take part in the evaluation process in school.

The evaluator is evaluated, too. In schools it is part of the daily routine for teachers as well as students to write self-assessment reports. We shall soon see how detailed this evaluation can be when both students' and teachers' qualities are scrutinized. The teacher evaluation form (*jiaoshi kaohe biao*) is also to include comments from all responsible persons at every office in the school administration.[16] Mutual teacher–student evaluation (*shisheng gongping*) is practised in some schools. It is also recommended that higher levels, as well as parents and students, should evaluate the class teacher who is in charge of the evaluation process in school.[17] Cadres too are thoroughly evaluated; and their evaluation, like that of teachers, is important background material for their further selection for jobs—or for purges or rehabilitations in political campaigns, for that matter. Evaluation concerns everything from moral and political world outlook down to matters of whether primary schoolchildren keep their schoolbags tidy, or wash their hands properly.[18] As there is a small-group network at the basic levels, there is also an evaluation network outside the smaller unit. China might not be a society of 'perpetual penalty', as Foucault expressed it, but it certainly is one of perpetual evaluation.

Self-evaluation is regarded as the basis for other people's evaluations. Students and employees, teachers, cadres, and leaders should all undertake self-evaluation. One should constantly check and reflect over one's own attitude toward the norms. Self-improvement and social improvement are presumed to go hand in hand, and self-improvement is said to strengthen control and administration.[19] Self-improvement is first and foremost about restraining oneself, and acting in accordance with the collective rules. Self-evaluation has since time immemorial been institutionalized in the formal theatre of self-criticism. This type of behaviour is in itself a good measure of *biaoxian*, in displaying the correct attitude towards one's superiors. Even if self-criticisms are honest reactions, what is displayed in such (often written) formulas are frequently pledges of loyalty and submission.

Self-improvement and self-criticism often take the form of a direct criticism of self. Self stands in the way of exemplary norms; since the class teacher is to lead students over the 'ideological boundaries of communist morality' (*gonchang zhuyi de sixiang jingjie*),[20] he or she has to fight against the display of self. In China 'self' (*ziwo*), 'self-centredness' (*zisi*), and 'freedom' (*ziyou*) all are concepts bearing a connotation of something negative, something hidden from view, going against the collective norms. The *zi* of self, and even the 'I', stand for something hidden from the social gaze, and thereby represent chaos and danger. In one example from an evaluation session, the discussion of self illustrates the attacks on the exemplary rules directly:

There are too many rules, I can't stand it,' says one student. The class teacher comments the matter for the entire class: 'The student always talks about himself', and takes up the problem of his 'I' (*wo*)' . . . 'What is the problem of "I" about?' Students: 'About liberalism, about individualism, about an undisciplined work style'.[21]

The debate takes the form of a mutual evaluation on the basis of a discussion of fixed moral rules. Control, restriction, and 'anger control' (*zhinu*) are prescribed ways to behave so as to curb modern illnesses of the undisciplined, unrestrained, and arrogant type.[22] Confucius himself is often quoted to underline this point.

Evaluation has to be carried out constantly, as a daily, continuous, ever-present process. For many in China, it is experienced as a completely natural way of organizing things, not only in schools, but in all types of organized activity. Evaluation almost seems to have become one of the 'learning how' experiences of socialization. The groups are parts of a larger organizational model, and even the Party functions through a *xiaozu*—or small-group network. Martin King Whyte has pointed out that one of the assets seen from the authorities' point of view is that smaller groups of activists can dominate the network.[23] In schools the principle of self-surveillance is normally used in mobilizing a group of activists (*jiji fenzi*) and class cadres (*xuesheng ganbu*) who work under close supervision of the class teacher. These activists are propagandists representing the exemplary standards set by the authorities themselves, and they see to it that members participate in the formation of these standards. Activist student cadres even serve as 'score-keepers' (*jifenyuan*), keeping track of the moral marks in class. Whyte emphasizes the control aspect of the *xiaozu* network, and its links to authority. The idea is that the *xiaozu* network can prevent the emergence of autonomous primary groups, and thereby prevent unauthorized standards from establishing themselves, and cliques and factions from developing. Groups should evaluate each member in order to set the standards in each individual, to solve problems, and to restore the collective unity. Whyte sees in them 'a slim parallel' to Western sensitivity groups, but with the difference that they are embedded in an authority structure which their Western equivalents lack.[24]

There are obvious psychological processes active in the small-group evaluation. 'Evaluations represent a process of moral experience', one textbook contends, a process where 'guilt and shame' are factors active in the formative process.[25] The authority structure in which the small group is embedded is undoubtedly an important side of the *xiaozu* network, but the limits of control should also be emphasized. That control is not absolute has been indicated by several informants I interviewed. Students picked out as exemplary and given positions or titles of honour against the will of other students are soon stigmatized by the informal collective that is always there outside the 'formalized informal' structures:

If a student was 'put on the list' and elected class cadre, a 'three-good student', etc., because the class teacher had overruled student decisions, the student would be even more hated than the teacher by the other students.[26]

It is correct, as Whyte says, that the small-group network is embedded in an authority structure, but it is equally correct to say that it is not absorbed by that structure. Another interviewee held that there was a kind of 50–50 balance of power between the informal student collective and the authority structure.[27] Even if there is a balance of power here, control through small groups remains a very powerful organizational basis for evaluation of individuals.

Appraisal through discussion is the most common method used in small-group evaluation, and in the larger sessions following up small-group discussions. The process of 'comparing and assessing' individuals, or *pingbi*, has a high profile, and is regarded as the most effective means of improvement. For many years his method was discredited, as it was claimed it destroyed the basic spirit of unity among students.[28] However, it was reintroduced in all schools in the early 1980s, to 'strengthen moral education', as it was formulated.[29] The process is now described as one of friendly competition, and is said to constitute an important moral education process in itself. Instead of pure meritocratic competition for marks, this process is meant to represent a competition for honour (*rongyu*).[30] According to one encyclopedia of education, *pingbi* means 'to examine, evaluate and compare students' thoughts and *biaoxian*, and represents a method of moral education'.[31] Further, the book explains, there are two main types of *pingbi*. The first is concerned with individual competitions—as in following the rules, observing hygiene, performing the setting up exercises, etc. The second is collective or all-round *pingbi*, as in competing to be 'advanced units', 'advanced classes', etc. '*Pingbi* is a method for uniting and helping everybody advance . . . reach results and overcome weaknesses, for praising good people and good deeds, and making everybody strive for the best.' *Pingbi* is here presented as a process of perfection rather than control. Comparison here has less to do with the distribution around an average, and more with conformity to the exemplary norm. Control and surveillance are here both seen in the picture of improvement. Some Chinese observers examining this particular kind of morality competition, however, have instead with acclaim identified the function of pure behavioural control.[32]

The freezing of *biaoxian* into written documents can take the form of homework, written exam results, investigation reports, and the like. Individual comments (*pingyu*) are to be written down for each student. The small group writes a brief evaluation summary (*xiaojie*). Both leaders and led, students and teachers, are required to take part in the process of evaluating morality. Summaries are also to be written by the representatives of the work-unit or the political organizations, like the Party or the Youth League. In addition, class teachers and tutors enter their comments on a consultation form (*zixun biaoge*).[33] In line with the renewed stress on the role of the class teacher, the latter has the final say over the students' own decisions when class teacher and student committee re-examine the judgements together. Control does not stop here: the evaluation goes up to the school bureaucracy for reassessment.

Thus, the evaluation process becomes an integrated part of the administrative routine in schools and work-units. In some schools, the student cadres are responsible for checking on work attendance and reporting their findings to the student section (*xuesheng ke*) weekly. The class teacher inspects the situation in the classes daily. The student union (*xuesheng hui*) collects the statistical material on moral conduct from every class weekly, and delivers three written reports: one to the deputy leader of the school administration (*xiaowu fujiaozhang*), one to the education administrative section (*jiaowuke*), and the original draft which they keep themselves.[34] In other schools the re-examined results from the *pingbi* process are announced to the students via the administrative committee for student work (*xuesheng gongzuo weiyuanhui*). The committee reconsiders the report from the class teacher and gives the final judgement. In the end, a seal is put on the final document; one copy is sent to the parents, one to the students, and one is kept by the committee for student work for reference.[35]

The final seal signifies that the process of evaluation has now been subsumed under the logic of bureaucracy. What started out as a 'method of education' now focuses on the written results of the process rather than on that process itself. *Pingbi* has been redefined and made into a measurable output of spiritual civilization, following the administrative logic of that movement. The 'output' are the evaluations presented in the final 'graduation appraisal' (*biye jianding*), which has something of the character of a pure 'morality diploma'.

Various 'morality diplomas' have become widely used. Titles of honour, too, have begun to appear in ranked order, forming a hierarchy of rewards for good and heroic deeds. For instance, 'three-good student' (*san hao xuesheng*), the best-known and most used title of them all, indicating good school results, good moral conduct, and good health, can now be given at different levels. In Anhui province, 358 'three-good' titles and 162 higher titles of honour were awarded to individual students and classes, while 62 were awarded collectively. These provincial-level titles of honour were awarded to those selected from among the 2.33 million secondary-school children in the province.[36] Titles exist all the way down to the local county school or even classroom levels, serving as an important proof of *biaoxian* written into the morality diploma. We may note the signs of a 'morality-diploma disease' in which the diploma as such assumes greater importance than actual morality. There also seems to be a bureaucratic burgeoning of reports and documents that go to make up the final morality diploma. Since 1987, a spate of new reports on political behaviour and moral conduct, etc., has been put into the student files; at the same time, the various titles of honour have been given a more prominent place in the file system.[37]

The *pingbi* process was interpreted as a friendly competition for honour. Increasingly, the system has become linked to material rewards—money premiums, stipends, allocation of jobs, and a host of other privileges. Stipends can still be given to needy students. The class teacher is in charge of selecting stipend levels on the basis of each family's financial situation. However, stipends are more and more linked to merit and to the registration of moral–political conduct, and are used as a means of disciplining the students. Money can be withheld for one month or taken away altogether in case of irregularities, and there are often detailed rules for the giving and withholding of stipends. Coming late to class or leaving early more than a certain number of times a month or being absent from collective activities can lead to monthly loss of stipends. Economic rewards can also be given for doing good deeds—showing an exemplary discipline, taking part in campaigns in an active way, or having a good labour assessment record. It is certainly a paradox when students gain individual money bonuses and personal privileges for showing a spirit of thrift and collective consciousness. Of course, academic achievements can also win material incentives, stipends, and money awards. Similarly, some categories of students are not eligible for stipends, for example those who break laws and regulations, cheat on exams, are absent too often, or have lost a certain number of moral points in the course of a month. In some schools the evaluation of stipends is discussed in class and reconsidered every semester by the class teacher.[38]

Morality diplomas and titles of honour have also become highly relevant in the search for jobs. Material from surveys issued by the Ministry of Finance concerning middle schools specializing in economy and management studies gives enough details relating to both titles of honour and job allocations to enable us to adduce a clear connection between the two. The surveys cover some fifty-seven such schools throughout China, some of which provide information on both matters. Material from one school in Anhui province shows that, out of 503 students who graduated between 1979 and 1983, 48, or 9.5 per cent of the total, had been awarded the 'three-good student' title; a further 16 received the title of 'excellent student cadre' (*youxiu xuesheng ganbu*), while 12 received the less elevated 'excellent member' (*youxiu tuanyuan*) of the Youth League. In all, 76 students, or 15.1 per cent, had received prominent titles of honour at this school; 59 others had received smaller rewards in 'learn from Lei Feng' campaigns, though these were not regarded as having the same status as the other 76. All the students obtained their jobs through the state job allocation system. The best jobs were defined as those of cadre on the provincial level, which were of two kinds: those in the Provincial Economic Office (*sheng caizhengting*) and those in the department directly responsible for the province (*sheng zhi zhuguan bumen*). Fifty-six students were appointed to these two work-units on the principle of selecting the best students for the best jobs (*zeyou fenpei*). Of these, 34 had been granted one of the three leading titles of honour. Thus 60.7 per cent of the top jobs went to students with such titles, while only 39.3 per cent went to students without titles of honour or with only minor titles. To sum up, while almost 45 per cent of students with leading titles of honour secured the best jobs, only just over 5 per cent of students without such titles were able to get that far. The chances of landing a top job in the provincial administration were nine times higher for those with such titles than for those without.[39]

All students can express their opinions in the written evaluation report (*pingyu*), but many refrain from doing so to avoid commenting on their fellow students in public. There is a resistance to enhancing the visibility of friends, colleagues, and classmates. Moral–political evaluation is a matter one does not embrace without considerable caution, and is full of hidden conflicts. At Beijing University I was told that, while students and teachers frequently agreed on the meritocratic abilities of the candidates, they were often in complete disagreement when it came to evaluating their morality. This is why class teachers are asked not to take the results of the small-group discussions among students too seriously in preparing their final evaluations; for these reports from activists and fellow teachers together with the class teacher's own opinion are what counts.[40]

The moral improvement process is linked to a system of punishment and rewards. This represents the type of virtuocratic competition which Susan Shirk describes as regimes that 'have tried to control society by controlling the distribution of career opportunities and by awarding the best opportunities to those who exemplify the moral virtues of the movement'.[41] When ideological orientation or attitude towards the exemplary norm is used as a starting point for the distribution of social mobility, we can speak of virtuocratic evaluation and virtuocratic mobility. In contrast to meritocratic processes, such evaluation is characterized by a low level of measurability; it follows subjective criteria for evaluation, and draws diffuse and flexible lines for the definitions of who can be regarded as worthy of receiving the scarce rewards. In China today, nothing less than an individual of high 'human quality' is seen as a worthy receiver. The reliance on moral conduct and *biaoxian* to evaluate individuals and allocate rewards can be precisely described as such a virtuocratic process. The dangers of linking morality to an organized system of rewards were anticipated by Durkheim, who warned that this would lead to an instrumentalization of morality. The particularistic and diffuse character of the process represents a problem for the Chinese authorities, and instrumentalization of morality is part of that problem. The disappointing answer given by Chinese educators, however, seems merely to be that morality is not being measured *well enough*. The problem thus becomes how to use 'scientific methods' to measure this morality *in a better way*. A process of 'objectification' and 'scientification' has become the technocratic answer.

On Objective Evaluation

'Comprehensive' (*zonghe*) is a word often used in the ongoing campaigns for spiritual civilization. There is both comprehensive control
(*zonghe zhili*) and the propagation of a comprehensive appraisal
(*zonghe ceping*). The use of the word reflects a wish to coordinate and
systematize old approaches to control in a comprehensive, modern, organized way. For instance, a 'comprehensive appraisal system for student
quality' is set up. Indexes of the moral, intellectual, and physical quality of students are established and claimed to be an objective way to
judge values. The underlying idea is to disaggregate moral quality into
points or marks reflecting a person's moral–political manifestations or
biaoxian in school, in the dorms, in the family, in the work-unit, or in
social life. A comprehensive appraisal system restricts and overcomes
the random character of evaluations, setting a relatively fair objective
standard for evaluation, the moral administrators claim.[42]

Evaluation starts with observance of behaviour; it ends in registration and written files, some of which will later be used as standards
defining the fixed and exemplary point from which further evaluations can start. The process follows an increasingly bureaucratic logic,
where the emphasis on quantification, techniques of measurement,
and the organizational methods more and more come to have a life of
their own. To arrive at an understanding of each individual's human
quality for the sake of improving it, evaluation must be utilized as a
systematic and continuous process of reform and improvement, Su
Weichang and Zhang Dimei claim. The two use a kind of 'pseudo-
behaviourism' in their book 'Techniques of educational evaluation', and
stress that behaviour is the main starting point for measuring the moral
quality of a person:

> The object to be measured consists of knowledge, feelings, wills, beliefs and
> behaviour. Behaviour is the end point of the other factors, and a sign for meas-
> uring the moral quality of a person. To see whether moral quality is in accord-
> ance with the evaluation goals, one [should] mainly look at behaviour.[43]

Behaviour repeated over and over again (*fanfu*) forms habits, the book
contends, and habit is a natural behaviour that does not need any
further supervision. When behaviour (*xingwei*) is tamed into habit
(*xiguan*), potentially unrestrained behaviour has been tamed. Evaluation constitutes and guarantees correct behaviour, so comprehensive
surveillance should be carried out everywhere. The individual's behaviour in school, in society, and in the family should be observed, guided,

and evaluated. In evaluating people, several methods should be used. Basically, one should observe and report on an individual's *biaoxian* wherever it is manifested, not just in the classroom or the work-unit. A teacher's evaluation should measure not only the results of tests and questionnaires, etc., to see whether a student's political level is high or low: account must also be taken of the student's *biaoxian* in general. Less emphasis on ideology and more on conduct is the medicine prescribed.[44] There is much talk of a large network of surveillance involving school, family, and society.

Since the measuring of *biaoxian* becomes the only gauge of the efficiency in moral education, the evaluation procedures and the accuracy in measuring *biaoxian* become crucial. Chinese textbooks give frequent examples of wrong ways of implementing evaluation. Individual differentiation is important. Some evaluators do not take evaluation seriously, and treat all in the same way (*qian ren yi mian*) as if there were no differences between them.[45] Even Confucius is quoted for having emphasized individualization and differentiation.[46] Refusing to use individualization in the evaluation process destroys the hierarchy of moral behaviour that develops around the exemplary norm, and questions the whole fundament of moral–political evaluation. This is the type of problem described in the method of merely rotating the honours of 'model workers'. The argument about differentiation and individualization is interesting because, contrary to those who claim that in China there is no individuality, it points to a particular way of individualizing the populace. Evaluation and criticism should be differentiated because students come from different backgrounds and have different personalities and problems.[47] It is a well established principle in China that 'individualization (*getihua*) and socialization (*shehuihua*) should be in balance'.[48] The evaluation process actually creates a form of individuality within the collective. This is clearly not the 'self-actualizing' individual of the West, or that of which some Chinese reform-minded thinkers talk. But the concept of the individual is not at all absent from the Chinese scene. It is there for improvement and disciplining—only it is a different concept of the individual.

Individuals should be evaluated constantly. Daily evaluation is recommended in schools. The results of evaluation are to be summed up every week or fortnight in a systematic scale with discussions and written reports. An overall appraisal is made in the end; in schools this is based on all the quantified results from the entire semester. Textbooks issue a strong warning against subjective evaluation, stressing that 'objective standards of evaluation' should be used.[49] A whole literature on the damage done by vague evaluation has appeared in recent years. Vague standards of evaluation by words only (*wenzi biaozhun*) should be avoided at all costs.[50] One should look at the different characteristics of students, and not make sweeping generalizations.[51] Others complain that a special code for polite formulas of evaluation has developed to avoid offending students and parents. In evaluating students, expressions like 'active' (*jiji*) or 'serious' (*renzhen*), 'relatively serious' (*jiao renzhen*) or 'still active' (*shang jiji*), are used to sum up the type of *biaoxian* displayed. It is felt by some that nobody can learn much from such statements. They simply do not give any directions for further improvement.[52] The class teacher should avoid empty talk (*konghua*) and polite or covered talk (*taohua*) in assessing students since it only leads to conflicts with those being evaluated.[53] Some teachers avoid doing thorough evaluation work because they think it can only injure their students. For them, the term 'moral evaluation' is a mere formality. Their evaluations contain more and more polite formulas and patterns, like 'has a praiseworthy sacrificing spirit', 'has established a communist view of life', or 'is capable of resisting all kinds of wrong thinking'; neither these rosy labels, nor equally negative labels such as 'has a bad style' or 'is arrogant and complacent' should be used.[54] Many of these articles are written in support of the evaluated student, and support a more democratic and objective style of evaluating. Li Wenxiang complains that some teachers only write a moral evaluation without using marks.[55] Such approaches can be confused and muddled, and do not distinguish properly between the students, a practice that could lead to all sorts of distortions and malpractices. Fixed standards of evaluation should be implemented. Moral and political quality can be measured only through *biaoxian*, so to measure the fixed standard, a marking of *biaoxian* should be attempted. The existence of objective norms and standards must be accompanied by an equally objective expression of behaviour. Students' political quality should be measured and marked in terms of their knowledge of dialectical materialism, their situation of political improvement, whether they have applied for Youth League and party membership, whether they display enthusiasm in political campaigns, or whether their attitude towards criticism and self-criticism and toward their studies is good. They should also be positively evaluated if they resist the 'freedom wave' of the capitalist classes, and if they accept their state placement in the job allocation process. Moral level is to be measured and marked in terms of results on the moral knowledge exam, attitudes towards collectivism, and respect for elder people as well as for comrades and friends in general. Work attitude is important, as is a civilized language and behaviour. Results on the law exam, attitudes towards rules and regulations in general, and in dorms in particular should also be noted. Finally, the students' attitude towards participation in military exercises, and to the protection of public property, should constitute the standard for setting marks on *biaoxian*. Marking should be based on a graded scale.[56]

In fact, Li's attempt to attain an exact measurement of *biaoxian* is among the more moderate solutions. The quest for exact measurements of the efficiency of moral education is accelerating as the bureaucracy comes to be more and more desperately in need of legitimating the output of its spiritual civilization. The methods of material civilization, with their exact measures of input and output, loss and profit, are increasingly becoming the model also for the sphere of 'moral economy'. Thus, in evaluating individuals, the professional evaluator should be 'scientific and objective'; favouritism and one-sidedness should be banned, subjective evaluation should be eschewed, and strict objectivity maintained.[57] Once again, the 'scientific method' provides the ultimate solution. The class teacher should *know*, not suppose, when evaluating moral achievement.[58] Thereby can class teachers as well as other evaluators fulfil the positivist ideal of the neutral scientist, or the scientific educator. Eureka! The subjective process of morality has become scientific.

The keyword in this process is 'quantification', or *shulianghua*; here it stands for the quantification of *biaoxian* and the precise measurement of moral behaviour. Objective evaluation seems to be the solution to all moral problems, and the measuring of objective *biaoxian* is the way to attain objectivity. 'Objective principles are reached with truth as the basis and statistics as the tool. Only when scientific judgements are carried out, can evaluation fit reality,' says Xin Yang. In order to legitimate the quantification of morality, Xin typically finds support in the symbols of socialism and science: 'Marx held that a science could only reach perfection when it successfully applied mathematics. Only then can personal experience and subjective [evaluation] be avoided.'[59] Quantification of morality is directly linked to the improvement of individuals, and in the much-used book 'Principles of Moral Education' Hu Shoufen states: 'Quantitative measurement of evaluation is a tool for advancing the students' character.'[60]

Not all are equally happy about the quantification drive. My impression from interviews among teachers is that the quantified evaluation is seen as relatively objective, but that it is also regarded with some scepticism. Class teachers at a secondary school in Beijing told me that a person cannot be evaluated fully through these measures, even if the teachers had long experimented with moral quantification, and had worked out quantified evaluation forms that were used in the school.[61]

You can evaluate people's behaviour, but not their thinking, they claimed. A university political instructor (*fudaoyuan*) told me that the deeper thoughts of a person cannot be evaluated, and that quantified marking could easily give a false impression. The general impression one has of a student is very often correct, he continued; the general evaluation might not be perfect although it would not be entirely wrong. The quality of a person cannot be expressed in points. One person with 80 points might be entirely different from another person with 80 points. Giving marks in the evaluation process is not a good idea because it means labelling the student.[62]

Hu Shoufen also admits that quantifying an abstract entity like a student's 'learning attitude' is difficult. Such measurements might produce smaller or larger errors. However, overall the conclusion is that in today's situation one has to rely on such methods. The aim is 'to find concealed or vague tendencies' of moral behaviour through the measurements.[63] It is all about enhancing knowledge, and making the invisible visible. The search for vague tendencies in each individual's overall *biaoxian* leads Zhang Yutian to use the concept 'vague mathematics' (*mohu shuxue*) as a description of the quantified moral evaluation system.[64] In Zhang's moral mathematics, an aggregate (v) is made up of ideological (x) and moral (y) 'systems' to form a quantified expression of *biaoxian*. Zhang's moral mathematics is of course a disciplinary technique that belongs to the technocratic discourse on human quality.

The quantification also links the evaluation procedure to the principle of micro penalty that we noted in Foucault's analysis. As indicated in Chapter 6, not only infractions of rules, but also failure to fulfil tasks or even failure to fulfil them in the right spirit are now matters for an improving disciplinary system. In one example of the measurement of 'attitudes towards the collective', the mark A stands for 'active concern', B is 'capable of concern', C signals 'neither cold nor hot', and finally D stands for 'self-centred'. Different norms do not have the same weight or importance. In Zhang's moral mathematics, a specific system of weighting marks should be used to perfect the process of measuring moral character.[65] Thus, there are not only exemplary norms and standards, there are also hierarchies of good and bad within those standards which are open for measurement, and there are gradings of the different levels.

Several techniques of marking an individual's *biaoxian* are practised. Perhaps the most widespread form is a four-grade scale which divides *biaoxian* into 'excellent' (*you*), 'good' (*liang*), 'average' (*zhong*), and 'bad' or 'not up to standard' (*cha*). Numbers or points are often used in connection with such marking. In one example the evaluators operate with ten main standards for moral evaluation, and all of these are then divided into four different grades, where grade A gives five points, B four, C three, and D only two. The ten standards are also divided into levels of perfection where 'actively . . .' and 'relatively . . .' stand for the difference between the A and the B mark. The C mark characterizes behaviour that is passable, and D indicates that *biaoxian* is flawed or not up to standard.[66] Various other systems are known, some using marks with up to several decimal places, like the one where excellent (*youxiu*) is an average mark of higher than 4.029 based on complicated scales and indexes of moral behaviour.[67] There are also collective marks (*pingbanfen*) allotted to groups of students or whole classes.[68] Such collective points are allegedly given to strengthen the collectivist spirit and the collective honour of classes or groups.[69]

A system of merits and demerits is introduced on all school levels, and in evaluation procedures in other units as well. Such practices have become increasingly widespread during the reform period. Plus-points (*jiafen*) and minus-points (*jianfen* or *koufen*) are used. Here we see the beginning of a system of moral rewards against which Durkheim argued. It takes the form of a micro penalty of privileges and impositions, exactly as in the examples discussed by Foucault. A percentage system for the weighting of marks (*baifenzhi jifen*) is employed by some units. It is quite usual for the 100-grade scale normally used in schools to also be used in the evaluation of *biaoxian*.

Table 2 shows an example of an evaluation table where *biaoxian* marking is linked to the fixed standards and rules of a particular secondary school. There are four main marks, and the point allocation is based on a 100-point scale. The evaluation form is divided into four main areas. The first relates to students' participation in social and political–ideological activities organized by the school. Some of these are 'voluntary' activities of social practice (*shehui shijian*), where participation is necessary to secure the 'actively and on one's own initiative' definition demanded to reach the highest mark. The second aspect concerns attitude towards school rules and discipline; the third checks attitudes towards physical labour; and the last evaluates students' dress and personal style. The example given in the table is from a Harbin specialized secondary school in 1987.

In Beijing in 1991 I found quite liberal attitudes among university teachers towards matters of personal style, clothes, makeup, etc. It was explicitly said that such matters were seen as 'expressions of individuality', and that outward appearance was irrelevant for evaluation. In secondary schools, however, there was still considerable control. High-heeled shoes, jewellery, and rings were not allowed. Dressing

TABLE 2 Evaluation table for students' *biaoxian*[a, b]

Mark	Specific evaluation standards (*pingding biaozhun*)				Points per month
	Activity participation	Keeping discipline	Physical labour	Dress/make-up	
Excellent (*you*)	Actively (and on one's own initiative) taking part in all activities organized by the school and the class, showing clear achievement in the activities (27–30 pts)	Following the laws of the state, the rules of the school, and the school regulations, the discipline of the Student Union and the hygiene inspection in an exemplary way; minus points for the whole month not to exceed 5 (27–30 pts)	Actively taking part in physical labour organized by the school and the class; not coming late, not leaving early; having an outstanding *biaoxian* in physical labour and keeping labour discipline (18–20 pts)	Dress and make-up in accordance with the status of a student (18–20 pts)	90–100
Good (*liang*)	Actively participating in all kinds of activities organized by the school, and having a average *biaoxian* in these activities (24–27 pts)	Same as above, but not done in an exemplary way as demanded in the top grade; minus points for the whole month not to exceed 10 (24–27 pts)	Taking part in the physical labour organized by the school and in class, occasionally coming late or leaving early; having an average *biaoxian* in physical labour (16–17.5 pts)	Dress and make-up basically in accordance with the status of a student (16–17.5 pts)	80–89

Average (zhong)	Participating in all kinds of activities organized by the school and the class, often coming late or leaving early, muddling through the activities only (21–24 pts)	Same as above, but done in a basic way only; minus points for the whole month not to exceed 15 (21–24 pts)	Participating in the physical labour organized by the school and the class; quite often coming too late, leaving early, taking sick-leave, and leave to attend to private affairs (14–15.5 pts)	Dress and make-up not quite in accordance with the status of a student (14–15.5 pts)	70–79
Bad (not up to standard) (cha)	Able to participate in the activities organized by the school and the class; sometimes absent without reason; showing behaviour that obstructs the normal order of the activities (19–21 pts)	Not following the laws of the state, the rules of the school, and the school regulations, the discipline of the Student Union, and the hygiene inspection; minus points for the whole month not to exceed 20 (17–21 pts)	Absent without reason in the labour organized by the school and the class; showing fear of dirty or hard work during practical labour; making accidents occur (11–13.5 pts)	Dress and make-up overstep the status of a student (11–13.5 pts)	60–69

[a] The moral and ideological requirements that students should follow are: actively take part in the building of spiritual civilization; love the CCP, the motherland, the socialist system, science, and physical labour; thoroughly study Marxism–Leninism–Mao Zedong's thoughts; and be capable of consciously resisting the corruption of bourgeois ideology.

[b] To get the overall achievement for the whole school term, add the points from all months and divide by the number of months.

Source: 'Ha'erbin shi shangye xuexiao guanli zhidu' (The administrative system of Harbin business school), Harbin (internal school document), 1987, pp. 132–3.

fashionably was regarded as a violation of the moral values of thrift and having a simple life-style.[70]

There are even more detailed examples of point allocation. At the risk of a monotonous listing of norms, sanctions, and rewards, let us look at one example in detail,[71] which is representative of many reports on merit systems. A lot of local circumstances seem to define the various standards and gradings, although they all concern school rules, moral conduct, and problems of a general nature. In the example given here, each student starts at 80 points at the beginning of each semester. A mark of 90 and over is excellent, 80–89 is good, 60–79 is average, and less than 60 is not up to standard. Point allocation and deduction are supervised within the student collective by the class cadres. After their inspection work, the results of moral *biaoxian* are handed over to the class teacher and written into the register form (*dengjibiao*). The small-group network is meant to use the system of quantitative evaluation for their own discussions and decisions.

Plus-points are allotted as follows. Outstanding *biaoxian* means taking an active stand against moral evil, active participation in different moral campaigns, or the student being praised or rewarded at the school level. This type of *biaoxian* earns as much as 5 points. Receiving praise from the school plenary meeting (*xuexiao dahui*) merits 2 points, praise from the class committee (*banweihui*) in charge of moral spirit can incur from 1 to 3 points. Observing the daily schedules, like not being absent from class without leave (*kuanke*), not coming late (*chidao*), or leaving early (*zaotui*), etc., can earn a student up to 3 points. Not violating the school discipline merits 2 points, and active squealing can earn as much as 5 points for 'exposing violations of the school discipline'. Doing a good job as class cadre, Youth League member, or activist in the Young Pioneers is worth from 1 to 3 points.

Demerits are in the form of minus-points. There is a deduction of 3 points for absence without permission; for tardiness an accumulated period of one lost hour leads to a 1-point deduction from the total *biaoxian* mark; disturbing the class order and getting criticized for it takes away 1 point; cheating on tests and exams loses a student 5 points, fighting as much as 10. Vulgar speech results in a deduction of 1 point each time, quarrelling 2 points, smoking 5 points, and not taking part in cultural or sports activities arranged by the school deducts 1 point from the overall *biaoxian*.

The standards involved in the counting of merits and demerits can be of a quite specific character. For example, playing ball inside the school building, skipping rope outside school, or kicking the ball against the school wall all mean a 2-point deduction. Writing graffiti on the wall takes as much as 5 points off the total mark, and neglecting sanitation and hygiene merits a 1-point deduction. Littering, pouring out dirty water, or spitting on the floor earns a demerit of 3 points. Pilfering and being singled out for disciplinary action can lose a student as much as 10–20 points. Damaging public property has great symbolic value, and takes away as much as 20 points even if the 'public property' can be a trifle like a blackboard eraser or some other small item. Damaging flower beds and trees means a 5-point demerit. Not taking part in social activities and campaigns for the public good arranged by the school or class means a loss of 3 points. Not taking the setting-up exercises seriously is a 1-point demerit. Since class cadres can earn extra points, there are also special demerits for those of them who neglect their duties. In such cases they should have their demerit points doubled. Finally, those who violate the rules and refuse to obey the teachers, to admit their mistakes, and to accept criticism, and students who deliberately provoke those who are checking on their attendance and behaviour, should also get their demerit points doubled.

The system of merits and demerits is closely linked to the disciplinary hierarchy of moral errors that represent the prelude to criminal offence. This disciplinary hierarchy is something well known to all Chinese; even if it is difficult for an outsider to understand what error is categorized under what level, among Chinese there is a certain 'feeling' for how far one can go and still be categorized under a specific level. The mildest form is disciplinary sanction (*xingzheng chufen*), and there are five levels here before one comes to the level of criminal sanction (*xingshi chufa*).

Crime prevention is in fact said to be one of the most important tasks of evaluation and the disciplining of *biaoxian*. First there is disciplinary warning (*jinggao*), of which the mildest form is oral warning (*kou jing*). Second comes the recording of a demerit (*jiguo*); not going to class or taking part in fights are examples of errors on this level. The third level is the recording of a major demerit (*jidaguo*), and the fourth level is being detained (at school or in the work-unit) to undergo examination (*liu (xiao/chang) chakan*). The fifth and final form of disciplinary sanction is expulsion (*kaichu*); some informants also refer to this level as *chuming*, meaning to remove somebody's name from the rolls. One of my informants mentioned the case of a student who had beaten up an activist 'three-good student' as an example of an error which evoked this most severe form of disciplinary sanction, the final level of sanctions before an error is categorized as a crime. All types of disciplinary sanction, with a possible exception of the mildest, are recorded in the student or personnel file.[72]

In some indexes of *biaoxian* marking, explicit reference is made to disciplinary hierarchies. In one such example, the first level of disciplinary sanction—the warning—is divided into two parts. A normal warning means 1 *koufen*, or minus point; a serious warning means minus $1\frac{1}{2}$ points. An error on the second level—the recording of a demerit or *jiguo*—loses a student 2 points, on the third level $2\frac{1}{2}$, and an error of the fourth level of disciplinary sanction—the examination—takes 3 points off the record of accumulated marks.[73] In yet another example it is noted that a person who has been evaluated as backward or not up to standard (*cha*) for two successive semesters will be granted leave and exposed to disciplinary sanction. Those who are evaluated as backward for three successive semesters can be asked to leave school.[74] The points of the different systems cannot be directly compared with each other as they follow different procedures of point-setting.

The practice of marking *biaoxian* can also be said to constitute a self-referential system. To gain different titles of honour, you need a certain number of points, but the title itself also conveys additional points. In the previous example from a Harbin specialized secondary school, the title of 'three-good student' (*san hao xuesheng*) merits 15 points. You can earn as much as 50 points if you are elected three-good student on the city level (*shiji san hao xuesheng*). Titles like 'excellent class cadre' (*youxiu bangan*), 'excellent League cadre' (*youxiu tuangan*), and excellent League member (*youxiu tuanyuan zhe*) and other titles of honour also give extra points. Collective titles such as 'excellent school class' (*xiao youxiu banji*) give 5 points. It is also one of the privileges of holding administrative student posts that points are awarded for it; the leader of the student union (*xueshenghui zhuxi*), and the deputy secretary of the Youth League committee (*tuanwei fushuji*) get 15–20 points; members of the student union, the Youth League committee, the class sponsor (*banzhang*), the league branch secretary and those responsible for students' mass organizations (*xuesheng shetuan zuzhi fuze ren*) get 10–15 extra points; and members of the class committee and the Youth League branch get 5–10 points each.[75] School cadres even get an additional 2 points on normal exams.[76]

That holding an administrative post is itself a point-earning activity seems to break with the principle of using moral behaviour as the sole criterion. Holding such posts, however, shows an activist attitude that is highly valued, and is seen as a proof of good *biaoxian* in itself. Since *biaoxian* is not a fixed quality, but has to do with a relation between the leaders and those who are led, it seems only logical that such manifestations are rewarded as they uphold discipline. Rather than representing a breach of the rules, the practice reflects the true nature of *biaoxian*. The subjective and relational character of *biaoxian* and the fixity of the exemplary norm is of course a constant paradox of the Chinese evaluation process. At times the heavy emphasis on objective standards may seem to indicate a permanent bad conscience for a reality already well known to all. The explanation is of course far more complex than that.

The Bureaucratic Logic of Overmeasurement

The belief in a scientific and objective way of measuring *biaoxian* is linked to the narrative of progress and modernization. Many see in the measurement new assurances in a time of change. Fixing behaviours to the stable norm, the trend is clearly linked to the 'civilizing' of society. The measurement of *biaoxian* is a direct part of the overall strategy of 'spiritual civilization'. *Biaoxian* points are called 'points for civilized behaviour' (*wenming xingwei fen*),[77] and the terms 'civilized' or 'civilization' (*wenming*) dominate the discourse on the disciplining of *biaoxian*. For instance there are 'civilized class assessments' (*wenming ban pingbi*),[78] and during the daily hygiene competitions in schools titles of 'civilized dorms' (*wenming sushe*) are awarded.[79] A student can even earn points by 'showing prominence in the building of two civilizations'.[80] Apart from the alleged improvement of individuals, the measurement gives bureaucrats in charge of spiritual civilization a measure of efficiency, it gives school cadres a chance to succeed, and it gives the reform technocrats a legitimacy rooted in science.[81] The roots of this scientism are deeply embedded in past practices, so again we see legacies from the past reappearing in the present.

The late Ming/early Qing period has long been identified as a time of intense social and economic change in China. The use of a type of moral account books, or ledgers of merit and demerit, during that period was an attempt to seek moral assurities in numbers. This reliance on numbers goes even further back. In ancient China, from around the third century BC, number-mysticism was an important means for understanding and organizing nature and society for at least 1,500 years.[82] The ledger of merit and demerit was a kind of morality book to be used for the improvement of individuals, and to encourage good and exemplary deeds while discouraging bad behaviour. It was assumed that the gods rewarded and punished human behaviour according to certain established moral standards. These books list good and bad deeds, using merit and demerit points to enable the user to measure his or her moral standing in a precise way.

Belief in the system of merit and demerit can be traced back to pre-Han times. For a period (parallel to the belief in number-mysticism) from the third century BC to the late twelfth century, when the first ledger of merit and demerit was produced, the system served primarily a religious purpose: in Daoist texts it was seen as a means of earning immortality; in Buddhist texts, rebirth in a higher level of existence.[83] Later, the ledgers served a more secular purpose, as a means of attaining social and career goals such as success in the examinations, official positions, etc. Still later, the ledger system was adopted by the educated elite as an instrument for strict moral and social discipline. By the eighteenth century the ledgers were commonly incorporated into the collections of moral instructions frequently published by gentry officials.

The belief in the salutory effect of good deeds listed in the ledgers is still very much a part of Chinese moral education. Since bureaucrats rather than priests were in charge of human improvement, it was only natural that ledgers rather than prayer books served the task of upholding moral order. And, as one of the ledger authors said, instead of praying to gods or sacrificing to heaven, performing five hundred, a thousand, three thousand, five thousand, and ten thousand meritorious deeds is more effective: as soon as the promised number of meritorious deeds is accomplished, your wishes will be granted. This awareness of the distinction between overt behaviour and covert motivation is a common feature of morality books since the late Ming.[84]

The ledgers were also used as a means to guarantee the Confucian principle of self-awareness and self-cultivation, or 'being cautious when alone' (*shendu*)—when hidden from the public gaze. The instructions given in the ledgers resemble the procedures for measuring *biaoxian*. The ledgers contain a list of standard good and evil deeds and mark their value in positive and negative figures. The reader is provided with blanks for listing demeritorious and meritorious deeds, and for calculating the balance: first the month should be entered, then the day of the month; under each day, one should make two columns, one for merits (*gong*) the other for demerits (*guo*); just before retiring for the night, one should write down the good and bad things done during the day, consulting the ledger for the points for each deed, and recording them on the sheet. These instructions were given in the famous Song dynasty work, the *Gong guo ge* (Ledger of merits and demerits).[85] The character *ge* has the meaning of 'standard' and 'regulation', and the book was intended as a guide to exemplary morality. But *ge* also means a frame, a limit, a pattern, or ruled lines for writing. The practitioner of this system is urged to keep an account of everyday behaviour. In this sense *ge* has been appropriately translated as 'ledger', and the most striking feature of the moral ledger is its quantification of morality. By keeping a daily tally of merits and demerits based on a system of points, and by taking monthly and yearly inventories, one was always able to determine the standing of one's moral account.[86]

The reappearance and popularity of these old morality books is yet another example of how the memories of the past reappear during modernization. It was recently stated that about 150,000 copies of ancient morality books sold out immediately after they were republished.[87] The ledgers might be seen as methods devised by bureaucrats to classify the populace, and some of their methods might have had some influence on popular morality. A study of the exemplary standards listed in these books has been found illuminating for the understanding of Chinese moral values, and I think a renewed look at the modern version of standard construction will serve the same purpose. In the moral ledgers and in the modern measuring of *biaoxian*, we see a general trend whereby buraucratic rationality was taking over other sectors such as education, morality, etc. Already the imperial exam system was a career system rather than a pedagogical system, with education geared more towards this aim than towards learning as such. Similarly, the quantified recording of morality has more to do with administrative classification and disciplining the populace, and with the administration of moral and social order, than with ethical matters in any strict sense.

Biaoxian marking is closely linked to the debate about the exemplary norm. In one example of the distribution of overall morality marks among university students, we see that the distribution of results does not follow a normal distribution curve. Instead, it opens up towards the exemplary end, with few really low marks, and considerably more marks in the upper echelons. Of the 65 students in this example, only 4 (6.1 per cent) did not pass or reach the 60-point mark; 24 students (37 per cent) got an average mark of 60–70 points, 21 (32.3 per cent) got good marks of 70–80 points, and 16 (24.6 per cent) achieved more than 80 points, and were termed excellent.[88] This small example may serve as an illustration of a much-stated 'fact of life' in debates on moral evaluation: that marking is meant to encourage and inspire, to improve the quality of individuals. Beijing teachers also told me there were no upper quotas for 'three-good students' even if there were stiff requirements for obtaining that title of honour: everybody should have the chance, and again no normal distribution-curve was found.[89] There is, however, another and less optimistic explanation. A survey about school leaders' attitudes towards political education showed that they were cynical about such education, but needed high moral–political marks because their schools are evaluated by the results they produce.[90] The diffuse character of such education made it easier to produce high scores in this subject.

As I have mentioned, there are obvious traces of the past in the present measurement of *biaoxian*. It is far from a modern phenomenon alone. On the other hand, the tendency is embedded in a bureaucratic rationality which has been brought about by an administration's need to legitimate its own activities by making moral–political activities comparable. Administrative and political cadres in charge of spiritual civilization work simply need a measure to show that their work is efficient. Of course, they realize that moral–political evaluation is a diffuse substance characterized by low quantification. Since that type of matter cannot be made visible in a bureaucratically rational way, measurability simply has to be forced on it. The problem is an important one indeed: that of trying to overcome the subjective methods of judgement inherent in the virtuocratic process. But the process of modernizing or rationalizing virtuocracy has often proved to be nothing but a scientistic trap. Instead of being preoccupied by *what* is actually measured in the process of judging morality, one is diverted to the question of *how* it is measured. In the language of methodology, this means concentrating on the reliability more than on the validity of the process. Methodology textbooks in the social sciences tell us that, once the scientist has failed to establish validity, he no longer knows what he has measured. As one sociologist puts it,

The chances of such failure are increased by the interaction between the researcher and his subjects, the imposition of his definition on theirs, their ability to interpret and adjust to his motives, and their skill in managing their responses.[91]

At the same time, in the process of evaluation, the very method of evaluating insists on the closest possible relations between the individuals involved in the process. What we see in the measuring of *biaoxian* is an attempt to measure objectively a process that demands subjectivity. Not only is there an attempt to measure and quantify, the process even tends to develop into overmeasurement. For example, in schools the administration pushes its bureaucratic rationality on the teachers in ways that make it difficult to fulfil tasks of education. To understand this, we have to make a short detour to consider the organizational setup of schools in China.

There are three organizational levels in addition to the grass-roots level, and the class teacher stands in between the school administration on the one side and parents and students on the other. The class teacher is a power-holder in some senses, and the title—*banzhuren*—literally means 'class chairman'. But the realm of the *banzhuren* is the class only. In many senses there is a relative powerlessness in the the class teacher's role, as he or she is squeezed in between the administration and the students and their parents. The highest organizational level in school is the 'school' level (*xiaoji ceng*) and is made up by the headmaster (*xiaozhang*) and the party secretary (*dangzhibu shu*). Then comes the administrative or management level (*chuji ceng*), where there are several leaders. The instruction director (*jiaodao zhuren*) is in charge of educational affairs, and is the direct leader of the class teachers. Here we also find the director in charge of general affairs (*zongwu zhuren*), the school factory director (*xiaoban zhuren*), and the person responsible for the Youth League (*tuandui ziren ren*). Then comes the third and lowest level in the hierarchy, the class level (*banji ceng*). This is no purely administrative level, even if teachers also have administrative tasks; it mainly concerns the day-to-day teaching. The class teachers and the 'responsible' teachers (*renke jiaoshi*) are represented in this level.

The class teacher, in other words, represents the basic level (*jizeng*) in the school organization, and is in charge of moral education. The *banzhuren* is defined as the person who 'establishes ideological and moral quality', the moral entrepreneur of spiritual civilization. There are a lot of rosy characteristics used to describe the sizeable tasks of a class teacher. Class teachers 'represent the relation to the people's and nation's future generations, and [determine] whether they will achieve a good or a bad quality, a high or a low level'. The class teacher is the school's face to the world, and a 'link between school, family, and society'—the so called 'bridging effect' (*qiaoliang zuoyong*). The class teacher receives orders and directives from above, and is responsible for carrying out the educational instructions of the headmaster. The *banzhuren* might be regarded as a foot-soldier of moral education, or a sergeant or a foreman. Placed 'in between', they have to obey instructions, and the main directive is to 'keep order in class'.[92] Despite the relative power class teachers have on the class level, powerlessness defines their relation to the school bureaucracy. Social status is also low.[93] The position of class teachers is important to understand because it shows the power of the school administration, and explains why a bureaucratic rationality can dominate schools even if teachers are not particularly enthusiastic about the quantification drive.

Complaints from teachers are often heard, and these complaints are understandable. The high demands on teachers can be seen through one example of the evaluation they themselves undergo. The following example also illustrates the bureaucratic moral quantification game, and a part of the 'human quality' technology that has been rapidly spreading in recent years.

As so much of the technocratic literature of the reforms, this model of teacher evaluation is inspired by the discourse of cybernetics or 'control theory' so popular in China during the last decade.[94] 'System' (*xitong*) is a most celebrated expression of that tradition, and the word has come to signify a scientific approach as such. One typical model operates with an 'ideological and moral quality system', a 'scientific and cultural quality system', and a 'bodily and psychological quality system'. In the elaborate table of 'teacher quality evaluation', ideological–political quality is the most important standard, accounting for as much as 45 per cent of the total quality evaluation. Scientific and cultural quality counts for 35 per cent, and physical and psychological quality for 20 per cent.[95] Particularly outstanding quality characteristics should be rewarded with extra 'advantage points' (*quanfen*). Within each quality system 11 such points can be given. In all, 33 advantage points can be obtained. Table 3 describes an evaluation with four grades: excellent, good, pass, and not qualified (or not up to standard) (*you, liang, jige, bu hege*). The quality marking has been written as A, B, C, D, with the additional extra points. The table gives a detailed description of the standards for 'teacher quality' as well as for 'human quality' in general.

TABLE 3   Evaluation form for class teacher quality

Structural system	No.	Most important features (sub-systems)	A	B	C	D	Extra points	Total points
Ideological and moral quality A = 45 B = 36	1	Attitude and standpoint towards the four basic principles	15	13	12	10	5	
	2	Study of Marxist theory	12	9	8	6	2	
	3	Educational ideology and attitude	8	7	6	2	2	
	4	Teacher's moral cultivation and exemplary effect	8	6	5	4	2	
								45
Scientific and cultural quality A = 35 B = 27	5	Knowledge of scientific educational theory	5	4	3.5	3	2	
	6	Specialized basic	5	4	3.5	3	2	

TABLE 3 *(cont'd)*

Structural system	No.	Most important features (sub-systems)	A	B	C	D	Extra points	Total points
		knowledge and general cultural knowledge						
	7	Observation and thinking power	5	4	3.5	3	2	
	8	Language expression ability	5	3.5	3	2.5	1	
	9	Ability in organizing education	5	3.5	3	2.5	1	
	10	Moral ability	5	4	3	1.5	1	
	11	Handling and operating ability (labour attitude and technical ability)	5	4	3.5	2.5	2	
								35
Bodily and psychological quality A = 20 B = 16	12	Bodily shape and function	5	4	3.5	3	2	
	13	Knowledge and ability in hygiene and health protection	5	4	3.5	2.5	2	
	14	Personal preferences (aesthetic sentiment)	5	4	3.5	3	3	
	15	Will and temperamental characteristics	4	3	3.5	2.5	3	
								20

Note: If one adds up all the figures, there seems to be a slight inconsistency in the sum of single marks and the calculated total marks. The table is taken directly from the source as presented there.

Source: Xin Yang (ed.), *Zhongguo banzhurenxue* (Chinese class teacher studies), Changchun, Jilin jiaoyu chubanshe, 1990, p. 189.

TABLE 4   Example of all-round class teacher quality evaluation

| | Evaluating instance (trait no.) | | | | | | | | | | | | | | |
	1	2	3	4	5	6	7	8	9	10	11	12	13	14	15
School leader	A	B	A	B	B	A	C	C	A	B	C	C	C	A	B
Students	A	B	B	A	A	A	C	C	B	B	C	C	B	A	A
Teachers	A	B	B	B	B	A	B	C	B	A	B	B	C	B	C
Self-evaluation	A	A	B	B	B	A	C	B	B	B	C	C	B	A	B

Source: Xin Yang (ed.) (see Table 3), p. 191.

An excellent grasp of the 'four basic principles' gives the highest score of all the 'sub-systems' in Table 3. These principles directly reflect Deng Xiaoping's guidelines for reform based on supporting the road to socialism, the dictatorship of the proletariat, the party leadership, and Deng's version of Marxism–Leninism–Mao Zedong thought. Since the leadership defines the criteria, the principle is strictly about loyalty. The Confucian stress on loyalty (*zhong*) thus seems to come back as the main standard for modern technocratic approaches of 'human quality'. In many ways, this corresponds to the relational definition of *biaoxian* as well. The main standard that, paradoxically, defines all the 'object-ive standards' is the subjective attitude towards one's leaders. As can be seen in Table 3, the diffuse character of some standards is well in line with the description of virtuocratic evaluation. The final point-setting lies in the hands of the administration as represented by the school leader, but it is recommended that students as well as other teachers take part in the evaluation and give marks. A self-evaluation rounds off the evaluation procedure, and adds up to a final mark. The all-round model of mark-setting is illustrated in Table 4.

For the sake of simplicity, the marks are made equal for all fifteen of the sub-systems in Xin Yang's example, even if there are different point scores for each item. The various weights of the different evalu-ators are not commented on, but normal practice is that the evalu-ation of the school leader is the final input. I have kept some of the original's emphasis on numbers, Xs, and Σs to illustrate the symbolic effect they have in pedagogical literature. They are signs of modernity, even if the calculations are very simple indeed. In all, we have 60 marks, of which 18 are graded A (excellent); this makes $18 \div 60 = 30$ per cent; 27 are graded B (good), making $27 \div 60 = 45$ per cent; 15 are graded C (passed), which means $15 \div 60 = 25$ per cent. A-marks are given a weight of 100, B-marks a weight of 80, and C-marks a weight of

60, while there are no disqualifying D-marks in the example. In the above example, this gives A = 30% × 100 = 30, B = 45% × 80 = 36, and C = 25% × 60 = 15. The total grade for this teacher will then be 30 + 36 + 15 = 81. By summing up the total grades of each teacher in school, we get the total school performance in the formula:

$$M = X_1 + X_2 + \ldots + X_n/n = \Sigma X_n/n.$$

To put it more simply, if there are four teachers and they get the point sums 81, 67, 84, and 73, the school average teacher quality will be the total of these marks, 305, divided by the number of teachers: 305 ÷ 4 = 76.25. On each of the three 'structural system' standards, the extra points should be added to make up the total score. The number of 'qualified' (*hege*) teachers is said to be 30 per cent among the 5.5 million teachers in primary school, 23.5 per cent among the 2.16 million teachers in lower secondary school, and 39.6 per cent among the 460,000 teachers in upper secondary school. A teacher in the C-bracket with between 60 and 74 points is characterized as *jige*—one having passed the exam.[96]

The school administration can give very detailed orders to the class teacher about daily classroom work. In the logic of bureaucracy, classroom order must be measured if it is to make sense and to be proved effective. Some class teachers have offered strong arguments against the bureaucratic rationalization of educational work, since it directly interferes with their classroom teaching.

Commenting on the reform of class teacher administration, Si Ren points out the flaws of the growing bureaucratization of morality and indirectly also of the entire teacher role.[97] The class teacher becomes a petty bureaucrat, and a master of ceremonies for intricate 'scientific' methods of evaluation. The administrative work of the class teacher has become too minute and too rigid; mark-setting is too frequent and too detailed. Some teachers also have regulations about how to use basic points (*jiben fen*), plus points (*jiafen*), minus points (*koufen*), and reverse minus points (*dao koufen*) in addition to recording their daily impressions. All this makes the school atmosphere quite tense. Assessments are loaded with trivial details, and the over-elaborate procedure of examination and assessment has many disadvantages but few advantages. The system destroys the creativity of both teachers and students. One main criticism is that, with too many rules and regulations in the evaluation process, many class teachers cannot but adopt an administrative approach towards education. The result is that ideological work becomes very difficult to carry out. The second main criticism is that the complicated evaluation systems are not rational. For instance, through a 'merry go round' of casual or ritual drop-ins at parents' homes you can manage to reach your 'quota' (*zhibiao*), since quality is here measured by frequency. Doing thorough family education work during home visits, however, makes you fall behind; it cannot be measured by the frequency norms of fulfilling class teacher's quality quotas. The result is a stifling system that prevents rationality instead of promoting it. Furthermore, the class teacher cannot leave the class for one second because he or she is too busy doing the *pingbi* work of comparison and assessment. These methods also hinder other types of social work and family education work and obstruct the flow of normal teaching.

The reply to Si Ren's criticism merely states that the reform should allow different programmes to develop, and to drop those that fail to prove successful. The class teacher has to follow up the directives about evaluation; here the pressure is great since the teacher's own evaluation depends on the evaluation of the students. Si Ren's attack supports the impression I gained from interviewing teachers, namely that enthusiasm about a quantified moral evaluation was not particularly high among them.

Another example of the irrationality of bureaucratic measurement concerns control in class, and shows the irrationality of some disciplinary techniques based on registration. Filling in forms (*tian biao*) is a favourite pastime of Chinese bureaucracy, and the practice is imposed on teachers as well. Methods of registration and the mark-setting of *biaoxian* must, of course, rely on observation; for this purpose the taking of observation notes (*canguan jilu*) is recommended for the class teacher.[98] All types of behaviour in class are to be noted and immediately written down. The recommended method is to use a 'regular observation record' (*an shijian de guancha de jilu*), in which the teacher notes down name and time for the occurrence of 'small movements' (*xiao dongzuo*) or other minor violations of classroom order throughout the fifty minutes of the class period. This observation record is a good indication of the constant observation and total visibility sought in the evaluation process.

A scale for observance made on a form is shown in Table 5. The class teacher is to observe anyone making 'small movements', or teasing others, looking out of the window, etc., for each five-minute interval. Each incident of small violation should be marked with an 0 for the student in question, and an all-round 'score' indicated at the top of the form. This recording method can also be made more systematic by naming the violation, like writing an A for 'small movements', B for teasing, C for looking out of the window. For each pupil there is to be a form with his or her name.

TABLE 5   Example of a 'regular observation record'

Name...   Total score.........................

5	10	15	20	25	30	35	40	45	50
0					0				0

Source: Hu Shoufen, *Deyu yuanli* (Principles of moral education), rev. edn., Beijing, Beijing shifan daxue chubanshe, 1989, p. 391.

In addition to this type of observation record, an additional 'anecdote record' (*yishi jilu*) should be used. The anecdote record is less quantitative, and there are forms of describing the problem with an additional space for interpretation. For this purpose special report cards (*kapian*) or 'ledger records' (*fenhu jilu*) are to be used. Behaviour frequency should be systematically written into these records. Fact description and fact interpretations should be recorded separately in the space provided for such notes. Both unusually good and bad behaviour should be observed, and a special 'behaviour frequency measure' (*xingwei pinlü de celiang*) should be used to give a 'clear and mathematically accurate picture' of the situation measured in an hour–behaviour ratio. For instance, if the period of observation has been half an hour, and the observed behaviour has occurred three times, this yields an hourly frequency of $3 \div 0.5 = 6$, and so on. Other disciplinary frequencies and ratios are also listed. One has only to imagine a class teacher at his desk in front of maybe fifty or more children, trying to give them moral education, and at the same time observing and writing down which of them are making small movements or looking out of the window, to see that bureaucratic rationality is not educational rationality. Apart from the obviously comical aspect of that poor class teacher, one can understand the frustration of class teachers faced with a bureaucracy with a logic alien to their own.

The problem concerns the organized 'imperialist' character of bureaucratic systems. In regulating education, a bureaucracy transforms that education in its own image, disregarding the needs of education. The problem is also one of overmeasurement caused by the administration's needs to legitimize its spiritual civilization work. Amitai Etzioni explains this phenomenon thus:

Most organizations under pressure to be rational are eager to measure their efficiency. Curiously the very effort—the desire to establish how we are doing and to find ways of improving if we are not doing as well as we ought to do—often has quite undesired effects from the point of view of the organizational goals. Frequent measuring can distort the organizational efforts because, as a rule, some aspects of its output are more measurable than others. Frequent measuring tends to encourage over-production of highly measurable items and neglect the less measurable ones.[99]

The quantified *biaoxian* record is undoubtedly an effective control mechanism. However, as in bureaucratic organizations, the result of such evaluation is as described by Peter Blau: 'the quantitative evaluation system led to the neglect of other phases of operations and sometimes directly interfered with employment service'.[100] In China the problem is even more acute since the object of measurement is morality and 'human quality' as such. Despite the obvious problems, statistical records of performance have in general proved themselves an effective mechanism of bureaucratic control,[101] but for various reasons it just might not be really possible to 'operationalize' morality into statistical records the way China has been attempting. The much-touted 'spiritual civilization' might turn out to be nothing more than a mere myth of scientism.

Evaluation, Surveillance, and Democracy

Textbooks on evaluation repeatedly see the process as something 'natural' and all-embracing. Evaluation is also directly linked to the issue of democracy. Some enthusiastically claim that 'evaluation develops a democratic consciousness'[102] among people, while others see the power and coercion of that process. Su Weichang and Zhang Dimei's textbook on evaluation discusses the fact that evaluation can be misused as a means of power. Evaluation can be viewed as the 'trump card' of coercion. The threat of the person in power could typically be: 'If you don't change your ways, I'll write a negative conduct evaluation report about you.' There is, however, no discussion of this aspect, merely a comment that this is the wrong way of using evaluation. In the particularistic society of organized dependence—described by Walder and discussed in Chapter 2—this is of course a problem of considerable dimension, illustrated not least by the subjective character of *biaoxian*. Petty bureaucrats or others in authority representing the exemplary standards have the freedom to change the evaluations arrived at from the individual reports and small-group assessments; for instance, in schools, the class teacher can adjust (*tiaozheng*) the evaluations of the others.[103]

In a description of her reforms of moral evaluation techniques, model-teacher Ren Xiao'ai presents a microcosm of the evaluating and controlling techniques in a system based on a moral responsibility principle.[104] Ren's articles on evaluation reform are interesting because they stress the connections between control and participation, and indirectly tell us a great deal about a view of democracy alien to a Western eye. Democracy in this connection is linked to the objectivity of norms, and is focused on the principle of self-management or self-supervision (*ziwo guanli*). Ren feels that teachers should foster abilities in self-supervision among students 'to fit the needs of society', and should not resort to the 'nursing and policing' styles and methods previously used. Such an approach would contribute to human improvement and 'create a new self' among the participants.

Ren's suggestion for reform builds on quite traditional ideas about regulation through written records. Democracy through participatory self-surveillance, in her view, rests with the written registration of behaviour; families should also be involved in this recording process. The method she suggests are meant to enhance the scope of information, find hidden abilities, and open up the evaluation process. The first stage is to establish a 'contact transmission record' (*lianxi chuandi bu*), regulating the contact between school and home. The parents' meetings should continue at regular intervals, and the already widespread practice of home visits by the teacher should be upheld. The contract transmission record should ambulate between school and home every week. It should carry notes on the students' moral behaviour, the rules of study, attendance record, test record, level of hygiene, delivering of homework, etc. Students themselves should bring the book home every Saturday; parents should use the weekend to go through teachers' evaluations, and carefully write down the students' *biaoxian* at home; each Monday the students should bring the record back to school. The teacher could then inspect it, and direct education towards any specific problems. This 'connection record' (*guanxibu*), the home visits, and the parents' meeting (*jiachang hui*), used together, could gather the best information possible about the students.

In Ren's view, there is an assumption linking the evaluation process to the Durkheimian concept of 'autonomy'. Freedom and democracy are part of a moral science based on the reliable knowledge of the moral order; and this is precisely the knowledge offered through the evaluation process. The message seems to be that democracy lies in accurate information, but also in finding the correct way to utilize the surveillance potential of the evaluated individuals themselves. As a way to overcome the contradictions between activists and the others, Ren suggests an activist rotation system, and this idea can stand as an example of a more general trend in Chinese disciplinary technology. Here again she bases her ideas on *ziwo guanli*, the crucial principle of self-supervision. While not opposing the traditional system of activists in any way, Ren suggests an additional 'system of fixed rotation of class cadres' (*ban ganbu dingqi lunhuan zhi*) to utilize the resources of control and surveillance from the whole class collective, and to try out more democratic methods of participation. This system has received due support in educational journals, and has found its way into schools and textbooks of pedagogy and evaluation techniques.

A 'two-day class teacher system' (*er ri banzhuren zhi*) and a 'one day hygiene supervisor system' (*yi ri weisheng jiandu yuan zhi*) should alternate every other month. The 'two-day class teacher system' would allow an elected student to read other students' diaries, make home visits, give notes to the parents, correct homework, and write remarks in the students' records (*jilu*) for two days. The class leader can set up his or her own 'cabinet' during this time. He or she should be addressed as 'teacher', and not by his or her given name, by both students and parents. After the two days are over the 'class teacher' would be evaluated by fellow students who would give marks for the two-day performance. These remarks would later be entered into the school file. The 'one-day hygiene supervisor', again an elected student, should check hygiene in general, including hairstyle, fingernails, clothes, and oral hygiene, whether fellow students use a civilized vocabulary or whether they swear and use dirty words. Bad behaviour should be criticized in the small group. If serious mistakes are reported, negative marks should be given.

Ren's idea here is that the class will be easier to control if the resources of the students themselves are used to help keep control. At the same time, it would develop each student, provide them with a better understanding of class teacher work, and underline the necessity of authority.

The rest of Ren's suggestions are in line with the normal practices of organizing evaluation through *pingbi* with its different reward systems, plus and minus points, titles of honour, material rewards, etc. She suggests a weekly overall appraisal (*zongping*), and stresses the collective feeling of honour (*jiti rongyu gan*) in the group, suggesting the use of an honour roll (*hongbang*) where collective as well as individual good deeds can be displayed.[105] In the university each department would post a notice of commendation (*tongbao biaoyang*) or criticism. The list would be circulated for school cadres to check.[106]

The democratic character of evaluation is often emphasized. Each individual is evaluated in small groups. Students can dissent if they wish;

they can reconsider decisions, and re-examine a case through these discussions in a democratic way. Self-understanding and democracy are thus promoted, and students can regulate their behaviour better, bringing it in accordance with the objective norms.[107] Often, however, the type of democracy discussed in the literature on evaluation indicates a very important distinction between Chinese and Western conceptions of 'democracy'. In China, evaluation is said to represent an 'objective' democracy where the exact knowledge of objective norms and standards forms the basis of the process. Evaluation entails insight into necessity.

The Chinese 'democracy of evaluation' is contrasted to a Western 'democracy of election'. An interesting article by Jin Rong discusses the importance of '*ping*'—evaluation or appraisal—and the uselessness of '*xuan*'—selection or election. Jin criticizes the fact that certain work-units have recently neglected the systematic evaluation of their employees. Instead of evaluation (*ping*), the units have used election (*xuan*) procedures to find the right persons for the right tasks, etc. Elections are used instead of evaluation, ballots instead of judgement. The educational aspects inherent in evaluation disappear from the process in such cases. Some people simply vote according to their own likes or dislikes, whether they are related to people, whether they have connections or *guanxi* with them, etc. Jin says that if elections are used instead of evaluation, the unity and stability of the work-units will disappear. Some prefer the new electoral procedures because they are so much faster, and avoid the quarrels associated with the evaluation procedure. Some people might have had bad experiences with the evaluation process, Jin admits, but their reactions are exaggerated and, 'like someone who is one day bitten by a snake, they get afraid of the rope to the well for three years'.[108]

It is interesting to note that the argument of rampant nepotism is cited against elections, and that factional infighting is blamed on them, since some of the arguments *for* elections go in the same direction. The explanation for Jin's outburst is easy to spot. The lack of a standard against which to judge people is evident in an election; elections are thus unprincipled and chaotic. Furthermore, elections are not objective because they are not linked to an exemplary standard; in fact, they are not linked to any standard at all, and there is no element of improvement or education in an election. Surely, it is wrong to be able to choose whomever you like for this or that post or purpose. The educative aspect as well as the building order lies in *ping*, in evaluation. Jin's argument indicates some of the traditional Chinese scepticism towards elections and representative democracy in general, and goes some way to explain the immense importance of evaluation in all walks of Chinese everyday life. Many authors have taken up the theme of evaluative democracy. Instead of emphasizing the ballot box and the ballot paper, the *xiaozu* network is presented as the stage on which democracy is intended to develop. A typical comment in the journal 'Shanghai education' formulates the idea explicitly: 'Small group evaluation develops a democratic consciousness.'[109] We can call this type of evaluative democracy an 'objective' or 'exemplary' democracy in line with the idea of moral science lying at the root of the argument.

The editor of the journal 'Research in higher education' shares the concern over elections to select candidates for the title of 'three-good student', claiming that appraisals are often carelessly done through secret ballot. Behind the concern lies the fear that the strictly regulated standards for the 'three-good student'—good study results, good moral conduct, and good health—could be tampered with. Critical to elections, the article signals its adherence to reform in another way, by suggesting a much wider use of material incentives as an end-product of the evaluation process. Material rewards should be allowed, and both cash awards and bonuses are suggested. Awards for excellent studies (*xuexi youxiu jiang*) should be graded, and those for making progress in study (*xuexi jinbu jiang*) should also be introduced.[110] Reform-minded articles are often much more likely to support reforms concerning material incentives than notions of elective democracy on any level.

Evaluation also seems to be a more regulated and less chaotic alternative to competition. Some have warned against the mounting problems of 'blind climbing' on the reform ladder of consumption and status. Evaluation through comparison should not be performed in order to show off one's wealth and self, but to compare oneself against a moral standard.[111] Order lies in evaluation compared against a standard, chaos in the unprincipled election.

The 'building' character of evaluation should be understood not only in terms of individual improvement. It concerns the building of the entire civilization, and is seen as a means to enhance both science and democracy. Evaluation procedures not only reflect the narrative of order, but also touch upon the narrative of progress, as does the spiritual civilization movement itself. In the standards of evaluation the themes of work ethic, thrift, and professional knowledge also appear. It is explicitly said that the evaluation process is closely connected to the four modernizations and economic development.[112] 'Only communist morality fits the needs of the development of the socialist mode of production,' says Wang Xingzhou. Such morality is an important factor in promoting the development of society and 'the basic and objective standard for the moral evaluation of people's behaviour'.[113]

Such general statements, however, are not accurate enough for the systematic and 'scientific' approach to the construction of standards that has emerged during reform. Long lists of measurable standards have been set up, as in Hu, Tang, and Ouyang's moral quality index system. There is now an attempt to include values of modernity in those long lists. These authors have constructed an index where morality is operationalized into forty-seven items, broken down into eleven main items, where 'seeking knowledge' is regarded as the most important.[114] The index emphasizes productive values, but the authors nevertheless underline the importance of morality. Moral quality is an even more important measure than age, social status, etc., they claim.[115] Both traditional and modern values are used in this index, but the aim here is to introduce modern standards within the same frame of ledgers used for the same type of evaluation as we have now discussed. The 'seeking knowledge' part of the index concerns the qualification of the work-force and includes such attributes as study habits, self-strength, creativity, and effectiveness. Other items are also related to a high work ethic.[116] Modern change is again controlled through the construction of fixed but orderly and gradually adapting standards, approached through an orderly process of objective evaluation. The attitudes towards the norms are ordered or frozen into written files, to which we now turn.

Notes to Chapter 7

1. Xie Hongmao and Chen Weifeng, 'Daxuesheng suzhi zonghe ceping tansuo' (Exploring the comprehensive appraisal of university students), *Fujian gaojiao yanjiu*, No. 1, 1991, p. 64.
2. Hu Wei, 'Xiandai deyu pingjia de tedian ji gongneng' (The characteristics and functions of modern moral evaluation), *Shanghai jiaoyu*, No. 7–8, 1987, pp. 16–17.
3. Wang Keqian, 'Shilun jiazhi he pingjia' (On values and evaluations), *Shehui kexue jikan*, No. 1, 1990, pp. 17–23.
4. Ibid., p. 18.
5. Hu Wei, p. 17.
6. Wang Keqian, pp. 19–21.
7. Zhang Yutian *et al.* (eds.), *Xuexiao jiaoyu pingjia* (Evaluation in school education), Beijing, Zhongying minzu xueyuan chubanshe, 1987, pp. 236–7.
8. Sun Longji, *Zhongguo wenhua de shenceng jiegou* (The deep structure of Chinese society), Hong Kong, Jixian she, 1983, p. 81.
9. Liu Guangming, 'Talü: zhongguoren xingge zhong de beiju' (Other-ruled: the tragedy of Chinese nature), *Qingnian xuezhe*, No. 1, 1989, pp. 50–1.
10. Zhang Yutian, *et al.* (eds.), p. 237.
11. Interviewees nos. 4, 5, 6, Beijing, 1991.

12. See Xie Hongmao and Chen Weifeng, p. 64.

13. Ding Ruxu, 'Guanyu banzhuren gongzuo yu jiating jiaoyu jiehe de xin tansuo' (New explorations of integrating class teacher work and family education), *Banzhuren*, No. 2, 1988, p. 30.

14. Ibid.

15. Ibid., p. 32.

16. 'Ha'erbin shi shangye xuexiao guanli zhidu' (The administrative system of Harbin business school), Harbin (internal school document), 1987, p. 90.

17. Xin Yang (ed.), *Zhongguo banzhurenxue* (Chinese class teacher studies), Changchun, Jilin jiaoyu chubanshe, 1990, p. 185.

18. Xia Daoxing, 'Gaige sixiang pinde ke kaocha de changshi' (An attempt to examine the reform of ideology and morality classes), *Jiaoxue yanjiu (xiaoxue ban)*, No. 4, 1987, p. 38. For a detailed description of evaluation of 'labour requirements' for primary school children, see Li Yuqi and Xie Yupu, 'Sheji laodong kepian shanghao laodong ke' (Planning a good labour class by using a labour card), *Hebei jiaoyu*, No. 10, 1989, p. 14.

19. Liu Jianyuan, 'Zengqiang ziwo pingjia yishi cujin jiaoyu gaige' (Strengthen the consciousness of self-evaluation, promote educational reform), *Xinjiang jiaoyu*, No. 4, 1989, pp. 10–11.

20. Ding Rong, 'Banhui huodong zhong jiaoshi de zhudao zuoyong yu xuesheng de zhuti zuoyong' (The guiding function of teachers and the subject function of students in class meeting activities), *Beijing jiaoyu*, No. 4, 1986, p. 18.

21. Ibid., p. 19.

22. Ibid., p. 20.

23. Martin King Whyte, *Small Groups and Political Rituals in China*, Berkeley/ Los Angeles, University of California Press, 1974, p. 11.

24. Ibid., p. 15.

25. Shanghai shi jiaoxian zhongxiaoxue deyu xiezuo yanjiu hui (eds.), *Nongcun zhongxiaoxue banzhuren gongzuo zhidao* (Directions for class teacher work in rural primary and secondary schools), Shanghai, Shanghai kexue jishu chubanshe, 1990, p. 104.

26. Interviewee 11, Beijing, 1991.

27. Based on interview material from Beijing, 1986; see Børge Bakken, *Kunnskap og moral* (Knowledge and morality), Report No. 1, Department of Sociology, University of Oslo, 1989, p. 197.

28. Ibid., p. 120.

29. *Zhongguo baike nianjian 1982* (China encyclopedic yearbook 1982), Beijing, Zhongguo dabaike quanshu chubanshe, 1982, p. 577.

30. *Zhongguo baike nianjian 1985* (China encyclopedic yearbook 1985), Beijing, Zhongguo dabaike quanshu chubanshe, 1985, p. 232.

31. Zhang Nianhong (ed.), *Jiaoyuxue cidian* (Dictionary of education), Beijing, Beijing chubanshe, 1987, p. 251.

32. See Yin Anren, 'Shilun xuesheng xingwei de kongzhi yu tiaojie' (On the control and regulation of student behaviour), *Shehui*, No. 5, 1985, p. 6.

33. Li Wenxiang, 'Xuesheng deyu zhiliang de lianghua pingjia' (The quantitative evaluation of students' moral quality), *Gaodeng jiaoyu yanjiu*, No. 2, 1986, p. 93.

34. 'Ha'erbin shi shangye xuexiao guanli zhidu', pp. 124–5.

35. Xie Hongmao and Chen Weifeng, p. 65.

36. *Zhongguo jiaoyu bao*, 1 April 1986, p. 2.

37. Ibid., 30 June 1987, p. 3, gives details about this 'morality diploma inflation', and specifies which reports were supposed to be in the files.
38. 'Ha'erbin shi shangye xuexiao guanli zhidu', pp. 131–5; see also *Zhongguo jiaoyu bao*, 25 March 1986, p. 4.
39. Caizhengbu renshi jiaoyu (ed.), *Wei hao caizheng zhongzhuan jiaoyu wei sihua jianshe peiyang rencai* (Fostering talent for good finance in secondary school education for the building of the four modernizations), Beijing, Zhongguo Caizheng jingji chubanshe, 1983, pp. 257–60.
40. This information is based on interviews with students from Beijing University in Beijing in 1986.
41. Susan Shirk, *Competitive Comrades: Career Incentives and Student Strategies in China*, Berkeley/Los Angeles, University of California Press, 1982, pp. *ix–x*.
42. Xie Hongmao and Chen Weifeng, pp. 63–66.
43. Su Weichang and Zhang Dimei (eds.), *Jiaoyu pingjia jishu*, p. 126.
44. Huang Zhifa, 'Yi ge xuesheng tou che tuanhuo fanzui xinli qianxi' (An analysis of the criminal psychology of a student involved in a bicycle stealing gang), *Qingshaonian fanzui wenti*, No. 5, 1986, pp. 39–40.
45. Su Weichang and Zhang Dimei (eds.), p. 129.
46. Shanghai shi jiaoxian zhongxiaoxue deyu xiezuo yanjiu hui, pp. 139–40.
47. Xiao Hongming, 'Piping de yishu' (The art of criticism), *Banzhuren*, No. 1, 1989, p. 24.
48. Shanghai shi jiaoxian zhongxiaoxue deyu xiezuo yanjiu hui, p. 137.
49. Su Weichang and Zhang Dimei (eds.), p. 131.
50. Xin Yang (ed.), p. 185.
51. Yu Fuchang, 'Caoxing pingyu qianshuo' (Elementary introduction to student conduct), *Banzhuren*, No. 1, 1989, p. 17.
52. Li Zhuoran, 'Pinde pingyu de yuyan yishu' (The art of moral evaluation language), *Banzhuren*, No. 5, 1990, p. 40.
53. Zhu Yagao, 'Tantan xie pinde pingyu' (On writing moral evaluations), *Shanghai jiaoyu*, No. 6, 1985, p. 12.
54. Peng Shiqiang, 'Cong "yueding chufang" shuoqi' (Talking about 'agreeing on a prescription'), *Shanghai jiaoyu*, No. 6, 1985, p. 12.
55. Li Wenxiang, p. 90.
56. Ibid., pp. 90–2.
57. See *Zhongguo jiaoyu bao*, 11 August 1984, p. 1; 19 April 1986, p. 3.
58. Huazhong shifan xueyuan jiaoyu xi *et al.* (eds.), *Jiaoyuxue* (Pedagogy), Beijing, Beijing jiaoyu chubanshe, 1985, p. 303.
59. Xin Yang (ed.), p. 184 (both quotations).
60. Hu Shoufen, *Deyu yuanli* (Principles of moral education), rev. edn., Beijing, Beijing shifan daxue chubanshe, 1989, p. 383.
61. Beijing shida er fuzhong (Beijing Normal University No. 2 Attached Secondary School), *Xuesheng xingwei guifan kaohe banfa: shixing cao'an* (Measures of examining student norms and behaviour: preliminary plan), Beijing, internal school material dated 19 March 1989 (6 pages).
62. Interviewee nos. 4 and 5 and interviewee no. 1, Beijing, 1991.
63. Hu Shoufen, p. 386.
64. Zhang Yutian *et al.* (eds.), p. 240.
65. Ibid., p. 237.
66. The ten standards for moral evaluation in this example are: (1) Uphold the four basic principles. (2) Be concerned with seeking truths from facts, and to

advance forward. (3) Take part in collective activities, show solicitude for the collective. (4) Attitudes towards studies. (5) Respect the national laws and the school rules. (6) Respect the teacher. (7) Treat one's fellow students well. (8) Treat correctly the difference between right and wrong. (9) Be loyal and honest. (10) Handle well work and other duties (see Su Weichang and Zhang Dimei (eds.), pp. 130–1.

67. Hu Wei, Tang Yuan, and Ouyang Hongsen, 'Guanyu pinde pingding zhibiao tixi de yanjiu' (On the study of moral quality index systems), Part 4, *Shanghai jiaoyu*, No. 12, 1986, p. 12.

68. Interviewees nos. 4 and 5, Beijing, 1991; no. 2, Beijing, 1991.

69. Gu Xinmei, '"Qingshaonian xiuyang" chengji pingding gaige de zuofa he tihui' (Methods to reform the evaluation of the achievements in 'youth cultivation' and its experiences), *Zhengzhi jiaoyu*, No. 11, 1987, p. 31.

70. Interviewee no. 4, Beijing, 1991.

71. Zhang Yutian *et al.* (eds.), pp. 237–43.

72. The information on disciplinary sanctions is based on interviews from two different Chinese work-units in 1991–2. The two main informants had both been university students earlier, and their independent explanations are much in accord with one another.

73. Xie Hongmao and Chen Weifeng, p. 65. The points in this example cannot be compared directly with those found in Zhang Yutian's example above. Here it was indicated that having disciplinary action taken against one could result in as much as 10–20 points each time. The markings are based on different total marks, and the overall setup and techniques for marking vary greatly from school to school, and from work-unit to work-unit. In another example, a warning (*jinggao*) leads to a deduction of 50 points, and the recording of a demerit (*jiguo*) to as much as 100–150 points' deduction. A sanction on the level of examination would cost 250 points (see 'Ha'erbin shi shangye xuexiao guanli zhidu', p. 126.

74. Zhang Yutian *et al.* (eds.), p. 239.

75. 'Ha'erbin shi shangye xuexiao guanli zhidu', p. 126.

76. Ibid., p. 134.

77. Interviewee no. 5, Beijing, 1991.

78. Interviewee no. 4, Beijing, 1991.

79. Xie Hongmao and Chen Weifeng, p. 66.

80. By showing prominence in this movement 15–20 points could be won: see 'Ha'erbin shi shangye xuexiao guanli zhidu', p. 126.

81. For a bureaucrat's administrative approach to the building of spiritual civilizations, see Xing Yu, 'Yong mubiao guanli fangfa jinxing jiceng danwei de jingshen wenming jianshe' (Use goal directed management methods in building spiritual civilization in basic level work-units), *Jingshen wenming jianshe*, No. 4, 1990, p. 28. Xing describes spiritual civilization as a language of 'checks and balances', 'meetings', 'diagrams', and 'evaluation points'.

82. Colin A. Ronan and Joseph Needham, *The Shorter Science and Civilization in China*, Vol. 1, Cambridge, Cambridge University Press, 1978, pp. 157 ff.

83. Cynthia Brokaw, 'Guidebooks to social and moral success: the morality books in 16th and 17th century China', in *Transactions of the International Conference of Orientalists in Japan*, No. 27, 1982, pp. 137–41.

84. Yü Chün-fang, *The Renewal of Buddhism in China: Chu-hung and the Late Ming Synthesis*, New York, Columbia University Press, 1981, p. 113.

85. Ibid., p. 121.

86. Yü Chün-fang has noted that in theory and practice this system of merits and demerits bears a strong resemblance to the ritual complex of merit-making in contemporary societies where Theravada Buddhism is practised. One accumulates merit or demerit, and, once acquired, it entails automatic consequences. This ideology of merit-making is clearly shared by the compilers of morality books. Merit is similar to money. For instance, the Burmese do careful merit bookkeeping in order to 'calculate the current state of their merit bank'. A quantified prayer practice is shown by the masters of the Buddha-beans who count beans for mentioning the name of the Buddha in prayers; see Yü Chün-fang, pp. 121–2, 128.

87. *Wenhui bao*, quoted in *China Daily*, 29 February 1992, p. 4.

88. Xie Hongmao and Chen Weifeng, p. 64.

89. Interviewee no. 7, Beijing, 1991. My experience is that there are seldom less than 5% and seldom more than 20% in the category of 'three-good student'.

90. The survey found that school leaders did not care much about political education; they only concentrated on getting high marks in political education because of the positive marking the school or they themselves would get from such results. Only 8% cared about political education, while 27% said they had no interest in such education at all. More than 50% paid ritual heed to such education. See Li Shuli, 'Cong chongyang diaocha kan wo sheng zhengzhi jiaoshi duiwu' (Looking at the political teachers in our province through a sample survey), *Zhengzhi jiaoyu*, No. 10, 1986, pp. 33–5.

91. Marten Shipman, *The Limitations of Social Research*, London, Longman, 1982, p. *xi*.

92. Xin Yang (ed.), pp. 62–5.

93. Even if the *banzhuren* normally have somewhat higher wages than regular teachers, their wages are still low, and the title ranks very low on lists of student's job preferences. Teachers in general have a low social status in China. The class teacher's alleged model function also suffers under this in the era of reform, where money counts more and more. The relative power of a class teacher is first and foremost evident in secondary schools. At the university level the title is sometimes even seen as a punishment, and some would say 'he can only do a class teacher's job'. This information is based on several interviews with both practising and former class teachers in Beijing in 1991 (interviewees nos. 3, 4, 5, 8).

94. Xin Yang (ed.), pp. 189–90.

95. Such strong emphasis on moral quality is perhaps demanded only from class teachers, cadres, party and Youth League members. Far less emphasis on moral–political criteria is found in examples from the job allocation process (*fenpei*) of students. In one such example, intellectual achievement (marks) should count 70%, moral conduct and moral education 20%, and physical condition 10%: see 'Ha'erbin shi shangye xuexiao guanli zhidu', p. 126.

96. Ibid., pp. 191–2. There exist vastly different figures for the number of teachers qualified for various school levels, and it would seem as if several different ways of arriving at these numbers are used.

97. Si Ren, 'Banzhuren guanli gaige bieyi' (A different opinion on the reform of class teacher administration), *Shanghai jiaoyu*, No. 6, 1985, p. 13.

98. Hu Shoufen, pp. 389–92.

99. Amitai Etzioni, *Modern Organizations*, Englewood Cliffs, NJ, Prentice-Hall, 1964, p. 9.

100. Peter M. Blau, *The Dynamics of Bureaucracy: A Study of Interpersonal Relationships in Two Government Agencies*, rev. edn., Chicago, University of Chicago Press, 1973, p. 56.

101. Ibid.
102. Hu Shoufen, p. 184.
103. Su Weichang and Zhang Dimei (eds.), p. 129.
104. Ren Xiao'ai, 'Jianli tuanjie, minzhu, pingheng, hexie de shisheng guanxi: xin shiqi banzhuren gongzuo chuyi zhi yi' (Build a united, democratic, balanced, and harmonious relation between teachers and students: my humble opinion on class teacher work in a new era, Part one, *Beijing jiaoyu*, No. 9, 1988, pp. 37–8; Part four, *Beijing jiaoyu*, No. 12, 1988, pp. 16–17.
105. See Ren Xiao'ai, Part four, pp. 16–17. *Hongbang*—literally, 'red roll' or 'red list'— is also called *guangrong bang*.
106. Xie Hongmao and Chen Weifeng, p. 65.
107. Ibid., pp. 63–6.
108. Jin Rong, 'Yi "xuan" dai "ping" bu kequ' (Substituting 'evaluations' with 'elections' is not to be recommended), *Renshi yu rencai*, No. 3, 1989, p. 25.
109. Hu Wei, Tang Yuan, and Ouyang Hongsen, Part 4, pp. 11–12.
110. Editorial article, 'Gaoxiao "san hao" xuesheng pingding gongzuo you dai wanshan' (The evaluation work of 'three-good' students in universities must be handled well), *Gaodeng jiaoyu yanjiu*, No. 3, 1986, pp. 98–9.
111. Shi Jun, 'Mangmu "panbi" bu keqi' (Blind 'climbing' is not desirable), *Renshi yu rencai*, No. 8, 1990, p. 38.
112. Zhou Lu, Yang Ruohe, and Hu Ruyong, *Qingshaonian fanzui zonghe zhili duice xue* (Studies in how to deal with comprehensive control of juvenile crime), Beiing, Qunzhong chubanshe, 1986, p. 211.
113. Wang Xingzhou, 'Guanyu daode pingjia de jiu ge wenti' (On some problems of moral evaluation), *Dongbei shida xuebao (zhexue shehui kexue ban)*, No. 3, 1987, pp. 3–4.
114. The 47 items are: (1) hygiene habits, (2) individual habits, (3) public welfare work, (4) house work, (5) study habits, (6) habits of collective life, (7) civilized language habits, (8) approach to public affairs, (9) thrift, (10) self-respect, (11) self-love, (12) self-dignified conduct, (13) self-confidence, (14) self-criticism, (15) independency, (16) self-support, (17) self-strength, (18) self-control, (19) sense of pride and dignity, (20) respect for parents, (21) respect for teachers, (22) friendliness towards fellow-students, (23) respect for working people, (24) reliability, (25) to decline modestly (*qianrang*), (26) modesty, (27) honesty, (28) feelings of sympathy, (29) understanding, (30) making a clear distinction between right and wrong, (31) loving the collective, (32) cooperation and unity, (33) democratic feeling, (34) respect for discipline and law, (35) duty and feelings of responsibility, (36) concrete (no empty words) in matters relating to work, (37) thirst for knowledge, (38) will-power, (39) decisive character, (40) creativity, (41) effectiveness, (42) ability to form social relations, (43) consciousness of participation, (44) uniting strength, (45) power of leadership, (46) ability to adjust to change, (47) aesthetic judgement (Hu Wei, Tang Yuan, and Ouyang Hongsen, 'Guanyu pinde pingding zhibiao tixi de yanjiu' (On the study of moral quality index systems), (Part 1), *Shanghai jiaoyu*, No. 9, 1986, pp. 13–14.
115. Hu Wei, Tang Yuan and Ouyang Hongsen, 'Guanyu pinde pingding zhibiao tixi de yanjiu' (On the study of moral quality index systems), (Part 2), *Shanghai jiaoyu*, No. 10, 1986, p. 8.
116. Hu Wei, Tang Yuan, and Ouyang Hongsen, Part 3, p. 14.

8

'Human Quality' Preserved into Files

'THE management of the modern office is based upon written documents ("the files")', Max Weber once remarked.[1] In China, the file or
dang'an characterizes the whole of society, with the discipline of regulation channelled through it. The file is an institution in China, representing both the result and the continuation of the evaluation process.
Even if the file is not formally regarded as a part of the evaluation system, there is a very close link between the two. The processes of evaluation and registration must be regarded as interlinked disciplinary
techniques. The file serves to 'freeze' morality and 'human quality' into
written documents, and is used as 'proof' of such quality. As Peter M.
Blau has explained, statistical reports of various kinds constitute an effective method for evaluating operations well suited to the administration
of large organizations: 'Dehumanized lists of cold figures correspond
to the abstract, impersonal criteria that govern bureaucratic activities.'[2]

For China, the significance of the file to bureaucratic organizations,
and the usefulness of statistical reports, is very great indeed. However,
in contrast to the 'dehumanized lists of cold figures' described by Blau,
the 'frozen' products of *biaoxian* evaluation are strikingly 'humanized',
and Chinese bureaucracy is remarkably 'face-to-face' oriented. While
the formalistic impersonalism of Western bureaucracies can also be
discerned, Chinese bureaucracy is so much under the pressure of
informal social and interpersonal relationships that it has adapted to
their influence. Particularism seems to have infiltrated universalism,
and flexibility to have challenged inflexibility in Chinese bureaucracy.
Furthermore, there is in China an educative function of bureaucracy
that makes of the impersonal, hidden bureaucrat a highly visible figure
who can be likened to a patriarch or teacher. Proximity rather than distance dominates the relation of power towards subordinates, at least
on some levels.

There is another side to this 'humanized' picture. The file, and in
particular the 'personnel file' (*renshi dang'an*), has increasingly become
concerned with the 'human quality' of each individual. That the file
represents a regulating and disciplining force in society is beyond

doubt: but this goes further than to mere disciplinary regulation. The file is legitimized much in the same way as was evaluation. Deng Shaoxing and He Baorong, in their 'Studies in file administration', make this point clear: 'The task of the file is to foster and select in order to understand and make use of people.'³ Again, improvement, selection, and understanding or knowledge are emphasized. The file is not only a disciplinary measure, but also contributes to the improvement of individuals. Thus, it is linked to the exemplary as well as the disciplinary, and, again, education and discipline form a unity. The notion of 'fostering'—*peiyang*—is a recurrent theme in Chinese social engineering strategies, and the file is no exception. Foucault saw the file as a type of disciplinary regulation where power was hidden from view. This is also the case in China—but only to a certain extent. Nor does the regulative power of the file form a contrast to the power of spectacle. On the contrary, it can itself be part of that spectacle; both in its regulating and in its spectacular form, it is a part of the programme of education and improvement. The powerful 'keeper of files' is partly bureaucrat, partly policeman, partly teacher—sometimes even the patriarchal father-figure.

The Personnel File

As noted in the preceding chapter in support of Dutton's critique, disciplinary technologies of regulation are not bound to any particular mode of production. Files are not metaphors of the modern. It has been claimed that China can cite forerunners to a filing system as far back as the Xia dynasty (*c.* 2100–1600 BC). These were so-called intelligence files (*pudie dang'an*), a form of genealogical tables kept to ensure the appropriateness of court officials and noblemen. This was a highly relevant system of 'job allocation' at a time when hereditary appointment was the rule. These Xia dynasty files can be described as the very first kind of personnel files in China, with functions much like those of a modern file.⁴ In 1930 an inscribed bamboo slip was found containing a full fledged file from the Han dynasty. This 2,000-year-old file contained the name of a nobleman, listing his ranks or titles of nobility (*juewei*), place of work, his native place, age, address, stature, etc. More important, there was also a report on his previous history and life experience (*liji*), his exam results (*kaoji*), his merits and accomplishments (*laoji*), and work appraisal (*gongzuo jianding*).⁵ Other types of file have existed throughout the dynasties, in particular since the imperial examination system made the recording of individual files more and more important.

Of course, files have been extended and modernized since that time; but they do not represent anything fundamentally new, e.g. marking the coming of a novel disciplinary era, as Foucault claimed took place in Europe.

In the People's Republic of China the file has continued to be important, and the personnel offices where the files were kept were the first to be stormed by the Red Guards during the Cultural Revolution. The offices held great symbolic importance, and the rebels executed a *de jure* 'power seizure' by occupying them and opening the files.[6] It is reported that many of them were surprised by the information they found; all kinds of slander and gossip had insinuated their way into the files. Often, however, material from the files found its way to the walls through the *dazibao*—the big-character posters of that period.[7] Walder describes the scene:

One common activity of rebel groups was the storming of factory offices in search of official documents, especially the personnel files containing evaluations of worker behavior (*dang'an*). The rebel groups sometimes published lists of informers and released materials to other workers to illustrate the kinds of suspicions and undocumented charges that could find their way into personnel files. Sometimes they removed such 'black materials' and destroyed them. When rebels raided personnel offices in search of *dang'an*, they were attacking not just a symbol, but a central institutionalized prop of the enterprise power structure.[8]

It is hardly surprising, then, that the present system takes pains to emphasize 'objectivity and truth' as the main criteria for what should enter the files.[9] On the other hand, the secrecy with which the file is handled goes back in part to the chaos of the Cultural Revolution, and the need to prevent a return to those days.

There are many different types of file or *dang'an* in China. I already mentioned the one most important for us in this connection, the personnel file. A central regulation from 1980 reintroduced the use of the personnel file on a general scale,[10] and the file is now part of the whole work-unit system in China, including the school system. The three main sections of a personnel file are the cadre files (*ganbu dang'an*), the worker files (*gongren dang'an*), and the student files (*xuesheng dang'an*). Here I will pay particular attention to the development of the student file and its incorporation into the personnel file.[11] There are further categories under these: among them we have already noted the teacher file (*jiaoshi dang'an*).

The personnel file is an individual personal file listing all kinds of historical information on a member of a unit, e.g. a factory, a school, a hospital, etc. There is even a moral point-system and a file for criminals, a case file (*anjian dang'an*).[12] For higher cadres in particular there exists a double file system. Two files are held on the same individual, one an important and highly confidential file (*zhengben*), and the other a shorter and less confidential file (*fuben*).[13]

The written document is important in any bureaucratic structure. In order to produce such documents, there is a need to take notes. According to one dictionary of 'talent studies', taking notes is of utmost importance for fostering talents. The file is to be be filled with everyday routine notes (*changgui jilü*), notes on achievements (*chenggou jilü*), inspection notes (*kaoke jilü*), appraisal notes (*jianding jilü*), and the recording of '*de, zhi, cai, xue, ti*'—that is, morality, political attitudes, talent, study performance, and physical health. The file is here seen as a scientific information system for use in job placement, etc.[14] Figure 5 shows a ten-point checklist for material included in a personnel file.

First comes the report on 'personal details' on education and work experience (*lüli biao*). This detailed description is not written by the individual in question, as is the second point on the checklist, the personal 'curriculum vitae' (*zizhuan*)—personal experiences, family situation, social connections, etc. Third is a column for appraisals (*jianding*); fourth, material on exam results and proficiency assessments (*kaohe cailiao*); fifth, a long list of 'material of political history' (*zhengzhi lishi cailiao*) with appeals to higher authorities (for rehabilitation, etc.), official answers, enclosed 'survey reports', proofs and testimonies, self-criticisms, and additional conclusions from higher levels. Sixth come materials on membership in the Party and Youth League (*dangtuan cailiao*); seventh, material on awards such as titles of honour, model positions, heroic deeds, etc. (*jiangli cailiao*). Point 8 lists disciplinary sanctions and punishments (*chufen cailiao*) including much of the same procedures as listed under point 5 with self-criticisms, etc.; under this point also comes material concerning cancelled punishments and re-examination of cases. Ninth is appointments and removals from positions, wage levels, technical levels, retirements, etc. (*ren-mian, gongzi*, etc.). The tenth and final point is simply a column for 'other' (*qita*), where any type of material can be entered. This of course confers an open-ended power, signalling that there is no limit to what type of 'knowledge' can be regarded as useful for the file.

The file not only lists all kinds of personal information, it also follows each individual from secondary school to the grave. When the subject finishes school, the file accompanies him or her to the work-unit. In case of transfer from one unit to the other, the file follows. The

人事档案材料底帐卡片

（正面）

档号　　姓名　　正本底帐卡片　　籍贯　　（　　）

履历表	自传	鉴定	考核材料				政治历史材料							党团材料	奖励材料	处分材料						任免工资等	其他
			学习成绩	创造发明	业务评定	其他	上级批复	结论	调查报告	证明材料	检查交待	申诉	其他			上级批复	决定	调查报告	证明材料	检查交待	其他		

FIGURE 5   Original checklist for materials included in a personnel file

Source: Deng Shaoxing and He Baorong (eds.), *Dang'an guanlixue* (Studies in file administration), 2nd edn., Beijing, Zhongguo renmin daxue chubanshe, 1990, p. 388.

principle is not to spread the material from the file over several different units; it is assumed that this would make the material inaccurate and would prevent the administration from getting a correct picture of a person's all-round situation. 'The file follows the person who is leaving' (*dang sui ren zou*). A person without a file should be checked through his contacts, his family, his place of residence or *hukou* registration at the public security bureau etc.[15] In addition, a system of identity cards (*shenfenzheng*) has been introduced in China recently, intended among other things to keep tabs on the transient population from the rural areas who are outside the system of work-units and files.[16]

Transfers are dependent on what is in your file. It might be difficult to transfer to another job if the material is negative, or if you have some black spot, or 'problem' (*wenti*) in your file material. There are at least four main types of problem. The first is 'historical problems' (*lishi wenti*) concerning political behaviour and organizational affiliations throughout life. Second, political problems (*zhengzhi wenti*) refer more directly to political mistakes made during your lifetime. Third, problems of style (*zuofeng wenti*) list personal sins, such as drunkenness, wife abuse, or in particular problems of promiscuity of all sorts. Finally, family problems (*jiating wenti*) concern misdeeds of a political, criminal, or other nature committed by your relatives.[17] Once a 'problem' enters the file, it can be hard to get rid of; sometimes it sticks with you for life, causing all sorts of problems.[18]

Despite the problems attached to such file-keeping, the system obviously has many supporters including at the grass-roots level. According to some observers, fears of conflict and chaos have led many Chinese to conclude that social order can be upheld only through the external controls of social organization, in which the individual is, in Richard Solomon's words, 'boxed in' by the combined forces of group obligations and social ties, and the authority of a strong leader. In the disciplinary techniques of evaluations and files, both can be found; indeed, one of Solomon's interviewees expressed the feeling that 'Everything has to be well organized . . . They ought to have a file on every person from the age of eight, so if, for example, he comes to a job we will know just what he has done.'[19] It is firmly implanted in most Chinese that all individual behaviour is evaluated, and linked to files and rewards. Walder describes such behaviour linked to the filing system as 'habitual, almost second nature'.[20]

The Student File and its Forerunners

The student file, a subfile of the personnel file, is introduced from the first year in upper secondary school. This was originally quite a simple file, containing the results of exams, health checks, school achievements, and the class teacher evaluation. Now the student file is expanding its domain, as we will see below, with the introduction of 'quality files'. Students' leisure time has become a part of the file. In the early 1990s, the Propaganda Department of the CCP Central Committee, the State Education Commission, and the Central Committee of the Communist Youth League wanted to formalize the social activities of students during the holidays. From the summer of 1992 on, students participating in so-called voluntary social practices in their spare time were to fill out a 'social practices registration form'. Such 'voluntary' practice was already an issue for gathering *biaoxian* points; now it enters the file in a more organized way. The form is to provide information about the time of participation, the projects chosen, and the achievements. Recipient units should also state their comments in the form. The form will become part of the student's file, and the information in it will serve as a basis for the school to assess students' performance—whether they should receive scholarships, whether they are qualified for titles of honour, whether they should be recommended for further studies, and where they will be assigned to work after graduation.[21]

To begin with, the student file mainly reflects constructive assessments intended for encouragement, I was told by class teachers. These are pupils who are growing and maturing, and obstacles should not be put in their way at this stage of development. This was expressed even by political inspectors at the university level. Bad students who commit crimes in secondary school might change into good persons later. Class teachers emphasized the educative and improving effect of the files above all.[22] At the university level, however, the student file seemed to be a much more serious thing. I had the opportunity to read some of the many forms included in the student file at one university. In one form, a normal registration form for entering the master's degree examinations, there were questions on whether the applicant had any 'historical problems'. The category of 'family problems' was also mentioned in the form, and there were columns to fill in about any friends, family or other social connections with 'serious historical problems'. It was also asked whether the applicant had been the target of any 'investigations' (*shencha*), whether there had been any punishment, etc.[23] The picture I got was far less innocent than that given me by the people in charge of evaluations for the student file. This impression—that the form was something quite different from merely a system of encouragement—was also confirmed by all the unofficial interviewees with whom I spoke, both in 1986 and in 1991.

Even if the formal official file system (*dang'an zhidu*) does not start with a personal file until secondary school, the idea of Solomon's interviewee quoted above has come closer to reality in recent years. I already mentioned Ren Xiao'ai's 'contact transmission record' to regulate the contact between home and school through written documents ambulating between parents and teachers. Some now go further, and, as previously noted, suggest that class-teachers' home visits should be linked to the establishment of a formalized student family file.[24] Guo

Zhao describes how home files can prevent juvenile crime, thus forming part of the 'comprehensive control' programme against juvenile delinquency introduced in China in the mid-1980s.[25] The home file should coordinate the pupil's behaviour at home and at school. Investigations show that juvenile criminals deal with their parents and with their schoolteachers in quite different ways. As long as school and family life are kept separate, nobody takes any notice of the delinquents' criminal behaviour. Family education and school education should therefore be coordinated.

There are several examples to indicate that the adjustment to written records and files starts back in primary school. An 'account book for good persons and good deeds' (*haoren haoshi jizaiben*) is used in some primary schools to record instances of exemplary virtue. This is an early adaptation to the later use of files. Children are to be praised and criticized, according to how frequently they are mentioned in this prototype of moral ledger.[26]

A model class teacher in a Beijing primary school told me about another early adaptation of a file system. As part of their moral education, pupils at this school were educated to be 'small helpers' (*xiao bangshou*), doing housework for their parents. It is important that they should have a household task to do every day in order to develop good working habits and show respect for their parents. These might be minor tasks like clearing the table, taking out rubbish, sweeping the floor, washing the dishes, etc. At the end of every week, the parents then have to write an evaluation report on the behaviour of the child, and hand it over to the teacher, commenting also on whether the children are polite and well-behaved at home. Some pupils obey and respect their teachers, but often disregard their parents' advice. Most parents appreciate the importance of this education, and are glad to write the weekly report since it has proved effective. To begin with, children behave well only because of the home evaluation report; after some time, however, good behaviour and respect for parents develop into a habit because of the early use of reports and files.

As in the pedagogical literature, we see here a belief in the repetitive process of habit formation, and that control repeated over time will automatically lead to improvement. The principle of moulding through 'imperceptible influence' has also been emphasized in this connection. The idea of such a file is to bind methods of evaluation and socialization to a written document. It is intended to strengthen the pedagogical effect of other methods as well. Sometimes when a child behaves badly at home, the parents discuss whether or not the naughtiness should be mentioned in the evaluation report. The child then often promises not to be naughty any more—and the parents respond by not entering the infraction on the report. Sometimes they may not record the infraction, but will tell the teacher about it secretly, to keep her informed. The teacher praises before the class those who have behaved well at home, while bad behaviour is condemned without giving names. This procedure is repeated every week, and there is a weekly praising and criticizing session at school to sum up the contents of the file.[27] These early files are focused on the improving character of such records, and are said to represent an educational process just as was argued in defence of evaluation. Through these proto-files, children are in fact exposed to a bureaucratic reality of socialization from early on— a process highly relevant for later life.

The official files have been considerably strengthened since the start of the reforms. Since the 1980s, the evaluation of political and moral behaviour among pupils and students has become an important part of the documents entering the personnel file. This material is used in the official job allocation (*fenpei*) process after graduation, and is described as 'very important for the recruitment of new students, and one of the basic grounds on which work-units can recruit new labour power'.[28] Since the class teacher, the *pingbi* process of evaluation, the moral grading game, and the school files were all abolished during the Cultural Revolution, in the early 1980s new regulations were imposed to reinstate and develop the system. In 1981 a regulation was issued on strengthening the task of compiling such files on pupils and students. It deals in detail with the content of the files, which are to contain all end-of-term examination results, health cards, reports and notes about the pupil/student made during school years, reports on material rewards, disciplinary sanctions, etc.[29] In 1984 the then Ministry of Education issued another regulation, stating that these files were to be consulted as part of the procedure for recruiting students for higher education. The task of setting up these files was at the time expected to be accomplished by 1987. The files were also to be given a more important role in job recruitment after graduation. They were to provide information on the student's family situation, and to list any political, economic, or legal 'problems' faced by each student. Particular stress is on the importance of the evaluation report (*pingyu*) and the graduation appraisal (*biye jianding*)—the very documents mentioned above in the discussion of *pingbi*.[30]

The file is also to contain a special section for any 'titles of honour' or other rewards achieved by the pupil or student. In practice, the class teacher is the main person in charge of collecting such information. Once again, objectivity is stressed: trifles and irrelevant information are to be weeded out so that the material may correspond to reality and give a true picture of the student. One might well wonder, however, whether this quest for objectivity is in fact upheld as long as criteria like having a 'disgusting character' (*pinzhi e'lie*), or being 'morally degenerate' (*daode baihuai*) are given as official reasons for refusing individuals access to a particular line of education or a specific job.[31] It is incumbent on the party committees at the different schools or universities to check such criteria before recruiting students.[32] Anything that goes against the rules of the school is to be entered in the file. On the other hand, I was told at a secondary school in Beijing that the student file is not so important for job allocation. The work-units look mainly at behaviour, and not at the file.[33] All the same, behaviour is frozen into the file; and a former class teacher who had a 'problem' after his activities during the Beijing spring of 1989 could tell quite another story. If you do not have a good *guanxi* or connection somewhere in the Party or the administration, your titles of honour and the evaluation report are regarded as important documents by many work-units. If you have a good *guanxi*, many do not read the files at all, but when there is no personal connection attached, the first thing a class teacher does when he or she gets new students is to read their files.[34] The file is then used for the selection of class cadres. In particular, this applies to the class leader (*banzhang*) and the Youth League secretary, since they must be selected immediately after joining university. The file is the basis of selection all the way from the start of the first school year.[35] Since there exists a double file system in society—one for cadres and one for the others—there should also be such a system in the schools, according to Zhang Yunqin; and, as there is a lack of good student cadres, a file over outstanding school cadres (*youxiu ganbu dang'an*) should be established.[36]

When it comes to the work-units' use of the files, some of them, particularly in the non-state sector, silently sabotage the regulations about paying heed to files when hiring personnel, regarding them as little more than irrelevant records of the past.[37] With the growing importance of an economic sector outside state control, this means that recruitment policies might gradually come to be more difficult to control. Whether this would also mean the abolition of the use of files in that sector is another question; it is quite possible that the result might just be another type of file. Even if some clearly do circumvent the official regulations, it is obvious from the official statements that regulation through files has been stepped up considerably since the start of reform. Some put a lot of emphasis on the files, others do not. One of my informants told me that his own hopes for a job were stopped after the personnel department at the unit in question had gone through his file. As in the above example, this descision was taken because of involvement in the demonstrations in 1989.[38]

Bureaucracy and the Art of 'Knowing People'

The person in control of the files is a person with an extraordinarily wide range of power. Each work-unit has a personnel office (*dang'an shi*) with a responsible person, or a personnel group (*renshi zu*), organized as a sub-section to the political office (*zhengzhi chu*). The personnel office takes care of administrative work regarding transfers within and between work-units; and it handles salary arrangements for the employees and other administrative tasks linked to personnel matters. This office is also in charge of the personnel files. In particular, the leader of the office, the registrar or 'keeper of files', is important here. In one specific example from a work-unit, the administrative cadre heading this office is described as a seemingly grey person with relatively low wages. This same cadre, however, had in his hands a great deal of power to make desicions about transfers, promotions, recruitment for jobs, etc. His most important power base was the almost exclusive control over the files, since they contained the information on the basis of which personnel decisions were made. Thus, his power exceeded that of his formal authority, and also gave him great *discretionary* power, which in turn created opportunities for favouritism and discrimination.[39] The potential benefits of maintaining good personal relations with these keepers of files cannot be underestimated, and the game of 'flattering the cadre' (*taohao ganbu*) is widespread. One must even flatter and establish good relations with the non-cadre women at the office, according to one informant.[40]

In schools the class teacher plays the part of registrar. As we have seen, the class teacher's power is weak in formal terms. In practice, however, the daily control of evaluation work gives the class teacher much of the same discretionary power as the registrar. In both cases we might talk of a face-to-face rule of the petty bureaucrat. Also in schools, evaluations and disciplinary sanctions are linked to the file in ways that make the class teacher an important object for flattery, since he or she is a 'maker of file reports'. Strategies of 'apple-polishing' or flattering the teacher are widespread, especially during the final year of upper secondary school.[41] As we have noted, the class teacher writes an evaluation report every school term, and the report is entered in the file. If the students are given a punishment (*chufen*) of some sort according to the disciplinary sanctioning system, it can be erased from the file (*chejiao*).[42]

There is another bureaucratic technique of socialization that functions like a drama of real-life experiences: the person who gets a punishment can apply to have it removed from the class teacher's report. The class teacher is the first to evaluate whether the *chufen* is to be deleted or not. He or she makes a report to present to the school authorities. The school has the final power to decide the fate of the *chufen*. In practice, only a few punishments are actually reported in the file. The practice of applications and withdrawals of reported punishments from the file is mainly an educative practice, according to my informants, and students and parents pay much heed to this. Allegedly, this is not primarily because the process is linked to future opportunities with regard to jobs, etc., but because it is linked to 'face'. The manipulations as to which 'black spots' should enter or be omitted from the files thus serve as a type of shaming technique highly effective in the Chinese cultural setting. The *banhui* or class meeting is also involved in the process of applications for having punishments deleted. This involves a process of showing repentance, in the same way as applying for Youth League and party membership can be seen as good expressions or manifestations of correct attitude; conversely, failing to apply regularly for party membership is seen as a lack of such attitude. Applications and petitions linked to the file are seen as important parts of an 'improvement technology', and the method is also used as a very effective means for controlling cadres. Basically, this type of penitential exercise is all about the bureaucratic reality of showing a good, or loyal, *biaoxian*.[43]

A political instructor at the Beijing Normal University claimed that the file contains mostly positive things about the student; bad things are recorded only if they come up to the fifth level of disciplinary sanction—*kaichu*—being expelled from school. If students take part in fights, etc., this is not entered into the file 'because such things will follow you for the rest of your life'. Taking part in fights is normally a violation on the low second level of disciplinary sanction. The political instructor held that only 'matters of principle' should be recorded in the file.[44] Another informant gave a somewhat different story. A boy in his school had beaten up one of his classmates, and the incident was recorded in his file. The boy's mother wanted to have the report excised from her son's file, and handed over money to the class teacher as a bribe, whereupon the teacher tore the report up and threw it away. In general, however, it seems that reports from incidents in school are not regarded as very important later in life even if they are recorded in the file. Filed 'problems' are mostly of another and more serious character, like that informant's own political problem dating from 1989.[45]

Bureaucracy is supposed to require a 'formalistic impersonality', to ensure precision and correctness of performance. In China perhaps more than anywhere else, this ideal behaviour comes under heavy pressure from the surrounding environment. The principles of formalistic impersonality have long been clearly recognized in Chinese bureaucracy; one of the Qing dynasty platitudes about officials was that 'the official entertains no personal friendship'.[46] To remain impersonal, however, the official had to resist not only the pressures from the environment but also a highly ethically valued principle of human conduct based on family relations and social connections. The latter was in fact the only medium the common people had for getting things done and surviving in society. Yang has described the dilemma constantly facing the official:

The pressure from social groups—stable circles of friends, fraternal bodies, localistic associations, and above all, kinship organizations—was usually a matter of claiming privileges from a member who had achieved official rank by appealing to the sense of obligation recognized among members of such groups. An official who refused to honour such claims or requests risked alienating himself from the whole system of social relations based on the informal personal bond.[47]

The official thus found himself in a never-ending conflict between two incompatible organizational systems, owing loyalty to both. Chinese bureaucracy has always been confronted by the reality of what Liang Shuming once called China's 'relation-based' (*guanxi benwei*) culture.[48] One remedy suggested was the so-called 'rule of isolation' (*guan fang*), by which a magistrate's aides were cut off from personal contacts with the outside world while serving in the magistrate's office.[49]

Today the segmentary structure of Chinese society in general and the insistence on imposing control by face-to-face or primary group interaction, as we saw it in the small-group network, still forces informal and personal conduct on the official. Even the alleged objective product of evaluation, a person's *biaoxian*, is a product heavily defined by personal relations, and particularism still seems to be the rule. Sometimes it looks as if confidence in the objectivity of evaluation, the quantified expressions of a person's *biaoxian*, and the written file material itself serve to compensate for the lack of impersonality of the bureaucrat. The objectivity argument is also heavily emphasized in the works on file regulation. Since the file is based on the objective evaluation process, it is also held that 'the personnel file . . . is an objective report of a person's objective aspects or features'.[50] This is to apply whether the file concerns cadres, workers, or other individuals; the objective features to be reported are the individual's moral, political, intellectual, and work abilities, rewards and punishments, etc. It is explained that the file represents a full reflection of a person's past and present situation; in particular, it is emphasized that the file is 'a proof of the education a person has got under the leadership of the Party'.[51] The file objectively measures the distance from the exemplary and objective norm for each individual.

'The personnel file should reflect and record the manifestations of each person's experiences and moral abilities,' Deng and He explain.[52] To obtain this type of knowledge about the populace, there is no need for a dehumanized type of control that is distant from the individual in question. In China, where class teachers are bureaucrats and bureaucrats are teachers, a closer relationship is needed than the one offered by formalistic impersonality. Particularly since the methods of *biaoxian* statistics and 'vague mathematics' are used, there is no need for a dehumanized and impersonalized controller: on the contrary, the controller is strikingly personalized or humanized. The crucial qualification of the person in control of the files should be 'to know persons' (*zhi ren*). This means knowing and understanding persons in the unit—their experience, abilities, morals, and entire *biaoxian*.[53] The relation between such a power-holder and those over whom he wields power is again a face-to-face relation. Such a 'knowing person' should be seen as a teacher, but also in a way as an ever-present, omnipotent patriarch with the techniques of modern measurement at his disposal. These 'objective' hard facts merely have to be applied correctly by the one who knows. The expression characterizing this knowing person— *zhi ren*—is also found in *zhi ren shan ren*, meaning (of a leader) to know one's subordinates well enough to assign them jobs commensurate with their abilities. We find another in *zhi ren zhi ming*, meaning the ability to appreciate a person's character or capability, or simply to have keen insight into a person's character. The 'knowing person' is one who knows everything about you, and has a great deal of power to act on the basis of this knowledge. Of course, this knowledge represents all the functions of the file; the knowing and understanding is in order to further educate and improve, and the final selection based on this knowledge is to benefit the civilizing of society. This selection function is emphasized. The file material should help to give people work suited to their abilities, to assign jobs to people according to their abilities, and to give an all-round understanding (*quanmian de liaojie*) of the employees and their history. It is a question of finding persons of talent for continuing the process of modernization.[54]

Here lies an obvious paradox between the quest for objectivity and the personal rule with which the registrar and other cadres or class teachers handle the files. Part of the explanation of the dilemma about the 'knowing person' is the belief in the objectivity of 'individual quality' (*geren suzhi*). It is constantly repeated that individual quality should be improved, and that this is highly important for the administrative staff. In particular, the political and professional quality of the personnel administration cadres should be improved.[55] The 'knowing person' is supposed to be of very high quality. Since quality in this respect means representing exemplary norms and standards, this type of alleged 'personal objectivity', together with the objectivity of the working tools, *biaoxian* evaluation, and files, is supposed to solve the paradox of the 'knowing' cadre: his or her knowledge is objective knowledge, and the problem of nepotism is thereby minimized. At least that must be so in the eyes of the administration. Of course, that type of objectivity is seriously questioned in China by other groups, and still 'the winner is always the party that has a "connection" or "acquaintance" '.[56] Of course the 'knowing person' is also a person who is well known among the employees in the work-unit. As was the case with the class teacher, the registrar is highly visible, and represents a power that is not impersonalized and removed from its subjects.

While the power-holder is far from hidden, the file itself in some important ways corresponds to the hidden character of registration described by Foucault. It is clearly stated that the material should be confidential: the cadre file is the 'confidential document of the Party and the Nation' (*dang he guojia de jimi*). If this confidence is broken, it could be used against the interests of the Party, and could harm the unity and stability in society.[57] In one unit I visited in Beijing, the people in charge of the files were not party members themselves, and only the files of cadres and party members were regarded as secret material. In such units, the party people over the personnel department are the real figures of power. In units where there *are* many employees with a party status, cadres, or military personnel, the people at the personnel office must themselves be party members.[58] It is emphasized that cadres should guard against revealing official secrets through carelessness, thereby betraying 'confidential matters' (*xiemi*). The emphasis is not on protecting individuals against bureacratic surveillance, but on protecting official secrets from the very individuals that such secrets concern.

The files are consulted for transfers, appointments, removals, trips abroad, applications to join the Party and the Youth League, and not least for the game of rehabilitations and 'mishandled cases' (*pingfan*). To understand each person, the file must be consulted on such matters.

People are not allowed to read their own files or those of relatives. Without the permission of their leaders, personnel file cadres are not able to read the files of cadres at the same or at a higher level, either. For others to check the file, they need a letter of introduction (*jieshaoxin*) from leading bodies. Party members' files can be read only by other specified party members. Lower levels are not allowed to check the files of higher levels. Nobody in the unit is allowed to check the file of the unit leader; they may look at parts of it in special cases, but only after following specific regulations. To be allowed to check parts of the leader's file, the unit has to formally apply to upper levels. Those with knowledge of a file are not allowed to reveal its contents to outsiders. They are not allowed to use the material to brand others, to slander, or misuse the files in other ways. Nor are they allowed to change anything in the file, damage it, take information out of it, etc. Copies of parts of the file can be made, but they have to be checked and given seals of approval.

Detailed regulations follow on how to practise such procedures.[59] Most research has confirmed that the rule about keeping files a secret is obeyed. Walder concludes from the work-units he investigated that workers had no right to see their files.[60] My own interviews also revealed that students were not allowed to look at their personal files. Not even a former university student union leader had heard about any students legally looking into their own files.[61] Suzanne Pepper, however, was told that various practices existed at the universities.[62] Of course, the files could be opened through the 'back-door' (*houmen*), the door that always opens when others are closed in China. One interviewee told me that he saw his own file at a time when he had good connections in the personnel office, but that this was before he had a 'problem' written into it.[63] In another case an employee, also with a 1989 'problem', actually had his 'problem' openly presented to him with the conclusion that his political *biaoxian* was not up to standard. A copy of what was recorded in the file on that particular subject was in this case also given to the person in question.[64] The rule is, however, that a file must be hidden from view, even if there seem to be some openings in the system. Is it then not correct to say that power is hidden from view as in Foucault's example, that the regulating discipline of the file is juxtaposed to the spectacles of pain and virtue?

Not entirely, and here the connection between education and discipline again enters the picture. I have already described the processes of modelling and evaluation as important education and control techniques of the exemplary society. The file was also said to have an educative function. And it continues the educative process started in modelling and evaluation. The file is not buried, but is 'recycled' in ways that take it away from its strong policing function and make it into an educative spectacle of virtue. Even if some 'spectacles' were made out of the files confiscated by the Red Guards during the Cultural Revolution, there is now a bureaucratically regulated way of making them into spectacles. This point is evident in Deng and He's chapter on 'the organization of files for people that have passed away'. The files of dead persons constitute a hierarchized 'life after death'. The files of high cadres and party members, people who were famous (scientists, artists, professors, etc.) on the national level, are considered especially interesting from the point of view of moral education. The files of particularly dedicated heroes and model figures as well as other famous public figures should be kept by the original work-unit for five years, and then turned over to the central archives to be kept permanently (*yongjiu baocun*). Other people's files could also be turned over to the central or local archives from the original unit to be kept for a long time (*changqi baocun*), for the sake of producing models or for posthumous rehabilitation, criticism etc. Files at other and lower levels are also kept for a long time.

There is a hierarchy of central, provincial, prefectural and county-level archives with differently regulated periods for how long files should be kept; for instance, at the county level files are supposed to be kept for three years. The files of other personnel or staff should be kept by the original unit and destroyed by the work-unit. This hierarchy of dead heroes and famous figures is utilized in local as well as nationwide campaigns. Here the written document comes out of hiding and is transformed into spectacle. As noted earlier, most heroic and exemplary figures are dead. In fact, all the articles written about them are based on material gathered during evaluation and later kept in files. When the diaries of soldier-hero Lei Feng are republished over and over again, it is because they were kept in his military unit as part of files based on constant evaluation, self-cultivation, and self-criticism. Even if they might have been tampered with later on, there is no need to assume that they were false documents, as some have asserted. When Jiao Yulu, the sacrificing cadre who died while serving the people back in 1964, rose to prominence in the early 1980s, it was because his files had been kept and the contents regarded as suitable for current needs. Files and spectacles are no longer juxtaposed, and meet in this practice of exemplary 'recycling' of files and parading of 'frozen' virtue. In this way, the written document, the result of the evaluation process, turns into the starting point of a new moral–political campaign constituting a new standard for new rounds of evaluation, in turn making up the materials for new documents and files. Such is the production cycle of exemplary individuals. Here we experience the paradoxical situation of a parading of formerly secret files.

Modernizing Files: The 'Human Quality' Files

Computerization represents a real modernization of the filing system.[65] And yet, when there is talk of modernizing the file, it is 'human quality' rather than computerization that has been the hottest issue. Technocrats in favour of theories about 'human quality' have seen the file as suitable for their engineering projects, and some have suggested that an additional 'quality file' should be added to the personnel file.

According to Da Li, one should establish a quality file (*suzhi dang'an*) to reflect rationally both the static and dynamic state of each employee.[66] The personnel file includes material and data on each person's social history, political features, etc. Those who work abroad have a so-called 'professional work file' (*yewu dang'an*) with detailed material on technical qualifications; but there is no file that sums up the broader issues of 'quality' in a systematic and scientific way. Such a 'quality file' should focus on physical and psychological traits, spiritual quality, personal temperament and disposition, personality, ability, intelligence, and knowledge. This file should be added to the other types of file, so that the combined files can reflect both outer and inner characteristics and lay the groundwork for a new science, an 'anthropology of quality' or a 'study of human quality' (*renlei suzhixue*). 'Human quality' includes key elements of both spiritual and material factors. 'Personal quality' (*geti suzhi*) includes inborn as well as achieved qualities, physical as psychological, political as cultural. The inborn qualities focus on various inherited characteristics which can be measured through genetics, eugenics, physiology, etc. These sciences should be combined to create the new scientifically based file.

'Physical quality' is here defined as inherited diseases of various kinds, and should also be listed in the file. The body becomes a subject for direct surveillance, something to be recorded in written documents. Birth control campaigns, hygiene, and sports campaigns should contribute to the improvement of such bodily quality. But quality concerns both body (*shen*) and heart (*xin*) in China. Psychological quality should focus on traits such as stability, interests, temperament, abilities, and special psychological dispositions. A quality file should also include material on political quality, even if this is included in detail elsewhere in the personnel file. It is unclear whether Da Li thinks of this as additional material, or the result of combining the quality file and the information kept in the ordinary personnel file. Political quality should include material on moral and ideological quality, collective qualities, worldview, value concepts, concept of happiness, and views on responsibility, duty, honour, conscience, general outlook, and integrity. Again, various sciences should be mobilized. Philosophy, law, ethics, sociology, and ideological and political work are basic in dealing with this material.

'Cultural quality' should report on the results of study and of the process of inculcation. It should include cultural, arts, science, and technological qualifications, and abilities in music, painting, and the fine arts. Material from educational studies, talent studies, and creativeness studies (*chuangzaoxue*) should support such an evaluation. This 'anthropology of quality' merges the aspects of all kinds of science. Typical of this genre is the lack of a theoretical explanation of how to systematize this type of overall quality science.[67] Such 'multi-science' approaches represent a popular trend in China, at least within the technological–political literature. Often such ideas seem to resemble some sort of bureaucratic scientism where the numbers of the sciences listed count for more than their contents, and the mere names of the sciences for more than their concrete substance. The administrative and educational system that hold this quality science together should work to raise the quality of the whole Chinese nation, inspiring people's work spirit as well as their enterprising spirit.

The quality file is not a mere concept on the drawing board, according to *Zhejiang ribao*. As early as 1985 Zhejiang province had set up a cadre quality file based on an elecronic computer system. 'The information shows that setting up a quality file is no longer false talk or idle dreams, mere fantasy. It is already a practical fact,' it is proudly explained.[68] Rational use of 'the modern spiritual quality of the quality file to promote socialism and make society more advanced to benefit its heroic one billion large people' has already been achieved. However, a potentially positive initiative to oversee the mental and physical health of students and others runs the risk of turning into part of a bureaucratic file system serving the technocratic strategies of social engineering. 'Transformation', 'cure', and 'surveillance' become concepts not easily distinguishable from each other.

The CCP Central Committee document No. 14, 1988, states that 'moral value feelings' and 'psychological quality' should be emphasized more strongly in moral education.[69] In today's China, deviance is often seen as illness, and moral–political work is seen as hygiene work. Moral–political educators often talk in medical terms such as 'diagnosis' (*zhenduan*) to see 'whether students are good or bad, true or false', as one textbook presents it. Diagnosis is for the sake of 'strengthening' (*qianghua*), a word often used in explaining 'the process of improving character (*pinzhi*) in order to restrain evil (*yi e*)'.[70] This strengthening process is an improvement of both body and 'heart'. 'In the fast-moving society the development of psychological hygiene (*xinli weisheng*) is important', it is explained. Since balance is perhaps the central catch-word of Chinese socialization as such, it is also stated that the psychological level as well as the psychological balance (*xinli pingheng*) should be improved. Psychological balance should make people more effective in study and work, and teachers and moral–political workers should work to prevent mental illness from occurring among their students. Mental hygiene is explained in the words of the civilization campaigns as 'spiritual hygiene' (*jingshen weisheng*), to emphasize the overall build-ing political aspect of such work. Quoting statistics from the World Health Organization showing that 75 per cent of youth are normal, 20 per cent have defects, and 5 per cent are mentally ill, the aim of psychological evaluation and file work is outlined as a process 'to prevent psycho-logical pollution (*xinli wuran*) among youth'.[71] Psychological hygiene is one of the new and important methods of moral education work. Improving the mental health of students also raises the level of their political thinking and their overall moral quality. The textbooks talk about strengthening three kinds of 'self': the first is the physiological or physical self, including the body and its condition; the second is the individual self concerning interests, abilities, feelings, consciousness, etc.; while the third is the social self in roles, statuses, responsibilities, etc. Strengthening all these 'selves' or aspects of self aims at raising the effectiveness of moral education. For this purpose, a more accurate 'student psychology file' (*xuesheng xinli dang'an*) should be established, to enhance an understanding of students' consciousness.[72]

In ancient China there was an awareness of the connection between *xin* and *shen*—mind and body. '*Ti jian shen shuang*'—'When the mind is at ease, the body feels comfortable'—was one of the maxims of the classical period. Mental hygiene education and physical exercise should be closely knitted together. We have also seen from the teacher's evalu-ation form shown in the last chapter that 'bodily balance' counts in the overall picture of 'human quality'. 'Bodily shape and function' was one of the fifteen criteria for teacher evaluation.[73] For instance, a phys-ical handicap has until recently been seen as disqualifying for univer-sity attendance, even in spite of high examination results. Further, it is particularly important to prevent psychological 'blocking' (*zhang'ai*). A stable mood among students is the aim of mental hygiene work;

and, to arrive at a correct understanding of the students' mental situation, the question of objectivity is put on the agenda. Psychological measuring methods should help to uncover latent spiritual abilities and find the positive aspects of student psychology. The methods to use in mental strengthening resemble the well-known methods of ordinary evaluation work. Self-diagnosis should be used to strengthen self-consciousness, but political treatment might also be needed in this type of improvement work. In many ways, this new psychological 'human quality' evaluation and file work brings such activities several steps closer to Whyte's comparison between the Chinese *xiaozu* network and Western sensitivity groups.

As in all kinds of evaluation procedures in China, the psychological hygiene diagnosis enters the world of written documentation. This new form is meant to give a report on the hygiene of the whole group as well as of the individual. A 'student psychological hygiene file' (*xuesheng xinli weisheng dang'an*) should be established as an objective foundation of assessment.[74] The basic individual student psychological registration form is shown in Table 6. The form is to be filled in by class teachers without any formal training in psychology. The textbook here quoted from is aimed at rural teachers; it starts with a warning against rural class teachers stealing ducks and chickens from the peasants, and thereby destroying their own abilities to serve as model examples for their students.[75] It is in this perspective that we should view the described psychological hygiene work. Rural class teachers themselves often have an educational standard only slightly above their own pupils. Many of them have never attended an institution of higher learning, and scarcely any of them have any training in psychological theories or consultation work.

The textbook in question has been compiled by a Shanghai research unit in moral–political work among primary and secondary schools. They identify three types of psychological condition: mental health, mental defects, and mental illness. Different character defects are listed for class teachers to use for their registration work, and 'scientific methods' are listed for curing the different defects. A so-called 'split character' should be treated by expanding the friendships of the student. Apathy should be cured by reading widely, establishing more social contacts, and a strengthening of self-consciousness. Depression is to be cured through participation in collective campaigns. General misadaptation should also be cured by teaching students to take a more active part in social activities. It is interesting to note that collective activities seem to be a kind of universal remedy for psychological defects of many various kinds. For the 'feeble minded' (*dineng*), however, special education is needed.

TABLE 6   Example of a student psychological registration form

Name............ Sex............ Age............ Study results............ IQ............		

Family structure	Family education level	Parents' special characteristics	Parents' report
Favourite interests	Strong points	Possessing/not possessing ideals and aims	

Temperament type
and stimulation

Character traits

Self-knowledge

Situation of
psychological blockage,
psychological defect, and
psychological illness

Situation analysis

Educational training and
opinion on recovery (cure)

Effect

Year.......Month.......Date.......Person in charge of registration......................

Source: Shanghai shi jiaoxian zhongxiaoxue deyu xiezuo yanjiu hui (eds.), *Nongcun zhongxiaoxue banzhuren gongzuo zhidao* (Directions for class teacher work in rural primary and secondary schools), Shanghai, Shanghai kexue jishu chubanshe, 1990, p. 128.

The psychological defects and illnesses mentioned concern modern dangers facing children and youth during reform. But the description equally strongly reflects the dangers represented by children and youth challenging exemplary norms and values. The problems described follow an age-old tradition of Chinese emphasis on filial piety and chastity, core concepts and archetypes of bodily and social balance. The dangers of early puberty and sexual 'chaos' are addressed in particular. Such dangers form part of the foundation for evaluation and registration work linked to moral education. Even the only child poses a danger. A so-called spoiling syndrome, or '421 syndrome' (*421 zonghe bing*) concerns the only child and the new situation of its having four grandparents and two parents to itself. These children should be encouraged to recognize their own spoilt character in order to correct their wilfulness and their self-centredness. Fear of learning (*kongxuezheng*) and a so-called examination syndrome among students are also mentioned as typical illnesses that should be recorded; less rigorous study demands should be imposed on such students. A general nervous state when faced with tests and exams can often be observed in students; the remedy here is to get rid of the excessive pressure from school and family, and to provide a training in self-control.

In these examples, the end-effects might be positive, contributing to a lessening of the overall burdens in school. Other illnesses mentioned are neurasthenia, hysteria, dementia praecox, and sexual hypertension. Those suffering from the last category have excessive inner feelings, indulge in sexual imaginings, and feel daily sexual desire. Such an illness has a negative influence on the development of study and school work. The prescribed cure is better education about puberty problems, raising the level of sexual moral knowledge, developing a healthy sexual moral feeling, and teaching good conduct in relations towards the other sex.

The final aim of this psychological hygiene work is linked to the narratives of order, and is explained as the importance of creating balance or equilibrium among individuals, and thereby in society in general.[76] Psychological hygiene registration work is not about curing the ill only: it is also about 'rectifying the defect, and raising the level of psychological hygiene among the healthy'.[77] In the final instance this improvement work is linked to the narratives of progress. To emphasize psychological hygiene is to emphasize 'training talents for the building the four modernizations'. A central theme in Chinese theories of socialization—the transformation of the 'biological person' (*shengwu ren*) into a 'social person' (*shehui ren*)—is also addressed. Nature should be conquered by society; better mental quality also means independence, better self-control and a stronger will for each individual. Psychology also provides improvement by transforming the bad and unbalanced into the good and balanced. As there are black and white, exemplary and deviant, there are also two types of student, it is contended. One type is psychologically stable; the other is unstable, and because of their unstable condition they develop bad behaviour. Bad moral behaviour develops into criminal behaviour. There is a close connection between such bad tendencies and psychological instability, defects, and illness.[78]

This psychological addition to the personnel file has already been introduced in some units. A recent report in the *Renmin ribao* could tell that 'psychological inspection' (*xinli jiancha*) has been in operation at the Beijing University of Science and Engineering since 1991. It has been found that as many as 34.3 per cent of the students here suffered from some sort of psychological disturbance. The inspection system has been linked to a 'psychology file' (*xinli dang'an*), and there is hope that the system will develop into a nationwide administrative system of psychological files for all university students. Mental health protection should be taken care of in a counselling service linked to the file.[79]

There is undoubtedly a need for a psychological counselling service at Chinese universities. However, linked to the social engineering techniques and control of the file, the system opens the gates for an even stronger surveillance of students. The system should also be seen in the perspective of increased control over students so evident in recent years.

In discussions on evaluation, a frequent theme has been the notion of democracy. Evaluation and the practices of file work are both seen as processes of participation—and such participation is both scientific (in the specific definition of moral science) and democratic in character, according to some of the Chinese advocates of those methods. There is, however, another side to the system that questions its democratic character. Both the file and its foregoing evaluation are processes that require individuals to develop strategies for manifesting properly compliant attitudes and behaviour. For each individual, such strategies might represent flexibility in an inflexible construction of fixed and exemplary norms. For collective action, however, the system is an effective mechanism of control. Walder has seen the system of files as a system of surveillance where, in his case, the workers were demobilized as a political force.[80] Both workers and students constantly have to 'qualify' themselves by playing individual games of loyalty to the petty bureaucrat, whether s/he is a registrar at a factory personnel office or a class teacher at school. This, then, is the particularistic twist of the alleged objective and universal exemplary norms and standards in today's China.

Notes to Chapter 8

1. Max Weber, *Essays in Sociology*, trans. H. H. Gerth and C. W. Mills, New York, Oxford University Press, 1946, p. 197.
2. Peter M. Blau, *The Dynamics of Bureaucracy: A Study of Interpersonal Relationships in Two Government Agencies*, rev. edn., Chicago, University of Chicago Press, 1973, p. 36.

3. Deng Shaoxing and He Baorong (eds.), *Dang'an guanlixue* (Studies in file administration), 2nd edn., Beijing, *Zhongguo renmin daxue chubanshe*, 1990, p. 367.
4. Unsigned article, '"Pudie" zui zao de renshi dang'an' ('Intelligence files' were the very first personnel files), *Renshi yu rencai*, No. 2, 1990, p. 31; originally published in *Xingzheng yu renshi*.
5. Ibid., p. 31.
6. See Marc J. Blecher and Gordon White, *Micropolitics in Contemporary China: A Technical Unit during and after the Cultural Revolution*, London, Macmillan, 1980.
7. Andrew Walder, 'Organized dependency and cultures of authority in Chinese industry', *Journal of Asian Studies*, No. 1, 1983, pp. 51–76.
8. Andrew G. Walder, 'Communist social structure and workers' politics in China', in Victor C. Falkenheim (ed.), *Citizens and Groups in Contemporary China*, Michigan Monographs in Chinese Studies, Vol. 56, Ann Arbor, University of Michigan Press, 1987, p. 84.
9. *Zhongguo baike nianjian 1985* (China encyclopedic yearbook 1985), Beijing, Zhongguo dabaike quanshu chubanshe, 1985, p. 449.
10. Deng Shaoxing and He Baorong (eds.), p. 370.
11. In Europe there were also attempts to develop student files as a means of discipline and education. In the 18th cent. the pedagogue Johann Basedow suggested that a file (*Protocoll*) should follow each student, with its contents kept a secret. It should also be used for allocating jobs: 'Beim Abschied der Schüler wird von den Pädagogen ein "Protocoll" geschrieben, "welches allen Privatpersonen unsichtbar bleibt", und das auf Verlangen der öffentlichen Behörden vorgelegt wird. Ein "Staatscollegium" entscheidet dann mit der Hilfe dieser Protokolle, die an allen Bürgerschulen, Gymnasien und Universitäten angefertigt werden sollen, über die Vergabe öffentlicher Ämter, die Gelehrten vorbehalten sind.' Basedow also suggested that every class should have a moral teacher, an 'educator', in much the same way as the Chinese now have a class teacher. See Johann P. Basedow, *Vorstellung an Menschenfreunde und vermögende Männer über Schulen und ihren Einfluß in die öffentliche Wohlfarth*, Hamburg 1768, p. 119; quoted from Wolfgang Dreßen, *Die pädagogische Maschine*, Frankfurt, Ullstein Materialen, 1982, p. 144.
12. For example, each of the inmates in a women's prison in Zhejiang had a 'medical record card' (*bingli ka*), actually a 'case history journal' where inmates' thoughts, what they say, the result of re-education, etc., were to be recorded. The small-group structure and the methods of evaluation are also used in prisons. See Zhang Jian and Zhang Wenbang, 'Dui Zhejiang sheng nü fanzui fuxing qijian de tuanhuo huodong fenxi' (Analysis of the gang activities of female prisoners in Zhejiang province during the period of imprisonment), in *Zhongguo qingshaonian fanzui yanjiu nianjian 1987*, p. 418. Since the early 1980s, a system of points has been generally adopted by all Chinese reform-through-labour institutions for assessment and determination of reward and punishment, wherein day-to-day behaviour of the prisoners as they undergo reform is translated into points. On the basis of a fixed number of points, those who show a positive attitude towards reform will be awarded additional points, and those who show indiscipline or who break regulations will have points deducted, with results of additions and deductions of points made public every month. See *SWB-FE*/1458, 13 August 1992, p. C1/8.
13. Wang Faxiong, *Renshi dang'an guanli gailun* (Introduction to file administration), Hubei renmin chubanshe, 1984, pp. 15–16, 172–7, quoted from Michael R. Dutton, *Policing and Punishment in China: From Patriarchy to 'the People'*, Cambridge, Cambridge University Press, 1992, p. 223.

14. Liu Rongcai (ed.), *Rencaixue cidian* (Dictionary of talent studies), Chengdu, Sichuan sheng shehui kexue yuan chubanshe, 1987, p. 23.
15. Deng Shaoxing and He Baorong (eds.), pp. 368, 399–400. On *hukou*, see Michael R. Dutton, pp. 189–239.
16. By March 1992, 780 m resident identity cards had been issued in China, accounting for 93% of the total who should have such cards; see *SWB-FE*/1333, 19 March 1992, p. B2/12–13.
17. Marc J. Blecher and Gordon White, p. 95.
18. In 1986 a film titled 'The Incident of the Black Cannon', a comedy by Huang Jianxin after a story by Zhang Xianling, gained considerable popularity in China. The film ridiculed the question of 'problems' in a satirical way, for which it was received with much acclaim by the audience I shared the experience with in Beijing. For a far more serious account of the consequences of 'black spots' in files, see Feng Jicai, ' "Wenge" jinxing le liangqian nian', in *Yibai ge ren de shinian* (The ten years of one hundred people), Jiangsu wenyi chubanshe, pp. 272–86; trans. as 'The "Cultural Revolution" has been underway for two thousand years', in *Chinese Sociology and Anthropology*, No. 1, Fall 1993, pp. 92–103.
19. Richard H. Solomon, *Mao's Revolution and the Chinese Political Culture*, Berkeley, University of California Press, 1971, pp. 132–3.
20. Andrew G. Walder, 'Communist social structure and workers' politics in China', p. 74.
21. 'Opinions of the Propaganda Department of the CCP Central Committee, the State Education Commission and the Central Committee of the Communist Youth League on Unfolding Extensive Deep-Going and Sustained Social Practice Activities Among Students of Institutes of Higher Learning', *SWB-FE*/1427, 8 July 1992, pp. B2/3–5 (4).
22. Interviewees nos. 2, 4, 5, and 6, Beijing, 1991.
23. *1986 Baokao gongdu shuoshi xuewei yanjiu dengjibiao* (Registration form for entering the 1986 master's degree examinations), Beijing, 1986.
24. Ding Ruxu, 'Guanyu banzhuren gongzuo yu jiating jiaoyu jiehe de xin tansuo' (New explorations of integrating class teacher work and family education), *Banzhuren*, No. 2, 1988, p. 30.
25. Guo Zhao, 'Shilun huanjing yingxiang yu diling fanzui' (A tentative discussion on the influence of the environment on minors' crime), *Qingshaonian tantao*, No. 4, 1990, pp. 19–20.
26. Xia Daoxing, 'Gaige sixiang pinde ke kaocha de changshi' (An attempt to examine the reform of ideology and morality classes), *Jiaoxue yanjiu (xiaoxue ban)*, No. 4, 1987, p. 37.
27. Interviewee no.7, Beijing, 1991.
28. Qiu Guang, 'Caoxing pingding' (Behaviour evaluation), *Zhongguo dabaike quanshu: jiaoyu* (The great Chinese encyclopedia: education), Beijing, Zhongguo dabaike chubanshe, 1985, p. 25.
29. *Zhongguo baike nianjian 1982* (China encyclopaedic yearbook 1982), Beijing, Zhongguo dabaike quanshu chubanshe, 1982, pp. 572–3.
30. The Ministry of Education was later renamed the Educational Commission. At the Beijing Normal University I was told that the annual evaluation report is not kept in the file, but only the final report from the class teacher.
31. *Zhongguo baike nianjian 1985*, pp. 448–9.
32. *Zhongguo jiaoyubao*, 3 April 1984, p. 3.
33. Interviewee no. 6, Beijing, 1991.

34. Interviewee no. 8, Beijing, 1991.

35. Interviewees nos. 1, 2, and 8, Beijing, 1991.

36. Zhang Yunqin, 'Zenyang peiyang xuesheng ganbu' (This is the way to foster class cadres), *Beijing jiaoyu*, No. 12, 1985, p. 7.

37. Information from student interviews, Beijing, 1986.

38. Interviewee no. 10, Beijing, 1991.

39. Marc J. Blecher and Gordon White, p. 23.

40. Interviewee no. 12, Beijing, 1991.

41. Interviewee no. 8.

42. Interviewees nos. 4, 5.

43. Interviewee no. 6.

44. Interviewee no. 2.

45. Interviewee no. 10.

46. Li Jiannong, *Zhongguo jin bai nian zhengzhi shi* (Chinese political history in the last hundred years), Shanghai, 1947; quoted by C. K. Yang, 'Some characteristics of Chinese bureaucratic behavior', in David S. Nivison and Arthur F. Wright, *Confucianism in Action*, Stanford, Calif., Stanford University Press, 1959, p. 156.

47. C. K. Yang, pp. 157–8.

48. Liang Shuming distinguishes Chinese culture from what he calls individual-based (*geren benwei*), team-based (*tuanjie benwei*), and society-based (*shehui benwei*) cultures: instead, China is a morality-based (*lunli benwei*) and relation-based (*guanxi benwei*) type of culture. The focus here is fixed not on any particular individual, but on the specific nature of the relations between individuals who interact with each other: Liang Shuming, *Zhongguo wenhua yaoyi* (The essential points of Chinese culture), Xianggang, Jizheng tushu gongsi, 1963, p. 94.

49. C. K. Yang, p. 135.

50. Deng Shaoxing and He Baorong (eds.), p. 367.

51. Ibid., p. 368.

52. Ibid.

53. Ibid.

54. Ibid., p. 372.

55. Ibid., pp. 371, 374, 379.

56. See Jian Xiong, 'The "acquaintanceship" atmosphere: a kind of social disease', *Shehui*, No. 10, 1991, pp. 45–6; also in *JPRS-CAR-92-007*, 18 February 1992, pp. 43–5.

57. Deng Shaoxing and He Baorong (eds.), pp. 371, 393.

58. Interviewee no. 12.

59. Deng Shaoxing and He Baorong (eds.), pp. 393–4.

60. Andrew G. Walder, 'Communist social structure and workers' politics in China', p. 68.

61. Student interview, Beijing, 1986.

62. Suzanne Pepper, *China's Universities: Post-Mao Enrollment Politics and their Impact on the Structure of Secondary Education. A Research Report*, Michigan Monographs in Chinese Studies, Ann Arbor, Mich., 1984, p. 53.

63. Interviewee no. 8.

64. Interviewee no. 10.

65. On the standardization and computerization of files in higher education, see *Gaodeng jiaoyu yanjiu*, No. 3, 1986, p. 100.

66. Da Li, 'Ren du suzhi chutan' (Initial exploration of human quality), *Shehui*, No. 2, 1985, pp. 4–7.

67. Ibid., p. 5.

314 *Norms, Discipline, and Exemplary Order*

68. Ibid., pp. 6–7.
69. Shanghai shi jiaoxian zhongxiaoxue deyu xiezuo yanjiu hui (eds.), *Nongcun zhongxiaoxue banzhuren gongzuo zhidao* (Directions for class teacher work in rural primary and secondary schools), Shanghai, Shanghai kexue jishu chubanshe, 1990, p. 119.
70. Ibid., p. 104.
71. Ibid., p. 116.
72. Ibid., p. 117.
73. Xin Yang (ed.), p. 189.
74. Shanghai shi jiaoxian zhongxiaoxue deyu xiezuo yanjiu hui (eds.), pp. 120–7.
75. Ibid., p. 2.
76. Ibid., pp. 129–35.
77. Ibid., p. 136.
78. Ibid., pp. 136–7.
79. *Renmin ribao (haiwai ban)*, 1 November 1993, p. 3.
80. Andrew G. Walder, 'Communist social structure and workers' politics in China', p. 69.

IV

Modernity, Deviance, and Dangers

9

Manifestations of Deviance and Modern Dangers

THE character *liu* which I have used to illustrate this part of the discussion implies 'drift' or 'flow'; 'to move', 'to wander'. These connotations of movement can be interpreted both in the positive and in the negative (as 'changing for the worse' or 'degenerating'). The character illustrates the movement of modernity, in which there is both hope and danger. While the focus of growth is on hope, the focus of order is on danger—the danger of modernity. In the process of socialization, there are several such dangers that have to be controlled.

In today's China we can note the suspicion with which modern change is regarded. Links are perceived between the modern and the deviant or the criminal in a way also found in the West's own traumatic early experiences with modern insecurities. As Berman has pointed out, Charles Baudelaire was one of the first to see clearly 'The spectacle of fashionable life (*la vie élégante*) and the thousands of floating existences . . . that drift about in the underworlds (*souterrains*) of a great city'.[1] Modern life emerges in conflict; central here is Baudelaire's use of fluidity ('floating existences') and gaseousness ('envelops and soaks us like an atmosphere') as symbols for the distinctive quality of modern life— a modernity Beaudelaire welcomed, hailing the 'fugitive, fleeting beauty of present-day life'.[2] Fluidity and vaporousness were later to become primary qualities in the modernist painting, architecture and design, music and literature, style and fashion that emerged at the end of the nineteenth century.[3] In Baudelaire's work deviance and modernity intermingle in a powerful intimation of the change to come. China has seen such tendencies lately; modernism in art and architecture still involve a great deal of the danger of novelty perceived earlier in the West.[4]

Baudelaire's modern fluidity is of course what the Chinese *liu* is all about. Here we may also recall Marx's words on the securities of the past that evaporate or 'melt into air' in the confrontation with modernization. Baudelaire's 'underworld' is discussed in China today as the underworld or underground (*dixia*) of a criminal culture, but the expression is also used for the new youth cultures that have challenged the norms, standards, and values of society. The elegant life is found in fashion, and even if style and fashion have been seen as progress, the notion of danger is never far away.

A discussion by Peng Xincai on the connection between fashionability and crime illustrates the broader issue of the problem of modern socialization.[5] Danger lies in the midst of progress, Peng says; it is produced by progress, and order must be recreated as part of that progress. Fashionable (*shimao*) clothes, consumer goods, entertainment, art, value concepts, and behaviour all tend to be popularized. In eating, drinking, dress, and recreation, we see a mad frenzy to follow the fashion (*gan shimao*). Undoubtedly this originates in earlier poverty, and can be seen as a rebellion against what was a dull and drab life; but following the fashion puts people under great psychological and financial pressure. With the focus on acquiring things, some become pessimistic and world-weary, and neglect their body and their health. Some turn to crime. The new (*xin*), the special (*te*), and the strange or odd (*qi*) are attributes of fashionability. Young people are unstable and full of contradictions, and they lack the ability to analyse and control themselves. Some seek the superficial appearance wrought by fashionable clothes and hair styles, imitating film and TV stars' life styles; others loaf about doing nothing. The organic, sexual, and social development of youth is no longer in balance. Fashionability leads to a high consumption fever (*gao xiaofei re*). This trend has developed at a rapid pace, and youths no longer get enough correct education or guidance. They become profit-seeking; they are decadent, vulgar, and have egotistical attitudes, wanting only to have fun (*wan*). Since it is hard to fulfil their insatiable needs, such youths put their own needs before the law, and end up as deviants.[6] Life-style is not 'handed down' and copied, as in the old society: rather, it is 'adopted' or 'created' from models that are foreign and alien. More than ever before, identity comes through outward appearance and personal experience. Everything is in flux; young people seek identity in things with no standards, and their behaviour signals disorder and danger.

'First Times' and the Chain Narratives of Danger

To explain the dilemma of modern dangers, let us return to the norm. A norm is not a point or a line, but rather can be explained through the image of a zone. A 'permissive zone' may exist around the most fixed of norms, allowing manifestations of over- or underconformity to take place.[7] The strict definition of exemplarity does not allow such ambiguity, and there are ways to restrict the zone and force it back into a linear configuration. The exemplary norm is a thin line of correct behaviour. Strengthening this analogy somewhat, we can regard the line as a boundary line where transgression is no longer permitted. These are not real lines or real zones; rather, we are speaking of a narrative that involves the modern relocation of social boundaries.

In China, even small infractions of the norm are perceived in the picture of greater narratives of order, making them into symbols or forewarnings of dangers to come. Since the norm as a line is really only an exemplary ideal, the 'zone' has to be controlled and guarded. To chain it to the exemplary norm, the hierarchy of infractions is linked together in a longer chain attached to the grand narrative of exemplary order. We have already discussed the existence of smaller and larger violations as accurately defined in disciplinary hierarchies. But the violations are also linked to each other so as to form a continuum of danger. This process can be explained by the concept of 'chain narratives': each link represents a specific form of behaviour or a situation where A leads to B, which leads to C, and so on. The first link in such a chain can be of a fundamental nature; if you say A, then the whole alphabet follows, so the crucial step in controlling a chain narrative is to either encourage or control this first link. In terms of controlling violations, the task will be to prevent individuals from doing A, thus breaking the chain at the earliest stage possible. There can be different degrees of causality between the different links in the chain, but the most effective strategy is to attack the first basic link.[8] Our actions are linked to such early beginnings—or 'first times' (*di yi ci*), to use the Chinese expression. This chain narrative is a dominant paradigm in Chinese analyses of criminology as well as in socialization theory and practice. Texts as early as Han stress the importance of examining the 'minutiae' (*wei*) stage of deviance while it can still be contained.[9]

We clearly see this chain narrative in Xu Deqi and Wu Zaide's theory of how a 'criminal clique' (*fanzui jituan*) develops. It all starts with the development of an 'unhealthy play group' (*buliang youxi qunti*), where children seek unconstructive amusements, are noisy and quarrelsome, and 'loaf about' (*youdang*). These early signs of non-adaptation then develop into the second link—a mischief-perpetrating group (*lieji qunti*) where children flock together, have parties, and stir up trouble, disturbing the public order. The third link follows when the wrongdoers develop into a criminally conscious group (*fanyi qunti*), in which they deliberately assist each other in misdeeds and petty crime. The next link is the criminal gang (*fanzui tuanhuo*), where criminal acts are carried out on a larger and more organized scale. Further development leads to the professional criminal circle of organized crime. The chain has found its end outside society, in an alternative threatening criminal society with norms the exact opposite of the exemplary.[10]

In another article, the same authors stress the importance of early education in curbing crime.[11] It all starts with the development of bad habits. 'Bad moral character' (*pinde buliang jieduan*) develops when individual thoughts fail to conform to the rules and norms of society. This can be seen in 8- to 12-year-olds, who may develop a whole series of bad habits (*buliang xiqi*). They are fond of eating but hate to work and study; they act selfishly, hankering after petty gains; they lie and fool people; they fight and swear, bullying the weak and the small; they hurt people for fun, stay out late, or run away from home; they smoke and gamble, copy 'yellow' books, or even start pilfering. Such individual bad habits are the buds that may develop into crime. One-quarter of a group of gang leaders who were investigated were only children who had been petted and spoilt by their families when they were small.

Youth prison personnel warn against the 'first time' (*di yi ci*) a child or youth stays out late or runs away from home (*taoye*). Some run away on their own, some in pairs or groups, and then there is the 'romantic runaway', when a boy and a girl run away together. The runaway makes a powerful narrative in itself: the very picture is symbolic of the breaking away from society. The runaway is the core of youthful breaking away, and signals the coming of an unstable society. The runaway challenges the family and family stability. Typically, discussions of this 'runaway chain' conclude with the theme of limitlessness which we can recall from Durkheim's discussion on morality. Youths who run away 'will be without scruples, and as boundless as the sea and the sky (*haikuotiankong*), unrestrained and far-reaching'.[12] The description of where this chain will end is a narrative of the lost battle. The runaways have transgressed the boundaries; now that they are outsiders challenging the normal order, they will develop into criminals.

The thought model represented by the chain narratives leads to an extraordinary preoccupation with so-called *analogous behaviour*. In criminology this is used to describe non-criminal behaviour that is closely connected to criminal behaviour, i.e. pre-criminal behaviour. The theme of self-control predominates. Here it is interesting to note that modern Western criminological theory also is much concerned with self-control. Gottferdsson and Hirschi's *General Theory of Crime* is very 'Chinese' in its core argument.[13] The criminal forecast often takes analogous behaviour as its starting point; the loss of balanced behavioural patterns is often the step that precedes the loss of control and the start of crime. Analogous behaviour is very closely connected to the notion of seemingly innocent 'first times', describing the A's in the alphabet of chain narratives.

'Bad' behaviour can be a mere trifle or rule violation, but such violations may develop into what Matza and Sykes call 'subterranean values'.[14] This is behaviour seen as delinquent for young people, even if not necessarily for grown-ups. Matza describes such values as

status offenses, activities which are expressly prohibited for juveniles but which may be performed by adults, within limits, with legal impunity. This includes truancy, drinking, gambling, driving cars, runaway, indulgence in sex, and, in some jurisdictions, smoking, swearing, staying out late, and a host of vaguely defined forms of misconduct.[15]

Matza and Sykes contend that the values underlying much juvenile delinquency are far less deviant than commonly portrayed. Existing alongside the official, dominant values of society, the conflicting set of subterranean values frequently relegated by adults to leisure-time pursuits belongs to the real existing 'zone' that defines social norms. There is no room for such values in the exemplary definition of the norm; but it does show that deviance and 'normalcy' are not the black-and-white dichotomy produced by Chinese moral control technology. Subterranean values might include a disdain for work, identification with the masculinity of aggressive behaviour, and the search for fun, thrill, and adventure. The juvenile deviant emphasizes society's subterranean values, but instead of relegating them to after-hours activities he makes them a way of life, a code of behaviour. Such deviants have not evolved an original set of values but have only taken over one aspect of those held by most people within the 'zone' of norms that oppose the dream of exemplarity.

Matza makes it clear that, while these activities may be officially delinquent, the law—particularly at the level of police enforcement—exhibits considerable discretionary tolerance with regard to youngsters who exhibit these forms of behaviour if they are otherwise law-abiding.[16] In China, however, such behaviour is not handled with the same discretionary tolerance; it is instead seen as a 'first chain' in the narrative of danger. We have seen how detailed the measuring of *biaoxian* is, and how important the detail is for the evaluation practices behind that measurement. Linked to the exemplary norm and a chain narrative of danger, we see the details of daily misbehaviour in a new and far more important light. Through the logic of 'first time', no detail is too small to be excluded from the narrative of danger.

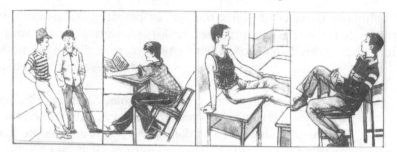

FIGURE 6 Examples of wrong standing and sitting positions among secondary school students

Source: Yan Dacheng (ed.), *Yangcheng jiaoyu: zhongxuesheng richang xingwei guifan zhidao* (Education for cultivation: norm instructions for secondary school students' daily behaviour), Beijing, Kexue chubanshe, 1991, p. 5.

We remember the frustrated teacher who had to measure 'small movements' and note minor infractions of classroom order in a 'regular observation record'. These small movements are often described in books and articles on pedagogy and criminology, and interviewees remembered being criticized for them during their own school days. Such 'small movements' might serve as a core symbol of analogous behaviour and 'first links' in the chain of deviance. We find many variations of this preoccupation with bodily movements, which also signals the tendency to incorporate the body in disciplinary terms. The small movements come back in descriptions of methods for reading effectively. 'Do not make any kind of movements (*dongzuo*) while you read' is one of the rules given here. You should only move your eyes, one book prescribes, making this robot-like effectiveness of reading into a specifically modern strategy of behaviour.[17]

We find this stress on the early disciplining of the body also in the rules for proper ways of sitting in school. Your hands should be tucked firmly against your back to give you an upright position at your desk. Irregular ways of sitting are seen as forewarnings of potential dangers farther down the chain of narration. Figure 6, taken from an instruction book on secondary school students' daily behaviour, shows deviant postures of sitting and standing. The signal to be looked for is disorder, and the pictures speak for themselves.

These positions will look familiar to anyone who has been to school. The two boys standing in the schoolyard may not strike one as particularly offensive. However, the violations are small but important: leaning against the wall, hands in the pocket, legs crossed. A 15-year-old boy in secondary school comments on the crossing of legs:

When you talk to the teacher, if you sit like this with your legs crossed, he'll say that you are outrageous and unruly. But how can that be outrageous and unruly? It's just comfortable! The teachers themselves like to sit with their legs crossed.[18]

He is of course right, but his innocent example focuses on a first-chain violation and touches upon the themes of both analogous and subterranean behaviour. Grown-ups are allowed to do such things, and the act in itself may not be so important; it is more a matter of learning self-control, and how to behave and obey. The principle of disciplining the body is at the core of the issue; it also finds more severe expression, for example in prisons. Here a way of disciplining the body is found in the method of the five regularities (*wuguding*). It is for the purposes of regulating and ordering the criminal body that this method was instituted:

The *wuguding* was designed to regularize sleeping berths, study places, eating positions, work stations and one's place in queues. With *wuguding*, every move became a potentially assessable step . . . This disciplining of the body . . . was designed to inculcate within the prisoner a valuing of regularity and orderliness in life. Such values replaced erstwhile criminal habits, which relied upon and created chaos and anarchy, with new values, which stressed order and discipline.[19]

Any form of bodily deviation must be checked and reordered. Bodily control involves self-control, developing good habits, and adapting to collective authority. Individualist tendencies are seen as causes of crime. Naturally, anything that could establish a difference along these lines is banned in prisons.

Various kinds of bodily ornamentation or adornment are seen as small signs of transgression. In one article, tatooing is condemned in the language of 'spiritual civilization' as a 'phenomenon contrary to modern civilization'.[20] It is something engaged in mainly by wayward youngsters, and is a clear example of analogous behaviour. Tatoos are 'an insult to the body' and to the collectivity. Memories of feudal banditry are activated by the fact that tatoos are today sometimes used to mark attachment to the criminal group or criminal gang, signalling deviant solidarity.[21] These examples indicate how even small tokens and insignia can come to have significant meaning once a community begins to label its deviants.

There is also firm control over style. While schools tend to be relatively permissive in Beijing, a report from the countryside outside Beijing is different: 'In our school there is a girl who dresses up, who puts on make-up, uses oil in her hair, and wears pointed leather shoes.' Her school results are very bad, the report assures us, and adds with relief that 'there are not many of her kind, although they do have some influence'.[22] Dressing up and using make-up clearly signify individualism, and a distancing from the collective.

Disagreement over the right to personal adornment is a hot issue of reform, and a line of demarcation between reformers and non-reformers, old and young, moderns and traditionalists. A secondary schoolteacher at the National People's Congress placed make-up in the perspective of moral education. Putting on make-up (*huazhuang*), love and sex, fighting and violent murder in real life and on TV—all belong to the package of modern dangers.[23] The contrast to the class teacher is found in a youth magazine which suggests 'dressing up to make yourself happy'. By wearing make-up you become happy; you can even 'make a new individuality for yourself by making yourself prettier'. You will immediately be more open and energetic, the article claims. Wear perfume and nice clothes, and you will soon be in a better mood. This does not mean trying to imitate other people, since you cannot change yourself into this other person, but you can instead become another by developing your own style.[24] Here identity and happiness are sought through style, make-up and fashion. This article represents a new trend in China where style is put before standards, posing a threat to the exemplary order.

The point about controlling the body becomes clearer when understood in the overall picture of social order and devotion to the collective. Alberto Melucci has grasped some of this phenomenon in his discussion on self, identity, and modernity. Melucci regards the body as a powerful symbol and instrument of identity and communication: 'the body is the channel for affects which refuse to be wholly neutralized in the rituals of social interchange'.[25] The body appears as a secret domain, to which only the individual holds the key, and to which he or she can return to seek a self-definition unfettered by the rules and expectations of society:

The body is seen as unique and inalienable 'property' which is capable of resisting and opposing the pressures of social order. For these reasons, we should not underestimate the conflict potential of the search for identity based on the body: it carries an enormous charge of cultural innovation and social transformation.[26]

However, it is also important to realize that there exists a deep ambiguity in the 'liberation' of the body. There is no reason to embrace what Foucault refuted as the 'repressive hypothesis',[27] since bodily satisfaction can also be an effective guarantee of social order. Melucci explains that in the West the body has become an object of consumption and thereby also an instrument of control. Market manipulation of the body is thus matched by a growing exploitation of the body as a resource of social control.[28] In China we might see more of this type of control when the market reforms have developed further, and the commercialization of Chinese society is more firmly established.

Youth, Movement, and Modern Dangers

In his description of subterranean values, Matza mentions bohemianism as a 'hedonistic withdrawal from public life'.[29] Given the Chinese condemnation of individualism and its stress on collective order, such hedonistic withdrawal is naturally also a main theme in the Chinese descriptions of modern dangers. Everything that sets a person apart from the norms is viewed with suspicion, and political as well as biological explanations are offered for the dangerous change China is now perceiving. He Xin, philosopher and protagonist for the present regime, claims that the 'anti-norm' (*fan guifan*) style of Mao Zedong was the main reason for the chaos during the Cultural Revolution. Mao's line was an all-out attack on the norms and standards of society. It led to a total destruction of etiquette and norms that every Chinese should have learned from infancy. These norms serve as a coagulating force holding society together, and they should not be tampered with, says He Xin.[30]

The Cultural Revolution led to a weakening of social adaptation abilities (*shiying nengli*) among youth, concludes a book compiled by the Shanghai Academy of the Social Sciences. It links together the themes of chaos during that period, claiming that this formed the basis of the growing egoism during the reforms.[31] The roving bands of Red Guards thus depict terrifying yesterdays even in the description of today's unrestrained youth. A political stamp is then given to the fears of modern dangers, and a worst-possible scenario is given as to what might happen unless the situation is once again brought under control.

Most Chinese commentators agree that a special characteristic about young people is their unbalanced character.[32] Youth, however, can also be used as 'a thermometer reflecting social change', one article claims.[33] The behaviour of youths both forecasts and promotes change; thus it is vital to observe the young. Young people are like 'strong winds and sudden rain', and their eruptive character tells us much about the modern fluctuation of norms. Youths nowadays admire selfishness and look down on social honour; a 'social restrictive force' (*shehui yueshu li*) should be mobilized against such tendencies. Here it is interesting to note the frequent appeals to honour, and the fact that honour is set up against individualism. As we have noted, the notion of honour is a recurring theme in evaluation work, and the process of comparison and assessment—the *pingbi*—was seen as a competition for honour. Peter Berger has analysed honour as a traditional trait threatened by the movements of modernity. His description leads us once again to think about exemplarity, and the relational and segmentary structure of Chinese society:

In a world of honor, the individual discovers his true identity in his roles, and to turn away from the roles is to turn away from himself . . . The social location of honor lies in a world of relatively intact, stable institutions, a world in which individuals can with subjective certainty attach their identities to the institutional roles that society assigns to them.[34]

In China, honour is still a means to achieve identity, and provides attachment to the collective. It is seen as particularly useful in upholding social standards, preventing the alienation that sets in as a result of modernization. Honour is not so much a question of traditional 'rudiments' as it is one of order. Again we experience a 'repetition with a difference', a memory of order used for the purposes of curbing the upheavals of modernization. Honour is seen as an effective means to give the young in particular the reliable identities that they so need. The stress on honour is in line with Durkheim regarding the honour of the class as a binding element in the constitution of the social bond.[35] In China collective honour is in fact still regarded as the most important trait, along with discipline and self-control, in the socialization of soldiers.[36]

In the Chinese 'Yearbook of sociology', youth is linked to growth and order. It is stated that young people affect both production and social order and stability in society, which is also cited as the reason why the study of youth is of such crucial importance. Particularly stressed by the Yearbook is the problem of the emerging new and uncontrollable youth cultures. 'Youth disturbances' and 'spontaneous youth riots' (*qingnian saodong*) are discussed. The sociologists underline the need to strengthen formal organizations to cope with such problems.[37] The reform period has seen a wave of unauthorized behaviour and organizations; and following such developments, 'the task of youth sociology is to secure social stability and unity through improving the social adaptation ability among youth'.[38]

An ability to adapt becomes particularly important in a modern society in a state of approaching *anomie*. A value-vacuum after the

Cultural Revolution gave people a feeling of being lost (*shiluo gan*), claims Liu Qing, a Youth League Propaganda Department writer.[39] In particular this was a problem for youth. The decadent tendency has become a cultural form, and now constitutes a whole sub-culture, he continues, a sub-culture shared by many more than bad students only. Liu Qing, seemingly well-read in Western theory, uses Margaret Mead's concept 'cofigurative culture' (*tongyu wenhua*) to explain the present stage of Chinese society. Today, culture is being transmitted inside the youth generation, no longer controlled from authoritative organizations, he explains.[40] This sub-culture has come into being because of the value-vacuum. First there is the situation of *anomie* (*shifan*). Liu emphasizes the importance of fixed standards, and quotes Durkheim, explaining that, if there are different norms for behaviour that is diffuse and mutually inconsistent, then people fall into a state of destructive *anomie*.

Liu proceeds to characterize the students. They have no basis in either traditional or contemporary thinking, and they no longer have any feelings of responsibility. With self as their focal centre, they superficially adopt contradictory positions and ideas. New immoral trends in personal behaviour are the result, and this phenomenon can be seen in the prevailing trend to strive for pleasure. Students also use new expressive symbols (*baoyi xiangzheng*) representing their own unauthorized values, beliefs, and norms. Examples are literature, music, slang, clothes, hair styles, and new kinds of amusement. Everything is governed by waves and trends, with no fixed moorings. Since the young are not yet taking part in society, they are also not highly regarded among people and come to feel that they are worthless and that life is meaningless. The student demonstations are explicitly seen as 'a result of the state of *anomie*',[41] and the importance of fixed norms and rules is again emphasized.

Both old traditions and the socialist tradition are being challenged by Western ideas. The result, claims Feng Yunxiang, is a state of cultural *anomie* (*wenhua shifan*).[42] The new youth culture is established on the basis of cultural *anomie*. Deviance and deviant behaviour (*nifan xingwei*) are rampant, and students no longer want to be 'good children' (*hao haizi*) or 'good students' (*hao xuesheng*). It is accurate to speak of the 'badness' (*huai*) of the new youth culture, Feng asserts. Cui Jian's popular rock-song '*Yi wu suo you*' (We have nothing to our names) became a top hit among Chinese youngsters during the late 1980s, and the title has repeatedly been quoted as being at the very core of the new youth culture. *Yi wu suo you* is nothing but a 'mad cry' (*kuang huluan*), Feng explains, and the song must be understood as cultural *anomie*. There is a 'deviant tinge' to youth culture that consists in challenging the social norms. This 'campus upheaval' (*xuechao*) should be criticized, concluded Feng, shortly before the spring of 1989. In this connection, it is interesting to note that in both Liu and Feng's analyses of the student upheaval there are references to Durkheim. The affinity to Durkheimian viewpoints is thus no longer of a theoretical character alone. Chinese sociologists and politicians have now moved towards a more active use of Durkheimian theories in upholding the social order.

Liu and Feng's analyses find much support in the literature of youth and the modern dangers of socialization. The 'hedonistic withdrawal' in China mentioned by Matza is first and foremost painted in a language of 'fun' (*wan*), stimulation (*ciji*), or 'evil stimulation' (*exing ciji*) and pleasure (*xingle*). It represents a withdrawal from collective and social obligations. This trend is found not only among students. A survey of young workers showed that they wanted more holidays and a more colourful life; they did not want a life of sacrifice, and their work-ethic was far lower than in Japan, where a parallel survey was conducted. In big factories the assembly line and the fixed work discipline were seen as restricting the workers' abilities to lead more colourful lives. A majority considered work dull and uninteresting.[43]

Young people are described as unfinished persons, not yet belonging to society and not yet having established the correct world-views and knowledge about life. They are one-sided and undialectical, and are not yet aware of the moral facts of life.[44] Youth is like an uncarved stone, and in jade the beauty lies in the carving and the polishing. The word for 'adult' or 'grown-up' in China is *chengren*, literally 'an established or fully developed person'. The unruliness of youth, however, is not just a modern phenomenon. On the basis of an analysis of classical historical records, Tatsuo Masubuchi has pointed out that unruliness, bravery, and hooliganism were classical connotations of the present Chinese word for 'juvenile'—*shaonian*:

[S]uch lawless hooligans as Fan K'uai is expressed with the word '*shaonian*' in *Shi ji* (chap. 8, p. 17). It is worthy of attention that the expression *shaonian* used in *Shi ji* and *Han shu*, had the special meaning of a 'young brave outlaw', 'a brave hooligan'.[45]

This link between 'juvenile' and 'hooligan' is evident in today's Chinese literature, in general socialization theory, and in criminology. 'Youth' stands for something unfinished and thereby potentially deviant and dangerous. The upheavals of modernity and change are often linked to discussions on deviance and crime. This is precisely the case with youth and youthful behaviour. Joseph Kett has noted similar trends in a Western context. It should be clear that the mentality that created the delinquent as a type resembled that which created the adolescent as a type, Kett remarks. However flawed the logic, the idea that the psychological or social constituents of adolescence caused delinquency and crime first arose during the first half of this century: 'It established that boys and girls, regardless of social class, were potentially delinquents and hence needed close supervision during adolescence.'[46]

To indulge in pleasures and seek stimulation is the creed among hooligans and sex delinquents, according to an investigation of such young people.[47] Their aim in life is to have everything, and to let nobody prevent them from having it. Such delinquents are uncultivated and uncivilized; their aesthetic sensibilities are defective, and they can no longer distinguish beauty from ugliness. Their feelings lean heavily towards direct sensory perception only. The aim of 'eat, drink, and have fun' (*chi-he-wan-le*) dominates their thinking entirely. Among juvenile criminals in Guangxi, these precise characteristics were found. A great majority 'act wilfully and do whatever they like' (*wei suo yu wei*). They also think that to 'have fun' (*xun kai*) is the most important aim in life,[48] or they simply hang around 'giving vent to their animal desires' (*faxie shouyu*).[49] The juxtaposition of their strong bodies and their weak controlling functions is another typical description of juvenile criminals, signifying the theme of nature against civilization, brawn against brain.[50]

It is vital to define criminals as people apart from society, to treat them as 'others'. In the criminological literature the 'different' is nearly always emphasized when a criminal is described. Many commentators stress that hooligan gang leaders had an unconventional life-style (*shenghuo shang de fangdang xing*). They are different from the 'crowd' (*zhong*). In dressing, they seek the odd (*guai*); in food, they seek the rare or peculiar (*qi*); in entertainment they strive for the crazy and wild (*kuang*). In every word and action, they try hard to expose themselves to the full (*xianlu*) in order to become noticeable. This is an unauthorized visibility, a visibility of vice. Gang leaders' unconventional lifestyles are manifested not only on the surface, in their quest for eating, drinking, and having fun, for the frivolous and the unusual, the vulgar and the lowly; but in particular are focused on their shameless and lewd sexual lives. In short, hooligan gang leaders are different, cruel, and want to stand out from the collective.[51]

Li Xihai takes the more extreme position that criminals are not part of a 'counter-culture', because they have no culture at all.[52] Li condenses his theory into a simple formula: 'a human being is animal plus culture' (*ren = dongwu + wenhua*). Here we see the criminal defined as outside of culture altogether, and the 'otherness' of the deviant is firmly established. In deviance lies the germ of the death of culture and a return to animal instincts. This animal character makes the criminal neglect the interests of others or of society. If man receives no education he will land on the road to crime. State education will in the end eradicate crime, just as cultural characteristics eradicate animal characteristics. We need to adopt comprehensive control, improving the cultural environment as well as the entire 'national cultural quality' (*minzu de wenhua suzhi*). 'If unconventional life and behaviour are not examined, they can pollute the pure souls of children, and even lead them into crime', Li concludes.[53]

In a description of local rural hooligans in Hubei who were executed for their criminal activities, we read that they did not work, but instead led a life of 'fun'. They wore flared trousers, had cigarette-stubs dangling from their mouths, had a liking for strange clothes, and travelled from place to place (*you shan wan shui*) to amuse themselves. The last aspect—travelling—has become a standard phrase in the literature on crime and is seen as a sign of disorder.[54]

'Travelling around' indicates movement, and the preoccupation with travelling as either a modern virtue or criminally analogous behaviour is often addressed in the literature on youth and deviance in China. The expression '*liulang*'—'to roam about' or 'to lead a vagrant life'— is also a recurrent theme in rock music as well as in the enormously popular *pizi* or *liumang* literature, where hooligan anti-heroes are the real heroes of the story.[55] Language again illustrates the connections between movement, deviance, and danger. *Liumang*—hooligan—is one such word. As mentioned, the character *liu*—to flow—also has the negative connotation of 'degeneration'. The original meaning of the character *mang*—people—was *zi bi lai ci zhi min*, 'the kind of other people coming here from the outside', or *jiaoye zhi min*, 'people coming from outside the boundaries', 'from the wilderness', or simply 'from the countryside'. Later it took on the connotation of 'non-reliable', 'non-dependent', or simply 'bad elements'.[56] We may note similar developments in Western languages. The German word for hooligan, *Pöbel*, comes from the latin *popolus*, meaning people. In Spanish people or *pueblo* originally stood for 'village'. In Europe the word 'hooligan' took on a negative connotation, of someone coming from the outside or the wilderness, even being lawless. In these connotations we might discern the beginning migration of industrialization and the traditional fear of the stranger. At least, the play with words illustrates real problems of modernization and the real fears linked to those problems.

Some use the expression '*liuluo*', meaning 'to wander about desti-tute and without aims', when describing juvenile criminals in general. Others see the phenomenon of travelling youngsters as an activity commensurable to 'hooligan sexually promiscuous activities'. It is a part of the dangerous liberalization wave in society, and an expression of Western 'civilization'.[57] The quotation marks are Dai's own, and the fear of young people travelling brings forth both pictures of all-round Westernization and memories of roving Red Guards.

Zhang Yingzhi does not incorporate travelling into a narrative of danger, but sees it instead as a positive expression of modernity. The travelling craze is a result of the higher incomes earned by many young people, but mainly it is an expression of the lively outlook of the young, he explains. More and more people have realized that travel can have a positive function, as it increases knowledge, streng-thens the physical constitution, and exerts a positive influence on feelings and values. Instead of the penniless vagrant, Zhang notes that the higher the educational level, the greater is the wish to travel; as much as 51 per cent of those who travel have a university education. This shows that travel is 'a spiritual pleasure and an act of cul-tivated character'. It even strengthens patriotic feelings. Travelling is also seen as educative—a modern way to grasp information, and a way to work and live independently.[58] Zhang's article is typical of the more positive tones about the elements of modernization to be found in China in the mid-1980s, and his definition of travelling is confined to tourism. Travelling in China today, however, has far more to do with the social and geographic mobility brought about by modernization.

Travelling (*youyong*) corrupts the young, one report on juvenile gang crime contends.[59] Chinese criminology emphasizes the roving charac-ter of gangs who are said to have a 'mobile character' (*liudong xing*).[60] Typical are the many descriptions of highway and train robberies. This notion of gang movement has interesting parallels in Western criminology. Bloch and Niederhoffer argue that a 'highly non-mobile and stationary nature' now characterizes the gang in Western research, but they also note that this was not always so:

Thrasher, frequently regarded as an outstanding authority on the sociology of the gang because of his . . . pioneering work in this area, has added the idea of *movement* to the concept of the gang as an important associated character-istic. In this, he may have been influenced by the etymology of the term, since it is generally regarded as being derived from the Anglo-Saxon *gang* signify-ing the process of moving or 'going'. The gang, as an integrated and highly *mobile* unit, has frequently been taken for granted.[61]

Dong means movement, and also stands for change and alteration. The character describes the main situation for China during modernization; like *liu*, it represents both hope and danger. It is perhaps more than a coincidence that the demonstrations and the final crackdown in June 1989 are described as *dongluan*—'turmoil' or 'disturbance'. The word indicates movement (*dong*) and chaos (*luan*); the 'turmoil of 1989' in many ways confirmed the most terrifying scenarios of the chain narratives of danger and movement. We may discern a symbolic connection between the *xiao dongzuo*, or small bodily movements in the classroom, via the movement of travelling, and large-scale population migration, all the way to the social movement or *dongluan* of rebellion. These are both real and imagined dangers in a society undergoing vast change. At least, the *luan* and the *dong* of floating and movement can stand as symbols of the dangers of modernization. Rapid and unauthorized movement are definitely causes of fear in Chinese society. But 'floating' and 'movement' are not about fears only: it is also a matter of temptations, hopes, and possibilities, just like in Baudelaire's 'fluidity' and in Marx's 'evaporation'.

The biggest fear, however, is another type of movement. I am talking of 'movement' in another meaning—of organized movements challenging the power of the authorities. This fear is evident in much of the literature on the emerging youth culture (*qingnian wenhua*) in China. We may recall the emphasis on 'environmentalism' in improving the campus-culture of the universities in the wake of student unrest. Lately, the unauthorized campus-culture among students has been widely commented upon. Yang Xiong, trying to trace the 'long-wave' cycles of Chinese youth culture, claims that 1986–7 represented the period when the 'campus culture' (*xiaoyuan wenhua*) grew up, and a large number of 'confused mass organizations' emerged on the campuses and among young people in general.[62] Expressions like youth sub-culture (*qingnian ya wenhua*), and unorthodox culture (*fei zhengtong wenhua*) became widespread from the late 1980s; sub-culture (*ya wenhua*), and system culture (*zhidu wenhua*) were contrasted with one another.[63] Gang crime had long been on the agenda for spiritual civilization work: now fear of another type of 'organized deviance' had emerged.

One manifestation of this tendency was the so-called 'salons' (*shalong*) that developed among young people during the 1980s. All kinds of small groups (*xiao qunti*)—challenging the official 'small-group' (*xiaozu*)—emerged during this period, as youngsters came together to discuss all sorts of issues. Youth culture represented an important part of an emerging 'civil society'. Xie Dexin explains that there are now four different types of such group organization in China. Some groups centre around a person, forming the traditional master–pupil type of relationship. Other groups form because of common interests. Third are the different interest groups organized from above, like trade unions and the Youth League. The fourth type of organization is represented by the relatively loosely organized 'salons'; such groups discuss art and literature, amusement of different kinds, or are general discussion groups.[64] The third type mentioned is of course regarded as the authorized and orderly way of organizing youth culture. There have been attempts to strengthen this type of leadership, or at least to control the unauthorized groups in various ways. Such control does not necessarily mean banning them altogether, but assimilating them and controlling them from within. In an overall programme for youth sociology, the control of unauthorized youth groups has high priority. All functions of such groups 'must be led and developed by official organizations' (*zhengshi zuzhi*). This is crucial to the stabilization of society, since 'social life must adapt to the national character, reform, open door policy, the four modernizations and socialism'.[65]

Insubordination, Secret Societies, and the Social Bond

Young people are winning spaces of marginal freedom for themselves in today's China—often spaces bordering on the illegal or deviant, in mobility, in unauthorized organization, in fashion and in self-expression. Deviants are described as rebels and criminals as people who 'have a mentality full of revenge against society'.[66] If the 'first time' has been given much attention as the origin of crime, the defiant 'last word' from executed criminals has gained status as a sign of the dangers of failed correction, or as a sign of defiant heroism in much of the youth culture. One 20-year-old sentenced to death for murder exclaimed before his execution: 'In the face of death I laugh; a free person cannot be killed.' Such last words are about taking revenge on society, and about extreme Western liberalization, criminologists contend.[67]

In his childhood recollections, He Xin emphasizes the extreme importance that is placed on submission and obedience as early as kindergarten. You can break the windows, you can fight and lie, He Xin claims: the kindergarten 'aunties' think such behaviour can be disciplined. But under no circumstances can they tolerate that a child will not obey (*bu tinghua*). You can do bad things in secret, but the first thing asked from you is to obey (*tinghua*). This means to submit (*fucong*) to a rule, a norm, or an authority. At least on the surface, there must be submission. When you submit you are a good person, a *hao ren*. If you do not, you are naughty or mischievious, a bad guy (*da huaidan*) who deserves to suffer. 'In China the most terrible crime is not to obey', he states. Because of He's disobedience he was punished through isolation from the other children, through exclusion from the collectivity.[68]

This emphasis on obedience is important also in Chinese criminal law. There is a long tradition of viewing a confession as a sign of restoration of order; confession should lead to more lenient punishment.[69] Conversely, a declaration of innocence or an appeal by a prisoner is often considered 'not acknowledging one's crime' (*bu ren zui*). Refusing to admit guilt is regarded as highly offensive behaviour, likely to cause even more trouble for oneself.[70] In prison redemption work, a crucial sign of 'reform' (*gaizao*) from an 'old self' (*jiu wo*) to a 'new person' (*xin ren*) is confession and admission of guilt. Admitting guilt is seen as a process of virtuous display, helping the offender to 'recover' (*fusu*) and return to society from his former egoistic and anti-social hiding place.[71] This process is often described in quasi-religious terms reminiscent of the confessional Catholic Church. The 'six-character principle' of redemption work is *jiao-yu, gan-hua, wan-jiu*—to educate, persuade, and save—the criminal.[72] For this work of 'rescue' or 'salvation' various methods are used, and here the parading of virtue finds its use in prison work. Mobile report teams (*xunhui baogao tuan*) and former criminals who have confessed and turned into good people visit prisons and street committees to get prisoners to confess and to make wayward youngsters realize the wrongness of their evildoings.[73] In one example, an inmates' brigade at a juvenile reformatory in Shanghai 'wrote and mailed 337 letters of repentance (*chanhui xin*) after having been educated to plead guilty'.[74] The criminological literature, and not least the youth magazines, are full of reports of 'recovered' criminals and bad persons who have experienced a 'sudden realization of truth', and have turned into good persons. There are also plenty of stories of 'fallen' good persons—individuals who used to be exemplary and then suddenly fell into the abyss of crime.[75]

Disobedience is perhaps more important than the criminal act or deviant behaviour as such, because obedience concerns the relocation of boundaries, and the restoration of cosmic order. This is a process mapped out by Kai T. Erikson in quite another context: the Puritans' reactions against the Quakers in seventeenth-century New England when, for the first time, a new religious faith challenged the fixed truths of Puritan belief. The Puritan authorities were very much concerned about the outward forms of the Quaker unrest. The mistake of the Quakers seems to have been to live within the Puritan world without really becoming a part of it. They did not attend religious services regularly, and when they did they were apt to disturb the congregation by offering unsolicited remarks of their own from the audience. They acted like outsiders, and Puritans reacted with violence. The Quakers also did not follow the New England custom of showing special deference to persons of religious authority; they wore hats in the presence of magistrates, and—since everyone was thought to be equal in the eyes of God—they defied normal polite conventions of speech by using terms like 'thee' and 'thou' when speaking to them. None of these offences would seem serious enough to warrant the harsh measures taken against them—there were floggings and executions of those who refused to submit to authority. Erikson explains that these Quakers represented a threat to the Puritans because they seemed to suggest a conscious lack of respect for the Puritan concept of authority. The very act of being an outsider had to be corrected.

In the very act of living apart from the rest of the community, the Quakers had ignored a fundamental responsibility by failing to share in what Durkheim called the 'collective conscience' of the group—that sense of firm ideological commitment, that willingness to participate fully in the rhythms of group life, that feeling of common heritage and common destiny which gives every society its underlying cohesion.[76]

So long as the Puritan elders suspected any Quaker of that basic betrayal, they would regard almost everything that person said and did as a form of sin. The process we see here is neatly summed up in Major General Dennison's threat against the Quaker deviants: 'If ye meet together and say anything, we may conclude ye speak blasphemy.'[77] It really did not matter what was said, for by the very fact of acting like strangers and remaining aloof from the ideological consensus of Puritan community, Quakers proved themselves to be blasphemous creatures simply refusing to obey rules of Puritan exemplarity.

It is worth noting that 'contempt of authority' was a specific crime in old England.[78] The Essex County Court in the sixteenth century criticized and punished not only persons who violated the law, but also those who infringed the customs of the group and who 'lived a scandalous life, who dressed in inappropriate clothes or let their hair grow too long, who swore, bragged, or talked too much, who disobeyed their parents, or engaged in frivolous games'.[79] In our Western societies too, there was formerly less of a difference between norms and the law. In Puritan New England as well as in sixteenth-century Essex, we see a tight wall of exemplary norms not so unlike the situation in present-day China where *de* and *fa*—morality and law—are still intertwined in many complicated ways, and where the legal system and the official norms are still linked to a definition of the exemplary that makes any form of deviance, insubordination, or breaches of norms suspect. Hooligan crime is defined not only as a crime against persons, but as a direct crime against norms and public order. Hooligan crimes of disturbance (*raoluan*) are seen as directed against the social order as such.[80] The situation in seventeenth-century New England and today's China also resemble each other in another respect. In both examples we see societies experiencing rapid change, challenged by a non-predictable shift in norms and values. Erikson has termed the situation a 'boundary crisis'; I will later return to other examples of such boundary crises in further detail in the story of wayward 'premature' youth.[81]

In China there is at present a struggle between authorized and un-authorized images and insignia. Authorized images of exemplarity have begun to wither, doubt has spread about their appropriateness in wide circles, and the young—the barometer of the future—are the most critical. In China today's younger generation has been called the 'image generation' (*yingxiang yidai*).[82] Eisenstadt has explained that young people are experiencing a period of 'role moratorium', of experiment in which they may assume different roles without definitely choosing any. The growing discontinuity between private and 'outside' worlds leads to attempts to react to the stresses of the new society by forming autonomous youth groups and youth cultures.[83] This means seeking new images and new heroes as alternatives to those officially set up. This might seem unremarkable in a Western setting, but in China the emergence of distinct youth sub-cultures and a search for alternative images is relatively recent, at least on the scale China is now experiencing.

The politics of the youth culture is a politics of metaphor, explains Dick Hebdige; it deals in the currency of signs and is always ambiguous.[84] Through several examples I have tried to show that the strait-jacket of exemplarity produces its own resistance. Sub-culture forms in the gap between surveillance and the evasion of surveillance; it translates the fact of being under scrutiny into a pleasure in being watched; it is opacity and visibility combined. Such youthful defiance of the norms is viewed as a severe danger in today's China. Thus, we should note that the sub-cultural response to exemplary society is neither simply affirmation nor total refusal or 'genuine revolt'. The stress on deviance and modern danger in the description of youth sub-cultures found in

China does not fit the reality of youth. To some extent, what we see is a declaration of independence, of otherness; a refusal of anonymity and of subordinate status. It would be correct to say that what China is experiencing is a youthful insubordination, rather than an all-out rebellion. All the new images adopted by the younger generation can be interpreted as an attribution of meaning, as an attempt to flee from exemplary evaluation and to gain control through creating an alternative knowledge opposing the 'scientific' knowledge of *biaoxian* measurement. In this sense, the Chinese authorities are right in assuming that youth subculture is a symbolic act of self-removal from society. Youth want to hide, but still they want to be seen. This process of 'hiding in the light' is dangerous—because of the opacity caused by the hiding, and because of the visibility of self and of unauthorized virtues paraded openly.[85] In challenging the exemplary norms, such virtues of course are reduced to vice by the authorities.

The step away from society, however, is not as great as the authorities would have us believe, and even young people are often more traditional than they are modern. John Gillis argues that the term 'tradition' seems most appropriate to describe the youth cultures that have evolved over time. By 'tradition', Gillis means an 'experientially based set of values that permit youth to perceive and act on the world'.[86] The traditions of the young can be described as sub-cultures—but they are also linked with particular adult cultures, making them less alien than in the most alarmist descriptions of their danger. Even the rebellious Red Guards resorted to 'exemplary' and rigid traditionalist behaviour. They recited the truths from Chairman Mao's little red book, and cut off all trousers which were wider than six *cun*, together with inappropriate hairstyles or permed hair.[87]

What is at stake may be not so much collectivism as such, but rather the exemplary collectivism controlled from above through disciplinary techniques. The example of Japan is illustrative in this respect. Robert Lifton has found it useful to think in terms of the interplay between inertia and flux in cultures and individual people.[88] In Japan one discovers that inertia, maintained by traditional psychological patterns, and flux, stimulated by pressures towards change, can both be extremely strong—that individual change is at the same time perpetual and perpetually resisted. Underneath the emerging modern Japanese ideal of self,

[O]ne can frequently detect an even more profound craving for renewed group life, for solidarity, even for the chance to 'melt' completely into a small group, a professional organization, or a mass-movement, even at the cost of nearly

all self-assertion. Those most concerned with selfhood . . . Japanese of all ages,
in virtually any situation, have a powerful urge toward group-formation . . .
One feels this tension between the ideal of individualism and the need for the
group in the concern of young people.[89]

Whether the situation in Japan today is the same as in the 1960s is
quite another case, but suffice it to say that Japanese culture is still far
more collectivist than any of the Western capitalist countries, despite
Japanese modernization. In the capitalist globalization in which China
has now begun to take part, the Western cultural model might not prove
dominant. Collectivism seems likely to prevail despite the sudden
popularity of 'self' and 'freedom'. Chinese young people are still the
'marginal persons' described at the start of my discus ion, caught between
flux and inertia.

The importance of the social bond is also emphasized in Western
social control theory. In the influential formulation of Travis Hirschi,
delinquent behaviour becomes more likely as an individual's bond to
society or family becomes weaker.[90] In some ways we might see the
whole disciplinary technology in China, from its moral–political education to its executions, as a huge social control theory. The principle
of 'attachment to the group' as a fundamental aspect of morality comes
back not only in moral education, but even in practical crime prevention work.

Chinese deviance is not in any fundamental way different from that
in the West, and China's attempts to 'define the deviant out' of the
entire culture do not fit the reality of the deviant or the criminal. The
deviant is rather a 'drifter', in the sense that Matza has defined it:

Drift stands midway between freedom and control. Its basis is an area of
the social structure in which control has been loosened, coupled with the abortive-
ness of adolescent endeavor to organize an autonomous subculture, and thus
an independent source of control, around illegal action. The delinquent tran-
siently exists in a limbo between convention and crime, responding in turn
to the demands of each, flirting now with one, now the other, but postponing
commitment, evading decision. Thus, he drifts between criminal and conventional action.[91]

The relationship between the sub-culture and the wider culture cannot be accurately summarized by 'opposition'. The relation is subtle,
complex, and sometimes devious. A sub-culture will rarely be simply
oppositional, precisely because it exists within a wider cultural milieu
which affects it and which it in turn affects. Sometimes the isolation
and enmity may be so great as to divide society fundamentally. As we
saw in the discussion of 'subterranean' values, however, conventional

culture does not consist simply of ascetic puritanism, exemplary morality, or high-score deeds of *biaoxian*. The sub-culture of delinquency consists of precepts and customs delicately balanced between convention and crime. The 'drift' of the deviant resembles the drift experienced by the 'marginal person' in modern society. Both the deviant and the marginal person are in a state of 'betwixt and between'.

Young people and deviants have a strong urge to hide from the gaze of the exemplary society. In China a particularly good hiding-place has been the secret society (*hei shehui*). The secret society has its roots in traditional Chinese society, but during modernization a wave of new secret societies has been observed, creating imitations of old forms of deviance. Chinese criminology sees the secret society as the ultimate disavowal of society into an alternative one, far removed from normal social rules and bonds.

Simmel has found in secret societies a certain duality. He sees in their widespread diffusion a proof of public un-freedom, of a tendency towards police regimentation and political oppression. First of all, there is in every secret society an element of freedom which the structure of society at large does not have. 'The [secret] society lives in an area to which the norms of the environment do not extend.'[92] Undoubtedly, the secret society is an effective hiding-place from the law as well as from the exemplary norm. Rather than being a negation of society, however, this is an escape into an imitation of it:

[T]he secret society makes itself into a sort of counter-image of the official world, to which it places itself in contrast. Here we find the ubiquitous sociological norm: that structures which resist larger, encompassing structures through opposition and separation, nevertheless themselves repeat the forms of these structures . . . The kind of organic self-sufficiency by virtue of which the same stream of life flows through all group members, is borrowed by the group from the larger whole, to whose forms the members had been adapted. The smaller structure can meet this whole most viably, precisely by imitating it.[93]

As secret society members seek freedom, they are confronted by rootlessness. Simmel claims that, while freedom and autonomy are important aims of the secret society, the consequences of leaving the general normative order may easily be rootlessness and the absence of a norm-giving basis. A secret society is full of rituals, and Simmel sees in the rigour of ritual a help to overcome this lack of normative order. The interrelationship between the need for freedom and the need for a bond operates here, and the freedom from all otherwise valid norms is brought into equilibrium by a submission and renunciation of the will, through the fixed ritual. The alternative bond found in the secret society is also manifested through its members' hostility towards outsiders. In these cases, says Simmel, 'secrecy and mystification amount to heightening the wall toward the outside, and hence to strengthening the aristocratic character of the group'.[94] This exclusion of everything outside the group defines what Simmel calls 'group-egoism' at the same time as it contributes to levelling the individuality inside the group, a process of 'de-selfing' (*Entselbstung*), in Simmel's words.[95] The small circle is a controlling element among the insiders of a group.

The smaller the circle which forms our environment and the more limited the relationships which have the possibility of transcending the boundaries, the more anxiously the narrow community watches over the deeds, the conduct of life and the attitudes of the individual.[96]

Simmel's description of the secret society is in many ways relevant to Chinese reality. Fleeing from the small circles of work-unit surveillance and small-group evaluation, secret society members enter another small circle with fixed rules and regulations. Chinese criminal gangs operate as an imitation of the traditional segmentary structures found in China in the form of feudal trade associations (*fengjian hangbang*) and black societies. They keep up the traditional forms of blood sacrifice, smearing their lips with sacrificial blood (*shaxue*) during their initiation rites. They also practise kowtow rituals and take oaths (*mingshi*).[97] Much has been written in recent years particularly about the kind of 'criminal solidarity' found in these gangs; it is often claimed that the *germen yiqi* or *jianghu yiqi*—the criminal code of brotherhood— is the pillar of gang crime. The origins of the present code of brotherhood can be found in the old society, but it cannot today be fully explained by reference to that tradition. Gang members call each other 'brothers' (*chengxiong-daodi*). Some drink blood and wine to 'become blood brothers' (*bai bazi*), and swear that they will 'share troubles in life and death' (*tong sheng si gong huannan*).[98] To outsiders the gangs show an excluding (*paichi*) behaviour. This 'exclusiveness' strengthens their inner solidarity and unites the group, comments one report on gang crime: 'they are like brothers, even closer than brothers'.[99] Thus, the group-egoism described by Simmel can be found in the gangs of present-day China.

The imitation of mainstream culture is also evident. The 'exclusiveness' of the *zijiren*—the mechanism of 'us' against 'them' that characterized Chinese society—is found to be duplicated in the secret society. Even China's disciplinary technology is built on the principle of the small circle. We may recall Fei Xiaotong's description of Chinese society as concentric circles of family and social relationships, organized

into 'rings' or 'spheres' of relations. The criminologist Shao Daosheng
has described criminal gangs in a similar way, like an inverted mirror
of Chinese society. Shao explains that membership in these gangs forms
an 'overlapping chain of rings' (*lianhuan taoshi*).[100] The most conspicuous characteristic of the criminal culture, however, is the 'familist' structure of the gangs. Shao describes the phenomenon as a 'one family,
one consciousness' (*yijia yishi*) ideology based upon a 'quasi family–clan
system' (*zhun jiazu zhidu*).

A clear example is the imitation of blood relationships, harking back
to consanguinity ceremonies and rituals, and building quasi-family relationships within the criminal culture; there are parent–son relations (*qinzi
guanxi*), uncle–nephew relations (*shuzhi guanxi*), and brother relations
(*xiongdi guanxi*), and the organization takes the form of 'feudal' patriarchal hierarchies in the predominantly male gang culture. Building
intimate 'family' relations inside the organization also builds up natural
support and interdependent relations in the gang, and strengthens the
absolute loyalty towards the organization on the part of its members.
There are strict rules and norms to restrict behaviour; violence is used
both inside and outside the gangs to enforce the rules.[101]

In a report from a labour prison camp, we see another cultural characteristic of mainstream society duplicated in the gang organization.
Within the prison culture, gangs form according to principles strikingly
similar to those of society outside the prison walls. In a discussion on
factionalism and regionalism in gang formation, the central segmentary principle of *tong* is reformulated on the prison scene. Gangs are
formed on connections such as involvement in the same criminal
case (*tong'an*), or membership in the same gang (*tonghuo*), with 'small
brothers' as the core. These operate as small groups within bigger gangs,
where smaller leaders accept control by chief leaders. Just like in the
greater society (*tong*) or the 'same village' (*tongxiang*), it is the regional
organizing principle that underlies the illegal prison gang. The legal
prison organization comes fully equipped with evaluations of 'reform
work', *biaoxian* marking, activists, and petty bureaucrats. The principle
of *tong* is even used by prison inmates to cultivate relationships with
prison staff, in the hopes of gaining petty advantages from them.[102]

Preventing Deviance and Crime

We noted that prevention of the 'first time' of bad behaviour is widely
discussed in Chinese criminology.[103] Prevention is an age-old principle
in China; the value of education, according to Confucius, resides in its

power to prevent evils before they occur and to arouse respect in trifling matters.[104] Today a totally clean environment is impossible, Xu Jian maintains; all preventive measures have a limit. It is unrealistic to keep youth in a 'safe' to protect them, but, since the protection of youth also means the protection of society, one should aim at the best prevention possible.[105] Crime prevention starts with small observations, turns into evaluation work, to small-scale prevention work, and develops into a whole social network of crime prevention. The observation lists for analogous behaviour form the starting point of any chain narrative of danger, and there are many such lists in circulation. They are popular in the emerging new 'industry' of early education and family education.

One such list was drawn up by the Department of Sociology at the Chinese Academy of the Social Sciences,[106] with the aim of preventing the first sexual criminal offence among girls. This can be done by close observation of their behaviour in the home. The first dangerous sign is that the girl is easily distracted, walks frequently in and out of the house, and has difficulty concentrating. The second sign is when she demonstrates that she thinks the warnings and advice from older people are unnecessary; that she is openly disgusted with their talk and moral exhortations. The third signal is when the girl starts to show an abnormal attitude towards her siblings; she may be very impatient with them, but then suddenly turn very nice. If she has an elder sister, she may keep close to her to hear about her love affairs, etc. (Of course, this particular sign of danger gets increasingly difficult to observe in the age of the only child). A fourth sign is that such girls no longer want to do housework; if forced to do it, they do it inadequately; they also cook badly and do not clean properly. It is a cause for extra suspicion when they clean and iron their own clothes well, however. The fifth signal of danger is when the girl spends a lot of time alone in her room, rather than with the rest of her family; she may daydream, have fantasies, and think about personal matters, ignoring other family members.

In addition, such girls also develop singular interests, five of which are listed as particularly important. A crucial prewarning is when girls develop a liking for stories about relationships between men and women; they read a lot of love stories, watch love movies, and look at 'pornographic material', paying special attention to stories about criminal cases that have to do with pornography, etc. The second such interest is in clothes and make-up. They want to wear fashionable clothes and other modern Western items. They 'blatantly show off' (*zhaoyao guo shi*), and 'swagger through the streets in a conspicuous (*yin ren zhumu*) way'. The third interest involves the well-known danger of movement. They like to move around (*ai dong*); they adore the variable and the changeable; they make a big fuss over small things, are affected and pretentious, and again like to show off (*xianshi ziji*). Fourth, they develop strange cravings for snacks, and they like to spend money. They want to smoke and drink, and are not interested in food served in the family. If interests of this kind become deeper and stronger, they will develop into abnormal behaviour and insatiable needs (*tan de wuyan*). The fifth and last type of strange behaviour is that such girls love to gain small advantages; sometimes they even steal things. They are greedy and easily get into fights. Also, they do not care about the social and moral rules of society. Their sexual behaviour is often deviant.

A network of 'comprehensive control' (*zonghe zhili*) is about to be set up in China, and some of the initiatives for such work can be seen in the detailed network of community-organized crime prevention. In the following I note just a few examples of this network, to indicate the importance with which crime prevention is regarded in China.

A concept often used in Chinese criminology and in evaluation work is 'crime forecast' (*fanzui yuce*).[107] If crime can be prevented when the young person is at the bad habits stage (*buliang xiqi*), it is like getting a two-fold result from half the effort. Such prevention, however, is just one side of the criminal system. The principle of 'beating one to warn a hundred' (*da yi jing bai*) should supplement the first type of prevention through educational deterrence. In other words, there is crime prevention both in techniques of regulation and in spectacle. Punishment and prevention should supplement each other and be linked to each other. This applies both to general prevention (*yiban yufang*) and special prevention (*zhongdian yufang*). General prevention is exemplified by the strengthening of moral education, law education, etc. It is the basis for special prevention.

There are two types of special prevention. In early prevention (*zaoqi yufang*), the 12–15 year age group is important. Their minds are naive, their temperaments vigorous, and they are highy receptive to bad influences. Bad habits and malevolent misdeeds (*lieji*) define the reverse side of the good deed or the heroic deed (*shiji*) so much promoted in model learning. Such wrongdoing is found among some 1–3 per cent of the population. The number of registered 'wrongdoers' is thus around ten to fifteen times greater than that of criminals.[108] Bad habits or misdeeds are here defined according to the lists of subterranean values discussed earlier: smoking, drinking, fighting, swearing, gambling, pilfering, etc. Such wrongdoing can rapidly escalate into stealing, gang fights, assaulting and robbing, etc. These youngsters quickly develop into a new crop of criminals since they already suffer from the 'non-adapting sickness' (*bu shiying bing*). Very frequently, such wrongdoers are school dropouts.

Special prevention is directed towards those who have already taken the first step into the fringes or margins of criminal activity. Such youngsters have often served time in a reform-through-labour centre. They should be prevented from sliding even deeper into the abyss through methods of marginal prevention (*bianyuan yufang*). Moral campaigns are also directed towards those who live on the fringes of crime, or do petty crime. Marginal prevention is directed particularly against seven types of illegal and criminal behaviour: (1) pilfering, snatching, specualtion, swindling, smuggling, and gambling; (2) light forms of hooliganism, showing pornographic material, etc. (3) fighting, provoking fights, hiding weapons, disturbing the social order; (4) sheltering small amounts of stolen goods, selling or making use of stolen goods; (5) being expelled from school or from undergoing examination or observation (in other words, those who are punished after the fourth and fifth scale on the hierarchy of disciplinary sanction are being subject to marginal prevention); (6) listening to enemy radio, and wanting to cross the border; (7) others. Exempt from these marginal prevention procedures are those who have for more than six months avoided committing crime, those who have taken part in crime accidentally, and those who have broken rules, norms, and discipline only.[109]

Early prevention starts by creating a good family atmosphere.[110] Campaigns for selecting 'five-good families', and for children to respect their parents, etc., are all seen as early preventive measures. To help erring youth back to society, the small group is extended to the neighbourhood community. So-called 'help-education small groups' (*bangjiao xiaozu*) should be set up, consisting of parents and relatives, teachers or leaders, and colleagues or classmates. In addition, retired cadres and prestigious elders in the neighbourhood, and policemen in charge of household registration should be responsible for following up young people on the fringes of crime. These neighbourhood forces come together to create a special educative environment (*jiaoyu huanjing*) aimed at preventing crime. In 1989 it was reported that in Beijing there were already more than 6,000 such groups with more than 30,000 members, and the network is said to have grown since then. Such preventive measures are not regarded as a punishment; nor is this a system of disciplinary sanction (*xingzheng chufen*). It is a special education measure for erring youngsters that should be carried out on a national scale, supplementing the methods of sanctions and punishments.

China's work–study schools (*gongdu xuexiao*) are of a more coercive character, but are still regarded as special education organizing youngsters who have been involved in illegal (*weifa*) or criminal (*fanzui*) behaviour to live in a strict and collective way. The policy of such schools is to 'save the children and train them to become talented persons' (*wanjiu haizi, zaojiu rencai*). It is reported that 80 per cent have changed their bad habits after such schools, while 10 per cent have become advanced workers and backbone elements of production. Some have even become 'three-good students'.[111]

A range of community crime prevention initiatives should be organized. So-called civil administration work (*minzheng gongzuo*) should be strengthened. And a 'guardian' (*jianshu ren*) network should be established, in which two or three guardians follow up an errant youngster, teaching him/her good morals and giving them a feeling of responsibility. There should also be an inspection system (*fudao zhidu*) to look after children from families where both parents are at work when the children come back from school. One must seek to prevent such children from developing bad habits. The small groups for help and education already mentioned should in particular take care of families where youngsters have been involved in illegal behaviour. Those who have returned from reform-through-labour programmes should be helped and supervised, through a cooperative network involving the local police station, the street committee, the school or work-unit, and the parents. Particularly in the countryside, the family is a vital community factor. In the rural areas, but also in the cities, 'patriarchy' rather than 'the people' is mobilized in crime prevention work, and plays an important role in the overall 'comprehensive control'.[112]

Comprehensive control should be linked to the ideological campaigns of 'spiritual civilization'. In one survey a normal group of young people is compared with a group of criminal youths.[113] Some of the findings concern the 'purification of environment' and the effect of moral education and *biaoxian* evaluation in schools. Table 7 shows that 'civilized street' (*wenming jie*) or 'civilized village' (*wenming cun*) activities had an improving effect on the crime rate, as four times as many in the normal group lived in such streets compared with those in the criminal group. Unfortunately, the data do not permit us to look for spurious findings or flaws in the methodology used.

Table 8 shows the marked effect of ideological education on the social order. Schools with a high profile of daily moral and ideological education proved to have law-abiding students.

In Table 9 the authors have found a measure on the effects of *biaoxian* measurement and the usefulness of evaluation. In several types of analogous behaviour linked to school attendance, the survey shows that such behaviour can effectively predict later crime. For instance,

TABLE 7   Has the street or village where you live developed the building of civilized street or village activities? (%)

	Normal group	Criminal group
Yes	44	10
Not sure	38	52
No	18	38
Sum	100	100

Source: Zhou Lu, Yang Ruohe, and Hu Ruyong, *Qingshaonian fanzui zonghe zhili duice xue* (Study in how to deal with comprehensive control of juvenile crime), Beijing, Qunzhong chubanshe, 1986, p. 178.

TABLE 8   Does your school carry out ideological education daily? (%)

	Normal group	Criminal group
Daily	54	21
Occasionally	38	56
Very little	9	13
Sum	100	100

Source: Zhou Lu, Yang Ruohe, and Hu Ruyong (Table 7), p. 198.

TABLE 9   *Biaoxian* discipline in school (%)

	Normal group	Criminal group
Not coming late or leaving early	69	19
Occasionally coming late	24	31
Frequently coming late	1	3
Occasionally absent without leave	6	30
Frequently absent without leave	1	17
Sum	100	100

Source: Zhou Lu, Yang Ruohe, and Hu Ruyong (Table 7), p. 214.

69 per cent in the normal group did not come to school late or leave early, while only 19 per cent of the criminal group had shown such exemplary conduct. Seventeen times as many in the criminal group had been 'frequently' absent from school without leave.

The authors summarize by stating that school is the most fundamental line of defence against crime, and that crime prevention is closely connected to moral, intellectual, bodily, and aesthetic factors. 'Education is the most profound way of criminal prevention', they maintain.[114] In particular, moral education is crucial both in terms of economic development and in terms of upholding the social order, linking the narratives of order and progress to the 'dangers of modernity'.

Notes to Chapter 9

1. From Baudelaire's 'Heroism of modern life', quoted from Marshall Berman, *All that is Solid Melts into Air: The Experience of Modernity*, London, Verso, 1983, p. 143.
2. Charles Baudelaire, *The Painter of Modern Life and other Essays*, trans. and ed. Jonathan Mayne, London, Phaidon Press, 1964, p. 40.
3. Ibid., pp. 143–4.
4. For a stimulating presentation of the different manifestations of this modern culture, see Geremie Barmé and Linda Jaivin, *New Ghosts, Old Dreams: Chinese Rebel Voices*, New York, Times Books/Random House, 1992.
5. Peng Xincai, 'Shimao yu qingshaonian weifa fanzui' (Fashion and juvenile criminal offence), *Qingshaonian fanzui yanjiu*, No. 10, 1988, pp. 23–5.
6. Ibid., p. 23.
7. The picture of norms as a 'permissive zone' was suggested in Robin M. Williams, Jr, *American Society: A Sociological Interpretation*, New York, Alfred A. Knopf, 1951, p. 348.
8. The concept of 'chain narrative' I have derived from discussions with Ivar Frønes at the Department of Sociology, University of Oslo.
9. The *Shuowen jiezi*, ch. 4b, pp. 2b–3a, defines *ji* ('the embryonic') as *wei* ('minutiae'). See Anne Behnke Kinney, 'Dyed silk: Han notions of the moral development of children', in Anne Behnke Kinney, *Chinese Views of Childhood*, Honolulu, University of Hawaii Press, 1995, pp. 28, 56.
10. Xu Deqi and Wu Zaide, 'Guanyu tuanhuo fanzui yu qingshaonian buliang jiaowang de diaocha fenxi' (Survey analysis of gang crime and the bad contacts of juveniles), in *Zhongguo qingshaonian fanzui yanjiu nianjian 1987*, Beijing, Chunqiu chubanshe, 1988, pp. 185–7.
11. Xu Deqi and Wu Zaide, 'Shi xi qingshaonian liumang tuanhuo touzi de texing ji jingcheng huangbian' (Tentative analysis of the characteristics and patterns forming and developing hooligan gang leaders), in *Zhongguo qingshaonian fanzui yanjiu nianjian 1987*, Beijing, Chunqiu chubanshe, 1988, p. 401.
12. Zhang Panshi, 'Dui shaonian "taoye" xianxiang de diaocha' (Investigation of the 'runaway' phenomenon among juveniles), in *Zhongguo qingshaonian fanzui yanjiu nianjian 1987*, Beijing, Chunqiu chubanshe, 1988, pp. 226–7. On sexual crime and the runaway, see Yu Qihong and Yin Zhijing, 'Bu yukuai–taoye–xing cuizuo' (Unhappy–running away–sexual criminal mistakes), *Dangdai qingnian yanjiu*, No. 1, 1988, pp. 10–11.
13. See Michael R. Gottferdsson and Travis Hirschi, *A General Theory of Crime*, Stanford, Stanford University Press, 1990.
14. David Matza and Gresham M. Sykes, 'Juvenile delinquency and subterranean values', *American Sociological Review*, Vol. 26, No. 4, October 1961, pp. 712–19.

15. David Matza, 'Subterranean traditions of youth', *Annals of the American Academy of Political and Social Science*, No. 338, November 1961, p. 109.
16. Ibid.
17. Wang Yanfeng, 'Xiandai ren de yuedu zhanlüe' (The reading strategies of modern persons), *Qingnian shidai*, No. 7, 1989, p. 27.
18. Quoted from an interview in Ann-Ping Chin, *Children of China: Voices from Recent Years*, Ithaca, NY, Cornell University Press, 1989, p. 143.
19. Michael R. Dutton, *Policing and Punishment in China: From Patriarchy to 'the People'*, Cambridge, Cambridge University Press, 1992, p. 311. Dutton bases his information on Gao Zhongxuan *et al.*, *Zuifan gaizao shouce* (Handbook in criminal reform), Shanxi, Shanxi renmin chubanshe, 1987, pp. 48, 51.
20. Wang Yuezhong, 'Weishen cizi luokou de yeman xingwei' (Tatooing is a backwards and uncivilized behaviour), *Banyuetan*, No. 3, 1991, p. 41.
21. Shao Daosheng, *Dangdai shehui de bingtai xinli* (The morbid psychology of today's society), Beijing, Shehui kexue wenxian chubanshe, 1990, p. 243.
22. Feng Changshui, 'Nongcun zhongxue banzhuren gongzuo chutan' (Preliminary discussion on class teacher work in the countryside), *Beijing jiaoyu*, No. 12, 1985, p. 15.
23. *Zhongguo jiaoyu bao*, 9 April 1991, p. 3. The Party has sought to adapt to the changing values on this field and assimilate the trend by linking cosmetology to health. A new journal was recently started in Beijing by the Ministry of Hygiene called *Jiankang yu meirong* (Health and cosmetology). The journal runs columns on methods of cosmetology, cosmetology courses, and how to live longer: see *Renmin ribao (haiwan ban)*, 9 December 1992, p. 3.
24. Chen Zhuo, 'Shenghuo yu meirong' (Life and cosmetology), *Shidai qingnian*, No. 2, 1992, p. 15.
25. Alberto Melucci, *Nomads of the Present*, Philadelphia, Temple University Press, 1989, p. 123.
26. Ibid., p. 124.
27. Michel Foucault, *The History of Sexuality*, Vol. 1, *An Introduction*, New York, Vintage Books, 1990, pp. 17–49.
28. Alberto Melucci, p. 124.
29. David Matza, 'Subterranean traditions of youth', *Annals of the American Academy of Political and Social Science*, No. 338, November 1961, p. 111.
30. He Xin, 'Gudu yu tiaozhan: qisihua yu mogui zhi pi' (Loneliness and challenge: the flower with seven colours and the skin of the devil), *Zixue*, No. 2, 1989, p. 39.
31. Zhongguo shehui kexueyuan shehuixue yanjiusuo, (ed.), *Qingshaonian fanzui xinlixue* (The psychology of juvenile delinquency), Shanghai, Shanghai renmin chubanshe, 1985, p. 102.
32. Li Zhaohong, 'Guanyu daxuesheng xinli fazhan bu pingheng xing chengyin tantao' (A discussion of factors causing the unbalanced psychological development among university students), *Qingshaonian tantao*, No. 3, 1988, pp. 31–4.
33. Liu Zhixue, 'Bodong yu pingheng' (Fluctuation and balance), *Qingnian yanjiu*, No. 9, 1990. pp. 37–8.
34. Peter L. Berger, 'On the obsolesence of the concept of honor', *Archives Européennes de Sociologie/European Journal of Sociology*, No. 2, 1970, pp. 343, 345.
35. Émile Durkheim, *Moral Education*, trans. Everett K. Wilson and Herman Schnurer, New York, Free Press, 1973, p. 241.
36. Li Shiqing and Zhang Xinxing (eds.), *Junshi shehuixue* (Military sociology), Beijing, Junshi kexue chubanshe, 1990, p. 194.

37. Zhongguo shehui kexueyuan shehuixue yanjiusuo (ed.), *Zhongguo shehuixue nianjian 1979–1989* (China Yearbook of sociology 1979–1989), Beijing, Zhongguo dabaike quanshu chubanshe, 1989, p. 130.

38. Tan Jianguang, 'Qingnian shehuixue de lilun yaodian' (Main theoretical aspects of youth sociology), *Qingshaonian yanjiu*, No. 2, 1987, p. 4; also in C4 *Shehuixue*, No. 5, 1987, p. 25.

39. Liu Qing, 'Shidai xingge de fumian: lun dangdai daxuesheng de jingshen tuifei', in Gongqingtuan zhongyang xuanchuanbu (Propaganda Department of the Youth League Central Committee) (ed.), *Dangdai qingnian lilun dachao* (The theoretical wave of contemporary youth), Beijing, Nongcun duwu chubanshe, 1989, pp. 3, 6.

40. The Young Pioneers and the Youth League during the 1950s and 1960s, until the Cultural Revolution started, had full control over the youth generation, much like youth movements in the Soviet Union were controlled through the Komsomol.

41. Liu Qing, pp. 6–9.

42. Feng Yunxiang, 'Wenhua shifan yu qingnian yuegui' (Cultural *anomie* and youth transgressions), *Qingnian yanjiu* No. 6, 1990, pp. 34–36, 41.

43. Chen Xiaochuan, 'Qingnian gongren de shenghuo taidu yu shenghuo sheji' (Life approaches and life plans among young workers), *Qingnian yanjiu*, No. 11, 1987, pp. 22–3, 15.

44. Zhang Panshi, 'Lüe lun qingshaonian de zisha wenti jiqi yufang' (Brief discussion of youth suicide and its prevention), *Shanghai qingnian yanjiu*, No. 7, 1986, pp. 26–7.

45. Tatsuo Masubuchi, 'The Yu Hsia (*yuxia*) and the Social Order in the Han Period', *Annals of the Hitotsubashi Academy*, Vol. III, No. 1, 1952, p. 90. Masubuchi mentions several examples from the classical books like in *Shi ji* ch. 129, pp. 28–9; ch. 124, pp. 12 and 13; ch. 7, p. 8; ch. 89, p. 4; ch. 55, p. 6; ch. 56, p. 4; ch. 92, p. 3; in *Han shu*, ch. 90, p. 11a; ch. 83, p. 30; *Hou han shu*, ch. 11 (mem. 1), p. 8b; ch. 77 (mem. 67), p. 7a. A partial translation of *Shi ji* is found in Ssu-Ma Ch'ien (Sima Qian), *Records of the Historian: Chapters from the Shih chi of Ssu-ma Ch'ien*, trans. by Burton Watson, New York, Columbia University Press, 1969. James Liu has found Masubuchi's translation 'hooligan' a little too strong, and instead suggests 'unruly youths': see James J. Y. Liu, *The Chinese Knight-Errant*, Chicago, University of Chicago Press, 1967, p. 209.

46. Joseph F. Kett, *Rites of Passage: Adolescence in America 1790 to the Present*, New York, Basic Books, 1977, pp. 255–6.

47. Zhongguo shehui kexueyuan shehuixue yanjiusuo (ed.), *Qingshaonian fanzui xinlixue* (The psychology of juvenile delinquency), Shanghai, Shanghai renmin chubanshe, 1985, pp. 250, 253.

48. Mo Dong, 'Guangxi qingshaonian weifa fanzui qingkuang de diaocha' (An investigation of the situation of juvenile criminal offenders in Guangxi), *Qingshaonian tantao*, No. 1, 1990, p. 26.

49. Zhongguo shehui kexueyuan shehuixue yanjiusuo (ed.), p. 255.

50. See e.g. Guo Zhao, 'Shilun huanjing yingxiang yu diling fanzui' (A tentative discussion on the influence of the environment on minors' crime), *Qingshaonian tantao*, No. 4, 1990, p. 16.

51. Xu Deqi and Wu Zaide, 'Shi xi qingshaonian liumang tuanhuo touzi de texing ji jingcheng huangbian', p. 399.

52. Li Xihai, 'Wenhua, wenhua huanjing yu qingshaonian fanzui' (Culture, cultural environment, and juvenile delinquency), *Qingshaonian fanzui yanjiu*, No. 4–5, 1991, pp. 34–6.

53. Ibid., p. 35.

54. Xu Qiancheng, 'Hubei Jingzhou diqu nongcun "tuliuzi" fanzui diaocha' (An investigation of crime among local thugs in Hubei's Jingzhou area), in *Zhongguo qingshaonian fanzui yanjiu nianjian 1987*, Beijing, Chunqiu chubanshe, 1988, p. 156.

55. Geremie Barmé, 'Wang Shuo and Liumang ("Hooligan") Culture', *Australian Journal of Chinese Affairs*, No. 28, July 1992, pp. 23–64.

56. Gao Ge, 'Dui liumang fanzui de bijiao yanjiu' (On the comparative research of hooliganism), *Jilin daxue shehui kexue xuebao*, No. 3, 1986, pp. 54–9; also in *D41 Falü, Fuyin baokan ziliao*, No. 8, 1986, p. 71.

57. Dai Fukang, 'Ziyouhua sichao yu qingshaonian fanzui' (The liberalization wave and juvenile crime), *Qingshaonian fanzui yanjiu*, No. 3–4, 1990, p. 3.

58. Zhang Yingzhi, 'Wo guo qingnian lüyou re' (The Chinese travelling craze), in Gongqingtuan zhongyang yanjiushi (ed.), *Zhongguo daqushi yu dangdai qingnian* (Chinese megatrends and contemporary youth), Jinan, Shandong renmin chubanshe, 1989, pp. 103–10.

59. Guo Xiang and Ma Changmiao, 'Lun qingshaonian tuanhuo fanzui' (On juvenile gang crime), in *Zhongguo qingshaonian fanzui yanjiu nianjian 1987*, Beijing, Chunqiu chubanshe, 1988, p. 377.

60. Ibid., p. 382.

61. Herbert A. Bloch and Arthur Niederhoffer, *The Gang: A Study in Adolescent Behavior*, New York, Philosophical Library, 1958, p. 6. Thrasher's classic work on gang crime mentioned here states that 'Locomotion (or wanderlust) for its own sake— interest in mere change and movement—is an extensive activity in the undirected gang, where it readily assumes the character of vice': see Frederic M. Thrasher, *The Gang*, Chicago, University of Chicago Press, 1927, p. 171.

62. Yang Xiong, 'Lun dangdai qingnian wenhua de "changbo" xianxiang' (On the phenomenon of 'long wave' youth culture), *Qingnian yanjiu* No. 2, 1990, pp. 1–6.

63. Zhongguo shehui kexueyuan shehuixue yanjiusuo (ed.), p. 157.

64. Xie Dexin, 'Qingnian de guannian bianhua he qingnian yeyu wenhua de xin qushi' (The change in youth concepts and the new trends in youth leisure time culture), in Gongqingtuan zhongyang xuanchuanbu (ed.), *Dangdai qingnian lilun dachao* (Theoretical waves on contemporary youth), Beijing, Nongcun duwu chubanshe, 1989, pp. 143–53.

65. Tan Jianguang, pp. 27–29.

66. Shao Daosheng, p. 239.

67. Dai Fukang, p. 3.

68. The 'aunties' in the kindergarten thought that He Xin's naughtiness meant that he was harming their honour on purpose. They claimed he was free, selfish, unorganized, and without discipline. Because he did not obey he was constantly punished by isolation from the other children. The 'aunties' told the children that He Xin was a naughty little boy with his head full of bad thoughts that could not be cured. They hinted that they would contact the 'uncles' from the police who would send him to education through labour. They warned all his little classmates that they should not pay any attention to the deviant, and that they should not play with him since they would learn bad things and be taken away by the police. The 'aunties' called disobedient He Xin a 'horse that harms the group' (*hai qun zhi ma*). See He Xin, 'Gudu yu tiaozhan: wo shengming de yuanzui' (Loneliness and challenge: my original guilt in life), *Zixue*, No. 1, 1989, pp. 15–16.

69. See W. Allyn Rickett, 'Voluntary surrender and confession in Chinese law: the problem of continuity', *Journal of Asian Studies*, No. 4, 1971, pp. 797–814.

70. Hongda Harry Wu, *Laogai: The Chinese Gulag*, Boulder, Colo., Westview Press, 1992, p. 97. For an account of female prisoners refusing to admit guilt, see Zhang Jian and Zhang Wenbang, 'Dui Zhejiang sheng nü fanzui fuxing qijian de tuan-huo huodong fenxi' (Analysis of the gang activities of female prisoners in Zhejiang province during the period of imprisonment), in *Zhongguo qingshaonian fanzui yanjiu nianjian 1987*, Beijing, Chunqiu chubanshe, 1988, pp. 413–19.

71. Liu Ruifeng, 'Lun gongdu xuexiao dui qingshaonian fanzui de zaoqi ganyu' (On the early intervention of the work–study school on juvenile delinquency), in Yantai daxue faxuesuo (ed.), *Zhong Mei xuezhe lun qingshaonian fanzui* (Juvenile delinquency and its treatment by Chinese and American scholars), Yantai, Qunzhong chubanshe, 1989, p. 97.

72. Zhang Shaoxia, 'Wo guo bangjiao gongzuo de lilun yu shijian' (The theory and practice of Chinese help-education work), in Yantai daxue faxuesuo (ed.), *Zhong Mei xuezhe lun qingshaonian fanzui* (Juvenile delinquency and its treatment by Chinese and American scholars), Yantai, Qunzhong chubanshe, 1989, p. 84.

73. Ibid., p. 88.

74. Xiang Zhongyu, 'Lun wo guo dui weifa fanzui shaonian de jiaoyu yu wanjiu' (On the education and redemption of juvenile delinquents in China), in Yantai daxue faxuesuo (ed.), p. 49.

75. Zhang Shaoxia, p. 88. On a 'fallen' former 'three-good student' turned criminal, see Ge Fang, 'Zou xiang huimie de "san hao xuesheng"' (A 'three-good student' walking towards destruction), *Qingnian shidai*, No. 11, 1988, pp. 24–5. Another 'three-good student' in Nanjing read an obscene novel, and afterwards raped and murdered a neighbourhood girl: see Dai Fukang, p. 5.

76. Kai T. Erikson, *Wayward Puritans: A Study in the Sociology of Deviance*, New York, John Wiley, 1966, p. 130.

77. Ibid., p. 131.

78. Ibid., p. 171.

79. Ibid., p. 168.

80. See Gao Ge, p. 75. and Liu Hua, 'Liumang zui' (Hooligan crime), in Zhongguo xingfa cidian bianweihui (ed.), *Zhongguo xingfa cidian* (Chinese encyclopedia of criminal law), Shanghai, Xuelin chubanshe, 1989, pp. 700–3.

81. Kai T. Erikson., p. 68.

82. Ye Xiaoping and Yin Jianhua, ' "Yingxiang yi dai" biaozheng ji duice chutan' (Initial discussion of the illnesses of the 'image generation' and its countermeasures), *Qingnian yanjiu xuekan*, No. 1, 1991, pp. 38–41.

83. Sergei N. Eisenstadt, *From Generation to Generation*, New York, Free Press, 1971, pp. *xiv, xvi–xvii*.

84. Dick Hebdige, *Hiding in the Light: On Images and Things*, London, Routledge, 1988, p. 35.

85. The expression is taken from Dick Hebdige's book-title, and points to the duality of youth cultures in general.

86. John R. Gillis, *Youth and History: Tradition and Change in European Age Relations, 1770–Present*, expanded student edn., New York, Academic Press, 1981, p. 219.

87. He Xin, 'Gudu yu tiaozhan: huangdan er kongbu de hong bayue' (Loneliness and challenge: absurd and terrorizing red August), *Zixue*, No. 11, 1989, p. 9. (One *cun* is 3.33 cm.)

88. Robert Jay Lifton, 'Youth and history: individual change in postwar Japan', in Erik H. Erikson (ed.), *The Challenge of Youth*, Garden City, NY, Anchor Books, 1965, pp. 260–90.

89. Ibid., p. 273.
90. Travis Hirschi, *Causes of Delinquency*, Berkeley, University of California Press, 1969.
91. David Matza, *Delinquency and Drift*, new edn., New Brunswick, NJ, Transaction Books, 1990, p. 28.
92. Georg Simmel, 'The secret society', in Georg Simmel, *The Sociology of Georg Simmel*, trans. and ed. Kurt H. Wolff, New York, Free Press, 1964, p. 30; from *Soziologie: Untersuchungen über die Formen der Vergesellschaftung*, 1908.
93. Ibid.
94. Ibid., p. 371.
95. Ibid., p. 373.
96. Georg Simmel, 'The metropolis and mental life', in Georg Simmel, *On Individuality and Social Forms*, Chicago, University of Chicago Press, 1971, p. 333; from *Soziologie: Untersuchungen über die Formen der Vergesellschaftung*, 1908, p. 333.
97. Zhonghua renmin gongheguo gonganju, 'Wo guo qingshaonian fanzui de qushi he yufang' (The trends of juvenile crime in China and their prevention), in *Zhongguo qingshaonian fanzui yanjiu nianjian 1987*, Beijing, Chunqiu chubanshe, 1988, p. 43.
98. Guo Xiang and Ma Changmiao, pp. 379–80.
99. Xu Deqi and Wu Zaide, 'Guanyu tuanhuo fanzui yu qingshaonian buliang jiaowang de diaocha fenxi', p. 183.
100. Shao Daosheng, p. 232.
101. These rules and norms are stipulated in explicit terms. For example, members should not betray their 'brothers' in trials; they should show loyalty towards fellow members; they should not reveal gang secrets; they should not take possession of the gang's achievements or profits single-handedly; they should not defect from the gang; etc. Rigorous punishment awaited anyone who broke the rules (Shao Daosheng, pp. 241–2).
102. Dang Guoqing, 'Laojiao renyuan jiehuo fan gaizao wenti de pouxi' (Analysis of the problems of ganging up and going against reform among the inmates of re-education through labour institutions), in *Zhongguo qingshaonian fanzui yanjiu nianjian 1987*, Beijing, Chunqiu chubanshe, 1988, p. 407.
103. See e.g. Zhou Lu, Yang Ruohe, and Hu Ruyong, *Qingshaonian fanzui zonghe zhili duice xue* (Studies in how to deal with comprehensive control of juvenile crime), Beijing, Qunzhong chubanshe, 1986, p. 161.
104. See T'ung-Tsu Ch'ü, *Law and Society in Traditional China*, Paris, Mouton, 1961, p. 249.
105. Xu Jian, 'Lun wo guo baohu qingshaonian lifa de xin fazhan' (New developments in the legislation of juvenile protection in China), in Yantai daxue faxuesuo (ed.), *Zhong Mei xuezhe lun qingshaonian fanzui*, pp. 113–23.
106. Zhongguo shehui kexueyuan shehuixue yanjiusuo (ed.), *Qingshaonian fanzui xinlixue* (The psychology of juvenile delinquency), Shanghai, Shanghai renmin chubanshe, 1985, pp. 260–2.
107. Zhou Lu, Yang Ruohe, and Hu Ruyong, pp. 72–5.
108. According to self-reports, deviant behaviour is far lower in China than in Japan and the USA. There is also a higher awareness among Chinese that certain acts are wrong. On the basis of a survey of about 5,600 young people in the three countries, Wu Qingxiang compiled statistics on attitudes and manifestations of bad behaviour among young people from USA, Japan, and China's Shanghai region (see Table N1). It should be noted that, while the Japanese interpreted the question about staying out late as 'coming home after midnight', the Chinese

TABLE N1

Type of bad behaviour	Has taken part in such behaviour			Regards this as wrong behaviour		
	American	Japanese	Chinese	American	Japanese	Chinese
Stealing	20.7	6.6	0.9	97.1	84.5	100.0
Beating, swearing, teasing teacher	5.4	2.5	0.3	95.1	80.1	99.4
Taking drugs	11.1	2.1	0.0	95.5	83.1	99.5
Cutting classes	17.9	7.5	2.5	91.4	77.5	98.6
Cheating friends	52.3	48.7	11.1	94.4	64.2	96.2
Staying out illegally	18.1	5.6	1.0	90.9	74.7	95.9
Smoking	28.2	10.1	3.5	93.2	80.8	95.8
Destroying public property	12.2	20.0	13.4	95.6	80.7	95.5
Standing up to the teacher	45.4	25.0	8.6	83.1	60.9	88.8
Staying out late	30.1	10.4	25.1	86.7	76.7	77.2
Coming late to class	56.1	35.3	37.3	87.4	52.6	75.5

interpreted it as 'coming in late for dinner'. The Chinese also had much stricter definitions of 'public property' than both Japanese and Americans. See Wu Qingxiang, 'Riben, Meiguo, he wo guo Shanghai diqu qingshaonian cuicuo yuanyin de bijiao fenxi' (Comparative analysis of the origins of criminal mistakes among youth in Japan, the United States, and the Shanghai area in China), in *Zhongguo qingshaonian fanzui yanjiu nianjian 1987*, Beijing, Chunqiu chubanshe, 1988, pp. 540–4.

109. Ibid., pp. 76–82.
110. Wang Luosheng, 'Lun wo guo qingshaonian fanzui yufang' (On the prevention of juvenile delinquency in China), Yantai daxue faxuesuo (ed.), pp. 32–6.
111. Ibid., pp. 36–8.
112. Zhou Lu, Yang Ruohe, and Hu Ruyong, pp. 172–4.
113. Other tables show the importance of not spoiling children, teachers' attitudes toward their students, whether love affairs between students go on in school, etc. Strict education, good teacher–student relations, and fewer love affairs are all found to contribute to the maintenance of social order and the prevention of crime. Unfortunately, and regrettably, as usual, Chinese surveys do not provide enough information about the methods of measuring, definitions of variables, etc., for us to say much about the validity or reliability of the findings presented.
114. See Zhou Lu, Yang Ruohe, and Hu Ruyong, pp. 207–10.

10

'Never for the First Time':
'Premature Love' and Social Control

In China, the initial transgression of social boundaries, 'the first time' (or in this connection 'the first love' (*chulian*)), is seen as vastly import-ant, the first link in the chain narrative of danger. 'Sexual disorder' has increasingly come to be seen as a social problem. One phenomenon that has led to a veritable obsession is that of 'early love' or 'premature love' (*zaolian*). Here I propose to examine the official discourse on 'purity and chastity' as a product of the fear of social disorder. Some anthro-pologists have interpreted ideologies of purity as symbolic systems express-ive of social change and cultural tension, in which the physical body is used to symbolize the social body.[1] If the physical body is seen as threatened by uncontrollable forces, then presumably the society in ques-tion is one that fears change.

China is currently experiencing a 'boundary crisis'.[2] A primary objective of the authorities has become a strengthening of the primary social boundaries which are rapidly eroding as a result of modernization. Official exemplary norms and standards of 'normality' and 'abnormality' are promoted, and warnings are issued about social deviance. Para-doxically, the young are regarded both as China's hope for a modernized future, and as a marginal group with a strong tendency to transgress moral and ideological boundaries.

As Carroll Smith-Rosenberg has pointed out, historians of religion study theology not to learn about the nature of God, but to learn about the nature of the culture that has produced that theology.[3] Similarly, one should not take Chinese reports and data on 'premature love' at face value, but rather should seek the cultural bias underlying such data. 'Disorderly' sexuality has become a symbol of the threat to the collect-ive identity. It goes against the aim of *anding tuanjie* (social stability and unity), which is the very essence of the official political line.[4] The exag-gerated concern with 'sexual disorder' fits Stan Cohen's description of a 'moral panic':

[A] condition, episode, person or group of persons emerges to become defined as a threat to societal values and interests. Such threats are presented in a stylized and stereotypical fashion by the mass media as well as by the moral educators.[5]

Admittedly, the earlier onset of puberty and the growth in liberal ideas among young people in China during the last decade may very well have caused an increase in early love affairs. In addition, the 'one-child policy' may have increased the fear of unwanted births. Nevertheless, the enormous attention attached to this subject seems exaggerated when compared with the actual behaviour of youth. Sexuality has increasingly been subsumed under a scientific (and pseudo-scientific) discourse of medicine, psychology, pedagogy, criminology, etc., as a subject of a discourse on power, 'human improvement', and purification. 'Premature love' is said to debase human quality, and obstruct the building of a new spiritual and material civilization; it is regarded as a threat to modernization itself.

Although several surveys have been undertaken to investigate the problem of *zaolian*, there is every reason for scepticism, as with Chinese surveys in general. The survey method is popular, but many surveys seem to break every rule in the survey methodology book.[6] They show a systematic cultural bias, and would appear to have been designed and conducted merely to affirm a predetermined conclusion. Precisely because of such bias, these surveys are of particular interest. The bias tells us a great deal about popular stereotypes and cultural myths.

An analysis of the discourse on 'premature love' reveals basic symbols, myths, and mechanisms of the current boundary crisis or moral panic. It will demonstrate that gender inequality and the moral double standard remain strong in China: public discourse has especially turned against the independent, sexually active girl as being mainly responsible for today's sexual disorder.

The Mounting Crisis of 'Premature Love'

The 'whisperings of love' are no longer heard only in universities. They are also heard in lower secondary schools, even in primary school. While traditionally such love affairs were looked upon as something shameful, embarrassing, or even illegal, 14-year-old girls now regard having a boyfriend as something to boast about. A national survey recently found that half of the children under 14 had boyfriends and girlfriends.[7] The more it is prohibited, the more it spreads, sounds the anguished cry of one teacher.[8]

There are also biological reasons for the phenomenon of 'premature love'. Chinese children are reaching physiological maturity much earlier than before. A survey conducted among schoolgirls in Beijing in 1963–4 showed that the average age of first menstruation was 14.4 years;[9] in 1989 it had fallen to 13.0 years, and was not uncommon among 10-year-olds.[10] It was recently found that as many as 91.5 per cent of Chinese girls had experienced their first menstruation by the age of 14.[11] The average age is now close to that of Japan and the United States.[12] Most surveys show that the physical maturation of boys takes place about two years later than that of girls, and argue on this basis that boys have reached a relatively higher degree of psychological maturity when they become physically mature. This is taken to mean that the sexual awakening of boys is less dangerous to society than that of girls. The feeling of crisis is accentuated by the parents' ignorance of sexual matters. A typical story is that of a 13-year-old girl who was severely beaten after her first menstruation. The mother, who had been 18 when she herself had had her first period, suspected her daughter of being involved in some 'unnatural sexual relation'.[13]

Sex education had long been neglected, and even in 1988 only about 7,000 of the more than 90,000 secondary schools had started courses in 'sexual science'. In 1992 sex education was offered in just about one-quarter of the colleges in the country.[14] Such education is not compulsory in secondary schools, and there are very few textbooks. Interestingly, those in favour of sex education use the argument of social order to legitimize their standpoint. Sex education is said to be effective in reducing 'premature love' among schoolchildren, and in improving the quality of their work and the school ethos.[15] Many teachers, however, are hostile to sex education and even sabotage the distribution of textbooks.[16] A survey of secondary schoolchildren from Shanghai (a national model for sex education) showed that only 4.6 per cent of the boys, and 28.4 per cent of the girls, received their sexual information from either the school or their parents.[17] Parents find it embarrassing to discuss sexual matters with their offspring.[18] Even many secondary school students are ignorant of the simplest facts of life, such as where babies come from.[19]

In China millions of rural youngsters have left their villages to work in the cities.[20] The city, with its new migrant population and rapidly changing social norms, is perceived as a threat to the young and the unwary. Modern city life and the dangers of sexuality are regarded as interlinked phenomena of dangerous 'movement':

The cities do not only represent the magnificence of modern civilization, but they also have their filthy nooks and crannies . . . Everything in the city no doubt appears 'sexy' to those who are away from home. The marginal figures now invading the modern city are said to possess 'the psychology of the traveller', characterized by 'sexual hunger' and a tendency to stir up social disorder.[21]

The authorities firmly believe that there is a direct connection between mobility and 'sexual disorder'. Thus, while on the social level independence is gaining momentum, there is a strong urge to restrain this process on the moral level. The term 'sexual disorder' (xingluan)[22] comprises a whole range of undesirable phenomena. The definition of 'sexual crime' includes numerous types of behaviour that would not be regarded as criminal acts in most other countries. For example, a new regulation from the Ministry of Civil Affairs stated that 'cohabitation without official marriage registration' would be treated as illegal.[23] AIDS and venereal disease are also seen as symptoms of social disorder, and 'careless attitudes toward sex by some young people seeking "sexual liberation" and "sexual freedom"' are often blamed for the rise of venereal disease.[24] Also, the rising divorce rate is regarded as a sign of disorder and instability.[25]

The extreme importance attached to 'early education' (zaoqi jiaoyu) in China is paralleled in the fear of early deviance. In 1977 it was still forbidden to 'talk of love' (tan lianai) at universities. Student couples were tailed at night, and partners were often allocated jobs in different regions after graduation. During the 1980s, the official policy towards student love affairs changed from prohibition (jinzhi) to 'not encouraging' them (bu tichang). The authorities took an attitude of 'neither suppression, nor letting things drift'. A 'positive guidance' was introduced to encourage students to concentrate on their studies and to avoid love affairs.[26] In some universities it has been written into the rules of discipline that students are 'not allowed to smoke or drink, or have love affairs during their time of study; they are also not allowed to marry. Those who do will have to leave university.'[27] In some institutions, there was a return to prohibition after 1989. In October 1991, Beijing University decided to ban hugging and kissing on campus. A system of warnings and fines was introduced to make the regulation effective.[28] The exemplary norm prescribes a narrow framework for love and marriage. Interestingly, there is also a problem of 'postmature love': 'older unmarried youths' (daling weihun qingnian) in their late twenties and early thirties have been described as a direct 'threat to social stability'.[29]

Liu Dalin, in his recent large-scale study of sexual behaviour in China, concludes that teenagers are sexually precocious compared with earlier times.[30] Such findings have unintentionally triggered off several alarmist reports on the insatiability of youthful sex. Not all reports indicate

precocity among the young, however. A large-scale survey from Shanghai found that only 10.77 per cent of university students were found
to have had any 'sexual experience' (*xing xingwei*).[31] The figure is supported by data from an investigation among Beijing students in 1991,
which found that only about 9 per cent held a positive attitude toward
'sexual liberation'. The number of male students with a positive
attitude was twice as high as that of female students; between 65 and
70 per cent of both sexes, however, were 'actively against' such trends.
A clear majority also held that cohabitation was immoral.[32]

Although the current perception of a 'sexual disorder' is a reaction
against recent changes in sexual mores and behaviour, this need not
mean that these changes are really of the magnitude described or feared
by the authorities. For example, statistics do not indicate any widespread occurrence of early marriage. The percentage of married females
under 18 declined steadily during the 1980s, from 5.2 per cent in 1980
to only 1.9 per cent in 1987.[33] Nor is the current moral panic in
proportion to the number of births to young couples.

Seen from the authorities' point of view, the general picture of disorder was aggravated by those intellectuals who advocated 'sexual freedom'.[34] It was said that under their influence some students held that
having a love affair was a sign of 'historical progress toward the liberation of individuality'.[35] Wuer Kaixi, the 1989 student leader, declared
that democracy for Chinese students implied sexual liberation.[36] In
the 1980s many intellectuals argued that sexual freedom would benefit
Chinese society as a whole. One theorist, Xing Yihai, claimed that,
because the Chinese have no sexual desire, there is no sexual selection
in society, and this has led to the backwardness of the Chinese nation;
the reasoning was that only reproduction through sexual desire breeds
people of quality.[37] We might see Xing's social Darwinist assumptions
as a counter-imitation of the authorities' view that 'human quality' can
be guaranteed only by sexual restriction and self-control. The main
premiss—the desirability of creating 'human quality'—seems to be the
same for both views.

The scholar Wen Yuankai has criticized the powerful sexual myth
of female chastity, which lies at the very core of Chinese sexual mythology. This is reflected, as Wen pointed out, in the old story about the
woman who cut off her arm to preserve her purity after it had been
touched by a man,[38] and the popular sayings 'to die of hunger is a small
thing, but to lose your virginity is a big thing' (*e si shi xiao, shi jie shi
da*), and 'under the influence of his beautiful words, the girl sacrificed her most precious thing' (*xianchu le ziji zui baogui de dongxi*). Wen
comments:

For a young girl of the 1980s, isn't the most precious thing high revolutionary ideas, extensive and profound knowledge, a good attitude toward society and other people, intelligence and abilities, instead of merely chastity?[39]

Wen attacks the cultural myth that 'the first time' (*di yi ci*) can destroy a person's whole life; that it can cause psychological wounds that can lead to moral degeneration, insanity, even suicide.[40] In fact, one Chinese survey published in 1992 concludes that 72.6 per cent of males and 78.4 per cent of females believe that 'virginity is a girl's most valuable possession'.[41]

'Premature Love', 'Human Quality', and the Wayward Girl

A survey conducted in Shanghai showed that, among 946 pupils in upper secondary classes, 44 had love affairs, a total of 4.65 per cent. The survey also provides valuable information on cultural prejudice, as it is based on the assumption that there is a connection between early love affairs and school results, 'moral quality', and home discipline.[42]

According to Table 10, students involved in 'premature love' are low achievers: 11 out of 94 with the lowest marks make up 11.7 per cent of this group, compared with only 6 out of 207, or 2.9 per cent, of those with excellent marks. Furthermore, from Table 11 we see that only 1.6 per cent of those with 'first-grade moral quality', and as many as 19.44 per cent of those in the 'third grade', have love affairs. It is interesting to note that in Table 12 an implicit attack is made on insufficient discipline at home. Apparently, it is assumed that lack of discipline makes a student's involvement in love affairs more likely. A majority, 547 students, are subject to a strict discipline at home, and only 21 of them, or 3.84 per cent, have love affairs; of the 34 who receive 'non-strict discipline', 6, or 17.65 per cent of the group, are involved

TABLE 10   Students involved in 'premature love' (*zaolian*), and school results

Type of school results	No. of students	No. of students	% of students
Excellent (*yongdeng*)	207	6	2.9
Good (*liangdeng*)	268	11	4.1
Medium (*zhongdeng*)	377	16	4.24
Bad (*chandeng*)	94	11	11.7

TABLE 11   Students involved in 'premature love' (*zaolian*), and moral quality

Type of 'moral quality'	No. of students	No. of students	% of students
1st grade (*jiadeng*)	375	6	1.6
2nd grade (*yideng*)	495	24	4.85
3rd grade (*bingdeng*)	72	14	19.4
4th grade (*dingdeng*)[a]	4	n.a.	n.a.

[a] Three of the four pupils in the 4th grade category had already been transferred to part-work/part-study schools (*gongdu xuexiao*) for moral improvement and were not part of the survey.

TABLE 12   Students involved in 'premature love' (*zaolian*), and home discipline

Type of home discipline	No. of students	No. of students	% of students
Relatively strict (*bijao yan de*)	547	21	3.84
Normal (*yiban de*)	365	17	4.66
Not strict (*bu yan de*)	34	6	17.65

in love affairs. There is also an assumed connection between family discipline, petty crime, and love affairs. A survey of the family situation of students committing petty crime showed that in 48 of the 100 families surveyed there was support for or tacit consent to 'too close contact between the sexes'.[43]

In summary, then, the young lover is depicted as a person of low achievement and low moral quality, who is not sufficiently disciplined at home, and who has a tendency towards petty crime. A clear indication that young love is even seen as the *cause* of crime is found in material published by the Chinese Public Security Bureau. Here, it is openly stated that 'premature love is a very important factor in bringing about criminal activities in the secondary school student'. An investigation of 33 students involved in premature love affairs showed that a full 31 were also involved in criminal activities; by contrast, a control group of 300 students not involved in early love affairs had only 2 criminal offenders.[44]

Few would seem to oppose the theory that 'premature lovers' are persons of low quality. Sociologists Zeng Tao, Wei Xiaohong, and Lan

Yue, however, claim that there is no reason to exaggerate the dangers involved in premature love. They maintain that such youths are in fact resourceful individuals, and are 'high quality rather than low quality students'. It is emphasized that they are students who are class cadres or Youth League cadres; they are characterized by being intellectually 'above average' in class, and by having wide social contacts, a cadre or intellectual family background, and a good upbringing. In short, they conclude, there is no basis whatsoever for the cultural stereotypes about such young people.[45]

Opponents of young love have been particularly hostile towards the young girl. Nowadays, it is said that it is often the girls who take the initiative (*zhudong xing*) and 'launch the first attack'. They are described as 'lacking in self-control and reason, running around doing completely as they please'.[46] The double standard is also revealed in the statistics on 'sexual crime'.[47] At one detention centre, 10 per cent of the boys had been arrested for 'sexual crimes' (*xing fanzui*), as against 95 per cent of the girls.[48] Statistical material for the whole country shows that as much as 90 per cent of all crime among young girls is defined as 'sexual criminal mistakes' (*xing zuicuo*).[49] This way of criminalizing young female sexuality and sexualizing female crime is also found in far more permissive cultures. Both in China and the West, the deviant behaviour of boys is perceived as the result of their violent activities and their wish to 'get rich fast', while girls are accused of deviant behaviour by not adapting to a 'healthy feminine role'. There is less tolerance for girls transgressing social and moral boundaries. There are 'sex-girls' but no 'sex-boys', as Gustav Jonsson puts it in a Swedish study.[50]

The violent and unstructured element of sexual activity is a common point of departure in all kinds of moral systems dealing with the disruption of order. In the West, our own Victorian heritage is based on a belief-system built around bodily controls and purity regulations. Other common themes in the discourse of bodily symbols and social disorder are the 'insatiability' and the 'unrestrained individualism' of sexual deviants, as described in detail by advocates of Victorian purity.[51] In one description of the inmates of a girls' prison, their 'insatiable desire' (*tanyu*) for food, clothes, luxury, and sex is stressed: 72 per cent of the girls were said to have an insatiable desire for food; as a cure, they were allowed to buy a few snacks to supplement their coarse prison fare once a month.[52] Unrestrained individualism is displayed, it is said, by a strong tendency to 'become visible', or 'manifest oneself' (*xianlu ziji*). Such 'self-parading' goes against the exemplary parading of virtue. 'Extreme egoism, unrestrained squandering, pleasure seeking, and sexual freedom'

TABLE 13   Girls with a record of sexual crime compared with student girls without criminal records

	Introverts		Extroverts	
	Stable emotions	Unstable emotions	Stable emotions	Unstable emotions
Sex criminals (N = 36)	4 (11%)	8 (22%)	7 (20%)	17 (47%)
Non-criminals (N = 13)	4 (30.8%)	5 (38.4%)	4 (30.8%)	0 (0%)

are the 'catalysts of hooligan crime', and the standard expression 'to eat, drink, and have fun' (*chi-he-wan-le*) is now almost *de rigueur* in descriptions of crime in general, and sexual crime in particular.[53]

A survey of one hundred girls convicted of 'sexual crime' repeats many of these stereotypes.[54] In the first place, it points out the girls' lack of a proper moral education: they had been either spoilt, or beaten and scolded by their parents. As one variable, the survey employs Eysenck's distinction between extrovert and introvert personality,[55] another variable is stable versus non-stable emotions. On the basis of these two variables, 36 girls convicted of 'sexual offences' are compared with 13 girl students without criminal records (Table 13).

The survey shows that 67 per cent of the sexual criminals are extroverts. Girls who are both extrovert and of an unstable character account for 47 per cent of all those with a sex crime record, as compared with none in the control group of 'normal' student girls; in this group, we find as many as 69.7 per cent introverts. Although the survey contained only 13 'normal' girls, the author concludes that a *passive* girl is a normal girl—again, much in accordance with culturally accepted norms. He comments that the 'fallen' girls are victims of their insatiable physical needs, which has led them to 'completely degenerate to the animal stage'. There has been an imbalance between their physical and psychological development from the age of 11 or 12 onwards. Especially dangerous is a 'too liberal' discipline at home, and early moral education is the means of preventing the low 'inner quality' found in sexual criminals.

For persons who suffer from 'sexual hyperfunction' (*xing kangjin de ren*) and 'sexual addiction' (*xing pi de ren*), education is insufficient. In these cases, psychological and medical treatment should also be applied. Medical treatment is needed to regulate the sex hormones, in order to transform the deviants' 'defective mental structure' and rectify their 'evil individuality'.[56] Typically, only girls are said to suffer from 'illnesses' like 'hyperfunction' and 'addiction'; the labels are simply ways of describing girls with a 'too active sex life'.

An 'unhealthy sexual psychology' is listed as one of the 'major, object-ive factors leading to crime'.[57] One researcher argues both that juven-ile crime leads to premature love affairs, and that the latter are a cause of crime. He claims that early love causes endocrinopathy, i.e. internal secretion disorder (neifenmi shitiao); this leads to 'violent physical impulses in the form of sexual hyperfunction', which in turn leads to social disorder. He notes that 67 per cent of the girls in part-work, part-study schools were found to lead lives of 'sexual disorder', after having been raped or involved in 'unlawful sexual intercourse'.[58] This assumed connection between social disorder and physical ailment is com-mon in Chinese criminological literature.

The dance hall has only recently made its reappearance in China, and its bad reputation must be seen in the context of 'locating vice', typical of periods of rapid social change. Marginal figures and institu-tions are, by their very nature, perceived as dangerous to social order.[59] The independent girl is portrayed as a sexual criminal, and the dance hall as a 'temple of evil'. Numerous stories of 'fallen' teenage girls in youth magazines and educational publications start at the dance hall. In one story, we see a young couple visiting dance halls and 'roaming around in the parks'. They stay away from school and eventually fail their exams. Their love means 'forgetting to care about others', a sign of egoism in which they distance themselves from society and reject collective and exemplary norms.[60] It is stated that dance halls are 'a morbid environment offering a fertile soil for juvenile delinquency', and that 'the virus of crime multiplies easily in crowded places of enter-tainment such as cinemas, parks and dance halls'. It is felt that 'in the absence of correct guidance and proper outlets, their pent-up energy and needs will outgrow the social codes'.[61]

Controlling the Wave of 'Premature Love'

Some scholars have called Chinese culture, with its emphasis on mod-eration, balance and self-control, a 'cult of restraint'.[62] Today, the em-phasis on the need for restraint (zhi) is still strong. One article defines three types of control.[63] 'Control by leading' (daoxiang kongzhi) means providing positive role-models; educators should themselves be par-agons of virtue. A second form is 'process control' (guocheng kongzhi), involving a scientific understanding of the physical and mental develop-ment of youth. The third is 'control of circumstances' (tiaojian kongzhi), which is concerned with 'hiding evil'—i.e. protecting students from seeing love scenes in films, everyday scenes of couples 'nestling together in the parks', etc., since this might easily 'overexcite young people's brains'. Instead, young men and women should concentrate on work, study, and physical exercise, and read stories of positive heroes like Ostrowsky's 'How the Steel was Tempered'.[64] Such sublimation is one of the most frequently cited remedies for young love. A competition conducted by the magazine 'Hubei youth' invited its readers to write about love. Among the entries cited were 'edifying stories' describing the positive effect of platonic love, love of work, the Party, and the mother-country. One participant said: 'It doesn't matter whether you love a person, a great cause, or your motherland . . . true feelings are the motivating force to forge ahead.'[65] The aim was to turn the potentially dangerous power of love into a positive social force.

Despite help from the official media, educators are faced with increasing difficulty in preventing 'premature love'. The harsh methods of *du* and *jin*—oppression and prohibition—i.e. of scolding, beating, and humiliation in front of others should, however, be avoided.[66] Discretion is recommended, particularly when handling cases concerning loss of chastity. Teachers should instead guide and engage in heart-to-heart talks with the girls.[67] This often poses a generational problem. One schoolgirl who had had an abortion, instead of professing regret for what she had done, criticized the Chinese view that chastity is sacred as being demeaning for women. She dismissed her teacher's question about what she would do if her future husband should discover that she is not a virgin: if her husband respected her, they would stay together. 'There is no law saying that the wife's virginity belongs to the husband', she concluded.[68]

Although the educational literature emphasizes that the process of change during adolescence is 'perfectly natural', it also stresses the need for self-control (*zikong*).[69] Some describe premature love as a kind of illness, characterized by symptoms like dizziness and lack of concentration. It is, moreover, regarded as contagious: it 'spreads rapidly throughout schools and youth communities'. Young people are advised to 'cut the strings of love' in order to be able to grow up in a healthy way. The aim is to develop a state of healthy and platonic 'pure friendship' (*chunzhen youyi*) between classmates of both sexes.[70]

An analysis of how Chinese youth magazines in the 1980s dealt with the problem of young love provides illuminating insights into the widening generation gap. The problem was one of the most frequently discussed in these magazines. Often we recognize the cultural myths and stereotypes of love and sex much as we found them described by

Wen Yuankai. Some were presented in the form of young girls' letters to the editor under headlines like: 'I experienced premature love: how can I ever be happy again?'[71] There were also critical letters—such as the one written by the secondary school student who described his class teacher as a feudal lord, infringing upon the freedom of his students. They were not even allowed to dance during school performances. The class teacher was accused of reacting against 'something perfectly normal', and making the lives of his students boring and unhappy. The student demanded that young people should be allowed to lead a happier life.[72]

There is a typical story from the magazine 'Youth world' about a 17-year-old girl, Wenwen, who was expelled from school and forced to sign a 'love contract' (aiqing xieyi shu) after having been involved in a love affair with a boy who was not a pupil at the school. The lovers had to subscribe to the following conditions:

On the basis of information obtained from teachers and parents, we have come to understand that love affairs at too young an age affect study and work. We have come to the mutual agreement to study, live and work according to the following articles:

(1) While the girl is finishing upper secondary school, the boy is not allowed to distract her from her studies.
(2) While the boy is working, the girl is not allowed to distract him from his work.
(3) The two parties should stimulate and support each other in study and work, and transform their love into a motivating force.
(4) If one party changes his or her feelings towards the other, the other party is not allowed to try to change his or her mind. The free will of the other party should be respected.[73]

Her love-affair destroyed, Wenwen is eventually allowed back in school again. Far from improving her behaviour, she changes for the worse. The formerly simple, lively girl now starts meeting boys in dance halls and putting on earrings and heavy make-up. She even has her hair permed, neglecting 'her natural beauty', the principle taught in aesthetics class. She no longer listens to advice from her teachers and even writes a letter to her class teacher saying:

I'm seventeen years old, and I have ideas and thoughts of my own. In your eyes, love only seems to be invented for adults. We are also human beings, why shouldn't we be allowed to love and be loved? If love makes people bad, then aren't you also bad?

The teacher's reaction is that Wenwen is 'very extreme, very childish'. Wenwen simply comments that 'our lives are not the same', succinctly summing up the generation gap.[74]

Cautionary Tales, Small Beginnings, and 'First Times'

Another kind of story which also serves the aim of moralizing social control is the cautionary tale. According to Honig and Hershatter,

cautionary tales, a genre of popular literature intended specifically for adolescent girls and young women, laid out in merciless detail the consequences for women who gave in to their own sexual feelings and suffered the depredations of men.[75]

Such tales in particular describe the process of '*duoluo*', or degeneration, in young girls. The stories often claim to be based on police files, but they have obviously been reworked in a sort of literary fashion. They are rich in detail, especially regarding descriptions of the activities of sexually active young girls. The narrators assume the detached pose often used in traditional Chinese pornographic tales, never failing to warn their readers against evil. These stories are good indicators of the moral and social boundaries in today's China. At the same time, they are written chain narratives, complete from their accounts of innocent 'first times' to the programmatic disastrous consequences.

It is noteworthy how much importance is attached to a deviant's first *faux pas*. It is assumed that early deviation, even if it seems relatively harmless, will gradually develop into crime and catastrophe unless nipped in the bud. 'Never for the first time' should be read as a central phrase in the disciplinary discourse of today's China. It should be understood not only in its obvious sexual meaning, but in the broader context of social disorder in general, and the initial transgressing of given social boundaries in particular. 'Premature love' is a very small beginning that threatens to debase 'human quality' and thereby undermine the social order. One report presents several such cautionary tales.[76] The first tale begins by quoting police sources stating that 74 per cent of all 'fallen' girls started their downward path by staying out late.[77] The report then goes on to present the stories of several young girls who started on their downward path this way and now find themselves standing 'by the gates of hell' (*guimenguan*).

The first story emphasizes the immense and devastating effect of 'the first time' and the subsequent loss of virginity. The girl in question, we are told, loved fun and hated work, although she came from a good cadre family. Her parents did not put any pressure on her, and only wanted her to finish school and find a job as a worker. She often left home in the company of hooligans, and eventually found herself in bed with a stranger. The story emphasizes how normal the girl's family was, as if to say to the readers: 'This could happen to you too if you don't stay at home at night.' The story comments that, after having 'sacrificed her chastity, a young girl's most precious thing' (*xianchu le shaonü zui baogui de zhancao*), she loses everything. All her 'face' and self-respect are gone, and she ends up selling herself on the streets.[78] Her parents have no alternative but to have the police put her in an educational reform programme (*jiaoyu gaizao*) for up to five years.

The next story is about an independent and wayward young country girl who leaves home for the big city of Nanjing. Apart from presenting the familiar sexual myths and stereotypes, the story also repeats the traditional moral of 'not aiming too high', especially if you are a mere country girl. The moral of the tale is that a terrible fate awaits country girls who dare to rebel against authority and try 'to reach for something beyond their grasp' (*hao gao wuyuan*). The girl is described as 'too proud' and 'stubborn'. Not content with country life, she wants to experience the big world. It all begins in a 'small' way, by her staying out at night. The parents react by beating and scolding her. In the end she decides she has had enough, steals money from her parents, and sets off for the city. There she is seduced, and finds herself abandoned the next morning. She, too, then ends up in a circle of crime and sex, and is reported as lamenting: 'If only that one time (*na yi ci*) had not happened, a lot of other things would also not have happened, and I would not have degenerated to my present condition.'[79] An early indicator that she was on the road to ruin was the fact that she 'wanted to challenge her destiny and lead a life of pleasure'. In this cautionary tale, the criminological assumptions about premature love and the 'flaunting of self' (*xianshi ziji*) are confirmed.[80]

The third story is about a bright, active, but spoilt 13-year-old girl from a rich family. She decides that she wants to see more of life, stays out at night, and frequents restaurants and other places of entertainment. After getting drunk at a party, she wakes up in bed with one of her hooligan friends, who is still caressing her naked body. She realizes that she has lost her virginity against her will, and leaves enraged and deeply depressed, lamenting:

I have lost so much, I have lost the treasure of my youth, I have lost a young girl's most precious thing (*shiqu le shaonü zui baogui de dongxi*), and I have lost my personal dignity. I will bear this shame for the rest of my life . . .

The moral commentary admonishes young girls to let this girl's sad destiny serve as a reminder that they should 'value the beautiful treasure of youth'.[81]

It is important to note that the girl believes that, by losing her virginity, she has also lost her personal dignity and has become a social outcast. To use the Chinese term, she has 'lost her body', or 'lost herself' *(shi shen)*. The expression *shi shen* is the antonym of *an shen*, which means that one's body or one's self is at ease. It also means 'to settle down' or 'make one's home'—in short, it is about finding a place in society.[82] Thus, the meaning of *shi shen* can also be interpreted as 'loss of morality', with a strong connotation of 'losing one's place in society'. The seduced girl has become an outcast, a potentially dangerous 'non-social' or 'asocial' person. Such discussion of marginality would seem an essential component of cautionary tales. Sociological analysis also indicates that in China girls with a 'sexual history' are in fact shunned on the marriage market and thrown out of their homes by angry parents.[83]

As we have seen, young love is associated with low achievement in school, moral inferiority, a lack of discipline, and a tendency towards petty crime as well as psychological and physical illness. Focusing on the panic about 'premature love', I have sketched the contours of a belief-system originating in a culturally based and distorted perception of social danger. I have argued that today's concern with bodily controls must be interpreted as a reaction against the rapid social change that has occurred in the reform period. There is a clear parallel between the bodily 'loss of balance' brought about by early puberty and the loss of balance in Chinese society during the present period of reform and modernization. The 'loss of balance' *(shi heng)* and the 'loss of self' *(shi shen)* have become central concepts in discussions of both society and youth in general, and 'premature love' in particular. *Shi heng* is also a keyword in Chinese discussions on socialization. Belief in purity can be seen as an attempt to come to terms with the powerful forces of the modern Juggernaut, and to regain a lost balance. The concern about the 'first time', 'bodily imbalance', 'unrestrained individualism', and the 'insatiability of bodily needs' is the result of the fear of young people transgressing social boundaries. This seems to be a near-universal reaction to social change, in many cultures and periods. It makes little difference whether the aim is to create a God-fearing citizen through the means of the Bible and Sunday schools, as in Jacksonian America, or a high-quality 'new person' under the regime of a 'spiritual civilization' movement, as in contemporary China.[84]

We have seen that in present-day China, the independent young girl is labelled a sexual deviant. In return, many girls start to identify with the label and live up to it.[85] Labelling theory sees deviance as a product of the social control process itself. The deviant's response to societal reaction leads to a secondary deviation, by which the person defined as a deviant comes to accept a self-image of someone locked within a deviant role. Such a production of deviance is another effect of the Chinese exemplary chain narratives. The 'fallen' girls simply live their narrative to the end, failing to distinguish between narrative and reality. The process is summed up in a Chinese saying, about 'fallen' girls who become criminals after their fall, 'Once they are already in the water they float ten thousand li' (*yidan chuci xia shui bian yi xie qian li*).

The analysis of 'premature love' also shows the persistence of the double standard and inequality between the sexes in China. Traditionally, girls have been more strictly supervised than boys, so that when a girl breaks out of her social confinement, she becomes an easy target. In the symbolic or emotional logic as described here, we see social behaviour only through a filter of cultural beliefs. Such belief systems have always had their scapegoats and their witch-hunts.[86] The 'fallen' girl has become a convenient scapegoat in today's China. The facts show that girls are actually the least likely to lead a promiscuous life, but the most likely to be accused of it. In traditional Chinese literature, the independent girl was often portrayed as an evil 'fox spirit' (*huli jing*); she now appears in the guise of a new 'folk devil', the target of a 'moral panic'.[87]

In recent years, early love has been regarded as symptomatic of the 'psychology of defiance' of young people: 'if this psychology of defiance among the young is allowed to spread, it can even lead to setbacks in the national economy and social civilization'.[88] The struggle against 'premature love' becomes a struggle against 'spiritual pollution' and for 'spiritual civilization'. The terms may be Chinese, but the phenomenon is universal, occurring when the Establishment seeks to preserve order by employing a discourse of purity in order to combat 'the pollution' concomitant with the process of social change. In short, we have seen a combat between what Mary Douglas has called 'purity' and 'danger'.

Notes to Chapter 10

1. See Victor Turner, *The Forest of Symbols: Aspects of Ndembu Rituals*, Ithaca, NY, Cornell University Press, 1967; Victor Turner, *Dramas, Fields, and Methaphors*, Ithaca, NY, Cornell University Press, 1974; Mary Douglas: *Natural Symbols*, London, Barrie & Rockliff Cresset Press, 1970; Mary Douglas, *Purity and Danger*, London, Ark, 1984. In *The Forest of Symbols* Victor Turner discusses the polarization of meaning in symbols in the division between an 'ideological pole' and a 'sensory pole' (pp. 28 ff.).

2. Kai T. Erikson, *Wayward Puritans: A Study in the Sociology of Deviance*, New York, John Wiley, 1966. Erikson uses the term to describe the crisis of moral and social order and the 'creation' of deviance and 'moral crime'.

3. Carroll Smith-Rosenberg, 'Sex as symbol in Victorian purity: an ethnohistorical analysis of Jacksonian America', *American Journal of Sociology*, no. 84 (Supplement), 1978, p. 214.

4. It is also not without reason that the theme of unity and stability is used as a justification of research in the introduction to the nationwide investigation of sexual behaviour in China in 1989–90; see Shanghai xing shehuixue yanjiu zhongxin (Shanghai research centre for sexual sociology), 'Xiandai Zhongguo ren de xing wenti' (Sexual problems of today's Chinese), *Minzhu yu fazhi*, No. 10, 1990, p. 30; trans. in *Chinese Education*, Vol. 25, No. 1, Spring 1992, pp. 56–67.

5. Stan Cohen, *Folk Devils and Moral Panics*, Oxford, Martin Robertson, 1980, p. 9. For a theoretical overview on moral panics see Erich Goode and Nachman Ben-Yehuda, *Moral Panics: The Social Construction of Deviance*, Oxford, Blackwell, 1994.

6. A US delegation of sociologists and anthropologists visiting China in the mid-1980s concluded that methodology still did not 'satisfy the professional sociologist' because reports 'seldom provide sufficient detail on methodology of a research project'. See CSCPRC Sociology/Anthropology Delegation Report: Sociology', *China Exchange News*, Vol. 12, No. 4, 1984, p. 7. Stanley Rosen presents an overview of the methodological problems of Chinese surveys in: 'Value change among post-Mao youth: the evidence from survey data', in Perry Link, Richard Madsen, and Paul G. Pickowicz (eds.), *Unofficial China: Popular Culture and Thought in the People's Republic*, Boulder, Colo., Westview Press, 1989, esp. pp. 194–200.

7. Yang Xin, 'Chuzhong nüsheng de zaolian ji jiating jiaoyu de zhidao' (Premature love among female lower secondary school pupils and family education), *Beijing Jiaoyu*, No. 12, 1987, p. 8; and *China Daily*, 18 May 1990, p. 5.

8. Ding Yu, 'Tantan ruhe zhengque chuli zhongxuesheng "zaolian" de wenti' (On how to handle correctly the problem of 'premature love' among secondary school pupils), *Renmin jiaoyu*, No. 3, 1988, p. 21.

9. A similar survey conducted in 1979–80 showed that the average age had dropped to 13.6 years, although in cities like Shanghai and Nanjing the average age was slightly higher, at 13.9 and 13.8 years respectively. See Yuan Fangfu and Wu Jieping: *Xing zhishi shouce* (Handbook of sexual knowledge), Beijing, Kexue jishu wenxie chubanshe/Renmin weisheng chubanshe, 1988, pp. 61–2.

10. See Wang Ruoye and Han Shuyuan (Beijing shi jiating jiaoyu yanjiu hui) (Beijing municipality research association for family education), 'Dui Beijing 200 ming zhong-xue-sheng de shenghuo huanjing ji xing shengli yishi de diaocha baoguo' (Investigation report on the living environment and the sexual physiology and sexual awareness among 200 secondary school pupils), *Beijing Jiaoyu*, No. 11, 1989, p. 42.

11. *Minzhu yu fazhi*, No. 10, 1990, p. 30.

12. Over the past 100 years, menarche in Europe has been occurring ever earlier, by between three and four months per decade. Better standards of living may well account for part of this, although no one has yet given a full explanation. See Peter Laslett, 'Age at menarche in Europe since the eighteenth century', *Journal of Interdisciplinary History*, No. 2, 1971, p. 222.

13. Jin Ge, 'Yongdong de chunqing: qingshaonian chunqi wenti caifang sui gan' (Stirrings of love: thoughts after gathering material on puberty problems among youth), *Xinjiang qingnian*, No. 10, 1989, p. 12.

14. It was not until 1988 that the first training course in sex education in China was arranged at the People's University in Beijing (see *China Daily*, 25 May 1988, p. 3, and 5 May 1992, p. 3). The situation is, however, reported to have improved somewhat after 1990, particularly in the more economically and culturally developed major cities (see *Zhongguo Tongxun She*, 16 January, in *Joint Publications Research Service Report: China*, *JPRS-CAR-92-012*, 9 March 1992, p. 90). In 1992 it was reported that about 1,000 researchers in China were working on sex-related matters (see *China Daily*, 3 August 1992, p. 3). For a short introduction to sexual education in China, see Fang Fu Ruan, *Sex in China: Studies in Sexology in Chinese Culture*, New York/London, Plenum Press, 1991, pp. 171–8.

15. For a review of such literature, see Zhongguo shehui kexueyuan shehuixue yanjiusuo, *Zhongguo shehuixue nianjian 1979–1989* (China yearbook of sociology 1979–1989), Beijing, Zhongguo dabaike quanshu chubanshe, 1989, p. 176.

16. Jin Ge, p. 12, describes such a teacher in detail.

17. A total of 1,693 students were surveyed (ibid.). Similar results were found in *Minzhu yu fazhi*, No. 10, 1990, p. 32; here it was found that 13.5% had obtained their sexual information from parents or teachers.

18. Yang Xin, p. 9.

19. Wang Ruoye and Han Shuyuan, pp. 41–2.

20. The example of the new economic zone of Shenzhen strongly illustrates this point. Women make up as much as 70% of the labour force in the zone. The policy is also to recruit young workers, preferably under 35 and single. The absence of family households with their restrictions and obligations has weakened traditional control and authority. The absence of parental and familial pressure has led girls in this zone to experiment with their newly won freedom. In other words, the zone has been an experiment not only economically, but socially as well. The promise of wealth and modernization seems mixed with the danger of social chaos and disorder. See Phyllis Andors, 'Women and work in Shenzhen', *Bulletin of Concerned Asian Scholars*, Vol. 20, No. 3, 1988, pp. 22–41.

21. Zhang Yiquan gives a sociological analysis of this phenomenon and the roots of prostitution in *Shehui*, No. 68, 20 October 1990, pp. 38–40; see also *JPRS Report: China*, *JPRS-CAR-91-005*, 31 January 1991, pp. 62–5.

22. The categories of 'sexual crime' and 'sexual disorder' overlap, but the latter is more associated with 'premature love', pre- and extramarital relations, and sexually transmitted disease, i.e. behaviour mainly associated with breaking the norms rather than the law.

23. By 1991, the regulation had been submitted to the Legislative Bureau under the State Council to become law. A national marriage registration file system is also being introduced to control 'illegal marriage practices', according to *China Daily*, 19 June 1991, p. 3. Previously, if a cohabiting unmarried couple fulfilled the conditions for marrying according to the Marriage Law, they would normally receive some education through criticism (*piping jiaoyu*) before being asked to marry; it was not directly regarded as a crime, even if it was described as 'going against the spirit of the marriage law'. Such matters were handled by the Court for Social Morality (*shehui daode fating*) (see Liu Xiaoping, 'Weihun tongju wenti chushen' (Initial reflections on the problem of living together unmarried), *Shandong Qingnian*, No. 5, 1986, p. 35). There is not only a moral, but also an economic, aspect to the new and officially condemned practice of cohabitation. In the countryside some local authorities demand up to 600 yuan, more than a year's average income for a peasant, for the issue of marriage certificates (see *China Daily*, 5 March 1990,

p. 3). The sky-high expenses of traditional weddings is another factor that encourages cohabitation (see *China Daily*, 5 February 1990, p. 4; 4 January 1991, p. 3, and *China Daily (Business Weekly)*, 19 February 1990, p. 2).

24. There is a latent AIDS peril in China because of an emerging drug problem and poor hospital conditions resulting in the re-use of syringes and surgical instruments and a lack of strict sterilization procedures for medical equipment. Of the 493 people who tested HIV-positive up to 1991, however, only 5 had developed AIDS (see *China Daily*, 24 July 1991, p. 3). In 1996 1.74 million cases of sexually transmitted disease were reported, a dramatic increase from the 400,000 cases reported in 1990. The actual number of cases has been estimated to reach 3 m. (see *SWB-FE* 2794, 13 December 1996, p. G/10, and *China Daily*, 14 December 1990, p. 3). By 1998 only 9,970 cases of HIV/AIDS were reported, although scientists held that the actual number of AIDS cases in China might be as high as 200,000 (see *SWB-FE* 3221, 8 May 1998, p. G/8).

25. The 1991 national divorce rate of 1.38 per 1,000 of total population was nearly four times as high as in 1978. This increase is due mainly to the 'alienation of affection' clause in the Marriage Law introduced in 1980: see *China Daily*, 11 June 1991, p. 3, and Gao Jiansheng and Liu Ning (eds.), *Lihun wenti mianmianguan* (Looking at the problems of divorce), Henan renmin chubanshe, 1988, pp. 69, 96. For international comparison, see Collection ministère de la justice, *Le divorce en Europe Occidentale* (Divorce in Western Europe), Paris, La documentation française, 1975. Only 54% of the divorce-applicants in China were actually divorced in 1989.

26. Zou Xiaohong, 'Daxuesheng lianai chengfeng bu xunchang' (Student love is becoming unusually common), *Zhongguo jiaoyubao*, 8 September 1988, p. 3.

27. 'Ha'erbin shi shangye xuexiao guanli zhidu' (The administrative system of Harbin business school), Harbin (internal school document), 1987, p. 124.

28. Associated Press report from Beijing, October 1991.

29. Daling qingnian jiehun diaochazu (The study group of marriage among older youth), 'Daling qingnian de jiehun wenti dui shehui de yingxiang' (The marriage question of older youth and its impact on society), *Qingnian Yanjiu*, No. 5, 1985, pp. 40–51.

30. Liu Dalin (ed.), *Zhongguo dangdai xing wenhua* (Sexual behaviour in modern China), Shanghai, Shanghai sanlian shudian, 1992; English edn, Liu Dalin, Man Lun Ng, Li Ping Zhou, and Erwin J. Haeberle, *Sexual Behaviour in Modern China: Report from the Nationwide Survey of 20,000 Men and Women*, New York, Continuum, 1997. See also interview with Liu in *China Daily*, 18 May 1990, p. 5. A survey from Beijing stated that '90% or more' began to practise sex before being lawfully wedded, but we should be very critical of this statement. Large figures such as the above are probably the result of collective exaggeration or collective misunderstanding. As social scientists know well, young people tend to over-report actions that enjoy a certain status within the frame of a youth culture. The idea may in fact be more popular than the action itself. Zou Ping, 'Beijing shi bufen weihun qingnian rengong liuchan qingkuang de diaocha' (An investigation of abortion among some unmarried young people in Beijing), *Qingnian yanjiu*, No. 10, 1985, pp. 57–61.

31. *Minzhu yu fazhi*, No. 10, 1990, p. 32.

32. Feng Junshi and Li Hua, 'Xiaoyuan lian'ai wan hua jian' (Ten thousand flowering love letters on campus), in *Daxuesheng*, No. 4, 1991, pp. 40–3.

33. *Zhongguo shehui tongji ziliao 1990* (The social statistics of China 1990), Beijing, Zhongguo tongji chubanshe, 1990, p. 37.

34. The philosopher Li Zehou was one of those who explicitly saw sexuality in the light of 'liberating individuality' (*gexing kaifang*) in the 1980s; see Huang Lipin, 'Li Zehou tan nan huan nü ai' (Li Zehou on love), *Mingbao yuekan*, No. 5, 1988, pp. 56–7. In Liu Xiaobo's writings we see sexuality as a natural and primitive rebellious force taken to extremes. Liu is 'stressing to the extreme' the desire for 'sex and money' to save China; see Liu Xiaobo, 'Xin shiji wenxue mianlin weiji' (The literature of the new period faces a crisis), in Xianggang daxue xueshenghui guoshi xuehui (ed.), *Zhongguo sixiang jiefang wenji: gaige husheng* (Collected articles on the liberation of thought in China: the voice of reform), Hong Kong, Jixian shuju, 1988, p. 205. The article was originally published in *Shenzhen qingnianbao*, 3 October 1986.

35. Zou Xiaohong, 'Daxuesheng lianai chengfeng bu xunchang' (Student love is becoming unusually common), *Zhongguo jiaoyubao*, 8 September 1988, p. 3.

36. See Lee Feigon, 'Gender and the Chinese student movement', in Jeffrey N. Wasserstrom and Elisabeth J. Perry, *Popular Protest & Political Culture in Modern China: Learning from 1989*, Boulder, Colo., Westview Press, 1992, p. 127.

37. Xing Yihai, 'Zhongguo chuantong wenhua fan jinhua de tezhi ji qi weiji yu chulu' (The anti-evolutionary character, the crisis of Chinese traditional culture, and the way out), *Zhongshan daxue yanjiusheng xuekan (Sheke pian)*, No. 1, 1987, p. 11, in *Fuyin baokan ziliao, Wenhua yanjiu*, No. 4, 1987, p. 36. Such wild evolutionary theories have been seen before in China. Wu Zhihui and Qu Pu gave the most wildly romantic contribution to the science of eugenics around the time of the Republican Revolution in 1911. Wu insisted that love itself was eugenic. In advocating 'promiscuous copulation', Qu Pu had advocated love matches; for they, he insisted, would produce the best seed. And Wu Zhihui agreed: 'Women who mate, become pregnant, and give birth because of love will definitely have better sons than those who mate because they are forced to' (see James Reeve Pusey, *China and Charles Darwin*, Cambridge, Mass., Harvard University Press, 1983, pp. 381–2).

38. T'ien Ju-k'ang, *Male Anxiety and Female Chastity: A Comparative Study of Chinese Ethical Values in Ming–Ch'ing Times*, Monographies du T'oung Pao, Vol. 14, Leiden, E. J. Brill, 1988, pp. *xii–xiii*, shows a phenomenon akin to the one discussed here. Reports about virtuous female suicides during the Ming dynasty did not so much reflect the occurrence of such acts as bear a close correlation to the number of male scholars experiencing the bitterness of repeated failure in the official examinations. In other words, concerns about the social and moral state of society served to determine such reports more than did virtuous suicidal behaviour as such. See also Wen Yuankai, *Zhongguo chuantong wenhua qian jiegou de gaizao. Wen Yuankai tan gaige* (Remoulding the hidden structure of the Chinese traditional culture. Wen Yuankai on reform), Shanghai, Shanghai renmin chubanshe, 1988, p. 55.

39. Wen Yuankai, p. 56.

40. Ibid., p. 57.

41. Zha Bo and Geng Wenxiu, 'Sexuality in urban China', *Australian Journal of Chinese Affairs*, No. 28, July 1992, p. 9. Ray Tannahill, *Sex in History*, London, Hamish Hamilton, 1980, pp. 374, 423–4, gives interesting figures illustrating this phenomenon also in Japan and the USA.

42. Wang Xiaoling, 'Zhongxuesheng lianai qingkuang de diaocha' (An investigation of the situation of love affairs among secondary school pupils), *Shanghai jiaoyu*, No. 2, 1986, p. 12.

43. Wang Guozhen and Zhang Maiyu, 'Bai ming weifa qingshaonian de jiating qingkuang diaocha' (An investigation of the family situation of one hundred juvenile criminals), *Wei le haizi*, No. 5, 1988, p. 19.

44. Li Guofang, 'Guanyu zaolian yu zhongxuesheng weifa fanzui de diaocha' (An investigation of premature love and crime among secondary school students), in *Zhongguo qingshaonian fanzui yanjiu nianjian* (Yearbook on Chinese juvenile delinquency studies), Beijing, Chunqiu chubanshe, 1988, p. 215.

45. Zeng Tao, Wei Xiaohong, and Lan Yue, 'Zhongxuesheng zaolian bu juyou pubian xing' (Premature love among secondary school students is not widespread), in *Qingnian yanjiu*, No. 4, 1987, pp. 18–21.

46. Yang Xin, p. 8.

47. 'Sexual crime' can be defined as everything from 'seductions at dancing parties' (the so-called 'seductive character' (*yinyou xing*) of sexual crime) that are 'seldom reported', to prostitution, to rape and gang rape (or the 'forced character' (*qiedao xing*) of sexual crime): see Pi Yijun, 'Lun fanzui tuanhuo anjie de tedian' (A discussion of the characteristics of criminal gang cases), in *Zhongguo qingshaonian fanzui yanjiu nianjian 1987*, p. 390. There is no fixed definition of the term, neither in the criminal law nor in the extensive '*Chinese Dictionary of Criminal Law*'. See *The Criminal Law and the Criminal Procedure Law of the People's Republic of China* (in Chinese and English), Beijing, Beijing Languages Press, 1984, and *Zhonghua xingfa cidian* (Chinese dictionary of criminal law), Shanghai, Xuelin chubanshe, 1989.

48. Yuan Jinhua, 'Qingshaonian fanzui yu xuexiao jiaoyu de guanxi de diaocha' (Survey on the connection between juvenile crime and school education), *Jiaoyu yanjiu*, No. 11, 1986, p. 60. In another institution, 59% of the boys had been 'involved in sexual crime', and 98% of the girls: see *China Daily*, 17 July 1989, p. 4.

49. Cao Manzhi (ed.), *Zhongguo qingshaonian fanzuixue* (The criminology of Chinese juvenile delinquency), Beijing, Qunzhong chubanshe, 1988, p. 261.

50. Gustav Jonsson, *Flickor på glid: en studie i kvinnoförtryck* (Slipping girls: a study of the repression of women), Borås, Tiden Folksam, 1977, p. 39; and Gustav Jonsson, *Flickor på glid: en studie i kvinnoförakt* (Slipping girls: a study of the contempt for women), Värningby, Tiden Folksam, 1980, p. 28. Jonsson points out that research at the detention centre for juvenile criminals at Skå in Sweden found that 70% of the 94 girls at the centre had made remarks about sexually deviant behaviour in their journals, compared with 10% of the boys. The 'main reason' for being at the detention centre was 'sexually deviant behaviour' for 52% of the girls, and for *none* of the boys. The sexualizing of crime among girls has been documented in international criminological research. It has been found that girls reporting the same type of crime as boys have been treated differently from boys by the law. Their promiscuity defined the law's attitude towards them, in contrast to boys with the same behavioural pattern: see Lesley Shacklady Smith, 'Sexist assumptions and female delinquency: an empirical investigation', in Carol Smart and Barry Smart (eds.), *Women, Sexuality and Social Control*, London: Routledge & Kegan Paul, 1978, pp. 74–88.

51. See Carroll Smith-Rosenberg, pp. 212–47.

52. Zhang Jian and Zhang Wenbang, 'Dui Zhejiang sheng nü fanzui fuxing qijian de tuanhuo huodong fenxi' (Analysis of the gang activities of female prisoners in Zhejiang province during the period of imprisonment), in *Zhongguo qingshaonian fanzui yanjiu nianjian 1987*, Beijing, Chunqiu chubanshe, 1988, p. 414.

53. Shao Daosheng, *Dangdai shehui de bingtai xinli*, (The morbid psychology of today's society), Beijing, Sheshui kexue wenxian chubanshe, 1990, p. 238; see also *Fazhi ribao*, 11 June 1990, p. 3.

54. Zheng Yunzhen, 'Xing fanzui nü qingshaonian de gexing pianqing he tiaozheng' (Individual character deviation and the correction of young sexual criminal girls), *Jiaoyu lilun yu shijian*, No. 1, 1986, p. 60.

55. The Chinese researcher here is obviously basing his analysis partly on Hans Eysenck, *Crime and Personality*, London: Routledge & Kegan Paul, 1964.

56. Zheng Yunzhen, pp. 61–3. (In the original Chinese table on p. 60, the number of girls described as 'sex criminals' is wrongly written as 35 instead of 36.) This is a modern form of the traditional Chinese idea that physical and psychological harmony in the individual are prerequisites for establishing harmony in society; see Confucius's 'Great Learning' (*Daxue*), in James Legge (trans.), *The Four Books (Sishu)*, Taipei, Culture Book Co./Wenhua tushu gongsi, 1983, pp. 4–7.

57. See *Fazhi ribao*, 13 February 1997, p. 6.

58. Li Guofang, p. 217.

59. Such 'vice-locating' processes are common reactions in periods of modernization and rapid social change; they are typically found in new and yet little-known institutions or phenomena. In the USA W. I. Thomas observed in 1923 that 'The automobile is connected with more seduction than happen otherwise in cities together.' Park adds that 'The newspaper and the motion picture show, while not so deadly, are almost as demoralizing.' See W. I. Thomas, *The Unadjusted Girl*, quoted in Robert E. Park *et al.*, *The City*, Chicago, University of Chicago Press, 1925, p. 108. On marginality and danger in general, see Carroll Smith-Rosenberg, p. 230, Victor Turner, *The Forest of Symbols*, pp. 93–111, Mary Douglas, *Purity and Danger*, pp. 95–7.

60. Liang Xuezhang and Liu Ruqin, 'Banzhuren chuli zaolian wenti de yuanze he fangfa' (Principles and methods for the class teacher to handle the problem of premature love), *Renmin Jiaoyu*, No. 2, 1988, p. 28.

61. *Zhongguo fazhi bao*; quoted from *China Daily*, 21 July 1987, p. 4.

62. See Ambrose Y. C. King and Michael H. Bond, 'The Confucian paradigm of man: a sociological view', in Wen-Shing Tseng and David Y. H. Wu, *Chinese Culture and Mental Health*, London, Academic Press, 1985, pp. 34–5.

63. Xin Yang, 'Banzhuren zai jiejue "zaolian" wenti zhong de zuoyong' (The function of class teachers in solving the problem of 'premature love'), *Renmin jiaoyu*, No. 1, 1988, p. 37.

64. Liang Xuezhang and Liu Ruqin, p. 29.

65. Editorial article, 'Dangdai qingnian zai aiqing zhong de lixiang zhuiqiu' (Ideals and the pursuit of love among today's youth), *Hubei qingnian*, No. 4, 1986, pp. 14–15.

66. Huang Zhifa, 'Zenyang duidai zaolian zhong de xuesheng' (How to handle students who are involved in premature love), *Shanghai jiaoyu*, No. 2, 1986, p. 13.

67. Liang Xuezhang and Liu Ruqin, p. 29.

68. Bo Yin and He Xiangqing, 'Zaolian: xiaoyuan "malasong"' (Early love: the 'marathon' of the school-yard), *Qingnian Shijie*, No. 9, 1989, p. 34.

69. Ding Yu, p. 21.

70. See Liang Xuezhang and Liu Ruqin, p. 28; Ding Yu, p. 21, Xiao Tulin, 'Chuli zaolian wenti "shifa"' ('Ten methods' for handling problems of premature love), *Renmin jiaoyu*, No. 10, 1988, p. 28.

71. 'Xiao nühai gaobie zaolian' (Young girls, bid farewell to premature love), *Dongfang qingnian*, No. 9, 1989, p. 21 (letter to the editor).

72. Qing Shu, 'Banzhuren fengjian' (The class teacher is feudal), *Dangdai qingnian*, No. 10, 1986, p. 11.

73. Bo Yin and He Xiangqing, p. 34.

74. Ibid., p. 36.

75. A 'cautionary tale' is defined as a genre of 'popular literature intended specifically for adolescent girls and young women' and dealing with the consequences of yielding to their feelings in such cases as mentioned here; see Emily Honig and Gail

Hershatter, *Personal Voices: Chinese Women in the 1980s*, Stanford, Calif., Stanford University Press, 1988, pp. 63–7.

76. Gu Zhaosen, 'Shao nümen, weishenme liulang' (Young girls, why are you roaming about), *Hubei qingnian*, No. 8, 1989, pp. 34–6.

77. It is no coincidence that the Chinese character for 'peace' or 'order' (*an*) depicts a woman under a roof, or a woman inside the house.

78. Gu Zhaosen, p. 34.

79. Ibid., p. 35.

80. Zhongguo shehui kexueyuan shehuixue yanjiusuo (ed.), *Qingshaonian fanzui xinlixue* (The psychology of juvenile delinquency), Shanghai, Shanghai renmin chubanshe, 1985, p. 261.

81. Gu Zhaosen, pp. 35–36.

82. See Sun Longji, *Zhongguo wenhua de shenceng jiegou* (The deep structure of Chinese society), Hong Kong, Jixian she, 1985, pp. 9, 20 on the social meaning of *anshen*.

83. Zhang Yiquan, pp. 38–40 (62–5).

84. Paul Boyer, *Urban Masses and Moral Order in America, 1820–1920*, Cambridge, Mass., Harvard University Press, 1978, and Joseph F. Kett, *Rites of Passage: Adolescence in America 1790 to the Present*, New York, Basic Books, 1977, can both be read as descriptions of how purity beliefs attempt to cope with processes of change and disorder.

85. One survey conducted among 50 girls at a psychiatric hospital in Henan showed that they had all 'become mentally deranged as a result of losing their virginity'. The girls looked upon sex as something dirty and sinful. One girl had become insane after she was raped and was subsequently thrown out of home by her father. In another incident, Chen Suhua, a rural girl, became mentally ill because of the ridicule she suffered as a nude model at the Nanjing College of Arts (see Wen Yuankai, p. 58, and *China Daily*, 2 June 1988, p. 4).

86. On the connection between boundary crises and witch-hunts, see Kai T. Eriksson, *Wayward Puritans*.

87. Stan Cohen, p. 9.

88. Xu Ming, Chu Xian, Song Defu, and Qiang Wei (eds.), *Sixiang zhengzhi gongzuo daoxiang* (Guidance in ideological-political work), Beijing, Kexue chubanshe, 1990, p. 193.

11

Crime, Juvenile Delinquency, and Deterrence Policies

IN today's China, the danger of crime has become a narrative also about the dangers of youth. In the 1980s China began to witness a substantial increase in criminal activity, mainly as a consequence of rapidly growing juvenile delinquency. Chinese deterrence policy vastly overreacted to this perceived threat to social order, in an effort to demonstrate the government's defence of moral and cultural values at a time of dramatic economic and social change. The mid-1950s in China are still remembered as a time when 'doors were unbolted at night and no one pocketed anything found on the road' (*ye bu bi hu, duo bu shi yi*). In recent years, complaints about corruption and social disparities have become prevalent, with people harking back to the honesty and sense of unity that reportedly prevailed during those early years of the People's Republic—a period when society displayed, one criminologist has asserted, a standard of behaviour seldom seen in history.[1] The 1950s are now regarded by adult Chinese as a 'golden age'.

At the same time, there is much uncertainty about the accuracy of official crime statistics. There is every reason to regard the official figures with due scepticism. Different sources give different figures, and it is not entirely clear how the official figures have been established. This scepticism should be applied to the historical material as well as today's figures.[2] My discussion here is based primarily on the official material, but despite the uncertainty I hope to give an indication about developments on the Chinese crime scene.

Crime rates fell after the new regime took power, but soared thereafter as a consequence of the political campaigns against Rightists. In 1956 the total crime rate was a mere 23 cases per 100,000 population.[3] In 1958 it rose to 120, largely owing to political arrests; 'counter-revolutionary crime' that year accounted for 45.8 per cent of all cases.[4] However, recently published historical statistics on crime in China seem to omit such categories of crime, and report a low 32 crimes per 100,000 population for 1958.[5] The total number of 'counter-revolutionary criminals' for the whole period from 1949 until the end

TABLE 14   Crime rates in the People's Republic of China, 1950–1995 (criminal cases per 100,000 population)

Criminal cases per 100,000 population

1950	93	1961	35 (64)	1977	58	1988	77.41
1951	59	1962	62 (48)	1978	55.30	1989	181.49[c]
1952	42	1963	36	1979	64.80	1990	200.90
1953	50	1964	35 (31)	1980	76.30	1991	209.44 (215)
1954	65	1965	33 (30)	1981	89.37	1992	138.60[d]
1955	37 (53)[a]	1966–72	40–60[b]	1982	74.02	1993	140.30
1956	23 (29)	1972	46	1983	59.81	1994	142.83
1957	58 (46)	1973	60	1984	49.91	1995	144.04
1958	120 (32)	1974	57	1985	52.06	1996	135.12
1959	35 (30)	1975	52	1986	51.91	1997	134.98
1960	33	1976	53	1987	54.12		

[a] Kang Shuhua and Xiang Zexuan's more recent figures are given in parentheses throughout the table in cases where they differ from previously used material by more than 1%. They differ considerably from earlier statistical material during the mid- and late 1950s and the early 1960s. The considerably lower 1958 figure probably omits any reported counter-revolutionary crime, while the considerably higher figure for 1961 is not accounted for. I have used the different figures as a reminder of the caution with which we have to handle official and semi-official crime statistics in the PRC.

[b] The estimate of 40%–60% for the Cultural Revolution period is based on a range of figures in the Chinese criminological literature. The Cultural Revolution saw a breakdown in the public security system; thus, no statistical material on a national level exists from this period, only rough estimates derived from local data. Details on how this estimate was arrived at are given only generally in material from the Chinese Ministry of Security, which bases its estimates on 'typical examples' from selected areas and has set the rate at 40%.

[c] The sudden increase in crime cases in 1989 was due mainly to a national reorganization of the statistical standards used to define a criminal case.

[d] From 1992, the apparent fall in crime rates is due entirely to a new revision of the criteria of how to define a law case; in particular, this concerns cases of theft. Comparable crime rates went up 5% from 1991 to 1992. With an annually reported increase in crime of 2.41% from 1991 to 1995 (see *SWB-FE*/2447, 30 October 1995, p. G/12), and with correction for annual population increase, the likely approximate figure for 1995 comparable to the standard used before 1992 would be about 222 cases per 100,000 population. Disregarding the statistical redefinitions, the crime rate has shown a steady increase since 1984–5. In the Interpol statistics the overall crime rate is reported as slightly lower—124.38 for 1992 and 127.75 for 1993 (see Organisation Internationale de Police Criminelle, *Statistiques Criminelles Internationales* 1993, p. 18; 1994, p. 28.

Sources: Xin Ming (ed.), *Fanzui xue* (Criminology), Chongqing, Chongqing chubanshe, 1991, pp. 86, 130, 132, 138; Cao Manzhi (ed.), *Zhongguo qingshaonian fanzuixue*, Beijing, Qunzhong chubanshe, 1988, pp. 177–8; Shao Daosheng (ed.), *Zhongguo qingshaonnian fanzui de shehuixue sikao* (Sociological reflections on Chinese juvenile crime), Beijing, Shehui kexue wenxian chubanshe, 1987, pp. 9–13; Kang Shuhua and Xiang Zexuan, *Qingshaonian faxue xinlun* (New discussions on juvenile law), Beijing, Gaodeng jiaoyu chubanshe, 1996, pp. 94–104; Zhonghua renmin gongheguo gonganbu (PRC Ministry of Public Security), 'Zhongguo qingshaonian fanzui de qushi he yufang' (Trends in Chinese juvenile delinquency and its prevention), in *Zhongguo qingshaonian fanzui yanjiu nianjian 1987* (Yearbook on Chinese juvenile delinquency studies 1987), Beijing, Chunqiu

of 1966 was reportedly 956,000 persons, an average of about 8–9 a year per 100,000 inhabitants,[6] and thus the 'non-political' crime rate up through the 1960s was even less than the low figures cited in Table 14.

In comparison with the early 1950s, the early 1980s witnessed something of a 'crime wave'. This period also saw a sudden increase in the population of young people, as the baby-boomers of the Cultural Revolution came of age, accompanied by a rise in juvenile delinquency. The 'Severe Blows' *(yanda)* campaign of 1983 was meant to halt this trend, rid society of its core of hard criminals through harsh penalties and executions, and frighten the rest off criminal involvement. Capital punishment was used extensively.

The crime rate of the late 1980s demonstrates that this draconian campaign did not manage to achieve any long-term effects. From a low 514,000 cases in 1984, or 49.9 per 100,000 population, the rate had risen to 77.4 by 1988. The number of criminal cases investigated by the police in 1990 went up sharply from 827,000 cases in 1988 to nearly two million in 1989, and reached a peak of 2.37 million—nearly 210 cases per 100,000 population—in 1991.[7] This sudden increase in reported crime in 1989 is due mainly to a national reorganization of the statistical standards used to define a criminal case. The reformulation of standards led to a systematic rise in the reported number of crime cases, in some categories up to 30–40 per cent according to official estimates.[8] The stress on public order and crime prevention was further intensified after 1989; this also explains some of the increases in crime rates from 1989 onwards. Talk about 'dealing a blow to crime' has again been stepped up. A new national 'Severe Blows' campaign started in April 1996 in order to 'change the situation of poor social order . . . deter crimes and develop the legal system'.[9] A 'winter crackdown' followed, and a 'spring action' continued this campaign style of policing in 1997.[10] There are, however, critical voices even among the security forces against this campaign model. This criticism is not necessarily

chubanshe, 1988, pp. 41–7, 48; *Zhongguo falü nianjian* (The law yearbook of China), 1988, p. 820; 1989, p. 1084; 1990, p. 996; 1991, p. 942; 1992, pp. 861, 872; 1993, pp. 940, 951; 1994, pp. 1033, 1041; 1995, pp. 1069, 1075; 1996, pp. 963, 971; 1997, pp. 1061, 1069; 1998, pp. 1244, 1251, Beijing, Zhongguo falü nianjian she; *Zhongguo 1982 nian renkou pucha ziliao* (Mateials from the 1982 population census of China), Beijing, Zhongguo tongji chubanshe, 1985; *Zhongguo renkou tongji nianjian 1990* (China population statistics yearbook 1990), Beijing, Kexue jishu wenxian chubanshe, 1991; *National Population Census Office under the State Council, Major Figures of the Fourth National Population Census of China* (in Chinese and English), Beijing, China Statistical Publishing House, 1991; and *Zhongguo shehui tongji ziliao 1990* (China's social statistics 1990), Beijing, Zhongguo tongji chubanshe, 1990.

against the 'hardness' of the 'Strike Hard' concept, but a criticism of the fact that such repeated 'educative campaigns' do not mean effective police work. Some claim that the *yanda* is 'impractical', 'not worth its name'; that it is wearing out the police force, and that the repeated campaigns are taking time away from ordinary police work.[11]

The public security system, meant to be a tool of 'proletarian dictatorship' in the 1950s, was not designed for the 'normal' crime that is now on the upsurge. The old public security system was dismantled in the 1980s to make way for a new and more 'professional' system. The mass public security network was also in disorder: in 1988 it was reported that only 20 per cent of the local security committees (*zhibaohui*) were efficient.[12] Even if there are attempts to strengthen this network, a comprehensive community control system is almost totally out of the question today, according to some Chinese officials.[13]

The Chinese 'Crime Wave' in Perspective

International statistics on crime such as those compiled by Interpol are virtually unannotated, leaving us completely uninformed about national differences with respect to reporting practices, laws, different methods of calculation, or definitions of crime. Nevertheless, the Interpol data provide a rough indication of where China stands internationally in terms of crime.[14] Reports from 113 countries between 1985 and 1988 on rates of crime ranked China 111th.[15] In comparison, a group of Western countries had an average crime rate nearly 140 times higher than China's during that period; the reported crime rate in China has increased during the period of reform, but the latest Interpol statistics still show reported crime rates more than 60 times higher than that of China among this group of countries.[16] A more reliable measure than overall crime rates is provided by homicide statistics. Internationally, homicide reports follow a fairly uniform pattern, as most countries view it as a very serious crime. The Chinese homicide rate in 1986 was 1.1 per 100,000 population, giving it a ranking of 103rd among the 113 countries reported. In 1990 it stood at 1.92, and despite reaching 2.18 in 1997, this is still low in a global perspective.[17]

Other materials that focus specifically on international differences also indicate very low crime rates in China. In 1977, for example, the United Nations compiled data from 64 countries on the reported instances of major crimes per 100,000 population. The UN comparison of world crime rates in the period 1970–5 with Chinese crime rates for the 'crime wave' year of 1981 shows that China suffered only 1.2 per cent as many

TABLE 15   World crime rates, 1970–1975, and Chinese crime rates, 1981, per 100,000 population

	World average crime rates, 1970–5	Chinese average crime rates, 1981	Chinese crime rates relative to world crime rates (%)
Intentional homicide	3.9	0.96	24.6
Assault	184.1	2.16	1.2
Sex crimes	24.2	3.09[a]	12.8
Kidnapping	0.7	0.01[b]	1.4
Robbery	46.1	2.24	4.9
Theft	862.4	74.72	8.7
Fraud	83.3	2.04[c]	2.4
Illegal drug traffic	9.8		
Drug abuse	28.9	0.3[d]	0.8
Alcohol abuse	67.8	n.a.	n.a.
Total	1,311.2	89.37	6.8

[a] Includes only rape.
[b] Figures from 1990.
[c] Including counterfeiting and forgery (0.17%).
[d] Figures from the late 1980s for 'drug-related crime' include both illegal drug trafficking and drug abuse.

Sources: Report of the Secretary-General on Crime Prevention and Control, *UN Report* A/32/199, 22 September 1977, p. 9; James Q. Wilson and Richard J. Herrnstein, *Crime and Human Nature* (see n. 12), p. 441; *Zhongguo qingshaonian fanzui yanjiu nianjian 1987*, p. 48; Gonganju wuju bangongshi (Public Security Bureau Office No. 5), 'Jinnian lai wo guo qingshaonian fanzui de jiben zhuangkuang tedian' (The basic situation and characteristics of juvenile delinquency in our country during recent years), *Qingshaonian fanzui yanjiu*, No. 3, 1991, pp. 1–4; *China Daily*, 16 July 1991, p. 4.

assaults as the world average (Table 15). Serious assault, however, has increased in China during the 1990s.

Even homicide, which ranks highest in China as a percentage of the world average, was four times less likely to occur there. The purportedly higher reliability of homicide as a measure of overall crime rates suggests that other types of crime in China are under-reported, though it is notable that the ratio between homicide rates and other types of crime in China is somewhat similar to that of other countries that are poor and predominantly rural. Wilson and Herrnstein have observed that higher per capita productivity (or gross national product) is usually accompanied by more property offences (particularly theft), fewer murders, and a net overall increase in crime.[18]

'Sex crimes' also seem relatively high in China compared with other types of crime, particularly since only rape is included in the Chinese figures. The strong tendency of the Chinese penal system to focus on sex crimes partly reflects a general emphasis on moral order rather than the prevalence of the crime itself; the definition of what constitutes rape is wider in China than in most other countries.[19] In China explanations of rape have overwhelmingly emphasized the moral responsibility of the offender and his deviation from social norms.[20]

Overall, it is clear from the UN survey that China's crime rate in 1981 was extremely low, only 6.8 per cent of the world average. On the other hand, the Chinese rate of juvenile delinquency ranks high among all the countries reported. Countries using 18 years as an upper limit for juvenile crime report that this group committed 7.7 per cent of all crimes in 1985.[21] In China in 1985, 14- to 18-year-olds committed nearly one-fourth of all reported crimes.[22] Although the percentage fell to 12.6 in 1993, partly owing to redefinitions of crime, China would seem to have a very low overall crime rate but a high proportion of juvenile crime.

The economically developed countries generally exhibit higher overall rates of crime, a disproportionate number of property offences, and more female and juvenile crime.[23] China belongs to the 'traditional' or 'developing' category in terms of its low crime rate overall, but in terms of its high rate of juvenile delinquency it is 'modern' or 'developed'. China seems closer to the crime profiles of developed countries in terms of the ratio of crimes against persons and against property. With its overall share of 83 per cent crimes against property, it is comparable to the 82 per cent average for the developed world; the developing country average was 49 per cent.[24] According to recent UN data, however, it is getting increasingly more difficult to term trends in international crime as having a 'traditional' or 'modern' profile.[25]

During the 1980s China had a considerably lower proportion of drug-related crime compared with both categories of countries, at only around 0.3 per cent. During the 1990s, however, this situation has been rapidly changing; and, particularly in provinces like Yunnan, Guangxi, and Sichuan, the problem is now about to reach 'world standards'. Drug cases now make up 2.3 per cent of the total number of crime cases in China.

Economic progress may partly explain the rising crime rates, but it cannot account for the contradictory traits China exhibits with regard to the 'developing–developed' dichotomy. China in fact defies the assumptions attaching to level of economic development, and both cultural and structural factors may account for this.

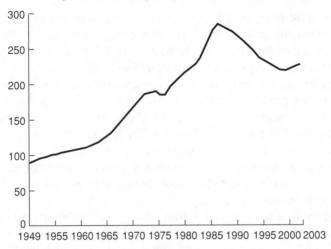

FIGURE 7 The population of 14- to 25-year-olds in China, 1949–2000 (millions)
Source: Population statistics for 1982 and 1990.

Age and Danger: Does a Youth Boom Mean a Crime Wave?

Criminology has long known that criminal behaviour is to a large extent youthful behaviour. Some early criminologists even went so far as to conclude that the age distribution of crime conforms to a 'law of nature'.[26] Modern criminologists have abandoned such notions of a 'law', but many still talk about an 'age invariance effect'. For instance, Blumstein and Cohen have declared that, while numbers of arrests have changed in absolute magnitude over time, 'the same pattern has persisted for the *relative* magnitudes of the different age groups, with fifteen- to seventeen-year-olds having the highest arrest rates per population of any group'.[27] If this is true, then China's high juvenile delinquency rates can be explained mainly by demographic data. What we do know is that the overall picture of Chinese crime in the early 1990s fits the description given by 'age invariance' theoreticians, and that its crime curve fits the 'ageing out' effect described in the criminological literature.[28] The 'baby boom' of the Cultural Revolution years would be expected to produce increased crime rates as the baby-boomers grew into their teens (see Figure 7). Criminologists have also predicted that, as the overall crime rate increases, the peak of criminal activity will occur at a younger age.[29] To understand China's juvenile delinquency rates, however, we first need to study Chinese population statistics.

It is notable that the 14–25-year age group increased rapidly in the 1980s. From 90 million in 1949, this group grew to 137 million at the beginning of the Cultural Revolution in 1966. The youth boom in China rose to a peak of 282 million in 1987, the early 1990s witnessing a decline as the baby-boomers began entering their late twenties. Thanks to the present restrictive birth-control policy, by the year 2000 the group will have declined to 215 million. It will then start expanding again, reaching about 225 million in 2003.[30] At first glance, 'age invariance' theory would seem to fit the Chinese case. The 'crime wave' and the youth boom were both distinct characteristics of the 1980s, and the most striking development during this period was the rapid growth of juvenile delinquency.

The early 1950s witnessed a uniquely low rate of youth delinquency. From only 18 per cent of all crime in 1956, however, the rate increased to 32.3 per cent in 1957. This percentage remained relatively stable up to 1965. Most estimates for youth delinquency during the Cultural Revolution period stand at 40–50 per cent of the total crime rate. Local surveys indicate that the crime rate for 14- to 25-year-olds peaked around 1973, and by 1975 it was only slightly higher than the pre-Cultural Revolution figure for 1965. A new upsurge occurred after the beginning of the reform process in the late 1970s, as both national and provincial statistics suggest.[31] In 1979, youth delinquency accounted for 47.6 per cent of total crime on a national scale, but rose sharply to a peak of 75.7 per cent in 1988; since then it has decreased with the waning of the youth boom and reportedly stabilized at 65 per cent from 1991 to 1993 (see Table 16).

As Table 17 shows, the juvenile group of under-18-year-olds also accounted for an increasingly larger proportion of the total crime rate of the early 1980s. From a near zero rate in the 1950s and 1960s, it rose to just to 1.4 per cent in 1977. By 1985, however, this age-bracket was committing 23.8 per cent of all crimes, and there was a rapid drop in the age of first offence. This figure has since fallen to 12.7 per cent, as the proportion of this group in the population as a whole has declined and as the definition of theft has changed in the statistics.[32] As we shall see, however, this does not mean that criminal activity has decreased among minors.

The curves in Figure 8 suggest that demographic factors have influenced crime rates among young people but cannot account for more than a part of the increase. The best correlation is between curves (1) and (2)—youth crime rates (14–25) and the population of that age group as a percentage of their elders—from the mid-1950s until the late 1970s. However, in the early and mid-1950s youth delinquency was under-represented in criminal statistics; youths simply committed

TABLE 16   Youth delinquency (14- to 25-year-olds) as a percentage of total crime, 1952–1993

Year	%	Year	%	Year	%
1952	20.2	1975	37.0[b]	1986	72.5
1955	22.0	1979	47.6	1987	74.4
1956	18.0	1980	61.2	1988	75.7
1957	32.3	1981	64.0	1989	74.1
1961	30.0	1982	65.9	1990	69.7
1964	30.0	1983	67.0[c]	1991	65.0
1965	35.0	1984	63.3	1992	65.0[d]
1966–74	40–50[a]	1985	71.3	1993	65.0[d]

[a] Average estimates by Chinese criminologists.
[b] Derived from data in Cao Manzhi (ed.), *Zhongguo qingshaonian fanzuixue*, Beijing, Qunzhong chubanshe, 1988, p. 178. (Total criminal cases rose 3.2 times from 1975 to 1983.)
[c] Earlier official sources claimed it was 60.2% in 1983, a figure that has been corrected in more recent official material.
[d] Estimates.

Sources: Xin Ming (ed.), pp. 86, 130–8; Cao Manzhi (ed.), pp. 177–8; Shao Daosheng (ed.), p. 16; Gonganju wuju bangongshi, p. 1; *Zhongguo qingshaonian fanzui yanjiu nianjian 1987*, p. 48; Du Hangwei, p. 5; Jiang Liu, Lu Xueyi, and Shan Tianlun (eds.), *1993–1994 nian Zhongguo: Shehui xingshi fenxi yu yuce* (Analysis and forecast of the social situation in China 1993–1994), Beijing, Zhongguo shehui kexue chubanshe, 1994, p. 287; and population censuses for 1982 and 1990. One source claims that the rate was as low as 18.1% in 1972 and 31.2% in 1976. Since the 1972 rate is based on incomplete statistical material from the Cultural Revolution, I have not included it in the overall statistics. See Zhou Weixin, 'Zhongguo chengshi fanzui xianzhuang pouxi' (Analysis of the situation of urban crime in China), *Shehui*, No. 5, 1988, pp. 14–15.

TABLE 17   Juvenile delinquency (14- to 18-year-olds) as a percentage of total crime, 1950s–1993[a]

Year/s	%	Year	%	Year	%
1950s–60s	0.2–0.3	1983	18.0	1990	16.3
1977	1.4	1984	20.4	1991	14.6
1978	2.2	1985	23.8	1992	13.5
1979	3.3	1986	22.3	1993	12.7
1980	7.0	1987	21.6		
1981	13.3	1988	21.0		
1982	19.6	1989	19.9		

[a] Until 1982, percentages referred to number of cases (*xingshi anfan*). For 1983–5, some sources use 'cases' while others use 'persons involved' (*xingshifanzui zuo'an chengyuan*) or 'number of crimes' (*fanzui shu*) as their basis. As gang crimes are usually prevalent among juveniles, this makes a difference. For example, in one investigation of 104 gang cases, 182 people were arrested (see Pi Yijun, p. 388). Thus, the difference from 1977 to 1989 might be less sharp than depicted here. The figures from 1992 and 1993 are taken from the Interpol statistics, which report slightly lower overall crime rates than the official material used in China.

Sources: Cao Manzhi (ed.), p. 255; Xin Ming (ed.), pp. 140, 231; *Zhongguo qingshaonian fanzui yanjiu nianjian 1987*, pp. 43, 316; Gonganju wuju bangongshi, pp. 1–2. Du Hangwei, p. 6; Organisation Internationale de Police Criminelle, *Statistiques Criminelles Internationales* 1993 (International Criminal Statistiques 1993); Le Secrétariat Général de l'OIPC–Interpol, Lyon, 1993, p. 18; 1994 statistics, p. 28.

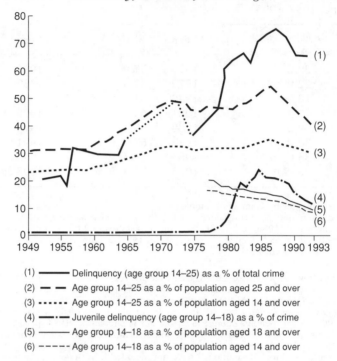

(1) ———— Delinquency (age group 14–25) as a % of total crime
(2) — — Age group 14–25 as a % of population aged 25 and over
(3) •••••• Age group 14–25 as a % of population aged 14 and over
(4) —••— Juvenile delinquency (age group 14–18) as a % of crime
(5) ———— Age group 14–18 as a % of population aged 18 and over
(6) – – – – Age group 14–18 as a % of population aged 14 and over

FIGURE 8   Chinese delinquency (14–25 and 14–18-year-olds) as a percentage of total crime, compared with the relative population size of different age groups, 1949–1993

Notes: Local reports of the upper age level for Chinese delinquency were as high as 30 years in the 1950s, and 28 years up to 1975. It is not clear to what extent these figures have been corrected for overall delinquency rates for this period.

Delinquency is represented here by curves (1) and (4). Population curves (2) and (5) show the youth groups as a percentage of the population, aged respectively 25 and over and 18 and over. This is normally regarded as a more accurate measure of the connection between age group and crime than population curves (3) and (6), which show the age group as a percentage of the entire criminally responsible population over 14. These two curves, however, show the actual over-representation of crime within the respective age groups in a 1:1 relation when compared with curves (1) and (4). Population curves (5) and (6) for the age group 14–18 show that the crime rate had been entirely unaffected by increases or decreases in the relative population of this group between 1949 and the late 1970s.

Sources: see Tables 16 and 17. Population data are estimated from the censuses of 1982 and 1990.

fewer crimes than adults in absolute as well as in relative terms. This finding runs quite counter to the 'age invariance' theory, which holds that youths in their late teens or early twenties will dominate crime statistics at all times and in all cultures.[33]

Figure 9 shows the connection between age, crime, and population factors for 1956 and 1988. In 1956, as can be observed, 14- to 25-

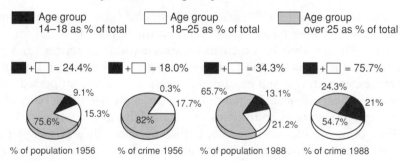

FIGURE 9   Relative size of the age groups 14–18, 18–25, and 25 and over as a percentage of total population over 14, and as a percentage of total crime rates in China in 1956 and 1988

Source: based on data given in Figure 8.

year-olds accounted for nearly one-fourth of the total population group over 14, but they committed less than one-fifth of all crime; in 1988, the same age group represented slightly over one-third of the population, but committed more than three-fourths of all crime.

The age invariance hypothesis is even less applicable to the 14- to 18-year-old age group. From 1956 to 1988, this group increased in size from 9.1 to 13.1 per cent of the over-14 population; over the same period, their share of crime increased from a mere 0.3 to as much as 21 per cent of the total.[34] The percentage went down to 12.7 in 1993, but despite this fact, crime among that age group increased in absolute terms, and the crime rate among the population group has increased since the mid-1980s. This very obviously cannot be explained at all on the basis of demography and the relative size of that age group. Whereas for the whole 14–25 age group demographic factors provide part of the explanation, they appear invalid in the case of the 14–18 age group. The earlier onset of physical maturity than in previous decades largely explains the decreasing average age of delinquents.[35]

Crime, Mobility, and the New Industrial Revolution

We have already noted the importance of 'movement' in the Chinese narratives of danger. While 'movement' has been understood symbolically as a sign of disorder, during the period of modernization a real social and geographical mobility has set in. 'Mobility' should here be understood to include both population migration and value change. On one side is the disorder or *dongluan,* as represented by the new migrant population and their *liudong* (mobility); on the other side is the fear of modern Western ideas and their influence on youth, as represented by the fear of the *liumang*—the Chinese hooligan. Movement and mobility represent both real and imagined dangers. In the reform period, the country has experienced the painful effects of a process of mobility and 'drift' which stands in contrast to the age invariance hypothesis.

The young are the most mobile, both geographically and sociologically, and China's rising crime rate can be seen as an unbidden guest who has slipped in through the open door of reform. There is also another tendency in some Chinese criminological literature to view juvenile delinquency as a relic from the feudal past or as a product of the Cultural Revolution.[36] Yet the reform period and its heightened mobility and crime can in many ways also be seen as a Chinese version of the nineteenth-century Industrial Revolution in the West. An Industrial Revolution style of migration from the rural areas to the cities is in progress, and such factors as the abolition of the rustication programme and the reorganization of the school system also actively contributed to the increased mobility of the 1980s. The rustication programme sent nearly twenty million youths from the cities 'up to the mountains and down to the villages' (*shangshan xiaxiang*) in the 1960s and 1970s. At the end of the programme, hordes of young people were suddenly pouring back into the cities. At the same time, the educational system was being thoroughly reshuffled. While the secondary schools in the countryside might have been of poor quality, they at least had kept many young people at school. The new educational policy stressed quality rather than quantity and resulted in an exodus of youth, particularly rural youth, from school, spurred on by a desire to work on contracted family land instead. Rural secondary schools disappeared at an alarming rate, or were turned into primary schools. Dropout rates increased sharply during the initial years of reform.[37] This new army of dropouts (*liushisheng*) constituted a group at high risk of turning to crime.

In several regions the data for dropout rates and the percentage of dropout inmates in prison showed a clear correlation.[38] In Tianjin the crime rate among school dropouts was found to be 15.6 times higher than for young people still in school.[39] It is true that dropping out of school does not necessarily alter law-breaking behaviour, and some have even found that dropping out can be beneficial, reducing peer-group opportunities to engage in illegal activities.[40] But the scope of the dropout problem in China—in the order of millions—was very different from that of the much milder scenarios described in Western investigations. In China dropping out was not restricted to the group of 'double-poor students' (*shuangchasheng*), i.e. those with poor school results and poor conduct. Dropouts also included a vast number of 'single-poor students' (*danchasheng*), i.e. those of formerly good conduct who had dropped out because of poor academic performance alone. In the case of Tianjin, although the first group outnumbered the second, accounting for 31.8 per cent of all prison inmates, as many as 15.8 per cent of the inmates belonged to the latter group. That they turned to crime could in many cases be attributed to their having left school.[41] The cities were unable to absorb the large numbers of youths who had come on to the job market. The expression *daiye qingnian*—'youths waiting for jobs'— was the euphemism for unemployed young people. In 1978, 47 per cent of the jobless were young people, but by 1984 this had risen to over 83 per cent. In addition to the returned rusticated urban youth, vast numbers of rural surplus labourers flowed into the cities looking for work, many in vain.[42] This flood of mostly young people into the cities from the countryside contributed to the emergence of a new group of people on the fringes of urban society.[43]

The onset of agricultural reform and the return to household farming made evident the extent of surplus labour power in China's rural areas: calculations range from 100 million to more than 200 million out of the total rural work-force.[44] Judging by China's present economic growth rate, only 120 million agricultural jobs will be available in the next ten years, and so a further 120 million will become jobless.[45] An official number of 80 million of these joined the 'floating population' (*liudong renkou*), migrants registered as temporary urban residents, and only 44 million of them are registered with the public security organs as temporary residents.[46] There is in addition an 'army' of unregistered vagrants, mostly from the rural areas, who go under the name of the 'blindly floating population' (*mangliu renkou*). The influx of jobless wanderers and temporary workers has been so large that officials have begun to warn against the dangers of slums arising on the outskirts of some cities.[47] The migrant population consists of many groups, from vagrants and beggars to jobless people, temporary workers (*linshi gongren*), self-employed people (*getihu*), and others who come under little official supervision. The seasonal migration of job-seekers has also posed a problem.[48]

Popular opinion tends to brand the whole migrant population as a dangerous, criminal force. Exaggerated and discriminatory as such claims undoubtedly are, they are not entirely baseless. In Shanghai non-natives accounted for one-third of all offenders arrested in 1990.[49] This rate was double their share of the population—although, given that most offenders are young and that migrant groups are composed mostly of young people, the figures are less dramatic than they look. However, people 'with three no's', i.e. without valid identification cards, fixed residences, and proper jobs, dominate crime statistics.[50] Similarly, trades dominated by the 'mobile and scattered' (*liudong fensan*) are over-represented in the crime statistics.[51] The evidence is that crime rates are higher among the migrant population, although some of the reports appear exaggerated and alarmist, reflecting a general fear of migrants as 'roving criminals'. Such alarmist reports are not only reflecting the fear of crime. Dorothy Solinger has pointed out that the floating population has a dual function: it is threatening the stability of society and 'reinforcing the state' by providing 'cheap and vulnerable labour' at the same time as it strengthens popular acceptance of the police force.[52]

Despite the frequent claim in various Chinese criminology textbooks that the 'socialist system does not produce crime',[53] the 1980s saw the emergence of a new lumpenproletariat in China. The authorities take care to describe the *liumang* or hooligans, and the *youmin* or 'drifters' who 'blindly flood' into the cities, as remnants of the old society. Argument has it that such elements had traditionally constituted a criminal class that formed gangs to oppose Kuomintang bureaucrats and 'evil landlords'. Oppressed and forced into crime, they nevertheless had adopted the viewpoint of the oppressor classes. But today, so the argument goes, there is no social basis for such phenomena.[54] From this argument derives the remarkably strong emphasis in Chinese criminology on the open choice facing criminals: they know what they do; they know it is wrong: they should therefore be punished.

In today's China, large groups of young people have greater freedom since they now live away from the influence of their families, and in many cases outside the economic structure as well. We have seen that such circumstances provide grounds for the fear of disorder and the moral indignation that commonly accompany traditional beliefs about marginalized people. Anthropologists have pointed out generally that marginal figures or groups easily become symbols of a social or moral decay eating away at the very fabric of society.[55] It is worth remembering, however, that Chinese youths are in fact generally law-abiding, compared with the youth populations of nearly all other countries. The new situation is that they have now moved beyond the order and control experienced in the traditional or rural society.

Even if this new freedom has still not touched the majority of young people in China, the example set by the new migrants and marginals has led to a change of the very *Zeitgeist*. The life-styles of the new generation have stirred up anxieties among their elders in much the same way that similar youth groups have done in the West. The fear of gang crime is linked to the tendency of youths to place their horizontal allegiance to peers above their vertical allegiance to authorities. Such allegiances and attitudes challenge the exemplary standard, signalling danger and the death of the exemplary society. We have seen similar fears of social and moral pollution in our own societies. The rising rates of crime and disorder during the first decades of the nineteenth century prompted Americans and Europeans to develop an array of voluntary associations and institutions designed to develop character and teach self-control. That period also witnessed puritan and Victorian attacks on the evils of modernization, much like the attacks made in China today.[56]

As we saw in Chapter 10, young independent women in particular have come to typify the 'loose morals' that accompany modernization. This point is vividly illustrated by the criminologist Cao Manzhi, who claims that the ratio of female to male offenders provides a 'measure of the moral level in society'.[57] According to Cao, the increase in this rate from roughly 1 : 100 before the Cultural Revolution to 1 : 10 in the 1980s represents a clear quantitative measure of growing moral disorder. The Ministry of Public Security estimates that girls comprised 10 per cent of total juvenile delinquency arrests in 1983, a figure reported to be nearly doubled only two years later.[58] The overall percentage of criminal offences in China committed by women and reported to the Interpol was, however, as low as 3.5 per cent in 1994.[59]

American research has linked increased numbers of female crime in the United States almost entirely to increased property offences, with the relative proportion of females involved in violent crimes remaining constant at about 10 per cent and those involved in property crimes at about 22–6 per cent.[60] In China the picture is different, for as much as 90 per cent of all crimes among young girls are defined as 'sexual transgressions' (*xing zuicuo*).[61] The frequent use in China of administrative detention of females for 'sexual transgressions' must be seen in the light of the protection of moral boundaries. As such, female sexual crime is probably the prime example in China of 'constructed crime'.[62] What is 'criminal' for females is not necessarily so for males.

Deterrence Policy and the Failure of the 'Severe Blows' Campaign

The campaign of 'Severe Blows against Serious Criminal Activities' (*yanli daji yanzhong xingshi fanzui huodong*), or the *yanda* campaign, was launched in 1983 to stop the 'crime wave' of the early 1980s. Ten years later, it was clear that the campaign was a useless and bloody affair, but it has provided important information about the effects of deterrence policy in general.

The 'Severe Blows' movement started as a political campaign, motivated not by increasing crime rates but by the need to do something about the prevailing general social disorder and the public's loss of confidence in the police force. It was more than mere coincidence that the campaign against 'spiritual pollution' (*jingshen wuran*) was launched in the same year as the negative counterpart of the 'spiritual civilization' movement.[63]

When the *yanda* campaign was launched in September 1983, the crime rate was in fact the lowest since 1979, but, as one criminologist commented, the falling crime rate 'did not fall fast enough'.[64] The traditional belief in China is that parading evil—or, rather, bringing evil to justice for all to see—will lead to a decrease in crime. Thus it was that the 'Severe Blows' campaign gave great importance to publicizing the many executions that took place. The campaign had as a main target the newly emerging gang crimes, and the gangs' leaders (*touzi*).[65] The aim also was to prevent further recruitment of juvenile criminals—though it was unclear whether removing the most actively delinquent 'veterans' from gangs would indeed decrease significantly the recruitment of younger juveniles. Some Western criminologists conclude that we do not know enough about criminal networks to say what will happen if leaders are isolated—whether others will take over the leadership of the broken criminal network, or whether the gangs will dissolve.[66] The Chinese strategy of eliminating gang leaders by executing them did not have that latter consequence. The networks survived, the gangs multiplied, and there was a fall in the age of the youths involved. A report from the Ministry of Security based on material from several cities confirms this. In 1986 a record-high figure of 93.3 per cent of all gang members were 25 and under, almost half of them under the age of 18.[67] All over the country, gang crime grew and thrived in the wake of the 'Severe Blows' campaign. In the late 1980s gang crime accounted for 60–70 per cent of all criminal offences in China, which is somewhat similar to the figures for Western countries.[68]

Chinese criminologists and politicians, however, managed to conclude that the campaign had been a success. In one 1984 investigation of neighbourhoods all over China, researchers found the reassuring answers they had hoped for. Of the juveniles who had been engaged in illegal activities and petty crime, 89 per cent claimed that they had stopped. Neighbours who were asked about particular unruly youths claimed that 93 per cent of them now exhibited better behaviour as a result of the campaign. The investigation concluded that the campaign had been

TABLE 18 'Major, special, and serious crimes' (*zhongteda fanzui*) as a percentage of total crime in China, 1979–1994

Year	%	Year	%	Year	%	Year	%
1979	6.50	1982	8.55	1985	15.95	1988	24.54
1980	6.70	1983	n.a.	1986	19.00	:	n.a.
1981	6.90	1984	12.03	1987	21.40	1994	26.80

Sources: Xin Ming (ed.), p. 138, *China News Analysis*, No. 1536, June 1995, p. 3; *Zhongguo falü nianjian* 1995, p. 1069. After 1988, murder, assault, robbery, and rape increased rapidly. While rape showed a downward trend after 1993, robbery continued to rise sharply, from 36,000 cases in 1988 to 160,000 cases in 1994. Because several types of petty theft were omitted from the statistics in 1992, and were no longer termed 'criminal', the situation of 'major, special, and serious crimes' is not as bad as it looks when we compare 1994 with 1988.

effective in 'warning off unstable and dangerous elements in society' and had delivered a 'big shock' to juveniles who lived 'on the fringes of crime'.[69] Such shocks have been described before in the criminological literature, however, and in most cases have been only short-term.[70] The decreasing crime rate over the short run was due entirely to a fall in theft and petty crime. In fact, serious theft tripled from 1982 to 1986, and violent crime increased.[71]

The capture and execution of gang leaders and other 'principal criminals' after summary trials was the most conspicuous feature of the 1983 'Severe Blows' campaign. One problem, however, was the low age of some of these criminals. Article 44 of the then 'Chinese Criminal Law' stated that: 'The death penalty is not to be applied to persons who have not reached the age of eighteen at the time the crime is committed.' The Article goes on to say, however, that 'Persons who have reached the age of sixteen but not the age of eighteen may be sentenced to death with a two-year suspension of execution if the crime is particularly grave.'[72] This right to hand down the death penalty for juveniles under 18 was used extensively during the campaign. In keeping with this, in 1985 the legal age of criminal responsibility was lowered, making 14- to 16-year-olds criminally responsible for a number of serious crimes.[73] In the draft amendments to the new Criminal Law, the death penalty was changed to life imprisonment for juvenile criminals aged 16–18. This change, however, met resistance from some deputies at the National People's Congress in March 1997. They claimed that the new measures would 'not help combat crime'.[74]

Table 18 shows that between 1979 and 1988, 'major, special and serious crimes' quadrupled as a percentage of total crime. The rate has been relatively stable since then, but reached 26.8 per cent in 1994 and has since risen to well over 30 per cent.[75] The use of explosives had become more common, and murders, rapes, and robberies reportedly involved greater brutality. The taking of hostages had also become a much more common practice among criminals.[76] Moreover, in 1989 a record-high 73.1 per cent of the violent crimes such as homicide, rape, assault, and armed robberies were committed by youths.[77]

Furthermore, the average age of juveniles involved in crime continued to fall in the years following the 1983 'Severe Blows' campaign. In Beijing, in 1984, when the deterrent effects of the campaign were reportedly at their strongest, a record-high 10.8 per cent of all crimes by minors under 18 years of age were committed by delinquents of 13 or younger.[78] There were reports too of gangs of juvenile delinquents with an average age of 10 years, and some as young as 7.[79] 'Young and violent' became the new characteristics of criminals.

In light of the brutalization that followed the 'Severe Blows' campaign of 1983, some started to criticize the campaign openly, stating that, in terms of deterring crime among under 18-year-olds, it had had very little effect. Some appealed for the use of different means of reducing crime rates, such as early education and other preventative controls.[80] Others, however, argued that, while early education and preventative methods are indeed important, they should be combined with a strict deterrence policy rather than used as a substitute for it.[81]

Deterrence theory holds that increasing the penalty for an offence will decrease its frequency, while decreasing the penalty will result in increased violations. As many criminologists critical of deterrence theory and capital punishment have pointed out, however, a brutalizing effect is the more likely outcome, as confirmed by the findings after the 'Severe Blows' campaign.[82] Yet in China the 'iron fist' method and the parading of convicted criminals have remained in vogue. The short-term effect on petty crime and theft is used to justify their continued use. A particularly cynical tactic is *youdou*, when the 'big stick' (*da paizi*) is displayed in public places just before holidays such as the Chinese New Year and National Day, or prior to festivals. By executing a few criminals in public at such times, the authorities aim not only to show who is in control, but also to make the streets safer for the public during the festivities. It is also common practice that persons with a 'problem' of some sort in their file are 'for educational reasons' the first to be sent from their work-units to be spectators at sentence pronouncement or execution rallies.[83] In one case in Kunming, a rally was held to pronounce death sentences on a number of criminals 'to greet the third China art festival and maintain public security and social order'.

The sentences were carried out immediately.[84] Shortly before the 14th Party Congress in 1992, mass executions of criminals in a sports stadium in Chengdu were shown on Sichuan television.[85] The method is effective over the short term, as criminologists are likely to confirm; but, if all the murders that have followed in the wake of the 'Severe Blows' campaign teach us anything, it is that deterrence does not work over the long term.

During the recurrent deterrence campaigns after 1983, extensive use was made of the death penalty for looting, drug trafficking, and serious robbery.[86] Recent reports also tell of death penalties for embezzling, car theft, grave-robbery, and even for relatively small-scale theft in the case of repeat offenders.[87] The *liuhai* 'Six Evils' campaign that started in late 1989 adopted the same methods as the 'Severe Blows' campaign.[88] In 1990 China decreed the death penalty for printing, selling, or trafficking in obscene books, photographs, or tapes.[89] During the 'Special Struggle against Theft' launched in 1991, many scores of thieves and others involved in economic crime were executed.[90]

On the other hand, there are developments in an opposite direction. Chinese scholars and human rights experts recently called for the abolition of the practice of public executions, and Guangdong province in 1997 decided to stop such executions and the public parading of convicts although an exception from this rule was made for 'major and serious cases'.[91] People in academic circles now advocate lighter treatment of criminals, and some have even suggested abolishing capital punishment altogether.[92]

However, the harsh treatment of criminals enjoys considerable public support; a recent survey of 15,000 people showed that nearly 60 per cent thought the state's handling of criminals was 'too lenient' (*guokuan*), while only 2 per cent thought it was 'too strict' (*guoyan*).[93] The popularity of 'public rallies to pronounce sentences' would appear to confirm these findings. At one such rally in Lanzhou, where eleven criminals were sentenced to death, it is reported that 'over 10,000 people attending the rally could not help but clap and cheer'.[94] In another incident, thirty-five drug dealers were sentenced to death 'before the eyes of 40,000 people who attended a grand public trial held in Kunming'.[95] A report on hooligan gangs in the rural areas (*tuliuzi*), which had been one of the main targets of the 'Severe Blows' campaign, concluded that 'a few of the most evil among them should be resolutely executed to avoid the indignation of the common people'.[96] Such statements are clearly more than mere propaganda.

While most Chinese criminologists and authorities alike maintain that continued use of the 'iron fist' policy is based on rational calculation of its effects on crime, it may also be viewed more as having educational value and as a dramatization for the masses of the ancient theme of retribution. The regime needs to exhibit the criminal to parade wrongdoing and to demonstrate publicly its ability to uphold social order. Chinese criminologists are clearly aware of the close connection between education, social control, and deterrence. Zhu Genxiang sees control as a continuum from ideological education to deterrence, and in such a perspective even executions can be seen as a form of education.[97] Executions in particular have become symbols of social order, and of the power to uphold it, as illustrated by the following report about the execution of two criminals in Guangzhou for procuring women for prostitution:

The two criminals were immediately taken to the execution ground and shot by a bullet to the head. Some people might ask: since the criminals . . . have not committed a crime as serious as murder or robbery, why have they received such severe punishment? This reflects, no doubt, a lack of understanding about the harmfulness of prostitution. Prostitution erodes people's souls, poisons the social atmosphere, destroys happy families and harms future generations. Moreover, it can easily give rise to other crimes, such as theft, robbery, murder, and so on, seriously undermining social stability . . . Should we be lenient toward them, we would be unfair to both our ancestors and our future generations. Moreover, it would humiliate our great socialist system.[98]

The justification for killing juvenile delinquents is found not only in public displays and in stories meant to frighten potential wrongdoers, but also in edifying stories of repentance.[99] In addition, several reports of sensationally low recidivism or fallback rates have been published. Such stories are meant to be edifying stories in themselves, underlining the efficiency of the judicial system as well as the successful improvement of the criminals. From a prison in Beijing it is reported that 'only 5% of those freed after serving their terms return to their criminal ways. This is believed to be the lowest rate for any prison in the world.'[100] Even the average national rates for recidivism allegedly come close to this world record. Such figures would scarcely seem realistic, however, and higher rates have now begun to appear.[101]

This discussion of crime in China has to be complemented by cultural analysis of the symbols of danger. The 'youth effect' of the Chinese crime scene has not been one of 'age invariance', an automatic criminal response of a specific demographic age composition of the population. I have focused on the rise of juvenile crime rates as an unintended consequence of modernization, caused partly by the increased mobility and marginality of youth. This increased marginality implies a threat to the social fabric. The harsh reactions to such dangers that typify traditional societies undergoing change are also apparent in China. However, the process there has been linked to the 'pernicious influence of Western bourgeois ideology', with its decadence, hedonism, and egoism. In this respect, the 'construction' of crime and the harsh reactions of the public security system have contributed to China's rising juvenile delinquency rates.

I have tried to illustrate this point by discussing certain paradoxes in the Chinese crime scene. International comparison has highlighted the remarkably low rates of crime in China. The tough reaction there to all forms of crime cannot be rationally explained on the basis of these low rates. It may seem extraordinary that such rates can trigger such harsh and brutal methods of deterrence, particularly since these methods also fail to deliver. The many executions have served only to brutalize the crime scene. While massively arguing that people learn by exemplary models, and educating people about the dangers of breaking the social bond, the state seems oblivious to the fact that the government's own violence—both in the streets and on the execution ground—might be responsible for propagating further violence. To appreciate the seemingly irrational policies pursued in China over the past decade, it is necessary to view deterrence and execution as social and cultural spectacles, not as types of crime control or punishment only.[102] Such phenomena represent a highly structured cultural system of meaning. The criminal and his destruction become a symbol of both transgression and defence of social and cultural boundaries. The drama conducted by the public security organs is meant to show to a broader audience the themes of social order and cultural danger. Whether this produces more or less crime is in principle secondary to its symbolic meaning and its assumed overall educational effect.

The official Chinese crime rates are most probably too low. Some calculate that the real crime rates are as much as three to four times as high if all the criminal cases that do not reach the courts and are summarily dealt with by the police are included.[103] This is a general warning against crime statistics, and it is wise to remember that the process of gathering crime statistics is itself socially organized. Young people are generally under more rigorous systems of control and surveillance from families, schools, and society than are adults. Their actions are generally more publicly accessible and observable than those of adults, and they are less experienced and more easily caught. Juvenile subcultures are more easy to detect than economic and administrative or political subcultures of a criminal kind. Youths are mainly excluded from the type of 'hidden economy' or 'hidden social structure' that causes a phenomenon like corruption. This results in an unintended de-emphasis in the statistics of crimes committed by adults.

Viewed in an international perspective, the Chinese crime wave is but a mere ripple in a pond, but this comparative finding does not lessen the anxieties in China about crime and youthful deviance. We must realize that reactions against crime in Chinese society might not be rationally based on, or at least limited to, the wish to solve the problem of crime as such. They have to be seen in terms of defending the social and moral order in a society in the throes of rapid transformation. In this process, the harsh reaction to crime has become a problem in itself.

Notes to Chapter 11

1. Xin Ming (ed.), *Fanzui xue* (Criminology), Chongqing, Chongqing chubanshe, 1991, p. 130. The point about corruption is highly justified. The UN 'International Corruption List' for 1995 (not all countries are included) shows China with a score of 2.16 to be the second most corrupt country in the world, surpassed only by Indonesia; see *Inside China Mainland*, No. 10, October 1995, p. 11.

2. See Zhou Jianjun, Gan Yan, Yan Yujun, and Yang Shaohua, 'Dangqian xingshi anjian li'an bushi de biaoxian, yuanyin yu duice' (Today's unreliable registration of criminal cases: causes and counter-measures), *Gong'an daxue xuebao*, No. 3, 1996, pp. 5–8.

3. Xin Ming (ed.), p. 9. The definition of crime (*fanzui*) is by no means meant to account for all types of 'illegal activity' (*weifa xingwei*) in China. The latter covers a wide range of activity, from traffic violations and cohabitation among unmarrieds to a range of public order violations, etc. The rate for illegal activities has been estimated to have averaged 500–700 per 100,000 population in the 1950s, 600–800 in the 1960s, and an estimated 1,200–1,500 in the early 1980s (ibid., p. 86).

4. Cao Manzhi (ed.), *Zhongguo qingshaonian fanzuixue* (The criminology of Chinese juvenile delinquency), Beijing, Qunzhong chubanshe, 1988, pp. 177–8. When these arrests are discounted, the 1958 rate still came to about 65 crime cases per 100,000, a jump in non-political crime that can be traced to the economic and social disruptions of the Great Leap Forward. Notably, the crime rates of 1957 and 1958 are normally omitted from crime statistics in China today, apparently because of the extraordinarily high 'counter-revolutionary' bias; Cao's book is an exception. As of 1984, 'counter-revolutionary' crimes accounted for only 0.47% of all crime; see Xin Ming (ed.), p. 88.

5. Kang Shuhua and Xiang Zexuan, *Qingshaonian faxue xinlun* (New discussions on juvenile law), Beijing, Gaodeng jiaoyu chubanshe, 1996, p. 95. Kang and Xiang do not make any comment whatsoever on the former high figures given for 1958.

6. Yu Xinting, 'Dalu zhengzhi fan zhi duoshao?' (How much political crime exists in mainland China?), *Zhengming*, no. 12, December 1991, p. 14, bases these figures on an internal Chinese report issued in June 1991. The report further claims that there were 876,500 'counter-revolutionary criminals' between 1966 and 1972. The category of 'counter-revolutionary crime' is now defined as a common criminal offence under the revised criminal law. Officially only 2,026 people serve sentences

for 'jeopardizing state security' (terrorism and prison riots are mentioned as examples) in China today; see *SWB-FE*/2881, 1 April 1997, p. G/3.

7. *Zhongguo falü nianjian* (The law yearbook of China), Beijing, Zhongguo falü nianjian she, 1988, p. 820; 1991, p. 942; 1992, pp. 861, 872.

8. See *Zhongguo falü nianjian*, 1990, p. 996.

9. *Renmin ribao*, 29 April 1997, p. 1.

10. *SWB-FE*/2655, 4 July 1996, p. G/8.

11. See Huang Hong, 'Guanyu shenru kaizhan "yanda" douzheng de jidian sikao' (Some reflections on deeply developing the struggle of 'Hard Blows'), *Gong'an yanjiu*, No. 5, 1996, pp. 50–3. There is a certain fatigue in the police force concerning such 'educative campaigns'. The burden of ordinary policemen is summed up by policeman Guo Benli, who says: 'We just don't have a day off even on weekends, and some of the men can't even find time to see their wives if they're sick' (*SWB-FE*/2908, 2 May 1997, p. G/9).

12. *Liaowang*, 12 December 1988, pp. 11–13; quoted in *Inside China Mainland*, no. 123 (March 1989), p. 11. The security committees are mass organizations that maintain basic supervisory work at a street and work-unit level, find work for former inmates, organize mass public-security campaigns, etc. They are led by small groups of citizens cooperating with the police and other organs of the public security bureaus.

13. Meng Qingfeng, 'Jiaqiang jiceng wangluo jianshe, tigao shequ kongzhi nengli' (Strengthen the construction of basic level networks and increase the capacity of community control), *Qingshaonian fanzui yanjiu*, No. 11, 1992, p. 15. For the development of security committees, see *Zhongguo falü nianjian*, 1991, p. 947; 1992, p. 866; 1993, p. 946. The Yearbook stopped publishing such data in 1994.

14. See Organisation Internationale de Police Criminelle, *Statistiques criminelles internationales 1985–1986* (International criminal statistics 1985–1986), St Cloud, Secrétariat Général OIPC/Interpol, 1988; 1987–1988 statistics, Lyon, 1990. The numbers quoted in this article are based on the 1985–6, 1987–8, and 1991–2 statistics. (I have omitted the South African 'homelands' from this list.)

15. Only two countries—Mali with 11.08 cases per 100,000 population, and Nepal wilh 33.29 cases—had a lower reported crime rate than China's 51.9 cases per 100,000 population in 1986.

16. The 14 Western countries were: West Germany, England, Italy, France, Spain, USA, Canada, Belgium, Norway, Denmark, Sweden, Finland, New Zealand and Australia. The average crime rate for these countries was about 7,200 per 100,000 population; in the 1992–4 Interpol statistics the average had moved to nearly 9,000 per 100,000 population among these countries.

17. It shared the place with Finland. Only Saudi Arabia, Indonesia, Norway, Congo, Ireland, Camerun, Argentina, Burkina Faso, and Mali had lower reported homicide rates, ranging from Saudi Arabia's 1.02 to Mali's 0.01 at the bottom of the list. See also *Zhongguo falü nianjian*, 1995, p. 1069. The 1993 figures reported to Interpol claim the homicide rate was 0.2 per 100,000 population, or 2,553 cases. This is obviously wrong, and the Chinese official statistics report 25,380 cases and a rate of 1.57 for that year. See *Statistiques criminelles internationales*, Lyon, 1994, p. 28, and *Zhongguo falü nianjian*, 1998, p. 1244.

18. James Q. Wilson and Richard J. Herrnstein, *Crime and Human Nature*, New York, Touchstone, 1985, p. 442.

19. 'Sex crimes' can be defined as anything from 'seduction at dancing parties' and so-called crimes of a 'seductive character' (*yinyou xing*) to prostitution, and sex

crimes of a 'forced character' (*qiedao xing*) such as rape and gang rape. See Pi Yijun, 'Lun fanzui tuanhuo anjie de tedian' (A discussion of the characteristics of criminal gang cases), in *Zhongguo qingshaonian fanzui yanjiu nianjian*, 1987, p. 390. A rapist is one who 'by violence, coercion or other means rapes a woman', or one who has 'sexual relations with a girl under the age of fourteen'; see Art. 139 of the Criminal Law in *The Criminal Law and the Criminal Procedure Law of China*, Beijing, Beijing Languages Press, 1984, p. 49. 'Prostitution' probably has the widest definition of all sexual crimes, including 'promiscuous behaviour'. One investigation showed that only 45% of all female sex offenders had ever had sex for money or material gain. See Shanghai xing shehuixue yanjiu zhongxin, 'Xiandai Zhongguo ren de xing wenti' (Sexual problems of today's Chinese), *Minzhu yu fazhi*, No. 10, 1990, p. 34. Prostitution is often labelled as 'hooligan crime' (*liumang fanzui*). The number of convicted prostitutes rose from 25,000 to 200,000 between 1986 and 1990 (see *SWB-FE*/1141, 3 August 1991, p. B2/6).

20. Harold Tanner, 'Chinese rape law in comparative perspective', *Australian Journal of Chinese Affairs*, No. 31, January 1994, p. 16.

21. *New York Times Magazine*, 4 August 1985; quoted from Xin Ming, p. 231.

22. See Gonganju wuju bangongshi, 'Jinnian lai wo guo qingshaonian fanzui de jiben zhuangkuang tedian' (The basic situation and characteristics of juvenile delinquency in our country during recent years), *Qingshaonian fanzui yanjiu*, No. 3, 1991, p. 2.

23. See Preben Wolf, 'Crime and development: an international analysis of crime rates', *Scandinavian Studies in Criminology*, No. 3, 1971, pp. 107–20.

24. Figures adapted from *Report of the Secretary-General on Crime Prevention and Control*, UN Report *A/32/199*, 22 September 1977, p. 10. See also A. D. Viccica, 'World crime trends', *International Journal of Offender Therapy and Comparative Criminology*, Vol. 24, 1980, p. 270; cited in James Q. Wilson and Richard J. Herrnstein, pp. 442–3; *Zhongguwuo qingshaonian fanzui yanjiu nianjian 1987*, p. 48; *China Daily*, 22 June 1991, p. 1; 16 July 1991, p. 4.

25. See review of the Fourth United Nations Survey on Crime Trends and Operations of Criminal Justice Systems (1986–1990), in *Trends: United Nations Criminal Justice Information Network, Crime and Justice Letter*, No. 1/2, 1993. There is, however, one type of modern profile of reactions against crime that should be thoroughly studied in China. In contrast to the stereotypical image of public demand for imprisonment and harsh punishment, community service rather than imprisonment is seen in most developed countries in Europe as the suitable punishment for a recidivist juvenile criminal. In some developed countries, such as the USA, Canada and Australia, and, conspicuously, in all developing countries and the countries of eastern Europe, support for imprisonment and harsher treatment of criminals dominates.

26. Charles Goring, *The English Convict*, Montclair NJ, Patterson Smith, 1913; quoted in Michael R. Gottfredson and Travis Hirschi, p. 124.

27. Alfred Blumstein and Jacqueline Cohen, 'Estimation of Individual Crime Rates from Arrest Records', *Journal of Criminal Law and Criminology*, No. 70, 1979, p. 562.

28. See Michael R. Gottferdson and Travis Hirschi, *A General Theory of Crime*, Stanford, Calif., Stanford University Press, 1990, p. 131.

29. James Q. Wilson and Richard J. Herrnstein, p. 146. The ubiquity of the early peak in criminal activity may be steep or shallow, early or late. Societies that maintain strong parental or adult control should display a later peak.

30. This population projection is based on *Zhongguo 1982 nian renkou pucha ziliao*, pp. 272–81, and *Zhongguo renkou tongji nianjian 1990*, pp. 317–18. The population of youth age cohorts of the early years of the People's Republic is slightly higher than in this projection, because deaths in these cohorts have not been accounted for accurately in the statistical material, as the population has been projected back from 1982.

31. For example, in Liaoning province juvenile delinquency stood at 59.7% of total crime in 1977; by 1979 it had jumped to 78.7% and in 1980 it passed 80%; see Liu shengshi qingshaonian fanzui yuanyin diaochazu, 'Liu shengshi qingshaonian fanzui yuanyin diaocha' (Investigation of the causes for juvenile delinquency in six cities and provinces), in *Zhongguo qingshaonian fanzui yanjiu nianjian 1987*, p. 237.

32. Du Hangwei, 'Bashiniandaimo jiushiniandaichu wuguo qingshaonian fanzui de jiben zhuangkuang he tedian' (The basic situation and characteristics of Chinese juvenile crime at the end of the 1980s and the start of the 1990s), *Qingshaonian fanzui yanjiu*, No. 1, 1994, p. 6.

33. The 'counter-revolutionary crime' bias reported earlier might modify this picture; the overall figures on counter-revolutionary crime, however, do not indicate the age of the persons in question, and we are left to speculate about their effect on the age factor, leading us to modify our arguments against 'invariance' theory, as arrests in the 'counter-revolutionary' and rightist categories presumably focused on a somewhat older age group. However, the low youth crime rates of the early 1950s, as well as in 1956, occurred before the 'high tide' of counter-revolutionary and rightist crime of 1957–8. One source claims that 'there were three times more counter-revolutionary cases than ordinary criminal cases' in the 1950s, and that ordinary criminal cases were below 150,000. If that is the case, then juvenile crime rates might have been higher than assumed here. However, this would also mean that overall ordinary crime rates were even lower in the early 1950s than assumed here (see Lu Jian, 'Crime: a dilemma in the course of modernization', *Shehui*, No. 78, July 1991, pp. 44–6).

34. There are some inconsistencies in the Chinese statistics. Until 1982 the percentage shows number of cases (*xingshi anfan*). For 1983–5 different sources use the same figures, but some use 'cases', while others use 'persons involved' (*xingshi fanzui zuo'an chengyuan*) or 'number of crimes' (*fanzui shu*) as their basis. As gang crimes are usually prevalent among juveniles, this makes a difference. The percentage will be higher where there is talk of persons than where there is talk of cases, simply because more juveniles will be involved in each case than will criminals of a more mature age. For example, in one investigation of 104 gang cases, 182 people were arrested (see Pi Yijun, p. 388).

35. See Cao Manzhi (ed.), pp. 81–97.

36. See Xu Deqi and Wu Zaide, 'Shi xi qingshaonian liumang tuanhuo touzi de texing ji xingcheng huangbian' (Tentative analysis of the characteristics and patterns forming and developing hooligan gang leaders), in *Zhongguo qingshaonian fanzui yanjiu nianjian 1987*, p. 400. Such alleged influence is often postulated out of political convenience and does not seem confirmed by hard data; see Zhongguo shehui kexue yuan shehuixue yanjiusuo, *Qingshaonian fanzui xinlixue*.

37. I have discussed these developments in Børge Bakken, 'Backwards reform in Chinese education', *Australian Journal of Chinese Affairs*, no. 19/20, January 1988, pp. 127–63.

38. Zhang Jing *et al.*, 'Yige xin de yanzhong de shehui wenti' (A new important social problem), *Qingshaonian fanzui yanjiu*, no. 2, 1983, pp. 2–6, 24; also in 'Tianjin

shi liushisheng yu weifa fanzui de diaocha' (Investigation of dropouts and criminal offences in Tianjin), in *Zhongguo qingshaonian fanzui yanjiu nianjian 1987*,
pp. 222–6. See also ibid., pp. 43, 486; and Chen Xianrong, 'Beijing shi zhongxiao
xuesheng liushi yu weifa fanzui diaocha baogao' (The phenomenon of dropouts
and criminal delinquency among primary and secondary school students in
Beijing), *Shehuixue yu shehui diaocha*, no. 2, 1985, pp. 28–35. Chen's article is
translated in *Chinese Education*, vol. 20, no. 3, Fall 1987, pp. 86–110.

39. The official dropout rate in Tianjin rose from 0.6% to 11.9% in the period 1978–
81. During the same years dropouts as a percentage of inmates in Tianjin's
juvenile prisons increased from 13%, a figure relatively constant since 1974, to
50%; see Zhang Jing *et al.*, *Zhongguo qingshaonian fanzui yanjiu nianjian 1987*,
pp. 222–3.

40. James Q. Wilson and Richard J. Herrnstein, p. 278, quote some of these findings.

41. Zhang Jing *et al.*, *Zhongguo qingshaonian fanzui yanjiu nianjian 1987*, p. 223.

42. Erhard Louven, 'Anmerkungen zur Arbeitslosigkeit und zum Arbeitsmarkt in der
VR China' (Remarks on joblessness and the job market in the People's Republic
of China), *China Aktuell*, no. 8, 1988, pp. 650–4. Official estimates on unemployment are a mere 3.5 per cent for the whole country, but 9 per cent in the
cities. Affecting fifty million households, the unemployment rate now stands three
times as high as in 1993. See *SWB-FE*/3261, 24 June 1998, p. G/9, and *SWB-
FE*/3402, 5 December 1998, pp. G./7–8. The official estimates are far too low
as many workers are never registered in those statistics, and since unemployed
workers 'waiting for jobls' (*daiye*) are not regarded as jobless according to the statistics. Even officially it is being admitted, however, that China's unemployment rate
is now the highest in fifty years. See *SWB-FE*/3155, 19 February 1998, p. G/13
and *SWB-FE*/3478, 9 March 1999, p. G/9.

43. Børge Bakken (ed.), *Migration in China*, NIAS Report 31, Copenhagen, NIAS, 1998.

44. *China Daily*, 21 June 1991, p. 4.

45. *SWB-FE*/2216, 1 February 1995, p. G/7.

46. *SWB-FE*/2362, 22 July 1995, p. G/9.

47. *China Daily*, 21 June 1991, p. 4.

48. In Beijing the floating population accounted for 22.03% of the total population
in 1991, in Shanghai 26.18%, in Wuhan 21.79%, and in Chengdu 24.88%; see
Gu Shengzhu, *Feinonghua yu chengzhenhua yanjiu* (A study of non-agriculturalization and urbanization), Hangzhou, 1991, p. 135; quoted from Li Cheng,
'Surplus rural laborers and internal migration in China: current status and future
prospects', in Børge Bakken (ed.), *Migration in China*. The spring migration in
particular has become a yearly problem of great dimensions. The migration is from
the poor areas to rich ones with more job opportunities. In 1992 it was reported
that nearly 150,000 travellers were trapped in railway stations in Hunan and Sichuan
alone. On the morning of 24 February, 40,000 job seekers were stuck in the
Zhengzhou railway station. One-third of them were headed for the Daqing oilfield
to seek seasonal jobs. At the same time, over 100,000 rural workers flooded into
Xiamen (one of the country's special economic zones) in one week as a result of
false rumours of a large recruitment drive in the city. The city called on the
governments in the labourers' home provinces to take action to stop the flow; see
China Daily, 26 February 1992, p. 3, and 21 February 1992, p. 3, *Renmin Ribao*
20 February 1992, p. 5.

49. *SWB-FE*/1085, 30 May 1991, p. B2/5.

50. The statistics from Tianjin seem serious, with official data showing that the crime
rate among the 'mobile population' there was as high as 9,330 per 100,000

population. In one district it reached 25,900, compared with a crime rate among permanent residents of 360 per 100,000 population; see He Jichuan, 'Concern about the floating population', *Zhongguo shehui bao*, 13 September 1991, p. 3. In Chengdu young rural women account for the majority of the city's prostitutes, while immigrant criminal rings dominate the crime scene, according to Zou Hanming and Li Hui, 'Chengdu shi qingshaonian weifa fanzui diaocha' (An investigation of juvenile delinquency in Chengdu), *Qingshaonian fanzui yanjiu*, no. 10, 1990, p. 9. In Guangdong 80% of the arrested criminals in 1994 were outsiders (see *SWB-FE*/2236, 24 February 1995, p. G/7). Investigation of the juveniles responsible for murder and assault in Hubei revealed that more than 70% of the murderers hailed from rural areas according to Wang Xinpan, 'Dui 416 ming qingshaonian xiongsha, shanghai fanzui de diaocha' (Investigation of 416 juvenile murderers and assaulters), in *Zhongguo qingshaonian fanzui yanjiu nianjian 1987*, p. 165; see *also SWB-FE*/2638, 14 June 1996, p. G/13 on a Guangdong drive to clear out people 'with three no's'.

51. In branches such as post and telecommunications, instrument factories and the electronics industry, the crime rate is relatively low at 80–100 per 100,000 population. In the machine-building and electrical machinery industries the total crime rate is also a relatively low 100–200. These are also the trades with the most stable work-forces. The trades with the highest crime rates among their workers are construction, transport, and commerce, with rates of 210–400. The new class of temporary workers is found in the first two industries, and the self-employed are strongly represented in commerce; see Xin Ming (ed.), p. 217.

52. Dorothy J. Solinger, *China's Transients and the State: A Form of Civil Society?* Hong Kong, Hong Kong Institute of Asia-Pacific Studies, 1991, p. 26.

53. Quoted from Cao Manzhi (ed.), p. 167.

54. This line of argument is used by Gao Ge, 'Dui liumang fanzui de bijiao yanjiu' (On the comparative research on hooliganism), *Jilin daxue shehui kexue xuebao*, No. 3, 1986, p. 56.

55. For anthropological discussions of marginality and socially perceived 'danger', see Mary Douglas, *Purity and Danger*, London, Ark, 1984, and *Natural Symbols*, London, Barrie & Rockcliffe, 1970; and Victor Turner, *The Ritual Process*, Chicago, Aldine, 1969.

56. See Paul Boyer, *Urban Masses and Moral Order in America, 1820–1920*, Cambridge, Mass., Harvard University Press, 1978; Joseph F. Kett, *Rites of Passage: Adolescence in America 1790 to the Present*, New York, Basic Books, 1977; and John C. Burnham, *Bad Habits: Drinking, Smoking, Taking Drugs, Gambling, Sexual Misbehaviour, and Swearing in American History*, New York/London, New York University Press, 1993.

57. Cao Manzhi (ed.), p. 261.

58. In 1985 girls made up 18.6% of total juvenile delinquency, or a total of 13.3% of all persons involved in criminal cases. Even so, youth delinquency has accounted for only 54.8% of all female crime, which is considerably less than for the case of males: Zhonghua renmin gongheguo gonganbu, 'Zhongguo qingshaonian fanzui dequshi he yufang' (Trends in Chinese juvenile delinquency and its prevention), in *Zhongguo qingshaonian fanzui yanjiu nianjian 1987*, p. 44. Some reports present other figures. One source claims that the female crime rate was only 4% in 1986, but the same source also stated that the female proportion of youth delinquency was 30%—an impossible combination, since youth delinquency made up 72.5% of the total that year: see Kang Shuhua, Liu Lanpu, and Zhao Ke, *Nüxing fanzui lun* (Discussions on female crime), Lanzhou, Lanzhou daxue

chubanshe, 1988, pp. 17, 26. Xin Ming, p. 86, estimates female crime at the beginning of the 1980s to be 24% of the total crime rate, and even claims implausibly that the percentage has gone down since the 1950s and 1960s—yet another reminder about the need for caution in handling Chinese crime statistics.

59. Organisation Internationale de Police Criminelle, *Statistiques criminelles internationales 1994*, p. 28.

60. James Q. Wilson and Richard J. Herrnstein, p. 107. In the USA 9.9% of homicides and 25.6% of all theft cases were related to women according to Interpol in 1994: see Organisation Internationale de Police Criminelle, *Statistiques criminelles internationales 1994*, p. 37.

61. Cao Manzhi (ed.), p. 261.

62. For an account of the Chinese 'construction' of female crime, see Nicole Hahn Rafter, 'The social construction of crime and crime control', *Journal of Research in Crime and Delinquency*, vol. 27, no. 4, 1990, pp. 376–89.

63. The much-publicized case of the *erwang*, the 'two brothers Wang', is relevant in this respect. The two brothers killed several policemen, repeatedly escaping the law and humiliating the public security forces. The army was mobilized against them, and the two 'kings of crime' (*wang* also means king in Chinese) were finally killed in a shootout. It was vital for the authorities to regain face, and this case in particular became a catalyst for the campaign.

64. Xin Ming (ed.), pp. 136–7.

65. While some regard gangs as vestiges of a feudal past, others date the birth of gang crime as 'the second half of 1981': see Cao Manzhi (ed.), p. 278. Others locate the origins of such crime in the Cultural Revolution. On the treatment of the *touzi*, see Xu Deqi and Wu Zaide, pp. 398–406, and Zhonghua renmin gongheguo gonganbu, p. 43.

66. Jerzy Sarnecki, 'Delinquent networks in Sweden', *Journal of Quantitative Criminology*, vol. 6, no. 1, 1990, pp. 31–50, esp. pp. 47–9.

67. Zhonghua renmin gongheguo gonganbu, p. 43. An investigation in Zhejiang province found that 89.97% of all delinquents under 18 were gang members: see Kang Shuhua, 'Lun qingshaonian dilinghua de yuanyin' (On the origins of decreasing age among juvenile delinquents), in *Zhongguo qingshaonian fanzui yanjiu nianjian 1987*, p. 483. The same result (90%) was found in Qingdao: see Bai Gang and Jin Yonghua, 'Fanzui dilinghua yanjiu zongshu' (Summary of the research on the decreasing age among juvenile delinquents), in *Zhongguo qingshaonian fanzui yanjiu nianjian 1987*, p. 319. In Shenzhen 95.8% of those arrested for gang crime were juvenile delinquents. In Harbin and Xian 75.5% and 75.6% of all criminals arrested over the last few years were gang members. In Tianjin less than 9% of juveniles committed their crime alone, according to another survey: see Zheng Zhang, 'Wo guo dangqian qingshaonian weifa fanzui de qungkuang he tedian' (The present situation and characteristics of juvenile delinquency in China), *Qingshaonian fanzui yanjiu*, No. 10, 1990, p. 6.

68. Kang Shuhua, p. 483. The phenomenon of juvenile delinquents operating in groups seems universal. Western criminologists have found that the proportion of arrested juveniles who had committed their offences in groups was never less than 50% and for most property offences was well over 70%. Several such findings are quoted in James Q. Wilson and Richard J. Herrnstein, p. 292.

69. Zhou Lu, Yang Ruohe, and Hu Ruquan, *Qingshaonian fanzui zonghe zhili duicexue* (Studies in how to deal with comprehensive control of juvenile crime), Beijing, Qunzhong chubanshe, 1986, pp. 102–8.

70. In examining changes in the number of homicides immediately following publicized executions in London in the period 1858–1921, D. P. Phillips found that there were declines: the greater the publicity, the greater the decline. The decline lasted for about two weeks, followed by an increase in the weeks thereafter. The deterrent effect was temporary indeed. The same tendency has also been found in America immediately after highly publicized executions or life sentences: see D. P. Phillips, 'The deterrent effect of capital punishment: new evidence on an old controversy', *American Journal of Sociology*, no. 86, 1980, pp. 139–48. See also the debate between Steven Stack, 'Publicized execution and homicide 1950–1980', *American Sociological Review*, vol. 52, 1987, pp. 532–40, and William C. Bailey and Ruth D. Peterson, 'Murder and capital punishment: a monthly time-series analysis of execution publicity', *American Sociological Review*, Vol. 54, no. 5, 1989, pp. 722–43, where Bailey and Peterson criticize Stack's methodology and point out that the deterrent effect 'is very slight and short term, and essentially a zero-effect'. More recent campaigns in China have shown similar effects. Reports from Xuzhou municipality in Jiangsu showed that crackdowns in December 1990 and January 1991 brought crime rates down in February, but that this was followed by a new rise in the succeeding months: see *Renmin ribao*, 11 June 1991, p. 5.

71. Violent rape, which accounted for 3.5% of all crimes in 1981, increased in 1984 to 8.7%. Homicide rates stabilized in 1984, but increased steadily in 1985 and 1987 in both relative and absolute terms (*Zhongguo qingshaonian fanzui yanjiu nianjian 1987*, p. 48). By 1997 homicide had reached a high of 1.62%, while rape had declined in proportional terms to 2.52% (calculations based on *Zhongguo qingshaonian fanzui yanjiu nianjian 1987*, and *Zhongguo falü nianjian*, 1988, p. 820; 1998, p. 1244).

72. The new criminal law was published in 1997: see Quanguo renda weiyunhui fazhi gongzuo weiyuanhui xingfashi (ed.), *Zhonghua renmin gongheguo xingfa. Zhonghua renmin gongheguo xingshi susongfa* (The criminal law and the criminal procedure law of the People's Republic of China), Beijing, Falü chubanshe, 1997, p. 21.

73. Zhao Bingzhi, 'Lun wo guo xingfa dui weichengnian ren fanzui congkuan chufa de yuanze' (On the principle of treating under-aged criminals with leniency in Chinese criminal law), *Zhengzhi luntan:—Zhongguo zhengzhi daxue xuebao*, no. 1, 1989, p. 22.

74. See *SWB-FE*/2869, 17 March 1997, p. S1/11.

75. Lu Jian, p. 38; *China News Analysis*, No. 1536, 1 June 1995, p. 3. Local reports also tell of increasingly brutal crimes after 1984. In Guangxi even property crimes were dominated by violence in 1988: as much as 85.3% of all theft cases were reported to have included violence. See Mo Dong, 'Guangxi qingshaonian weifa fanzui qingkuang de diaocha' (An investigation of the situation of juvenile criminal offenders in Guangxi), *Qingshaonian tantao*, No. 1, 1990, p. 25. In 1997 'serious theft' alone stood for 27.8 per cent of all crime, up from 21.4 per cent in 1994. See *Zhongguo falü nianjian 1995*, p. 1069; 1998, p. 1244.

76. Gonganju wuju bangongshi, pp. 3, 4.

77. Ibid., p. 3.

78. Kang Shuhua, p. 483. An investigation of cities in Henan Province showed that 18.9% of all the arrested juvenile delinquents under 18 were 14 or younger: see Guo Zhao, 'Shilun huanjing yingxiang yu diling fanzui' (A tentative discussion on the influence of the environment on minors' crime), *Qingshaonian tantao*, No. 4, 1990, p. 15.

79. Bai Gang and Jin Yonghua, 'Fanzui dilinghua yanjiu zongshu' (Summary of the research on the decreasing age among juvenile delinquents), in *Zhongguo qingshaonian fanzui yanjiu nianjian 1987*, p. 316.

80. Jin Yonghua, 'Lüelun zaoqi jiaoyu zai fanzui yufang zhong de zuoyong' (A brief discussion on using early education in the prevention of crime), *Qingshaonian fanzui yanjiu*, no. 5, 1988, p. 46.

81. Official policy represents a combination of crime prevention and deterrence methods through what is called a system of 'comprehensive control' (*zonghe zhili*) of social order. The policy was summed up by Qiao Shi at the 'National Conference on Improving Social Order' in January 1991: 'We must adhere to the principle of combining "severe blows" with other measures related to a comprehensive program to improve social order, in order to prevent crimes and reduce the crime rate' (see *SWB-FE*/0976, 22 January 1991, p. B2/4).

82. The same brutalizing effect was illustrated on a wider scale by Dane Archer and Rosemary Gartner; their evidence from a cross-national sample also showed, in contrast, that abolition of capital punishment was in most cases followed by absolute *decreases* in homicide rates, not by the increases predicted in deterrence theory: see Dane Archer and Rosemary Gartner, *Violence and Crime in Cross-National Perspective*, New Haven/London, Yale University Press, 1984.

83. Interviewee no. 13, Beijing, 1991.

84. *SWB-FE*/1189, 28 September 1991, p. B2/4.

85. See Klaus Pan, 'Was Kinkel in China nicht sah', *Die Tageszeitung*, 7 November 1992, p. 9.

86. *SWB-FE*/1353, 11 April 1992, p. B2/4. On a special 'anti-drug day' in Yunnan in October 1991 as many as 88 people were sentenced to death for drug dealing in 14 different prefectures (see *SWB-FE*/1215, 29 October 1991, p. B2/1).

87. On death penalties for embezzling, see *SWB-FE*/1187, 26 September 1991, p. B2/4. One criminal, released after a prison term, was executed after he helped steal two cars from companies in Shenzhen and Guangzhou (*SWB-FE*/1193, 3 October 1991, p. B2/8). Another thief who stole cars and motorcycles in Shenzhen was also executed (*SWB-FE*/1381, 15 May 1991, p. B2/6). On grave-robbers executed in Changsha, see *SWB-FE*/1419, 29 June 1992, p. B2/4. A criminal who stole state power equipment was sentenced to death in Harbin (*SWB-FE*/1189, 28 September 1991, p. B2/4). In Xian two thieves from Shaanxi were executed after several incidents of theft averaging slightly over 1,000 yuan (or less than US$200), and for stealing 25 tons of grain (*SWB-FE*/1158, 23 August 1991, p. B2/5).

88. The 'six evils' are pornography, drugs, gambling, prostitution, abduction of women and children, and feudal superstition.

89. *Xinhua* report, quoted in *SWB-FE*/0819, 18 July 1990, p. B2/4.

90. For example, the Beijing municipal intermediate people's court executed 12 thieves following an open trial, and reports of similar occurrences have now become quite common (see *SWB-FE*/1279, 16 January 1992, p. B2/4; also *SWB-FE*/1289, 28 January 1992, p. B2/12).

91. See *SWB-FE*/2511, 17 January 1996, p. G/6; *SWB-FE*/2807, 3 January 1997, p. G/10; and *Bingguo ribao*, Hong Kong, 7 January 1997, p. A16; quoted from *SWB-FE*/2825, 24 January 1997, p. G/8.

92. *Xinhua* news report, in *SWB-FE*/2866, 13 March 1997, p. S1/6.

93. Gonganbu gonggong anquan yanjiusuo (ed.), *Ni ganjue anquan ma?* (Do you feel safe?), Beijing, Chunzhong chubanshe, 1991. pp. 46, 250 ff.

94. *SWB-FE*/0991, 8 February 1991, p. B2/6. Such public support for official violence is of course not solely a Chinese phenomenon. Surveys in the USA also show extremely widespread public support for violence committed by police—for shooting looters during riots and for shooting political protesters in general (see Dane Archer and Rosemary Gartner, p. 63–4).

95. *SWB-FE*/1215, 29 October 1991, p. B2/1. A set of regulations governing trials of juvenile delinquents require that trials of youths over 14 and below 16 years of age should not be held in public and that trials of 16- to 18-year-olds should be held in public only in special circumstances (*SWB-FE*/0971, 16 January 1991, p. B2/5).

96. Xu Qiancheng, 'Hubei Jingzhou diqu nongcun "tuliuzi" fanzui diaocha' (An investigation of crime among local thugs in Hubei's Jingzhou area), in *Zhongguo qingshaonian fanzui yanjiu nianjian 1987*, p. 157.

97. Zhu Genxiang, 'Lun shehui kongzhi yu sixiang zhengzhi gongzuo' (On social control and political/ideological work), *Hubei dangxiao xuebao*, No. 6, 1987, pp. 30–2.

98. S*WB-FE*/0928, 22 November 1990, p. B2/7.

99. In Zhang Siqi's 'Prisoners are young', the theme of repentance, the justification of the death penalty, and the 'good warden' are described in almost religious terms: 'Hou Jiancheng is sentenced to death for killing two persons. On the eve of his execution, he howls like a wolf in his cell. He cries out that he has been "wronged". Seeing this, the warden asks the guard to unlock his handcuffs and helps to bathe the prisoner, who suffers from a skin disease. The warden then excoriates Hou for killing two innocent persons. With a deep sigh, Hou admits that he deserves death. In the early morning, Hou writes a long letter of farewell to his father, a letter soaked with tears of regret. His guilty soul will probably rest in peace after death' (quoted from an article by Yu Wentao in *China Daily*, 30 July 1990, p. 5).

100. *SWB-FE*/0985, 1 February 1991, p. B2/8. A recidivist is in China defined as a person who commits crime again less than three years after release from prison.

101. In the 1950s recidivists constituted 2%–4% of the total number of criminals. In the 1960s it went up to 5%–7%, and in the early 1980s to 7%–10% (Xin Ming (ed.), p. 86). The official 'White Paper' on crime from 1992 operates with a rate of recidivism of 6%–8% (see *Renmin ribao (haiwai ban)*, 12 August 1992, p. 3, and *SWB-FE*/1458, 13 August 1992, pp. C1/2). There is reason to doubt those numbers, and criminologists in private tell of rates of recidivism of up to 60% in poor areas and in some of the new economic development zones. In one incident known to this author, such findings were not allowed to be published.

102. One might say with Roland Barthes's famous statement, 'Wrestling is not a sport, it is a spectacle', that deterrence policy and executions are not methods of punishment, they are spectacles: see Roland Barthes, *Mythologies*, London, Paladin, 1973, p. 15. The original was issued in French in 1957.

103. Between 1986 and 1988, a national research project was undertaken to determine the real crime rates in China. The authors concluded by stating that the actual crime rates were three to four times as high as in the official statistics: Dai Wendian, 'Dui wo guo xianjieduan fanzui wenti yanjiu de yixie sikao' (Some reflections on the research into current problems of crime in China), in *Zhongguo xianjieduan fanzui wenti yanjiu (di yi ji)* (Research into crime in today's China), pp. 1–11; quoted from Michael Dutton and Lee Tianfu, 'Missing the target? Policing strategies in the period of economic reform', *Crime & Delinquency*, No. 3, 1993, p. 318.

V

Theatre and Simulation

12

'Ways of Lying': Concluding Remarks on the Erosion of Control

WE have seen an exemplary society of a segmentary character embedded in a bureaucratic face-to-face structure of control. The system is intended to give optimal visibility over the population, and the exemplary norm is further meant to form the foundation of a 'building' order of transformation and improvement of the populace. From the viewpoint of the regime and its bureaucracy, this is the 'exemplary' way to plan both social order and the improvement of human quality as a means of halting the Juggernaut of modernity. However, this system also bears a price tag—that of hypocrisy. Here I am not thinking primarily of a moral hypocrisy, but rather of the structural 'ways of lying' inherent in an exemplary society that forces people to behave in prescribed ways, and to follow exemplary 'objective' standards. This 'lying' is a counterproductive consequence of exemplarity: a type of forced behaviour leading to a potential lack of predictability and a disintegration from within the control system itself. Together with these internal contradictions of the exemplary society, the monster of modernity represents the threat from outside the exemplary.

Overt obedient behaviour is highly prized in the exemplary society. We recall that the Chinese word for imitation is *mofang*, while a model is *mofan*. Overt behaviour and the imitative–repetitive Chinese cultural setting based on 'face' and modelling, however, breed another type of culture, that of simulation. *Moni* is another Chinese expression which can be translated as both 'imitation' and 'simulation', and the two processes are closely interlinked. Durkheim pointed to the destruction of morality and the 'degrading commercial air' which a moral reward system would necessarily lead to. Not only does morality suffer from the 'simulating' tendencies of overt and feigned 'exemplary behaviour'; the possibility for rational calculation and planning on a larger scale is also destroyed.

It might seem odd for me to conclude my discussion of the exemplary society with notions of 'hypocrisy' and 'lies'. Such concepts are meant not to denote moral judgements, but to serve as signals of disintegration, signals pointing to the internal contradictions of the system and the limits of exemplary control. Outwardly, the 'culture of hypocrisy', or rather the 'culture of simulation', might give the impression of a society resting on unity and stability. An order based on simulation, however, is a superficial one, and the art of ruling loses its power by leaning too heavily on the mechanisms to elicit formal overt obedience.

We see a paradox of order here, since form only manages to cover conflicts with a thin veneer of order. The prevalence and ubiquity of violence in China has been seen as a paradox, because China is also a society whose official norms value harmony and condemn conflict so thoroughly.[1] Underneath the veneer of formal obedience and apparent harmony, we discern eruptive conflicts that may suddenly break through the surface in surprisingly violent ways. The process was described by Jin Guantao in his discussions of the recurring peasant uprisings throughout Chinese history. There have also been sudden outbursts of conflict and violence during the era of the People's Republic, such as the Cultural Revolution, and the aftermath of the Beijing Spring of 1989. Waves of conflict are always close at hand in the apparent sea of tranquillity that is China's surface. The Confucian model exemplary person has been described as 'a person who stood so aloof from the conflicts of common people and was so committed to achieving harmony that he could be called a "weakling" (*ru*)'.[2] The expression was the original meaning of the word for 'Confucian'. In the same way as the socialization process here has been described as a mixture of transmission and resistance, the Confucian ideal of the obedient 'gentleman' also faces the *liumang* or hooligan of resistance summed up by Zhou Zuoren in his famous essay 'Two Demons': '[T]wo demons live within me . . . One is a gentleman, the other a *liumang* . . . I love the attitude of the gentleman and the spirit of the *liumang*.'[3] Zhou refused to abandon either of the demons, thus neatly summing up a latent tendency within Chinese culture, where apparent exemplarity suddenly bursts into explosions of disorder. We should not personify these 'demons'; rather, we should see in them the paradoxes of an exemplary society—a society producing demons of both order and disorder. In the exemplary society there lies both the promise of control and the possibilities of chaos and breakdown. What we have seen so far is an initial erosion of control.

'Culture Fever', Social Order, and the Importance of Overt Form

Starting in 1982, there was in China a major intellectual discourse, now called the 'culture fever' (*wenhua re*). Intellectuals of various shades have all debated the assets or the curses of Chinese culture as the most important hindrance or the most promising possibility for reform and modernization. Concepts like 'national cultural psychology' (*minzu wenhua xinli*) and 'national spirit' (*minzu jingshen*) or 'national character' (*minzu xing*) dominated the scene. Among the reformists in particular, much of this debate has taken the form of self-flagellation, where the flawed 'national character' and the 'deep-rooted bad habits' (*liegenxing*) of the Chinese are blamed for most of the evils in Chinese society. The improvement of 'human quality' must also be seen in this picture; the 'culturalist' approach to reform is found among the ortho-dox conservative as well as the liberal reformer, although they come to different conclusions about which 'national character' should be fos-tered. 'Civilization', in most debaters' conceptions, lies in the improve-ment of the imagined flawed cultural character of the Chinese. The Beijing University professor and historian Luo Rongqu has warned against what he terms the 'cultural determinism' (*wenhua juedinglun*) of this debate.[4] In criticizing the 'culture fever', Luo is attacking the reduc-tionistic and deterministic conception of culture prevalent in that debate —culture as feelings, moods, beliefs, values, thoughts, and morality directly explaining social development.

In line with the emphasis on 'moral science', the Chinese 'culture fever' has painted a picture of 'culture as morality'. Such 'moral cul-ture', however, is regarded as an objective entity as it is turned into a belief in the omnipotence of 'objective values' as social agents for stab-ility or change. Luo's criticism does not underscore the importance of culture, but I think it wise to look at the structural mechanisms of the exemplary society in combination with culture. By referring to 'struc-ture', I am not thinking of something opposing 'culture': I am rather looking at social structure and social organization as manifested in a segmentary China, with its work-units, family institution, party organ-ization, school system, bureaucracy, and the disciplinary structures and techniques of the exemplary society. These structures should be seen in close connection with the local and national cultural characteristics as they are manifested in concrete social practice. In current China, structure seems to be the forgotten element in the debate—perhaps because attacking structures is a risky business in the political sense.

My discussion of the origins of the disciplinary system of exemplarity is not far removed from Walder's view of the 'neo-traditional'. I advocate a non-deterministic approach to Chinese culture. While stressing here the impact of 'cultural traditions', I do not mean to imply that the exemplary control system is not yet 'modern'. The control system and its techniques are creatures of the present; much of this controlling structure is even of a fairly recent date, and cannot be termed as 'rudiments' of tradition. The notions of culture and tradition must be used carefully, and not as determinants of development or origin. The system is both 'traditional' and 'modern' at the same time. The transmission of culture and tradition is reflexive, not determinist, and there is nothing in tradition that forces the system into the pattern it forms today. I see, however, elements of the 'learning how' in Chinese culture that can explain why certain ways of control are implemented instead of others, and it is this mechanism that can be described as 'memory' or 'repetition with a difference'. Such 'memories' are not only about tradition: they also concern the adoption of effective mechanisms of control. The system cannot be described as fully 'intended' or 'rational'; there are also self-reinforcing elements in the present control system that seem scarcely amenable to the influence of individuals. Certain mechanisms underline the irrationality of the system; in the following paragraphs I will discuss these irrational aspects of the exemplary structure. Some of these mechanisms point in the direction of disintegration, as the Chinese 'way of life' turns into 'ways of lying' so as to fool the controlling system itself.

One of the cultural aspects debated in the climate of 'culture fever' is the Chinese tendency to emphasize outer form. This aspect has been associated with order and stability, but also with 'falseness' or 'hypocrisy' (*xuwei*) in the on-going debate. Yet, we should realize that the Chinese emphasis on outer form is nothing unique. All human beings, in all cultures, preserve a division between their self-identities and the 'performances' they put on in specific social contexts. But in some circumstances the individual might come to feel that the whole flow of his activities is assumed, or false.[5] In China this 'falseness' is a particularly strong trait, and it has been suggested that this 'culture of hypocrisy' can be found in Confucian ideology itself. In my opinion, this is far too simple an explanation. In fact, Confucius called the hypocrites 'thieves of virtue':

He who puts on an appearance of stern firmness, while inwardly he is weak, is like one of the small, mean people;—yea, is he not like the thief who breaks through, or climbs over, a wall? . . . Your good, careful people of the villages are the thieves of virtue.[6]

Zhu Xi, who formalized and institutionalized Confucian doctrines, also had nothing good to say about those who studied in order to beautify themselves in the eyes of beholders without changing the inner self in any way. It was not the learning pursued by men of antiquity, Zhu held; it was not true learning. He condemned the 'learning for the sake of others' prevalent in the world of learning in twelfth-century China.[7] There is thus nothing in the tradition of ideas as such that hails hypocrisy, and it can hardly be explained by reference to a flawed psychological 'national character'. On the contrary, it is a fact that Confucians believed that what kept people behaving properly was their inner sense of sincerity (*cheng*). The test of whether one was sincere was one's willingness to pay the price of practising good manners. The sincere man obeyed all the requirements of proper etiquette. Bad or crude behaviour suggested a lack of sincerity. Confucianism thus raised an issue still present in Maoism, i.e. whether the actual performance or the inner spirit of officials and the common people is more important to perfect government. Neither Confucius nor Mao Zedong believed that objective measures of behaviour should be the sole basis for evaluating the worth of people, and both stressed the importance of the inner state of mind and spirit. In contributing to the greater self of society, the need for a good 'inner self' should support the act. Mao attacks the hypocrites who parade their own 'deeds' for their own benefit, and contrasts them with the selfless sacrifice practised by Bethune—a 'true communist', compared with the first category, who 'cannot be counted as devoted communists'.[8] During both Confucian and Maoist regimes, however, the criterion for 'inner person' sincerity has been correct behaviour.[9] Such viewpoints spread the importance of overt behaviour even if they attack the hypocrite. An explanation of this phenomenon is that ideologies are weak in confrontation with bureaucracies, and that ideal intentions in the long run lose the battles with bureaucratic rationality. This is a variant on the theme of the primacy of structures over ideas.

It has been claimed that the tradition of learning from models gives rise to overtly proper behaviour, since this is presumed to be the ultimate indicator of one's own worth as well as the best guarantor of the proper behaviour of others.[10] Psychologists have pointed out that in Chinese culture individuals are remarkably able to maintain a separation of overt formalism and covert emotion. Overt compliance, however, by no means implies private acceptance, nor does it appear to engender it.[11] The stress on formalism and external compliance in school is found both in China and in Taiwan. This is what has been called the 'good boy' level of morality.[12] This 'good boy' morality is a result of the inculcation of moral standards or norms (*daode guifan de guan-shu*), Yuan Zhenhui claims, advocating the cultivation of moral feelings (*daode qinggan de peiyang*) as a modern approach to 'sincerity'.[13] As we saw from the debate on inculcation versus elicitation, however, the aim of sincerity found among advocates of elicitation methods is not necessarily the aim of the 'inculcators'. The two sides do not agree about whether sincerity or overt correct behaviour will lead to the most stable form of order. The Chinese *zuncong*—conformity—also means 'to obey' or 'to follow', and has a far more positive connotation than its English equivalent. Its two component words originally appeared separately, each meaning to follow, to obey, or to adopt. A person doing what is expected is well versed in human sentiments, is understanding, and has elegance—as distinguished from one who is socially clumsy, has no concern for others, and/or is obdurate. The problem for Chinese education has always been to make the individual live according to the accepted customs and rules of conduct, not how to enable him to rise above them.[14]

The emphasis on overt form is thus connected to social order, and can also be found in the many politeness campaigns. An article in the 'People's Daily' explicitly stresses the importance of surface behaviour as the 'outward sign of human civilization' and the 'external manifestation (*waizai biaoxian*) of human relations'. It goes on to point out the essential importance of politeness in 'protecting the normal social order'. Politeness is of course the prototype of overt behaviour, but such forms must be seen in connection with the quest for order, and should not be regarded as 'mere politeness'. Roland Barthes has discussed Oriental politeness from this perspective and asks:

Why, in the West, is politeness regarded with suspicion? Why does courtesy pass for a distance (if not an evasion, in fact) or a hypocrisy? Why is an 'informal' relation (as we so greedily say) more desirable than a coded one?[16]

Barthes's answer is that Occidental impoliteness is based on a certain mythology of the 'person'. Western man is reputed to be double, composed of a social, fictitious, false 'outside' and of a personal, authentic 'inside'; 'to be impolite is to be true' is logical enough in our Western morality, he claims.[17] Even if Barthes's observations are based on the Japanese culture, they link politeness to a collectivity that also fits China. It is bent on regulating the behaviour of the social person more than it is concerned with the individual. In this respect it would be ethnocentric for a Westerner to accuse the Chinese of 'hypocrisy'. Again, the Greco-Western roots of truth and falsity do not apply for China.

Formalism is also connected to the theme of nature versus society. Formal politeness concerns what Durkheim called the 'triumph over nature' and what Chinese criminologists called the abolishment of 'animal character'. The polite gesture is seen as something cultivated, something to counter the dangerous 'naturalness' of human beings, destroying their 'quality'.[18] Reactions against this formalism have been voiced increasingly in China. As we have seen, Chinese youth culture has become increasingly informalized. A group of Chinese researchers concludes that one characteristic of today's youth culture is that it stresses natural life without the falseness and the formal forms of politeness.[19] It is not only young people, however, who recognize the falseness and cynicism produced by the *biaoxian* approach towards social conduct in China. For instance, in a survey asking people to give their opinions about the reasons they assumed friends had in applying for party membership—an important manifestation of political correctness—4 per cent answered: 'They believe in Communism and want to make a contribution'; 59 per cent said: 'In reality they want a "party card" which they can use as capital to receive future benefits.'[20]

The hypocrisy reproduced by the stress on outward formal politeness has been ridiculed even in classical Chinese literature. The seventeenth-century author Li Ruzhen describes the country of the 'two-faced people' in his satirical book *Jinghua yuan* or 'Flowers in the mirror'—a Chinese equivalent to Swift's *Gulliver's Travels*. During a visit to the country of the 'two-faced people', Li's heroes discover that the inhabitants all wear turbans at the backs of their heads. In the words of Brother Tang,

I went up to some of them and had a nice talk. I asked them about the customs of the country, and they were all smiles and spoke to me most respectfully and in the most cordial manner. I thought they were a charming, lovely people . . . I sneaked around the back of one of these people, and stealthily lifted his turban. When I saw what was underneath, I received the shock of my life and screamed. There was an ugly face with rat's eyes, hooked nose and a furious expression on it, and when this face saw me, the bush-like eyebrows gathered in a deep frown. It opened its huge basin of a mouth, and stuck out its tongue at me. I was overpowered by an extremely vile smell which made me almost faint.[21]

The two-faced person revealed not only his other face, comments Li, but also his true self. Li's description of the 'two-faced people' is suggestive of the problem of overt politeness. However, to understand the exemplary society, we do not gain much by discussing the 'true self' of the Chinese. The 'extremely vile smell' felt by Li's Brother Tang must rather be understood in the perspective of social structure.

Identity, Social Theatre, and Social Stability

The American-based scholar Sun Longji claims that outside the 'we-group', or *zijiren*, the Chinese are totally without restrictions, and it is impossible to get people to keep order or show altruism.[22] This is why he emphasizes the 'making of a person', or *zuo ren*, as the most important way to uphold general social order. In Sun's conception, the Chinese can ignore what is going on behind the stage, always protecting their own back stage where the performance staged for the outsiders is contradicted as a matter of course.[23] Outside the we-group, order is upheld by showing tact or discretion towards the 'self-making' of others. Keeping a presentable surface is also a question of maintaining order. Politeness and decorum must not be seen as mere forms without purpose, nor as moral ends in themselves; there is more reason to regard them as instrumental acts of order maintenance, and the formalized action also gives a feeling of social security.[24] Thus, we can see that the discussion of 'hypocrisy' is closely linked to the issues of order and identity with which we started. Polite 'falseness' is a component of the very cement that holds society together.

In China we see a situationalist or 'situation-centred' form of behaviour where the situation defines an individual's action more than inner values do.[25] Chinese are not 'identical' or 'the same' (*tongyi*) in different situations; such situation-based behaviour is considered perfectly natural, and can even be seen as identity-giving behaviour.[26] Alexander and Lauderdale talk about a 'situated identity' where strict social definitions and forms of conduct make it easier to decide what to do or what to expect another person to do, on the basis of knowledge about what kind of person the other is or would want to become.[27] Situated identity might thus be seen as social maps according to which an individual can orient himself in an unknown social situation. Situated behaviour is not random behaviour; it is closely linked to the all-embracing 'standards'. In this sense, the 'standards' are not moral standards, but instrumental standards or standards of situational definition.

Chinese conformity is often a surface conformity where individuals are not subject to serious pressures for consistency between inner beliefs and outer behaviour. Individuals more often respond to the dictates of the situation than the dictates of their own selves. Such behaviour is not necessarily construed or hypocritical behaviour: rather, it is a culturally sanctioned mechanism enabling the individual to maintain a harmonious relationship with the external world. Formalistic conformity has a ceremonial function in maintaining social harmony, which was also the function of the classical *li*.[28] Even the moral rules are not absolute, but follow a hierarchy of relations in which such rules are applied or neglected. Honesty, for instance, is sacrificed to preserve the greater value of family harmony.[29] A similar reality forms the situation of the exemplary 'fixed standard' in China.

Not all commentators agree that overt situational behaviour provides stability. Zhang Zhixue, one of the many Chinese scholars who apply cybernetics, claims that moral conviction (*daode xinnian*) is the crucial force of what he terms the 'motivation system' (*dongji xitong*).[30] Moral conviction or moral belief is the spiritual pillar of people's moral behaviour, and the guiding system in everything an individual is doing. Zhang argues for the usefulness of the 'inner-directed' person rather than the person of situated identity. He claims that moral conduct has been taken as the only standard for measuring moral character. This is a one-sided approach, not effective in upholding social order. Some people behave in a morally correct manner just because of outer pressure. When the outer circumstances change, behaviour changes as well. Such behaviour lacks stability, while moral feelings and convictions stabilize a person's morality and guarantee good moral behaviour in accordance with the needs of society, even during periods of change. Improving the moral behaviour of youth is important, as social stability rests on the effectiveness of moral conviction among the younger generation.[31] Zhang attacks the dogmas of the alleged omnipotence of *biaoxian* measurement as the sole criterion of moral correctness; moral faith, he holds, is better equipped to halt the changes that follow in the wake of the modern Juggernaut.

The Chinese reality of socialization, however, is described in the maxim '*zhong zai biaoxian*', or 'the stress is on *biaoxian*'. He Xin claims that there is probably no other expression that can explain the acting character (*biaoyan xing*) and falseness of the Chinese better than that maxim. From their schooldays, Chinese are made into actors (*yanyuan*) who pretend to be good persons.[32] There is another word—*biaoyan*—that actually describes the process of *biaoxian* better, he continues. *Biaoyan* means to 'perform', to 'act', and can stand for 'performance' and 'exhibition'.[33]

Herbert Kelman has categorized socialization into three different types that correspond to the Chinese 'pyramid of morality' mentioned in Chapter 3. Socialization might be described as internalization, identification, or compliance. We have seen that a too strict and inflexible exemplary discipline seldom brings about internalization of values. It does, however, in many cases provide identification, described by Kelman as a situation providing identification with prescribed models, and 'control in a situation in which the individual is helpless, direction in a situation in which he is disoriented, or belongingness in a situation in which he is isolated'.[34] The Chinese segmentary and exemplary society does provide such belongingness, and thus provides social stability and control. The *biaoxian* and *biaoyan* reality of Chinese 'acting character' socialization, however, best fits Kelman's description of compliance:

Compliance can be said to occur when an individual accepts influence from another person or from a group because he hopes to achieve favourable reaction from the other. He may be interested in attaining certain specific rewards or in avoiding certain specific punishments that the influencing agent controls. For example, an individual may make a special effort to express only 'correct' opinions in order to gain admission into a particular group or social set . . . What the individual learns, essentially, is to say or do the expected thing in special situations, regardless of what his private beliefs may be. Opinions adopted through compliance should be expressed only when the person's behavior is observable by the influencing agent.[35]

Traditional Chinese culture was based on an 'other-ruled' (*talü*) orientation of 'doing the right thing' to become 'good' in the eyes of others, rather than doing what you find good for yourself—the so-called 'self-ruled' (*zilü*) approach to social life.[36] Zhao Tiantang elaborates the language of theatre even more than does He Xin when he describes the effects of this culture and what he terms the Chinese 'traditional personality' (*chuantong ren'ge*). A person's aim is to gain social prestige by behaving correctly, and showing correct *biaoxian*. This 'is only for other people to see' (*zuo gei ren kan*), says Zhao: it is only a staged show, in much the same way as an actor goes on stage (*xitaizi*) with theatre make-up and a mask (*mianju*).[37]

A peculiar mixture of Confucian 'sincerity' and the 'falseness' of parading can be seen from the fact that the best way 'to be seen' is in fact 'not to be seen'. Stories abound of sincere people who did good deeds without making them known to the public. In some instances these people have been 'seen' anyway, and their actions are then regarded as the highest form of moral behaviour. A political inspector in Beijing told me such a story about one of his students who had helped an ill person to hospital; he did not give his name to the hospital staff to get praised, but it was later found out anyway.[38] In terms of strategy, the best way of doing good deeds is to be 'accidentially discovered' while doing them. This theme even became part of the official propaganda when it was 'discovered' that the 'anonymous' person who had donated money to a poor school in Guangxi was Deng Xiaoping himself. The

'People's Daily' ran several articles about the Guangxi children praising and loving the 'anonymous' Deng afterwards.[39]

Zhao further discusses the traditional personality to describe the flaws of present-day China, regarding the social theatre as the 'tragic fate of feudal Confucian morality'. The Confucian ideology stresses 'harmony as the most highly valued' (*he wei gui*) aim of social life. The stress is on yielding to others, giving others face, and winning face for oneself through the performance of social theatre. Zhao explains the quest for order as something inherent in a traditional personality character that fears change and seeks stability and harmony. Stressing the stabilizing functions of this social theatre, however, he also sketches the limitations of acted social harmony. Its tragedy is that harmony is in reality confined to the small familiar circle (*shuren quan*). Harmony does not necessarily concern those outside the circle; the traditional personality does not care about strangers.[40] Social theatre applies a touch of hypocrisy when extended to the larger circle of society. The other-ruled theatre produces 'human reproductions' (*fanban ren*) only,[41] that is, reproductions of 'objective' exemplary models of the 'moral sciences'. Here we see the connection between 'other-ruled' social theatre and the characteristic Chinese imitative–repetitive culture: reproductions are always in some sense 'false'. It is important to note the two-faced character of an imitative–repetitive culture rather than look under the turban of a two-faced person. The reverse side of the coin called imitation is simulation, just as the reverse side of an imitative–repetitive culture is a culture of simulation.

Exemplarity: The Culture and Structures of Simulation

The phenomenon of social simulation of course is not specifically Chinese. While simulation has cultural and historical roots, in China we must also see it as something created by the very exemplary structure of the modern state. 'Hypocrisy' and 'falseness' are directly produced through the structures of the disciplinary techniques, among them the reward systems of the exemplary society, its evaluation procedures, and its regulation through files. Perez Zagorin has discussed the phenomenon of simulation in more general terms in his *Ways of Lying*,[42] suggesting an approach that may lead us to a conception of the 'structural lie'—a situation where one is forced to 'lie' to survive or cope with society.

Dissimulation is the subject-matter of Zagorin's book; his main question is how people in the early modern states armed themselves morally and ideologically to resist oppressive regimes, divinely appointed kings, and the Catholic Church. Religious dissimulation was found among the Reformation Protestants who, far from openly committing themselves to the new faith, dissembled their beliefs by a feigned conformity to Catholicism. 'The phenomenon of dissimulation is as widespread as the world and as old as nature itself', Zagorin maintains.[43] There is a difference between the terms 'dissimulation' and 'simulation', although the two constitute opposite sides of the same coin. In the Latin from which they derive, both have virtually identical meanings. *Dissimulatio* signified dissembling, feigning, concealing, or keeping secret; *simulatio* also meant feigning or a falsely assumed appearance, deceit, hypocrisy, pretence, or insincerity. The two words each denote deception, with the further possible connotation of lying. To be precise, Zagorin explains, we can say that 'dissimulation is pretending not to be what one actually is, whereas simulation is pretending to be what one actually is not'.[44] If we follow this definition in the example of present-day China, we see that dissimulation describes a process of hiding that is not so common as the process of parading virtue. Simulation more than dissimulation describes the practices of *biaoxian*, as individuals are rewarded for pretending to be some exemplary person they are actually not.

Simulation and dissimulation can serve as means to hide from view—a refuge from oppressive powers. Dissimulation has been central in all kinds of religious dissidence in the early modern era. The phenomenon is known as Nicodemism, and the term derives from 'Nicodemites', the name John Calvin gave the members of underground churches among Catholics whose congregations betrayed their faith by conforming outwardly to Catholic rites but in reality supported Protestantism. Its origin lay in the Gospel of John, which depicts the Pharisee Nicodemus as a believer in Christ who concealed his faith for fear of the Jews and came to hear Jesus secretly by night.[45] Historians have accordingly come to designate as Nicodemism the dissimulation used in self-protection by various sorts of Protestants and sectarians during the Reformation and Counter-Reformation. The Chinese practice of simulation is different from the dissimulation of Christian Nicodemism, but the aspect of self-protection from the visibility to rulers is common for both.

The practice of dissimulation is found not only in the Christian tradition. In China there is a long tradition of tactics and trickery; in Shi'ite teaching there is *taqiah*, which has been defined as 'the precautionary dissimulation of religious belief and practice in the face of persecution'; and in the European tradition we have the 'practical intelligence' (*metis*) of the Greeks and Machiavelli's book on the Prince, which of course is the work on dissimulation *par excellence*.[46] The practice was also described in well-known handbooks for courtiers and worldly men, such as the Spanish Jesuit Baltasar Gracián's *Manual of the Art of Discretion* from 1653. Gracián instructed his readers 'to think with the few and speak with the many' and to 'conceal your purpose' because 'the most practical wisdom consists in dissimulation'. The courts of princes were breeding grounds for such practices, and the maxim *Nescit vivere qui nescit dissimulare*—'He who does not know how to dissimulate does not know how to live'[47]—was frequently applied to courtiers. This principle might be seen as a necessary strategy for survival not only for medieval courtiers but also for survival in an exemplary society; as a counter-strategy produced by exemplarity itself.

Both the imitative–repetitive culture and the repressive character of Chinese exemplary society thus contribute to the widespread practice of simulation. Self-protection is an important element in today's China; and because of the fixity of the exemplary norm the 'ways of lying' are more or less forced into conquering spaces within what would have been the open 'zone' of norms in regimes with a less fixed norm structure. That China is currently a society out of touch with the ideals and standards prescribed for imitation strengthens the tendencies towards simulation. The phenomenon of *feng pai*—the 'style of the wind' faction—is illustrative of simulative social protection. By the time the 'Gang of Four', were purged, it had already become a rule that if the political wind happened to be blowing eastward then a person should lean eastward; if the wind happened to be blowing westward then a person should follow the westward direction. The best strategy of behaviour, in other words, was to follow the mainstream. The 'opportunist' strategy is for many the only active and 'natural' way to cope with the system.[48] The more inflexible the rules and standards of exemplarity tend to be, the more simulation the system produces.

Since the Chinese exemplary structure breeds simulation rather than dissimulation, social performance and theatre are not so much about hiding away as they are about presenting the expected exemplary surface—pretending to be what one is not. Theatre is part of the parading of norms, and is seen as part of the educative process of fostering and improving people. The play is well rehearsed, and the script is well-known to all. Even if the acts are theatre-performances, and even if everybody knows it is play-acting, the show goes on: not because people feel morally obliged to play the act, but because the acting is an important tool both for self-promotion and for 'getting things done', even in everyday life. Theatre and simulation represent flexibility within a system of inflexibility. The act of performing in terms of super-social norms is an integrated and crucial part of a career-ladder for positions and prestige in society. Rather than terming the phenomenon a 'culture of hypocrisy', we should talk of a 'culture of simulation' or even a 'structure of simulation', since the social theatre is a reaction to structures that force people to act in certain ways.

The well-organized and well-rehearsed 'campaign' or 'movement', the *yundong*, is a highly important part of this structure, occupying a very central place in the Chinese social fabric. Geremie Barmé has observed that the Chinese even organize time according to political campaigns and government-orchestrated purges. It is not uncommon to hear people periodizing their own lives according to the time-table of political campaigns—it is 'since the Cultural Revolution', 'after the Third Plenum', 'at the time of the campaign against spiritual pollution', and, since June 1989, 'after the turmoil'.[49] The classical Chinese approach of 'moral time' has found its equivalent in this modern 'campaign time'.

Political and moral campaigns, or *yundong*, form more than just a time-frame: they are the very foundations for political and public activity in China. Even during periods with a liberal political climate like the 1980s, there were constant 'civilization campaigns', politeness campaigns, public hygiene drives, and so on. It has been calculated that a major purge or a large-scale political campaign has taken place on an average every second year in the entire period of the People's Republic's forty-five-year-long history. Such campaigns again have links to larger political movements. As the then party general secretary Hu Yaobang said in 1982, 'Communism is, first and foremost, a campaign.'[50]

He Xin has divided the participants of campaigns into 'instigators' (*shandong*) and 'spectators' (*kanke*), and his categorization may help us understand the internal logic of the campaigns.[51] Some calculate that by playing the role of the instigator they can obtain personal advantage, become political activists, and perhaps attain prominent political positions. These strategists might not be so dominant in numbers, but they form a core of key participants. All sorts of behaviour might be turned into a campaign; we have even seen that 'voluntary social practices' are run as campaigns and become part of individuals' *biaoxian* score. 'Instigators' are also the most active gatherers of *biaoxian* points in the various campaigns, but there will always be many others taking part in the campaign on one level or other—these are the 'spectators'. The spectator is not necessarily a passive onlooker to campaign events, but his or her activities tend to be less calculated, and have less of a 'strategy' to them. Even if less enthusiasm has been shown for recent campaigns, it is wrong to state that enthusiasm has been absent from political campaigns as such. On the contrary, enthusiasm has led to one 'craze' after another—the history of the People's Republic is full of frenzied activities related to politics and ideology or some form of economic Great Leap Forward. For decades, Chinese society has been caught up in a cycle of repeated campaigns.

This does not mean that a campaign is an all-out theatre of strategies performed by all shades of hypocrites. Within a campaign, there may be more or less real enthusiasm and honest political and ideological belief. Such manifestations, however, cannot explain the inner logic of a campaign. Somewhat broadly, we might say that a campaign lies between craze and career. From their involvement in the exemplary reward system, instigators operating in a climate of hope or fear can set off crazes that are kept warm by the great numbers of spectators. The moral reward-system, the interlinked career-system, and the utilization of campaigns for private career purposes—these are crucial for understanding why so many campaigns end in crazes.

The *yundong* is a virtuocratic career-ladder for instigators and a battlefield of moral competition. Since morality lies in the doing, the logic for the instigator to follow is that of any effective bureaucrat. The more good deeds, the better; the faster fulfilment of the campaign's norms, the better. The instigators are the ceremonial masters of overt 'correct behaviour'—the models of super-social norms. The logic of campaigns might even explain the occurrence and existence of such super-social norms. The logic of better, bigger, more heroic, etc., is the driving force behind moral and political campaigns, and often such campaigns develop the mystique of sheer numbers. Each campaign has a 'target', and a 'quota' to be filled. It was even rumoured that during the *yanda* anti-crime campaign some work-units had to set quotas for the arrest of criminals; if there were too few or none, then, a criminal had to be produced to fill the quota.

Such rumours illustrate the logic of a campaign. There are two levels of rationality here. The effectivity of the campaign does not necessarily cause its halt or further its development; reward systems and career-ladders for activists and instigators do. By instigating a campaign that does not function you lose face, or you let your boss lose face. You need results at all cost, focusing on the 'more' and the 'better'. Instead of stopping a campaign that does not prove effective, instigators escalate it to reach their own aims. Such 'inner logic' of course may prove highly counterproductive; perhaps the most reputed example of a counterproductive campaign was the 'backyard steel furnaces' of the

Great Leap Forward in 1958, aimed at rapidly increasing the steel output of China. The steel was of inferior quality, agricultural production
was neglected, and the attempt to lift the country up—by the hair—
into industrial communism contributed instead to the famine years of
the early 1960s. The Great Leap was based on false reports from local
cadres who wanted to please their superiors and gain benefits for
themselves. Simulation is thus embedded in a structure of bureaucratic
careerism. The 'backyard furnaces', however, also represented a genuine craze of enthusiasm.

It is important to note the relation between panics and crazes. The
belief under which mobilization takes place distinguishes the two.
'Panic flows from a generalized projection of the negative possibilities
of an ambiguous situation, craze from a generalized projection of its
positive possibilities', according to Neil Smelser, who defines the
craze as a 'mobilization for action based on a positive wish-fulfillment
belief'.[52] In the Chinese *yundong*, wish-fulfilment beliefs are a driving
force in escalating the craze. Another expectation of wish fulfilment
among the few careerist instigators is the bureaucratic rational core
that gets the irrationality of the craze rolling. Political crazes tend to
develop into witch-hunts and violence, and we do not have to use the
now politically 'correct' example of the Cultural Revolution to find such
examples in China. The 'hard blows' of anti-crime campaigns serve the
same purpose, even if that connection is taboo in China 'after the Third
Plenum'—the start of the present reforms.

Even if the political campaigns are met with sinking enthusiasm and
soaring cynicism, China has nevertheless developed what Smelser
terms a 'get-rich-quick' mentality. This is described as an established
cultural belief that does not have to be created for every new speculat-
ive outburst. It is always present, and needs only to be excited by the
presence of other conditions.[53] Through the reform campaigns of 'getting rich first', set off by Deng Xiaoping in the early 1980s, such traits
have been institutionalized in China. To some extent, crazes thus seem
to have wandered from ideology to market over the last years. There
have been frequent reports on consumer fads or 'fevers' (*re*), and the
stock market turned into the scene of a hysteria when Chinese stock-
riots illustrated the point about broken wish fulfilment.[54]

A milder *ad hoc* variant of the campaign is *huodong*—various moral
and political 'activities' whereby exemplary morality is paraded in formalized and ritual ways. The Lei Feng activities often arranged in the
form of free service displays in the streets are illustrative examples. Free
haircuts, repairs, consultations, etc., are given in big moral drives; activists
put up their stalls on the street to the accompaniment of slogans, flags,

gongs, and drums. The do-gooder of such activities, however, now often runs into another problem, as illustrated by the story of Shandong soldier Zhang Yiju. He followed the call of 'learning from Lei Feng in serving the people and fostering unselfishness' by setting up a free repair stall for electrical appliances. His good deeds began backfiring on him, however, when the local traders turned on him for taking away their business. Zhang refused to close down, and the professional repairmen threatened to smash up his stall. In this instance the story ended happily, as some of the repairmen started to offer free services themselves.[55]

This problem was much discussed as a contradiction between interest and morality during the pre-1989 reform period. 'The World Economic Herald'—the voice of the new technocracy—saw the free service campaigns as an obstacle to economic progress. The debate developed into an ideological struggle between advocates of spiritual civilization and those stressing material civilization. Mao Yushi, borrowing the arguments of Adam Smith's invisible hand, claimed that doing something for the benefit of oneself was doing good for the other, and refuted the approach of 'serving the people' in doing good for others.[56] The struggle around the question of 'free service' also illustrates varying approaches towards the exemplary norm.

It is worth noting that the controversy over the exemplary do-gooder and the morality of 'serving the other' is also known from classical texts. It was again satirically described in Li Ruzhen's book 'Flowers in the mirror'. Li illustrates the consequences of taking the exemplary supersocial norm literally. In the 'Country of Virtuous Men' (*Junzi guo*) the novel's travelling heroes witness an episode in the marketplace:

When they came to the market, they overheard a soldier talking to a shopkeeper. He was holding something in his hand and saying, 'What a lovely thing this is! But you are charging too little for it! How could I deprive you of it? Please do me the favour of making it more costly, so that I may buy it with an easy conscience. If you refuse, it will only mean that you do not consider me your friend.' 'I suppose this is an example of what is meant by other people's interest mattering more than one's own,' whispered Tang Ao to Old Tuo. The shopkeeper replied, 'You know that we are not allowed to haggle here. All prices are one! I am afraid I shall have to ask you to shop elsewhere if you insist on paying more than the fixed price, for I cannot oblige.' 'You are putting me in an extremely difficult position by refusing to charge more,' said the soldier. 'I should not be kind if I agreed. How dare I take advantage of you?'[57]

The argument goes on, and the story ends with the soldier paying too high a price for goods of inferior quality and walking away. Since people on the street thought that he had not given the merchant a fair deal, he had no course but to come back, and exchange half of what he had taken for goods of the best quality.

For Mao Yushi, the question of individual interest becomes the crucial point. His question is whether society benefits when morality negates individual interest but affirms the interest of others. In Lei Feng activities the scene of free service for the masses is shown. People bring their broken items to be repaired. In the perspective of society as a whole, however, such use of labour and material resources for repairing worthless tools is a social waste, affecting both the exemplary norm and its parading. Modern society can undergo rapid economic progress only when each individual intelligently plans his or her own life. This planning is 'for oneself' (*wei le ziji*) and not 'for the other' (*wei le bieren*). The free-service phenomenon is not worth promoting even if we look at it only from the moral point of view, disregarding the economic side. The noble act of one individual does not attract people who come to learn noble acts: rather, it attracts people who wish to take advantage of the situation. Instead of describing an ethos of collectivism, he describes one of individualism; instead of describing people being improved by the parading of virtue, he describes cynical 'free riders' who take advantage of the free service offered. The communist moral concept of free service to others (*wei bieren fuwu*) is based on feudal tradition, he claims, and is not beneficial for raising social productivity.[58]

This illustrates my point about the 'learning how' of Chinese culture, as Mao develops the idea of 'campaigning' for modernity. Modern values can be promoted and 'fostered' in campaigns of human improvement, just like any other value. 'Creating income' activities on campuses were started in the mid-1980s, and even local anti-campaigns against the spirit of 'serving others' were launched by eager reformers. Activities of 'serving for payment' were promoted.[59] The basic purpose of a new morality established by commodity society is to maintain high efficiency, argues Mao Yushi, who goes on to claim that, while in the West 'private brutality' is more accepted, the privately brutal can be extremely polite in dealings with customers. China lacks such professional ethics. Lauding the exemplary deeds of service personnel does not focus on how to serve a large number of people, but only gives directions about how to 'do good' (*zuo haoshi*). Sometimes this means abandoning one's post and sacrificing the benefits of serving many to do good for one. A well organized society does not depend on individual virtuous acts by do-gooders, but instead needs a moral code of professional ethics. The 'extremely polite' but 'privately brutal' ideal of the Westerner with a high professional work-ethic describes the moral belief of the faction of Mao Yushi and the technocratic reformers. Since the whole success of commodity exchange lies in trustworthiness (*shouxin*) and not in cheating (*qizha*), this has to be developed as the standard of conduct.[60] The naive belief that social theatre, deception, and hypocrisy will disappear altogether once the market is in place is perhaps understandable from the fact that China has never experienced a fully fledged capitalist society, nor the 'deception of amiability' (*liebenswürdiger Schein*) seen in the capitalist sphere of consumption.[61] Instead, Mao Yushi makes the salesperson's overt 'extreme politeness' into an ideal of morality. Little seems to be won by his suggestions regarding the overtness and falseness in society. The lack of experience with a fully fledged capitalist society does not lessen the naivety of the reformers' dreams of a perfect capitalist society built over another exemplary dream of the 'invisible hand', while campaigning for 'service for payment' and 'creating income'.

Mao Yushi takes the consequences of the exemplary norm to its extremes. The exemplary norm might not be understood on an individual basis, however, as it does not apply for each one of us as a private ethic. Certain absolute norms and rules operate at the social level only; they are not commonly held as private norms or even as small-group norms. The Chinese exemplary norm is such a norm. In such instances moral wrongdoings have to be publicly manifested before there are sanctions. Robert Edgerton has pointed out that some norms operate on a 'now you see it, now you don't' type of basis. To restore the Bedouin family's honour, writes Edgerton, the husband or another member of the family had to kill his wife if she had sexual intercourse with anyone else than him, even if she had been raped. In many cases such family-honour homicides were reportedly actually carried out. Before such a killing for honour would occur, however, common knowledge about the case had to turn into a public challenge or complaint. Only when the breach of norms was seen by and actively disapproved of by the greater society would the punishment be enforced.[62] Similarly, the Chinese exemplary norm is a norm to be seen, a norm to be paraded, and a norm to be improved upon. If it is carried out on a private basis, people will often react with perplexity or rejection, as in the example in Chapter 5 of the disillusioned young worker who had tried to be an exemplary hero. Since I have called the exemplary norm a super-social norm, that expression must be modified by the notion of 'now you see it, now you don't'. The norm is 'social' only in another meaning than that we normally use—i.e. 'social' as contrasted to 'individual'.

Disintegration from Within and the Threat of the Juggernaut

The Chinese exemplary society is now under attack from two sides. Disintegration is developing from within the disciplinary system itself, and the threats of the modern Juggernaut are becoming increasingly acute. By using the Chinese prison regime as a picture or a microcosm of the exemplary society, I do not mean to imply that Chinese society is a prison. My emphasis here is not so much on prison as on the control system in general and on the interlinked phenomena of correction and improvement on one side and on performance, deception, and simulation on the other. The Chinese prison gives a good picture of the educative and disciplinary intentions of the exemplary society. At the same time, the inmates' use of the internal control system of the prison makes a mockery of the exemplary structure inside as well as outside the prison gate. The prison is a good example of the disintegration from within that is now facing the exemplary system.

Prison rehabilitation or redemption work is often a theatre of redemption only. It is reported that gang members in reform-through-labour institutions (*laogai*) for repeat offenders often fake active reform by adopting an outwardly correct behaviour. They either 'whitewash themselves' (*fenshi ziji*), or they 'make gestures' (*guzuo zitai*) toward the camp cadres to show that they are reverent and respectful; they always say 'yes' and answer 'OK'. When 'checking faults and crimes', these prisoners weep bitter tears of remorse, and seem to be emotionally moved. It is said to take some time to see through this sham. Before such prisoners can be unmasked, we are told, they have become small-group leaders and activists in the *laogai*. They eagerly try to be cited for meritorious service (*jigong*), and thereby get their penalty reduced. They also 'try to worm themselves into gaining the prison cadres' confidence', and exploit every opportunity to their advantage.[63]

In another example taken from a prison or reformatory of 're-education through labour' (*laodong jiaoyang*)—or *laojiao*—as many as half of the inmates are members of gangs.[64] Such criminals in China are often categorized in three levels, with the gang leader at the top. The gang's 'backbone elements' (*gugan fenzi*) constitute the intermediate level. They are regarded as the 'officers' corps' of gang crime—the tough guys in charge of gang justice in close contact with the ultimate leader. According to Chinese criminological research, these prisoners often obtain privileged positions within the internal prison reward system. They are often elected class leaders, small-group leaders, or scorekeepers (*jifenyuan*) in charge of the daily *biaoxian* routines of marking virtuous behaviour and good reform attitudes among fellow prisoners. New gangs form inside the prison walls, with the 'backbone elements' often in the position of class cadres and political activists in normal schools.[65]

Dang Guoqing studied two gangs inside one prison, led by gang leaders Yang and Huang respectively. Among the fourteen 'backbone elements' in Yang's gang, ten were leaders responsible for classes or small groups, and a further two were scorekeepers. In Huang's gang, six of the seven 'backbone elements' had class or group leader positions, while one was a scorekeeper. In the reformatory they enjoy privileges (*tequan*) for virtuous behaviour and good reform attitudes. Dang found that gang leaders and 'backbone elements' understand their wardens well and look for opportunities to influence and attain control over them. Stage 2 in the formation of a prison gang is the recruitment and development of members to consolidate the gang. The main means of control is through the exploitation of the legal power privileges given to them by the prison authorities through the moral reward system. This can mean the power to allocate light or hard prison work to their fellow inmates, to give extra work-points, to grant a day off, etc. The moral disciplinary system is thus directly used to consolidate gangs. Gang leaders also control the process of small-group evaluation through the group discussions (*pingjiang*). Those who work against them, who do not obey them, or who are not on close terms with the gang's 'backbone elements' are punished. The opponents get heavier work-loads, have to do the more dirty and tiring work, and are given fewer work-points. They are also criticized in small-group discussions for not confessing their crimes, for not reforming properly, etc. The 'backbone elements' take revenge on those who oppose them, maltreating them and blaming them for wrongdoing. Methods of blackmailing and 'paying tribute' are also found in prison, and the exemplary 'moral economy' is again utilized to this end. The backbone elements in 'virtuous' positions always recommend their fellow villagers—their traditional *tongxiang* loyalties—and their old criminal 'brothers' or *germen*.[66]

The prison culture and its theatre of redemption might stand as an extreme example of exemplary parading in the larger society. Chinese society is not a prison, however, and even if the 'carceral' or 'prison-like' is part of that society, the exemplary society defines another type of control than the 'total' and 'Orwellian'. I merely point to the fact that the moral control system as such is used for strategies of power-mongering and manipulation. The exemplary society is thus sabotaged from within. This is also a signal that the control mechanisms that used to operate so well have now atrophied considerably. It is a consequence of the exemplary disciplinary technique that it produces its own contradictions. This might be a moral problem, but first and foremost it is a problem of the structure and organization of exemplary discipline. When the system produces deception rather than virtue, then it becomes counterproductive to the very order it was meant to produce.

There is another problem brought about by the exemplary structure that is highly counterproductive for upholding the system. This concerns material civilization as much as spiritual civilization, and relates to the possibilities for planning. The 'ways of lying' are thus not only or not even primarily a question of morality. Alvin Toffler has grasped some of this problem in his description of the dilemma of the central planner. This dilemma neatly describes the problems of a bureaucracy built on an order of exemplarity:

> You can't make good decisions unless you can continually monitor their effects. For this you need people who are located on the periphery to tell you what's happening. You need information and you need it on time. You most especially need information about your errors. It is called negative feedback. But that's the last thing you, as a central planner, want to hear. You're always afraid your boss will punish you. Whole careers are built on denying error. So the people down below, not being stupid, sugar coat the information or just plain lie, or send in the truth too late, or play any number of other games with the information.[67]

If people cannot participate in making decisions and have no responsibility for them, their best strategy is to tell the leaders what they want to hear, give useless information, tell as little as possible, or simply lie. Every planner needs internal devil's advocates, critics, and 'nay-sayers' who have nothing to lose by talking back and opposing the planner. Since the alleged participatory system of evaluation is not actually a participatory system as much as it is a control system, the planner ends up in isolation, in a world of lies, illusions, and anachronisms. Whole economies can be destroyed as a result of this false information. The Great Leap Forward was partly such a career system built on yes-saying, denial of error, and the feigned 'overfulfilling' of production quotas. The overall irrationality of the bureaucratic system was linked to large-scale campaigns built on enthusiasm more than on rational calculation of possibilities.

If there was still considerable 'freshness' in the mass campaigns of the late 1950s, the situation is worse now that the formal skeleton of a mass movement is often all there is left of 'spiritual civilization'. Mass campaigns in China have become increasingly formalistic, and their stifling character no longer has the 'building' power of transforming people.

Standards are still overtly paraded, but covertly the same standards are more and more neglected. The limited effect of the moral campaigns now is that they are restrictive forces upholding order in a smaller group over a short interval of time.[68]

When simulation describes the very system of control, we also have the paradox that individuals can hide away while they are parading virtuous deeds. The system for keeping maximal visibility over the populace becomes one in which the populace can also hide away. When such visibility is no longer available, the control through outer form also collapses. What I have tried to show through the discussion of social theatre and structural 'ways of lying' is that the threat against the exemplary society comes not only from the outside, from the chaos created by the movements of the modern Juggernaut: it also comes from within. In fact, exemplary control and order produce their own non-exemplary uncontrollability and disorder. The type of disorder I am referring to is illustrated by Toffler's example above: this is the disorder of lacking predictability. Since predictability of behaviour was one of the prerequisites of control and the crucial point about habit formation, the resulting lack of predictability is a true paradox of exemplary order. This also means that a too tight grip of exemplary control produces the seeds of its own breakdown instead of describing a 'total' control. Exemplary society can be regarded as a thin veneer only, formalized and paraded to 'hold' a populace that is actually in constant movement. The disintegration from within points to the possibility that the very disciplinary system of 'moral science' and exemplarity might, in a slightly halting comparison, be seen as a Trojan horse in an alleged kingdom of order.

If the system is disintegrating from within, what about the outer threat it was meant to halt—the runaway engine of the modern Juggernaut? It is obvious that the current Chinese regime does not agree with Marx that the modern monster will make everything solid 'melt into air'. At least, Marx's image of how the modern monster should be tamed would not have included the 'moral control' prescribed in today's China. In the official Chinese conception, rather than melting into air or 'evaporating', the 'solid' character of culture and tradition must be made even more solid to curb the effects of the modern. The cohesive effects and the inertia of the traditional are building blocks of modern order. In this regard—with all the modifications we have already noted—the current Chinese regime is more Durkheimian than Marxist, more bent on cohesion than on conflict. Exemplarity is the answer to the mounting disorder of modernity. Instead of regarding the exemplary as rigid traditionalism confronting a dynamic modernity, it is seen as the most modern of all approaches. Exemplarity turns into a 'scientific' and 'objective' means to fix, bind, and order the norms and fluctuations of the modern. It is a great paradox that the cultural and historical approaches of the Chinese have turned into a scientistic monster where both culture and history have been subsumed under the regime of 'objective moral science'. One should keep the Chinese cultural and historical approach, but turn their 'exemplary objectivity' on its head in analysing the social and moral aspects of their society. This is done by showing that their very stress on 'exemplarity' and 'objectivity' is founded in their own culture and history.

With the memories of their own culture and history very much in mind, however, today's ruling elites gradually seem to be losing faith in their own exemplary control system, resorting to more open means of policing the populace. On the surface everything may look calm and stable, but underneath, eruptive resistance and potential breakdown are building up. That the exemplary society is fading and that it produces resistance, however, does not necessarily mean that it will produce its own breakdown; this is one scenario among others. The ruling elites are aware that the current 'silence' might be the lull before the storm, and that this storm might not easily be controlled by the methods of 'silent' disciplinary control described above. The image given by Jin Guantao's repeated but restorative rebellions haunts the minds of those in power.

Some party commentators envisage a scenario of great turmoil throughout all of China as a result of the development of reform over the next ten years. This will be a crucial period, they maintain, and a new and modernized version of 'ultrastability' reappears in the slogan: 'To keep the party's basic line unshakeable for 100 years, the key lies in keeping unshakeableness over the next 10 years.' For quite a long time to come, the country will experience a complicated and serious situation, and one must be prepared for problems during the coming years, according to official comments in 'China Youth'.[69] Modernization will not be smooth sailing. For a while the disadvantages of reform might even outweigh its advantages. In the process of establishing a market economy, it will be difficult to avoid social and structural disorder. This situation is bound to lead to 'mental imbalance' among a number of people. Discontent—even nationwide turmoil and unrest—may grow, social contradictions might sharpen in an acute way, and strikes and upheavals in parts of or even the whole country are likely to intensify, according to the Youth League paper, which also urges political leaders 'not to be panic-stricken'.

A well-known scenario of unrest is spreading. The traditional fear of peasant uprisings has not disappeared with modernity; on the contrary, the 'movements' of modern society have stirred up traditional peasant societies even more than before. As polarization sets in, and the peasants experience their 'double freedom' from the land and their freedom to sell their labour power, the officially '200 million jobless or potentially jobless peasants' will have to fight for survival.[70] In the rural areas the reality is described not by a large number of 'civilized villages' but rather by 'uncivilized'. Local peasant uprisings and workers' unrest have caused considerable worry among party leaders. In isolation, such uprisings and local riots might be effectively handled by the security forces. The scenario of fear is that the uprisings may get support from other groups, and 'the senior level in the central authorities . . . fears that a single spark can start a prairie fire'.[71]

Even if an order built on exemplary norms with increasingly weak social moorings may be a potential time-bomb, resistance and rebellion can be halted. The picture of armed insurrections overthrowing dynasty after dynasty is not likely to occur again, says Liu Binyan from his exile abroad. Instead, he suggests a scenario of disorder where the peasants make use of the weapons of the weak—pillaging and sabotaging the regime and the cities.[72]

Foucault has been criticized for claiming that there is no outside to power, or no place outside itself from which it can be resisted. What is left is just an all-embracing disciplinary technology. At least this is the case in Foucault's most rhetorical excesses on disciplinary society, although this assumption is gone in his later works on governmentality. In the exemplary society I see much more room for operating the system along the lines described by Michel de Certeau. In his account the panoptic script is no longer all-embracing and the hero of the story is no longer one of exemplarity. The latter was described as a dead hero, and this hero is dead in more than the literal sense. The hero of exemplary modernity also does not strike us as particularly healthy. Instead, according to de Certeau, there is an anonymous hero who is very much alive: 'This anonymous hero is very ancient. He is the murmuring voice of societies.'[73] The practices of everyday life open up numerous spaces of resistance, where subordinates 'consume', 'use' or 'make do' with the rules and regulations of the strong. Using Indian resistance against the Spanish colonizers as his example, de Certeau goes on to explain that the Indians 'made of the rituals, representations, and laws imposed on them something quite different from what their conquerors had in mind . . . [T]heir use of the dominant social order deflected its power . . . '[74] This line of thought fits in with the order of exemplary society as well. It has been commented, however, that de Certeau focuses on atomistic sources of resistance only. In his account we see individuals stripped of all weapons and fortifications except for

guile, ruse, simulation and deception. According to Tony Bennett, de
Certeau 'locates such practices in the domain of the ineffable' only;
those who lack power and 'are obliged to act constantly in the space
of the other'.[75] Bennett's observation is accurate, and de Certeau even
defines a tactic as something 'determined by the *absence of power*'.[76] He
is wrong not least because there are also the tactics and grand strategies of the powerful. Tactics are met by tactics, and strategies by strategies. The power of strategy has always been part of Chinese elite thinking
about government.[77]

Even if it were true that tactics were always based on the lack of power,
it would not mean that such tactics are powerless in their effects. The
sum total of everyday resistance represents a very important basis for
the waning of disciplinary and exemplary control. A system out of touch
with fundamental social norms will eventually break down because of
its lack of predictability and its ossified super-social character. The ways
of lying do represent important sources of everyday counter-power, and
often these ways of resistance represent the very breeding ground for
change. The ways of lying should not be regarded as mere atomistic
sources of resistance, but as reflections of the disorder and disintegration from within that characterizes the exemplary forms of discipline.
This type of resistance might have a 'slumbering' or 'murmuring'
character over long periods, but is also pregnant with the possibilities
of louder voices and sudden change. The experiences from Eastern
Europe and the breakdown of the Soviet Union are paid much heed
to in China today. We do not need to agree entirely with Solinger's
view of a civil society based on the new floating population, but there
is something about modern fluidity and the possibilities of movement
that adds to the argument of a 'murmuring background' ripe with
change.[78] More powerful groups, however, play by the same script, and
it is not only the weak or 'ineffable' who utilize the Chinese ways of
lying. Such techniques find their ways even into the apparatuses of power
and discipline as a hidden Nicodemus waiting for his day.

One should still listen to the warnings about the atomistic character
of simulation and deception. Resistance is an ambiguous category, and
the subordinate has many grounds for ambivalence about resisting the
relation to the dominant. In evaluation there are rewards, in the exemplary there are careers, and in the super-social there are possibilities
and power. As I have tried to point out, even the resister follows the
exemplary script during his strategies of deception and ways of lying,
and such lying is not utilized against the powerful only. There is no
reason to make romantic myths about resistance as such. Christine Pelzer
White has urged researchers to add the concept of 'collaboration' to

balance our views of resistance, and Sherry Ortner advises us to 'reveal the ambivalences and ambiguities of resistance itself'.[79]

This is precisely where the Foucauldian analysis so thoroughly fails. It does not understand the possibilities of resistance to control and opposition to power that lies in simulation, deception, and the everyday 'ways of lying'. The very same system that produces discipline, control, and 'docile bodies' simultaneously produces its own resistance as the 'bodies' resist docility through deception. The exemplary norm is pregnant with its own resistance, and 'lying' or 'operating' is the everyday practice of that exemplary norm; it has become a 'weapon of the weak'.[80]

In some ways, the Chinese system is also highly effective in bringing about order overall. The 'dangerous' fragmentation represented by the modern can be halted by another, 'ordering', fragmentation represented by the structures of a segmentary society. An observation by Walder points in this direction and underlines Ortner's advice. Noting that factionalism and private vendettas were the immediately striking features of worker involvement in the Cultural Revolution, Walder concludes:

It is highly unusual in industrial societies for the targets of workers' movements to be personalized to this extent. Collective demands are usually made to institutions and groups. Class hatreds are generalized animosities, but the hatreds of these workers were vented directly at specific individuals. In a very real sense, the ritualistic self-criticisms and personal humiliations endured by these officials were simply a mirror image of the self-effacement workers ritually performed in front of leaders in factory-meetings. This personalization of conflict was a direct outgrowth of the system of officially-organized patronage that personalized social control and rewards to an extent unusual in other industrial settings.[81]

Even if the exemplary order is in many ways an inflexible order, the simulation strategies fostered by the system provide flexibility within inflexibility. Private solutions to problems might be sought without the mobilization of collective support. Instead of the scenario of breakdown, we witness a scenario of overall order against a background of local conflicts. The system might prove effective not in keeping exemplary order, but in preventing collective action, easily wiping out local disorder wherever it occurs.

My task, however, has not been to offer scenarios of possible futures for China. Here I have mainly sketched the fabric of an exemplary society with all its confusing twists and turns, internal contradictions, and disciplinary techniques of control. In the description of how the Chinese regime goes about controlling the modern monster, it is important to note that the disciplinary control system has a Juggernaut momentum of its own.

Notes to Chapter 12

1. Jonathan N. Lipman and Stevan Harrell (eds.), *Violence in China: Essays in Culture and Counterculture*, Syracuse, NY, State University of New York Press, 1990.
2. Richard Madsen, 'The politics of revenge in rural China during the Cultural Revolution', in Jonathan N. Lipman and Stevan Harrell (eds.), p. 182.
3. Zhou Zuoren, 'Liangge gui' (Two demons), in *Zhou Zuoren zaoqi sanwen xuan* (Selected early prose of Zhou Zuoren), Shanghai, Shanghai wenyi chubanshe, 1984, pp. 98–9; trans. from Geremie Barmé, 'Wang Shuo and Liumang ("Hooligan") Culture', *Australian Journal of Chinese Affairs*, No. 28, July 1992, p. 29.
4. For Luo Rongqu's criticism, see *Renmin ribao*, 26 February 1989, p. 6.
5. See Anthony Giddens, *Modernity and Self-Identity: Self and Society in the Late Modern Age*, Cambridge, Polity Press, 1991, p. 58.
6. *Confucian analects (Lunyu)*, Bk XVII, ch. XII, in James Legge (trans.), *The Four Books (Sishu)* Taipei, Culture Book Co./Wenhua tushu gongsi, 1983, p. 324.
7. Chu Hsi (Zhu Xi), *Learning to Be a Sage: Selections from the Conversations of Master Chu*, trans. Daniel K. Gardner, Berkeley, University of California Press, 1990, p. 14.
8. Mao Tsetung (Mao Zedong), 'In memory of Norman Bethune', *Selected Works of Mao Tsetung*, Vol. 2, Beijing, Foreign Languages Press, 1965, p. 338.
9. Lucian W. Pye, *China: An Introduction*, 3rd edn., Boston, Little, Brown, 1984, p. 42.
10. Richard W. Wilson, *The Moral State: A Study of the Political Socialization of Chinese and American Children*, New York, Free Press, 1974, p. 48.
11. Paul J. Hiniker, 'Chinese reactions to forced compliance: dissonance reduction or national character', *Journal of Social Psychology*, Vol. 77, 1969, pp. 158, 175.
12. Chen Yinghao is a Taiwanese scholar quoted by Jeffrey F. Meyer, 'A subtle and silent transformation: moral education in Taiwan and the People's Republic of China', in William Cummings, S. Gopinathan, and Yasumasa Tomoda, *The Revival of Values: Education in Asia and the West*, Oxford, Pergamon Press, 1988, pp. 116–18.
13. Yuan Zhenhui, 'Lun jiaoyu zhong lixing yinsu yu fei lixing yinsu de hubu guanxi', *Zhongguo shehui kexue*, No. 2, 1987, p. 150; trans. as 'On the complementary relationship between rational and irrational factors in education', *Social Sciences in China*, No. 1, 1988, pp. 185–99.
14. Francis L. K. Hsu, *Americans and Chinese*, New York, Doubleday/Natural History Press, 1972, pp. 127–8.
15. Ren Zhongping, 'Lunjiang limao' (On paying attention to politeness) *Renmin ribao*, 25 January 1998, pp. 1, 3. In moral education, politeness is one of the 'five stresses' (*wu jiang*) together with decency, hygiene, order, and morality. See *Sixiang xiuyang xiao cidian* (Small dictionary of ideological cultivation), Shanghai, Shanghai cishu chubanshe, 1984, p. 36.
16. Roland Barthes, *Empire of Signs*, New York, Hill & Wang, 1982, p. 63.
17. Ibid., p. 63.
18. Zhao Zixiang, Li Shuliang, and Wang Zheng, 'Qingnian wenhua yu shehui bianqian' (Youth culture and social change), *Shehui kexue zhanxian*, No. 4, 1988, p. 112.

19. Ibid.
20. Stanley Rosen, 'Political education and student response: some background factors behind the 1989 Beijing demonstrations', *Issues & Studies*, No. 10, 1989, p. 19. Here, applying for party membership has become a formalized ritual, an input of good *biaoxian*—quite the contrary of the ideal promoted in Mao's article on Bethune.
21. Li Ruzhen, *Jinghua yuan* (Flowers in the mirror), Vol. 1, Beijing, Renmin wenxue chubanshe, 1986; quotations in English taken from Li Ju-chen (Li Ruzhen), *Flowers in the Mirror*, trans. Lin Tai-yi, London, Peter Owen, 1965, p. 89. The turban is of course a symbol of 'otherness' and the 'barbarian', but Li's book is nevertheless a parody of Chinese society.
22. Sun Longji, *Zhongguo wenhua de shenceng jiegou* (The deep structure of Chinese society), Hong Kong, Jixian she, 1983, p. 90.
23. Ibid., pp. 157, 160.
24. See the discussion on politeness and 'decorum', 'tact', and 'discretion' in Erving Goffman, *The Presentation of Self in Everyday Life*, Harmondsworth, Penguin, 1969, pp. 110, 223 ff.
25. Francis K. Hsu regards the Chinese as 'situation-centred' in his analysis. From a sociological standpoint, not only Chinese but also Japanese culture can also be considered as manifesting a situational ethic as opposed to the more universal ethic built around moral absolutes found in Western Christian thought. See George DeVos, 'The relation of guilt towards parents to achievement and arranged marriage among Japanese', *Psychiatry*, Vol. 23, No. 2, 1960, p. 288.
26. Interviewee no. 10, Beijing, 1991.
27. C. Norman Alexander Jr and Pat Lauderdale, 'Situated identities and social influence', *Sociometry*, Vol. 40, No. 3, 1977, p. 225.
28. Ambrose Y. C. King and Michael H. Bond, 'The Confucian paradigm of man: a sociological view', in Wen-Shing Tseng and David Y. H. Wu, *Chinese Culture and Mental Health*, London, Academic Press, 1985, p. 35.
29. Eng-kung Yeh, 'The Chinese mind and human freedom', *International Journal of Social Psychiatry*, Vol. 18, No. 2, 1972, p. 134. The classical example of the Chinese situational value hierarchy is the story of Confucius's attitude towards the stealing of sheep. The duke of Sheh informed Confucius, saying, 'Among us there are those who may be styled upright in their conduct. If their fathers have stolen a sheep, they will bear witness to the fact.' Confucius said, 'Among us, in our part of the country, those who are upright are different from this. The father conceals the misconduct of the son, and the son conceals the misconduct of the father. Uprightness is to be found in this.' Legge remarks that the expression used by Confucius does not absolutely affirm that this is an upright way of acting, but implies that this is a better principle than the conduct described by the duke of Sheh. See *Confucian analects* (*Lunyu*), bk XIII, ch. XVIII, 1, 2, in James Legge (trans.), p. 270.
30. Zhang Zhixue, 'Tan pinde xinli de jiegou' (On the structure of moral character psychology), *Jiaoyu Yanjiu*, No. 7, 1990, p. 39.
31. Ibid., pp. 39, 41.
32. He Xin, 'Gudu yu tiaozhan: Zai hei shehui de bianyuan qu' (Loneliness and challenge: on the edge of the black society), *Zixue*, No. 3, 1989, p. 17.
33. Ibid., p. 16.
34. Herbert E. Kelman, 'Processes of opinion change', *Public Opinion Quarterly*, Vol. 25, No. 1, 1961, p. 63.
35. Ibid., pp. 62–3.

36. Zhao Tiantang, 'Zhongguo chuantong renge de xiaoji yinsu ji qi chengyin' (The negative fators of the Chinese traditional personality and their causes), *Shehui*, No. 2, 1991, p. 9.

37. Ibid.

38. Interviewee no. 2, Beijing, 1991.

39. *Renmin ribao (haiwai ban)*, 26 November 1992, p. 3, and 3 December 1992, p. 1.

40. Zhao Tiantang, p. 9.

41. Ibid., p. 10.

42. Perez Zagorin, *Ways of Lying*, Cambridge, Mass., Harvard University Press, 1990.

43. Many plants and flowers use deceptions of colour or odour to lure the insects that pollinate them. An especially well-known instance of deception is the brood-parasitism of the cuckoo (Perez Zagorin, p. 1).

44. Ibid., p. 3.

45. See John 3: 1–2: 'There was a man of the Pharisees, named Nicodemus, a ruler of the Jews: The same came to Jesus by night, and said unto him, Rabbi, we know that thou art a teacher come from God: for no man can do these miracles that thou doest, except God be with him.'

46. On *taqiah*, see John L. Esposito (ed.), *The Oxford Encyclopedia of the Modern Islamic World*, Vol. 4, New York/Oxford, Oxford University Press, 1995, p. 186. The best known of the Chinese texts is of course Sunzi's (Sun Tzu), *The Art of War*, Oxford, Clarendon Press, 1963. For the European example, see Niccoló Machiavelli, *The Prince*, Toronto, Bantam Books, 1981. On the Greek strategies, see Marcel Détienne and Jean Pierre Vernant, *Les Ruses de l'intelligence: la mètis des Grecs* (The tricks of intelligence: the *metis* of the Greeks), Paris, Flammarion, 1974.

47. Here quoted from Perez Zagorin, p. 6.

48. See Godwin C. Chu, 'The emergence of the new Chinese culture', in Wen-Shing Tseng and David Y. H. Wu (eds.), *Chinese Culture and Mental Health*, London, Academic Press, 1985, pp. 20–1.

49. Geremie Barmé, 'Travelling heavy: the intellectual baggage of the Chinese diaspora', *Problems of Communism*, Nos. 1–2, 1991, p. 104.

50. Quoted from ibid., p. 104.

51. He Xin, *Dongfang de fuxing* (The revival of the East), Harbin, Heilongjiang jiaoyu chubanshe/Heilongjiang renmin chubanshe, 1991, pp. 285–6. Barmé, ibid., p. 106, quotes He's first approach towards explaining the campaign mentality in He Xin, 'Zhongguo dangdai beiwanglu: wode kunhuo yu youlü' (A contemporary Chinese cultural aide-memoire: my perplexities and concerns), *Jingjixue zhoubao*, 8 January 1989, p. 5.

52. Neil J. Smelser, *Theory of Collective Behavior*, New York, Free Press of Glencoe, 1963, p. 171.

53. Ibid., p. 173.

54. The so-called 'Shenzhen would-be investors riot' at the Shenzhen new economic zone's stock market took place in August 1992. During this incident, about 1.2 m people had lined up to buy share application forms, but only 10% were allowed to buy them following a lottery. Pandemonium broke loose as there proved to be an insufficient number of forms for the long lines of waiting would-be investors. The press report after the riots laconically commented: 'No deaths were reported, but witnesses saw a number of injuries' (*China Daily*, 12 August 1992, p. 2).

55. *China Daily*, 29 October 1990, p. 3.

56. Mao Yushi, 'Daodeguan: dui geren liyi cong fouding dao kending' (Moral concepts: from negation to affirmation of individual interest), *Shijie jingji daobao*, 29 February 1988, p. 7; summary trans. in *JPRS-CAR*-88-024, 23 May 1988, pp. 36–8.

57. Li Ruzhen (in Chinese), pp. 65–6; Li Ju-chen (in English), p. 58.

58. Mao Yushi attacks collectivism as cultural tradition rather than as communist ideology. This makes the task easier, because he can then refer to the positive task of rooting out the 'feudal dross' of tradition—a typical strategy of 'indirect attack' well known in China. Mao states that in the Confucian tradition, phenomena such as filial piety (*xiaoti*), overmodesty (*qianrang*), respect for elders (*zunzhang*), and selflessness (*keji*) all originate from *ren*—benevolence. To maintain control in society, the feudal ruling class built loyalty and patriotism on to this *ren*-centred foundation, yielding a complete traditional system of moral concepts based on *li*. When society developed into a commodity society, the complexity of human relationships expanded considerably. Mao describes a process whereby the traditional mechanical solidarity is taken over by a modern, organic solidarity. With the feudal moral concepts no longer adequate, a new set of moral concepts has to be developed in accordance with developments in production. We should organize the formation of modern concepts to benefit growth and production, he concludes (Mao Yushi, p. 7).

59. See *Inside China Mainland*, No. 133, January 1990, p. 26.

60. Mao Yushi, pp. 36–8.

61. See Klaus Ottomeyer, *Soziales Verhalten und Ökonomie im Kapitalismus* (Social behaviour and economy in capitalism), Giessen, Focus Verlag, 1976, p. 90 ff.

62. Robert B. Edgerton, *Rules, Exceptions, and Social Order*, Berkeley, University of California Press, 1985, p. 160.

63. Zhu Xiaomin, 'Shilun laogai fan zhong de fanzui tuanhuo' (Tentative discussion on criminal gangs among inmates in reform through labour institution), in *Zhongguo qingshaonian fanzui yanjiu nianjian 1987* (Yearbook on Chinese juvenile delinquency studies), Beijing, Chunqiu chubanshe, 1988, p. 411.

64. Dang Guoqing, 'Laojiao renyuan jiehuo fan gaizao wenti de pouxi' (Analysis of the problems of ganging up and going against reform among the inmates of re-education-through-labour institutions), in *Zhongguo qingshaonian fanzui yanjiu nianjian*, p. 406.

65. Ibid., p. 407.

66. Ibid., pp. 408–9.

67. Alvin Toffler, *Previews and Premises*, London, Pan Books, 1984, p. 97.

68. Sun Longji, pp. 90–1.

69. Liu Defu, '100 nian bu dongyao, guanjian shi 10 nian bu dongyao' (The key to 100 years of unshakeableness lies in the unshakeableness of the next ten years), *Zhongguo qingnian*, No. 1, 1993, pp. 15–17; see also *SWB-FE*/1668, 21 April 1993, p. B2/1.

70. This figure was mentioned by the Chinese Minister of Labour, Li Boyong, who added that urban labour 'waiting for employment' will reach 68 m in the next decade: see *China Focus*, Vol. 2, No. 1, 1994, p. 7.

71. In June 1993, 10,000 secondary school students from Chengdu voiced their support for peasants from Renshou county in Sichuan province who were rioting against the authorities because of the economic burdens levied on them. 'This peasant movement bears the danger of triggering a student movement', commented one observer. Armed forces were finally sent in against the peasants to quell the riots. See Jung Sheng, 'Great impact of agricultural issue: tracking the incident of peasant riots in Sichuan's Renshou county', *Xin Bao*, 10 June 1993; based on *Zhongguo xiaofeizhe bao* and quoted from *SWB-FE*/1713, 12 June 1993, pp. B2/1–4. Workers' unrest is increasing as millions of workers are being laid off in the state sector. In Jianxi in 1998 laid-off workers blocked trains, holding banners reading

'we want food and work'. Armed police were sent to suppress the workers' demonstrations. See *SWB-FE*/3244, 4 June 1998, p. G/6.

72. Liu Binyan, 'Another "Rural Encirclement of the Cities" campaign?', *China Focus*, No. 1, 1994, p. 4.

73. Michel de Certeau, *The Practice of Everyday Life*, p. v.

74. Ibid., p. xiii.

75. See Tony Bennett, *Culture: A Reformer's Science*, London, Sage 1998, pp. 175, 179. For a further discussion on de Certeau and Foucault, see Jeremy Ahearne, *Michel de Certeau: Interpretation and its Other*, Cambridge, Polity Press, 1995.

76. Michel de Certeau, *The Practice of Everyday Life*, p. 38.

77. Johnston in his book on the strategies of power does not talk about counter-strategies against everyday ways of lying, but discusses the grand strategies and strategic cultures of the powerful. He does so in the plural, pointing out that in Chinese history there have been multiple strategic cultures and disjunctures between strategic culture and strategic choice. There is also no clear cultural continuity as normally assumed from Sunzi to Mao Zedong, he claims. See Alastair Iain Johnston, *Cultural Realism. Strategic Culture and Grand Strategy in Chinese History*, Princeton, New Jersey, Princeton University Press, 1995.

78. Dorothy J. Solinger, *China's Transients and the State: A Form of Civil Society?*

79. Sherry B. Ortner, 'Resistance and the Problem of Ethnographic Refusal', *Comparative Studies in Society and History*, No. 1, 1995, p. 190, and Christine Pelzer White, 'Everyday Reistance, Socialist Revolution and Rural Development: The Vietnamese Case', *Journal of Peasant Studies*, No. 2, 1986, p. 56. This might also be used as a warning against a weakness in de Certeau's scholarship; the fact that his description is thin in terms of sociological, cultural and historical description.

80. This process is in many ways similar to the everyday forms of resistance described by Scott as weapons of the weak or relatively powerless, e.g. foot-dragging, dissimulation, desertion, false compliance, etc.; see James C. Scott, *Weapons of the Weak: Everyday Forms of Peasant Resistance*, New Haven, Yale University Press, 1985. I have already mentioned Michel de Certeau, *The Practice of Everyday Life*, Berkeley, University of California Press, 1988, whose 'ways of using' and 'ways of operating' describe similar processes.

81. Andrew G. Walder, 'Communist social structure and workers' politics in China', in Victor C. Falkenheim (ed.), *Citizens and Groups in Contemporary China*, Michigan Monographs in Chinese Studies, Vol. 56, Ann Arbor, University of Michigan Press, 1987, p. 84.

Bibliography

Abbot, Kenneth A., *Harmony and Individualism*, Taipei, Orient Cultural Service, 1970.

Ahearne, Jeremy, *Michel de Certeau: Interpretation and its Other*, Cambridge, Polity Press, 1995.

Alabaster, Ernest, *Notes and Commentaries on Chinese Criminal Law*, Taipei, Changwen Publishing Company, 1968, pp. 57–8.

Alchian, Armen, 'Uncertainty, Evolution and Economic Theory', *Journal of Political Economy*, Vol. 58, No. 1, 1950, pp. 211–21.

Alexander, C. Norman Jr and Pat Lauderdale, 'Situated Identities and Social Influence', *Sociometry*, Vol. 40, No. 3, 1977, pp. 225–33.

Allinson, Robert E., 'An Overview of the Chinese Mind', in Robert E. Allinson (ed.), *Understanding the Chinese Mind: The Philosophical Roots*, Hong Kong, Oxford University Press, 1989, pp. 1–25.

Anagnost, Ann, 'Socialist Ethics and the Legal System', in Jeffrey N. Wasserstrom and Elizabeth J. Perry (eds.), *Popular Protest and Political Culture in Modern China: Learning from 1989*, Boulder, Colo., Westview Press, 1992, pp. 177–205.

Andors, Phyllis, 'Women and Work in Shenzhen', *Bulletin of Concerned Asian Scholars*, Vol. 20, No. 3, 1988, pp. 22–41.

Archer, Dane and Rosemary Gartner, *Violence and Crime in Cross-National Perspective*, New Haven/London, Yale University Press, 1984.

Armer, Michael and Larry Isaac, 'Determinants and Behavioral Consequences of Psychological Modernity: Empirical Evidence from Costa Rica', *American Sociological Review*, Vol. 43, No. 3, 1978, pp. 316–34.

Aron, Raymond, *Main Currents in Sociological Thought*, Vol. 2: *Durkheim, Pareto, Weber*, Harmondsworth, Penguin, 1968.

Bai Gang and Jin Yonghua, 'Fanzui dilinghua yanjiu zongshu' (Summary of the research on the decreasing age among juvenile delinquents), in *Zhongguo qingshaonian fanzui yanjiu nianjian 1987*, Beijing, Chunqiu chubanshe, 1988, pp. 316–22.

Bai Yuntao, *Dangdai Zhongguo qingnian suzhi lun* (Discussions on the quality of contemporary Chinese youth), Shenyang, Liaoning renmin chubanshe, 1987.

Bailey, William C. and Ruth D. Peterson, 'Murder and Capital Punishment: A Monthly Time-series Analysis of Execution Publicity', *American Sociological Review*, Vol. 54, No. 5, 1989, pp. 722–43.

Bakken, Børge, 'Backwards Reform in Chinese Education', *Australian Journal of Chinese Affairs*, No. 19/20, January 1988, pp. 127–63.

—— 'Kinesisk sosiologi i dag: tiåring med tradisjoner' (Chinese sociology today: ten years after its reintroduction), *Tidsskrift for samfunnsforskning*, Vol. 30, No. 4, 1989, pp. 361–74, with a summary in English.

—— *Kunnskap og moral: Om utdanningsreformer i dagens Kina* (Knowledge and morality: on educational reforms in today's China), Report No. 1, Department of Sociology, University of Oslo, 1989.

—— ' "Never for the First Time": "Premature Love" and Social Control in Today's China', *China Information*, Vol. 7, No. 3, pp. 9–26.

—— 'Crime, Juvenile Delinquency and Deterrence Policy in China', *Australian Journal of Chinese Affairs*, No. 30, July 1993, pp. 29–58.

—— 'Prejudice and Danger: the Only Child in China', *Childhood*, No. 1, 1993, pp. 46–61.

—— (ed.), 'Juvenile Crime during the Reforms', *Chinese Sociology and Anthropology*, No. 3, Spring 1995.

—— (ed.), *Migration in China*, NIAS Report No. 31, Copenhagen, NIAS, 1998.

Bandura, Albert and Richard H. Walters, *Social Learning and Personality Development*, New York, Holt, Rinehart & Winston, 1963.

Barmé, Geremie, 'Travelling Heavy: The Intellectual Baggage of the Chinese Diaspora', *Problems of Communism*, Nos. 1–2, 1991, pp. 94–114.

—— 'Wang Shuo and Liumang ("Hooligan") Culture', *Australian Journal of Chinese Affairs*, No. 28, July 1992, pp. 23–64.

—— and Linda Jaivin, *New Ghosts, Old Dreams. Chinese Rebel Voices*, New York, Times Books/Random House, 1992.

—— *Shades of Mao: The Posthumous Cult of the Great Leader*, Armonk, NY, M. E. Sharpe, 1996.

Baron, Rueben M., 'Social Reinforcement Effects as a Function of Social Reinforcement History', *Psychological Review*, Vol. 73, No. 6, 1966, pp. 527–39.

Barthes, Roland, *Mythologies*, trans. Annette Lavers, London, Paladin, 1973.

—— *Empire of Signs*, trans. Richard Howard, New York, Hill & Wang, 1982.

Basedow, Johann P., *Vorstellung an Menschenfreunde und vermögende Männer über Schulen und ihren Einfluß in die öffentliche Wohlfarth*, Hamburg, 1768.

Baudelaire, Charles, *The Painter of Modern Life and other Essays*, trans. and ed. Jonathan Mayne, London, Phaidon Press, 1964.

Baum, Richard, *Scientism and Bureaucratism in Chinese Thought: Cultural Limits of the Four Modernizations*, Lund University Research Policy Studies Discussion Paper No. 145, Lund, Lund University, Research Policy Institute, 1981.

Beck, Ulrich, 'How Modern is Modern Society?' *Theory, Culture and Society*, Vol. 9, 1992, pp. 163–9.

—— *Risikogesellschaft: Auf dem Weg in eine andere Moderne*, Frankfurt am Main, Suhrkamp, 1986; published in English as *Risk Society: Towards a New Modernity*, trans. Mark Ritter, London, Sage, 1992.

Beijing shida er fuzhong (Beijing Normal University No. 2 Attached Secondary School), 'Xuesheng xingwei guifan kaohe banfa: shixing cao'an' (Measures of examining student norms and behaviour: preliminary plan), Beijing, internal school material dated 19 March 1989.

Benkan Pinglunyuan (Commentator's article), 'Lun guanshu' (On inculcation), *Qiushi*, No. 21, 1990, pp. 2–6.

Bennett, Tony, *Culture: A Reformer's Science*, London, Sage, 1998.

Berger, Peter L., 'On the Obsolesence of the Concept of Honor', *Archives Européennes de Sociologie/European Journal of Sociology*, No. 2, 1970, pp. 339–47.

—— Brigitte Berger and Hansfried Kellner, *The Homeless Mind*, Harmondsworth, Penguin Books, 1973.

—— *Facing up to Modernity*, New York, Basic Books, 1977.

—— 'An East Asian Development Model?' in Peter L. Berger and Hsin-Huang Michael Hsiao (eds.), *In Search of an East Asian Development Model*, New Brunswick, NJ, Transaction Books, 1988, pp. 3–12.

—— and Hsin-Huang Michael Hsiao (eds.), *In Search of an East Asian Development Model*, New Brunswick, NJ, Transaction Books, 1988.

Berman, Marshall, *All that is Solid Melts into Air: The Experience of Modernity*, London, Verso, 1983.

Blau, Peter M., *The Dynamics of Bureaucracy: A Study of Interpersonal Relationships in Two Government Agencies*, rev. edn., Chicago, University of Chicago Press, 1973.

Blecher, Marc. J. and Gordon White, *Micropolitics in Contemporary China: A Technical Unit during and after the Cultural Revolution*, London, Macmillan, 1980.

Bloch, Herbert A. and Arthur Niederhoffer, *The Gang: A Study in Adolescent Behavior*, New York, Philosophical Library, 1958.

Blumenthal, Eileen Polley, *Models in Chinese Moral Education: Perspectives from Children's Books*, Ph.D. dissertation, University of Michigan, 1976.

Blumstein, Alfred and Jacqueline Cohen, 'Estimation of Individual Crime Rates from Arrest Records', *Journal of Criminal Law and Criminology*, No. 70, 1979, pp. 561–85.

Bo Yin and He Xiangqing, 'Zaolian: xiaoyuan "malasong"' (Early love, the 'marathon' of the schoolyard), *Qingnian Shijie*, No. 9, 1989, p. 34.

Boas, Franz (ed.), *General Anthropology*, Boston, Heath, 1938.

Bond, Michael Harris (ed.), *The Psychology of the Chinese People*, Hong Kong, Oxford University Press, 1986.

Bourdieu, Pierre, *Outline of a Theory of Practice*, trans. Richard Nice, Cambridge, Cambridge University Press, 1977.

—— *In Other Words: Essays towards a Reflexive Sociology*, trans. Matthew Adamson, Cambridge, Polity Press, 1994.

Boyer, Paul, *Urban Masses and Moral Order in America, 1820–1920*, Cambridge, Mass.: Harvard University Press, 1978.

Brokaw, Cynthia, 'Guidebooks to Social and Moral Success: The Morality Books in 16th and 17th Century China', *Transactions of the International Conference of Orientalists in Japan*, No. 27, 1982, pp. 137–41.

—— *The Ledgers of Merit and Demerit: Social Change and Moral Order in Late Imperial China*, Princeton, Princeton University Press, 1991.

Bronfenbrenner, Urie, *Two Worlds of Childhood: US and USSR*, New York, Simon and Schuster, 1972.

Buckley, Christopher, 'A New May Fourth: The Scientific Imagination in Chinese Intellectual History, 1978–1989', unpublished paper, Australian National University, Canberra, 1989.

Burch, Betty, 'Models as Agents of Change in China', in Richard Wilson *et al.* (eds.), *Value Change in Chinese Society*, New York, Praeger, 1979, pp. 122–37.

Caizhengbu renshi jiaoyu (ed.), *Wei hao caizheng zhongzhuan jiaoyu wei sihua jianshe peiyang rencai* (Fostering talent for good finance in secondary school education for the building of the four modernizations), Beijing, Zhongguo caizheng jingji chubanshe, 1983.

Calhoun, Craig, *The Question of Class Struggle: Social Foundations of Popular Radicalism during the Industrial Revolution*, Chicago, University of Chicago Press, 1982.

Campbell, Joseph, *The Hero with a Thousand Faces*, Bollingen Series No. 17, Princeton, Princeton University Press, 1973.

Canguilhem, Georges, *On the Normal and the Pathological*, Dordrecht, D. Reidel, 1978.

Cao Jiongfang, 'Bangyang: daode renge yu pubian renge' (Models: moral personalities and normal personalities), *Nianqing ren*, No. 10, 1989, pp. 41–2.

Cao Manzhi (ed.), *Zhongguo qingshaonian fanzuixue* (The criminology of Chinese juvenile delinquency), Beijing, Qunzhong chubanshe, 1988.

Cell, Charles P., *Revolution at Work: Mobilization Campaigns in China*, New York, Academic Press, 1977.

Chan, Leslie W., *The Taching Oilfield: A Maoist Model of Economic Development*, Canberra, Australian National University Press, 1974.

Chan, Wing-tsit, *Religious Trends in Modern China*, New York, Octagon Books, 1969.

—— (ed.), *Chu Hsi and Neo-Confucianism*, Honolulu, University of Hawaii Press, 1986.

Chang, Iris, *Thread of the Silkworm*, New York, Basic Books, 1995.

Chang, Julia and R. W. L. Guisso (eds.), *Sages and Filial Sons: Mythology and Archaeology in Ancient China*, Hong Kong, Chinese University Press, 1991.

Chao Lin, *A Survey of Chinese (Han) Characters*, Hong Kong, Universal Book Company, 1968.

Chen Chuancai, 'Zhongguo minzu wenhua de tezhi yu biange' (The characteristics and change of Chinese national culture), in Zhang Liwen *et al.* (eds.), *Chuantong wenhua yu xiandaihua* (Traditional culture and modernization), Beijing, Zhongguo renmin daxue chubanshe, 1987, pp. 44–58.

Chen Jingpan, *Confucius as a Teacher*, Beijing, Foreign Languages Press, 1990 (originally University of Toronto Ph.D. dissertation, 1940).

Chen Kuiyan, 'Guanyu xiaoyuan wenhua de sikao' (Thoughts about campus culture), *Jiaoyu yanjiu*, No. 2, 1992, pp. 21–6.

Chen Sheng and Zhao Li, 'Dangdai qingnian de sixiang daode tedian jiqi chengyin' (The ideological and moral characteristics of modern youth and their cause of formation), *Jiaoyu yanjiu*, No. 7, 1990, pp. 61–5.

Chen Xianrong, 'Beijing shi zhongxiao xuesheng liushi yu weifa fanzui diaocha baogao' (The phenomenon of dropouts and criminal delinquency among primary and secondary school students in Beijing), *Shehuixue yu shehui diaocha*, No. 2, 1985, pp. 28–35; trans. in *Chinese Education*, Vol. 20, No. 3, 1987, pp. 86–110.

Chen Xiaochuan, 'Qingnian gongren de shenghuo taidu yu shenghuo sheji' (Life approaches and life plans among young workers), *Qingnian yanjiu*, No. 11, 1987, pp. 22–3, 15.

Chen Zhexian, 'Zai tigao nongcun laodongzhe suzhi shangxia gongfu' (Put all efforts into raising the quality of rural workers), *Qiushi*, No. 16, 1990, pp. 36–8.

Chen Zhizhao, 'Mianzi xinli de lilun fenxi yu shiji yanjiu' (The theoretical analysis and practical study of the psychology of face), in Yang Guoshu (ed.), *Zhongguo ren de xinli* (The psychology of the Chinese), Taipei, Guiguan tushu gongsi chubanshe, 1989, pp. 155–237.

Cheng Zhongying, 'Lun rujia xiao de lunli jiqi xiandaihua. Zeren, quanli, yü dexing' (On the Confucian ethic of filial piety and its modernization: responsibility, authority and virtue), *Hanxue yanjiu* (Chinese Studies), Vol. 4, No. 1, 1985, pp. 83–106.

Chen Zhuo, 'Shenghuo yu meirong' (Life and cosmetology), *Shidai qingnian*, No. 2, 1992, p. 15.

Chin, Ann-Ping, *Children of China: Voices from Recent Years*, Ithaca, NY, Cornell University Press, 1989.

Chu Bergsma, Lily, *A Cross-Cultural Study of Conformity in Americans and Chinese*, San Francisco, Robert D. Reed and Adam S. Eterovich, 1977 (*see also* Chu, Lily).

Chu, David S. K., 'Social Problems in Contemporary Chinese Society: Editor's Introduction', *Chinese Sociology and Anthropology*, Vol. 17, No. 2, 1984–5, pp. 3–38.

Chu, Godwin C., 'The Emergence of the New Chinese Culture', in Wen-Shing Tseng and David Y. H. Wu (eds.), *Chinese Culture and Mental Health*, London, Academic Press, 1985, pp. 15–29.

Chu Hsi (Zhu Xi), *Learning to Be a Sage: Selections from the Conversations of Master Chu, Arranged Topically*, trans. with a comment by Daniel K. Gardner, Berkeley, Calif., University of California Press, 1990.

Chu, Lily, 'The Sensitivity of Chinese and American Children to Social Influences', *Journal of Social Psychology*, Vol. 109, 1979, pp. 175–86 (*see also* Chu Bergsma, Lily).

Ch'ü, T'ung-Tsu, *Law and Society in Traditional China*, Paris, Mouton, 1961.

Chua, Beng-Huat, ' "Konfuzianisierung" in der Modernisierung Singapurs', in Joachim Matthes (ed.), 'Zwischen den Kulturen?' *Soziale Welt*, Vol. 8, Göttingen, Verlag Otto Schwartz, 1992, pp. 249–69.

Cihai (The ocean of words), Shanghai, Shanghai cishu chubanshe, 1985.

Ciyuan (The origin of words), Vol. 3, Beijing, Shangwu yinshuguan, 1984.

Cloud, Frederick D., *Hangchow: the 'City of Heaven'*, Shanghai, Presbyterian Mission Press, 1906.

Cohen, Stan, *Folk Devils and Moral Panics*, Oxford: Martin Robertson, 1980.

Collection ministère de la justice, *Le Divorce en Europe Occidentale*, Paris, La Documentation française, 1975.

Colson, Elizabeth, *Tradition and Contract: The Problem of Order*, Chicago, Aldine, 1974.

Confucian Analects, in *The Four Books (Sishu)*, (in Chinese and English), trans. James Legge, Taipei, Culture Book Co./Wenhua tushu gongsi, 1983.

Connerton, Paul, *How Societies Remember*, Cambridge, Cambridge University Press, 1989.

Contag, Victoria, 'Das Mallehrbuch für Personenmalerei des Chieh Tzü Yüan', *T'ong Pao*, Vol. 33, No. 1, 1937, pp. 15–90.

Cooley, Charles H., ' "Nature versus nurture" in the making of social careers', *Proceedings of the National Conference on Charities and Correction*, 1896, pp. 399–405.

Couvreur, S. J., *Chou king*, Hejianfu, 1897; reprinted Taipei, 1971.

Criminal Law and the Criminal Procedure Law of the People's Republic of China (in Chinese and English), Beijing, Beijing Languages Press, 1984.

CSCPRC, 'Sociology', Sociology/Anthropology Delegation Report, *China Exchange News*, Vol. 12, No. 4, 1984.

Cua, Antonio S., 'The Concept of *Li* in Confucian Moral Theory', in Robert E. Allinson (ed.), *Understanding the Chinese Mind: The Philosophical Roots*, Hong Kong, Oxford University Press, 1989, pp. 209–35.

Cui Chunbao, 'Cong chuantong guannian zhong jiefang chulai' (Liberation from traditional concepts), *Qingnian shidai*, No. 4, 1985, p. 7.

Cui Dashan, 'Xuesheng pinde pingjia chutan: Xingzhi, gongneng he biaozhun' (Preliminary discussion on students' moral character evaluation: nature, function, and standard), *Jiaoyu yanjiu yu shijian*, No. 3, 1986, pp. 70–6.

Cummings, William, S. Gopinathan and Yasumasa Tomoda, *The Revival of Values: Education in Asia and the West*, Oxford, Pergamon Press, 1988.

Da Li, 'Ren du suzhi chutan' (Initial exploration of human quality), *Shehui*, No. 2, 1985, pp. 4–7.

Dai Fukang, 'Ziyouhua sichao yu qingshaonian fanzui' (The liberalization wave and juvenile crime), *Qingshaonian fanzui yanjiu*, No. 3–4, 1990, pp. 1–7.

Dai Mucai, 'Lüelun jingshen wenmingxue' (Brief discussion on spiritual civilization studies), *Shehui kexue jikan*, No. 2, 1991, pp. 13–17.

Daling qingnian jiehun diaochazu (The study group of marriage among older youths), 'Daling qingnian de jiehun wenti dui shehui de yingxiang' (The marriage question of older youths and its impact on society), *Qingnian Yanjiu*, No. 5, 1985, pp. 40–51.

Dang Guoqing, 'Laojiao renyuan jiehuo fan gaizao wenti de pouxi' (Analysis of the problems of ganging up and going against reform among the inmates of re-education through labour institutions), in *Zhongguo qingshaonian fanzui yanjiu nianjian 1987*, Beijing, Chunqiu chubanshe, 1988, pp. 406–11.

'Dangdai qingnian zai aiqing zhong de lixiang zhuiqiu' (Ideals and the pursuit of love among today's youth) (editorial article), *Hubei qingnian*, No. 4, 1986, pp. 14–15.

d'Assigny, Marius, *The Art of Memory*, New York, AMS Press, reprint, 1985; first published in 1697.

de Certeau, Michel, *The Practice of Everyday Life*, trans. Steven Rendall, Berkeley, University of California Press, 1988.

DeFrancis, John, *The Chinese Language: Fact and Fantasy*, Honolulu, University of Hawaii Press, 1984.

Deng Hongxun, 'You'er jiaoyu shi peiyang yi ge xinren de dianji gongcheng' (Child education is an old process of fostering a new person), *Hongqi*, No. 11, 1987, pp. 30–3.

Deng Shaoxing and He Baorong (eds.), *Dang'an guanlixue* (Studies in file administration), Zhongguo renmin daxue chubanshe, 2nd edn., Beijing 1990.

Deng Xiaoping, *Selected Works of Deng Xiaoping (1975–1982)*, Beijing, Foreign Languages Press, 1984; Chinese edition: *Deng Xiaoping wenxuan (1975–1982)*, Beijing, Renmin chubanshe, 1983.

Détienne, Marcel and Jean Pierre Vernant, *Les Ruses de l'intelligence: la mètis des Grecs*, (The tricks of intelligence: the *metis* of the Greeks), Paris, Flammarion, 1974.

DeVos, George, 'The Relation of Guilt towards Parents to Achievement and Arranged Marriage among Japanese', *Psychiatry*, Vol. 23, No. 2, 1960, pp. 287–301.

Dewey, John, 'Intelligence and Morals' (1908), in John Dewey, *The Influence of Darwin on Philosophy*, Bloomington, Indiana University Press, 1965.

Dikötter, Frank, *The Discourse of Race in Modern China*, Hong Kong, Hong Kong University Press, 1992.

—— *Sex, Culture and Modernity in China*, London, Hurst, 1995.

—— *Imperfect Conceptions: Medical Knowledge, Birth Defects, and Eugenics in China*, London, Hurst, 1998.

Ding Dong, 'Qinggan lungang' (Outline of discussions on feelings), *Jinyang yuekan*, No. 6, 1987, pp. 95–103; also in *Fuyin baokan ziliao*, B4 *Xinlixue*, No. 1, 1988, pp. 28–36.

Ding Rong, 'Banhui huodong zhong jiaoshi de zhudao zuoyong yu xuesheng de zhuti zuoyong' (The guiding function of teachers and the subject function of students in class meeting activities), *Beijing jiaoyu*, No. 4, 1986, pp. 16–20.

Ding Ruxu, 'Guanyu banzhuren gongzuo yu jiating jiaoyu jiehe de xin tansuo' (New explorations of integrating class teacher work and family education), *Banzhuren*, No. 2, 1988, pp. 30–2, 18.

Ding Xiaodong, 'Jiaqiang jingshen wenming jianshe zujin daju wending' (Strengthen and promote the stability of the overall situation through the building of spiritual civilization), *Jingshen wenming jianshe*, No. 5, 1990, pp. 6–7.

Ding Yu, 'Tantan ruhe zhengque chuli zhongxuesheng "zaolian" de wenti' (On how to handle correctly the problem of 'premature love' among secondary school pupils), *Renmin jiaoyu*, No. 3, 1988, p. 21.

Doolittle, Justus, *Social Life of the Chinese*, 2 vols., Singapore, Graham Brash, 1986, Vol. 1; first published in New York in 1867.

Douglas, Mary, *Natural Symbols*, London, Barrie & Rockliff/Cresset Press, 1970.

—— *Purity and Danger*, London, Ark, 1984.

Dreßen, Wolfgang, *Die pädagogische Maschine: Zur Geschichte des industrialisierten Bewußtseins in Preußen/Deutschland*, Frankfurt, Ullstein Materialen, 1982.

Du Hangwei, 'Bashiniandaimo jiushiniandaichu wuguo qingshaonian fanzui de jiben zhuangkuang he tedian' (The basic situation and characteristics of Chinese juvenile crime at the end of the 1980s and the start of the 1990s), *Qingshaonian fanzui yanjiu*, No. 1, 1994, pp. 5–9.

Duan Mingjun, 'Peiyang xuesheng zijue zili zixue' (Foster students self-consciousness, abilities in taking care of themselves, and self-studies), *Nei mengge jiaoyu*, No. 1, 1988, pp. 11–12.

Dube, E. F., 'A Cross-Cultural Study of the Relationship between "Intelligence" Level and Story Recall', unpublished doctoral thesis, Cornell University, Ithaca, NY, 1977.

Dubs, Homer H. (trans.), *The Works of Hsüntze*, Taibei, Ch'eng-wen, 1966.

Dunning, Eric, 'Comments on Elias's "Scenes from the Life of a Knight"', in *Theory, Culture and Society*, Vol. 4, 1987, pp. 366–71.

Durkheim, Émile, *Sociology and Philosophy*, trans. D. F. Pocock, London, Cohen & West, 1965.

—— 'Introduction à la morale', *Revue Philosophique*, Vol. 89, pp. 79–97; translation quoted from Steven Lukes, *Émile Durkheim: His Life and Work, A Historical and Critical Study*, London, Penguin, 1973.

—— *Moral Education*, trans. Everett K. Wilson and Herman Schnurer, New York, Free Press, 1973.

—— *The Elementary Forms of Religious Life*, trans. Joseph W. Swain, London, George Allen & Unwin, 1976.

—— *The Division of Labour in Society*, trans. W. D. Halls and with an introduction by Lewis Coser, London, Macmillan, 1984.

—— *The Evolution of Educational Thought*, trans. Peter Collins, London, Routledge & Kegan Paul, 1985.

Dutton, Michael R., *Policing and Punishment in China: From Patriarchy to 'the People'*, Cambridge, Cambridge University Press, 1992.

—— and Lee Tianfu, 'Missing the Target? Policing Strategies in the Period of Economic Reform', *Crime & Delinquency*, No. 3, 1993, pp. 302–20.

Eckensberger, Lutz H., Walter J. Lonner and Ype H. Poortinga (eds.), *Cross-Cultural Contributions to Psychology*, Lisse, Swets and Zeitlinger BV, 1979.

Edgerton, Robert B., *Rules, Exceptions, and Social Order*, Berkeley, University of California Press, 1985.

Eisenstadt, Sergei N., *From Generation to Generation*, New York, Free Press, 1971.

Elias, Norbert, *The Civilizing Process*, Vol. 1, *The History of Manners*, trans. Edmund Jephcott, Oxford, Blackwell, 1978.

Elkins, David J. and Richard E. B. Simeon, 'A Cause in Search of its Effect, or What does Political Culture Explain', *Comparative Politics*, No. 11, 1979, pp. 127–45.

Elster, Jon, *The Cement of Society: A Study of Social Order*, Cambridge, Cambridge University Press, 1989.

Elvin, Mark, 'Female Virtue and the State in China', *Past and Present*, No. 104, 1984, pp. 111–52.

Erikson, Erik H. (ed.), *The Challenge of Youth*, Garden City, NY, Anchor Books, 1965.

Erikson, Kai T., *Wayward Puritans: A Study in the Sociology of Deviance*, New York, John Wiley, 1966.

Esposito, John L. (ed.), *The Oxford Encyclopedia of the Modern Islamic World*, Vol. 4, New York/Oxford, Oxford University Press, 1995.

Etzioni, Amitai, *Modern Organizations*, Englewood Cliffs, NJ, Prentice-Hall, 1964.

Eurich, Nell, *Science in Utopia: A Mighty Design*, Cambridge, Mass., Harvard University Press, 1967.

Ewald, François, 'Norms, Discipline, and the Law', *Representations*, No. 30, Spring 1990, Special issue: 'Law and the Order of Culture', ed. Robert Post, pp. 138–61.

Eysenck, Hans, *Crime and Personality*, London: Routledge & Kegan Paul, 1964.

Falkenheim, Victor C. (ed.), *Citizens and Groups in Contemporary China*, Michigan Monographs in Chinese Studies, Vol. 56, Ann Arbor, Mich., University of Michigan Press, 1987.

Farquhar, James Douglas, *Creation and Imitation: The Work of a Fifteenth-Century Manuscript Illuminator*, Fort Lauderdale, Fl, Nova/NYIT University Press, 1976.

Fei Xiaotong, *Xiangtu Zhongguo; Xiantu chongjian; Chongfang jiangcun* (Rural China; Rebuilding the countryside; Revisiting a village by Changjiang), Hong Kong, Wenxue chubanshe, 1948 (facsimile of the 1947 Shanghi edn.), pp. 22–30; excerpts trans. as 'Chinese Social Structure and its Values', in J. Mason Gentzler (ed.), *Changing China: Readings in the History of China from the Opium War to the Present*, New York, Praeger, 1977, pp. 210–14.

Fei Xiaotong (Fei Hsiao-tung), 'An interpretation of Chinese social structure and its changes (1946)', in Fei Hsiao-tung, *Chinese village close-up*, Beijing, New World Press, 1983, pp. 124–57.

Fei Xiaotong, *From the Soil*, Berkeley, University of California Press, 1992.

Feigon, Lee, 'Gender and the Chinese Student Movement', in Jeffrey N. Wasserstrom and Elisabeth J. Perry, *Popular Protest and Political Culture in Modern China*, Boulder, Colo., Westview Press, 1992, pp. 125–35.

Feng Changshui, 'Nongcun zhongxue banzhuren gongzuo chutan' (Preliminary discussion on class teacher work in the countryside), *Beijing jiaoyu*, No. 12, 1985, pp. 14–15.

Feng Jicai, ' "Wenge" jinxing le liangqian nian', in *Yibai ge ren de shinian*, Jiangsu wenyi chubanshe, pp. 272–86; trans. as 'The "Cultural Revolution" Has Been Underway for Two Thousand Years', in *Chinese Sociology and Anthropology*, No. 1, 1993, pp. 92–103.

Feng Junshi and Li Hua, 'Xiaoyuan lian'ai wan hua jian' (Ten thousand flowering love letters on campus), in *Daxuesheng*, No. 4, 1991, pp. 40–3.

Feng Quanxin, 'Chuantong jiaoxue yu qifa shi jiaoxue shi maodun de' (Traditional education and elicitation education are contradictory), *Zhengzhi jiaoyu*, No. 3, 1986, pp. 37–8.

Feng Youlan, 'Why China has no science: an interpretation of the history and consequences of Chinese philosophy' (in Chinese), *Zhongguo zhexue shi bu* (Further historical studies of Chinese philosophy), Shanghai, Wang ling wu, 1924, pp. 9–40.

Feng Yunxiang, 'Wenhua shifan yu qingnian yuegui' (Cultural anomie and youth transgressions), *Qingnian yanjiu*, No. 6, 1990, pp. 34–6, 41.

Feng Zusheng, Lin Yingnan, *Kaifang yu fengbi: Zhongguo chuantong shehui jiazhi quxiang ji qi dangqian liubian* (Openness and closedness: the value orientation in traditional Chinese society and its present change), Shijiazhuang, Hebei renmin chubanshe, 1987.

Feuerabend, Rosalind and Ivo Feuerabend, 'Aggressive Behaviour within Politics, 1948–1962: A Cross-National Study', *Journal of Conflict Resolution*, No. 10, 1966, pp. 249–71.

Foucault, Michel, *Discipline and Punish: The Birth of the Prison*, New York, Vintage Books, 1979.

—— *The History of Sexuality*, 1, *An Introduction*, New York, Vintage Books, 1990.

Fung Yu-lan (Feng Youlan), *Chuang Tzu: A New Selected Translation with an Exposition of the Philosophy of Kuo Hsiang*, Beijing, Foreign Languages Press, 1989 (enlarged from the 1931 Commercial Press edn.).

—— *A History of Chinese Philosophy*, Vols. 1–2, trans. Derk Bodde, Princeton, Princeton University Press, 1952.

Gan Yang, 'Chuantong, shijianxing yu weilai' (Tradition, temporality and future), *Dushu*, No. 2, 1986, pp. 3–10.

Gao Ge, 'Dui liumang fanzui de bijiao yanjiu' (On the comparative research on hooliganism), *Jilin daxue shehui kexue xuebao*, No. 3, 1986, pp. 54–9; also in *D41 Falü, Fuyin baokan ziliao*, No. 8, 1986, pp. 71–6.

Gao Jiansheng and Liu Ning (eds.), *Lihun wenti mianmianguan* (Looking at the problems of divorce), Henan renmin chubanshe, 1988.

Gao Ming (ed.), *Guwen zi leibian* (The written types of old characters), Beijing, Zhonghua shuju, 1982.

Gao Zhongxuan *et al.*, *Zuifan gaizao shouce* (Handbook in criminal reform), Shanxi, Shanxi renmin chubanshe, 1987.

'Gaoxiao "san hao" xuesheng pingding gongzuo you dai wanshan' (The evaluation work of 'three-good' students in universities must be handled well) (editorial article) *Gaodeng jiaoyu yanjiu*, No. 3, 1986, pp. 98–9.

Ge Fang, 'Zou xiang huimie de "san hao xuesheng"' (A 'three-good student' walking towards destruction), *Qingnian shidai*, No. 11, 1988, pp. 24–5.

Geertz, Clifford, *The Interpretation of Cultures*, New York, Basic Books, 1973.

—— *Negara: The Theatre-State in Ninteenth-Century Bali*, Princeton, Princeton University Press, 1980.

Geist, Beate, 'Vorbilder in Revolution und Reform: Die Modellierung des Menschen in der Volksrepublik China', unpublished manuscript, Ludwig-Maximilian-Universität, Munich, 1989.

—— 'Lei Feng and the "Lei Fengs of the Eighties"', *Papers of Far Eastern History*, No. 42, September 1990, pp. 97–124.

Gellner, Ernest, *Culture, Identity, and Politics*, Cambridge, Cambridge University Press, 1987.

Gentzler, J. Mason, (ed.), *Changing China: Readings in the History of China from the Opium War to the Present*, New York, Praeger, 1977.

Giddens, Anthony, *Capitalism and Modern Social Theory: An Analysis of the Writings of Marx, Durkheim, and Weber*, Cambridge, Cambridge University Press, 1971.

—— *The Constitution of Society: Outline of a Theory of Structuration*, Cambridge, Polity Press, 1984.

—— *The Consequences of Modernity*, Stanford, Calif., Stanford University Press, 1990.

—— *Modernity and Self-Identity: Self and Society in the Late Modern Age*, Cambridge, Polity Press, 1991.

—— 'Commentary on the Reviews', *Theory, Culture and Society*, Vol. 9, 1992, pp. 171–4.

Gillis, John R., *Youth and History: Tradition and Change in European Age Relations, 1770-Present* (expanded student edn.), New York, Academic Press, 1981.

Gluckman, Max, 'Tribalism in Modern British Central Africa', *Cahiers d'Etudes Africains*, Vol. 1, 1960, pp. 55–70.

Goffman, Erving, *The Presentation of Self in Everyday Life*, Harmondsworth, Penguin, 1969.

—— *Strategic Interaction*, Oxford, Basil Blackwell, 1970.

Gonganbu gonggong anquan yanjiusuo (ed.), *Ni ganjue anquan ma?* (Do you feel safe?), Beijing, Chunzhong chubanshe, 1991.

Gonganju wuju bangongshi (Public Security Bureau Office No. 5), 'Jinnian lai wo guo qingshaonian fanzui de jiben zhuangkuang tedian' (The basic situation and characteristics of juvenile delinquency in our country during recent years), *Qingshaonian fanzui yanjiu*, No. 3, 1991, pp. 1–4.

Gongqingtuan zhongyang xuanchuanbu (Propaganda Department of the Communist Youth League Central Committee) (ed.), *Dangdai qingnian lilun dachao* (Theoretical waves on contemporary youth), Beijing, Nongcun duwu chubanshe, 1989.

Gongqingtuan zhongyang yanjiushi (Research Office of the Communist Youth League Central Committee) (ed.), *Zhongguo daqushi yu dangdai qingnian* (Chinese megatrends and contemporary youth), Jinan, Shandong renmin chubanshe, 1989.

Goode, Erich and Nachman Ben-Yehuda, *Moral Panics: The Social Construction of Deviance*, Oxford, Blackwell, 1994.

Goring, Charles, *The English Convict*, Montclair, NJ, Patterson Smith, 1913.

Gottferdsson, Michael R. and Travis Hirschi, *A General Theory of Crime*, Stanford, Calif., Stanford University Press, 1990.

Gouldner, Alvin, *The Coming Crisis of Western Sociology*, London, Heinemann, 1971.

—— *The Future of Intellectuals and the Rise of the New Class*, New York, Seabury, 1979.

Gracián, Baltasar, *The Oracle: A Manual of the Art of Discretion*, by L. B. Walton, London, Dent, 1953 (orig. 1647).

Gramsci, Antonio, *Selections from Prison Notebooks*, New York, International Publishers, 1971.

Greenblatt, Sidney L., Richard W. Wilson, and Amy Auerbacher Wilson (eds.), *Social Interaction in Chinese Society*, New York, Praeger, 1982.

Grendler, Paul F., *Schooling in Renaissance Italy: Literacy and Learning 1300–1600*, Baltimore, Johns Hopkins University Press, 1989.

Gu Liping, 'Shi lun bangyang zai jiaoyu zhong de zuoyong' (On the effect of models in education), *Jiaoyu yanjiu*, No. 5, 1988, pp. 41–3.

Gu Mingyuan (ed.), *Jiaoyu da cidian* (Great encyclopedia of education), Vols. 1 and 2, Shanghai, Shanghai jiaoyu chubanshe, 1990.

—— and Huang Ji (eds.), *Jiaoyu xue* (Pedagogy), Beijing, Renmin jiaoyu chubanshe, 1987.

Gu Shengzhu, *Feinonghua yu chengzhenhua yanjiu* (A study of non-agriculturalization and urbanization), Hangzhou, 1991.

Gu Shudong, 'Dui peiyang xuesheng sixiang suzhi de yizhong renshi' (On understanding the fostering of students' ideological quality), *Shanghai jiaoyu*, No. 1, 1985, pp. 13, 25.

Gu Xinmei ' "Qingshaonian xiuyang" chengji pingding gaige de zuofa he tihui' (Methods to reform the evaluation of the achievements in 'youth cultivation' and its experiences), *Zhengzhi jiaoyu*, No. 11, 1987, p. 31.

Gu Zhaosen, 'Shao nümen, weishenme liulang' (Young girls, why are you roaming about), *Hubei qingnian*, No. 8, 1989, pp. 34–6.

Gumbrecht, Hans Ulrich, 'Modern, Modernität, Moderne', in Otto Brunner, Werner Conze, and Reinhart Koselleck (eds.), *Gesellschaftliche Grundbegriffe*, Vol. 4, Stuttgart, Klett-Cotta, 1978.

Guo Xiang and Ma Changmiao, 'Lun qingshaonian tuanhuo fanzui' (On juvenile gang crime), in *Zhongguo qingshaonian fanzui yanjiu nianjian 1987*, Beijing, Renmin chubanshe, 1988, pp. 374–88.

Guo Zhao, 'Shilun huanjing yingxiang yu diling fanzui' (A tentative discussion on the influence of the environment on minors' crime), *Qingshaonian tantao*, No. 4, 1990, pp. 15–20.

Guojia tigaisuo (State Institute of System Reform), 'Zhi you tongguo gaige gongjian: caineng huan lai shehui wending' (Only through reform one can assault fortified positions: ability brings social stability), *Shijie jingji daobao*, 29 August 1988, p. 7.

Habermas, Jürgen, 'Modernity versus Postmodernity', *New German Critique*, No. 22, 1981, pp. 3–14.

—— and Niklas Luhmann, *Theorie der Gesellschaft oder Sozialtechnologie: was leistet die Systemforschung?* Frankfurt am Main, Suhrkamp, 1971.

Ha'erbin shi jingshen wenming jianshi huodong weiyuan hui, 'Kaizhan "san wenming" huodong: tuijin wenming chengshi jianshe' (Develop 'three civilizations' activities: carry forward the building of civilized cities), *Wenming xiangdao*, No. 1, 1991, pp. 21–2.

'Ha'erbin shi shangye xuexiao guanli zhidu' (The administrative system of Harbin business school), Harbin (internal school document), 1987.

Hahn Rafter, Nicole, 'The Social Construction of Crime and Crime Control', *Journal of Research in Crime and Delinquency*, Vol. 27, No. 4, 1990, pp. 376–89.

Han Yu, *Yuan Hsing* (An enquiry into human nature); quoted in Chen Jingpan, *Confucius as a Teacher*, Beijing, Foreign Languages Press, 1990.

Hangzhou daxue jiaoyu xi (ed.), 'Deyu de fanfu xing' (The repetitive character of moral education), in Hangzhou daxue jiaoyu xi (eds.), *Jiaoyu cidian* (Encyclopedia of Education), Nanchang, Jianxi jiaoyu chubanshe, 1987.

Hansen, Chad, 'Chinese Ideographs and Western Ideas', *Journal of Asian Studies*, Vol. 52, No. 2, 1993, pp. 373–99.

Hao Zhilun, 'Lun "jiao" zhi chuantong wenhua yiyun' (Discussing the meaning of '*jiao* (to teach') in traditional culture), *Jiaoyu yanjiu*, No. 3, 1990, pp. 49–51, 77.

Harriman, Norman F., *Standards and Standardization*, New York, 1928.

Hawkins, John (ed.), *Education and Social Change in the People's Republic of China*, New York, Praeger, 1983.

He Bi, 'Lun jia sai' (On jumping the queue), *Daxuesheng*, No. 11, 1990, pp. 42–3; also in *JPRS-CAR*-91–007, 8 February 1991, pp. 72–4.

He Jichuan, 'Concern about the floating population', *Zhongguo shehui bao*, 13 September 1991, p. 3; quoted from *JPRS-CAR*-91–060, 30 October 1991, pp. 55–6.

He Xin, 'Gudu yu tiaozhan: wo shengming de yuanzui' (Loneliness and challenge: my original guilt in life), *Zixue*, No. 1, 1989, pp. 7–16.

—— 'Gudu yu tiaozhan: qisihua yu mogui zhi pi' (Loneliness and challenge: the flower with seven colours and the skin of the devil), *Zixue*, No. 2, 1989, pp. 35–43.

—— 'Gudu yu tiaozhan: zai hei shehui de bianyuan qu' (Loneliness and challenge: on the edge of the black society), *Zixue*, no. 3, 1989, pp. 13–22.

—— 'Gudu yu tiaozhan: Huangdan er kongbu de hong bayue' (Loneliness and challenge: absurd and terrorizing red August), *Zixue*, No. 11, 1989, pp. 3–11.

—— 'Zhongguo dangdai beiwanglu: wode kunhuo yu youlü' (A contemporary Chinese cultural aide-memoire: my perplexities and concerns), *Jingjixue zhoubao*, 8 January 1989, p. 5.

—— *Dongfang de fuxing* (The revival of the East), Heilongjiang jiaoyu chubanshe, Harbin, Heilongjiang renmin chubanshe, 1991.

Hebdige, Dick, *Hiding in the Light: On Images and Things*, London, Routledge, 1988.

Hiniker, Paul J., 'Chinese Reactions to Forced Compliance: Dissonance Reduction or National Character, *Journal of Social Psychology*, Vol. 77, 1969, pp. 157–76.

Hirschi, Travis, *Causes of Delinquency*, Berkeley, University of California Press, 1969.

Ho, David Yau-fai, 'On the Concept of Face', *American Journal of Sociology*, Vol. 81, No. 4, 1976, pp. 867–83.

—— 'Psychological Implications of Collectivism, with Special Reference to the Chinese Case and Maoist Dialectics', in Lutz H. Eckensberger, Walter J. Lonner, and Ype H. Poortinga, *Cross-Cultural Contributions to Psychology*, Lisse, Swets and Zeitlinger BV, 1979, pp. 143–50.

Hofstede, Geert, 'Value Systems in Forty Countries: Interpretation, Validation, and Consequences for Theory', in Lutz H. Eckensberger, Walter J. Lonner, and Ype H. Poortinga (eds.), *Cross-Cultural Contributions to Psychology*, Lisse, Swets and Zeitlinger BV, 1979, pp. 389–407.

Honig, Emily and Gail Hershatter, *Personal Voices: Chinese Women in the 1980's*, Stanford, Calif., Stanford University Press, 1988.

Howard, Pat and Roger Howard, 'China's Enterprise Management Reforms in the Eighties: Technocratic versus Democratic Tendencies', paper presented at the Sino-Australian conference on 'China 40 Years after the Revolution', Research Institute for Asia and Pacific, University of Sydney, September 1989.

Hsü Cho-yün, 'Comparisons of Idealized Societies in Chinese History', in Julia Chang and R. W. L. Guisso (eds.), *Sages and Filial Sons: Mythology and Archaeology in Ancient China*, Hong Kong, Chinese University Press, 1991, pp. 43–63.

Hsu, Francis L. K., *Americans and Chinese*, New York, Doubleday Natural History Press, 1972.

Hsü, James C. H., 'Unwanted Children and Parents: Archaeology, Epigraphy, and the Myths of Filial Piety', in Julia Chang and R. W. L. Guisso (eds.), *Sages and Filial Sons: Mythology and Archaeology in Ancient China*, Hong Kong, Chinese University Press, 1991, pp. 23–41.

Hu, Hsien Chin, 'The Chinese Concept of "Face" ', *American Anthropologist*, Vol. 46, No. 1, 1944, pp. 45–64.

Hu Shoufen, *Deyu yuanli* (Principles of moral education), rev. edn., Beijing, Beijing shifan daxue chubanshe, 1989.

Hu Wei, 'Xiandai deyu pingjia de tedian ji gongneng' (The characteristics and functions of modern moral evaluation), *Shanghai jiaoyu*, No. 7–8, 1987, pp. 16–17.

—— Tang Yuan, and Ouyang Hongsen, 'Guanyu pinde pingding zhibiao tixi de yanjiu' (On the study of moral quality index systems): Part 1, *Shanghai jiaoyu*, No. 9, 1986, pp. 13–14; Part 2, *Shanghai jiaoyu*, No. 10, 1986, pp. 8–9; Part 3, *Shanghai jiaoyu*, No. 11, 1986, pp. 14–15; Part 4, *Shanghai jiaoyu*, No. 12, 1986, p. 12.

Hu Yaobang, 'Create a New Situation in All Fields of Socialist Modernization: Report to the 12th National Congress of the Communist Party of China on 1 September, 1982, in *Beijing Review*, Vol. 25, No. 37, 13 September 1982; on the theory of spiritual civilization, see particularly pp. 21–6.

Hu Yinsheng and Wang Li (eds.), *Jiaoyu xue* (Pedagogy), Beijing, Renmin chubanshe, 1987, p. 286.

Huadong liu sheng yi shi jiaoyu xueyuan xiezuo (ed.), *Xuexiao jiaoyuxue* (School pedagogy), Zhejiang jiaoyu chubanshe, 1987.

Huang Lipin, 'Li Zehou tan nan huan nü ai' (Li Zehou on love), *Mingbao yuekan*, No. 5, 1988, pp. 56–7.

Huang Xiting, Zhang Jinfu, and Zhang Shulin, 'Wo guo wu chengshi qingshaonian xuesheng jiezhiguan de diaocha' (Investigation of the values of Chinese adolescent students in five cities), *Xinli xuebao*, No. 3, 1989, pp. 274–83.

Huang Zhifa, 'Yi ge xuesheng tou che tuanhuo fanzui xinli qianxi' (An analysis of the criminal psychology of a student involved in a bicycle stealing gang), *Qingshaonian fanzui wenti*, No. 5, 1986, pp. 39–40.

—— 'Zenyang duidai zaolian zhong de xuesheng' (How to handle students who are involved in premature love), *Shanghai jiaoyu*, No. 2, 1986, p. 13.

Huazhong shifan xueyuan jiaoyuxi *et al.* (eds.), *Deyu xue* (Moral education), Xi'an, Shaanxi jiaoyu chubanshe, 1966.

—— (eds.), *Jiaoyuxue* (Pedagogy), Beijing, Beijing jiaoyu chubanshe, 1985.

Humboldt, Wilhelm von, *Ansichten über Ästhetik und Literatur: Seine Briefe an Christian Gottfried Körner*, ed. Fritz Jonas, Berlin, 1880.

Inkeles, Alex, 'The Modernization of Man', in Myron Weiner (ed.), *Modernization: The Dynamics of Growth*, New York, Basic Books, 1966, pp. 138–50.

—— *Exploring Induividual Modernity*, New York, Columbia University Press, 1983.

—— and Donald B. Holsinger (eds.), *Education and Individual Modernity in Developing Countries*, Leiden, E. J. Brill, 1974.

—— and David H. Smith, *Becoming Modern: Individual Change in Six Developing Countries*, London, Heinemann, 1974.

Jacobs, J. Bruce, *Local Politics in a Rural Chinese Cultural Setting: A Field Study of Mazu Township, Taiwan*, Contemporary China Papers, Canberra, Australian National University, Research School of Pacific Studies, 1980.

—— 'The Concept of *Guanxi* and the Local Politics in a Rural Chinese Setting', in Sidney L. Greenblatt *et al.* (eds.), *Social Interaction in Chinese Society*, New York, Praeger, 1982, pp. 209–37.

Jian Xiong, 'The "Acquaintanceship" Atmosphere: A Kind of Social Disease', *Shehui*, No. 10, 1991, pp. 45–6; also in *JPRS-CAR*-92–007, 18 February 1992, pp. 43–5.

Jiang Haohua and Zhang Lin, 'Dui bangyang jiaoyu fangfa de zai renshi' (Towards a new understanding of model education), *Qingnian yanjiu*, No. 2, 1987, pp. 6–9.

Jiang Jiqing, 'Guanshu shi he qifa shi ying you ji jiehe' (Inculcation and elicitation must be organically combined), *Zhengzhi jiaoyu*, No. 3, 1986, p. 38.

Jiang Zemin, 'Xiang Lai Ning xuexi: zuo shehui zhuyi shiye jieban ren' (Learn from Lai Ning: become successors to the socialist cause), *Fudaoyuan*, No. 11, 1990, pp. 4–5.

'Jiji kaizhan lunlixue de yanjiu' (Actively develop the study of ethics: speech at the opening of the National Conference on ethics), *Zhexue yanjiu*, No. 6, 1980, pp. 3–5; trans. in *Chinese Studies in Philosophy* Vol. 13, No. 1, 1981, pp. 37–44.

Jin Ge, 'Yongdong de chunqing (Qingshaonian chunqi wenti caifang sui gan)' (Stirrings of love. (Thoughts after gathering material on puberty problems among youth)), *Xinjiang qingnian*, No. 10, 1989, p. 12.

Jin Guantao, *Zai lishi de biaoxiang beihou: dui Zhongguo fengjian shehui zhao wending jiegou de tansuo* (Behind the phenomenon of history: a discussion of the ultrastable structure of the Chinese feudal society), Chengdu, Sichuan renmin chubanshe, 1983.

Jin Rong, 'Yi "xuan" dai "ping" bu kequ' (Substituting 'evaluations' with 'elections' is not recommended), *Renshi yu rencai*, No. 3, 1989, p. 25.

Jin Yonghua, 'Lüelun zaoqi jiaoyu zai fanzui yufang zhong de zuoyong' (A brief discussion on using early education in the prevention of crime), *Qingshaonian fanzui yanjiu*, No. 5, 1988, pp. 46–9.

Johnston, Alastair Iain, *Cultural Realism. Strategic Culture and Grand Strategy in Chinese History*, Princeton, New Jersey, Princeton University Press, 1995.

Jonsson, Gustav, *Flickor på glid: en studie i kvinnoförtryck* (Slipping girls: a study of the repression of women), Borås, Tiden Folksam, 1977.

—— *Flickor på glid: en studie i kvinnoförakt* (Slipping girls: a study of the contempt for women), Värningby, Tiden Folksam, 1980.

Jun Feng and Yu Miao, 'Xican de zhishi yu lijie' (Etiquette and knowledge of Western food), *Shidai qingnian*, No. 2, 1991, p. 38.

Jung Sheng, 'Great impact of agricultural issue: tracking incident of peasant riots in Sichuan's Renshou county', *Xin Bao*, 10 June 1993; based on *Zhongguo xiaofeizhe bao* and quoted from *SWB-FE*/1713, 12 June 1993, pp. B2/1–4.

Kahl, Joseph A., *The Measurement of Modernism: A Study of Values in Brazil and Mexico*, Austin, Tex., University of Texas Press, 1968.

Kang Shuhua, Liu Lanpu, and Zhao Ke, *Nüxing fanzui lun* (Discussions on female crime), Lanzhou, Lanzhou daxue chubanshe, 1988.

—— and Xiang Zexuan, *Qingshaonian faxue xinlun* (New discussions on juvenile law), Beijing, Gaodeng jiaoyu chubanshe, 1996.

Kao Ming, 'Chu Hsi's Discipline of Propriety', in Wing-tsit Chan (ed.), *Chu Hsi and Neo-Confucianism*, Honolulu, University of Hawaii Press, 1986, pp. 312–36.

Karlgren, Bernhard, *Grammatica Serica*, in *Bulletin of the Museum of Far Eastern Antiquities* (Stockholm), Vol. 12, 1940.

Kelman, Herbert E., 'Processes of Opinion Change', *Public Opinion Quarterly*, Vol. 25, No. 1, 1961, pp. 57–78.

Kett, Joseph F., *Rites of Passage: Adolescence in America 1790 to the Present*, New York, Basic Books, 1977.

King, Ambrose Y. C. and Michael H. Bond, 'The Confucian Paradigm of Man: A Sociological View', in Wen-Shing Tseng and David Y. H. Wu, *Chinese Culture and Mental Health*, London, Academic Press, 1985, pp. 29–47.

Kinney, Anne Behnke, 'Dyed Silk: Han Notions of the Moral Development of Children', in Anne Behnke Kinney, *Chinese Views of Childhood*, Honolulu, University of Hawaii Press, 1995, pp. 17–56.

Kleinmann, Arthur and Tsung-Yi Lin (eds.), *Normal and Abnormal Behaviour in Chinese Culture*, Dordrecht, D. Reidel, 1981.

Kwok, D. W. Y., *Scientism in Chinese Thought, 1900–1950*, New Haven, Yale University Press, 1965.

Lai Yangchun, 'Xuexiao daode jiaoyu yu shehui daode pingjia de fancha' (The contrast between moral education in school and moral evaluation in society), *Zhengzhi jiaoyu*, No. 11, 1987, p. 44.

Laslett, Peter, 'Age at Menarche in Europe since the Eighteenth Century', *Journal of Interdisciplinary History*, No. 2, 1971, pp. 221–36.

Legge, James (trans.), *The Four Books (Sishu)* (in Chinese and English), Taipei, Culture Book Co./Wenhua tushu gongsi, 1983.

Lei Feng, *Lei Feng riji* (Lei Feng's diaries), Beijing, Jiefangjun wenyi she, 1966.

—— *Lei Feng riji shi wenxuan* (Selections of Lei Feng's diaries and poems), Beijing, Zhanshi chubanshe, 1982.

Lenin, V. I., 'What is to be done?' in *Collected Works*, Moscow, Progress Publishers, 1975; written between 1901 and 1902.

Lerner, Daniel, *The Passing of Traditional Society*, Glencoe, Ill., Free Press, 1965.

Levenson, Joseph R., *Confucian China and its Modern Fate: The Problem of Intellectual Continuity*, Vol. 1, Berkeley and Los Angeles, University of California Press, 1958.

Lévi-Strauss, Claude, *Structural Anthropology*, Vol. 1, trans. Claire Jacobson and Brooke Grundfest Schoepf, New York, Basic Books, 1963.

LeVine, Robert A. and Merry I. White, *Human Conditions: The Cultural Basis of Educational Development*, New York/London, Routledge & Kegan Paul, 1986.

Li Boxi, 'Peiyang qingnian ren: yingjie ershi yi shiji' (Educating young people, welcoming the 21st century), in Gongxingtuan zhongyang yanjiushi (ed.), *Zhongguo daqushi yu dangdai qingnian* (Chinese megatrends and contemporary youth), Jinan, Shandong renmin chubanshe, 1989, pp. 125–33.

Li Cheng and D. Bachman, 'Localism, elitism and immobilism: elite formation and social change in post-Mao China', *World Politics*, No. 42, 1989, pp. 64–94.

—— and Lynn T. White III, 'China's Technocratic Movement and the World Economic Herald', *Modern China*, Vol. 17, No. 3, 1991, pp. 342–88.

—— 'Surplus Rural Laborers and Internal Migration in China: Current Status and Future Prospects', in Børge Bakken (ed.), *Migration in China*, NIAS Report No. 31, Copenhagen, NIAS, 1998.

Li Guangda, 'Wanjiu jiaoyu gongdu xuesheng de wu ge jieduan' (Five stages of redemption education for work-study schools), in *Zhongguo qingshaonian fanzui yanjiu nianjian 1987*, Beijing, Chunqiu chubanshe, 1988, pp. 764–6.

Li Guofang, 'Guanyu zaolian yu zhongxuesheng weifa fanzui de diaocha' (An investigation of premature love and crime among secondary school students), in *Zhongguo qingshaonian fanzui yanjiu nianjian*, Beijing, Chunqiu chubanshe, 1988, pp. 215–18.

Li Guoshi, 'Siwei fangshi yu xiandaihua' (Modes of thinking and modernization), *Lanzhou xuekan*, No. 4, 1988, pp. 50–5; also in *Fuyin baokan ziliao*, B4, *Xinlixue*, No. 10, 1988, pp. 19–24.

Li Jiannong, *Zhongguo jin bai nian zhengzhi shi* (Chinese political history in the last hundred years), Shanghai, 1947.

Li Jidong, 'Fubai yu xiandaihua de bianxing' (Corruption and the deformation of modernity), *Shehuixue yu shehui diaocha*, No. 5, 1989, pp. 12–14, 19.

Li Jinquan, 'Zhengque dudai chuantong wenhua daode yichan he jianshe shehui zhuyi jingshen wenming de guanxi' (The relation between correctly handling the moral heritage of traditional culture and the construction of socialist spiritual civilization), *Zhongshan daxue xuebao* (*Zhexue shehui kexue ban*), No. 1, 1990, pp. 31–6.

Li Ju-chen, *Flowers in the Mirror*, trans. Lin Tai-yi, London, Peter Owen, 1965; *see also* Li Ruzhen.

Li Junjie, *Fanzui jiaoyuxue* (Criminal pedagogy), Beijing, Qunzhong chubanshe, 1986.

Li Qiang, *Zhongguo dalu de pinfu chabie* (Differences between rich and poor in mainland China), Tianjin, Zhongguo funü chubanshe, 1986.

Li Ruzhen, *Jinghua yuan* (Flowers in the mirror), Vol. 1, Beijing, Renmin wenxue chubanshe, 1986; *see also* Li Ju-chen.

Li Shiqing and Zhang Xinxing (eds.), *Junshi shehuixue* (Military sociology), Beijing, Junshi kexue chubanshe, 1990.

Li Tisheng, *Xunzi zhishi*, Taipei, Xuesheng, 1979.

Li Weiwei, 'Shehui xuyao yingxiong, yingxiong xuyao shehui baohu' (Society needs heroes, heroes need society's protection), *Nianqing ren*, No. 9, 1989, p. 4.

Li Wenxiang, 'Xuesheng deyu zhiliang de lianghua pingjia' (The quantitative evaluation of students' moral quality), *Gaodeng jiaoyu yanjiu*, No. 2, 1986, pp. 90–3.

Li Xihai, 'Wenhua, wenhua huanjing yu qingshaonian fanzui' (Culture, cultural environment and juvenile delinquency), *Qingshaonian fanzui yanjiu*, No. 4–5, 1991, pp. 33–6, 12.

Li Xiulin *et al.* (eds.), *Zhongguo xiandaihua zhi zhexue tantao* (Approaching the philosophy of Chinese modernization), Beijing, Renmin daxue chubanshe, 1990.

Li Yuqi and Xie Yupu, 'Sheji laodong kepian shanghao laodong ke' (Planning a good labour class by using a labour card), *Hebei jiaoyu*, No. 10, 1989, p. 14.

Li Zhaohong, 'Guanyu daxuesheng xinli fazhan bu pingheng xing chengyin tantao' (A discussion of factors causing the unbalanced psychological development among university students), *Qingshaonian tantao*, No. 3, 1988, pp. 31–4.

Li Zhuoran, 'Pinde pingyu de yuyan yishu' (The art of moral evaluation language), *Banzhuren*, No. 5, 1990, pp. 40, 48.

Liang Shuming, *Zhongguo wenhua yaoyi* (The essential points of Chinese culture), Xianggang, Jizheng tushu gongsi, 1963, p. 94.

Liang Xuezhang and Liu Ruqin, 'Banzhuren chuli zaolian wenti de yuanze he fangfa' (Principles and methods for the class teacher to handle the problem of premature love), *Renmin Jiaoyu*, No. 2, 1988, p. 28.

Lieberthal, Kenneth G., *Revolution and Tradition in Tientsin, 1949–1952*, Stanford, Calif., Stanford University Press, 1980.

Lifton, Robert Jay, 'Youth and History: Individual Change in Postwar Japan', in Erik H. Erikson (ed.), *The Challenge of Youth*, Garden City, NY, Anchor Books, 1965, pp. 260–90.

Lin Yueh-Hwa (Lin Yaohua), *The Golden Wing: A Sociological Study of Chinese Familism*, London, Kegan Paul, Trench, Trubner, 1948.

Link, Perry, Richard Madsen and Paul G. Pickowicz (eds.), *Unofficial China: Popular Culture and Thought in the People's Republic*, Boulder, Colo., Westview Press, 1989.

Lipman, Jonathan N. and Stevan Harrell (eds.), *Violence in China: Essays in Culture and Counterculture*, New York, State University of New York Press, 1990.

Liu Binjie, 'Ren de jingshen suzhi xiandaihua', in Gongqingtuan zhongyang xuanchuanbu (Propaganda department of the Youth League Central Committee) (ed.), *Dangdai qingnian lilun dachao* (Theoretical waves on contemporary youth), Beijing, Nongcun duwu chubanshe, 1989, pp. 12–25.

Liu Binyan, 'Another "Rural Encirclement of the Cities" Campaign?' *China Focus*, Vol. 2, No. 1, 1994, pp. 1, 4.

Liu Bo, 'Xuehui "mofang" ' (Learn 'imitation'), *Zhongguo qingnianbao*, 19 April 1991, p. 4.

Liu Dalin (ed.), *Zhongguo dangdai xing wenhua* (Sexual behaviour in modern China), Shanghai, Shanghai sanlian shudian, 1992. English edition by Liu Dalin, Man Lun Ng, Li Ping Zhou, and Erwin J. Haeberle, *Sexual Behaviour in Modern China: Report from the Nationwide Survey of 20,000 Men and Women*, New York, Continuum, 1997.

Liu Defu, '100 nian bu dongyao, guanjian shi 10 nian bu dongyao' (The key to 100 years of unshakeableness lies in the unshakeableness of the next ten years), *Zhongguo qingnian*, No. 1, 1993, pp. 15–17; *see also SWB-FE*/1668, 21 April 1993, p. B2/1.

Liu Feng, 'Shehui huaijiu xintai toushi' (Perspectives on the nostalgic mentality in society), *Shehui kexue*, No. 7, 1990, pp. 21–8.

Liu Guangming, 'Talü: zhongguoren xingge zhong de beiju' (Other-ruled: the tragedy of Chinese nature), *Qingnian xuezhe*, No. 1, 1989, pp. 50–5.

Liu Guojie, 'Lun kexue zhishu, wuzhi shenghua yu daode de guanxi' (The relationship of scientific technology and material life to morality), *Zhexue yanjiu* (Philosophical research), No. 6, 1980, pp. 12–18; trans. in *Chinese Studies in Philosophy*, Vol. 13, No. 1, 1981, pp. 3–21.

Liu Hua, 'Liumang zui' (Hooligan crime), in Zhongguo xingfa cidian bianweihui (ed), *Zhongguo xingfa cidian* (Chinese encyclopedia of criminal law), Shanghai, Xuelin chubanshe, 1989, pp. 700–3.

Liu In-Mao, 'Chinese Cognition', in Micheal Harris Bond (ed.), *The Psychology of the Chinese People*, Hong Kong, Oxford University Press, 1986, pp. 73–105.

Liu, James J. Y., *The Chinese Knight-Errant*, Chicago, University of Chicago Press, 1967.

Liu Jianyuan, 'Zengqiang ziwo pingjia yishi cujin jiaoyu gaige' (Strengthen the consciousness of self-evaluation, promote educational reform), *Xinjiang jiaoyu*, No. 4, 1989, pp. 10–11.

Liu Ke *et al.* (eds.), *Deyu zhishi cidian* (Dictionary of moral knowledge), Shanghai, Shanghai jiaotong daxue chubanshe, 1987.

Liu Qing, 'Shidai xingge de fumian: lun dangdai daxuesheng de jingshen tuifei', in Gongqingtuan zhongyang xuanchuanbu (ed.), *Dangdai qingnian lilun dachao* (The theoretical wave of contemporary youth), Beijing, Nongcun duwu chubanshe, 1989, pp. 1–11.

Liu Rongcai (ed.), *Rencaixue cidian* (Dictionary of talent studies), Chengdu, Sichuan sheng shehui kexue yuan chubanshe, 1987.

Liu Ruifeng, 'Lun gongdu xuexiao dui qingshaonian fanzui de zaoqi ganyu' (On the early intervention of the work-study school on juvenile delinquency), in Yantai daxue faxuesuo (ed.), *Zhong Mei xuezhe lun qingshaonian fanzui* (Juvenile delinquency and its treatment by Chinese and American Scholars), Yantai, Qunzhong chubanshe, 1989, pp. 92–101.

Liu shengshi qingshaonian fanzui yuanyin diaochazu, 'Liu shengshi qingshaonian fanzui yuanyin diaocha' (Investigation of the causes for juvenile delinquency in six cities and provinces), in *Zhongguo qingshaonian fanzui yanjiu nianjian 1987*, Beijing, Chunqiu chubanshe, 1998, pp. 236–43.

Liu Shugong, 'Yanjiu xiandaihua lilun, tansuo xiandaihua daolu' (Researching modernization theory, approaching the road of modernization), *Lilun yu xiandaihua*, No. 1, 1989, pp. 12–24.

Liu Wei, *Yi ge sifenkesi zhi mi de qiujie* (Striving to understand the mystery of a sphinx), Beijing, Renmin chubanshe, 1988, pp. 21–5, 33.

Liu Xiang, *Gu lienüzhuan*, juan 1, Kap. 11 (*Zou Meng Ke mu*), in *Congshu jicheng*, Shanghai, Shangwu yinshuguan, 1936; trans. in A. R. O'Hara, *The Position of Women in Early China, according to Lieh nü chuan, 'The Biographies of Eminent Chinese Women'*, Washington, Catholic University of America Press, 1965, pp. 39–42.

Liu Xiaobo, 'Xin shiji wenxue mianlin weiji' (The literature of the new period faces a crisis), in Xianggang daxue xueshenghui guoshi xuehui (ed.), *Zhongguo sixiang jiefang wenji: gaige husheng* (Collected articles on the liberation of thought in China: the voice of reform), Hong Kong, Jixian shuju, 1988.

Liu Xiaoping, 'Weihun tongju wenti chushen' (Initial reflections on the problem of living together unmarried), *Shandong Qingnian*, No. 5, 1986, p. 35.

Liu Xiuming, 'Ping Jin Guantao de "chao wending jiegou" shiguan' (Evaluating Jin Guantao's 'ultrastable structure' view of history), *Qiushi*, No. 11, 1990, pp. 13–21.

Liu Yuelun, Li Jiangtao, Chen Zhenhong, and Guo Weiqing, *Xiandairen xue* (Modern person studies), Guangdong, Guangdong renmin chubanshe, 1988.

Liu Zhixue, 'Bodong yu pingheng' (Fluctuation and balance), *Qingnian yanjiu*, No. 9, 1990, pp. 36–40.

Louven, Erhard, 'Anmerkungen zur Arbeitslosigkeit und zum Arbeitsmarkt in der VR China', *China Aktuell*, No. 8, 1988, pp. 650–4.

Lu Feng, 'Danwei: Yizhong teshu de shehui zuzhi xingshi' (The work-unit: a specific form of social organization), *Zhongguo shehui kexue*, No. 1, 1989, pp. 71–88.

Lu Jian, 'Crime: A Dilemma in the Course of Modernization', *Shehui*, No. 78, July 1991, pp. 44–6; also in *Joint Publication Research Service* (hereafter, *JPRS Report*) *JPRS-CAR-91-061*, 4 November 1991, pp. 37–9.

Luhmann, Niklas, 'Sinn als Grundbegriff der Soziologie', in Jürgen Habermas and Niklas Luhmann, *Theorie der Gesellschaft oder Sozialtechnologie: Was leistet die Systemforschung?* Frankfurt am Main, Suhrkamp, 1971.

Lukes, Steven, *Émile Durkheim, His Life and Work: A Historical and Critical Study*, London, Penguin, 1973.

Luo Rongqu (ed.), *Cong 'xihua' dao xiandaihua* (From 'westernization' to modernization), Beijing, Beijing daxue chubanshe, 1990.

—— 'Lun xiandaihua de shijie jincheng' (On the world-wide process of modernization), *Zhongguo shehui kexue*, No. 5, 1990, pp. 107–26.

Lyman, Stanford M. and Marvin B. Scott, *A Sociology of the Absurd*, New York, Appleton-Century-Crofts, 1970.

Lyotard, Jean-François, *The Postmodern Condition: A Report on Knowledge*, Manchester, Manchester University Press, 1984.

Ma Shaoning (ed.), 'Wenming cun jianshe de yige chuangzao: henan sheng Xingyang xian kaizhan zhengchuang "shixingji wenming nonghu" jiaoyu huodong de jingyan (zhi yi)' (A creative way to build civilized villages: experiences from the educational activities on carrying through the competition in creating 'ten star-grade civilized households' (Part one)), *Jingshan wenming jianshe*, No. 10, 1990, pp. 15–16.

—— 'Wenming cun jianshe de yige chuangzao: henan sheng Xingyang xian kaizhan zhengchuang "shixingji wenming nonghu" jiaoyu huodong de jingyan (zhi er)' (A creative way to build civilized villages: experiences from the educational activities on carrying through the competition in creating 'ten star-grade civilized households' (Part two)), *Jingshan wenming jianshe*, No. 11, 1990, pp. 18–19.

Machiavelli, Niccolò, *The Prince*, Toronto, Bantam Books, 1981 (first published in 1513).

MacIntyre, Alasdair, *After Virtue: A Study in Moral Theory*, 2nd edn., Notre Dame, Ind.: University of Notre Dame Press, 1984.

Madsen, Richard, 'The Politics of Revenge in Rural China During the Cultural Revolution', in Jonathan N. Lipman and Stevan Harrell (eds.), *Violence in China: Essays in Culture and Counterculture*, New York, State University of New York Press, 1990, pp. 175–201.

Mair, Lucy, *Witchcraft*, New York, McGraw-Hill, 1969.

Mallee, Hein, 'China's Household Registration System under Reform', *Development and Change*, No. 1, 1995, pp. 1–29.

Mannheim, Karl, *Ideologie und Utopie*, 3rd edn., Frankfurt/Main, Verlag G. Schulte-Bulmke, 1952; quotations in English taken from *Ideology and Utopia*, trans. Louis Wirth and Edward Shils, New York, Harcourt, Brace & World, 1936.

Mao Tsetung (Mao Zedong), 'In Memory of Norman Bethune', *Selected Works of Mao Tsetung*, Vol. 2, Beijing, Foreign Languages Press, 1965, pp. 337–8.

Mao Yushi, 'Daodeguan: dui geren liyi cong fouding dao kending' (Moral concepts: from negation to affirmation of individual interest), *Shijie jingji daobao*, 29 February 1988, p. 7; summary trans. in *JPRS-CAR*-88-024, 23 May 1988, pp. 36–8.

Marx, Karl, 'Manifesto of the Communist Party', in *Capital: The Communist Manifesto and Other Writings of Karl Marx*, ed. Max Eastman, New York, Carlton House, 1932, pp. 315–55.

—— *Die Frühschriften*, Stuttgart, Alfred Kröner Verlag, 1971.

Masubuchi, Tatsuo, 'The Yu Hsia (*yuxia*) and the Social Order in the Han Period', *Annals of the Hitotsubashi Academy*, Vol. III, No. 1, 1952, pp. 84–101.

Matza, David, *Delinquency and Drift*, new edn., New Brunswick, NJ, Transaction Books, 1990.

—— 'Subterranean Traditions of Youth', *Annals of the American Academy of Political and Social Science*, No. 338, November 1961, pp. 102–18.

—— and Gresham M. Sykes, 'Juvenile Delinquency and Subterranean Values', *American Sociological Review*, Vol. 26, No. 4, October 1961, pp. 712–19.

Mead, Margaret, *Culture and Commitment: A Study of the Generation Gap*, New York, Natural History Press/Doubleday, 1970.

Mei, Yi-Pao (trans.), *The Ethical and Political Works of Motse*, London, A. Probsthain, Hyperion Press, 1929; reprinted 1973.

Melucci, Alberto, *Nomads of the Present*, Philadelphia, Temple University Press, 1989.

Mencius, 'The Works of Mencius', in *The Four Books (Sishu)* (in Chinese and English), trans. James Legge, Taipei, Culture Book Co./Wenhua tushu gongsi, 1983.

Meng Qingfeng, 'Jiaqiang jiceng wangluo jianshe, tigao shequ kongzhi nengli' (Strengthen the construction of basic level networks and increase the capacity of community control), *Qingshaonian fanzui yanjiu*, No. 11, 1992, pp. 15–18.

Merton, Robert K., *Social Theory and Social Structure*, rev. edn., Glencoe, Ill., Free Press, 1957.

Metzger, Thomas, *Escape from Predicament: Neo-Confucianism and China's Evolving Political Culture*, New York, Columbia University Press, 1977.

Meyer, Jeffrey F., 'A Subtle and Silent Transformation: Moral Education in Taiwan and the People's Republic of China', in William Cummings, S. Gopinathan, and Yasumasa Tomoda, *The Revival of Values: Education in Asia and the West*, Oxford, Pergamon Press, 1988, pp. 109–30.

Minson, Jeffrey, *Genealogies of Morals*, London, Macmillan, 1985.

Miyazaki, Ichisada, *China's Examination Hell: The Civil Service Examinations of Imperial China*, New York/Tokyo, Weatherhill, 1976.

Mo Dong, 'Guangxi qingshaonian weifa fanzui qingkuang de diaocha' (An investigation of the situation of juvenile criminal offenders in Guangxi), *Qingshaonian tantao*, No. 1, 1990, pp. 25–7.

Mozi jian gu (Mozi with separate explanations), Beijing, Zhonghua shuju, 1986.

Mu Guangzhong, 'Renkou suzhi xinlun' (New discussion on human quality), *Renkou yanjiu*, No. 3, 1989, pp. 55–8; also in *Fuyin baokan ziliao*, C5, *Renkouxue*, No. 5, 1989, pp. 90–3.

Mu Shuhuai, 'Zhengque duidai zhongxuesheng lian'ai xianxiang' (Correctly handle the phenomenon of premature love among secondary school students), *Ningxia jiaoyu*, No. 1–2, 1989, pp. 15–16.

Mumford, Lewis, *The Story of Utopias: Ideal Commonwealths and Social Myths*, London, George G. Harrap, 1923.

Munakata, Iwao, 'The Distinctive Features of Japanese Development: Basic Cultural Patterns and Politico-Economic Processes', in Peter L. Berger and Hsin-Huang Michael Hsiao (eds.), *In Search of an East Asian Development Model*, New Brunswick, NJ, Transaction Books, 1988, pp. 155–78.

Munro, Donald J., 'The Chinese View of Modeling', *Human Development*, Vol. 18, No. 5, 1975, pp. 333–52.

—— *The Concept of Man in Early China*, Stanford, Calif., Stanford University Press, 1969.

Naisbitt, John, *Megatrends: Ten New Directions Transforming Our Lives*, New York, Warner Books, 1984.

National Population Census Office under the State Council, *Major Figures of the Fourth National Population Census of China* (in Chinese and English), Beijing, China Statistical Publishing House, 1991.

Needham, Joseph, *Science in Traditional China: A Comparative Perspective*, Hong Kong, Hong Kong University Press, 1981.

Nettleship, R. L., *The Theory of Education in Plato's Republic*, Oxford, Clarendon Press, 1935.

Neuner, Gerhart, 'Kommunistische Erziehung der Persönlichkeit: komplexer Gegenstand wissenschaftlicher Forschung' (Communist education of personality: a complex subject of scientific research), *Sitzungsberichte der Akademie der Wissenschaften der DDR Gesellschaftswissenschaften*, No. 5/G, 1976, pp. 5–19.

Ning Decong, 'Zai fuxi zhong gonggu zhishi, peiyang nengli, fazhan zhili: yuwen di ba ce de fuxi yaodian he jianyi' (Consolidate knowledge, foster abilities, develop intelligence through repetition: suggestions on the main points of repetition for Chinese language textbook no. eight), *Beijing jiaoyu*, No. 2, 1986, pp. 38–9.

Nivison, David S. and Arthur F. Wright, *Confucianism in Action*, Stanford, Calif., Stanford University Press, 1959.

Norman, Dorothy, *Hero: Myth/Image/Symbol*, New York, Anchor Books Doubleday, 1990.

O'Hara, A. R., *The Position of Women in Early China, according to Lieh nü chuan, 'The Biographies of Eminent Chinese Women'*, Washington, Catholic University of America Press, 1965.

Organisation Internationale de Police Criminelle, *Statistiques Criminelles Internationales* 1985–1986 (International Criminal Statistiques 1985–1986), Le Secrétariat général de l'OIPC–Interpol, Saint Cloud, 1988, and statistics 1987–1988, Lyon, 1990.

Ortner, Sherry B., 'Resistance and the Problem of Ethnographic Refusal', *Comparative Studies in Society and History*, No. 1, 1995, pp. 173–93.

Ottomeyer, Klaus, *Soziales Verhalten und Ökonomie im Kapitalismus* (Social behaviour and economy in capitalism), Giessen, Focus Verlag, 1976.

Pan, Klaus, 'Was Kinkel in China nicht sah', *Die Tageszeitung*, 7 November 1992, p. 9.

Pan Shu (ed.), *Jiaoyu xinlixue* (Educational psychology), Beijing, Renmin jiaoyu chubanshe, 1982.

Park, Robert E., Ernest W. Burgess and Roderick D. McKenzie, *The City*, Chicago, University of Chicago Press, 1925.

Paulsen, Friedrich, *Geschichte des gelehrten Unterrichts auf den deutschen Schulen und Universitäten vom Ausgang des Mittelalters bis zur Gegenwart*, 2 vols., Leipzig, 1919, 1924.

Peng Shiqiang, 'Cong "yueding chufang" shuoqi' (Talking about 'agreeing on a prescription'), *Shanghai jiaoyu*, No. 6, 1985, p. 12.

Peng Xincai, 'Shimao yu qingshaonian weifa fanzui' (Fashion and juvenile criminal offence), *Qingshaonian fanzui yanjiu*, No. 10, 1988, pp. 23–5.

Pepper, Suzanne, *China's Universities: Post-Mao Enrollment Politics and their Impact on the Structure of Secondary Education*, a Research report, Monographs in Chinese Studies, Ann Arbor, University of Michigan Press, 1984.

Perrault, Charles, *Parallèle des anciens et des modernes en ce qui regarde les arts et les sciences*, ed. Hans Robert Jauss, Munich, Eidos Verlag, 1964; first published in 1688/97.

Peshkin, Alan and Ronald Cohen, 'The Values of Modernization', *Journal of Developing Areas*, No. 2, 1967, pp. 7–21.

Phillips, D. P., 'The Deterrent Effect of Capital Punishment: New Evidence on an Old Controversy', *American Journal of Sociology*, No. 86, 1980, pp. 139–48.

Pi Yijun, 'Lun fanzui tuanhuo anjie de tedian' (A discussion of the characteristics of criminal gang cases), in *Zhongguo qingshaonian fanzui yanjiu nianjian 1987*, Beijing, Chunqiu chubanshe, 1988, pp. 388–91.

Plato, *The Republic*, trans. Benjamin Jowett, Oxford, 1894.

Popper, Karl R., 'Epistemology without a knowing subject', in *Objective Knowledge: An Evolutionary Approach*, rev. edn., Oxford, Clarendon Press, 1979, pp. 106–52.

Power, Edward J., *Evolution of Educational Doctrine: Major Educational Theorists of the Western World*, New York, Appleton Century-Crofts, 1969.

' "Pudie" zui zao de renshi dang'an' ('Intelligence files' were the very first personnel files), *Renshi yu rencai*, No. 2, 1990, p. 31.

Pusey, James Reeve, *China and Charles Darwin*, Cambridge, Mass., Harvard University Press, 1983.

Pye, Lucian W., *China: An Introduction*, 3rd edn., Boston, Little, Brown, 1984.

Qian Hang and Xie Weiyang, ' "Zongzu wenti": Dangdai Zhongguo nongcun yanjiu de yige shijiao' (The question of clans: a view from today's Chinese rural studies), *Shehui kexue*, No. 5, 1990, pp. 21–4, 28.

Qian Mingfang, 'Bangyang jiaoyu xiaoying ruohua de yuanyin yu duice' (The weakening of the model education effect and its countermeasures), *Pujiao yanjiu*, No. 3, 1990, pp. 12–13.

Qian Xuesen, 'Zhongshi kexue wenhua fazhan "di si chanye"' (Pay attention to science and culture and the development of a 'quaternary industry'), *Renmin ribao*, 17 June 1981, p. 3.

—— 'Yanjiu shehui zhuyi jingshen caifu chuangzao shiye de xuewen: wenhuaxue', *Zhongguo shehui kexue*, No. 6, 1982, pp. 89–96; trans. as 'Culturology: Study of the Creation of Socialist Spiritual Wealth', *Social Sciences in China*, Vol. 4, No. 1, 1983, pp. 17–26.

—— and Wu Jiapei, 'Zuzhi guanli shehui zhuyi jianshi de jishu: shehui gongcheng' (Social engineering: a technique for the organization and administration of socialist construction), *Jingji guanli*, No. 1, 1979, pp. 5–9.

—— and Sun Kaifei, 'Jianli yishi de shehui xingtai de kexue tixi' (Build a scientific system of ideological social formation), *Qiushi*, No. 9, 1988, pp. 2–9.

Qiao Lin, 'Gaige kaifang yu shehui xinli' (Opening, reform, and the social psychology), *Shehui*, No. 3, 1988, p. 11.

Qin Shuli, 'Nongcun shehui zhuyi jingshen wenming jianshe de yi zhong hao xingshi: xingyang xian "shixingji wenming nonghu" huodong diaocha' (A good way of building socialist spiritual civilization in the rural areas: investigation of 'ten star-grade civilized peasant household' activities in Xingyang county), *Qiushi*, No. 17, 1990, pp. 30–6.

Qing Shu, 'Banzhuren fengjian' (The class teacher is feudal), *Dangdai qingnian*, No. 10, 1986, p. 11.

Qingnian yingxiong de gushi (Stories about young heroes), Beijing, Zhongguo qingnian chubanshe, 1978.

Qiu Guang, 'Caoxing pingding' (Behaviour evaluation), *Zhongguo dabaike quanshu: jiaoyu* (The Great Chinese Encyclopedia: Education), Beijing, Zhongguo dabaike chubanshe, 1985, p. 25.

Qiu Ling, 'Yi zhong burong hushi de xianxiang' (A phenomenon one is not allowed to ignore), *Beijing jiaoyu*, No. 4, 1986, pp. 20–1.

Qiu Shaoyun, *Jiti zhuyi de yingxiong* (Heroes of collectivism), Shanghai, Renmin chubanshe, 1971.

Quanguo renda weiyuanhui fazhi gongzuo weiyuanhui xingfashi (ed.), *Zhonghua renmin gongheguo xingfa. Zhonghua renmin gongheguo xingshi susongfa* (The criminal law and the criminal procedure law of the People's Republic of China), Beijing, Falü chubanshe, 1997.

Quetelet, Alphonse, *Sur l'Homme et le développement de ses facultés; ou, Essai de physique sociale* (On man and the development of his faculties; or, Essay on social physics), 2 vols., Paris, 1835.

—— *Du Système social et des lois qui le régissent* (Of the social system and the laws that govern it), Paris, 1848.

Reichard, Gladys A., 'Social Life', in F. Boas (ed.), *General Anthropology*, Boston, Heath, 1938, pp. 409–86.

Ren Xiao'ai, 'Jianli tuanjie, minzhu, pingheng, hexie de shisheng guanxi: xin shiqi banzhuren gongzuo chuyi zhi yi' (Build a united, democratic, balanced, and harmonious relation between teachers and students: my humble opinion on class teacher work in a new era: Part one, *Beijing jiaoyu*, No. 9, 1988, pp. 37–8; Part four, *Beijing jiaoyu*, No. 12, 1988, pp. 16–17.

Ren Zhongping, 'Lunjiang limao' (On paying attention to politeness), *Renmin ribao*, 25 January 1998, pp. 1, 3.

Rickett, W. Allyn, 'Voluntary Surrender and Confession in Chinese Law: the Problem of Continuity', *Journal of Asian Studies*, No. 4, 1971, pp. 797–814.

Ricoeur, Paul, *Lectures on Ideology and Utopia*, New York, Columbia University Press, 1986.

—— 'Life in Quest of Narrative', in David Wood (ed.), *On Paul Ricoeur: Narrative and Interpretation*, London/New York, Routledge, 1991, pp. 20–33.

Roethlisberger, F. J. and William J. Dickson, *Management and the Worker: An Account of a Research Program Conducted by the Western Electric Company, Hawthorne Works, Chicago*, Cambridge, Mass., Harvard University Press, 1947.

Ronan, Colin A. and Joseph Needham, *The Shorter Science and Civilization in China*, Vol. 1, Cambridge, Cambridge University Press, 1978.

Rosen, Stanley, 'Education and the Political Socialization of Chinese Youths', in John Hawkins (ed.), *Education and Social Change in the People's Republic of China*, New York, Praeger, 1983, pp. 97–133.

—— 'Political Education and Student Response: Some Background Factors behind the 1989 Beijing Demonstrations', *Issues and Studies*, No. 10, 1989, pp. 12–39.

—— 'Prosperity, Privatization, and China's Youth', *Problems of Communism*, March/April 1985, pp. 1–28.

—— 'Value Change Among Post-Mao Youth: The Evidence from Survey Data', in Perry Link, Richard Madsen, and Paul G. Pickowicz (eds.), *Unofficial China: Popular Culture and Thought in the People's Republic of China*, Boulder, Colo., Westview Press, 1989, pp. 193–216.

Ryle, Gilbert, *The Concept of Mind*, London, Hutchinson, 1958.

Sahlins, Marshall, *Culture and Practical Reason*, Chicago, Chicago University Press, 1976.

Sarnecki, Jerzy, 'Delinquent Networks in Sweden', *Journal of Quantitative Criminology*, Vol. 6, No. 1, 1990, pp. 31–50.

Schwartz, Benjamin, *In Search of Wealth and Power: Yen Fu and the West*, Cambridge, Mass.: Belknap Press, 1964.

Scott, A. C., *The Classical Theatre of China*, London, George Allen & Unwin, 1957.

Scott, James C., *Weapons of the Weak: Everyday Forms of Peasant Resistance*, New Haven, Yale University Press, 1985.

Selznick, Philip, 'Sociological Theory and Natural Law', *Natural Law Forum*, No. 6, 1961, pp. 84–108.

Shacklady Smith, Lesley, 'Sexist Assumptions and Female Delinquency: An Empirical Investigation', in Carol Smart and Barry Smart (eds.), *Women,*

Sexuality and Social Control, London: Routledge & Kegan Paul, 1978, pp. 74–88.

Shanghai shi jiaoxian zhongxiaoxue deyu xiezuo yanjiu hui (eds.), *Nongcun zhongxiaoxue banzhuren gongzuo zhidao* (Directions for class teacher work in rural primary and secondary schools), Shanghai, Shanghai kexue jishu chubanshe, 1990.

Shanghai xing shehuixue yanjiu zhongxin (Shanghai research centre for sexual sociology), 'Xiandai Zhongguo ren de xing wenti' (Sexual problems of today's Chinese), *Minzhu yu fazhi*, No. 10, 1990, pp. 30–4; trans. in *Chinese Education*, Vol. 25, No. 1, Spring 1992, pp. 56–67.

Shao Daosheng (ed.), *Zhongguo qingshaonnian fanzui de shehuixue sikao* (Sociological reflections on Chinese juvenile crime), Beijing, Shehui kexue wenxian chubanshe, 1987.

—— *Dangdai shehui de bingtai xinli* (The morbid psychology of today's society), Beijing, Shehui kexue wenxian chubanshe, 1990.

Shapiro, Sidney, *The Law and Lore of China's Criminal Justice*, Beijing, New World Press, 1990.

Shehui xinlixue jiaocheng (The educational process of social psychology), Lanzhou, Lanzhou daxue chubanshe, 1986.

Shen Furong, 'Guanshu jiaoyu "zhuru shi"' (Inculcation education is different from the 'spoon feeding method'), *Zhengzhi jiaoyu*, No. 4, 1986, p. 36.

Shen Jianguo, 'Guanyu ren de shehuihua de ji ge wenti' (Some questions on the socialization of man), *Fujian luntan: jingji, shehui ban*, No. 5, 1987, pp. 47–50; also in *C4 Shehuixue, Fuyin baokan ziliao*, No. 4, 1987, pp. 47–51.

Shen Xiping, 'Xue yingxiong, xuyao yizhong jiankuang de shehui daoxiang' (Learning from heroes needs healthy guidance by society), *Nianqing ren*, No. 9, 1989, p. 5.

Sheridan, Mary, 'The Emulation of Heroes', *China Quarterly*, No. 33, 1968, pp. 47–72.

Shi Jinyao, 'Qiantan bangyang jiaoyu ying zunxun de yuanze' (On the principles to be followed in moral education), *Fudaoyuan*, No. 4, 1991, p. 24.

Shi Jun, 'Mangmu "panbi" bu keqi' (Blind 'climbing' is not desirable), *Renshi yu rencai*, No. 8, 1990, pp. 38–9.

Shils, Edward, 'Tradition', *Comparative Studies in Society and History*, Vol. 13, No. 2, 1971, pp. 122–59.

Shipman, Marten, *The Limitations of Social Research*, London, Longman, 1982.

Shirk, Susan, *Competitive Comrades: Career Incentives and Student Strategies in China*, Berkeley/Los Angeles, University of California Press, 1982.

Si Ren, 'Banzhuren guanli gaige bieyi' (A different opinion on the reform of class teacher administration), *Shanghai jiaoyu*, No. 6, 1985, p. 13.

Sichuan jiaoyu xueyuan (ed.), *Jiaoyu xue* (Pedagogy), Chengdu, Sichuan jiaoyu chubanshe, 1984.

Simmel, Georg, 'Fashion', in *On Individuality and Social Forms, Selected Writings*, ed. Donald N. Levine, Chicago, University of Chicago Press, 1971, pp. 294–323; first published in English in 1904, and in German in 1905.

—— 'The Metropolis and Mental Life', in Georg Simmel, *On Individuality and Social Forms*, Chicago, University of Chicago Press, 1971; from *Soziologie. Untersuchungen über die Formen der Vergesellschaftung*, 1908, pp. 324–40.

—— 'The Secret Society', in *The Sociology of Georg Simmel*, trans. and ed. Kurt H. Wolff, New York, Free Press, 1964, from *Soziologie: Untersuchungen über die Formen der Vergesellschaftung*, 1908, pp. 345–76.

—— 'The Stranger', in *On Individuality and Social Forms*, trans. and ed. Donald N. Levine, Chicago, University of Chicago Press, 1971, pp. 143–9; first published as 'Der Fremde', in *Soziologie*, Munich/Leipzig, Dunker and Humbolt, 1908, pp. 685–91.

Sixiang xiuyang xiao cidian (Small dictionary of ideological cultivation), Shanghai, Shanghai cishu chubanshe, 1984.

Skinner, G. William, 'Introduction: Urban Social Structure in Ch'ing China', in G. William Skinner, *The City in Late Imperial China*, Stanford, Calif., Stanford University Press, 1977, pp. 521–53.

Slotkin, James S., *Social Anthropology: The Science of Human Society and Culture*, New York, Macmillan, 1950.

Smart, Carol, and Barry Smart (eds.), *Women, Sexuality and Social Control*, London: Routledge & Kegan Paul, 1978.

Smelser, Neil J., *Theory of Collective Behavior*, New York, Free Press of Glencoe, 1963.

Smith-Rosenberg, Carroll, 'Sex as Symbol in Victorian Purity: An Ethnohistorical Analysis of Jacksonian America', in *American Journal of Sociology*, Vol. 84 (Supplement), 1978, pp. 212–47.

Solinger, Dorothy J., *China's Transients and the State: A Form of Civil Society?* Hong Kong, Hong Kong Institute of Asia-Pacific Studies, 1991.

Solomon, Richard H., *Mao's Revolution and the Chinese Political Culture*, Berkeley, University of California Press, 1971.

Song Huichang, 'Daode jianshe zhong de jige lilun wenti' (Some theoretical questions on moral construction), *Hongqi*, No. 10, 1987, pp. 34–40.

Song Xiren, 'Lun shehui zhuyi daode de jiben yuanze' (On the basic principles of socialist morals), *Qiushi*, No. 4, 1990, pp. 20–3, 31.

Song Xuewen, 'Meiyu dui fazhan qingshaonian xinli suzhi he renge wanshan teshu jiezhi' (The special value of aesthetics education in developing the psychological quality and the perfection of personality among youth), *Jiaoyu luncong*, No. 1, 1991, pp. 26–30.

Spence, Jonathan D., *The Memory Palace of Matteo Ricci*, Harmondsworth, Elisabeth Sifton Books, Viking, 1984.

Ssu-Ma Ch'ien (Sima Qian), *Records of the Historian: Chapters from the Shih chi of Ssu-ma Ch'ien*, trans. Burton Watson, New York, Columbia University Press, 1969.

Stack, Steven, 'Publicized Execution and Homicide 1950–1980', *American Sociological Review*, Vol. 52, 1987, pp. 532–40.

Stein, Aletha Huston, 'Imitation of Resistance to Temptation', *Child Development*, Vol. 38, No. 1, 1967, pp. 157–69.

Stone, Lawrence (ed.), *Schooling and Society: Studies in the History of Education*, Baltimore/London, Johns Hopkins University Press, 1976.

Strauss, Gerald, 'The State of Pedagogical Theory ca. 1530: What Protestant Reformers Knew about Education', in Lawrence Stone (ed.), *Schooling and Society: Studies in the History of Education*, Baltimore/London, Johns Hopkins University Press, 1976, pp. 69–94.

—— *Luther's House of Learning: Indoctrination of the Young in the German Reformation*, Baltimore/London, Johns Hopkins University Press, 1978.

Su Weichang and Zhang Dimei (eds.), *Jiaoyu pingjia jishu* (Techniques of educational evaluation), Changsha, Hunan jiaoyu chubanshe, 1988.

Su Xiaokang and Wang Luxiang (eds.), *Heshang* (River elegy), Beijing, Xiandai chubanshe, 1988.

Sun Longji, *Zhongguo wenhua de shenceng jiegou* (The deep structure of Chinese society), Hong Kong, Jixian she, 1983.

Sun Xiting, Jin Xibin and Chen Xiaobin, *Jianming jiaoyu xue* (Concise pedagogy), Beijing, Beijing shifan daxue chubanshe, 1985.

Sunzi (Sun Tzu), *The Art of War*, Oxford, Clarendon Press, 1963.

Tabboni, Simonetta, 'A Configurational Approach to the Study of Traditional Behavior', *Research of Social Movements, Conflicts and Change*, Vol. 10, 1988, pp. 225–33.

Tan Guangrong, 'Banzhuren gongzuo zhaji liang ze' (Two standard rules for class teacher work), *Zhengzhi jiaoyu*, No. 9, 1987, pp. 38–9.

Tan Jianguang, 'Qingnian shehuixue de lilun yaodian' (Main theoretical aspects of youth sociology), *Qingshaonian yanjiu*, No. 2, 1987, pp. 4–8; also in C4 *Shehuixue*, No. 5, 1987, pp. 25–30.

Tan Zhen and Hu Shouhe, 'Lun shehui jiazhi he ziwo jiazhi' (On social value and self value), *Wuhan daxue xuebao (shehui kexue ban)*, No. 3, 1988, pp. 46–51.

Tannahill, Ray, *Sex in History*, London, Hamish Hamilton, 1980.

Tanner, Harold, 'Chinese Rape Law in Comparative Perspective', *Australian Journal of Chinese Affairs*, No. 31, January 1994, pp. 1–23.

Tao Xincheng, 'Fumu suzhi yu jiating jiaoyu' (Parent quality and family education), *Fumu bidu*, No. 12, 1989, pp. 4–6.

Tarde, Gabriel, *The Laws of Imitation*, New York, Henry Holt, 1903; originally published in French in 1895 as *Les lois de l'imitation*.

Thomas, James H., Kathleen M. Due and Diane M. Wigger, 'Effects of the Competence and Sex of Peer Models on Children's Imitative Behavior', *Journal of Genetic Psychology*, Vol. 148, No. 3, 1987, pp. 325–32.

Thrasher, Frederic M., *The Gang*, Chicago, University of Chicago Press, 1927.

Tianjin qingnian bao (ed.), *Qingnian shouce* (Youth handbook), Beijing, Zhongguo zhanwang chubanshe, 1986.

T'ien Ju-K'ang, *Male Anxiety and Female Chastity: A Comparative Study of Chinese Ethical Values in Ming-Ch'ng Times*, Monographies du T'oung Pao, Vol. 14, No. 14, Leiden, E. J. Brill, 1988.

Tittle, Charles R. and Alan R. Rowe, 'Moral Appeal, Sanction Threat, and Deviance: An Experimental Test', *Social Problems*, Vol. 20, No. 4, 1973, pp. 488–98.

Toffler, Alvin, *Previews and Premises*, London, Pan Books, 1984.

Tomas à Kempis, *The Imitation of Christ*, trans. by Edgar Daplyn of the manuscript '*De Imitatione Christi*' from 1441, London, Lakeland, 1979.

Tönnies, Ferdinand, *Einführung in die Soziologie*, Vol. 2, Stuttgart, Ferdinand Enke, 1931.

—— *Soziologische Studien und Kritiken, Dritte Sammlung*, Jena, Verlag von Gustav Fischer, 1929.

Tseng, Wen-Shing and David Y. H. Wu, *Chinese Culture and Mental Health*, London, Academic Press, 1985.

Turner, Victor, *The Forest of Symbols: Aspects of Ndembu Rituals*, Ithaca, NY, Cornell University Press, 1967.

—— *The Ritual Process*, Chicago, Aldine, 1969.

—— *Dramas, Fields, and Methaphors*, Ithaca, NY, Cornell University Press, 1974.

Unger, Jonathan, *Education under Mao: Class and Competition in Canton Schools 1960–1980*, New York, Columbia University Press, 1982.

—— 'Internal Change in China: Commentary', in Stuart Harris and James Cotton (eds.), *The End of the Cold War in Northeast Asia*, Melbourne, Longman Cheshire, 1991, pp. 72–8.

Walder, Andrew G., 'Organized Dependency and Cultures of Authority in Chinese Industry', *Journal of Asian Studies*, No. 1, 1983, pp. 51–76.

—— *Communist Neo-Traditionalism: Work and Authority in Chinese Industry*, Berkeley, University of California Press, 1986.

—— 'Communist Social Structure and Worker's Politics in China', in Victor C. Falkenheim (ed.), *Citizens and Groups in Contemporary China*, Michigan Monographs in Chinese Studies, Vol. 56, Ann Arbor, University of Michigan Press, 1987, pp. 45–89, 263–79.

—— 'Factory and manager in an era of reform', *China Quarterly*, No. 118, 1989, pp. 242–64.

—— 'A Reply to Womack', *China Quarterly*, No. 126, 1991, pp. 333–9.

Wang Banghui and Zhang Zhifen, 'Zhuzhong deyu de qianyi mohua yingxiang' (Pay attention to the imperceptible influence of education), *Zaoqi jiaoyu*, No. 3, 1991, pp. 2–3.

Wang Faxiong, *Renshi dang'an guanli gailun* (Introduction to file administration), Hubei renmin chubanshe, 1984.

Wang Fengxian, 'Xuexiao deyu de zhudao zuoyong yu shehui huanjing de youhua wenti' (The leading role of moral education in today's schools and the perfection of environment for social education), *Jiaoyu yanjiu*, No. 8, 1989, pp. 3–8.

Wang Ge, 'Gaige yu shehui kongzhi' (Reform and social control), *Shehui kexue*, No. 9, 1987, pp. 34–8; also in *Fuyin baokan ziliao, C4 Shehuixue*, No. 5, 1987, pp. 91–6.

Wang Guorong (ed.), *Guannian xiandaihua yi bai ti* (One hundred concepts of modernity), Beijing, Yejin gongye chubanshe, 1988.

Wang Guozhen and Zhang Maiyu, 'Bai ming weifa qingshaonian de jiating qingkuang diaocha' (An investigation of the family situation of one hundred juvenile criminals), *Wei le haizi*, No. 5, 1988, p. 19.

Wang Jie, *Wang Jie riji* (Wang Jie's diaries), Beijing, Renmin chubanshe, 1965.

Wang Keqian, 'Shilun jiazhi he pingjia' (On values and evaluations), *Shehui kexue jikan*, No. 1, 1990, pp. 17–23.

Wang Luosheng, 'Lun wo guo qingshaonian fanzui yufang' (On the prevention of juvenile delinquency in China), ed. Yantai daxue faxuesuo, *Zhong Mei xuezhe lun qingshaonian fanzui*, (in Chinese and English), Yantai, Qunzhong chubanshe, 1989, pp. 32–6.

Wang Ruiying, 'Zhengdang "xiao mifeng"' (Seeking to be 'honey-bees'), *Zhongguo funü*, No. 9, 1980, pp. 32–3.

Wang Ruoye and Han Shuyuan (Beijing shi jiating jiaoyu yanjiu hui) (of the Beijing municipality research association for family education), 'Dui Beijing 200 ming zhong-xue-sheng de shenghuo huanjing ji xing shengli yishi de diaocha baoguo' (Investigation report on the living environment and the sexual physiology and sexual awareness among 200 secondary school pupils), *Beijing Jiaoyu*, No. 11, 1989, p. 42.

Wang Xiaoling, 'Zhongxuesheng lianai qingkuang de diaocha' (An investigation of the situation of love affairs among secondary school pupils), *Shanghai jiaoyu*, No. 2, 1986, p. 12.

Wang Xingguo, 'Tantan chuantong yu gaige' (Discussing tradition and reform), *Hongqi*, No. 12, 1987, pp. 28, 30.

Wang Xingzhou, 'Guanyu daode pingjia de jiu ge wenti' (On some problems of moral evaluation), *Dongbei shida xuebao (zhexue shehui kexue ban)*, No. 3, 1987, pp. 1–7.

Wang Xinpan, 'Dui 416 ming qingshaonian xiongsha, shanghai fanzui de diaocha' (Investigation of 416 juvenile murderers and assaulters), in *Zhongguo qingshaonian fanzui yanjiu nianjian 1987*, Beijing, Chunqiu chubanshe, 1988, pp. 164–9.

Wang Yanfeng, 'Xiandai ren de yuedu zhanlüe' (The reading strategies of modern persons), *Qingnian shidai*, No. 7, 1989, p. 27.

Wang Yuezhong, 'Weishen cizi luokou de yeman xingwei' (Tatooing is a backwards and uncivilized behaviour), *Banyuetan*, No. 3, 1991, p. 41.

Wang Zhiping, 'Explicating "Law": A Comparative Perspective of Chinese and Western Legal Culture', *Journal of Chinese Law*, Vol. 3, No. 1, 1989, pp. 55–91.

Wang Ziguang, 'Ye tan qifa shi jiaoxue' (On teaching by elicitation), *Beijing jiaoyu*, No. 7, 1986, pp. 40–1.

Wang Zongzhu, 'Guanshu–shudao–xunlian' (Inculcation–dredging–drill), *Pujiao yanjiu*, No. 5, 1990, pp. 23–4.

Wasserstrom, Jeffrey N. and Elizabeth J. Perry (eds.), *Popular Protest and Political Culture in Modern China: Learning from 1989*, Boulder, Colo., Westview Press, 1992.

Watson, Burton (trans.), *Hsün Tzu: Basic Writings*, New York, Columbia University Press, 1963.

Watson, James L., 'The Renegotiation of Chinese Cultural Identity in the Post-Mao Era', in Jeffrey N. Wasserstrom and Elizabeth J. Perry, *Popular Protest and Political Culture in Modern China*, Boulder, Colo., Westview Press, 1992, pp. 67–84.

Weber, Max, *Essays in Sociology*, trans. H. H. Gerth and C. W. Mills, Oxford/New York, Oxford University Press, 1946.

—— *Grundriss der Sozialökonomik*, Vol. 3, *Abteilung: Wirtschaft und Gesellschaft*, 3rd edn., Tübingen, Verlag von J. C. B. Mohr, 1947.

—— *The Religion of China*, trans. Hans H. Gerth, New York, Free Press, 1951.

—— *The Theory of Social and Economic Organization*, trans. A. M. Henderson and Talcott Parsons, New York, Free Press, 1964.

—— *Gesammelte Aufsätze zur Religionssoziologie*, trans. Paul Siebeck, Vol. 1, Tübingen, J. C. B. Mohr, 1986; first published in 1922.

Wei He, 'Guanyu xiaoyuan wenhua de jiu qian tantao' (Study of campus cultures), *Jiaoyu yanjiu*, No. 2, 1992, pp. 31–4.

Wei Lei, *Zhongguo ren de renge: Cong chuantong dao xiandai* (The personality of the Chinese: from traditional to modern), Guiyang, Guizhou renmin chubanshe, 1988.

Wei Xiuyi (ed.), *Zhongguo wenhua re* (The Chinese culture fever), Shanghai, Shanghai renmin chubanshe, 1988.

Weiner, Myron (ed.), *Modernization: The Dynamics of Growth*, New York, Basic Books, 1966.

Wen Hanjiang, *Xiandai jiaoxue lun yinlun* (Guiding discussion in educational theory), Tianjin, Tianjin jiaoyu chubanshe, 1988.

Wen Yuankai, *Zhongguo chuantong wenhua qian jiegou de gaizao: Wen Yuankai tan gaige* (Remoulding the hidden structure of the Chinese traditional culture: Wen Yuankai on reform), Shanghai, Shanghai renmin chubanshe, 1988.

Westney, Eleanor D., *Imitation and Innovation: The Transfer of Western Organizational Patterns to Meiji Japan*, Cambridge, Mass., Harvard University Press, 1987.

White, Christine Pelzer, 'Everyday Resistance, Socialist Revolution and Rural Development: The Vietnamese Case', *Journal of Peasant Studies*, No. 2, 1986, pp. 49–63.

Whyte, Martin King, *Small Groups and Political Rituals in China*, Berkeley/Los Angeles, University of California Press, 1974.

Williams, Robin M., Jr. *American Society: A Sociological Interpretation*, New York, Alfred A. Knopf, 1951.

Wilson, James Q. and Richard J. Herrnstein, *Crime and Human Nature*, New York, Touchstone, 1985.

Wilson, Richard W., *The Moral State: A Study of the Political Socialization of Chinese and American Children*, New York, Free Press, 1974.

—— 'Conformity and Deviance Regarding Moral Rules in Chinese Society: A Socialization Perspective', in Arthur Kleinmann and Tsung-Yi Lin (eds.), *Normal and Abnormal Behaviour in Chinese Culture*, Dordrecht, D. Reidel, 1981, pp. 117–35.

—— Amy Auerbacher Wilson and Sidney L. Greenblatt (eds.), *Value Change in Chinese Society*, New York, Praeger, 1979.

Wolf, Preben, 'Crime and Development: An International Analysis of Crime Rates', *Scandinavian Studies in Criminology*, No. 3, 1971, pp. 107–20.

Womack, Brantly, 'Review Essay. Transfigured Community: Neo-traditionalism and Work-Unit Socialism in China', *China Quarterly*, No. 126, 1991, pp. 313–32.

Wood, David (ed.), *On Paul Ricoeur: Narrative and Interpretation*, London/ New York, Routledge 1991.

Wouters, Cas, 'Formalization and Informalization: Changing Tension Balances in Civilizing Processes', *Theory, Culture and Society*, Vol. 3, No. 2, 1986, pp. 1–17.

—— 'Developments in the Behavioural Codes between the Sexes: The Formalization of Informalization in the Netherlands, 1930–85', *Theory, Culture, and Society*, Vol. 4, No. 2–3, 1987, pp. 405–27.

Wrong, Dennis H., 'The Oversocialized Conception of Man in Modern Sociology', *American Sociological Review*, Vol. 26, No. 2, 1961, pp. 183–93.

Wu, Hongda Harry, *Laogai: The Chinese Gulag*, Boulder, Colo., Westview Press, 1992.

Wu Huijing and Fu Wen, 'Jisi zhi luan hou de lengjun fensi: He Xin fang tanlu' (Stern reflections on the chaos of 1989: notes from a talk with He Xin), *Zhongguo Qingnianbao*, 6 December 1989, pp. 1, 3.

Wu Naitao, 'Su Ning: A Pace Setter', *Beijing Review*, Vol. 34, No. 28, 1991, pp. 27–8.

Wu Qingxiang, 'Riben, Meiguo, he wo guo Shanghai diqu qingshaonian cuicuo yuanyin de bijiao fenxi' (Comparative analysis of the origins of criminal mistakes among youth in Japan, the United States, and the Shanghai area in China), in *Zhongguo qingshaonian fanzui yanjiu nianjian 1987*, Beijing: Chunqiu chubanshe, 1988, pp. 540–4.

Wu Shenyuan, *Zhongguo chuantong wenhua de yichuan he bianyi* (Change and heritage in Chinese culture), Changsha, Hunan wenyi chubanshe, 1988.

Wu Xinjuan and Chen Ziliang, *Xuesheng xinli yu banji guanli* (Student psychology and class management), Beijing, Zhongguo kexue jishu chubanshe, 1991.

Wu Zhen, 'Ertong mofang de tezheng yu jiaoyu' (The characteristics and education of children's imitation), *You'er jiaoyu*, No. 10, 1986, p. 5.

Wu Zhuo, 'Guanyu xuexi Lei Feng de jiu ge shiji wenti shiyi' (Clearing up some practical questions about learning from Lei Feng), *Zhongguo gaodeng jiaoyu*, No. 10, 1990, pp. 23–4.

Xia Daoxing, 'Gaige sixiang pinde ke kaocha de changshi' (An attempt to examine the reform of ideology and morality classes), *Jiaoxue yanjiu (xiaoxue ban)*, No. 4, 1987, pp. 37–8.

Xiang Zhongyu, 'Lun wo guo dui weifa fanzui shaonian de jiaoyu yu wanjiu' (On the education and redemption of juvenile delinquents in China), in Yantai daxue faxuesuo (ed.), *Zhong Mei xuezhe lun qingshaonian fanzui* (Juvenile delinquency and its treatment by Chinese and American Scholars), Yantai, Qunzhong Chubanshe, 1989.

Xianggang daxue xueshenghui guoshi xuehui (ed.), *Zhongguo sixiang jiefang wenji: gaige husheng* (Collected articles on the liberation of thought in China: the voice of reform), Hong Kong, Jixian shuju, 1988.

Xiao Hongming, 'Piping de yishu' (The art of criticism), *Banzhuren*, No. 1, 1989, pp. 24–6.

'Xiao nühai gaobie zaolian' (Young girls, bid farewell to premature love), *Dongfang qingnian*, No. 9, 1989, p. 21.

Xiao Tulin, 'Chuli zaolian wenti "shifa" ' (Ten methods for handling problems of premature love), *Renmin jiaoyu*, No. 10, 1988, pp. 28–9.

Xiao Yuxiu and Yan Guocai, 'Shiji' (Memorization), in *Zhongguo dabaike quanshu: Jiaoyu* (The great Chinese encyclopedia: Education), Beijing, Zhongguo dabaike quanshu chubanshe, 1985, p. 322.

Xie Dexin, 'Qingnian de guannian bianhua he qingnian yeyu wenhua de xin qushi' (The change in youth concepts and the new trends in youth leisure time culture), in Gongqingtuan zhongyang xuanchuanbu (ed.), *Dangdai qingnian lilun dachao* (Theoretical waves on contemporary youth), Beijing, Nongcun duwu chubanshe, 1989, pp. 143–53.

Xie Hongmao and Chen Weifeng, 'Daxuesheng suzhi zonghe ceping tansuo' (Exploring the comprehensive appraisal of university students), *Fujian gaojiao yanjiu*, No. 1, 1991, pp. 63–6.

Xin Ming (ed.), *Fanzui xue* (Criminology), Chongqing, Chongqing chubanshe, 1991.

Xin Yang, 'Banzhuren zai jiejue "zaolian" wenti zhong de zuoyong' (The function of class teachers in solving the problem of 'premature love'), *Renmin jiaoyu*, No. 1, 1988, p. 37.

—— (ed.), *Zhongguo banzhurenxue* (Chinese class teacher studies), Changchun, Jilin jiaoyu chubanshe, 1990.

Xing Yihai, 'Zhongguo chuantong wenhua fan jinhua de tezhi ji qi weiji yu chulu' (The anti-evolutionary character, the crisis of Chinese traditional culture, and the way out), *Zhongshan daxue yanjiusheng xuekan (Sheke pian)*, No. 1, 1987, pp. 10–13; also in *Fuyin baokan ziliao, Wenhua yanjiu*, No. 4, 1987, pp. 35–8.

Xing Yu, 'Yong mubiao guanli fangfa jinxing jiceng danwei de jingshen wenming jianshe' (Use goal directed management methods in building spiritual civilization in basic level work-units), *Jingshen wenming jianshe*, No. 4, 1990, p. 28.

Xu Deqi and Wu Zaide, 'Guanyu tuanhuo fanzui yu qingshaonian buliang jiaowang de diaocha fenxi' (Survey analysis of gang crime and the bad contacts of juveniles), in *Zhongguo qingshaonian fanzui yanjiu nianjian 1987*, Beijing, Chunqiu chubanshe, 1988, pp. 185–7.

—— and —— 'Shi xi qingshaonian liumang tuanhuo touzi de texing ji jingcheng huangbian' (Tentative analysis of the characteristics and patterns forming and developing hooligan gang leaders), in *Zhongguo qingshaonian fanzui yanjiu nianjian 1987*, Beijing, Chunqiu chubanshe, 1988, pp. 398–406.

Xu Jian, 'Lun wo guo baohu qingshaonian lifa de xin fazhan' (New developments in the legislation of juvenile protection in China), in Yantai daxue faxuesuo (ed.), *Zhong Mei xuezhe lun qingshaonian fanzui* (Juvenile delinquency and its treatment by Chinese and American scholars), Yantai, Qunzhong chubanshe, 1989, pp. 113–23.

Xu Juefei, Shu Hongkang, Shao Mingzheng and Yu Qisheng, *Laodong gaizaoxue* (Studies in reform through labour), Beijing, Qunzhong chubanshe, 1983.

Xu Ming, Chu Xian, Song Defu, and Qiang Wei (eds.), *Sixiang zhengzhi gongzuo daoxiang* (Guidance in ideological–political work), Beijing, Kexue chubanshe, 1990.

Xu Qiancheng, 'Hubei Jingzhou diqu nongcun "tuliuzi" fanzui diaocha' (An investigation of crime among local thugs in Hubei's Jingzhou area), in *Zhongguo qingshaonian fanzui yanjiu nianjian 1987*, Beijing, Chunqiu chubanshe, 1988, pp. 154–7.

Xu Shen (ed.), *Shuowen jieci zhu* (Explanations and analysis of characters with commentaries), Shanghai, Shanghai guji chubanshe, 1981.

—— (ed.), *Shuowen jiezi* (Explanations and analysis of characters), Beijing, Zhonghua shuju, 1990.

Xu Sumin, 'Ren de xiandaihua' (The modernization of man), *Qingnian luntan*, No. 1, 1984, pp. 10–17.

Xu Weicheng, 'Create a Socialist Moral System with Chinese Characteristics', *Sixiang zhengzhi gongzuo yanjiu* (Research in ideological political work), No. 11, 1990, pp. 8–12; Part I in *JPRS Report*, *JPRS-CAR*-90-086, 21 November 1990, pp. 6–9; Part II in *JPRS Report*, *JPRS-CAR*-91-005, 31 January 1991, pp. 57–62.

Xu Yinglong, 'Ba meihao de qiwang zhuanhua wei haizi shangjing de lizhong', *Qiushi*, No. 16, 1988, pp. 10–12.

Xu Zhangsong (ed.), *Daxuesheng chengcai xiuyang* (Self cultivation for university students to grow into useful timber), Shanghai, Fudan daxue chubanshe, 1988.

Yan Zhimin, 'Guanyu lixiang de jiu ge bianzheng guanxi' (On some dialectical relations concerning ideals), *Hongqi*, No. 16, 1986, pp. 39–44.

Yando, Regina, Victoria Seitz and Edward Zigler, *Imitation: A Developmental Perspective*, New York, John Wiley, 1978.

Yang, C. K., 'Some Characteristics of Chinese Bureaucratic Behavior', in David S. Nivison and Arthur F. Wright, *Confucianism in Action*, Stanford, Calif., Stanford University Press, 1959, pp. 134–64.

Yang Deguang, 'Gaoxiao deyu ying juyou xiangdui duli diwei' (University moral education should have an independent status), *Renmin ribao*, 1 July 1989, p. 5.

Yang Fan and Lin Xiao (eds.), *Zhongguo minjian shejiao tongyong quanshu* (Encyclopedia of China's popular rules for social relations in common use), Nanning, Guangxi renmin chubanshe, 1990, p. 1.

Yang Guoshu (ed.), *Zhongguo ren de xinli* (The psychology of the Chinese), Taipei, Guiguan tushu gongsi chubanshe, 1989.

Yang, Mayfair Mei-hui, *Gifts, Favors and Banquets: The Art of Social Relationships in China*, Ithaca, NY, Cornell University Press, 1994.

Yang Wenrong, 'Xin shiqi deyu fangfa de tedian' (Characteristics of moral education methods in the new period), *Banzhuren*, No. 4, 1990, pp. 5–7.

Yang Xin, 'Chuzhong nüsheng de zaolian ji jiating jiaoyu de zhidao' (Premature love among female lower secondary school pupils and family education), *Beijing Jiaoyu*, No. 12, 1987, p. 8.

Yang Xiong, 'Lun dangdai qingnian wenhua de "changbo" xianxiang' (On the phenomenon of 'long wave' youth culture), *Qingnian yanjiu*, No. 2, 1990, pp. 1–6.

Yang Ye, 'Ku a! Zai ouxiang guanghuan li' (Oh bitterness! Inside the halo of an idol), *Nianqing ren*, No. 8, 1989, pp. 22–3.

Yantai daxue faxuesuo (ed.), *Zhong Mei xuezhe lun qingshaonian fanzui* (Juvenile delinquency and its treatment by Chinese and American scholars) (in Chinese and English), Yantai, Qunzhong chubanshe, 1989.

Ye Nanke and Tang Zhongxun, 'Lun xiandai renge zhuanxing' (On the changing character of Chinese personality), *Shanghai shehui kexueyuan xueshu jikan*, No. 1, 1990. pp. 122–8; also in *Fuyin baokan ziliao, C4 Shehuixue*, No. 3, 1990, p. 33.

Ye Xiaoping and Yin Jianhua, ' "Yingxiang yi dai" biaozheng ji duice chutan' (Initial discussion of the illnesses of the 'image generation' and its counter-measures), *Qingnian yanjiu xuekan*, No. 1, 1991, pp. 38–41.

Ye Zheng, 'Zhuru shi jiaofa fei gaibian bu ke' (Cramming methods of education must be revised), *Zhengzhi jiaoyu*, No. 5, 1986, pp. 38–9.

Yeh, Eng-kung, 'The Chinese Mind and Human Freedom', *International Journal of Social Psychiatry*, Vol. 18, No. 2, 1972, pp. 132–6.

Yi Changtai, 'Jingji gaige yu shehui xinli' (Economic reform and social psychology), *Zhongguo jingji wenti*, No. 3, 1987, pp. 1–6, 21; also in *C4 Shehuixue, Fuyin baokan ziliao*, No. 4, 1987, pp. 75–81.

Yin Anren, 'Shilun xuesheng xingwei de kongzhi yu tiaojie' (On the control and regulation of student behaviour), *Shehui*, No. 5, 1985, pp. 3–8.

Yin Lujun (trans.), *Ren de xiandaihua* (The modernization of man), Chengdu, Sichuan renmin chubanshe, 1985.

Yinghan jiaoyu cidian (English–Chinese dictionary of education), Beijing, Jiaoyu kexue chubanshe, 1982.

Yinghan shehuixue cihui (English–Chinese glossary of sociology), Nanchang, Jiangxi renmin chubanshe, 1983.

Young, Graham, 'The Fourteenth Congress of the Chinese Communist Party: Consolidation of Reformist Orthodoxy', *China Information*, Vol. 7, No. 3 (Winter 1992–3), pp. 1–8.

Yü Chün-fang, *The Renewal of Buddhism in China: Chu-hung and the Late Ming Synthesis*, New York, Columbia University Press, 1981.

Yu Fuchang, 'Caoxing pingyu qianshuo' (Elementary introduction to student conduct), *Banzhuren*, No. 1, 1989, pp. 17–18.

Yu Qiding, 'Zai lun suzhi: jian ping Hong Baoshu tongzhi de "shangque" ' (Discussing quality again: and evaluating comrade Hong Baoshu's 'Discussion'), *Jiaoyu lilun yu shijian*, No. 10, 1990, pp. 46–50.

Yu Qihong, Yin Zhijing, 'Bu yukuai–taoye–xing cuizuo' (Unhappy–running away–sexual criminal mistakes), *Dangdai qingnian yanjiu*, No. 1, 1988, pp. 10–11.

Yu Wujin, 'Lun dangdai Zhongguo wenhua de ji zhong beilun' (On some controversies in contemporary Chinese culture), *Renmin ribao*, 22 August 1988, p. 5.

Yu Xinting, 'Dalu zhengzhi fan zhi duoshao?' (How much political crime exists in mainland China?), *Zhengming*, No. 12, December 1991, p. 14.

Yuan Fangfu and Wu Jieping, *Xing zhishi shouce* (Handbook of sexual knowledge), Beijing, Kexue jishu wenxie chubanshe/Renmin weisheng chubanshe, 1988.

Yuan Huayin and Pang Shuqi, 'Tantan tizhi gaige yu shehui pingheng wenti' (On the problem of system reform and social equilibrium), *Shehuixue yanjiu*, No. 5, 1987, pp. 76–9; also in *C4 Shehuixue, Fuyin baokan ziliao*, No. 5, 1987, pp. 87–91.

Yuan Jinhua, 'Qingshaonian fanzui yu xuexiao jiaoyu de guanxi de diaocha' (Survey on the connection between juvenile crime and school education), *Jiaoyu yanjiu*, No. 11, 1986, pp. 60–2, 80.

Yuan Zhenhui, 'Lun jiaoyu zhong lixing yinsu yu fei lixing yinsu de hubu guanxi', *Zhongguo shehui kexue*, No. 2, 1987, pp. 145–56, 191; trans. as 'On the Complementary Relationship between Rational and Irrational Factors in Education', *Social Sciences in China*, No. 1, 1988, pp. 185–99.

Yun Pengju, 'Guanyu qingnian shehuihua de ji ge wenti' (On some problems concerning the socialization of youth), in Gongqingtuan zhongyang xuanchuanbu (eds.), *Dangdai qingnian lilun dachao* (The theoretical spring tide of modern youth), Beijing, Nongcun duwu chubanshe, 1989, pp. 163–76.

Zagorin, Perez, *Ways of Lying*, Cambridge, Mass., Harvard University Press, 1990.

Zeng Tao, Wei Xiaohong and Lan Yue, 'Zhongxuesheng zaolian bu juyou pubian xing' (Premature love among secondary school students is not widespread), *Qingnian yanjiu*, No. 4, 1987, pp. 18–21.

Zha Bo and Geng Wenxiu, 'Sexuality in Urban China', *Australian Journal of Chinese Affairs*, No. 28, July 1992, pp. 1–20.

Zhang Boxing, 'Yongyuan jicheng fayang jianku fendou de Yan'an jingshen' (Forever carry on the Yan'an spirit of plain living and hard work), *Qiushi*, No. 19, 1990, pp. 2–7.

Zhang Deqing, 'Zou chuqu, chengshou meihao huanjing de xuntao: xuesheng suzhi peiyang gongzuo zhi yi' (Go out, inherit the edifying effect of a beautiful environment: student quality development work, Part one), *Beijing jiaoyu*, No. 7–8, 1987, p. 46.

—— 'Zou chuqu, chengshou meihao huanjing de xuntao: xuesheng suzhi peiyang gongzuo zhi er' (Part two), *Beijing jiaoyu*, No. 9, 1987, pp. 14–15.

Zhang Guangbo (ed.), *Shehuixue cidian* (Dictionary of sociology), Beijing, Renmin chubanshe, 1989.

Zhang Jian and Zhang Wenbang, 'Dui Zhejiang sheng nü fanzui fuxing qijian de tuanhuo huodong fenxi' (Analysis of the gang activities of female prisoners in Zhejiang province during the period of imprisonment), in *Zhongguo qingshaonian fanzui yanjiu nianjian 1987*, Beijing, Chunqiu chubanshe, 1988, pp. 413–19.

Zhang Jilian, 'Bangyang jiaoyu youxiao tujing de bijiao yanjiu' (Comparative research on the effective ways of model learning), *Xinli xuebao*, No. 1, 1984, pp. 27–33.

Zhang Jing, Shao Daosheng, Yang Shufeng, Yang Ruohe, Zhang Hanying, and Zhou Lu, 'Yige xin de yanzhong de shehui wenti' (A new important social problem), *Qingshaonian fanzui yanjiu*, No. 2, 1983, pp. 2–6, 24; also in 'Tianjin shi liushisheng yu weifa fanzui de diaocha' (Investigation of dropouts and criminal offences in Tianjin), *Zhongguo qingshaonian fanzui yanjiu nianjian 1987*, Beijing, Chunqiu chubanshe, 1988, pp. 222–6.

Zhang Lifu, 'Xianjin yinggai shi huoshengsheng de' (Older people must keep active), *Zhongguo qingnian bao*, No. 20, 1981, p. 11.

Zhang Liwen *et al.* (eds.), *Chuantong wenhua yu xiandaihua* (Traditional culture and modernization), Beijing, Zhongguo renmin daxue chubanshe, 1987.

Zhang Mingyuan, *Zhongguoren de rensheng quxian* (The lifeline of the Chinese), Beijing, Zhongguo renmin daxue chubanshe, 1989.

Zhang Nianhong (ed.), *Jiaoyuxue cidian* (Dictionary of education), Beijing, Beijing chubanshe, 1987.

—— and Leng Hong'en (eds.), *Rencaixue cidian* (Dictionary of talent studies), Beijing, Nongcun duwu chubanshe, 1989.

Zhang Panshi, 'Dui shaonian "taoye" xianxiang de diaocha' (Investigation of the 'runaway' phenomenon among juveniles), in *Zhongguo qingshaonian fanzui yanjiu nianjian 1987*, Beijing, Chunqiu chubanshe, 1988, pp. 226–9.

—— 'Lüe lun qingshaonian de zisha wenti jiqi yufang' (Brief discussion of youth suicide and its prevention), *Shanghai qingnian yanjiu*, No. 7, 1986, pp. 26–8.

Zhang Shaoxia, 'Wo guo bangjiao gongzuo de lilun yu shijian' (The theory and practice of Chinese help-education work), in Yantai daxue faxuesuo (ed.), *Zhong Mei xuezhe lun qingshaonian fanzui* (Juvenile delinquency and its treatment by Chinese and American scholars), Yantai, Qunzhong chubanshe, 1989, pp. 83–91.

Zhang Xiaolin, 'Zhangxue bawo jingshen wenming yu shangpin jingji de jiu ge lilun wenti' (Several theoretical questions on correctly grasping the relationship between spiritual civilization and commodity economy), *Qiushi*, No. 9, 1990, pp. 38–43.

Zhang Xuemin, 'Zun lao jing xian yingdang chengwei shidai fengshang' (Respecting the old and the virtuous should become the practice of the times), *Shehui kexue jikan*, No. 4, 1989, pp. 29–32.

Zhang Yingzhi, 'Wo guo qingnian lüyou re' (The Chinese travelling craze), in Gongqingtuan zhongyang yanjiushi (ed.), *Zhongguo daqushi yu dangdai qingnian* (Chinese megatrends and contemporary youth), Jinan, Shandong renmin chubanshe, 1989, pp. 103–10.

Zhang Yunqin, 'Zenyang peiyang xuesheng ganbu' (This is the way to foster class cadres), *Beijing jiaoyu*, No. 12, 1985, p. 7.

Zhang Yusheng, 'Lei Feng jingshen shi yongheng de' (The Lei Feng spirit is eternal), *Hongqi*, No. 7, 1987, p. 47.

Zhang Yutian, *et al.* (eds.), *Xuexiao jiaoyu pingjia* (Evaluation in school education), Beijing, Zhongying minzu xueyuan chubanshe, 1987.

Zhang Zhanbing and Song Yifu, *Zhongguo: Mao Zedong re* (China: the Mao Zedong fever), Beijing, Beiyue wenyi chubanshe, 1991.

Zhang Zhilun, 'Shilun "guanshu"' (Tentative discussion on 'inculcation'), *Pujiao yanjiu*, No. 2, 1991, pp. 26–7, 33.

Zhang Zhixue, 'Tan pinde xinli de jiegou' (On the structure of moral character psychology), *Jiaoyu Yanjiu*, No. 7, 1990, pp. 37–41.

Zhang Zongke, 'Wo zheyang jinxing qimo fuxi' (This is how I conduct end-term reviews), *Xiaoxue jiaoxue yanjiu*, No. 6, 1991, p. 2.

Zhang Zuhua, ' "Sihua" yu guannian xiandaihua' ('The four modernizations' and the modernization of concepts), in Gongqingtuan zhongyang yanjiushi, (ed.), *Zhongguo daqushi yu dangdai qingnian* (Chinese megatrends and contemporary youth), Jinan, Shandong renmin chubanshe, 1989, pp. 42–52.

Zhao Bingzhi, 'Lun wo guo xingfa dui weichengnian ren fanzui congkuan chufa de yuanze' (On the principle of treating under-aged criminals with leniency in Chinese criminal law), *Zhengzhi luntan: Zhongguo zhengzhi daxue xuebao*, No. 1, 1989, pp. 19–25.

Zhao Lu, Yang Ruohe and Hu Ruquan, *Qingshaonian fanzui zonghe zhili duicexue* (Studies in how to deal with comprehensive control of juvenile crime), Beijing, Qunzhong chubanshe, 1986.

Zhao Tiantang, 'Zhongguo chuantong renge de xiaoji yinsu ji qi chengyin' (The negative factors of the Chinese traditional personality and their causes), *Shehui*, No. 2, 1991, pp. 8–11.

Zhao Xuehua, 'Xin shiqi peiyang mubiao de tedian' (The characteristics of fostering objectives in the new period), *Beijing jiaoyu*, No. 12, 1986, p. 6.

Zhao Zixiang, Li Shuliang and Wang Zheng, 'Qingnian wenhua yu shehui bianqian' (Youth culture and social change), *Shehui kexue zhanxian*, No. 4, 1988, pp. 109–16.

Zheng Xinran, 'Bangyang huodong yu ren de xinli fenxi' (A psychological analysis of education by model activities), *Qingnian chao*, No. 3, 1990, pp. 17–20.

Zheng Yunzhen, 'Xing fanzui nü qingshaonian de gexing pianqing he tiaozheng' (Individual character deviation and the correction of young sexual criminal girls), *Jiaoyu lilun yu shijian*, No. 1, 1986, pp. 59–63.

Zheng Zhang, 'Wo guo dangqian qingshaonian weifa fanzui de qungkuang he tedian' (The present situation and characteristics of juvenile delinquency in China), *Qingshaonian fanzui yanjiu*, No. 10, 1990, pp. 6–8.

Zhong Peizhang, 'Qingnian jiaoyu de kunhuo' (The perplexity of youth education), *Qiushi*, No. 5, 1988, pp. 22–4.

Zhonggong zhongyang Mao Zedong sixiang yanjiushi bianxiezu (ed.), *Sixiang zhengzhi gongzuo jiaocheng* (Lectures in political–ideological work), Beijing, Zhonggong zhongyang dangxiao chubanshe, 1987.

Zhonggong zhongyang zuzhibu zuzhiju (ed.), *Ru dang jiaocai* (Teaching material on entering the Party), Shanghai, Shanghai renmin chubanshe, 11th edn., March 1991; first published in 1989.

Zhongguo baike nianjian 1982, 1983, 1984, 1985, 1987, Shanghai, Zhongguo da baike quanshu chubanshe, 1982, 1983, 1984, 1985, 1987.

Zhongguo dabaike quanshu: jiaoyu (The Great Chinese Encyclopedia: Education), Beijing, Zhongguo dabaike chubanshe, 1985.

Zhongguo falü nianjian (The law yearbook of China) 1988, 1989, 1990, 1991, 1992, 1993, 1994, 1995, 1996, 1997, 1998, Beijing, Zhongguo falü nianjian she, 1988–98.

Zhongguo gongchandang zhangcheng (The regulations of the Communist Party of China), Beijing, Renmin chubanshe, 1982.

Zhongguo qingshaonian fanzui yanjiu nianjian 1987 (Yearbook on Chinese juvenile delinquency studies), Beijing, Chunqiu chubanshe, 1988.

Zhongguo renkou tongji nianjian 1990 (China population statistics yearbook 1990), Beijing, Kexue jishu wenxian chubanshe, 1991.

Zhongguo renmin jiefangjun zong zhengzhibu quncong gongzuobu (Mass Work Department, General Political Department, People's Liberation Army) (ed.), 'Jinyibu gaohao junmin gongjian jingshen wenming de huodong' (Do a still better job in building a spiritual civilization with Army-people joint activities), *Qiushi*, No. 15, 1990, pp. 17–21.

Zhongguo shehui kexueyuan shehuixue yanjiusuo (Department of Sociology, Chinese Academy of Social Sciences) (ed.), *Qingshaonian fanzui xinlixue* (The psychology of juvenile delinquency), Shanghai, Shanghai renmin chubanshe, 1985.

—— (ed.), *Zhongguo shehuixue nianjian 1979–1989* (China yearbook of sociology 1979–1989), Beijing, Zhongguo dabaike quanshu chubanshe, 1989.

Zhongguo shehui tongji ziliao 1990 (The social statistics of China 1990), Beijing, Zhongguo tongji chubanshe, 1990.

Zhongguo 1982 nian renkou pucha ziliao (Materials from the 1982 population census of China), Beijing, Zhongguo tongji chubanshe, 1985.

Zhonghua renmin gongheguo gonganbu (The PRC Ministry of Public Security), 'Zhongguo qingshaonian fanzui de qushi he yufang' (Trends in Chinese juvenile delinquency and its prevention), in *Zhongguo qingshaonian fanzui yanjiu nianjian 1987*, Beijing, Chunqiu chubanshe, 1988, pp. 41–7.

—— 'Wo guo qingshaonian fanzui de qushi he yufang' (The trends of juvenile crime in China and their prevention), in *Zhongguo qingshaonian fanzui yanjiu nianjian 1987*, Beijing, Chunqiu chubanshe, 1988, pp. 41–7.

Zhonghua xingfa cidian (Chinese dictionary of criminal law), Shanghai, Xuelin chubanshe, 1989.

Zhongxue zhengzhike shouce, 'Qingshaonian xiuyang' bufen (Political class manual for secondary schools, 'Youth self-cultivation' section), Beijing, Beijing shifan daxue chubanshe, 1984.

Zhongwen da cidian (The encyclopedic dictionary of the Chinese language), 7th edn., Vols. 4, 6 and 8, Taipei/Huakang/Yangmingshan, Chinese Culture University, 1985.

Zhongxue zhengzhike shouce, 'Qingshaonian xiuyang' bufen (Political class manual for middle schools, 'Youth self-cultivation' section), Beijing, Shifan daxue chubanshe, 1984.

Zhou Dechang, *Zhongguo gudai jiaoyu sixiang de piping jicheng* (Criticizing and inheriting ancient Chinese educational thinking), Beijing, Jiaoyu kexue chubanshe, 1982, pp. 87–121.

Zhou Lu, Yang Ruoquan, and Hu Ruyong, *Qingshaonian fanzui zonghe zhili duice xue* (Studies in how to deal with comprehensive control of juvenile crime), Beijing, Qunzhong chubanshe, 1986.

Zhou Luming, 'Ba gaoxiao sixiang zhengzhi gongzuo zuowei yi men kexue lai yanjiu' (Study ideological–political work in universities as a science), *Gaodeng jiaoyu yanjiu*, No. 4, 1985, pp. 88–9, 94.

Zhou Weixin, 'Zhongguo chengshi fanzui xianzhuang pouxi' (Analysis of the situation of urban crime in China), *Shehui*, No. 5, 1988, pp. 14–15.

Zhou Xiaozheng, 'Renkou suzhi shi wo guo renkou wenti de guanjian' (Population quality is the key to the problem of China's population), *Keji daobao*, No. 4, 1989, pp. 14–19, 28; also in *Fuyin baokan ziliao*, C5, *Renkouxue*, No. 5, 1989, pp. 83–90.

Zhou Zuoren, '*Liangge gui*' (Two demons), in *Zhou Zuoren zaoqi sanwen xuan* (Selected early prose of Zhou Zuoren), Shanghai, Shanghai wenyi chubanshe, 1984.

Zhu Genxiang, 'Lun shehui kongzhi yu sixiang zhengzhi gongzuo' (On social control and political/ideological work), *Hubei dangxiao xuebao*, No. 6, 1987, pp. 44–6, also in *Sixiang zhengzhi jiaoyu*, *Fuyin baokan ziliao*, G2, No. 2, 1988, pp. 30–2.

Zhu Jiang and Zhang Yaocan, *Daxue deyu gailun* (Introduction to university moral education), Wuhan, Hubei jiaoyu chubanshe, 1986.

Zhu Ruoqian and Xu Jiangjia, 'Jiaoyu shi tigao quan minzu suzhi de zhongyao shouduan' (Education is an important method of raising the quality of the whole nation), *Xiandaihua* (Modernization), No. 11, 1988, pp. 19–20; also in *Jiaoyuxue*, G1 *Fuyin baokan ziliao*, No. 1, 1989, pp. 53–4.

Zhu Xiaomin, 'Shilun laogai fan zhong de fanzui tuanhuo' (Tentative discussion on criminal gangs among inmates in reform through labour institution), in *Zhongguo qingshaonian fanzui yanjiu nianjian 1987*, Beijing, Chunqiu chubanshe, 1988, pp. 411–13.

Zhu Yagao, 'Tantan xie pinde pingyu' (On writing moral evaluations), *Shanghai jiaoyu*, No. 6, 1985, p. 12.

Zong zhengzhibu (ed.), *Lei Feng riji xuan* (Selections from Lei Feng's diaries), Beijing, Jiefangjun wenyi chubanshe, 1989.

Zou Hanming and Li Hui, 'Chengdu shi qingshaonian weifa fanzui diaocha' (An investigation of juvenile delinquency in Chengdu), *Qingshaonian fanzui yanjiu*, No. 10, 1990, pp. 9–12.

Zou Ping, 'Beijing shi bufen weihun qingnian rengong liuchan qingkuang de diaocha' (An investigation of abortion among some unmarried youth in Beijing), *Qingnian yan-jiu*, No. 10, 1985, pp. 57–61.

Zou Xiaohong, 'Daxuesheng lianai chengfeng bu xunchang' (Student love is becoming unusually common), *Zhongguo jiaoyubao*, 8 September 1988, p. 3.

1986 Baokao gongdu shuoshi xuewei yanjiu dengjibiao (Registration form for entering the 1986 master's degree examinations), Beijing, 1986.

Select Glossary

爱情协议书	aiqing xieyi shu	love contract
安定团结	anding tuanjie	stability and unity
暗示教育	anshi jiaoyu	suggestive education
帮教小组	bangjiao xiaozu	help-education small group
榜样	bangyang	model
榜样教育	bangyang jiaoyu	model education
班长	banzhang	class sponsor
班主人	banzhuren	class teacher
背诵	beisong	repeat the text from memory
崩溃修复	bengkui xiufu	collapse-restoration
变	bian	change
边际人	bianji ren	marginal person
边缘预防	bianyuan yufang	marginal prevention
表现	biaoxian	show, display, manifestation
表演	biaoyan	performance, act, exhibit
表扬	biaoyang	commend, praise
标准	biaozhun	standard
标准答案	biaozhun da'an	standard answer
毕业鉴定	biye jianding	graduation appraisal
不合格	bu hege	not qualified (grade)
不良习气	buliang xiqi	bad habits
不平衡	bu pingheng	unstable
不听话	bu tinghua	disobey
残疾人口	canji renkou	disabled population
差	cha	not up to standard (grade)
常规	changgui	routine, rule
忏悔信	chanhui xin	letter of repentence
超前消费	chaoqian xiaofei	premature consumption
超稳定	chao wending	ultrastability
超稳定的平衡	chao wending de pingheng	ultrastable equilibrium
差序格局	chaxu geju	differentially ordered configuration
城	cheng	sincerity
成人	chengren	adult, grown-up
逞凶到底	chengxiong daodi	intimate brothers
吃喝玩乐	chi-he-wan-le	eat, drink, and have fun
窗口单位	chuangkou danwei	window (exemplary) work unit

创新	chuangxin	innovation
创造	chuangzao	create
传统人格	chuantong renge	traditional personality
处分	chufen	punishment
刺激	ciji	(unhealthy) stimulation
大领未婚青年	daling weihun qingnian	older unmarried youth
档案	dang'an	file, dossier
挡案室	dang'an shi	personnel office
单位	danwei	work unit
单位性质	danwei xingzhi	work unit character
道德败坏	daode baihuai	morally degenerate
道德建设	daode jianshe	moral construction
道德沦丧	daode lunsang	moral decline
道德失落	daode shiluo	loss of morality
大同	datong	great harmony
大我	dawo	big me
打一警百	da yi jing bai	beating one to warn a hundred
德	de	morality
德育的效率	deyu de xiaolü	moral efficiency
德育教育	deyu jiaoyu	moral education
德育投资	deyu touzi	moral investment
典型	dianxing	model, typical example
底下	dixia	underground
地一次	diyi ci	the first time
动	dong	movement
动乱	dongluan	turmoil, disturbance
动作	dongzuo	(bodily) movement
二重性的人格	erchong xing de renge	double personality
耳濡目染	erru-muran	be imperceptibly influenced by
恶性	exing	evil stimulation
法	fa	law
反常	fanchang	unusual, strange, perverse
反潮流	fan chaoliu	going against the tide
反复	fanfu	rehabilitation, repeated practice
反复锻炼	fanfu duanlian	repeated exercise
反复教育	fanfu jiaoyu	education by repetition
方法	fangfa	method
反规范	fan guifan	anti-norm

翻身	fanshen	self-examination
范围	fanwei	sphere
反省	fanxing	introspection
犯罪教育	fanzui jiaoyu	crime pedagogy
犯罪集团	fanzui jituan	criminal circle
犯罪团伙	fanzui tuanhuo	criminal gang
犯罪预测	fanzui yuzi	criminal forecast
发现榜样	faxian bangyang	discover a model
发泄	faxie	letting off feelings
封建行帮	fengjian hangbang	feudal trade association
风派	feng pai	wind faction
分配	fenpei	job allocation
复	fu	repeat
辅导员	fudaoyuan	political instructor
复评	fuping	repeated evaluation
复苏	fusu	recovery
复习	fuxi	repetition
改造	gaizao	reform, transform, remould
改造环境	gaizao huanjing	transform (improve) the environment
干部档案	ganbu dang'an	cadre's file
赶时髦	gan shimao	follow the fashion
高消费论	gao xiaofei lun	theory of high consumption
高消费热	gao xiaofei re	high consumption fever
割肝	gegan	cut one's liver to show filial piety
割股	gegu	cut one's flesh to show filial piety
个人素质	geren suzhi	individual quality
哥儿们	germen	brothers, buddies
哥儿们义气	germen yiqi	(criminal) code of brotherhood
个体户	getihu	self-employed person
个体素质	geti suzhi	personal quality
公	gong	public
工读学校	gongdu xuexiao	work-study school
工具论	gongju lun	tool theory
工人档案	gongren dang'an	worker's file
工作鉴定	gongzuo jianding	work appraisal
怪	guai	odd, strange
关防	guanfang	'rule of isolation' (official seal)
灌输	guanshu	inculcation
关系本位	guanxi benwei	relation based

关系网	guanxi wang	connection net
骨干分子	gugan fenzi	backbone element, key member
规范	guifan	norm, standard, pattern, model, example
过度学习	guodu xuexi	'over-learning'
好	hao	good
好人好事记载本	haoren haoshi jizaiben	account book for good deeds and persons
好学生	hao xuesheng	good student
合格	hege	qualified
黑社会	hei shehui	secret society
合理的社会平衡	heli de shehui pingheng	rational social equilibrium
恒	heng	constant
和谐	hexie	harmony
后门	houmen	back door
化	hua	change
坏	huai	bad
黄帝	Huangdi	yellow emperor
皇冠主义	huangguan zhuyi	emperorism
环境陶冶	huanjing taoye	environmental moulding
环境文化	huanjing wenhua	environmental culture
会	hui	meeting
会馆	huiguan	trade guild
户口	hukou	household registration
狐狸精	huli jing	fox spirit, seductive woman
混乱	hunluan	confusion
活动	huodong	activity, movement
互评	huping	mutual evaluation
家常会	jiachang hui	parents' meeting
家访	jiafang	(a teacher's) home visit
加分	jiafen	plus points
监督	jiandu	control
减分	jianfen	minus points
艰苦朴素艰苦奋斗	jianku pusu jianku fendou	plain living and hard struggle
江湖义气	jianghu yiqi	(criminal) brotherhood
教	jiao	teach, instruct
教育	jiaoyu	education
教育改造	jiaoyu gaizao	reform through education
教育感化挽救	jiaoyu, ganhua, wanjiu	educate, persuade, and save
夹塞儿	jia sair	jump the queue

家庭问题	jiating wenti	family problem
价值	jiazhi	value
家族性	jiazu xing	clan character
介绍信	jieshaoxin	letter of introduction
激发	jifa	stimulate
记分员	jifenyuan	score keeper
及格	jige	passed (grade)
记功	jigong	cite someone for meritorious service
记过	jiguo	demerit
积极	jiji	active
积极分子	jiji fenzi	activist
记录	jilu	record
警告	jinggao	disciplinary warning
净化	jinghua	purification
精神滑坡	jingshen huapo	spiritual slide
精神素质	jingshen suzhi	spiritual quality
精神卫生	jingshen weisheng	spiritual hygiene
精神文明	jingshen wenming	spiritual civilization
精神文明学	jingshen wenmingxue	spiritual civilization studies
精神污染	jingshen wuran	spiritual pollution
精神支柱	jingshen zhizhu	spiritual pillar
禁止	jinzhi	prohibition
机械熟记	jixie shuji	mechanical memorization
记忆力	jiyili	memory (power)
君子	junzi	(Confucian) gentleman
君子国	junzi guo	Country of Virtuous Men
开除	kaichu	expel (disciplinary sanction)
抗药性	kangyaoxing	immunity and resistance
看客	kanke	spectator
考记	kaoji	exam result
可塑性	kesuxing	plasticity, flexibility
课学管理	kexue guanli	scientific management
孔教	kongjiao	Confucian religion
控制	kongzhi	control
控制论	kongzhi lun	cybernetics
狂	kuang	crazy, wild
劳动	laodong	work
劳动模范	laodong mofan	worker model
劳改	laogai	reform through labour
劳绩	laoji	report on merits and accomplishments
劳教	laojiao	reform through education

礼	li	rules of propriety or proper conduct
脸	lian	face
良	liang	good (grade)
两个文明	liang ge wenming	two civilizations
劣	lie	inferior
劣根性	liegenxing	deep rooted bad habits
劣迹	lieji	evil deeds
历绩	liji	report on life experience and history
礼论	lilun	theory of *li* (礼)
零素质	ling suzhi	zero quality
临摹	linmo	copy a model of calligraphy or painting
临时	linshi gongren	temporary worker
历史问题	lishi wenti	historical problem
流	liu	float, drift, wander
流动	liudong	mobility
流动人口	liudong renkou	floating population
六害	liu hai	six evils
流氓	liumang	hooligan
乱	luan	disorder, chaos
盲流人口	mangliu renkou	blindly floating population
漫灌	manguan	flood irrigation
冒险	maoxian	risk taking
毛泽东热	Mao Zedong re	Mao Zedong fever
面具	mianju	mask
面子	mianzi	face
民族的文化素质	minzu de wenhua suzhi	national cultural quality
民族精神	minzu jingshen	national spirit
民族文化心珶	minzu wenhua xinli	national cultural psychology
民族性	minzu xing	national character
民族自我	minzu ziwo	national self
模范	mofan	model
模仿	mofang	imitate, copy
模仿战略	mofang zhanlue	imitation strategy
模范教师	mofan jiaoshi	model teacher
模拟	moni	simulation, imitation
勺	nei	inner
内部	neibu	internal (material)
内部模仿	neibu mofang	internal imitation
逆反心理	nifan xinli	psychology of defiance
凝聚力	ningju li	coagulating force
奴才性	nucai xing	lackey character

排解性疏导	paijie xing shudao	mediative dredging
培养	peiyang	foster, cultivate
培养榜样	peiyang bangyang	foster a model
评	ping	evaluate, appraise, judge
评班分	pingbanfen	collective (class) grades
评比	pingbi	evaluate, appraise through comparison
评反	pingfan	mishandled case
评分	pingfen	evaluation points
痞子	pizi	hooligan, ruffian
奇	qi	odd, queer
潜移默化	qianyi-mohua	exert a subtle influence on someone
潜在的生产力	qianzai de shengchanli	hidden productive forces
潜在课程	qianzai kecheng	hidden curriculum
启发式	qifa shi	elicitation method
情感陶冶法	qinggan taoye fa	method of moulding feelings
青年文化	qingnian wenhua	youth culture
青年亚文化	qingnian ya wenhua	youth subculture
弃其糟粕 取其精华	qiqi zaopo, quqi jinghua	get rid of the dross, and adopt the essence
热	re	fever
人	ren	person, human
仁	ren	benevolence
人才	rencai	talent
人才学	rencaixue	talent studies
人的素质	ren de suzhi	human quality
人的现代化	ren de xiandaihua	human modernization
人类素质学	renlei suzhixue	human quality studies
人事档案	renshi dang'an	personnel file
人言可畏	renyan ke wei	gossip is a fearful thing
儒	ru	Confucian
三好学生	san hao xuesheng	three-good student
煽动	shandong	instigator
上山下乡	shangshan-xiaxiang	up to the mountains, down to the villages
少年	shaonian	juvenile
傻子	shazi	idiot
傻子村	shazi cun	idiot village
社会工程	shehui gongcheng	social engineering
社会监督	shehui jiandu	social supervision
社会控制	shehui kongzhi	social control
社会人	shehui ren	social person

社会实践	shehui shijian	social practice
社会形态	shehui xingtai	social formation
社会约束	shehui yueshu	social restriction
社会秩序	shehui zhixu	social order
身	shen	body
审查	shencha	investigation
身份证	shenfenzheng	identity card
生搬硬套	shengban-yintao	copy mechanically
生存的危机	shengcun de weiji	existential crisis
神化	shenhua	deification
渗透	shentou	infiltration
诗	shi	poetry
师表	shibiao	model (of exemplary learning)
师创生收	shi chuang sheng shou	teachers pass on knowledge, students merely receive it
失衡	shi heng	loss of balance
十年树木，百年树人	shi nian shumu, bai nian shuren	it takes ten years to grow a tree, and a hundred years to foster (good) people
师成	shicheng	master to disciples way of teaching
失范	shifan	*anomie* (lose limits)
示范作用	shifan zuoyong	exemplary effect
识记	shiji	memorization
失落感	shiluo gan	feeling of being lost
失去优势的危机	shiqu youshi de weiji	crisis of losing superiority
失身	shi shen	loss of self
师生公评	shisheng gongping	mutual teacher–student evaluation
适应能力	shiying nengli	social adaptation ability
适应性	shiying xing	adaptability
慎独	shendu	being cautious when alone
帅	shuai	emulate
双重价值系统	shuang chong jiazhi xitong	double value system
疏导	shudao	dredge
输而不作	shu er bu zuo	transmit, but not create
四书	sishu	Four books (of Confucian classics)
思想	sixiang	ideology
思想反复	sixiang fanfu	ideological relapse
思想建设	sixiang jianshe	ideological construction
思想素质	sixiang suzhi	ideological quality
思想政治教育	sixiang zhengzhi jiaoyu	political-ideological education

思想转化	sixiang zhuanhua	ideological transformation
速度	sudu	speed
素质	suzhi	quality
素质档案	suzhi dang'an	quality file
他律	talü	other-ruled
谈恋爱	tan lian'ai	talk of love
贪欲	tanyu	insatiable desire
套话	taohua	polite (covered) talk
桃李不言，	tao li bu yan,	peaches and plums do not
下自成蹊	xia zi cheng xi	have to talk, yet the
		world beats a path to them
陶冶法	taoye fa	method of infiltration
陶冶性	taoye xing	moulding character
逃夜	taoye	runaway
特	te	special
特权	tequan	privilege
填表	tian biao	fill in a form
天法	tian fa	laws of heaven
填鸭式	tianya shi	method of force feeding
听话	tinghua	obey
同	tong	common, same, alike
同案	tong'an	same criminal case
同构系统	tonggou xitong	common structure system
同化	tonghua	assimilate
同活	tonghuo	partner
同乡	tongxiang	same homeplace
同姓	tongxing	common surname
同心圆	tongxinyuan	concentric circle
同学	tongxue	fellow student
同志	tongzhi	comrade (common will)
头子	touzi	gang leader
土流子	tuliuzi	rural hooligan
外	wai	outer
玩	wan	fun
伪君子	wei junzi	false gentleman
危机感	weiji gan	crisis consciousness
为了别人	weile bieren	for the other
为了自己	weile ziji	for oneself
为人民服务	wei renmin fuwu	serve the people
稳定	wending	stability
文化	wenhua	culture
文化建设	wenhua jianshe	cultural construction
文化决定论	wenhua juedinglun	cultural determinism
文化热	wenhua re	culture fever

文化失范	wenhua shifan	cultural *anomie*
文化素质	wenhua suzhi	cultural quality
文化学	wenhuaxue	culturology
文明	wenming	civilization
文明村	wenming cun	civilized village
文明单位	wenming danwei	civilized work unit
文明街	wenming jie	civilized street
问题	wenti	problem
我	wo	I, me
物的现代化	wu de xiandaihua	material modernization
五固定	wuguding	five regularities (of prison discipline)
无规范	wu guifan	without standards or norms
五好家庭	wu hao jiating	five-good family
五经	wujing	five classics
五论	wu lun	five human relations (in Confucianism)
无意识教育	wu yishi jiaoyu	unconscious education
物质文明	wuzhi wenming	material civilization
显露自己	xianlu ziji	manifest oneself
先入为主	xian ru wei zhu	first impressions are strongest
显示自己	xianshi ziji	show off (self)
孝	xiao	filial piety
小动作	xiao dongzuo	small (bodily) movements
效法	xiaofa	learn from, model oneself from, imitate
效仿	xiaofang	school visit
小范围	xiao fanwei	small range
小人	xiaoren	small man
孝悌	xiaoti	filial piety and fraternal duty
小我	xiaowo	little me
校长	xiaozhang	headmaster
小组	xiaozu	small group
习惯	xiguan	habit
心	xin	heart, mind
新	xin	new
刑	xing	imitate
行	xing	do, perform, carry out
性亢进	xing kangjin	sexual hyperfunction
行乐	xingle	pleasure
性乱	xingluan	sexual disorder
性癖的人	xingpi de ren	sexually addicted person
刑事处罚	xingshi chufa	criminal sanction

行为	xingwei	behaviour
性行为	xing xingwei	sexual behaviour
行政处分	xingzheng chufen	disciplinary sanction
性罪错	xing zuicuo	sexual transgression
心理档案	xinli dang'an	psychology file
心理检查	xinli jiancha	psychological inspection
心理平衡	xinli pingheng	psychological balance
心理素质	xinli suzhi	psychological quality
心理卫生	xinli weisheng	psychological hygiene
心理污染	xinli wuran	psychological pollution
新人	xin ren	new person
信息论	xinxi lun	information theory
戏台子	xitaizi	stage
系统	xitong	system
系统理论	xitong lilun	systems theory
修复机智	xiufu jizhi	restoration mechanism
修养	xiuyang	self-cultivation
选	xuan	election
宣传榜样	xuanchuan bangyang	promote a model
选择	xuanze	select
学潮	xuechao	campus upheaval
学生干部	xuesheng ganbu	student cadre
学生会	xuesheng hui	student union
学院文化	xueyuan wenhua	campus culture
驯服工具	xunfu gongju	docile tool
熏染	xunran	exert a gradual, corrupting influence
熏陶	xuntao	exert a gradual, uplifting influence
虚伪	xuwei	hypocrisy, falseness
虚伪文化	xuwei wenhua	culture of hypocricy
严打	yanda	severe blows campaign
养	yang	educate and cultivate
阳奉阴违	yangfeng-yuwei	covert opposition (feign compliance)
严厉打击严重刑事犯罪活动（严打）	yanli dali yanzhong xingshi fanzui huodong	campaign of severe blows against serious criminal activities (yanda)
亚文化	ya wenhua	subculture
义	yi	righteousness
意	yi	meaning, idea
一般预防	yiban yufang	general prevention
以法代德	yi fa dai de	replacing morality with law
引导	yindao	guidance

映象一代	yingxiang yidai	image generation
英雄	yingxiong	hero
英雄事迹	yingxiong shiji	heroic deeds
引经据典	yinjing-judian	copying the classics
隐形文化	yinxing wenhua	hidden culture
隐一套，堂一套	yin yitao, tang yitao	show one behaviour in private, another in public
艺术陶冶	yishu taoye	artistic moulding
一统化	yitonghua	unification
医治	yizhi	treatment
以知代德	yi zhi dai de	replacing morality with education
优	you	excellent (grade)
游荡	youdang	loaf about
优胜学	youshengxue	eugenics
约束力	yueshu li	restraining and binding force
运动	yundong	campaign
载体	zaiti	carrier
早恋	zaolian	premature love
早期教育	zaoqi jiaoyu	early education
障碍	zhang'ai	blockage
正	zheng	upright
政	zheng	administration
正本	zhengben	original document (confidential file)
政治处	zhengzhi chu	political office
政治历史材料	zhengzhi lishi cailiao	material on political history
政治问题	zhengzhi wenti	political problems
知	zhi	knowledge
旨	zhi	purpose
制	zhi	restraint
治安委员会	zhi'an weiyuanhui	security committee
指标	zhibiao	quota
制怒	zhinu	anger control
知人	zhi ren	know people
知人善人	zhi ren shan ren	knowing one's subordinates well enough to assign them jobs that fit their abilities
忠	zhong	loyalty
中	zhong	average (grade)
重点预防	zhongdian yufang	special prevention
重特大犯罪	zhongteda fanzui	major, special and serious crime

注入	zhuru	cramming, spoon feeding, pour into
注入式	zhuru shi	spoon feeding method
子	zi	child, son
自发论	zifa lun	theory of spontaneity
自己人	zijiren	one of us, in-group
自控性	zikong xing	self-controlling character
自利	zili	self-interest
自律	zilü	self-ruled
自评	ziping	self-evaluation
自然人	ziran ren	natural person
自然素质	ziran suzhi	natural quality
自私	zisi	self-centredness, egoism
自我	ziwo	self, oneself
自我管理	ziwo guanli	self-supervision
自我控制	ziwo kongzhi (zikong)	self-control
自我牺牲	ziwo xisheng	self-sacrifice
自由	ziyou	freedom
自由泛滥	ziyou fanlan	overflow of freedom
自由化	ziyouhua	liberalization
自主探索复习	zizhu tansuo fuxi	self-exploring repetition
综合测评	zonghe ceping	comprehensive appraisal
综合模仿	zonghe mofang	comprehensive imitation
综合治理	zonghe zhili	comprehensive control or management
总评	zongping	overall appraisal
尊敬长辈	zunjing zhangbei (zunzhang)	respect for the elder generation
作风问题	zuofeng wenti	problems of style
作给人看	zuo gei ren kan	do only for other people to see
作好人	zuo haoren	make good people
作好事	zuo haoshi	do good deeds
作人	zuo ren	make (do, be) a person
作戏	zuo xi	play theatre

Index

coercion 99–100
  through evaluation 276
  through imitation 139
  see also deterrence
cognition, *see* knowledge; 'mind set';
    thought patterns
Cohen, Stan 354
collectivism 58, 106–11, 337
  attitudes towards 256
  and culture 416
  as discipline 109
  and environmentalism 160
  inculcation of 155
  informal 191
  loss of traditional 222
  or prevention of collective action 437
Colson, Elizabeth 73
communism 9–10, 54, 415, 426
  as campaign 424
  and economic development 280
Communist Party 39, 55, 290, 301, 417
Communist Youth League 136, 155,
    199, 269, 292
  membership application to 256, 262,
    264, 290, 298
community:
  control 100, 380
  and crime prevention 345
  principle of *tong* 31–4, 341
  see also particularism; segmentary society
competition 61
  and evaluation 280
  in Party statutes 171
comrade 31
  and *Genossenschaft* 33–5
confession:
  as restoration of order 334
conformity/conformism 109, 113
  in China and the US 227–9
  and comparison 216–17
  surface 418
Confucian classics 25, 42, 144–5
Confucian ethic 4, 6, 8
  and principle of benevolence (*ren*) 104
  and principle of self-cultivation 266
  reemergence of 24
Confucianism 8
  Communist Party's celebration of 18
  and gentleman (*junzi*) ideal 91–2,
    120, 178, 412
  and ideal society 72
  and malleability of human beings 85
  and loyalty (*zhong*) 272
  order and disobedience in 221
  and punishment 94

revival of 29
and virtuous models 169
Confucius 92
  on educational methods 131, 152
  on exemplary virtue 172
  on hypocrisy and sincerity (*cheng*)
    414–15
  on individualization and differentiation
    255
  on poetry 143–4
  on preventing evil 341–2
consumption 101, 280
  fads 426
  fever of 318
  premature 102–3
Cooley, Charles H. 128
craze 140
  and campaigns 425
  and 'get-rich-quick' mentality 426
creativity:
  in ancient Chinese painting 137
  and creative capacity 71
  and creativeness studies 305
  destroyed in schools 273
  and imitation 135–6
  in moral quality index 280
  suppression of 148
crime 377–98
  and age 383–7
  and beautification campaigns 159
  and 'criminal solidarity' 340
  drug related 382
  and economic development 20–1,
    381–2
  female 382, 391
  and feudalism 388
  and floating population 389–90
  forecast 343
  and individual instability 309
  international statistics on 380–2
  and moral error 26
  as moral quality 71
  organized 320
  pedagogy 145
  and 'premature love' 360, 363
  prevention 263, 341–4
  rates of the PRC 378–9
  and self-control 320–1
  sexual 357, 361–3, 382
  statistics and reliability 377–9, 390
  wave 379, 384
  as youthful behaviour 383
  see also anti-crime campaigns (*yanda*);
    homicide; hooligan(ism); juvenile
    delinquency

Cui Jian 327
cultural bias 11, 354–5
cultural determinism 2–3, 6, 9, 40, 50,
    413–14
culturalism 24
Cultural Revolution 17, 41, 51, 187,
    303
  and abolishment of school files 295
  and breakdown of norms 325, 327
  and juvenile crime 384, 388
  and storming of personnel offices 289
  and violence 412
culture 18, 56–8, 326–9
  assimilating character of Chinese 38
  campus 157–9
  construction of 18–19, 26, 58
  counter- 329, 332
  criminal 317
  and cultural chauvinism 109
  and cultural development 57
  and cultural engineering 53
  and 'cultural quality' 305
  and decadence 327
  fever 58, 413–14
  as 'fourth industry' 56
  of hypocrisy and simulation 412, 424
  imitative-repetitive 148–9, 228, 421,
    423
  imitative type of 128, 139
  inertia of Chinese 39
  and moorings of models 179–81, 197,
    200
  prison 431
  'relation-based' 299
  as repertoire of possibilities 2
  youth 318, 326–8
culturology 52–9
cybernetics 37, 269, 419
Cyrus the Great 150

Da Li 304
dangers 317–47
  'chain narratives' of 318–24, 342
  of deviance and sub-culture 336–7
  as fear of social and moral pollution
    391
  of 'hedonistic withdrawal' 325,
    329–30
  of marginality 363, 390
  of migrant population 389
  of modernity 1, 5, 103, 308, 317, 347
  of movement 330–2, 342–3, 435
  and the norm 318–19
  purity and 368–9
  of the runaway 320

of self-love 184
of sexuality 356–7
of youth 377, 390–1
Daoism 19, 94
d'Assigny, Marius 142
death 105
  and models 185–6, 435
  see also self *under* sacrifice
de Certeau, Michel 435–6
democracy 276–80
  and evaluation 276, 279–80, 310
  and modernization 237
  traditional scepticism towards 279–80
Deng Shaoxing 288, 300
Deng Xiaoping 51, 60, 426
  on modelling 173
  on morality and economy 96
  on repetition 147
  and strategy 420–1
  on thrift 103, 198
dependence 99
  in Chinese and Americans 228–9
  organized 34–5, 229, 276
de Pizan, Christian 138
deterrence 91, 94
  educative 343
  see also coercion
deviance 36, 42, 67, 317–47
  in 17th-century New England 334–6
  and analogous behaviour 320, 323,
    330, 342
  as 'fun' 320–1, 329–30
  among girls 369
  seen as illness 305
  and labelling theory 368–9
  and modernity 317–18
  rehabilitation of 145
  and 'subterranean values' 321, 339,
    343
  and tatoos 323
  and travelling 330–1
Dewey, John 158
disability 67, 71–2
discipline 42, 52, 96–9, 113
  based on norm 213–14, 237
  and deception 432
  and disciplinary sanction 263–4
  and disciplinary society 5, 8, 215
  and disciplinary technology 52, 200,
    214, 238
  and education 87–8, 288, 302
  and evaluation 287
  and 'first times' 319–21, 333, 341–2
  and 'love contracts' 365
  and modernity 235

Index